JEANNE DEVEREAUX

Show Biz

FROM VAUDE TO VIDEO

SHOW

by ABEL GREEN &

New York:

BIZ

from

VAUDE

to

VIDEO

JOE LAURIE, Jr.

Henry Holt and Company

To the muggs, past, present, and future—and the greatest Variety mugg of them all, *Sime,* whose book this really is.

Take-A-Bow Dept.

★

This is one book that was not written—it was rewritten. And often.

Compressing a rich and vibrant half century of show biz into 230,000 words called for a skilled assist from Jules Archer, who organized the vast material for us; the patience and understanding of a couple of hep editors such as Bill Raney and Ted Amussen; and one or two Seeing Eye Dogs who helped us wade through 50 years' accumulation of disa and data. There were times when the authors' notes to themselves reminded them of the old Hollywood wheeze: "Never mind producing the script, just shoot the footnotes and we've got enough for a serial!"

It was difficult for us to be completely objective about show biz and *Variety* because of the personality of its fabulous founder, Sime Silverman. That is why the book is part theatrical history and part biography.

Written in Varietyese, *Show Biz: From Vaude to Video* is intended to be breezy and gay as well as informative.

ABEL GREEN
JOE LAURIE, JR.

New York City
September, 1951

CONTENTS

Contents

PART THREE
Big Boom (1919–1929)

PART FOUR
Big Bust (1930–1932)

SIME'S SQUARE

★

Sime Silverman, founder-editor-publisher of *Variety,* died September 22, 1933. For almost 20 years now, usually on an Indian summer day, on the Wednesday nearest that date (Variety muggs' day off, following press day) a strange pilgrimage of showmen, from Broadway to Hollywood, from Jimmy Durante to Mary Margaret McBride, travels to Brooklyn's Salem Fields, to the Silverman mausoleum.

It's strange in many ways because, through the years, men and women who probably never pay the same reverence to their immediate families take time out from highly tensioned, busy schedules for this annual reunion in memory of the most unusual Variety mugg of them all. A list of these "pilgrims" would constitute a Who's Who of all the Seven Lively Arts.

Sime was so the personification of Broadway that Mayor Jimmy Walker was serious in wanting to rename that triangle from 46th to 47th Streets, known as Duffy Square, Sime's Square. *Time* magazine observed in 1934 that Wilfred John Funk named the 10 modern Americans who have done most to keep American jargon alive. Sime headed the list, followed by Mencken, T. A. (Tad) Dorgan, Walter Winchell, Bugs Baer, Ring Lardner, Damon Runyon, Gelett Burgess, George Ade, and Gene Buck.

Through the paper he founded and styled, Sime's impact is indelible, durable, deathless. The journalistic pattern of *Variety* as it approaches its half-century mark continues to be unique not only in American journalism but in world-wide impact. As Hollywood pix, Broadway legit, Yankee jazz, and the U. S. brand of radio-T-V spreads to all the world capitals, American show biz is best mirrored by and through *Variety*.

In the tradition of the great American journalists to whom he has been frequently compared, Sime was most articulate through his paper. He shied from public attention even within his immediate show biz orbit, even going to Havana and Mexico in 1931 with his wife Hattie to avoid publicity on the occasion of *Variety's* Silver Anniversary. This was the first time Sime left U. S. shores. Hattie was an inveterate globetrotter, but Sime never yenned to go abroad. Broadway was his home, his work, and his playground.

Sime remains indelible in memory to the surviving show biz veterans—the originals or scions of the Loews, Zukors, Schencks, Warners, Balabans, Zanucks, Goetzes, Selznicks, Mayers, Blumbergs, Kennedys, Aylesworths, Shuberts, Hammersteins, and the host of personalities such as Berlin, Cantor, Jolson, Benny, Hope, Allen, Jessel, Fairbanks, Chaplin, Pickford, Durante, Winchell—for his vigorous, forthright aggressiveness.

He didn't like vaudeville tycoons pushing actors around. He didn't like unthinking actors led and hoodwinked by professional organizers. *Variety's* championing of the rank-and-file worker in the theatre, from stagehand to star, is a historic and a continuing credo of the paper. He abhorred dishonesty. By his forthrightness he set a cardinal rule for his staffers' professional and private lives: *If you tell the truth even the people who don't like it must respect you.*

Sime hated phonies and could spot one as quick as the FBI. He also hated scavenger sheets. In the era of *Town Topics* which, by blind items, pecked away at socialites and finally expired of its own chicanery, there was a pseudo-theatrical sheet called *Broadway Brevities,* edited by Steve Clow. Not as "raw" was still another sheet, *Zit's Weekly,* sired by Carl F. Zittel which met its just desserts, being the carbon-copy we*a*kly that it was.

This man, for whom *Variety* continues a vibrant, evergreen monument, was destined for greatness among show biz people. Born May 19, 1873, in Cortland, New York, reared in Syracuse, Sime was stage-struck from youth. Possessed of an unusual mathematical mind, a heritage from his father's private banking business which he spurned, thus alienating all family sympathy and economic support, he hung around Syracuse theatres. When his father, Louis Silverman, owner of the Fidelity Bank, a loan institution at 140 Nassau Street, New York City, brought Sime to the Big Town in 1898 as an appraiser, he rebelled at the calling. Instead he somehow got to know Leander Richardson, theatrical commentator on the *New York Morning Telegraph,* through Joshua Lowe, Richardson's secretary. It's not generally known that Sime's journalistic career first started on *Daily America.* This short-lived newspaper was founded in 1903 by George Graham Rice, owner of a race track tipster service, in pique against the *Telegraph,* and its boss, Blakely Hall.

Rice retaliated by taking Richardson as his ace. Lowe, his secretary, remembered Sime's ambitions when it became necessary to establish a counterpart column in the new paper, and through them Sime got into newspaper work. Though no hero worshiper, Sime always respected Richardson in the same way he respected Elbert Hubbard and Napoleon, his two favorite heroes.

Sime became The Man In the Third Row, a signature identified solely with him on *Daily America,* and never on the *Telegraph,* as is Broadway legend. When he subsequently got a job on the *Telegraph,* he used a house signature "Robert Speare." Sime's glory was short-lived. *Daily America* was dissolved when Blakely Hall made peace with George Graham Rice; the latter returned his ads to the *Telegraph* and Richardson returned to the paper. Hall took back a couple of turf writers, but Sime was laid off. Despite this—and his father's banking business—he remained a familiar figure above Union Square, then the rialto.

Sime finally connected with the *Telegraph*. While the paper was still under Blakely Hall's direction, Lewis had put on B. C. Hart as advertising solicitor. Hall complained that he couldn't get ads for the Lewis Publishing Company "if the notices ran wild." An unwritten rule was that any act that regularly advertised in the special (Sunday) issues, or that took a Christmas ad, was a "good" act.

Sime had heard of the rule but it didn't mean a thing to him—at least, not for the moment—in his eagerness to land on the *Telegraph*. Despite that he started off in his characteristic hit-'em-hard style. His bosses raved and frothed for the first couple of weeks and Sime knew that his persistence could mean his job any edition.

For historians, therefore, it's as much to the credit of a knockabout comedy team, Redford & Winchester, as anything else, that *Variety* came to be. The team squawked to the paper about Sime's panning notice. In those days it was considered justifiable for an actor to rebuke a critic, and mild mayhem was a popular outdoor sport along the rialto. On a vaudeville trade paper it was particularly justifiable, as Redford & Winchester had placed a Christmas ad in the *Telegraph*. They canceled their ad, and Sime lost his job.

Thus, Sime started *Variety* December 16, 1905, on a lot of nerve and $1,500 cash. The $1,500 was borrowed from his father-in-law, Alderman George Freeman of Syracuse. It contained 16 pages and sold for a nickel. Sime had the vision not to call his paper *Vaudeville* or any other name that might limit its scope, and settled on *Variety* which he thought embraced all phases of show biz. Legend has it that while dining in Pabst's Casino in Harlem with his bride, Hattie doodled on the tablecloth and created the fancy flourishing "V" that distinguishes the *Variety* trademark today.

During the first 25 years running gags in Sime's columns were that "*Variety* never went to press, it went to the cleaners," "the sheriff was as permanent on the premises as the typewriters." It took virtually a quarter of a century for the paper to get into the black and Sime so recorded it in a memorable editorial: "For the first time in 24 years Variety got out of debt in 1929. May it keep out. Some years ago it was said on this page that when Variety paid off, if ever, it would be told. Here 'tis." With the same open-book nonchalance, the

Literati department apprised all that "With this note Sid Silverman
will learn he is now 50 per cent owner of *Variety*." Similarly, Sime
inducted the present editor one summer day in 1933 shortly before his
death by pointing to his desk and telling him, simply, "You sit there,
Abel."

At one time *Variety* muggs found themselves tripling on three
papers—*The Clipper, The Times Square Daily,* and *Variety.* Only
an acute loyalty and deep-rooted affection for their chief mugg could
have compelled such devotion.

Sime bought *The Clipper* in 1923 from Leo Feist, who had used
it as a mouthpiece for his song publications, to build it into a specialized outdoor newspaper as competition to *The Billboard.* Later
he dissolved it—at a personal loss of $120,000, largely through his
benevolence to the small mugg stockholders.

In founding *The Times Square Daily,* which was a gag sheet and
forerunner of today's Broadway gossip column, he set the pattern
for what became the present *Daily Variety* in 1933.

The paper's first *Annual Radio Directory,* a separate hard-covered
book numbering 1100 pages, appeared in 1937, and while the 4 an-
nuals published thereafter were successful, they were scrapped as
consuming too much time and effort. The best features continue
regularly in the parent weekly.

Variety's first two-room office was on 38th Street, just below the
old Casino and across the hall from Charles Dillingham. Later, when
Oscar Hammerstein built his Hammerstein's Victoria above 42d
Street, Sime moved beyond it, to 45th and Broadway. Later, learning that Madame Frances, a theatrical couturière, was moving to
Fifth Avenue and that Loew's State Theatre's stage entrance would
be approximately next door to 154 West 46th Street, Sime made a
deal with her and *Variety* got its own building, which it still occu-
pies. West 46th Street between Broadway and Sixth Avenue is known
far and wide as *Variety* Street. (Certainly no *Variety* mugg ever
calls it Avenue of the Americas.)

More theatrical history emanated from the fifth floor on top of
Variety's present office building than from many another theatrical
tycoon skull-practice session. Top names in show biz gathered upstairs for Sime's advice, interspersed with a drink. The top floor was
the champ free speakeasy in America. The initiates had their own

keys, but none came who didn't see the upstairs light which meant
that Sime was holding forth. The Old Boy had a special key made
for Jimmy Walker. Walter Winchell and Mark Hellinger had keys.
Winchell even wrote his notices for the *Graphic* in the *Variety* office.
The ice chest was always full of food and drink, and a specially
locked compartment contained chilled vintages for particular femme
company. When business was bad in the joints around town, it was
said, "Sime must be staging one of his brawls." They were not large
but they did take certain key spenders out of circulation.

An impressive figure, Sime Silverman was 5′ 10½″ in height,
weighed 210 pounds, dressed expensively but unostentatiously, and was
most memorable for his bow ties, generally solid brown or green in
color, and an unruly curly forelock. He had a good head of gray hair,
always wore brown suits sans vests, specially made shoes costing
$50-$60 (with a special arch support), a brown gabardine trench coat
and brown slouch hat to match; no breast pocket handkerchief, no
boutonniere. His prime personal extravagance was very fine linen,
oversized handkerchiefs.

He was a one-fit man and hated even that. A tailor would come to
his office or home, take his measurements, and that was that. His
shirts were silk and expensive, always with detached collar of matching cloth. He took little or no exercise but looked physically fit, sans
paunch, despite his irregular eating and drinking habits. The hacking
coughs through the years were ascribed to the strong cigarettes to
which he was addicted. At first none of us thought the cough was
serious, but with the years occasionally one of us would observe, "One
day we'll find the Old Boy keeled over up there," pointing to the
"throne" as the elevated platform with his desk was called.

His favorite Christmas present was a $20 gold piece, which he
distributed to the office wives, girl friends, cops, doormen, and waiters.
He was also a quarter jingler. Every morning the bookkeeper sent
down $10-$20 worth of two-bit pieces. Despite his seasonal penchant
for $20 gold pieces, Sime hated Xmas cards and deprecated the "Xmas
bonus" idea. He practiced a more realistic Yuletide spirit by putting
it on a 52-week good living wage basis. He discouraged Xmas "loot"
for himself, unless really personal. But despite his admonitions, loot
arrived and his private secretary, Betty Brown (who is still with the

paper), or the office boys often inherited the crates of fruit and the like. He shoveled hundreds of Xmas cards into the wastebasket unopened, but when told that one contained a business check, he instructed Betty to open them for subscriptions or checks; otherwise, into the basket as before.

He was also a complete martinet. You could have been out with him the night before, or just come back from lunch with him, but while you were in the office there was no palsy-walsy stuff with anyone, including his son, Sid, on whom he was even tougher.

To be fired at least once by Sime was par for the course. Abel made par. Apparently his coming to work at two and three P.M., despite the late speakeasy coverage, was too much for Sime. He rarely held mass office meetings, and he was *not* the traditional Front Page editor. His "I think" suggestion was more potent than a "You do it *this* way." But when he did stage a meeting, it was a lulu. Abel was "it" one time in an intra-office political wrangle which prompted him to say, "Well, if you feel that way about it, Mr. Silverman, I'll resign." He was quick to bark, "That's not necessary," indicating that the intent of the general bawl-out was psychological for morale and was now water under the bridge. Later that day he copyread one of Abel's stories and on his way out told him he was making it the No. 1 lead!

More often known as "Mr. Sime" around town to headliners and headwaiters alike, he abhorred formality within the office. Once he barked to Abel, "Cut out the Mister stuff. It's Sime!" To which he meekly replied, "Yes, Mr. Silverman."

Sime had inherent showmanship without flamboyance. His penchant for transmuting the argot of the circus, the tanbark, Tin Pan Alley, the stage and the screen, the Broadwayite and nitery hound into a common language found ready response within show biz. So did the original green cover on *Variety*. A holdover from those days is *Variety's* green stationery and the green cover used on the anniversary number. A green neon Variety once blazed over Times Square, in front of 1534 Broadway, now the present site of Loew's State Theatre Bldg. His same showmanship commanded a BRyant 1534 telephone number. Then, when other publications went in for kindred ballyhooey, Sime cooled and his staffers thereafter have let the paper's contents be its best advertisement. At 25¢ a copy *Variety* feels it must give the reader plenty of value.

His round table at the Hotel Astor was a glorified listening post, an extraordinary editorial vantage point. In those days the Astor's Hunting Room was the showmen's crossroads, a composite of the Hollywood and Beverly Hills Brown Derbies, Romanoff's and Chasen's, the Pump Room in Chicago, the Stork, 21, Toots Shor's, Lindy's, the Waldorf men's bar, and the Oak Room of the Plaza in New York. Any time the Astor's laundry couldn't add up over $27,000,000 off certain tablecloths, it was a sign show biz was bad.

Sime garnered more news in a lunch period than his entire staff in a day. The side pockets of his coat were his newsgathering depots. In the right pocket he kept a small 2-x-4-inch pad and a stub of a pencil. The left was for the single-word reminders which keyed important stories for him later. "Metpix" meant that a trend in filmusicals with Metropolitan Opera stars was brewing. "Zanuck Schenck 10/1" meant that Zanuck and Schenck were merging their 20th Century Films Corporation with Fox Films on a 10-1 stock exchange basis. It's the same system *Variety's* reporters still pursue when a pad and pencil can scare an informant into clamming up.

Sime was devoted to his mother, who was the Fannie Ward of the Silverman family and who loved poker to her death when she was in her nineties. Sime visited her regularly and got a bang out of her letters to him signed, "Your loving mother Rachel."

Sarah Loucks, the mammy of the Silverman home, was a soft touch for Sime. She always had folding money and somehow knew whether to disburse $200, $300, or $400 to him. Sime always sent it to her by messenger the next day.

He was adamant about having stewed tomatoes for lunch (actually brunch many times) "because it's anti-acid and good for you after drinking," he'd counsel. Plain garden spinach was his other favorite vegetable.

If any of the office wives were physically run down he'd send over Guinness' Stout or Bass Ale as a builder-upper. If a staffer left on vacation Sime's parting word was, "Be sure to wire or lemme know if you need anything." "Anything," of course, meant money.

His impatience with stupid office boys was legendary. "Go upstairs and get your money!" he'd snap when some unbright kid didn't know what he was doing. He scared the hell out of them all the time. One time he gave a kid $10. "Go out and buy me a hat." Luckily the kid knew enough to ask the men what size and shade they thought Sime wore. He brought it back, Sime put it on without looking up from his typewriter, grunted, "Keep the change," and continued as if he'd only sent him out for a pack of cigarettes.

Conversely, he'd do the darndest things for an office boy he thought looked peaked, upsetting Hattie and Sid at their Thousand Islands summer place. The office boy would suddenly find himself transplanted into a new world via a note from Sime. As Sid put it, "A kid would pop in at the Islands with the statement, 'Mr. Silverman sent me up.' There'd be a note from the Old Boy, 'Dear Sid: This is Eddie McCaffrey who needs a rest, so take care of him for a couple weeks.' I had to drop everything and take care of him. That was the Old Boy's way of making sure the kid got a vacation. Two weeks later the kid was just as apt to be fired for something the Old Boy didn't like."

Above everything else, *Variety* was Sime's mistress. Next to the paper and show biz, his deepest affections were for his son and his staff, the *Variety* muggs. The first is natural, the latter unique in a publisher's relations with newspapermen. *Variety's* staff turnover in all the offices (New York, Hollywood, Chicago, Washington, and London) has been relatively small. *Variety's* string correspondents have often expressed themselves that they like "knocking ourselves out for *Variety*" because they can speak freer than on the large dailies.

At the time a drunken actor took a shot at Sime through the *Variety* window he was cautioned that "perhaps Sid had better carry a billy." Sime laughed, "A man has been assigned to me, so don't worry." But the bodyguard was not from the West 47th St. Police Station. He was on Sime's personal payroll and his job was to keep an eye more on Sid than Sime.

Their relationship was Broadway legend. Underneath the hard-bitten exterior of *Variety's* No. 1 mugg was an affection for his only son which was unique without being sticky. He indulged him but didn't spoil him. If Sid was uncertain he would ask the Old Boy, "because I could never cross him." This applied to the time Sid thought maybe he had promised the Old Boy not to drink until he was 21. At a St. John's Manlius Military Academy function—where Sid was enrolled—Sid phoned Sime to tell him he was taking a drink but wanted to put himself on record that he wasn't breaking any pledge.

It wasn't until around the time Sid was 17 or 18 that the significance of religion asserted itself. St. John's had compulsory chapel. Sime told Sid, "Absorb what you want from chapel. It won't hurt you and the rest doesn't matter."

Sime set up charge accounts for Sid at Reisenweber's, Maxim's, Rector's, Healy's, the Golden Glades, the Plantation, Bustonaby's, and Shanley's but the boy never abused them. Sime was known for seeking unobtrusive tables but the only time he asked for the No. 1 table at Reisenweber's was on Sid's first date with the musical-comedy dancer, Marie Saxon.

Marie's death in 1941, at 37, preceded Sid's at 51 in 1950. Their son, Syd, now 19 and a Princeton undergraduate, has inherited *Variety's* dominant ownership. Equal minority shares were willed by Sime to business manager Harold Erichs and the present editor.

Sime really reached the peak of his hard playing and hard working in the Roaring Twenties. He maintained a fleet of three cars, all open jobs. Sid was more aesthetic in his cars, ranging from the Mercer of his Manlius days to an imported Isotta-Fraschini. (The same liking for fancy motors shows in young Syd.) Two sets of Negro chauffeurs always stood by. Sime gave them enough time to catch up on their sleep, and drove them as hard as he drove himself as he paid them well. Personally, he was a poor driver, with a murderous sense of direction, particularly when it came to pseudo-short cuts.

At the end of a hard day's work, he would signal two or three staffers and ask, "Got a date for tonight?" Few, if any, ever did have a date when Sime signaled for an excursion to Texas Guinan's or Westchester roadhouses. A born gambler, Sime lived the full life, gambling on himself and his personal judgment. Often he was wrong, mostly he was right. He thought he was right in spurning insurance actuaries, saying, "If a company is willing to bet on my life, why shouldn't I bet on it?" Yet he counseled his son and Harold Erichs and Abel Green to load up on insurance.

Gambling on himself, he may be said to have lost the percentage of life's span when he died at 60, yet Dr. J. W. Amey, his long-time friend and physician, observed, "Sime died at 120—he lived two full lives."

When he went out, Sime never brought his own liquor. The road-houses and niteries always saw that he and his boys and girls drank the best in the house. He was a fabulous check-grabber and a good tipper without being ostentatious.

He was a Scotch-and-Perrier man. Although he had never been to France, he knew that the *source gaz naturelle,* which distinguishes the French spa's *eau du Perrier,* was the best mixer. The Perrier importers asked, "Who is this man Silverman who is doing such a terrific job for us in all the places by requesting Perrier?" He spurned their offer of complimentary cases but approved being billed at wholesale prices for the caseloads that went to his home, his friends, and the famed "top floor" of the *Variety* building.

He would chide us, as he did others, for cocktails and "all those fancy drinks . . . you'll find you'll travel best on Scotch as you get older." He was right.

After roadhousing he'd bring us home for a nightcap and maybe watermelon, which, like stewed tomatoes, he felt was a great antidote to a rugged evening of drinking. He would always bawl out Sarah for being awake then. Looking alert and spic and span in her snow-white cap, she would say, "Well, Mr. Sime, I thought maybe you wouldn't know where to find the watermelon which is nice and cold tonight."

Sime didn't die at his desk. He died at the Ambassador Hotel in Los Angeles where he had gone the last two winters of his life to regain his health there and on the desert in Palm Springs.

That which was Sime was best summed up, strangely enough, by Steve Clow, ex-publisher of the blackmail sheet, *Broadway Brevities.* Clow was finally committed to Atlanta for using the mails to defraud. It was typical of Sime, who undoubtedly never regretted seeing Clow knocked out, not to kick a fellow when he was down. Clow, on the q.t., got regular financial aid from Sime while in prison. When he got out, Sime put him to work handling galleys and doing other innocuous chores in order to help him to possible rehabilitation.

Once Clow and I were alone in the office. He pointed to the platform containing Sime's desk and said, "You wanna know who's the only real Christian I know, Abel? It's that lovable Jew bastard up there on that throne!"

PART ONE

VAUDE SOCKO

1905 - 1913

1

Bubbling Crucible

★

When the curtain rose on 20th-century entertainment,
Variety was five years late in getting to its seat. One rainy afternoon
in December, it sauntered down the aisle of Broadway, nothing in
its pockets except hands. Coolly trampling on powerful toes in the
front row, Variety lifted a bored eyebrow at each scowl, threat, kick
and goose. Finally it sat down to review, and influence, the greatest
show on earth—Show Business.

Show business, in the hoopla years 1905-1913, largely meant vaudeville, whose king was Benjamin Franklin Keith. Two distinct

noises could be heard during the Keith dynasty. One was the ever-livelier bounce of silver at the box office. The second was the back-stage thud of rivals' heads as they fell under the agile sword of Keith's lord high executioner, Edward F. Albee.

There was frenzied bidding on the talent auction block. Deter-mined challengers of the Keith-Albee empire, such as William Morris, Klaw & Erlanger, the Shuberts, Martin Beck and Marcus Loew, offered astronomical salaries to corner the star market. *Nouveaux riches* headliners began buying Stutz Bearcats, gilt-edged bonds, and $150-to-$900-an-acre homesites in Freeport, Long Island.

The tug of war between theatre giants provided an embarrass-ment of riches for the bewildered but delighted public. Wooed with super-theatres, lavish productions and star-studded bills, it found such seduction irresistible. Theatre-going changed from a Saturday night event to a fixed American habit—two and three times a week.

Tony Pastor, last of the gemütlich showmen, had made vaude-ville respectable "for ladies and gentlemen" before his death in 1910. Incidentally, he died with very little personal fortune as against the estates left by other vaudeville tycoons. Now that Americans were going in for shows more frequently than baths, B. F. Keith deloused vaude further—"for women and children." Face scrubbed clean, satin bows in its hair, vaudeville could no longer be scorned as the saloon strumpet of yesteryear. The new skyrocket whooshed up so fast that stars of the legitimate stage, who formerly looked down their classic profiles at "vohdville," sought engagements with the two-a-day. In time divinities like Sarah Bernhardt and Lily Langtry were sharing bills with wirewalkers, contortionists, dog acts and midgets.

A 1910 nose-count showed America knee-deep in 2,000 smalltime hinterland theatres. Vaudeville toppers quickly plucked these plums for their flowering circuits. So many two-a-day chains flourished that one actor, booked for a circuit he had never heard of, asked his agent, "What is it? Smalltime, medium smalltime, big smalltime, little big time, medium big time or big time?" Just how big "little big time" could be was demonstrated by Charles F. Kohl, kingpin of the midwest Kohl & Castle circuit, who, when he died in 1910, left $7,000,000, all uninflated.

Variety reported "blah b. o." only once during this golden age, when show business felt the pinch of the financial panic in 1907. But after a short-lived depression, audiences sought the usual catharsis in laughter and thrills. Vaudeville, 1908-1913, was "socko."

In those unsophisticated days the corn was very green. Actors laid them in the aisles with such sparkling chestnuts as: "I sent my wife to the Thousand Islands for a vacation—a week on each island." . . . "Are oysters healthy? I never heard them complain." . . . "You can drive a horse to drink but a pencil must be lead." Parodies of popular songs, "coon-shouting," and any gag employing false teeth or hair, a wooden leg or a mother-in-law, panicked the house.

Sensationalism was an equally important keynote of the period. Every producer twisted himself into knots trying to offer more bizarre attractions than his rival. There was an epidemic of epidermis acts presenting Salomé and seven shedding veils, forerunner of the latter-day Sally Rand and Gypsy Rose Lee. Willie Hammerstein booked freaks from halfmen-halfwomen to gun molls. Audiences of the day were invited to goggle at Evelyn Nesbit, love angle of the Thaw murder case, and gasp at Annette Kellerman, in the first one-piece bathingsuit, diving into a tank.

In 1904 not a single nickelodeon sullied the land. But three years later, over 2,000,000 people a day, one-third of them children, were jamming into movie shows. Early nickelodeons were simply converted stores seating 299 (theatres seating 300 or more required an amusement license), and running from 12 to 18 shows daily.

By 1909 movies had become a first-class headache to veteran branches of show business. One legit road company touring New England revealed sadly that its baggage bill in one town was more than its boxoffice receipts. One-night stands all over the country (at 75¢ and $1 admissions) crumpled in the face of cheaper movie opposition.

Most vaudeville magnates quickly added pix to their bills. Reluctant dragons who despised this newfangled threat to flesh entertainment were rapidly forced to their knees by public demand.

The years 1905-1913 were Gold Rush days, for show business, with eager pioneers staking claims in what they hoped would prove the biggest lodes. Each frantic week spawned a new form, style or combination of entertainment. Spoiled by so much courting, the public was dangerously fickle—today you had 'em, tomorrow you didn't. Producers, in what time remained between feuds among themselves, flung fortunes into theatrical experiments. Actors—

many of them the Hollywood and radio headliners of today—had thousands of stages on which to rub off their raw edges and develop style.

The whole era was a period of glittering showmanship and gaudy showplaces, in a tradition later to be revived with such triumph by Roxy. But for every dazzling blueprint that came to life, 20 "ink-and-paper theatres" were washed off hotel dining-room table cloths. In 1911 Variety announced, "The biggest amphitheatre of its kind ever contemplated for indoors will be erected by the New York Central Railroad on top of its immense new Grand Central Station, now building. It is planned to accommodate all exhibitions, sporting events or circuses."

But no elephant ever did shake the ceiling above Track 32.

rowdyism and racial libels   In those days America was peeling off old restraints, right down to its woolen underwear. Skirts were climbing to an accompaniment of whistles. Stuffed birds rode gayly on umbrella-sized hats. Men of distinction wore peg-top pants, two-toned button shoes and spats. The waltz and two-step were gradually pushed off the dance floor by the ragtime tempo of sexy dances like the turkey trot, grizzly bear, bunny hug and the maxixe.

So many millions of Americans were new to theatregoing in the years 1905-1913 that it took a long while before they could be disciplined into the decorous role of an audience. The "Colonial clap" (audience counting out a performer in applause unison) and boos (forerunner of the "Bronx cheer" which was born at the National Theatre in the Bronx, New York)—earmarks of today's rugged fight fans—were stock expressions of audience disapproval in the youth of vaudeville.

"Rowdyism Must Stop!" thundered Variety in 1907. "Although one of the most select vaudeville theatres in the city, Percy G. Williams' Colonial holds terror to all artists playing there at the Monday matinee. Among the first audience of the week is a crowd of young roughs, who are accompanied by young women, nearly as badly behaved. . . . On the slightest provocation, hissing, cat-calls and the 'clapping' of hands will follow, 'breaking up' any act on the stage at the time. . . . Last Monday a special officer was placed in the theatre with instructions to watch out for the miscreants, and treat them as they deserved when found."

The stage of that era mirrored its audiences with remarkable fidelity. At first when Irish, German, Italian, Jewish and other immigrants poured through the gates of Ellis Island, each nationality had its stock prototype on the stage, usually portrayed at the level of the lowest common denominator. Thus Irish characters wore ear-to-ear chin beards, called sluggers or gallaways, carried dinner pails, drank whiskey from hip-bottle flasks, jigged and never spoke without saying "begorra." Stock Germans with padded stomachs wore chin whiskers, blond wigs, small brown derbys, checkered trousers, big shoes, fancy vests with heavy watchchains, and murdered the English language.

An interesting change took place. As each immigrant minority prospered during the boom years before World War I, it achieved a new economic and social dignity. It no longer cared to laugh at itself, or to have other nationalities laugh at it. Protests began to be heard from the most influential citizens of each minority, as in 1907, when the rabbis and priests of Cleveland united in condemning Jewish and Irish stage comics, threatening reprisals if show business did not withdraw these insulting portrayals.

Irish societies, increasingly more sensitive, hissed off the Russell Brothers and their "Irish Servant Girl" act at Hammerstein's. The Hibernian Society staged a riot when "McFadden's Flats" was performed. In San Francisco, when an actress named Pitkin depicted an Irish character drinking beer out of a can in "The Belle of Avenue A," she was driven off the stage with a shower of rotten eggs.

Such protests were not unfruitful. Gradually each burlesque Irishman, Jew, German, and Italian gave way on the stage to the "neat" comic—one well-dressed and attractive, who relied on his wit and talent for laughter and applause. Retaining a careful bit of the old brogue or dialect, he was much more popular than he had ever been in his slapstick impersonation.

(It is an interesting parallel that protests against burlesque dialect were registered in more recent times against radio comedians. There is accented nationalism the world over. Today there are no longer Mexican villains in films, in deference to good neighborliness and an eye on the rich tourist business south of the border. Comics like Groucho Marx joined columnist Walter Winchell's tirade against

Lapidus, Sambo (Negro) and kindred dialects, while protagonists of dialectic humor, such as Harry Hershfield and Peter Donald (of the "Can You Top This?" radio program) contended that humor in dialect, brogue or other accents, if wholesome, and purposeful for locale or native appreciation, was not offensive. So did the co-author of this book who also made a point in Variety that perhaps the most dialectically used and abused nationals were the Scots and the Swedes, who have never complained, to which Groucho Marx—like Winchell—countered that "the Sandy McPhersons and the Yonny Yohnsons were not a minority being subjected to oppression, restriction, segregation or persecution.")

that foreign touch   Then as now, "Great European Artists"—many neither great, nor European, nor artists—enjoyed a popular vogue on the theory that anything "imported" was far superior to the domestic brand. Americans were not the only audience afflicted with astigmatism. At the same time that "Great English Artists" were making a hit in New York, "Great American Artists" were knocking them dead in London in those pre-1913 days.

Any American actor with a foreign tour under his belt found his stock boosted at home. When he checked into a hotel without Continental labels to distinguish his luggage, he was obviously "small time." One shrewd printer of the day did a magnificent business selling home copies of European baggage stickers to all Americans on the road who wanted to create an impression.

Another cherished foible of audiences was the "obvious" superiority of the Negro dancer. It was unquestioned folklore that Negroes were born hoofing on the levee to the strumming of banjos. Consequently, many a second-rate sepia dancer was accorded a thunderous reception, which he encouraged by a great show of self-enjoyment, while first-rate white dancers, with less ability to "sell it," were allowed to limp off to faint applause. There were, of course, a few outstanding Negro hoofers in that era but not until the latter-day Bill (Bojangles) Robinson, John W. Buck (Buck & Bubbles), the Nicholas Brothers, Tip, Tap & Toe, the 3 Step Brothers, and the like, did the real Harlem legmania assert itself.

Although comedy found the quickest response in audience moods, pathos was not without its rewards. To be pathetic, an actor used a gold-painted, high class chair, on which he placed one foot, as the orchestra would strike up "Hearts and Flowers." Turning up his coat collar, and with a sad amber or blue spotlight on him, he would dejectedly recite some immortal classic concerning a mongrel dog, a pal that went back on you, a lost sweetheart, the kid's last fight, a dying baby, or the old folks at home. It never failed to whip out the handkerchiefs.

the salomé craze   The phoniest craze of all to hit show business was the Salomé dance. When New York went Salomé-mad, the nation followed. Maude Allen started it in London vaudeville, and it was brought to New York by Gertrude Hoffman. Vaudeville's leading female stars, including Eva Tanguay, either turned to Salomé acts, or incorporated the routine into their turns. Audiences were hit in the face with Salomé for something like five years, and loved it!

Reformers tore their hair. In Pittsburgh, when a dancer named Miss Deyo did Salomé for the Joe Weber Company, the WCTU passed a resolution calling upon all of its members to pray for one solid week for the soul of this lost woman. Astute publicity agents engineered the arrest of many a Salomé, with subsequent b.o. benefits. Some communities were genuinely hostile to the phenomenon. Yonkers audiences hooted Mlle. Froelich off the stage when she tossed them some Salomé in 1908. Fully 150 theatre managers in Ohio, West Virginia, Pennsylvania and Kentucky tabooed the dance. But long before John the Baptist's prop head was forced to garner dust, Salomé had garnered a fortune.

A sizeable percentage of early audiences had less interest in the theatre as an entertainment palace than as a classroom. Immigrants went to vaudeville and the movies to learn how to speak English. As a subtitle flashed across the screen, or a vaudeville comedian delivered a wisecrack, they poked elbows into progeny beside them and demanded, "What means this?" Loyal to odorous neighborhood theatres, they were suspicious of ornate showplaces which often charged identical prices. Besides, they were at home with an unwashed, haphazardly dressed audience that munched apples and sandwiches while enjoying the show.

More so in those days than these, audiences sought their own levels.

pre-1910 wisecracks Show business, never more than a polished reflection of the ordinary people of its time, took much of its color, tone, slang and humor from its audiences who, in turn, borrowed the verbal currency of show business. Slangsters of 1908 were very gay when they wisecracked, "Make a noise like a hoop and roll away," introduced by vaudeville's Bert Leslie who also inspired that class-A repartee, "Get under the sink with the rest of the pipes."

Some years later Alf Grant gave a classic example of the slang in vogue among show people of that day when asked if he had seen a certain actor. "Sure," he replied, "I saw him standing on Hope Island (in front of the Palace) on the waffle iron (subway grating on sidewalk) about ten minutes ago. He walked down Cripple Creek (47th Street, hangout for idle musicians) with a couple of turtles (laid-off actors, basking in the sun) headed for the Water Hole (Automat)."

Broadway was a lusty playground without cover charge, curfew or columnist (except "The Skirt" on Variety) to tell tales on who was seen celebrating at Rector's, Shanley's, Brown's, Churchill's, Bustonaby's or Keen's Chop House.

["The Skirt" incidentally, was Hattie (Mrs. Sime) Silverman, wife of the paper's publisher. She did a unique gossip and fashion column. It was true journalistic pioneering for the present-day Hoppers and Parsons, not to mention the general Broadway-Hollywood chatter. Done with an "inside stuff" outlook, The Skirt's nod on who was "the best dressed woman" of the week, whether at the Palace, in musical comedy or one of the lobster palaces, was a sort of sartorial Oscar.]

Broadway's side streets were brightened by singing waiters, resurrected from the old Paris cafe and Western saloon idea. Working for "throw money," the take was divided—or was supposed to be—evenly among entertainers and musicians at the end of the night. But more than one ingenious, tray-toting ballad singer hit upon the idea of surreptitiously collecting donations at the tables, and soundproofing his pants pockets with sawdust to allay the suspicions of his comrades. (Today most nightclub hat-check girls wear costumes without pockets.)

Actors went in for smoking saxophone-sized kalabash pipes and driving elongated automobiles. Martin Beck was arrested for speeding 18 miles an hour within New York City's limits in 1907. Daredevil actor Sidney Grant took a 300-mile auto trip, and was widely acclaimed as a pioneer, despite skeptics who refused to credit the news.

When burlesque producer Al Reeves bought a new car in 1912, Variety although obviously impressed, wrote facetiously: "Have you seen it? It passed up Longacre Square Tuesday. Even the baseball fans were hushed in awe. It's a limousine built along the general lines of a Queen Anne cottage, with latticed windows and everything flossy except a tennis court in the front yard. It anchored in front of the Columbia Theatre about noon and was surrounded by a crowd all day."

Some years later Carter De Haven and Flora Parker went Reeves one better by fixing up their car as a cottage on wheels, with windows bearing flower boxes and grass mats on the running boards. Tab show owner A. B. Marcus made heads turn about this time with his black-and-white checkerboard car.

Managers, too, went in for fancy baubles, comparable to the actresses with their flashy clothes. Big yellow diamonds were usually associated with the come-lately-just-struck-it-rich impresario. Besides, the "ice" was always hockable. Al Woods, for many generations the prime exponent of melodrama on Broadway, was particularly partial to a lurid "headlight" in his tie. Once, on a late and lonely night, in a Times Square side-street, he suspected two loiterers were about to waylay him. The resourceful Woods, instead of hastening his gait, approached them directly and offered to sell them the diamond "for a couple of bucks; I got no place to sleep." The potential foodpads chased him away as a phoney with a phoney diamond who would rook them for two or three dollars. Sid Grauman, the great California showman and impresario, recounted shortly before his death in March 1950, how he, too, thought a couple of guys on the Sunset Strip might have waylaid him. Thinking fast, Grauman turned up his collar, pulled his hat down, hunched over rather pathetically, put copies of the Los Angeles *Examiner* and *Times* under his arm, and pretended to be a newspaper hawker, and thus outwitted the suspicious characters.

Show people were in the forefront of the new interest in aviation. As early as 1906, Fields and Wooley—not W. C. Fields—were playing a comedy act in a prop airship. Houdini, in England, was winning headlines by jumping out of airplanes. Ralph Johnstone, a bike rider in vaudeville, held the altitude record of 7,303 feet in a Wright plane when he was killed in an air accident in 1910.

Stunt man Claude Graham-White collected $29,500 for 12 days' flying, all cash prizes in a Boston air meet, after which Keith booked him to appear at popular prices for one afternoon, flying a Bleriot monoplane and Franum biplane over Squantum Field. Grahame-White's *pièce de résistance* was shutting off his motor at 1,000 feet and gliding to earth. Grahame-White in later years married vaudeville headliner Ethel Levey, ex-wife of George M. Cohan.

inflaming nontipping actors   Theatre fires were a persistent, dreaded tragedy. One of the worst blazes occurred in 1908 when the Rhodes Theatre at Boyerton, Pennsylvania, burned to the ground with 169 patrons killed in the tragedy. Stricter fire laws followed, giving birth to a juicy new racket.

In some cities, especially Chicago, after the Iroquois Theatre fire, in 1903 the fire inspector would test an act's curtain drop by applying a blowtorch. No curtain of that, or this day, could be *that* fire-resistant. Stagehands, who were more than nodding acquaintances of the inspector, would then blandly offer to "fireproof" the drop with some salt solution—for a consideration. The helpless act either paid this blackmail, or was not allowed to use the drop.

Stagehands also had interesting ways of enforcing their unwritten law of the footlights that actors must tip them. When actors didn't —and many could scarcely afford to—sandbags had a habit of falling down from the flies, scoring near-misses; trunks were broken; and everything somehow went wrong with the act, especially if it used stage props.

When a nontipping act left for its next booking, its trunks were marked with some mysterious chalk cipher—in the fashion of hobo code—which passed the word on to the stagehands in the next town.

Percy Williams tried to stop the practice by raising the salaries of stagehands in all his theatres. But even this couldn't smash a tradition so firmly entrenched that it exists to this day.

Another lucrative racket of the 1906 era was ticket speculation. Dozens of parasites operated openly in front of theatres with hit shows. Hammerstein's finally put up a sign warning the public that tickets bought from speculators would not be honored at the door. Another producer hit upon the idea of sealing tickets in special envelopes as they were sold at the box office. To be valid, tickets had to be presented at the door in unopened envelopes.

These noble efforts to combat the evils of speculation received due and laudable publicity—which is what Hammerstein and the other producers were after. It is true that they sincerely wished to eliminate these unauthorized middlemen. But not because they wished to protect the public from being fleeced. It was purely a question of *who* would fleece the public—and the showmen saw no reason to let outsiders cut in on this racket. So they put their own "authorized" speculators out front. One of them, working with Willie Hammerstein, became famous later on. His name was Morris Gest, later the producer of such Broadway successes as *The Miracle* and *Chauve-Souris*.

Ticket speculators, and "ice" to b.o. treasurers, came to more heinous spotlighting in 1920, and even more so in 1949, when dozens of ticket brokers lost their licenses and a more stringent system for policing the scalpers was established. Shows like *South Pacific, Kiss Me Kate, Detective Story* and *Mister Roberts* caused New York's Commissioner of Investigations John M. Murtagh to summon the big and small Broadway managers, box office men and ticket agents to City Hall for probing. It resulted in a stricter code being set up. It also caused Oscar Hammerstein 2d and Richard Rodgers, the co-authors and co-producers of *South Pacific,* to express themselves that "the show just isn't that good, that everybody must want to see it at one and the same time and pay such fantastic premiums for a pair of $6 tickets." (They were getting $40 to $60 a pair, and sometimes more.)

South Pacific soon became a symbol of the problems attendant to seeing a hit. Cracks like "it was easier for the GIs to take the South Pacific than to get into *South Pacific*" were typical. A pal of Hammerstein's phoned, "Ockie, I just must get a pair for your show for my wedding night." Hammerstein assured his friend, "Of course, for such a sentimental occasion I'll see that you get my or Dick's or Pinza's or Mary Martin's house seats. Don't worry. When is the anniversary?" "You don't understand," said the pal, "When you get me a pair for *South Pacific* that's the night I'll get married!"

(Incidentally, the usage of the term "ice" to box office men revived the derivation of the euphonism. It stems from political funds for "Incidental Campaign Expenses.")

blue laws   The churches of America, hard hit by the growing competition of the theatre, made sure that most of 1905-1913 was blanketed under Sunday Concert, or blue, laws. These laws allowed singing or reciting, but no sketches, dancing, acrobatics or vaudeville which "reflected upon the sanctity of the day of rest." In most cities, however, a very lax interpretation of these laws was customary.

In New York, for example, much depended upon the extent of grease in the palms of police captains and inspectors. At the Olympia on 14th St., formerly the old Tony Pastor's, Sunday acts were strictly bound by all the taboos, including a ban on the use of makeup. Across the street at the Dewey Theatre, partly owned by one of New York's politicos, "Big Tim" Sullivan, the Sunday show was no different from the weekday version. The blue laws were a gravy train which no reformers' blasts could shake for more than a few weeks during which graft was suspended—but not ended.

In 1907 New York's Mayor George B. McClellan decided to order strict enforcement of the laws. All theatres promptly closed in protest. Restaurants were crowded, streets overflowed with New Yorkers who had no place to go. Broadway itself was deserted. After a few weeks of this, blistering public protest forced Mayor McClellan to call off his dogs. Producer Percy Williams sued the city to win greater freedom under the Sunday Concert laws. To Broadway's jubilation, the State Supreme Court gave him the verdict.

Another fighter against blue Sundays was a Yonkers theatre manager, Henry Meyers, who unfurled his banners by giving free Sunday performances. The program included a 40-minute monolog by manager Meyers on the inalienable rights of American citizens, which evoked tumultuous applause from the cuffo customers.

Indianapolis outwitted its Sunday laws, and slyly cut the ground from beneath church opposition, by admitting patrons "free." The managers guarded the exits with men carrying baskets, "soliciting" money for charity benefits as the audience filed out.

What clergyman could argue with that?

2

Absolutely Free—One Baby!

★

A producer might slap his wife around, bash his infant son on the skull, or gouge his best friend's eyes, but never would he risk the blow to his reputation of "bad showmanship." Actually, there weren't any bad showmen—not for long, anyhow.

Willie Hammerstein scored a triumph of 1907 showmanship when he arranged for the arrest of Gertrude Hoffman, who was writhing a mild form of the eternal Salomé for him. The judge helped the Hammerstein box office considerably by warning the dancer to wear ankle-length tights, and appointing a matron to examine her costumes at every show.

In 1909 Martin Beck installed 15-piece orchestras in all the Orpheum theatres on his vaudeville circuit to dignify his bills with a very classy overture. He also gave his pitmen strict orders not to stop playing in the middle of the exit march, while people were still in the theatre. Aware of the disenchantment of plodding through a silent, empty house, he commanded, "Play the last person out!"

Marcus Loew put a picture of himself on chewing gum wrappers, with a guarantee to jaw-waggers of its 5¢ rebate value at any Loew house. To sell more intermission lemonade, he lured 1911 audiences to the rear of his American Roof Theatre with luxurious gardens, complete with potted plants, running vines, a bamboo arbor, and a wooden deck for a view of the Hudson River and New Jersey. All that, and vaudeville too, at a popular price scale of 25¢-50¢-75¢! Today Radio City and the Empire State Building collect 70¢-$1.20 for the skyline view alone.

One small-time theatre showman cooked up a sensational scheme to bolster flabby Monday night business. On that night, he advertised, the theatre would give away—absolutely free—one baby. His publicity man saw to it that the police were properly agitated. When they rushed to the theatre to prevent this sacrilege, the manager baffled them by explaining that it was perfectly all right—"the mother doesn't object." The house was packed on Monday. And the showman lived up to his promise by giving away a baby pig!

how giveaways started   A minor skirmish of showmanship took place between entrepreneurs Percy Williams and F. F. Proctor in 1905. Proctor introduced the first intermission in a popular-priced New York City vaudeville theatre at his 58th Street showplace, lending an air of distinction to his bills. Actually, it served as a "chaser" to clear the house of patrons sitting through two shows, and helped boost candy sales in the lobby. Proctor also gave away dolls to girls at matinees, and ash trays to men on Monday nights. (Since then popcorn and candy sales have become more of a profit item to some theatres than the basic show, reaching the degree that film distributors demanded, but never got, a percentage of the side-income, arguing, not without some justification, that since the pictures stimulated the sale of cokes, chocolate bars and popcorn, they were entitled to a pro rata. Chains like National Theatres, comprising Fox-West Coast Theatres and other regional subdivisions in the Rocky Mountain and midwest areas, according to Charles P. Skouras, president of the giant circuit of cinemas, have made profits into the millions from popcorn and the like.)

When Williams opened his Colonial Theatre on Broadway at 63d Street, he borrowed the intermission idea. But he added a million-dollar touch by serving tea to the audience during that intermission. Thereupon Proctor promptly surpassed that by also having the tea served—by "genuine Geisha girls!"

Hurtig & Seamon combined vaudeville and delicatessen in 1907. The audience was handed neatly printed cards advising that a lunch counter in the rear of the Metropolis Roof would serve pigs knuckles, cold jelly and potato salad for a quarter. There was a 20-minute intermission as theatregoers satisfied the inner man to the lively serenade of Joe Ali and his musicians.

Klaw & Erlanger foreshadowed the elaborate lobbies of the Roxy and Radio City Music Hall that same year when they decorated their New York Theatre with fine sculpture and paintings they had borrowed from the Augustin Daly collection. E. F. Albee later copied the idea for his de luxe showplaces, such as the Palace in Cleveland, Keith's Memorial in Boston, and the Albee Theatre, in Brooklyn. He fancied himself an art connoisseur but was taken in for plenty.

Manager Max Faetkenheur, of the Cleveland Hippodrome, introduced special "automobile boxes" in 1907 for the convenience of patrons who stopped in from auto trips, dressed in touring clothes—goggles, caps, veils, gloves and dusters. The boxes allowed them to see the stage without the embarrassment of being on exhibit to the audience.

The manager of New York's Dewey Theatre made a shrewd bid for summer business in 1908. He advertised proudly that there were fully 25—count 'em—electric fans inside his theatre, making it the coolest show in the city.

Adolph Marks set a record of personal exploitation in 1908 when John J. Murdock opened his Olympia Music Hall in Chicago. Marks sent flowers for the lobby—flowers which made *his* name dwarf every offering beside it. His gift was a vast flower bed, fully 32 feet long and 3 feet wide, in the vein of the floral extravagances of the Cicero gangsters.

the most fabulous hammerstein   If E. F. Albee owned the body of vaudeville, Willie Hammerstein owned its heart and soul. No showman better exemplified the times than the father of Oscar Hammerstein 2d. With the passing of Tony Pastor, living symbol of vaudeville of his era, the two-a-day took its color from Willie Hammerstein until World War I.

Hammerstein's Victoria was built by Willie's equally famous father, Oscar I, on the world's busiest corner, Broadway and 42d Street. It became the greatest, most colorful vaudeville theatre to thrive under the administrations of McKinley, Roosevelt, Taft and Wilson. It finally shut down in 1915, after 17 booming years under the shrewd management of Willie. The Victoria grossed over $20,000,000, earning Hammerstein a clear profit of $5,000,000.

No manager of his time, before or after, ever won the headlines that Willie Hammerstein inspired with his lively showmanship. The lobby of the Victoria, where he sat in a crooked chair surrounded by his cronies—actors, press agents, playwrights, managers, wine salesmen, vaudeville agents, bookers, gamblers and screwballs—was his only office. Price of admission to this golden circle was a talent for being funny or "interesting." Tales of the Hammerstein clique are Broadway legend.

It was Willie who inaugurated the "freak" act in vaudeville. He booked all the prominent fighters, wrestlers, bicycle and running champions. He played the killers and near-killers. When two attractive girls, Lillian Graham and Ethel Conrad, placed bullets in the leg of W. E. D. Stokes, a social registerite, Hammerstein went their bail. While the case was still coining lurid headlines, he billed the ladies at the Victoria as "The Shooting Stars." Their inability to sing, dance or act being highly immaterial, they packed the house to the rafters. Asked what he thought of the ladies' act, noted monologist James Thornton opined, "They'll have to *kill* someone to get another week."

So many lady sharpshooters took their bow at Hammerstein's that every pawnshop gun sold to a woman practically carried the guarantee of a week's booking. Outstanding pistol-packin' mamas who played the Victoria were Nan Patterson, who received a $500 booking after wounding her boy friend, and Florence Carman, wife of a Long Island doctor, who shot one of her husband's femme patients at the lady's home. Florence's contribution to show business was a touching rendition of the song, "Baby Shoes."

the cherry sisters   Then there were the Cherry Sisters whom Willie billed at Hammerstein's as "America's Worst Act," spreading a net in front of the stage to catch the vegetables and hen fruit tossed from the audience. It's a show biz tradition to this day to term a nadir act "a road company of the Cherry Sisters."

(Some years later, when the Hearst columnist, Arthur (Bugs) Baer, essayed a vaudeville flyer, he wired his pals at the Friars Club, from Cleveland: "Opened today. I didn't know the Cherry Sisters had a brother.")

There was Lady Francis Hope, née May Yohe, who was once booked into the New York Theatre to sing a few songs and show the famous $100,000 Hope diamond. Willie hired her for $1,500 a week, providing her husband, Lord Francis Hope, would just stand in the lobby of Hammerstein's and pose. Years later, when bad times befell her, and there was no Hope (via the divorce court),

Willie booked her as plain May Yohe at $75 a week. In more recent times, Evalyn Walsh MacLean, the late Washington, D. C. newspaper publisher, owned the Hope diamond.

from dr. cook to phoney dancers   In the grotesque gallery of Hammerstein celebrities there were even polar explorers like the famous Dr. Cook, who delivered a discourse for Willie twice a day at $1,000 a week. He found the North Pole much warmer than the critical Victoria audience, which also chilled Bessie De-Voie, a lady in the headlines through her collection of love letters from multimillionaire Frank Gould.

"Countess" Swirsky jammed in the customers for Willie with a "classical" dance at $750 a week that had them guffawing derisively. The sensation for one entire summer was "Shekla, the Court Magician to the Shah of Persia." He was a Hindu whom Willie had found playing in a small London music hall. He conceived the idea of a new hoax and dispatched Morris Gest to Europe. Gest dressed him à la a titled Persian—at the least the Willie Hammerstein idea of Damascus nobility—hired a retinue of "native" servants who were more indigenous to the Soho, Whitechapel and Limehouse of London than the Dardanelles, and brought him across the Atlantic with a hoopla reception for benefit chiefly of the ship news reporters.

There was a "farewell" appearance for Carmencita, dancing idol of the gay blades of 1894. This was one of Hammerstein's most remarkable tours des force, inasmuch as Carmencita had been dead for six years when she appeared at the Victoria. It was, of course, an impostor who had been an obscure chorus girl next door at the Belasco only a few months before. Willie sent her to Europe, and arranged for cables back home to report her glowing "success." Then he re-imported her for the Victoria, and her reappearance made headlines. Dead or alive, if you were a great name you played Hammerstein's.

His flair for sensationalism—ably abetted by such fertile press agents as Abe Levy, Ann Marble, Nellie Revell, John Pollock, Joe Flynn and the ubiquitous Morris Gest—assured loyal patrons of Hammerstein's Victoria that they need not leave their seats for a closeup of every headline and trend of the period. In truth, any Hammerstein bill was practically a living newspaper of the more sensational news items.

When the Apache craze swept across the Atlantic, its first appearance was at Hammerstein's. After Will Rock had hurled Maude Fulton—later to click as a playwright—from stage pillar to post, audiences shrilly protested this shockingly unchivalrous demonstration. But they came back to shudder some more. Rock and Fulton, incidentally, had been rushed into the Victoria to beat the French originators to the American market.

A choice morsel of forbidden fruit was Hammerstein's booking of an excommunicated minister, the Rev. Alexander Irvine, in a sketch called "The Rector of St. Judes." It contained two "hells," one "damn," and a generous dose of socialist propaganda for good measure.

One of Hammerstein's biggest successes was Gertrude Hoffman, whom he persuaded to try the inevitable Salomé. He sent her to London to study Maude Allen's gyrations in the role at the Palace Music Hall. Upon her return, Miss Hoffman faced the objection of Willie's father: "But I've just engaged Mary Garden to sing Salomé at my opera house. We can't have *two* Hammerstein Salomés!"

Once the carriage trade had its fill of the polite version, however, Miss Hoffman was permitted to appear at the Victoria in "A Vision of Salomé." It was also a vision at the box office—22 solid weeks, a record run. If, as the late Channing Pollock once declared, Willie built Hammerstein's into an institution, he made quite sure that it wasn't an institution for the blind.

evelyn nesbit top b.o.　　　The greatest Hammerstein money-maker of all was ex-chorine Evelyn Nesbit, whose playboy husband Harry K. Thaw murdered architect Stanford White to "protect the purity of the wives and the homes of America," it says here. The murder occurred atop the old Madison Square Roof Garden at a performance of *Mlle. Champagne,* a very weak vintage distilled by Edgar Allen Woolf. Woolf's mother happened to be present the night that Thaw ventilated White. She made a quite natural assumption and cried, "My God—they've shot my son!"

As a result of the sensational publicity, Evelyn Nesbit was too hot for even Willie Hammerstein to touch immediately, so he sent her to Europe to cool off. When he finally brought her back to the Victoria, an incredible publicity break accompanied her first week's appearance.

Harry Thaw, who had been committed to Matawan for insanity, escaped. Willie promptly saw to it, of course, that Evelyn "feared for her life." He won a uniformed detail of police to guard her day and night, and the dancer became the most talked-about woman of 1913. Willie was uncharitably accused by envious rivals of having actually engineered Thaw's coincidental escape.

F. F. Proctor tried to steal some of Hammerstein's thunder by dickering with the owner of the escape car to exhibit the Packard at his Fifth Avenue Theatre. But the owner would not even allow the car to be photographed without cash being laid on the line. Miss Nesbit earned $3,500 a week, and Hammerstein made an $80,000 profit on her 8-week engagement, despite the star's petulant insistence that he change her billing from "Mrs. Thaw" to her maiden name.

Often mixed in with the man with the 17-foot beard, cows and beautiful milkmaids, armless and legless freaks and other miscellany that trod the boards at the Victoria was really fine talent which might have blossomed unseen but for the shrewd eye of Willie. One of these was a dancer named Radha, who was a $750 a week flop at Proctor's 23d Street. Hammerstein hired her a few years after that appearance, put his publicity battery to work for her, and paid her $2,000 a week for doing almost the same dance at the Victoria. She became one of America's greatest exponents of the dance—as Ruth St. Denis.

harems, giants and suffragettes   Hammerstein was at his best when perpetrating a gigantic fraud. The case of Abdul Kadar, Court Artist of the Turkish Sultan, and his three wives, was classic. Abdul was the inspiration of Willie at a time when Turkey was in the limelight with rumors of a Turkish revolution. Morris Gest was dispatched to Europe with orders to get a Turk with three wives, or reasonable facsimile. At a small variety house in Lucerne, Switzerland, Gest saw an artist named Adolph Schneider who did quick oil sketches on the stage. Schneider, Gest discovered with delight, was traveling with his wife, daughter and sister-in-law. A deal was quickly consummated. Gest took Abdul Kadar (nee Schneider) and his three "wives" to Adrianople to be outfitted with a Turkish wardrobe, vocabulary and demeanor. En route to New York with his harem, the Court Artist of the Turkish Sultan played in Paris and created a sensation. The imminence of their visit to New York was cabled, winning headlines.

On board ship, when passengers asked them any questions, Abdul and his wives would sink to their knees and pray to Allah. It made quite an impression, and spared them any possible slip in answering. Willie Hammerstein helped stir up more news by complaining to the immigration authorities under an assumed name. Abdul and his wives were detained at Ellis Island, while the official status of the wives was determined in Washington.

Willie finally put up a bond guaranteeing that the Turks would leave our shores in good time, without becoming a burden on the taxpayers, and sent them to the Waldorf-Astoria, where he made sure they would be refused accommodations. Reporters and photographers trailed the troupe around, with their 40 pieces of baggage, from one big hotel to another, as all refused to allow the Turk with three wives to sign the register.

Willie finally permitted Abdul and his harem to retire to the furnished apartment, which he had for them all the time.

When "the Court Artist" finally appeared at Hammerstein's, his three "wives" accompanied him on the stage, doing nothing except remove the sketches when they were finished. Little Adolph Schneider, his wife, daughter and sister-in-law were a sensation for many weeks, after which they bought a home in Atlantic City, and lived there for many years on the profits earned during their engagement by the amazing Willie.

Anything in the public eye was grist for the Hammerstein mill. In 1912 he put his shoulder enthusiastically to the wheel of woman suffrage. Setting aside a Woman's Suffragette Week at the Victoria, he allowed speeches to be made outside the theatre. Buttons and flowers were peddled for the cause to the audience. Onstage, Fola La Follette, daughter of the famous Wisconsin senator, spoke for 15 minutes with one hundred women in white dresses standing behind her. Willie gave them an impressive orchestral entrance to the tune of "Battle Cry of Freedom." The box office suffered badly that week, but Willie didn't care. He'd won another publicity bonanza.

Possibly nothing characterized Willie Hammerstein better than two methods he used to exploit the public's gullibility during hot weather. To induce customers to cool off in his theatre, he placed a thermometer in his lobby which supposedly indicated the interior temperature—except that it rested upon an exposed cake of solid ice. A blackboard recorded 70° on the hottest day and, to convince any skeptics, the message: "If you don't believe it—look at the thermometer!"

Then when convinced customers entered the elevator that took them up to the roof garden, they became acutely conscious of the sweltering weather. Willie ingeniously heated the elevator, so that when it finally dumped the customers out on the roof, the perspiring customers imagined that it *was* cooler up there.

hammerstein the first   Any Hammerstein saga would be fragmentary without at least a bare mention of the equally astonishing exploits of the senior Hammerstein, Oscar I, who made theatrical history with a deskless office, a bookless bookkeeper, a reversible plug hat, a gold-headed cane, a big cigar and a Van Dyke beard. Oscar I was the kind of man who would bet $100 that he could write a complete opera in 24 hours. He did exactly that, producing *The Kohinoor Diamond* with his own words and music. It flopped with a sickening, expensive thud—but Oscar proudly collected his $100.

The first American Hammerstein emigrated from Berlin at the age of fifteen to become first a cigar-maker, then the nation's greatest impresario of grand opera. Oscar I built the Harlem Opera House, the Columbia, the Manhattan Opera House, the Olympia, the Belasco (now the Republic)—the present Belasco on West 44th Street, opened many years later—the Victoria, and opera houses in Philadelphia, Chicago, Boston and London. Yet frequently Willie had to shove a $5 bill into the empty pocket of his father, to whom making money was a pastime; handling it a nuisance.

In 1910 the elder Hammerstein inaugurated a 24-act vaudeville show at the Manhattan Opera House, the first and only three-ring vaudeville bill. There were three "dumb" (nontalking) acts performing at the same time—a cycling turn, a cartoonist and wire-walking act. The show lasted from 7:30 to 11:50 P.M., when a film closed the bill. A stunned audience, groaning with headache, eye-ache and festive indigestion, turned thumbs-down.

Oscar Hammerstein's Olympia, later known as the New York Theatre, was the talk of the town when the great showman first unveiled it. For a 50¢ admission, he gave New Yorkers a combination theatre, music hall, roof garden, Oriental cafe, smoking room, billiard room and lounge.

But it was his son Willie who lingers longest, most fondly, in the memory of old-timers. Actors loved to play the "Corner," as they called the Victoria, which was to its heyday what the Palace later became to big-time vaudeville.

3

L Is for Lauder

★

In 1905 Bill (Bojangles) Robinson was teamed with an actor named Cooper in a comedy, song and dance routine called "Looking for Hannah." Willie and Eugene Howard withdrew two-thirds of the assets from an act named "The Messenger Boy Trio," and began their career that lasted more than a third of a century. Leo Carrillo, self-styled "Only Chinese Dialect Comedian," further demonstrated his dexterity by drawing cartoons for Variety on backstage politics. His views, and Variety's, were typified in a cartoon showing Eliza (vaudeville actors) pursued across the ice by bloodhounds (vaudeville managers). As a sideline Carillo drew sketches of actors' specialties, a crude type of proof against any imitators. He also sketched lobby displays.

Buster Keaton, spotted by Variety as a coming headliner, was part of The Three Keatons. New York's Gerry Society, which kept children under 16 off the stage, didn't know Keaton was a minor when he appeared at Proctor's 23d Street in 1905. Four years later he thumbed his nose at them with an ad in Variety: "Today I Am a Theatrical Man—Goodbye, Mr. Gerry!"

Charlie Chaplin, fresh from England as a minor comedian with a troupe who played "A Night In a Music Hall," was another budding talent for whom Variety signified a bright future. By 1910

Chaplin was chief comic in an act called "Karno's Wow Wows" at the Colonial.

Yet in 1913, when Alf Reeves sent Variety a photo of the cast in his Karno's Company, he didn't bother to identify Chaplin in the accompanying credits. Two years later Chaplin was the idol of the nation.

the astaires and jolson   Fred Astaire and his sister, Adele, barred from the New York stage because they were under-age, were kid hoofers out west in 1906 vaudeville, billed as "Juvenile Artists, presenting an electric (sic) musical toe dancing novelty." Jesse Lasky, who once trod the boards in a blackface cornet act with his sister, was a Chicago manager that year for William Morris.

When Al Jolson, up-and-coming, appeared at the Fifth Avenue Theatre (N.Y.) in 1909, Variety's reviewer, *Sime,* was surprised into reporting, "Haven't seen a demonstration for a single act, or any act for that matter, as was given Al Jolson."

After the mammy singer rejoined Lew Dockstader's Minstrels, he was next to closing in the olio of the show, wearing evening clothes which Variety noted as "taupe shade." This spot was formerly reserved for Dockstader himself, but the minstrel veteran yielded because the ovation for Jolson was so tremendous that nobody could follow him.

Jolson's star rose so rapidly that by 1912 he was giving those famous Sunday-night performances for show people at New York's Winter Garden. Called upon from the audience, he would take off his collar and tie onstage, declare, "This is just like playing pinochle," and hold his audiences with song and patter for a full hour.

The Shuberts paid him a bonus of $10,000 in 1913 to sign with them for seven years. He had started with them at $250 a week, was getting $1,000 a week and a 35-week-per-year guarantee, and at the expiration of his new contract, in 1920, would be earning $2,000 a week. And to prove his growing drawing power, when *Honeymoon Express* closed in 1913, he signed for a week at the Brighton Theatre for—and the Shuberts groaned—$2,500 a week!

Almost 40 years later, a kid named Larry Parks "brought Jolson back" in the Columbia film, *The Jolson Story,* which revived a wave of songs Jolson sang to fame.

w. c. fields, cantor, brice   The late W. C. Fields, who had been tossing Indian clubs in London, announced his return to America in 1909 in a Variety ad that had a black-mourning border. He was so highly regarded in show business that the great Sarah Bernhardt, whose 1912 contract with Martin Beck stipulated no animal acts or acrobats would be allowed on the bill with her, also honored Fields by making him the first and only juggler she ever permitted to appear on the same bill with her. The great Bernhardt played with him at the Palace in 1913, Fields coming on in the third spot.

Eddie Cantor, in 1910, was an unknown stooging a comedy bit for Bedini & Arthur in a burlesque of *Madame X* called "Madame 10" at Hammerstein's. His first ad appeared in Variety in 1912, to announce " 'The Kid Kabaret,' with Eddie Cantor."

Fanny Brice, fresh from burlesque, became an overnight sensation with her songs, "Lovie Joe" and "Grizzly Bear," in the *Ziegfeld Follies of 1910*. Leon Errol was bruising Stella Chatelaine in a rag dance with the "Jersey Lillies" Burlesque Company. Irving Berlin appeared in a Boston show called *Up and Down Broadway*. When Klaw & Erlanger featured Edna Wallace Hopper in Philadelphia, a printed slip in the program gave hasty added credit to her pianist for the songs she sang. His name was Jerome D. Kern.

In 1912 The (Three) Marx Brothers were doing an act with 19 actors in the cast, called "Mister Green's Reception." That year Variety featured an ad by Salisbury & Benny, the latter half of the act billing himself later that year as "Ben Benny, the Fiddlin' Kid." His fiddle is still serving him in good stead, but meantime he had changed the name to Jack Benny in order not to be confused with Ben Bernie.

Boston authorities, looking around for something to forbid in 1912, selected an actress in the Shubert play, *The Never Homes*. Reason: she was under age. Her name was Helen Hayes.

mae west's redolent s.a.   Another lady singled out for attention in 1912 was an actress playing the Model Theatre in Philadelphia. The ad plugging her act read: "She does a muscle dance in a sitting position. It is all in the way she does it, and her way is all her own." The performer sang a song called "Rag Rag

Rag," and would accompany it with some interesting movements while seated in a chair.

Her name was Mae West. She was a sensation even then. In 1912 she was getting into the public eye and making it blink. When she appeared with the Vera Violette show in New Haven, the Yale undergraduates attempted to tear down the house. And not from rage.

Sime reviewed her act when she went on alone at Hammerstein's. "There's enough of the act just now to pass," he suggested, "if Miss West can be taught how to 'get' an audience. (Sic!) She's one of the many freak persons on the vaudeville stage where freakishness often carries more weight than talent, but Miss West should be coached to deliver the full value of her personality."

Mae might have misinterpreted those last few words of *Variety's* advice. When she appeared later at the American Roof with the Gerard Boys, she wore a trick dress with a strap that broke easily, delivering the full value of her personality. The manager of the Roof would yell, "Don't you realize I've got a family audience?" Mae would calmly shrug and insist she couldn't help it when her strap broke. Variety summed up the matter gently by declaring, "The gal was always making a dress adjustment."

leonard, dressler, guinan, tanguay   Before Bing Crosby thought of tricking lyrics with "buh-buh-buh-boo," minstrel-man Eddie Leonard was panicking audiences as early as 1891 with a "wah-wah" style of singing—"One morn-orn-ing whan-an the morn-orning wahah break-ahn-ing. . . ." Like Jolson, whose style was not entirely uninfluenced by Leonard, he was told by his minstrel boss to cut it out because it "sounded foolish."

But Leonard was still stopping the show with it well after the turn of the century. When he took endless encores in "Roly Boly Eyes," telling the patrons, "Eddie is shoh glad to still be with you," Variety's Jack Lait chided him as "the Chinese philosopher—On Too Long, Bow Too Long."

Marie Dressler, later to win world renown with Wallace Beery in *Min and Bill* and *Tugboat Annie* roles on the screen, was already one of the few actresses of the time with both a great reputation and social standing. She was the guest of Mrs. Woodrow Wilson at the summer White House in 1913, and the President's family accepted an invitation to the Dressler villa. "Miss Dressler," commented Variety, "has a big society following."

Texas Guinan, firebrand hostess of the Golden 20s, first came to the attention of her "suckers" in 1908 when she was featured in an act called "The Gibson Girl," in which she displayed her figure and dispensed a song or two. The following year she inaugurated the stunt of singing from a basket over the audience, rhapsodizing such noble lyric sentiments as "Pansies Bring Thoughts of You." By 1913 she was one of the stars of *The Passing Show*. Her ads in Variety offered her own "Marvelous New Treatment for Fat Folks." A picture of herself in dazzling costume was captioned, "God's Masterpiece and the Most Fascinating Actress in America." Miss Guinan testified: "Mr. Shubert, on account of my glorious new figure, made me the star of *The Passing Show*—and mind you, this very same manager had said I was doomed to oblivion just a short time before when I tipped the scales at 204 pounds. . . ." In 1913 the Post Office prosecuted the promoter of the fat reducer to which Texas had lent her name.

Eva Tanguay, the Betty Hutton of her time, electrified audiences with the spectacle of a very beautiful, talented singer, clowning hoydenishly, showing her legs and ridiculing herself. Her salary shot from $250 to $2,500 a week as she sang herself to fame with numbers written specially for her—"Give An Imitation of Eva," "I Can't Help It," "Egotistical Eva," "Whistle and Help Me Along," (all Blanche Merrill songs) and her most famous hit, "I Don't Care."

(Miss Tanguay once risked her reputation by singing on Loew's National Theatre's amateur night in 1910, under the pseudonym, Lillian Doom. She was a great hit, incognito. Bert Williams, who tried the same stunt, failed dismally. Similarly, Gloria Swanson, at the height of her screen career, flunked a screen test, dressed in a blonde wig. Other stars like George M. Cohan and Willie Collier risked amateur night appearances, as a favor to Joe Schenck, then g.m. of Loew's Theatres—but *not* incognito. Will Mahoney essayed it at the Regent, but under an assumed name, was recognized generally by the audience, and did a solid half-hour act.)

In 1913 Miss Tanguay told Variety readers, "Our season with cyclonic vaudeville has commenced wonderfully well on the road, and from what I hear that is the place to be in vaudeville just now.

Inside information—the way to attract business is to have an attraction." This was by way of reprisal to the United Booking Office, which refused to pay her the $3,000 she asked. Miss Tanguay earned *more* than she had asked by touring with her own road show.

Among the great actresses of the time who oscillated between America and the Continent was "The Divine Sarah," Sarah Bernhardt. In 1911, when she concluded her second "farewell tour" of the United States, after five years' absence, her 284 performances in legit netted her $1,000,000. In 1912, opening at Chicago's Majestic Theatre for Martin Beck, the first week's gross was $25,000 and speculators were selling $1 seats for $3.

Back again in 1913, she opened in New York at the Palace, which raised its prices to $1.50 and $2. Many show people consider that it was this engagement—on May 9—which "put the Palace on the map." Earlier that year Bernhardt was in a slight auto accident in California while en route to the theatre. The Los Angeles Times carried a report to the effect that, when rescued by another car, she rode in the lap of a strange man, "and she enjoyed it."

The outraged Sarah took a huge ad in Variety, a replica of bills she ordered posted all over Los Angeles, which read: "OPEN LETTER to the Public. An article appeared Thursday morning . . . entitled, 'And She Enjoyed It,' and is unsigned. But I hereby declare that it has been written by a Liar and a Coward. Sarah Bernhar't." The Orpheum people for whom she was playing hastily ordered all these bills posted over.

After her great contemporary, Lillian Russell, condescended to step down from legit to vaudeville in 1905, Variety caustically commented, "The former favorite 'has went' to Europe. Lillian didn't want to go especially, but the disappointment of 'falling down' in vaudeville was too much for the fair one to endure. On the other side, amid balmy lands, a little thing like that may be forgotten."

theatrical royalty   Lily Langtry (The Jersey Lily) started a tradition in 1907 when she asked the manager of her theatre to lay a carpet from her dressing room to the stage, to keep the hems of her dresses clean. The carpet happened to be red. Shortly afterward, Anna Held made the same demand. From then on managers had their hands full with temperamental stars who wouldn't leave their dressing rooms without this tribute to theatrical royalty. Thus derived the saying, "Roll out the red carpet."

Will Rogers was on the way up in 1906 when he became the added attraction for the "New York Stars Burlesque Co." Booked for Philadelphia, the company staged a parade of four horses, 10 men with banners announcing Rogers' appearance, and finally Will himself on horseback. Three hours later the theatre was sold out, a week in advance—or so he advertised in Variety.

When Rogers introduced his new act in 1911, he told his audience: "I've been getting away with this junk for so long that I thought you would get wise to me sooner or later, so I went and dug up a little new stuff with which to bunk you for a few more years." Variety summed up the new act in which the cowboy imitated Fred Stone by stating: "Rogers is a surprise when he starts dancing, and gets away with it big."

lauder's american invasion   Producer after producer tried to lure Harry Lauder away from England. Despite the fact that he was being paid much less, in 1907, the canny Scot singer declined an offer of $1,500 a week in vaudeville. He declared he could not afford to risk his future bookings abroad by the chance of a failure in America, where it was possible the people would not appreciate his peculiar style.

Lauder finally succumbed to the blandishments of booking agent Clifford C. Fischer of the H. B. Marinelli office, on behalf of Klaw & Erlanger, and signed for a short tour at $2,500 weekly. He appeared later for William Morris, who paid him $3,000, and his London managers an extra $1,000 "royalties," at the American Music Hall in New York City in 1908. The theatre was so packed that campstools were placed onstage behind him. Over 300 patrons paid $1.50 each to look at Lauder's back.

His tour of America, in his own roadshow under William Morris management, set new vaudeville records everywhere. Philadelphia paid $5,000 for two performances; Detroit, $6,000; Chicago, $18,000 for six shows; and in Toronto, Lauder played to a $7,200 house in one day. He refused to perform on Sundays, insisting that the audiences he played to were religious. In later years he did work on Sunday for war benefits.

So inspired was the Lauder name by 1911 that when he was late in getting through quarantine, in a return trip to America, one audience at the Manhattan Opera House waited until past midnight. Lauder showed up at 12:30 A.M. and entertained his patient admirers until 2:20 A.M.

Lauder was earning $4,000 a week in 1913, which he insisted be paid in three $1,000 bills, one $500 note and the rest in small currency. Yet, canny Scotsman though he was, his integrity was a thing of wonder. When he was ill that year, and compelled to miss a few performances, he returned $3,000 to William Morris, stating that this represented money he hadn't earned and didn't want.

Playing for Morris with his own vaudeville show at the Casino Theatre, New York, in 1913, Lauder went on to new and greater heights—grossing $23,000 in one week. Yet, odd as it seemed at the time, this most successful artist of the era had actually been hooted off the stage in Glasgow three years earlier by Scotsmen who disliked him personally. There was no special reason for this other than a local ornery attitude, possibly born of the fact that Lauder was tasting the richest fruits of life and the national economic temper was such that it resented his international acclaim.

english thrushes and france's chanteuse   This was also the heyday of English songbirds who warbled "smart" *double-entendre* songs and slightly suggestive parodies. Vesta Victoria was the rage until she was supplanted in popularity by Alice Lloyd in 1907. The songs that swept Miss Lloyd to fame were "Stockings On the Line," "Never Introduce Your Bloke to Your Lady Friend," and "Who You Lookin' At?"

A later foreign importation by the Shuberts for the Winter Garden was France's Irene Bordoni in 1912. Engaged as a singer, she was cast instead in a pantomime dance with Agoust, which Variety described as N.S.G. Many years later she became a vaudeville and musical comedy star.

Sophie Tucker, in later years to be billed as "The Last of The Red-Hot Mammas," was appearing in Pittsburgh with the "Gay Masqueraders," in 1908, after heeding Tony Pastor's advice to abandon blackface. Blossom Seeley, another "red hot mamma," was coon-shouting "Put Your Arms Around Me, Honey," telling Negro dialect stories, and lustily hoofing a new rag dance called "Doing the Todelo" out in San Francisco.

eltinge, cook, wynn, and savo   One of the most peculiar vaudeville sensations of 1907 was Julian Eltinge, the female
impersonator, whose Salomé was one of the best. "Eltinge's act is
extremely high class," opined Variety, "which probably accounts for
his popularity; and as a club and private entertainer he undoubtedly
plays more private shows than any other vaudevillian in America."

When Eltinge appeared with Harry Lauder in 1910, his applause
eclipsed that of the great Scot himself. He was a hit for years, easily
the No. 1 female impersonator. Eltinge also clicked in pictures. A
canny showman, he never took his bows by stripping his wig and
thanking his audience in a studied *basso profundo* voice. Eltinge
had long since been presold by a staged fight in a 42d St. and 9th
Avenue saloon when he "cleaned up the joint" because some drunk
made aspersions about female impersonators. Eltinge was one of the
few players whose name graced a Broadway legit theatre in his lifetime, along with Maxine Elliott, Ethel Barrymore, Al Jolson (now
the Century), or the deceased Arnold Daly and Richard Mansfield.
In the main, managerial names like Belasco, Woods, Harris, Cohan
(although he was an actor-manager), Erlanger, Cort, Shubert
adorned the marquees unless it was a neutral billing like the Globe,
Lyceum, or Majestic.

Joe Cook, Ed Wynn and Jimmy Savo were among the funny men
of the day who later became big musical comedy names. Cook advertised his vaudeville act in Variety, 1909: "Master of All Trades.
Introducing in a 15-minute act, juggling, unicycling, magic, hand
balancing, ragtime piano and violin playing, dancing, globe rolling,
wirewalking, talking and cartooning. Something original in each
line—SOME ENTERTAINMENT."

Jimmy Savo's ad, a year later, read: "SAVO—JUGGLER. Juggling
everything from a feather to an automobile." Ed Wynn, already a
name in vaudeville, came further into the limelight by stealing the
show from its star, Harry Kelly, in the 1910 production, *Deacon
and the Lady.*

call of the films in 1910   The movies were beginning to claim some of Broadway's favorites. Trixie Friganza and
Blanche Ring were among the vaudeville stars signed up by Cameraphone in 1908 to do their acts for the screen. In Newark, Clara
Mathes was presenting *Camille* as it had never been done before.

She used a Pathe film starring herself for the first two acts. Then the movie sheet went up, and she hurried onstage to finish dying in person.

Two of the best-liked male dancers of the period were Fred Stone and Pat Rooney. *Skigie* (Sid Silverman), the 9-year-old son of Variety's editor and publisher, reviewing Rooney's act "The New Bellboy" in 1907, recorded for posterity: "Nearly everyone in the show could dance, but I didn't care for any of them except Pat Rooney and his wife, Marion Bent. They are the best in the business, and Pat looks like a real bellboy, and he sticks his finger in the coffee pot and says, 'Is it hot enough?' "

The era saw the split-up of one famous comedy team, Weber & Fields, in 1906 (although later reunited abortively) and the union of another, Gallagher & Shean, in 1910. Basically burlesque comedians, Ed Gallagher and Al Shean were destined to split and reunite for their greatest success, singing Bryan Foy's "Mr. Gallagher & Mr. Shean" doggerel in the *Ziegfeld Follies*. Both are now dead, along with Joe Weber and Lew Fields. Al Shean, uncle of Groucho Marx and frères, was the last to go. When Weber & Fields went their separate ways, the New York *Sun's* dramatic critic, John Corbin, asked hollowly, "Is low comedy doomed?" Abbott & Costello and Martin & Lewis gave the answer in a future era.

Although eclipsed by the rising comet of vaudeville, the legitimate stage was still thriving and producing great theatrical figures. Between 1905 and 1913 Broadway audiences acclaimed such stars as Nazimova, Mrs. Fiske, John Drew, Richard Mansfield, John and Lionel Barrymore, Otis Skinner, Fay Templeton, Billie Burke, Ellen Terry, E. H. Sothern, Julia Marlowe, Ethel Barrymore, Maude Adams, George Arliss, Douglas Fairbanks, Maxine Elliott, DeWolf Hopper, Eddie Foy, Alice Brady, David Warfield, Willie Collier, Jane Cowl, Elsie Janis and Laurette Taylor.

1910 salaries—but untaxed!   Variety shed an interesting light on the financial aspects of stardom in 1910 when it published a list of the highest weekly salaries in show business. Gertrude Hoffman (with a big company) led the field with $3,000, followed by Eva Tanguay (alone) with $2,500. A hypnotist named J. Robert Pauline was high up with $2,000; Annette Kellerman (the 1910 version of Esther Williams and Eleanor Holm), Julian Eltinge,

Alice Lloyd and the Gus Edwards ("School Days") Song Revue drew $1,500 each.

Elbert Hubbard, after making a hit in vaudeville in Chicago, abruptly ended his vaudeville career in Cincinnati when a gallery heckler angered him into leaving the stage and going home for good. Hubbard was in the $1,250 bracket at the time, as was the movies' Fatty Arbuckle who faded into obscurity years later after an unfortunate mess of notoriety attendant to a morals charge. Lionel Barrymore reflected legitimate stage salaries with $850, and in the $500 category were Pat Rooney, Fred Niblo (later to become a famous movie director), James J. Morton and Joe Welch.

The year 1912 saw Albertina Rasch, later to dominate the ballet field of musical comedy, doing a vaudeville act with her girls called "Le Ballet Classique." At the Brighton Beach (N.Y.) Theatre a new act was stopped by the Gerry Society—"Eddie Foy and His 7 Little Foys." The Society finally gave the Foy children permission, and Eddie Foy continued to convulse audiences by gazing at the kids, then assuring the audience, "If I lived in Flatbush, it would be a *city*."

Two interesting ads appeared in the Variety of 1913. The first was a full-page ad by the great singing comedienne Irene Franklin and Burton Green, her pianist-husband. The ad consisted of nothing but their names in giant black type. What made it unusual was that they were the first to print these oversized calling cards on the front cover of Variety.

When Gertrude Hoffman's new show opened that year at the Lyric Theatre in Philadelphia, her ad was replete with the new slang of the day, referring to the girls in the show as "chickens," "squabs" and "broilers."

"The merry chirping of our chickens from the 'Gay White Way'," it said roguishly, "is in no way disturbed by the sad cackle of passé old hens." Which was by way of reprisal to those who considered Miss Hoffman's show rather fowl.

But it didn't lay an egg, either.

4

They Did It First

★

If there is nothing new under the sun, there is certainly nothing new in show business. The "innovations" of each era, including our own, are invariably derivations from a past heritage. What we term "new" is simply fresh mayonnaise on old potato salad.

Before the first radio commercial ever plagued an ear, the eyes of 1905 audiences were outraged by vaudeville curtains plastered with screaming ads. A huckster named Lee Lash painted these, collecting from advertisers, and giving the curtains free to theatre managers, who promised to exhibit them for a certain number of turns.

Before the day of mammoth indoor ice shows, entertainment on ice was offered by two vaudeville ice skaters, Earle Reynolds and Romain King. As early as 1906 these performers froze the ice blocks on which they performed by a secret formula. King declared that his secret would revolutionize the entire artificial ice business.

Not too long ago, when the late comedian, Joe Penner rode to prominence on a catch-phrase, "Wanna buy a duck?" he might have had in mind the example of Al Reeves, who plagued 1906 sensibilities with a similar slogan, "Give me credit, boys!" That line and two banjos are carved on the tombstone of the man who also gave Broadway its first burlesque show without a blonde in it (a woeful failure, incidentally). Other catchphrase originators were Frank Fogarty ("Am I right, boys?") and the Dancing Brittons who would accentuate trick steps by asking the gallery, "How's that?" Jolson's "You ain't heard nothin' yet!" and Ted Lewis' "Is everybody happy?" later became trademarks. The male half of The Kemps popularized "Oh Lady, Lady!" as a catchphrase; Sam Sidman, the burlesque comedian, would exclaim "Hot Dawg!"; Bert Lahr's "gahng, gahng, gahng" is as identified with him as Lea is with Perrins; Joe Laurie, Jr. & Aleen Bronson popularized "let-ergo!"; and J. Francis Dooley & Corinne Sales made "Will yer, Jim?" famed wherever there was a vaudeville theatre.

Before Gene Krupa and others agitated the drum into a solo in-strument for fanatical hepcats, their spiritual ancestor (inspired in turn, no doubt, by tribal tub-thumpers) was the drummer in Anna Held's show *Miss Innocence*. During a stage wait he announced the curtain with a roll of drums—but the curtain refused to go up. After several unsuccessful cues, he finally broke out into a rash of drumming. This solo made such an immediate hit that it stayed as part of the show.

The Lambeth Walk captured the American imagination on stage and dance floors about 1938. This "sensationally new" song and dance was performed, under the same name, by Daphne Pollard, sister of the movie Keystone cop, Snub Pollard, in 1909.

The Hawaiian craze had its origin in 1910, with Toots Paka as its chief exponent. With her was a guitar player who produced a weird, exotic tone from his instrument by laying it across his lap and pressing on the strings with a piece of metal. He carried this metal with him, and refused to show it to curious vaudevillians who tried everything to get a peep at it.

One day an actor succeeded in getting the Hawaiian guitar player drunk and learned the secret of his metal piece. In one year there were more guitar players producing weird, exotic tones than could be ac-commodated in Madison Square Garden. And music stores were selling the metal gadget to amateur guitar players by the thousands.

double-talk, dance marathons, amateur nights
Contemporary entertainers who "introduced" double-talk as clever comedy have only to consult a 1910 Variety to find an ad by Collins & Hawley which read: "We have never narrasprafed and wafused and weir comfed when we dimffd but we never bever flivver."

The first marathon dance was staged by the famous Coast show-man (the late) Sid Grauman (owner of Hollywood's Grauman's and Chinese Egyptian theatres) in San Francisco in 1910. Dancers were not allowed to leave the floor, a handicap which led to some peculiar dancing postures. Three weeks later Grauman put on an-other one, which was stopped after 15 hours on the recommendation of doctors in attendance.

After Miner's copied the ideas from English music halls, the first vaudeville house in New York to imitate burlesque in offering amateur nights was Keeney's in 1905. Prizes totaled $20 in cash. Later variations of "give 'im the hook," which finally refined the old amateur night out of existence, included carrying ill-fated performers off in a stretcher and squirting them with seltzer bottles. H. C. (for Henry Clay) Miner originated the hook for acts that flopped and is also credited for creating amateur nites. Years later Major Edward J. Bowes, utilizing the wider medium of the radio for amateur opportunity contests, used the gong in lieu of the hook. Arthur Godfrey, even more recently, gives them jobs instead of money although, for a time, the touring Bowes Amateur Units employed some radio "winners" and, more often, "professional amateurs," or mediocre talent which, under the aura of trying to break in, took on new semblance and new values. Ted Mack's television talent quests result in job opportunities and ditto Horace Heidt with his sundry national amateur contests via radio and personal appearances.

bert williams—firsts   Among more firsts, Bert Williams, famous half of Williams & Walker, was the first to break loose from the standard formula of colored acts—the chicken-stealing, crap-shootin', gin-guzzlin', razor-totin', no-account. He was also the first Negro entertainer, since the early 1890's, to appear in an all-white show before ofay Southern audiences, taking pains to avoid provoking any incidents in public. In later years, when he traveled with the *Ziegfeld Follies,* he stayed at the best hotels, under the generally friendly aegis of either Flo Ziegfeld, Will Rogers, Eddie Cantor, Marilyn Miller or Fanny Brice. But Williams always insisted on coming in the back way and not embarrass the managements. A 1950 variation of this is the "Equity hotels" which Actors Equity Association aligned as an "approved" roster of hostelries across the country where Negro or white talent would not be embarrassed.

Another leading colored team of the time, Cole & Johnson, enhanced the dignity of the stage Negro of 1909 by doing their act in full-dress suits, an example soon followed by white monologists. Johnson & Dean were another colored team who dressed their act immaculately, he in tails and she in decolleté. They were the first to do the cakewalk.

Another first for Bert Williams is the fact that he is the first (and only) Negro to be buried with white Masons. His St. Cecil's Lodge, N. Y. City, got special permission from his lodge in Scotland.

In 1905 the first animated, off-diamond replica of a World Series was set up in the old Madison Square Garden. It visually reported play-by-play developments through the use of lights on a miniature field. Box-office apathy did not discourage the Manhattan Theatre from trying the experiment again in 1907, nor still others through the years, until radio and television turned the trick more vividly.

battle of billing   Klaw & Erlanger were the first producers in the legitimate theatre to wipe out bickering between stars by listing them on the program in the order of appearance, instead of prominence.

William Gane introduced the first (and last) All-Automatic Minstrels at the Manhattan Theatre in 1908. Outside of one live interlocutor, all the minstrels were dummies with gramophones concealed inside, telling jokes and singing songs upon cue. Real minstrel shows of those days were still going strong—Frank Dumont's Minstrels in Philadelphia were in their 54th consecutive season.

Advertising in the sky made its debut in 1908. A box-kite was flown into the Broadway sky, carrying a dummy on a trapeze and a banner advertising a show.

Modern night clubs were prophesied in 1907 when agent Jack Levy induced restaurateurs to present a few acts of vaudeville after show hours. These eateries soon became known as supper clubs, in the era of the "lobster palace," which gave way eventually to the speakeasy of Prohibition, and today's niteries.

As early as 1905 the public read its first cigarette testimonials by stars, when Fatty Arbuckle, comedian Harry Bulger and dramatic star John Mason extolled in ads the virtues of Murads. A first theatre oasis was Hammerstein's! Like the Sherry's bar of today in the Metropolitan Opera House, he served drinks at intermission in the balcony of his Victoria. The less tony downtown burleskeries, like Miner's and the London, served beer in the audience during intermission.

One of the most inspired ideas of 1906 occurred to George Huber when he transformed East New York's Zip's Casino to the Music Hall. He installed a beer room for men, and a nursery with cots where mothers could leave children while they enjoyed the show in rare peace, prototype of today's soundproof baby "cry rooms" in the deluxe movie palaces. Theatregoers of 1907 were offered the first special booth at which to buy reserved seats by Keith's in Boston. The first split skirt was daringly worn in 1907 by English songstress Chummie La Mara, whose singing was immaterial.

The first vampire slunk across the boards in 1910, when Katherine Kaelrcd sizzled fatal sex appeal in Robert Hillard's play, *A Fool There Was,* anticipating the movies' Theda Bara and Louise Glaum. Equally electrifying was Dr. Herman the Great, king spark of vaudeville's sudden flurry of electricity acts, who lighted bulbs with his teeth and sent flashes out of his fingertips.

What was claimed to be the first revolving stage in the United States, enabling five scenes to be set at once, spun in 1910 at the Liberty Theatre in Oakland, Calif.

The first showplace catering to an all-Negro audience appeared that year with the opening of the New Palace at 51st Street and 7th Avenue, New York City.

In 1912 W. C. Fields claimed to be originator of a comic bit for bows—walking off stage as the curtain rose, and coming back as it hurtled down. Joe Jackson, the tramp bike comedian, did the same bit, so did many other acts. Fields, as a matter of fact, claimed originality for many things which he didn't originate such as the "family Ford" (Tate's Motoring act first did so), the golf game (also Tate's), and others.

more famous firsts   The first act to be financed by an airplane company was "The Fly Girl" in 1913, featuring Berenetta Miller, the only woman in the United States of that year with an aviator's license. She flew for the Moisant Aeroplane Company in one of their models.

That year George Rector introduced afternoon teas, from four to six, at Rector's, which set the style for Broadway in the era of *thé dansantes* and the professional society dancer.

And that year a California theatre advertised the first—and only —"Hot and Cold Vaudeville." When the California weather was not raining orange juice, the shows were given in an open "airdrome." When the California weather turned "unusual" the show went on under cover. In actuality, the airdrome pioneered what is known to-day as the drive-in. A standing vaudeville gag for acts playing combination policy theatres (vaudfilm) was that they "couldn't play at the airdome because someone had their wash on the line."

those phoney feuds   Pseudo-feuds of contemporary show biz, like Jack Benny versus Fred Allen, Bob Hope-Bing Crosby, Walter Winchell and the late Ben Bernie, have paid off handsomely in laughs and Hooperatings. They paid off in 1909, too. Two vaudeville acts, Gray & Graham and the Four Musical Cates, utilized paid ads and all the free publicity they could wangle, to duel over who had the world's largest saxophone. Sharpshooting acts, dancers and magicians all challenged each other in Variety's ad columns, each claiming supremacy—"the best," and "the only and only." Frequently they would post fantastic money: "$1,000 to anyone who can duplicate our trick" was a familiar come on.

In 1913 even Variety columnists—Polin Mary and Tommy Gray —crossed words in verbal pseudocombat. Journalistic duels like Pegler-Winchell, Pegler-Pearson, Winchell-*Time* and *Life,* Winchell-O. O. McIntyre and F. P. A.-Bugs Baer, later became common occurrences.

Quiz programs today give away fabulous prizes (donated sur-lecuff for equally fabulous publicity), and movies arrange deals with firms who want their products flashed on the screen. Whenever you hear a radio script name-dropping the brand of some liquor, washing machine, hat, resort, airline, and the like, there is a generous payoff in merchandise and services in many quarters. Industrial shorts, in later years, got to paying exhibitors so much per thousand of film fans (the "circulation") to keep the name of an airline, an automotive product, or just an over-all industry like pineapples, oil, aviation and the like before the public. This is a pure echo of 1905, when companies gave vaudeville acts cases of whiskey and medicinal waters in return for an onstage plug. Burlesque was the worst offender. In many cases firms paid for an act's entire scenery to mortgage its soul. And the music publishers' subsidy of bands and singers to plug songs is an evil that continues today.

Olsen & Johnson gave audiences something "new" in *Hellzapoppin'* when they intermingled bald heads out front with choristers from the stage. So new that it eclipsed the memory of burlesque's "Sliding" Billy Watson, who in 1908 originated the idea of having the audience come onstage to waltz with *his* chorus girls. The earliest beginnings of audience participation shows, however, are believed to be the "unbiased committees from the audience" invited onstage by vaudeville magicians.

The use of films to teach school children history seems a very modern development. But in 1908, the Springfield (Mass.) Nelson Theatre presented the flicker, "Paul Revere's Ride," and offered a prize for the best composition written on that event by a public school student. "Public school officials," Variety reported, "welcome the opportunity, and the plan is widely approved."

Atomic warfare is of recent vintage, but its prophecy is at least as old as 1908, when the New York Hippodrome staged a spectacle called *Battle of the Skies.* A program note predicted that war would be fought 75 to 100 years from then "between the United States of Europe and the United States of America."

American airships, it went on, would "have radium guns which will be able to devastate any city to the ground." To demonstrate this horror, the Hippodrome moved a blimp across the arena on a wire cable, from which an actor "fired" colored rays of light, as the cast below "disintegrated." The actor who was supposed to climb a ladder into the blimp on opening night became dizzy, and refused to complete the ascent, whereupon the producer, R. H. Burnside, went up in his place to become the first prophet of Hiroshima.

When you think of an actor with an oversized mouth as his trademark, Joe E. Brown is the first name that suggests itself. But long before Brown or Martha Raye discovered boxoffice values in opening one's mouth—and wide—a comic named Billy Kersand was amusing audiences by inserting five soda crackers and a regulation cup and saucer in his mouth. That was in 1911—but it was a comeback for Billy, who had been doing it in the Gay Nineties.

And before Samuel L. Rothafel (Roxy) got around to making audiences' eyes pop by staffing his ushers in field marshal's uniforms, the Nixon Theatre in Pittsburgh presented its ushers to the public in 1912, dressed in English army mess uniforms. Sam S. Scribner was partial to Japanese ushers at his Columbia (burlesque) Theatre on Broadway and 47th Street (now the Mayfair); the Japs were Columbia University students. When Keith opened his Union Square Theater in New York City in 1893, he put Zouave uniforms on his ushers, and caps and aprons on the maids in the ladies' rooms.

Al Jolson created a sensation when he first jumped into theatre aisles to sing his songs intimately to the audience. But he wasn't the originator of the technique. The first to do it in 20th century show business was burlesque singer Dave Marion in 1912.

5

King Vaudeville

★

Lyman B. Glover, manager of Chicago's Majestic Theatre, is generally credited with coining the aristocratic nomenclature, "Advanced Vaudeville." Other showmen quickly followed with Refined, Fashionable and Polite Vaudeville. Willie Hammerstein topped them all with Colossal Vaudeville. Finally Charles E. Kohl offered a $100 reward for an entirely new name for the two-a-day to reflect its *nouveau riche* prestige. Plain vaudeville, with no patrician adjective, vanished even from New York's Third Avenue Theatre, where Six (6) Big Acts cost 5¢ (Reserved Seats 10¢).

By 1908 the Orpheum Circuit considered the single-sheet showbill too lowly a menu to offer vaudeville audiences. Its flattered patrons received instead attractive theatre programs, à la the "legitimate." Orpheum distributed over 5,000,000 of these in one season.

Another elegant touch was the introduction of a master of ceremonies. James J. Morton, one of America's first emcees, was paid $2,000 a week to do four shows a day at two different theatres, simultaneously. It was he who lent tone and glitter to the opening of New York's biggest vaude and film theatre of 1909, Loew's National, which at capacity could seat 2,800 people at once.

Vaudeville's breathless pace, compared to the majestic but turtle strides of the legitimate stage, was best interpreted by William Morris as early as 1906, when he told Variety: "I remember some years ago when my office expenses were $200 monthly. Now they are

$30,000 yearly. I didn't do it; it just naturally grew with the business."

Variety authenticated Morris two years later when it wrote, "Vaudeville has held up extremely well during the depression which has existed for over a year. In fact, all the variety forms of amusements (except summer parks) have passed through a period of depression in much superior form to the legitimate." Tolling a bell, it added significantly, "That bespeaks an underlying strength which the 'higher theatre' has not."

This was a natural, if woefully erroneous, assumption of those unsettled days. Al Woods, vet manager and producer of the legit, made it when he swung over to vaudeville in 1909 with the Liberty Theatre in Brooklyn's East New York section. So did Hyde Behman when they knifed melodrama in their ten-twent'-thirt' Bijou, Brooklyn, replacing it with six acts, a two-reel movie and illustrated song slides.

Loew's Circuit began that year when Joe Schenck, then general manager for Marcus Loew, booked 12 houses for the People's Vaudeville Circuit. Later Schenck went to Chicago to scour the city for "small-time" material suitable for New York. Asked by Variety what he got in Chicago, the future movie mogul sighed, "Not even a cold."

But there was plenty of talent—good, bad and terrible—enlivening the hinterland. Especially dancers—wooden-shoe dancers. At the turn of the century, there were few makers of wooden shoes. By 1907 a great many firms specialized in them; some made wooden shoes exclusively. And there were so many new stages for these shoes to clog on, that alarmed amusement managers held a rush huddle, agreeing to "discourage" the building of "unnecessary" theatres.

shades of milton berle   Top vaudeville entertainers of the era, Vesta Victoria, Eddie Leonard, Harry Lauder, Bert Williams, Anna Held, Eva Tanguay, Irene Franklin, to name but a few, were constantly outraged at the bland theft of smaller fry who stole their material under the guise of "imitations." There was only one Irene Franklin, with her oh-so-English monologs in song, but many more audiences applauded second-hand versions of the inimitable songstress than clapped for the original. There might only be one George M. Cohan, but dozens of vaudeville actors were getting sore wrists waving flags. Variety scornfully pigeonholed all of Cohan's mimics as "red-white-and-blue guys."

Annette Kellerman plunged her magnificent body clad in the first one-piece bathing suit, into stage tanks, and came up dripping with boxoffice gold. Orchestra leaders were soon splashed simultaneously in San Francisco, Chicago and New York. Showman William Morris was responsible for grooming at least one carbon-copy mermaid, when he lost the original lady diver to his arch-rival Albee.

Headliner Alice Lloyd, the English songstress, was the first actually to copyright a bit of stage business. Imitators were subsequently warned not to use her "protected" stunt of manipulating a mirror as she sang, and reflecting the spotlight onto bald heads in the audience. Mimics of Miss Lloyd, afraid to run afoul of the United States Government, carefully eschewed imitating her copyrighted glitter. Other actresses, Lottie Gilson among them, quarreled over who was the first to wear a costume made of mirrors. The Steward Sisters followed suit, going a step further by filing photographs of their dancing act. There was a picture for all poses in the routine, with captions to describe every movement. The dance was registered as a "pantomime presentation" under the label of dramatic composition.

Piracy was so flagrant that one Alexander Byers, who operated under the name of the Chicago Manuscript Company, privately referred to himself as a "dramatic pirate." He publicly offered to sell scripts of any current show or vaudeville act. Copyright laws couldn't touch him, because Byers actually sold only manuscripts, not the dramatic rights for performance.

The longest private cable filed up to the year 1912 was one sent to London by actor Edmund Hayes. Running 2,218 words and costing $246, it outlined his sketch and stage business. Hayes' idea was to protect his act from being pirated by English performers, using the cable as a method of international copyright.

The highest-priced act of 1907 was the English comic singer, Vesta Victoria, whom Keith signed for 20 weeks at $3,000 a week. Her top number was "Waiting at the Church."

The song team of Nora Bayes and Jack Norworth was popular enough to demand and get $1,750 a week. They later were paid as high as $2,250, and the Shuberts booked Nora Bayes solo for $3,000

in time. Queens of the coonshouting craze who all but buried sentimental ditties at the end of the era were Clarice Vance, May Irwin,
Elizabeth Murray, Sophie Tucker and Blossom Seeley.

gus edwards' 'school days' One of the biggest vogues
of vaudeville, at its height just before World War I, was the
"School Days" act. A 1913 Variety census showed 62 such turns
being booked. They were always surefire—with their inevitable
hand-raising, kid-writhing gags—and had the important advantage of being highly inexpensive. The only props were a few desks
and chairs. There were always stagestruck youngsters available to
sing and dance.

Of all the School Days acts, Gus Edwards' was pre-eminent both
by reason of his renown as a songwriter and his shrewd choice of
talented small fry (via school acts and otherwise), who included
Georgie Jessel, Georgie Price, Lila Lee, Herman Timberg, Eleanor
Powell, Groucho Marx, the Duncan Sisters, Jack Pearl, Ricardo
Cortez, Joan Sawyer, Eddie Buzzell, Walter Winchell, Mitzi May-
fair, Hildegarde, Jack Wiener, Eddie Garr, Mae Murray, Ray
Bolger, Eddie Cantor, Mervyn LeRoy, Helen Menken, Bert
Wheeler and many others. Jessel, Cantor, Winchell and Wiener
were in one of the earliest acts, later being joined or replaced by
Price and Lila (Cuddles) Lee, and so on. As the boys and girls grew
older the newcomers got their opportunities.

Proctor's Fifth Avenue and Loew's American Roof, both in New
York, were the most important "break-in" or tryout, houses for new
acts. Here fame or obscurity were courted by a nervous cavalcade
of minstrels, wirewalkers, acrobats, trapeze artists, contortionists,
opera singers, comedians, cello players, ventriloquists, dancers,
midgets, jugglers, leaping dogs, balancing acts, xylophone and sax
combinations, imitators, magicians, bike-riders, bag-punchers, shad-
owgraphers, sharpshooters, quartets, archers and boomerang-
throwers.

Comic novelty acts were very successful. The Lunatic Bakers,
imported from the Continent, delighted audiences with fast-paced
acrobatics in and out of ovens. Pièce de résistance of the London
Fire Brigade troupe was the loud disintegration of their prop fire
engine in a thunderous finale. The badge of the English comic was
a flaming red nose; of the American comic, tramp clothes.

Not that vaudeville was incapable of satire on a higher level. Actresses made hits, for example, with "I'm-a-poifect-lady-but" soubret roles. The most popular catchphrase among actors, later universal, was "Ain't it awful, Mabel?" This was a song refrain in one of the Jack Hazzard shows.

indigo humor   But for a long while vaudeville belonged to the pie-throwers and comics who fished for laughs with slightly "blue," or suggestive material. A liberal sprinkling of "hells" in dialog shocked some theatregoers, tickled others.

"Inclination of the audience is to favor the old straight variety act . . . a laughing act," Variety lamented in 1908. "Managers are hiring the slapstick act for the false laughter it brings—feeding oakum acts to oakum audiences. It is not helping vaudeville. Apt to undo what the object of the last five years in vaudeville has aimed at—a cleaner and better bill." (Oakum later became hokum, and eventually hoke acts. Still more lately, the idiom gave way to corny, icky, off-the-cobb and square-from-Delaware.)

Comedians and comic singers at first acknowledged enthusiastic applause (10 applauders and up) with a thank-you speech. Then more and more of them began to give encores. Finally, in a pattern later adopted by the burleycue stripteasers, they saved their best material for encores, into which they were coaxed with the greatest of ease. This enabled them to make their final dash into the wings a triumphant exit, instead of a limp bow-off to scattered applause.

Off-trail acts, built around personalities who were not actors, enjoyed a brief but emphatic vogue. Willie Hoppe, a billiards champion at 18, demonstrated his agility with a cue by means of a large mirror reflecting table shots. Jockey "Snapper" Garrison, prototype of the "Garrison finish"—a last-minute burst of speed—delivered a racetrack monolog, as did his rival Tod Sloan. Baseball's contributions to vaudeville include Tinker, Coombs, Marquard, Anson, Donlin, Mathewson, Schaefer, Morgan and Ty Cobb, just as in later years vaudeville, radio and video saw Al Schacht, Dizzy Dean, Babe Ruth, Joe Di Maggio and Jackie Robinson doing all right in show biz sidelines as a result of their athletic prowess.

Vaudeville also featured the greats of the prize ring, champion wrestlers, 6-day bike race winners, milers and marathon runners, even champ heel-and-toers, and others. (Television, of course, made the Gorgeous George brand of grunt-and-groaner a business in itself. TV also sparked roller derbies, bowling matches, and is largely credited with furthering the popularity of basketball and hockey.) "The reason football players don't go into vaudeville," explained Tommy Gray, a wagster of his day, "is because by the time their injuries are healed, the theatres are closed for the summer."

animal acts big fares   Animal acts enjoyed a warm place in the vaudeville sun. No one would suspect that America maintained free zoos, judging by audience enthusiasm for monkeys on the stage. "Drunken dog" acts brought down the house. When J. Al Coin of Coin's Dogs made "some very insulting remarks about what he pleases to term 'imitators' of his (?) act," Charles Barnold indignantly declared that *he* had first developed the intoxicated canine idea in 1904.

Barnold and his tipsy pet hit the jackpot in the battle for supremacy among vaudeville giants. Hammerstein was paying him $300 a week, but Klaw & Erlanger lured him away with an offer of $1,-000. This was the highest price paid for an animal act up to 1907, surpassing the previous record held by Lockhart's Elephants.

Big Jim, a dancing bear, was a big hit with audiences. His routine consisted of one wiggly dance, but it was frequently re-named after the current dance craze. Thus, in early years he would do his wiggles as the "Grizzly Bear dance," and much later on as the "Charleston."

Audiences eventually became jaded by ordinary thrill acts. Competition among breakneck artists stiffened as each sought new refinements on neo-suicide. One auto act thrill queen, Mlle. Bergerot, did a double somersault with an auto around a circular track. Manual Pacavento was crushed and killed during a performance when his automotive apparatus failed to function properly.

Lalla Selbini, "a wow on wheels," provided more than one kind of thrill when she juggled and did tricks on bikes, then stripped to full tights. Never the prude, *Sime* had definite attitudes on the "family" appeal of vaudeville, hence he waxed rather righteously indignant in his critique of Signorina Selbini by observing, "Well made up (the GIs call it 'well stacked'), Miss Selbini discards her costume, appearing as nature intended her with only a skin-tight piece of cloth separating her natural color from the gaze of the audience. Without the aid of corsets she presents a figure that excites admiration, and while riding a wheel assumes positions that leave little to the imagination. There are no laughs, only gasps. Miss Selbini is frankly indecent in her exhibition and will probably be talked about, become a drawing card thereby. As a 'living picture' she is immense."

Audiences soon became so blasé, and headliners so scarce, that by 1913 even prisons were being raided for new boxoffice sensations. Pantages gave a contract to Ed Morrell, youngest member of the Evans-Sontag outlaws in California, pardoned after he had finished 16 years of his sentence. Pantages also offered ex-forger George Schroder as "Convict 6630—The Man Who Sang Himself Out of the Penitentiary!"

"Clean-show" Albee waived the rules by booking Frank Keenan & Co. in a skit called "Vindication." Keenan, veteran star of the legitimate theatre, played a man seeking a gubernatorial pardon for his imprisoned son who, it seemed, had shown a picture of General Lee to a man. "He spit on General Lee's picture!" Keenan would quiver in outrage, "and GODDAM HIM—my son killed him!" The South, of course, loved the act. But many audiences gasped at the profanity, and complained.

6

Pix—Poor Man's Amusement

★

Moving pictures, patronizingly referred to in 1905 as "the tape" and "the poor man's amusement," slowly attracted a brand-new strata of theatre-goers who rarely, if ever, patronized flesh-and-blood entertainment. Nobody could ask for a bigger nickel's worth. Especially when the Nickolat Company generously threw in illustrated song slides furnished free by music publishers. After each half-hour performance an attendant would empty the store by shouting, "Show is over!"

Pioneer picture companies offered features to exhibitors—some as long as 768 feet—at 12¢ to 20¢ a foot. Most films were "chase" pictures, although Pathe offered travelogs, and 1905 audiences saw the very'first newsreel feature, *Vanderbilt Auto Races*. Film fare of that year included *Through the Matrimonial Agency, Escape From Sing Sing, Raffles, Servant Girl Problem* and *Sherlock Holmes*.

But film producers shrewdly realized that audiences would not be hypnotized for long by such featherweight novelties. To get out of the freak class, movies would have to offer more substantial emotional fare than custard pies (however superbly hurled) and miscellaneous fragmentia. So as picture stories became more ambitious, weighty themes were essayed, the like of which no modern Hollywood studio would dare offer its boy-meets-girl clientele.

One such was *The Fatal Love,* released in 1909 by Urban-Eclipse films, and reviewed in Variety with no mention of the players or calibre of acting. The play, obviously, was the thing in the throbbing, pulsative new business called The Pix Biz.

Any resemblance between the picture-making business of those days, and the later colossus of Hollywood, was not even coincidental. Epes Winthrop Sargent, who wrote skin-flaying reviews for Variety under the pseudonym *Chicot* (later *Chic*), once took a fling at it for Commodore J. Stuart Blackbon's old Vitagraph Co. He was hired as a $100-a-week picture company editor, "which meant I selected the scripts, wrote the continuities, edited the film, overlooked production and wrote the ads."

The first vaudeville houses added movies to their bills for highly unflattering reasons. Patrons usually walked out on the last act of a vaudeville bill, in the same way that today's audiences start for exits during the finale or last round of a fight. This was highly annoying to managers, who still had to pay last spot performers between $75 to $250.

They solved this dilemma by adding a $75 film to the bill. Customers could then indulge their curious habit of flight at the expense of a cheaper attraction. Commenting on the innovation, Variety cannily prophesied, "If patrons stayed, they would see some real excitement. . . . The picture machine is here to stay as long as a change of film may be had each week."

4,000-5,000 double-nickelodeons in 1907   Ten-cent movie houses spread through the West. By 1907 Variety reported "between 4,000 and 5,000 running and solvent, and the number is increasing rapidly. This is the boom-time in the moving picture business." Most of the new showplaces were called "family theatres," both because they catered to the whole family, and were also catered by a family. Father was manager, mother handled cash and tickets, daughter made use of her piano lessons, and son applied his mechanical talents to the projector.

By 1909 vaudeville was beginning to sit up and take notice of the new upstart in show business. There was unmistakable handwriting on the wall when one vaudeville manager complained that his show, costing him $300 a day to run, wasn't grossing even $200 a day—all because of cheap movie opposition.

Both the church and the Society for the Prevention of Crime were fiercely opposed to "the poor man's amusement." On the day before Christmas, 1908, they persuaded New York's bluenose Mayor George B. McClellan to revoke the licenses of 550 nickelodeons. To regain licenses, managers had to sign written pledges not to give Sunday performances, and to bar films tending "to degrade the morals of the community."

chi, the hollywood of 1910   One fifth of the world's movies in 1910 were made in Chicago, whose two large film factories ground out 10 productions a week, at a cost of some $1,000 each. The effect of this film colony on Chicago itself was evident in the jump from less than 100 theatres in the city in 1906 to over 12,-000, most of them converted stores, in less than four years.

Los Angeles, in the ugly duckling days before Hollywood, was far enough along by 1913 to encourage the organization of the Photoplayers Club. Its president, Fred Mace, accepted a political candidacy for mayor of Los Angeles to change the city from a "tight" to an "open" town.

Even the Federal Government acknowledged the astonishing hold movies were exercising over the public. As early as 1906, the Navy made a film showing the delights of a salt-water career—for recruiting.

If anyone doubted that the movies were rapidly becoming big business, a suit against a film patents trust in 1908 served as an eye-opener. The upshot was a combine of major producers into a new trust called the Moving Pictures Patent Company, and a regrouping of independents into the National Independent Moving Picture Alliance. In 1909 the big-league outfit alone leased out 5,000 movie machines, and rented 1,800 to 2,000 reels a week.

And that year Variety reported, "It was rumored about this week that showmen of means had become interested in the new devices for color photography as applied to moving pictures, and the new 'talking-singing' picture machine lately brought over to America from England."

pioneer pix personalities   There were few movie "stars" in the fledgling days of the silents. One of these few was Florence Lawrence, "The Girl With A Thousand Faces," who was given a life contract by the Imp Company at $15,000 a year—or so Imp's publicity department boasted. In 1910 the hydra-faced star made a glamorous personal appearance before a thrilled St. Louis vaudeville audience.

Early in the era top screen personalities to-be were still giving their personal regards to Broadway. In 1908 the fabulously funny John Bunny, who with Flora Finch became the Fibber McGee & Molly of the silents, was still merely "a member of the cast" in a vaudeville act called "The Love Waltz." But by 1913 he was headlined at Hammerstein's at $1,000 a week—as a famous "film star." And a film house was named the Bunny Theatre.

In 1911 Douglas Fairbanks was getting ready to leave the legitimate stage—but not for the movies. He was asking $2,000 a week for his debut in vaudeville. And in 1912 the greatest screen cowboy of all time, William S. Hart, was playing in a vaudeville skit called "Moonshine" at New York's Alhambra.

But stars were beginning to shine in the flicker of the projection room beam by 1913. Actors demanded screen credits. Most of the large film companies yielded by listing names of one or two (but seldom three) stars. To actors' pressure for increased cast credits, producers shrugged that exhibitors were complaining that too much footage was used for this purpose—a complaint still voiced by exhibitors today. The first pix company to give actors screen credit was Pathe through its Paris company, followed by Edison and Vitagraph in America.

With stars' names beginning to mean something to audiences, John Barrymore consented to let Daniel Frohman present him in the film, *American Citizen,* for Famous Players. Mary Pickford, then a Belasco star, signed at $5,000 a week, after winning film repute as "Little Mary." Her success was crowned by an offer from Belasco to star her in his play, *Good Little Devil.* Lillian Gish and Ernest Truex were her colleagues in the same Belasco show.

In the general grab for movie stars, Keystone signed Roscoe (Fatty) Arbuckle, who later became one of the custard-pie company's biggest money-makers until his sudden fall from grace. Dave Montgomery and Fred Stone set a record for devotion to the stage by refusing a $104,000 movie contract—$2,000 a week for a year—as well as a vaudeville contract for $5,000 a week, to remain under the management of the legitimate theatre's Charles Dillingham.

Despite the enormous public tapeworm for "the tape," movie houses did not shed their Cinderella rags at once. On New York's Avenue A, theatregoers were offered a deluxe film, soda pop and a smear of icecream "all for the price of one nickel, folks."

Where Gimbel's now hoards its secrets from Macy's, Gane's Manhattan Theatre used to present a one-hour show—two acts and three reels of film—for a dime. Instead of a spotlight, the Manhattan used the movie projector beam. And Mr. Gane, one storm eye peeled for Mayor McClellan, barred all films not guaranteed 99 44/100 per cent pure.

the first talkies—and first color pix   The first talking and colored movies in America won a twin debut in Cleveland in 1907. The process, called Chromophone, presented life-sized films in color with speech and other sounds fully synchronized to the feature. The first colored talkie consisted of a smattering of grand opera, a bull fight with loud snorts, and a political speech with an accompaniment of jeers and shouts. To present it, Max Faetkenheur spent $25,000 fixing up a dilapidated Cleveland family theatre that seated 600 open-mouthed, disbelieving spectators.

Later the same year Hammerstein introduced New York's first talking pictures at his Roof Theatre. It was a different process called Cameraphone, involving the use of victrola records. Cameraphone, alas for the 15 years its inventor claimed to have sweated over it, opened on Monday and closed on Tuesday.

Undaunted, the talkies invaded New York again the following year. Brooklyn's Orpheum Theatre, in addition to its silent feature, offered talking and singing screenings of famous stage acts, including Alice Lloyd, Eva Tanguay and James J. Morton. For permitting this vocal use of their shadows, Eva Tanguay collected $2,500 and Alice Lloyd $1,500. When Vitaphone, years later, made a talkie of Kitty Doner's act, she quickly regretted it upon discovering that her biggest across-the-street competition was often herself. Years later, other stars who had "sold themselves" to the movies made the same discovery.

Cameraphone won a laurel wreath in Chicago that year. It was offered in a large auditorium converted into a picture house. Three projectors were kept in constant operation, and 50 people were employed for special stage effects. The bill included a travelog, "Around the World," by Henry Lee, with sound; a fire-fighting spectacle (whooshing of water from the hose, crackling of fire and engine alarm bells); and similar audio-visual knicknacks. The biggest trouble with Cameraphone was locating the phonograph. This generally had to be put on one side of the stage, because placing it behind the screen produced wrinkles in the presentation.

Another film innovation appeared in 1910, as a result of the unhappy experience of managers presenting open-air movies. As though the hazards of rain weren't enough, the program was often impaired by an inconsiderate full moon, which beamed so brightly that nobody could see the pictures. When this happened to one Schenectady manager, he had to refund the money for an entire performance of his Jeffries-Johnson fight films.

The new invention was called Photoplane, which permitted movies to be screened in full light. The man who invented it was Samuel L. Rothafel, better known in later years as Roxy. He used it for a year in his own family theatre in Forest City, Pennsylvania, then gave it a test run in Philadelphia. Albee's right hand, J. J. Murdock, formed a corporation to push the device.

Murdock had his finger in another movie pie, the Urban Colored Film, which was backed with $6,000,000 in 1911 to push the black-and-white film off the nation's screens. He became general manager of the Kinemacolor Corporation of America, which Variety predicted "may eventually become the father of the moving picture industry on this side of the ocean." But Kinemacolor was never destined to achieve the Technicolorful glory that was the reward of Herbert and Natalie Kalmus.

On the other side of the ocean, colored films had already achieved such prestige that a three-hour spectacle of the Coronation of King George at Delhi as Emperor of India, was being prepared. Millions of breathless Americans, Variety gently scoffed, would be able to gasp at the rainbow pageantry "when George is regularly ordained a proper King through the gentle dissension along official channels of a coronet upon his cranium." In London the film was used to open its famed new showplace, the Crystal Palace. In New York it was presented at the Herald Square Theatre with an orchestra, pipe organ and backstage choir. "Kinemacolor has started something," Variety speculated, "that will keep the black-and-white pic manufacturers lying awake nights."

Kinemacolor did start to go places in 1913, with 700-foot features starring Willie Collier, Raymond Hitchcock and Flora Zabelle. When Kinemacolor added Anna Held to its roster, Variety's review declared, "She simulates sexual unrest with her eyes." Some enraged clergymen of the day would have said "stimulates."

Films and royalty made joint headlines again in 1913, when Lady Diana Manners, daughter of the Duke of Rutland, offended Queen Mary by a striptease bit she did in a film. "When the film was shown last Monday evening at Balmoral Castle," cabled the Variety mugg in London, "Queen Mary uttered a short, shrill exclamation of surprise, at a point in the reel where the titled dancer is revealed doffing her skirt, preliminary to the assumption of the complicated one-piece costume that Isadora Duncan and Gertrude Hoffman made popular for the pastoral style of terpsichore. After the show the Queen ordered the film destroyed."

France put in its bid for film attention in 1912 when Sarah Bernhardt received $30,000 for making two reels of *Camille* on French soil. Three reels were made of the nation's own Mme. Rejane in a picture titled *Madame Sans-Gêne*.

Home movie machines made their appearance in 1912. "Why go out in a storm and be jostled about in a moving picture theatre," demanded the ads, "when you can have a satisfactory substitute in your parlor?" The machines sold for between $18 and $20, and reels rented for $2.50 apiece.

The first animated cartoons were the work of Winsor McKay, who patented his device in 1911. Every film cartoon today pays a royalty tribute to the McKay estate.

Fight fans all over the country went to the movies to see fisticuff history re-enacted on the screen. The Fitzsimmons-O'Brien scrap was shown in 1905 movie houses—but it was a spurious re-enactment, with Fitzsimmons going through the motions against a boxer representing O'Brien. Few moviegoers realized the deception. When Hammerstein's showed 12 rounds of the 21-round Gans-Nelson fight in 1908, a professional referee was hired to interpret the battle round-by-round to the spellbound audience.

In the filmed Jeffries-Johnson fight (1910), every view of flying gloves had a tobacco ad as background. By an odd coincidence, there was a prior exchange of money between the film company and the tobacco company, whose ad was on the fight stadium's fence. Johnson subsequently received $5,000 for making a talkie about his gloved dispute with Jeffries. The American Cinephone Company film showed him in motion and avowed that "the talking end of the session will keep rhythm with the movements of his lips."

fans razz pioneer talkies A strange development occurred in the years 1912-1913—a determined struggle between Keith-Albee and the public. About $500,000 of Keith's bankroll had been sunk into promoting Thomas A. Edison's imperfectly synchronized talking pictures. The public, after a few weeks in which curiosity was satisfied, began resenting them vocally. But with half a million dollars at stake, Albee was in no mood to heed *vox populi*. Edison, incidentally, had frugally sought to persuade vaudeville stars to appear in his talkies gratis, with rewards in "prestige."

When first presented in Keith houses, the films were sandwiched in between two halves of the vaudeville bill. The lowering of the screen was the signal for jeers, boos and other insignia of disapproval. In 1913 Albee desperately tried the experiment of shifting the talkies to the tail end of the bill at Keith's Colonial in New York. The audience didn't boo or hiss this time—it merely walked out.

"The talking picture film has been forced upon vaudeville audiences in New York for several weeks," commented Variety, "excepting at Hammerstein's. This house, not exhibiting them at all, has been doing the biggest business of any variety theatre in town."

Marcus Loew was doing so well for himself, with a conservative combination of vaudeville and silent films, that he recapitalized his circuit $5,000,000 in 1911. Once he became outraged at Variety for what he claimed was a too derogatory report of Loew's, Inc. earnings. "You and your blankety paper," he fumed at Variety's editor. "I'm mad, Sime—good and mad! In fact, I'm absolutely stark mad!"

"Don't be silly, Marcus," Sime Silverman shrugged. "Why not take a page ad in Variety and show everybody that Variety was wrong?"

"At $400 a page?" Loew replied. "*That* mad I'm not."

Film houses were still being built so rapidly in 1913 that Variety reported the melancholy instance of a man who entered his favorite saloon after a week's absence, only to find that he was blinking at a movie instead of pink elephants. That year, Variety reported, there were 30,000 American movie houses, two-thirds of which were worth an average of $40,000 each. With about $200,000,000 tied up in pix companies, Variety estimated the total 1913 investment in movie enterprises was over $1,000,000,000.

As films grew more ambitious, prices grew more daring. When Rainey-Hunt gave the American hinterland a look at *Quo Vadis* it charged locals $1 a look—and got it. There was a new rush in 1913 to book Broadway theatres for superproductions. Universal beat Vitagraph to the Joe Weber Playhouse with *Traffic In Souls,* utilizing a cast of 800. A week later Vitagraph took over the Criterion Theatre with *The Christian.*

a pioneer presentation   The end of the prewar era also saw the beginnings of movie showmanship. Film exhibitors were learning from vaudeville. In San Francisco the manager of the Silver Palace Moving Picture Theatre built a balcony out front, dressed it with special scenery, then hired actors to reproduce dramatic scenes from the film being played inside. The stunt stopped traffic on Market Street.

Variety was very impressed with the 1913 premiere of *The Miracle,* which it declared superior in some respects to Max Reinhardt's pantomime production in London. Certainly the staging of the film was ambitious showmanship. Sound effects lent realism to a knock on the door and the church scenes.

Like vaudeville, films also began to go in for novelties and sensations. The Eclair Co. presented *The Sons of A Soldier,* which it
billed prophetically as "War with Japan, shown in three parts." Another film offered Jack Rose, Sam Schepps and Harry Valon, whose
evidence sent Police Lieutenant Charles Becker to the chair for the
murder of gambler Herman Rosenthal, in *The Wages of Sin.*

The year 1913 also saw the early rehearsal of a "public enemy"
film cycle, as boxoffice receipts jumped for "underworld" pictures.
Current cynicism, inflamed by the Rosenthal-Becker case, held that
there was unholy collusion between police and the underworld, inspiring a lively interest in crime.

early censorship   Spokane's mayor banned a film called
Tango Dancing Lesson because, as he explained wrathfully, "I
won't let my daughter do those dances!" Possibly the most high-
handed act of censorship, however, was enacted in the name of the
15,000 people of Woburn, Mass., whose legal guardians refused to
grant film exhibitors licenses to display "celluloid debauchery."

To head off further attacks, New York film magnates formed
an organization to combat censorship and bad legislation. The late
Carl Laemmle, then president of Universal and World's Best Film
Co., was elected to lead the fight. Movies were becoming big business and they found themselves in need of friends in high places;
in state capitals and Washington as well as on a local level. Eventually the Hays office was formed, with former Postmaster General
Will H. Hays as "czar" of the movies, and more recently succeeded
by Eric Johnston as president of the Motion Picture Association of
America.

By 1913 the film balloon had expanded so gaseously that it was
beginning to attract top-drawer talent. The best magazine writers
and novelists were wooed by Mutual Film Corp. The year saw screen
vehicles, readied for the megaphone of D. W. Griffith, by such
skilled writers as John Kendrick Bangs, Zona Gale, E. Phillips
Oppenheim, Mary Roberts Rinehart, Roy L. McCardell and Thomas
Nelson Page, then United States Ambassador to Japan.

Movie directors began to earn big money. Thomas Ince was paid
the highest salary, $500 a week, plus 20 per cent of the Kay-Bee
Company's receipts. Biograph paid D. W. Griffith $25,000 a year.

Top stars of Vitagraph were Florence Turner and Maurice

Costello, father of Dolores. Keystone had Mabel Normand and Fred Mace. King Baggott was king at Imp. On the lower levels, however, movie extras were not too happy about their treatment. Some companies paid for extras' meals and expenses while on location, but not for tobacco or liquor. The extras immediately conspired to have their smokes and drinks listed on dinner checks as "salad." The film producers retaliated by furnishing extras on location with "meals" in the form of sandwiches, a banana and a bottle of ginger ale. Both principals and extras immediately protested they wanted a place where they could buy their own food, and tobacco and beer.

Indian extras were paid between $7 and $8 a week, plus expenses. Indian chiefs, in their capacity as straw bosses of working crews, earned from $10 to $12 a week. Gags about Lo, the Poor Indian refusing to remain poor soon sprang up, such as the redskin who wanted $10 to play an Indian role. Despite his protestations that he was a full-bred Injun he was offered only $5. He accepted, reluctantly, but warned he'd only impersonate a half-breed.

Another western film star of 1913, George M. Anderson—(né Max Aronson) a cowboy from the Bronx—better known to palpitating youngsters of the day as Broncho Billy, created a riot by appearing in person in New York streets and restaurants. He was forced to flee from the ardent embraces of worshipful followers, not one of whom wore bobbysox.

Legit Pre-World War I

★

Many of the legit managers of the pre-World War I era were very bewildered gentlemen. Although doing nicely at the b.o., they blinked at the figures quoted by vaudeville magnates. There was something wrong somewhere.

The legit manager had to write out large checks for authors, scenic artists, actors, music, costume designers, stagehands, theatre staff, and all the et cetera that always made legitimate production such an expensive proposition. But the vaude manager didn't do anything except furnish a theatre, stagehands, boxoffice, orchestra and ushers. Actors obligingly brought their own wardrobes, music, material and usually scenery. And if one show laid an egg, the vaudeville manager could afford to shrug—he'd have a completely new show the following week.

Vaudeville could and did seduce such great figures as David Belasco into producing *Madame Butterfly* for the Orpheum Circuit, and Ethel Barrymore into playing James M. Barrie's *Twelve Pound Look,* and Sarah Bernhardt in *Camille* and other excerpts for the two-a-day. But many legit figures grimly stuck to their guns and the smaller money. They knew their business, and most had a deep conviction that what goes up in a hurry comes down in a hurry. Then there was always the intangible pride of tradition. There were quiet, self-satisfied smiles on Broadway in 1912 when Chicago's Palace, a two-a-day, ventured into musical comedy. But after a terrible b.o. beating, the Palace quickly returned to vaudeville.

Ten Nights In a Bar Room was still playing in 1905, but melodrama quickly gave way to dollar-top farce and comedy until 1912, when a blood-and-thunder item called *The Whip* scored a surprise success and touched off a new wave of mellers.

George Bernard Shaw enjoyed his greatest American vogue in the pseudo-sophisticated years of 1905 and 1906, when six of his plays were hurled at (or over) the heads of Broadway first-nighters. These were *Caesar and Cleopatra, Arms and the Man, John Bull's Other Island* (a flop), *Mrs. Warren's Profession* (which enraged newspapers and the clergy, and was banned by the police), and *Cashel Byron's Profession,* with Jim Corbett.

Another blow at propriety was hurled in 1906 with Charles Klein's thinly-disguised attack on John D. Rockefeller, *The Lion and the Mouse.* It struck a responsive chord among Americans of the time, in whom the trust-busting Theodore Roosevelt had stirred a latent animosity toward sanctimonious millionaires. The play ran for two years, with four companies touring on the road.

The success of other 1906 plays which butchered sacred cows was further indication of both the drama's and public's rejection of old-fashioned, middle-class values. *Chorus Lady* gave firstnighters Rose Stahl in a role that glorified a tough, loose-moraled showgirl as a heroine, through her endeavor to keep her sister's purity intact. And *The New York Idea* presented Mrs. Minnie Maddern Fiske in a very lighthearted treatment of divorce.

The season also offered such staples as Sarah Bernhardt in *Camille* and repertory; Nazimova in Ibsen's *Hedda Gabler* (another high-class shocker); and James O'Neill, father of the noted playwright Eugene, for 4,802 performances as Edmund Dantes in *The Count of Monte Cristo*.

As though in revolt against such heavy fare, the following year in the theatre was captured for gay musical items. Outstanding hit of 1907 was *The Merry Widow*, first of a long line of charming, tuneful, and amusing light operettas. *The Merry Widow* introduced a nostalgic note which actually gave the waltz a new lease on life in an age which doomed its tempo. The season also ushered in the first of the *Ziegfeld Follies*. And it was the year when Richard Strauss' musical drama, *Salomé*, was offered to Broadway. Where-upon J. P. Morgan, who denounced it as "revolting, disgusting," offered to pay for the whole production to stop it. Curiously, offense was not taken at the notorious Dance of the Seven Veils, but at the spectacle of a lady fondling a man's head without the rest of him attached.

sex in 1908 The two sexiest shows of the era turned up simultaneously in 1908. *The Easiest Way* featured the trials and tribulations of a "kept woman," and *The Girl From Rector's* was a bedroom farce.

The world's hokiest play, *The Old Homestead*, was offered again in dead earnest with Denman Thompson as Josh Whitcomb—newspaper ads promising "not a thing in the play has been changed or brought up to date."

On the credit side, Broadway presented Israel Zangwill's *The Melting Pot*, which drama dolefully prophesied the disappearance of the Jewish heritage as America's Jews were absorbed into the social fabric of the new world. And all of show business suddenly broke out into a metaphysical rash with vaude, film and legit productions starring Satan. Confusion was rampant with two versions of Ferenc Molnar's *The Devil* on the boards at the same time. One was realtor Henry W. Savage's production at the Garden Theatre. The other was Harrison Grey Fiske's Faustian epic at the Belasco, "featuring" George Arliss. After the first night, Arliss' billing changed to "starring." So many Americans were suddenly eager to view His Satanic Majesty that Savage decided what the hell, and sent four companies of *The Devil* out on a prosperous road tour.

There was a poor crop in 1909, with the most distinguished offering being Sir Johnston Forbes-Robertson in *The Passing of the Third Floor Back,* more sermon than play. Lillian Russell helped matters somewhat by opening in a vehicle called *The Widow's Might,* and there was a fairly competent problem play called *A Man's World.*

Douglas Fairbanks brightened the 1910 season in a farce called *The Cub* by Thompson Buchanan, while John Barrymore also used the light touch in *The Fortune Hunter.* Otis Skinner displayed perfect manners in *Your Humble Servant* by Booth Tarkington and Harry Leon Wilson. Producers became acutely title-conscious when a show called *We Can't Be As Bad As All That* folded in a week. Critics couldn't resist the opportunity to deny the titular assertion. Morton Singer decided to take no chances—he changed the name of his show in rehearsal, *The Belle of Bald-Headed Row* to *Miss Nobody From Starland.* And that year a tribute to the art of Sarah Bernhardt was paid by the Chicago booking of four of her cousins who were billed in exactly that capacity.

The New York stage that year presented some interesting extremes in success and failure. A succession of hits for the New Amsterdam Theatre, like *The Merry Widow* and *Madame X,* netted $125,000 for that house. While, for the first time on Broadway, two legit shows were actually stranded—Daly's New Grand Opera Company and *The Country Girl* company at the Herald Square. Salaries unpaid, chorus girls were appeased with costume shoes, stockings and dresses.

first cabaret-theatre a flop   A much more expensive failure was *The Folies Bergere* at the 46th Street Theatre, later called the Fulton. Variety described it as "a burly show of the highest type." The first of its kind in America, it offered a cabaret revue, food and drink. Even with James J. Morton as its m.c., it failed to click. Folding in the same year it opened, the *Folies* cost Jesse

L. Lasky, later to become a movie giant, and Henry B. Harris, $100,-
000. Years later, Clifford C. Fischer, Earl Carroll, Ziggy atop his
New Amsterdam Roof (the *Midnight Frolics*) clicked with the
same policies. In 1911 Lasky was ahead of the times.

As in the realm of vaudeville, the movies found bitter enemies
among legitimate producers. In 1911 Charles Frohman put a
clause in all his contracts pertaining to moving picture work. There
was no welcome mat at Frohman's for any stage actor who had
filled out a summer wait before the cameras.

At a later date, Keith-Albee was to emulate Frohman's example
in vaudeville, by refusing to book any acts which appeared on the
radio. Few dreamed of a day when $10,000-$25,000-a-week stars like
Benny, Hope, Cantor, Kaye and Sinatra could swing around easily
and profitably from stage to screen to radio to nitery.

synge and barry fitzgerald   Possibly the most notable achievement of the 1911 season was the importation of the
Irish Abbey Theatre Players from Dublin to open Boston's New
Plymouth Theatre. This was the famous group that was to give,
among other great names, playwright J. M. Synge and actor Barry
Fitzgerald to the world. When Synge's *Playboy of the Western
World* was first presented in Boston, New York and Philadelphia
in 1912, however, Irish societies led the public outcry against its
blasphemous tone.

The 1912 season was both terrible and wonderful. It was terrible
because of the worst summer in 20 years, closing theatres in all big
cities and stranding stock companies on the road. It was wonderful
because theatregoers were faced with a bewildering choice of 14
smash hits on Broadway. One of the biggest was *Within the Law,*
with the late Jane Cowl, which played to $156,000 in 13 weeks.

Many of the day's important actors were paid on a guarantee and
percentage basis. Famed wearers of the buskin like David Warfield,
William H. Crane, William Gillette, Francis Wilson, Julian Eltinge,
Maude Adams, John Drew, May Irwin, Dustin and William Farnum, and Willie Collier lived affluently on large estates. From stock
came Wagenhals & Kemper, the first an ex-leading man and Kemper an ex-stage director, and clicked big. In but a few years each

retired with $1,000,000 in an era when the purchasing power was at its highest level. They produced *Paid in Full, Seven Days,* and *The Man from Home,* all smash hits. They gained prestige with a revival of Tolstoy's *Resurrection,* starring Blanche Walsh. They owned the Astor Theatre on Broadway, truly a "house of hits," and a natural location midriff in the heart of Times Square.

sinking of the *titanic* The year that the *Titanic* sank (throwing a pall over the boxoffice for weeks afterward) belonged principally to musical comedy. The Winter Garden in that 1912 season offered the first *Passing Show,* starring Willie and Eugene Howard, with Trixie Friganza and Charlotte Greenwood.

Weber & Fields reunited for the opening of the new Lew Fields Music Hall, his solo venture. This was on the site of what later became the 44th St. Theatre (and Nora Bayes Roof), which in turn was razed in the late 1940s to give the New York *Times* additional space, backing up that paper's 43d St. plant. Fields, besides reuniting with Joe Weber, had a cast that included Marie Dressler, Nora Bayes, Jack Norworth, Frank Daniels and Bessie Clayton.

Business was so lush for Sam Bernard's *All For The Ladies* that he paid his show girls $50 a week, a record in 1912. Will Rogers, featured with Blanche Ring in *Wall Street Girl,* his first Broadway show, dryly confessed to the audience, "I knew it was all right for 50¢, but I was a little afraid at $2." The sixth *Ziegfeld Follies,* in the year Anna Held sued the producer for divorce, was again clicko with song lyrics by Gene Buck, who later produced many of Ziggy's *Follies* editions, plus 16 of his *Midnight Frolics.*

Gene Buck was to become perhaps a greater figure with the years as president of the American Society of Composers, Authors & Publishers, guiding that organization through some of its most critical fights on sundry legislative fronts, with theatre-owners objecting to paying a music tax, and the radio broadcasting interests ditto. Of ASCAP, more anon.

Two oddities of the 1912 legitimate scene were Max Reinhardt's play without words at the Casino Theatre, *Sumurun,* and Martin Beck's first unsuccessful attempt to invade legit as a producer with *The Glass House,* which closed in two days. When Beck, the great vaudeville figure, finally died, his monument on Broadway was, oddly enough, the legitimate theatre on West 45th Street which still bears his name.

It is the only legit house in New York west of 8th Avenue. When Beck built it, he dreamed of opening up 8th Avenue into a new Broadway, since the old Broadway was cramped for every inch of space. But as the years went on show business, unheeding, moved more east, in the direction of the Ziegfeld Theatre on 6th Ave. Another real estate venture of show business caught with its dividends down was the W. R. Hearst-Arthur Brisbane-Marion Davies boom for Columbus Circle, a large hunk of which was theirs. Hearst's Cosmopolitan Theatre, later the International, remained very much an old maid, because show biz just keep rollin' along, staying away from all off-trail doors. But with Television in 1950 it was to become a key NBC-TV playhouse. There was preliminary talk in 1951 of building a new Met op house in this locality—if the money can be raised.

The chorus of firm, polite applause in 1913 that greeted a light opera, *Firefly*, was significant. "There is not a coarse nor a vulgar thing in it," wrote Variety approvingly. Which was more than could be said for many of the shows of that year, especially *The Lure* and *The Fight*. Press agents helped out their "blue" shows by writing phoney letters of indignation to the newspapers to stir up spurious interest.

The season was otherwise fairly undistinguished by new offerings, except possibly for George M. Cohan's *Seven Keys to Baldpate*, Douglas Fairbanks in *Hawthorne of the U. S. A.*, *Potash and Perlmutter* (Barney Bernard and Alexander Carr), De Wolf Hopper in *The Beggar Student* and Elsie Janis and Montgomery & Stone in *The Lady of the Slipper.*

Within the Law was still going strong in New York with Jane Cowl, and no less than six companies on the road, a feat equaled by another attraction of that year, *Mutt and Jeff*. At the opposite pole was a comedy-drama called *Nancy,* which played three Pennsylvania towns to a gross of $86.10, of which the show's portion was $57.54—the lowest any show ever earned up to World War I. The gross might even have been lower, in keeping with the tendency of managers to exaggerate. A standing show biz joke has to do with the Shakespearean repertory troupe which did a $6 matinee. . . . but the manager couldn't resist. "We did $8," he said.

belasco and cohan   The two legitimate producers who engraved their names on the highest niche of the period were David Belasco and George M. Cohan. Belasco gave the stage its greatest impetus toward realistic staging. He tolerated no painted waterfalls—on Belasco stages either real water spilled or none at all. He was master of scenic and lighting effects, often so spectacular that they stole the show from the actors. In one play he enchanted audiences by having a cat walk onstage, stretch, then lay down to play with a ball of yarn in front of a fireplace. Belasco ensured this performance by cramping the cat in a small box for an hour before stage time and releasing it from the wings on cue. The yarn ball was smeared with catnip. It was also typical of the omnipotent Belasco that in 1912 he enraged actors by announcing he would open a sorely-needed school of acting.

Cohan, like all good showmen, enjoyed offstage practical jokes. Once he and Willie Collier, to stagger Louis Mann, who was a very serious man despite being a great comedian, cut cards for what they casually agreed would be "$1,000 a throw." After a few hours of this high-powered gambling in the presence of the awe-struck Mann, Collier "won" two theatres from Cohan, using a stacked deck. This was too much for Mann, who vainly pleaded with Cohan to stop and chokingly told Collier he was doing a terrible thing. They ignored him, and finally Collier "won" everything Cohan possessed. Tears welled in Mann's eyes. Finally Collier challenged his "impoverished" opponent, "I will now play you one cut for Sam Harris!"

Cohan, the producer, with his partner, Sam H. Harris, shared the honor of being the first showfolks to have their names on a dinner menu, when the Knickerbocker Hotel offered shirred eggs with livers under the guise of "Cohan & Harris Special Eggs." They also shared the second highest nest egg of 1911 legitimate profits, following William A. Brady and A. L. Erlanger, with earnings of $250,000. Cohan turned down $10,000 a week offered him by Marcus Loew to go into vaudeville in 1910, and the following year was paid more than Caruso to sing 10 songs for the Victor Talking Machine Company.

For many actors of the period it was hard to resist the big money in vaudeville. Two-a-day managers would watch musical comedies for signs of failure or termination of runs, then dash frantically to win headliners of these shows for vaudeville. Legit stars often drew smaller crowds than the regular vaudeville headliners, but they were in demand for "prestige" and the newer class of patrons they attracted.

In 1907 Tyrone Power, Sr., father of the 20th Century-Fox film star of today, firmly refused to do a try-out skit with his wife but he yielded six years later.

Between 1908 and 1910 the abduction of legitimate stars for the two-a-day was a widespread practice. Fannie Ward accepted $2,000 a week to appear at Percy Williams' Colonial in a scene from *Van Allen's Wife,* with a supporting cast that cost another $1,200 and included William H. Boyd, later of the films (not the "Hopalong Cassidy" Bill Boyd). So did the distinguished English actress, Mrs. Patrick Campbell, who played at the Colonial in "The Sword of Damocles" for $2,500 a week, and John Barrymore who made a hit in his skit, "His Wedding Morn," in 1913.

The Shuberts tried to reverse English in 1912 by tempting Al Jolson with a five-year starring contract that would "put his name in lights as big as Gaby Deslys'." They kept their word the following year by co-starring Deslys and Jolson in *Honeymoon Express.*

Few brighter stars shown in the prewar world of legitimate than Maude Adams, whose *Peter Pan* a woman confessed to sitting through an amazing total of 47 times. (Only Sinatra's bobbysoxers a third-of-a-century later approached that.) When Miss Adams opened in *Chantecler* at the Knickerbocker Theatre in 1911, one of the year's outstanding successes, there were no less than 22 curtain calls, only the last of which she acknowledged by herself. American actors of that day, incidentally, acknowledged curtain calls by bowing to the audience first, then to each other. English actors started a new vogue in 1912 by standing rigidly motionless at curtain calls, staring out into the audience like a group daguerreotype.

Among male actors, suave personalities rode the highest legitimate crests of the era. Audiences admired John Drew as much for his gentlemanly, "very classy" manner as for his sterling acting ability. Otis Skinner was respected for his "excellent elocution and graceful, florid style." George Arliss could do more with his eloquent nostrils than most actors could with every dramatic trick in the book. Willie Collier's comedy was polished along Ronald Colman lines, with smooth, ironic overtones. As against all these "gentlemen" actors,

however, David Warfield held his own with unabashedly sentimental, highly emotional, tear-jerking tactics, using such homely
material as a father's love for his child.

Warfield's "If you don't vant her, I vant her!" is still remembered.
Memories of many other great stars of the day are evoked by the
verbal trademarks of their curtain speeches. "That's all there is, there
isn't any more," was Ethel Barrymore's tagline. De Wolf Hopper,
regardless of the show he appeared in, inevitably took his bows
with a going-over of "Casey At the Bat."

There is an interesting story, never told till now, behind the most
famous curtain speech in all show business—George M. Cohan's,
"My father thanks you, my mother thanks you, my sister thanks
you, and I thank you." It was actually invented by Julius Tannen,
the monologist, who thought of it as a mock curtain line when
doing an imitation of Cohan at an amateur show put on by the
Armour meat company employees, while he was Armour's secretary. Cohan saw Tannen do the take-off that night, and borrowed
the tagline for as long as he appeared with members of his family.
Although Tannen later went into vaudeville, and worked for
George M. Cohan, he never once suggested that Cohan's famous
curtain speech was his own original idea.

8

Kickapoo and Bernhardt, Too

★

Broadway could no more absorb all the theatrical hopefuls
of 1905-1913 than it can today. But the road both could and did.
Hinterlanders were starved for the sight of anything that didn't
squeal, moo or cluck. Farmers would travel miles even to attend a
store demonstration of a new slicing machine. The road situation
was akin to the reply of the farmer who was reprimanded by his

wife for losing his money to a gambling table that was obviously crooked. "I know it's crooked," he drawled, "but, heck, it's the only game in town."

As an example of the contempt in which actors and shoestring producers held the road, a 1905 Variety ad stated baldly. "Who's got a new show to sell for $50? Anything will do as long as there is lots of printing, and suitable for playing small towns. State all first letter."

James Madison's *Budget* was a bestseller among road "actors" at $1 a throw, earning Madison between $15,000 and $20,000 a year. This was a paper-bound book with "acts" for two men, a man and a woman, sketches, minstrel shows, monologs, parodies, and the like. Professionals even used this material, which ran for 50 annual editions before Madison died. Most of the material was pure corn —but it was a blessing to the newcomer.

No actor wanted a road engagement if he could help it—but many couldn't help it. One-night stands in small towns, where curtains were hung with safety pins, were grueling ordeals. The "opry house" was usually a hall over a jail, or in the public baths, tabernacle or livery stable.

Most shows carried their own "paper," or billboard posters, to announce their "sensational" attractions. The Miner Lithograph Co. ran an ad in 1908 Variety which listed stock posters for sale, and stated: "You can use any script you have to fit the title." Which might explain why, in one small town, *Hamlet* was billed as "How A Step-Father Got His Dues."

In San Francisco's Pacific Street—called "Terrific Street"—the Thalia was still going strong in 1910 with the type of entertainment that first gave the Barbary Coast its reputation. Backstage, a list of prior-day regulations for honkytonk actors was still to be seen on one of the walls: "No vulgar language allowed in green room, boxes or dressing rooms. . . . Ladies and performers must turn down the gas every time they leave the dressing rooms. . . . All lady performers must wear tights. . . . Ladies are not allowed to run each other down to customers in the boxes . . . Performers are not allowed to guy or laugh in acts or turns. . . . Performers are obliged to do as many acts and specialties as requested by the managers. . . ."

As the era wore on, and rural audiences were offered a wider choice of entertainment in 5¢ and 10¢ movies, one-night stands became more and more unprofitable. The abrupt dearth of attractions caused theatres to put up "to let" signs. In Los Angeles "The 9¢ Theatre" advertised eight acts and 6,000 feet of film—at a bargain basement 9¢.

medicine showmen   In spite of cheap movie competition, however, some forms of roadshow business stood up rather well. In 1911 there were in the United States 180 stock companies playing Broadway hits to full hinterland houses. But the medicine shows were a business all their own. Salary expenses were low because so many roadshows were closing that actors for stock or for "selling the snake oil" were a drug on the market. Not all the stock companies were scrupulous about paying royalties. This slight oversight cost one Hilliard Wright a conviction for play piracy when he produced the Broadway success, *Paid in Full,* at Aberdeen, South Dakota, without benefit of prior legal sanction.

Eventually, even the bucolics got wise to the phoney purveyors of nostrums, yclept the medicine show. However, as evidence of the stability of the medicine show, when the Kickapoo Indian Medicine Co. went on the block in 1911, after 30 years roaming the American plains and hamlets, it still brought $250,000. At one time there were 150 medicine shows on the road, all of them featuring one or more Kickapoo Indians. The medicine show was the training school for many headliners and show figures.

'uncle tom's cabin'   "Tom" shows were still circulating in 1912 and 1913, and there were 13 big, successful minstrel troupes on the road, including Lew Dockstader's, Al Fields' and Dumont's. But the only real gold was mined by the top headliners of the era on tour—Harry Lauder, George M. Cohan and Sarah Bernhardt, the former with his own vaudeville show, the latter two with legitimate attractions.

Harry Lauder made road history in 1908 with his special Lauder Train, under the management of William Morris. Moving with startling speed for those times, he visited 15 cities, playing 50 shows in 26 days. At a daily salary and transportation expense of $2,500, the road engagement cost $65,000, but reaped a boxoffice fortune at a 50¢-$2 scale. The troupe consisted of a 15-piece orchestra, Scots pipers and a supporting cast for Lauder. Six advance men traveled ahead of the show, stirring up public enthusiasm and frothing it with a triumphant street parade.

George M. Cohan toured his *Yankee Prince* throughout the South and West in 1910, traveling in a special train as Lauder did. He boldly charged a $4-$5 price scale—known at that time as "Grand Opera Prices"—and made a grand opera cleanup.

The 1911 road tour of Sarah Bernhardt was a b.o. landslide, breaking all records, particularly in the West. The movements of the Divine Sarah were of such supreme interest that the month before she was scheduled to appear in Chicago, Variety reported, "The theatre she is to play in is being kept secret."

new circuits spring up   Some upheavals in show business of 1911-1912 had a peculiar effect upon "the road." When bigtime vaudeville became practically a monopoly, with the defeat of Martin Beck's attempt to compete with Keith in the East, its product suffered as all products must when competition is eliminated.

Actors, producers and other vital factors of bigtime vaudeville began to desert to other fields, angered by the highhanded tactics of the Keith-Albee eastern monopoly. Many went into musical comedy, and many more went with smaller chains which were booming as a result—the Pantages Circuit and the newer combine of Loew-Sullivan & Considine. These chains respected the actor, either playing acts as booked, or paying them off . . . no peremptory cancellations.

Some stars went out with vaude roadshows, giving their best performances in opposition to Keith-Albee houses. Eva Tanguay was one of those who had the satisfaction of kicking Keith-Albee hard in the boxoffice wherever she played. Other stars who took to the road in 1913 were Marie Dressler, Alice Lloyd and Weber & Fields, all of whom clicked. Anna Held's road tour earned more than enough for John Cort to compensate for the losses of his Lillian Russell roadshow.

Willard Mack and Marjorie Rambeau, stock faves of the West, came east in a skit called "Kick In," which he later elaborated into a hit legit meller. From that Mack developed into a topnotch actor-writer of melodrama, while Miss Rambeau scored in tough but-

goldenhearted roles on stage and screen. Mack's metier was the
red-coat Royal Mounted cop who always got his man; he was the
outstanding portrayer of the Canadian police officer.

To bolster flagging business in 1913, some road theatres began
to make deals with retail stores. At Westbrook, Maine, the manager
of the Scenic Theatre increased attendance 25 per cent by giving
away store trading stamps. And to open Chicago's new Colonial
Theatre with a bang, impresarios Jones, Linick & Schaefer permitted the Boston Store to sell admissions for the premiere at 1¢
a piece, jamming 10,000 Chicagoans into the Colonial's four performances.

In discussing the road situation just before the war period, Variety
disclosed that "many chiseling vaude managers were giving the
road a black eye through sharp practices." They would pay off acts
in dimes, nickels and quarters, just before train time, when actors
had no time to verify totals. When they counted up aboard the train,
they usually found themselves shortchanged.

the nabes   The public, disappointed by the declining calibre
of bigtime vaudeville, was turning to neighborhood smalltime theatres which gave them equally good, or better, shows at a 25¢ top.
Some began to offer bigger, finer shows than the desperate 12-act
bills Keith-Albee flung into the widening breach to hold their
ground.

Others, feeling vaudeville was on its way out, became outright
picture houses. "The high cost of living," Variety commented dryly
in 1912, "is the excuse for neighborhood houses cutting vaudeville
and just running pictures in Chicago." But it was obviously the high
cost of bigtime vaudeville—which didn't pay off at the boxoffice.
In a desperate effort to hold audiences, bigtime vaudeville managers
went to extremes in 1913. Proctor's started a 12-act bill on a four-a-
day basis, with no films. The New York Theatre topped that with
a 17-act policy, dished out in one matinee and two night shows.

Hammerstein's and the Palace offered lavish spectacle acts. Lew
Fields, opening his new Music Hall on 44th St., west of Broadway,
where the New York Times' presses now roar, fought his neighbors
with expensive $1.50 top productions. A typical bill offered Sam
Bernard in a scene from The Modiste Shop, using 44 people in the
act, and the Carmen Ballet, with a cast of 87.

tab shows Out of this turmoil came a new entertainment form—the "tabloid." This was an abbreviated musical comedy at the vaudeville level, which originated and had its greatest success in the Midwest. The career of tabs was short-lived but sensational.

In 1912 some 30 theatres abandoned vaudeville and offered nothing but tabs. Playing at a 10¢-20¢-30¢ scale, they earned bigger grosses than roadshows had attracted at $1.50 admissions. Profits for tabs reached $2,500 and $3,000 weekly.

Tab shows ran from 80 minutes to an hour and a half. The usual show, which was paid about $700 a week, consisted of four or five principals, seven or eight chorus girls, with one set of scenery. Transportation costs were borne by the manager. Although tab performers preferred to think of themselves as of musical comedy lineage, a healthy percentage of tabs were really junior burlesque shows.

The most successful tab show of the period was "The Duke of Bull Durham," which featured the Four Marks (later Marx) Brothers with their mother, Minnie Palmer, as manager. Other top tab shows were "The Suffragette," "The Princess," "Doings of Dorothy," "A Knight For A Day," and "Isle of Spice." A favorite bit of tab business, as a sample of the fare offered, had an actress sing a few mock opera notes, inquiring, "What do you think of my execution?" Whereupon the comic's rejoinder was: "I'm in favor of it."

Variety reported a rather pathetic incident concerning a man who owned a playhouse in Frigonia, North Dakota. He persuaded a tab show to play there by offering the first $1,000 receipts. But when the tab grossed only $800, its principals told the manager they were sorry he had played the show at a loss.

The manager merely smiled. "Me and the wife gets lonesome up here in the winter," he said. "We just wanted some nice company."

amusement parks There were many more thespians on the road than merely those in stock companies, vaudeville and tab shows. Thousands more had skip-and-jump bookings in amusement parks, circuses, Wild West shows, fairs and hippodrome spectacles. Mail was a serious problem for all of these, including the Ginsberg Indian Medicine Co. (sic) touring the West, even after Variety followed the old *Clipper* by inaugurating its theatrical post office in 1906. Mail sent via Variety would be forwarded to catch any actor on the road at his closest booking date.

Amusement parks offered actors valuable road and New York engagements throughout the 1905-1913 era. These first came into existence as an ingenious idea of the traction companies to induce more people to ride on streetcars. Coney Island's Luna Park started as "Sea Lion Park," where gay swains took their dates, via trolley, for a day at the "briny," plus hot dogs, beer garden refreshments, and a decorum-melting ride on the Giant Swing, forerunner of all thrill rides.

Luna Park in 1905 was offering such breathtaking *divertissement* as "A Trip to the Moon," Bostock's Animals, "Fire and Flames," and "The Igorrots Village," while Dreamland presented "Midget City" and "Piccolo Midgets." It was Dreamland which transfigured the old Coney from a shantytown of cheap shacks, tawdry shows, midway performers and disreputable hotels to a lavish, respectable playground. Dreamland's "Creation" show, a fig-leaf interpretation of Genesis, earned $226,000 that season.

That year White City, a $1,000,000 amusement park, opened in Chicago. In New York, Senator Chauncey M. Depew was rumored to be throwing a million into opening an amusement park at Brighton Beach which would turn empty beach and sand into a higher-class Coney Island. The plan fell through, but later on an enterprising showman utilized Brighton Beach to stage a head-on collision of wornout locomotives as a spectacle, and the staged crash played to a full open-air stadium.

Hundreds of amusement parks all over the country were offering vaudeville shows, musical comedies and brass bands. The bands, specializing in military marches, waltzes and cornet solos, included Pat Conway and his Ithaca Band, Ferulli, Brooks, Creatore, Ellery's, Kryl, Duss, Gargulos and Caliendos Venetian Band. In 1906, the king of bandleaders, Sousa, was offered $20,000 to play four weeks in White City Park, but refused to demean his art by performing at any establishment which only charged 10¢ admission. Vaudeville gradually replaced the band acts in the parks, despite the difficulties of open-air acoustics and the thundering competition of the roller coaster.

Reviewing the prospects of 1906 show business, Variety wrote, "Looks like a banner season for the parks. . . . 400 of 'em." And it was. There was an upsurge in thrill entertainment and spectacles —Rides of Death and Suicide Seekers, like Gadbins, who actually did die in a 90-foot high dive, when he struck a piece of the diving tower structure during his plunge. Dreamland did a fantastic business with a unique re-enactment of the San Francisco earthquake, requiring a tremendous cast both onstage and backstage.

Palisades Park in New Jersey was opened by the Schenck Brothers in 1908. It made their fortune and led to the eventual rise of Nicholas M. Schenck as president of Loew's, Inc., and Joseph M. Schenck as a film studio mogul at 20th Century-Fox and elsewhere.

The park specialized in an aeronautical atmosphere. It maintained a permanent airship experimental station, with daily flights for thrill-seekers in the big airship, "Boomerang," flown by airman Charles O. Jones. In 1910 the park sent Young Goodale in a little balloon dirigible, bannered with a Palisades ad flying over Broadway. Goodale sailed very low over the Times Building, and then over Hammerstein's, shouting down to the audience on the Roof Theatre and disrupting the performance. Exactly 36 years later, consciously or unconsciously, adman Howard Dietz paid Nicholas M. Schenck a handsome compliment when he publicized *The Yearling,* a Loew production, by advertising it on—that's right—a blimp over Broadway.

9

'I Hope It Rains Today'

★

Although burlesque was not the kingpin it had been in the Gay Nineties, it was doing very well for itself in the adolescent years of the 20th century. More than any other factor in show business, burlesque dealt the death blow to melodrama. Melo fans who still craved trussed ladies on railroad tracks and buzzsaw platforms turned to the movies.

Variety reviewed a typical burly show, "The New Century Girls of 1907," through the eyes of the editor's young son. *Skigie* declared, with all the candor of his nine tender years: "I can't tell what it's about, and I don't want to go any more. In the first act it's just all about Lillian Russell and Mansfield, and bye and bye a fellow gets shot and that's all I could make out. . . . All the chorus girls are homely, and sometimes they are wearing short dresses . . . and sometimes nothing at all (flesh tights). They make me sick when they have nothing on. Somebody is singing all the time, and they sang 'Schnitzelbank.' " (Because children were becoming an increasingly important boxoffice factor, Variety's founder, Sime Silverman, frequently let the trade see how its off-color wares impressed the juvenile minds.)

Anna Held had an upsetting influence on burlesque when she first appeared onstage in a musical with a beauty mark on her cheek. Almost overnight every lady in burlesque—as well as ladies offstage —broke out in a rash of beauty spots. These could be bought readymade, or put on with black plaster. Showgirls used them both to appear "exotic" and to disguise facial blemishes. Beauty spots gradually began to appear in the shape of stars and moons, growing successively larger. Distraught managers, worried lest the fad logically culminate with their showgirls in blackface, boycotted beauty spots into an eventual decline.

The first burlesque theatre to open on Broadway was the Columbia in 1909. The show, "Follies of New York and Paris," starred Charlie Howard.

"I hope it rains today" was the byword of burlesque business, which depended more on inclement weather than talent to bring in "floaters" to its matinees.

Most boxers today become restaurateurs upon retiring from the ring, but most ex-fighters of those days joined burlesque companies. The great John L. had his own John L. Sullivan Players in 1907. "He's with burly," Variety reported, "and keeping sober."

There were not only pugilistic gentlemen in burlesque, but also some two-fisted ladies. Miss Juno, a distaff version of Man Mountain Dean, offered $500 to any man her own weight she couldn't throw. There were also lady burlesque managers—Agnes Barry of Albany and Ora Dresselhaus of Cincinnati's Standard Theatre.

Burlesque had been cleaned up considerably at the turn of the century, but the passing years gradually restored its gleaming impurity. By 1907 the smutty shows were playing to much bigger grosses than denatured rivals. Some of the lid-lifting burly houses were breaking records. A femme named Odell set the pace by performing the first striptease at New York's American Theatre. Another, who called herself Atlanta, raised hair on bald heads by disrobing to tights on a high wire, at the old London Theatre in New York.

The air was so blue over Chicago that year that the police were forced to declare unconditional warfare on cooch dancers. But the fierce reform gale quickly expended itself, and the storm windows were just as quickly taken down. Writing of Chicago in 1910, a prominent smut-hunter of the day, Samuel Paynter Wilson, reported a scandalous state of affairs, indeed. "Absolute indecency reigns supreme," he thundered. "The performers (of burlesque), mostly women of the underworld, are paid to amuse the audiences by kicking up their heels. The higher they kick, the more they are paid. The hooche-kooche and the Salomé dances are here given in all their rottenness. Vulgar sayings and gestures are indulged in to a degree that is amazing even in this enlightened age. These shows are liberally supported by all classes of men. Price of admission is low, and the performance suited to the tastes of the audience."

The hootchy-kootchy, as the reformer phrased it, later became known as the cooch. "Little Egypt," the nautch dancer, started this at the famous St. Louis Exposition in 1904 with a relatively normal routine of gyrations of the torso. "Bumps" were added to this, also the spinning of the breasts and the rump. And eventually it proved the undoing of burlesque when the low comics gave way to lower grinds and strips. For a time Gypsy Rose Lee gave class to the striptease, accented by a "lady author" and pseudo-culture overtone that did as much to refine her showmanship as when Gene Tunney mixed up his fisticuffs with Shakespeare.

While burlesque continued to concoct its shows purely out of the physical differences in human gender, it nevertheless became infected with the same fever that was inspiring vaudeville to hang red velvet drapes behind singers for "class." By 1911 Variety was hanging out storm signals with the headline: "Burlesque Getting Too Classy; Conference May Result."

Officials of burlesque's "eastern wheel," the Columbia Amusement Co., were worried that burly managers had shot the bankroll too lavishly that season. Overproduction, they insisted, was getting away from the burly idea. Leaders who gilded the lily were forcing others to follow suit, with a consequent kick in the b.o. for everybody.

Two pieces and an olio—"the real burlesque"—was what the business needed, opined the Columbia wheel. The fancied-up version of 1911, with its "book" that entailed special music, lyrics and production numbers, was bringing burlesque into disastrous competition with road musical comedy combinations. So burlesque, instead of dressing, reversed gears and returned to the fine old formula of merely undressing.

Burlesque, dressed and undressed, suffered a decline toward the close of the prewar period. The Columbia wheel, searching for greener fields, hit upon New Haven as an ideal burlesque market. After all, college boys. . . . They decided to try the Yale environs for an experimental three days in 1912. When the show opened at the Hyperion Theatre, unruly undergraduates criticized the prima donna with a shower of unfresh vegetables.

Business was so bad at the Casino, Brooklyn, that the management resorted to audience giveaways. It coaxed patronage first with prize offers of coal, then hams, then a goat—and finally, in a frenzy of desperation, a live horse. A wit suggested that Miner's then offer a $100 reward to anyone who would take the burly show off its hands.

Miner's 8th Avenue, in Manhattan, closed in 1913 for repairs. When it reopened, it was no longer a burlesque house. That year both the Columbia and Western wheels fought to hold their ground against the opposition of a new chain, the Progressive Burlesque wheel, which controlled 21 houses at a 50¢ admission scale. And to make matters worse, a new burly circut sprang up in Chicago, offering actors a 9-week booking in theatres that played to a 10¢ admission.

Burlesque needed more than "rain today." It needed a monsoon—and the monsoon came with the war years.

birth of the cabarets   Entertainment-while-you-eat was not exactly a new idea when cabaret, forerunner of the speakeasy and night club, popularized it starting about 1911. Combination eye-ear-and-mouth feasts existed for many years before, in one hybrid form or another.

Early in the century, the talents of Jimmy Durante and Eddie Cantor were consumed at Coney Island cafes along with steins of foaming beer and thick rye sandwiches. And an exclusive form of cabaret was given three nights a week at the Cafe Beaux Arts on West 40th Street, near 6th Avenue, where headliners gave ad lib performances before an audience of professionals who attended by invitation only. In 1909 Farbacher of New Orleans introduced "acts while you eat," and Saratoga and Boston restaurants began offering vaudeville between courses.

But the cabaret really got up steam with the appearance of the ill-fated *Folies Bergere* venture in 1911. Born before the general public was ready for it, the *Folies* ironically aroused an interest in cabaret that began to spread only after its demise. Acts that had formerly appeared in rathskellers went into vaudeville, singing ragtime, and audiences whistled in approval. Then the rathskellers gave vaudeville its coon-shouters, and more eyes began to turn toward the new cradle of talent.

The rathskeller was not slow to realize its opportunity. To suit its newly-acquired prestige, it changed its name to "cabaret," a Parisian term for cafe entertainment. The better Broadway cafes followed suit, and even the *Folies Bergere*—before its death, adopted the name for its midnight variety performance.

Cabaret shows were already costing $1,000 by 1912. The biggest New York palaces of gastronomic art and mirth, like the truly Parisian Louis Martin's, along with Maxim's and Shanley's, were taking in staggering weekly rewards ranging from $15,000 to $25,000. Smaller cabarets, many with singing waiters, began to pay more attention to their stage than to their kitchen.

how ascap was born It was because of this eating-to-music-and-entertainment that Victor Herbert conceived the idea of ASCAP (the American Society of Composers, Authors and Publishers). An habitué of Shanley's, then in the rear of the Putnam Building on 43d St. and Broadway (now the Paramount Building), he was struck with the idea that Tom Shanley got his fancy prices for his viands and vintages, because of the general "atmosphere." Said atmosphere included music, and if the performance of his (Herbert's) operetta music, along with excerpts from Friml, Kerker, Hoschna and Hirsch musicals, which he heard regularly while dining at Shanley's, was b.o. for the swank eatery then, figured Herbert, the songsmith rated a fee for the use of that music commercially. Herbert took his problem to his friend and counselor Nathan Burkan and thus was ASCAP cradled.

The cabaret craze spread so rapidly in 1912 that New York was offering drink-eat-and-be-merry shows at the Cafe Boulevard, Fleischman's, College Inn, Berry's Cafe, Cafe Revu, Pabst's 125th Street, Empire Hotel, Carlton Terrace, Fleischman's (Bronx), Rector's, Joel's, Ritz Grill, Healey's 125th Street, Sonntag's Summer Garden, Poodle Dog, Max Voll's Alhambra Rathskeller, Raub's (Brooklyn), Hickey's (Brooklyn), Churchill's, Garden, Frolics, Old Vienna, Faust's, Lincoln, Pekin and many others.

Cabaret on two floors, à la Gay Nineties, was offered at Hickey's. Ten singers, a dance orchestra plus a novelty banjo orchestra, were featured at Faust's. Lincoln's and Pekin's started the cabaret vogue of having entertainers mingle with patrons. Many of the brightest gems in the diadem of show business were first cut and polished in cabarets. Among them were Irving Berlin, Blossom Seeley, Sophie Tucker, George Whiting, Harry Fox, and of course, Durante and Cantor.

Although cabaret earned a quick admission into theatre society of the East, in the West it was more suspect because of its honkytonk origins. The police commissioner of San Francisco compelled cabaret and cafe entertainers to be photographed and numbered at police headquarters. In his zeal to keep careful tabs on the worst dives, he did not overlook the best. The custom persists nationally today in respect to night clubs.

Even the Winter Garden bowed to the craze by introducing its Palais de Danse Cabaret, later the Lido (Prohibition era) and in recent years a chowmeinery. But not every restaurant joined the exodus—some even put stiff signs in their windows to advise music-hating epicures: NO CABARET HERE. Further distinctions were made between "dancing" cabarets and "restaurant" cabarets. The situation became so confused that one could not be sure of simply eating, dancing, hearing or seeing a show. If the appellation "cabaret" meant anything, it inferred merely that *something* was offered besides meals.

Cabaret quickly became "smart" for the smart set. Cabaret dancers also became social lions—and social lions became cabaret dancers.

Lew Quinn, pet of the Four Hundred, sent Joan Sawyer's salary soaring by dancing as her partner. Irene and Vernon Castle, appearing in Chicago, danced "The Castle Walk" down the aisle of the city's first "tango wedding," uniting Florence Eizendrath and L. Montefiore Stein in terpsichorean but legal wedlock. The Castles had their own cabaret—Sans Souci Restaurant.

The famous ballerina, La Poukouwa, decided there was a brighter future in cabaret, so she made the switch by dancing the Turkey Trot. Mae Murray scored a hit in cabarets as substitute partner for Carlos Sebastian, doing the Barcarole Dance. John Murray Anderson, now the well-known director, and Señorita Tencitor gave lessons at the Hotel Astor's Tango Teas. Other well-known society dancers included Martin Brown and Rozicka Dolly (Dolly Sisters), Hale & Paterson, Hyson & Dickson, Harry Wallace & Kathryn Hatfield, Fontaine & Fischer, John Mason & Lois Whitney, Mrs. Ralph Hertz & Lester Sheehan and Al Davis & Bonnie Glass.

All of them were no little disturbed by the imposition of a one-o'clock curfew, aimed to keep New York's cabarets within "respectable" bounds. Cabarets were barred entirely in—of course—Boston.

european invasion   The pre-World War I years were lush ones for show business overseas as well as at home. 1905-1906 began a virtual invasion of England by American talent. W. C. Fields juggled at Manchester in a pantomime called "Cinderella," Houdini broke manacles and records all over Europe, including England. Barton & Ashley were a big hit in their act, "Canal Boat Sal."

To keep up with its ocean-hopping readers, Variety put on seven-league boots only one year after its inception. It proudly announced in 1906 that the paper could be purchased in Canada and all the capitals of Europe. Which was very pleasing news to such Variety fans as Will Rogers, who was then booked at Berlin's Winter Garden for a solid year, making a big hit among Deutschlanders with his 90-foot rope.

The two-way traffic of actors across the Atlantic persisted right up to the outbreak of the First World War. In 1907 steamship agent Paul Tausig sold 200 passages going over, and brought 100 acts from Europe.

Not every American feature clicked with English audiences. The

fast-talking monologist, Julius Tannen, laid an egg in London because his machine-gun wit poured round after round of blanks
over the heads of the bewildered English. But laying an egg was
better than being hit by one, the sad fate of Carrie Nation, "The
Anti-Souse Queen," when she appeared at London's Canterbury
Theatre in 1909. Upon the collision of the egg and Carrie, she indignantly ripped up her contract and went home.

The English theatre was operated on much more ethical standards
than its American cousin. An English contract was as good as gold.
If cancellations were necessary, artists were paid in full. In 1912,
when an act was lucky to get a 10-week booking in America, one
English manager booked a run-of-the-mill actor, Charles Stevens,
for eight solid years in advance, 52 weeks each year. The English
liked to buy their acts wholesale—at wholesale prices—which explained why Harry Lauder had been tied up for years on long-term
contracts at a modest—for him—salary.

from diabolo to tango   Like America, England was
seized with sudden crazes which were quickly reflected in the theatre. In 1907 London had an attack of the spinning bobbin, or
"Diabolo," acts. In 1911 ragtime swept the country, and London's
Hello Ragtime Review became a smash hit. In 1912 England suddenly evinced a tremendous interest in minstrel revivals, and burnt
cork sales shot up. At the very close of the prewar period, Variety
reported, "England Tango Mad."

Paris also made show news in 1912, by paying its highest vaudeville salary to Gaby Deslys and Harry Pilcer, the American who
became the French star's dancing partner. When Paris' Jap actor,
Kowakami, learned he was ailing that year, he asked to be taken
onstage, where he proceeded to take his final curtain surrounded by
his company.

English opera stars throughout the prewar years were very big
business in London vaudeville. In 1910, the manager of the Palace,
Alfred Butt, paid $5,000 for a week's engagement of prima donna
Lina Cavalieri, only offering half that for Anna Held. Viennese
composer Oscar Straus made his first vaudeville appearance at London's Coliseum Theatre in 1912 accompanied by a 42-piece orchestra.

Mascagni scored a triumph that year with his *Cavalleria Rusticana*
at the London Hippodrome. The show was paid $7,000 a week for

its 65-piece orchestra and company of 50. The cast, which was changed at every performance, employed three entire companies. The Hippodrome also offered Leoncavallo, composer of *Pagliacci,* with an orchestra, at a cost of $5,000 a week.

Despite the fact that a 1910 Variety survey showed more theatres in New York than in London, Paris and Berlin together, overseas bookings kept increasing astronomically until 1913, when over 700 acts were either booked or playing abroad. One of them was Irving Berlin, who was paid $1,000 weekly to sing the songs he had written. He gave Londoners a special treat by writing a special song to appeal to them the day before his opening—"The International Rag."

Wilkie Bard, who had made a hit at Hammerstein's some years before, accepted a $3,250 booking at the Palace in 1913. He was a famous English comedian whose songs, "Night Watchman," "Hail Smilin' Morn," and "Chrysanthemums," were immensely popular in London. Bard opened at a Monday matinee—and quit in disappointment over his poor reception. Before he could take the boat back, however, *Sime* in Variety pointed out that his only mistake was in trying to ape American comedians instead of sticking to his own very fine Welsh humor. The constructive criticism caused Albee to offer, and Bard to accept, another chance three days later. He stayed for four weeks, an overwhelming boxoffice success.

Broadway producer Charles Frohman had first call on almost every comedy and drama written by a European author. In 1913 Klaw & Erlanger rivaled his franchise by taking 5-year options on every Continental writer of musical comedy.

Show business was so international by 1913 that Variety opened a world-wide "information bureau," offering a Dun & Bradstreet type of lowdown on any figure of the entertainment world. Any request accompanied by $2, or a $100 annual subscription permitting 200 requests, would provide an inquirer with a full dossier on any theatrical notable from New York City to Calcutta. Variety today offers the same service, somewhat abbreviated, gratis.

op boff b.o.   Although grand opera was a somewhat remote branch of show business to Variety, it reflected some of its triumphs and curiosa in those early days of glitter. It never failed to report the doings of Enrico Caruso, opera's most glamorous figure—particularly when they affected vaudeville, as in 1911 when Keith's in Boston offered its patrons Caruso (on the phonograph) with a full house orchestra accompaniment.

It was, above all else, interested in Caruso's boxoffice accomplishments. Thus we learn that the great tenor upped his $3,000-per-concert take in the United States with a record South American tour in 1912 that paid him $84,000, at $8,000 a night in Buenos Aires, and $7,000 a night elsewhere. Returning from his triumphant tour, Caruso gathered some Broadway friends at his apartment and celebrated by singing, "Has Anyone Here Seen Kelly?" Offered $15,000 for three performances in Puerto Rico the following year, Caruso accepted on condition that his expenses be paid, including a retinue of 12 people and a throat doctor. They didn't sign Caruso.

Good or bad, opera of that day had one advantage no other type of show business enjoyed—a Social Register audience who used it as a frame to set off jewels, tiaras, furs, and other external manifestations of blue blood. Consequently, when orchestra seats rose in price from $5 to $6 in 1911, it was a matter of supreme indifference to the clientele. Who quibbles over a buck where social prestige is involved?

10

Morris Worries the Fox

★

The backstage drama of show business, 1905-1913, was often more absorbing than the entertainment out front. In many respects it was pure melodrama—with Keith-Albee as dual villains in sideburns, and William Morris as the hero. Viewed today, the conflicts behind the proscenium seem rather like profane farce comedy.

Vaudeville had been profitable in the heyday of Tony Pastor, but those times were nothing like the treasure chest it became during Variety's swaddling days. America's pockets were filling rapidly, and Americans—being Americans—wanted to empty them on the good things of life, which for millions meant sex, liquor and entertainment.

Opera and the drama held little appeal for this new strata of theatregoers. That entertainment was too high-priced, too difficult to understand, too "tony." It wasn't necessary to dress up for vaudeville; the audience was plain people, like yourself.

To win control of this immense, mass Croesus, showmen fought each other without morals, scruples or mercy. Giants like Keith-Albee ringed their empire with barbed wire, signing truces with one set of enemies to stave off attack from the rear, while at the same time they attempted to destroy another challenger at their flanks.

As a subplot to all this blood-and-thunder, the actors fought their own private skirmishes against the warring titans. Showmen were delighted when thieves fell out, and each side wooed actors' support with dazzling salary offers. They benefited by the circuit empires set up by rival showmen, which offered artists better bookings and steadier employment. Not content with these incidental crumbs from the bosses' table, actors waged organized warfare against all producers and managers by uniting in primitive types of trade unions.

keith & albee's ubo   At the center of almost every theatre storm of the period stood vaudeville king B. F. Keith and his Richelieu, E. F. Albee. Both were shrewd ex-circus men who frankly considered the domain of vaudeville theirs by inheritance. The United Booking Office, which had a practical monopoly on booking all acts for all theatres, was ruled by Albee with a hand no less free than iron.

Opposing Keith-Albee at every turn, worrying the fox from unexpected directions, rising up as often as he was crushed, was the amazing William Morris, a booking agent turned promoter and producer. Had he been less independent, less courageous, he would have ended as an office boy for Albee, as so many of Albee's enemies did. When the old master couldn't beat them, he bought them out. But he could do neither with the indestructible William Morris.

Although it often crippled Variety's editor financially, he constantly egged on and cheered every Albee opponent. In retaliation, Keith-Albee finally imposed its famous boycott of Variety in 1913.

Any actor who advertised in or was caught reading the paper was
blacklisted.

albee versus martin beck   One of Albee's first and
major feuds was with Martin Beck, an ex-waiter who spoke seven
languages, had impeccable taste in opera and music, and was not
unaware of his accomplishments. In 1905 Beck was vaudeville king
of the West. He controlled 16 to 18 theatres on his Orpheum Circuit chain. Albee at first tried to neutralize Beck's influence by
forcing him to sign a truce, setting Chicago as the dividing boun-
dary of empire. But Beck was ambitious. No bonds existed between
the two, however, except the Chicago line agreement. And that
quickly dissolved in the mutual dislike of Beck and Albee.

In 1906 Beck warned that the skyrocketing of stars' salaries,
touched off by producers' frantic bidding against each other, "would
drive the small vaudeville manager out of business." But that didn't
deter him from joining a plot against Albee by paying fabulous
sums to European stars with whom the conspirators intended to
stage a blitz invasion of vaudeville east of Chicago.

Beck went abroad with Orpheum's president, Morris Meyerfeld,
Jr., and foreign booking agent Clifford C. Fischer, to hook one of
the biggest satellites in all the show business firmament—Sarah
Bernhardt. Returning, Beck surveyed Broadway for the best spot
to build the first link of his projected eastern chain. He built New
York's famous Palace Theatre, soon to become the mecca of bigtime vaudeville.

Albee was furious. This was open treachery—the worse for being
open, so that all of show business knew a challenge had been flung.

Albee's revenge against Beck, Fischer and William Morris came
quickly. Beck, to extend the Orpheum's new eastern wheel, arranged to buy out six houses owned by Percy Williams. The deal
was all set, with Meyerfeld and Williams present and ready to
sign, but Beck, for some obscure reason, failed to show.

Both Williams and Meyerfeld were disgusted. Albee, learning of
the fiasco, quickly offered Williams a figure above the Beck bid.
Williams accepted. Angry at Beck, and tired of the hurly-burly
which vaudeville had become, Meyerfeld also sold the delighted
Albee his 75 per cent of the Palace, leaving Beck under Albee's
thumb with the former's minority holding of 25 per cent.

One hitch developed. By acquiring the Palace, Albee found himself in the embarrassing position of not being able to use his own acts from the United Booking Office. He had already sold the neighborhood franchise of UBO to Oscar Hammerstein, so he bought back the franchise from Hammerstein for $200,000. With this money the latter promptly built his Opera House in London, England. Hammerstein took the cash in lieu of one-third of the profits from the Palace offered by Albee, because he didn't believe the Palace would last.

Temporarily defeated, Beck left the Orpheum Circuit and vaudeville to produce and direct legitimate plays for Klaw & Erlanger. While he never completely relinquished his control of western vaudeville, his role became increasingly negligible after 1912. That year Keith-Albee pushed him out of Chicago by purchasing the Majestic Theatre, and finally, years later, swallowed up the entire Orpheum Circuit as well.

bill morris versus albee   Albee's sworn enmity toward Morris grew more bitter each year from 1904 to 1907, during which the agent acquired, through Clifford C. Fischer and the H. B. Marinelli Agency, such glittering foreign talent as Vesta Victoria, Karno's "Night in an English Music Hall" (with Charlie Chaplin), Alice Lloyd and Lily Langtry.

Morris' chief support, besides Percy Williams, was F. (Frederick) F. (Freeman) Proctor, an old-time foot juggler. Proctor was essentially a business man who viewed the vendettas of vaudeville with distaste, and wished to stand apart from them. Seldom going backstage, he concentrated on keeping his houses filled and counting his pennies. When he decided to stop booking his acts through Morris and switched to Albee's United Booking Office, in 1906, it was purely business.

The effect on Morris was near disaster. "The secession of Proctor came at a panic time in vaudeville," Variety declared sadly, "and had the moral effect of throwing the other managers booking through the Morris office into a monetary state of collapse." Now Keith-Albee could offer actors 34 weeks on the road in the East, while Morris could only guarantee 20 weeks, other than amusement park bookings. And in New York, Morris could only offer time for big acts, while Keith-Albee could book them all.

Proctor's scalp tucked safely in his belt, Albee set out after Percy Williams, whose early career included medicine shows and managing fighter Bob Fitzimmons. When Morris scored a triumph for Williams by signing Lily Langtry to a three-week run, Albee promptly stole Williams' thunder, and made him look like a second-run operator. He persuaded "The Jersey Lily" to appear also at Proctor's Harlem Opera House *in advance* of her Williams booking.

Such chicanery was as nothing compared to what followed. The Comedy Club, an early organization of actors, was seriously worried by the rapidly dissipating opposition to Albee. Actors, it feared, would shortly be at his uncontrolled mercy. To keep Percy Williams from being swallowed by the Keith-Albee octopus, the Comedy Club pledged all the 100 comedy acts it represented to the Williams banner for the following season.

In keeping with the ethics of the day—or the lack of them—Williams promptly showed this trophy to B. F. Keith. Keith calmly swallowed him into United Booking Office by giving Williams a lucrative share of UBO. Later, in 1912, Keith acquired complete ownership of all the Williams houses for five or six millions.

That beat Morris—temporarily. With Proctor and Williams knocked out from under him, he had no circuits left on which to book his acts. Keith-Albee won Round 1. The indefatigable Morris soon won the ear of Abe Erlanger, who headed the United States Amusement Corp., in which the Shuberts were partners with (Marc) Klaw & (A.L.) Erlanger. Until Morris stirred them up, however, both the Shuberts and Klaw & Erlanger had been content to remain in the legitimate field.

Now Morris proposed a bold alternative. Why shouldn't K. & E. open a circuit of vaudeville theatres all over the country in opposition to Albee? He would get the talent for them without much difficulty, since almost every actor without exception hated Albee. Give audiences something new—"Advanced Vaudeville"—star-spangled shows to make Albee's bills old-fashioned.

K. & E., fronting for the United States Amusement Corp., agreed. Morris was jubilant, and so was Variety. *Sime* cheerfully thumbed his nose at Albee—again—and climbed aboard the Klaw-Erlanger-Morris bandwagon.

Morris' old friend, Clifford C. Fischer, went into high gear again and brought over the greatest stars from the Continent, including

Harry Lauder, who opened for K. & E. at the New York Theatre in November 1907. While the proposed K. & E. Circuit was still on paper, Albee thoroughly aroused took drastic steps to effect a miscarriage of the plan.

He called a meeting of all managers who booked acts through his UBO, and coerced a pledge from them to boycott any Morris' act which signed for K. & E. Penalties were provided for any manager who violated this boycott, and Albee made it clear that any actor who signed with Morris would automatically be blacklisted from all Albee-controlled theatres.

But Morris had two trumps up his sleeve. The first was the hatred which actors nursed for Keith-Albee. The second was the unlimited treasury at his disposal, i.e., K. & E.'s permission to dazzle actors with as much gold as the dazzling required. "Vaudeville by wholesale," Morris blithely told Variety, "is what we're going to have." And it was. He spent almost $1,000,000 to solidly book 75 acts.

Albee was jarred. He was jarred further at K. & E.'s bland announcement that they had entered into an agreement with the Shuberts to form a $100,000,000 company to build and operate theatres, including control of Europe's vaudeville houses. Albee was flabbergasted when the first head-on collision between K. & E. and Keith-Albee took place in Philadelphia.

"Advanced Vaudeville" opened at the Chestnut Street Opera House with an unheard-of bill of headliners, $4,850 worth of talent. It featured the Four Mortons at $1,000, with eight other acts, none of which cost less than $300. Less than one block away on Philadelphia's Chestnut Street was B. F. Keith's Theatre. The Keith house, offering Vesta Victoria, appealed for help. Albee responded grimly by spending $1,500 to advertise the bill at B. F. Keith's. K. & E. promptly spent $3,000 to promote the Chestnut Street Opera House bill.

Albee groaned in horror at what happened the following week. The fighting mad K. & E.-Morris combination gave Philly a show costing $10,000, the first time in vaudeville history that so much money had been poured into a single week's bill.

Then a curious thing happened. Erlanger and Morris had a bitter argument. The exact subject of the dispute is not clear, but it is probable that Morris suddenly understood the hidden motive in the spectacular spending of K. & E. to assault the Keith-Albee citadel. K. & E. never seriously attempted to challenge the might of the Albee dynasty. They had never seriously intended to finance a rival circuit. From start to finish they had used Morris as their pawn in a gigantic, "legitimate blackmail" stunt. They didn't care how they spent money in snatching Albee's stars or battling him at the box-office, because they knew that eventually they would get back every cent—with a tremendous bonus. The lesson of Percy Williams was not lost to them. Their fireworks had one purpose—to force Albee to buy them out. And they succeeded. In 1907 Albee paid the required price—a $1,000,000 profit—and William Morris was out in the cold. Albee was once again undisputed monarch of show business east of Chicago.

And once again Variety's founder-editor sighed. He was not in the least surprised when Albee set up a rival show business paper, the New York *Star,* specifically designed to put Sime Silverman out of business. It was then, in an effort to crush Variety and replace it with the *Star* that Albee issued an edict at the UBO that any actor who gave Variety an ad would be refused bookings. With Albee in sole control of eastern vaudeville, this was as good as a death warrant for any actor who dared value self-respect more than three square meals a day.

Disregarding the motives of K. & E., it must be admitted that they did a great deal for show business during the short time they were setting the pace in vaudeville. They advertised extravagantly, boosted the earnings of actors to their highest level, and improved the quality of bills all over the country. Once K. & E. had wrought those changes, Albee had no choice but to perpetuate them.

down for the count—again   On the canvas again at the end of Round 2, William Morris shook his head groggily, and decided that the trouble lay with the men in his corner. He could trust no one but himself. So Morris incorporated himself for $500,-000, and for the first time stepped out into the vaudeville ring with managerial gloves, late in 1907.

Gathering as many headliners as he could once more under his banner, including Harry Lauder, he booked them where he could. With Morris once again a threat, Keith-Albee hastily signed a letter sent to the Vaudeville Comedy Club and White Rats of America, then the two key vaude actors' organizations, promising "better conditions" and declaring that there "shall be no blacklist, and that all old scores should be wiped out." They knew only too well the knight-in-shining-armor fascination Morris held for actors, in comparison with the ogre represented by the UBO.

Wherever Morris had a top star who could not be seduced away, Albee encouraged his actors to pirate the star's material or duplicate his act. Conversely, when Albee did steal Annette Kellerman, Morris promptly duplicated her act and booked his carbon copy. She was 15-year-old Rose Pitnof who swam from the Charleston (Massachusetts) Bridge to Boston lighthouse. Chief asset in Morris' years as independent manager was the great Lauder, who was S.R.O. wherever he played. Of course, Variety once again was in Morris' corner.

He was held in such high regard by actors that the White Rats made him guest of honor at a dinner in 1909.

The following year Morris got together with Tim Sullivan, owner of the American Theatre in New York and established a new circuit, to buck Albee. Morris introduced a sensational 22-act, $8,000 show at the American Music Hall as his initial thrust at Albee.

There was great cheering in 1911 when Orpheum, not yet fallen to Albee, agreed to book some of the new circuit's acts in Chicago, despite Morris' being opposition for Martin Beck. Once more Albee hastily (and temporarily) lifted the UBO blacklist, because too many acts were deserting to the Morris banner. The general jubilation was not dampened by a repetition of Morris' usual fate —a quarrel between him and Tim Sullivan, who subsequently withdrew his financial support from the circuit. But there was no disaster this time. Marcus Loew stepped into Sullivan's place, and paid Morris' creditors and gave him one-third control of the business. The omens were good. They looked even better when Loew introduced $1,500 and $2,000 shows in his normally "small-time" theatres.

This was the beginning of the end for the Albee dynasty. But, ironically, the pilot was dropped before the new victorious combination reached its destined port. Loew bought Morris out of the new circuit, which was the most gentlemanly exit through which Morris' ill-fated string of partners had ever kicked him.

On his own again, Morris puttered around. In 1913 he opened the New York Theatre as "Wonderland," giving Broadway the 10¢

admission steeplechase idea. Wonderland offered freaks, a merry-go-round, and sideshows which Morris later replaced with a dance floor. He also opened the Wonderland Picture Theatre, presenting nine acts and Kinemacolor pictures on a three-a-day basis, at a 10¢-20¢ price scale. But his heart wasn't in such trivia. Without a giant to battle, half the fun was gone. Morris went back to the booking agent business.

now it's the shuberts vs. k. & e.   But Albee wasn't the only storm center. His enemies fought as frequently among themselves. In 1909 Variety reported that "the knife is out between the Shuberts and Klaw & Erlanger." The Shuberts began to threaten K. & E. with one-night roadshows. K. & E. retaliated with threats that before they were finished, they would own every legitimate booking. To keep the pot boiling, Keith-Albee dropped dark hints that they planned to invade legit.

The Shuberts and K. & E. buried the hatchet in 1911, and Variety reported that K. & E. were supposedly negotiating with "Wall Street people" for a gigantic new corporation.

With the emergence of small-time vaudeville in 1909, Marcus Loew became an important figure. At that time Pantages was fighting Sullivan & Considine for control of small-time in the West, and Loew was fighting a battle with his rival, William Fox, for small-time supremacy in the East.

Both showmen mustered their forces for a showdown in 1911. Fox controlled 11 small-time vaudeville houses in Greater New York, and it was rumored that he would pick up another 15 from Klaw & Erlanger. Loew had 20 theatres and booked more. The fight began in earnest when Fox opened the New York Theatre with pop-priced vaudeville. Loew countered by a consolidation with Sullivan & Considine in the West, giving him a coast-to-coast circuit hookup as bait for actors.

Variety helped break the scandal of UBO operations in 1912. UBO for many years was nothing more than a gigantic swindle of both actor and agent. Albee's organization, when booking acts for Keith-Albee theatres, deducted 5 per cent of the actors' money and took half of the agents' 5 per cent commissions. One UBO subsidiary, headed by Albee's son, took in $200,000 a year in such fees, at an annual office expenditure of only $2,000. This was very thick gravy for the juicy spoils of the Keith-Albee chain.

Albee's right-hand man, John J. Murdock, proved to be the Achilles heel of Albee, much as Albee was of his boss, B. F. Keith. While Albee schemed to wrest power from his employer's hands, Murdock countermaneuvered to outwit Albee. Murdock scored after acting as Albee's agent in buying the Kohl & Castle Circuit of Chicago from the two ex-circus men. A very pleased Albee, in a moment of generosity, gave Murdock a reward of an option for holdings in the Keith-Orpheum Circuit. Murdock years later sold this option to Joseph P. Kennedy, who represented the Radio Corporation of America. This was the origin of the Radio-Keith-Orpheum Circuit—the move which finally and completely unseated E. F. Albee.

A grim figure in the show business of that day, Albee had an unconscious humorous side. It was revealed in the dilemma of his Boston manager, Grady, who was having his hands full with the devil-may-care vaudeville team, Jimmy Duffy and John Sweeney. At one matinee, Sweeney showed up but Duffy didn't. Grady told Sweeney to do a single turn. That night Duffy showed up, but Sweeney was "lost." So Duffy did a solo. This kept up for two days. Finally in desperation Grady phoned New York and told Albee what was happening at B. F. Keith's in Boston.

"When you get them together," Albee ordered seriously, "cancel them."

11

'Asking Albee a Question'

★

Variety's private war with Keith-Albee waged almost from its first issue. One of the tactics that drove Albee and his rivals insane was the astute editor's use of red herring to drag across the paths of the great in an effort to smoke out real news. Variety in its early days might carry a rumor that Martin Beck was going to move in on the eastern realm of Albee. Albee might be goaded into a stinging retort which, in turn, might actually prod Beck into making Variety's wild guess a reality. As more producers' doors opened to Variety after the first year or so, Sime Silverman won access to the behind-the-scenes news that he had originally been forced to acquire by shrewd surmise.

Throughout the era Variety needled Albee with open challenges, exposes and denunciation. Typical of its attacks, indirectly urging managers to oppose Keith-Albee, was one which quoted "a vaudeville artist of high standing." The anonymous artist stated: "It is not only the artist who has to fear Keith. The managers booking through the Keith Agency may well look out for themselves if B. F. Keith ever becomes the boss of vaudeville."

When Albee pulled his blacklist act on Variety in 1913, he left no stone unturned to see that it packed a solid wallop. In addition to forbidding actors and agents to read or advertise in Variety, he even warned music publishers to withdraw their ads, or he would not allow their songs to be sung in Keith theatres.

Keith theatres denied Variety staffers the usual press courtesies. Undisturbed, the paper's reviewers paid their way to Albee's shows, just as they did to Shubert houses, many years later. Albee further forbade any manager or employee to bring a copy of Variety in the Keith-Albee offices. His sergeant-at-arms, John J. Murdock, enforced the taboo on advertising in Variety. Murdock boasted that they kept $15,000 worth of ads out of Variety's Anniversary Issue. Many years later, however, *Sime* and Murdock became great friends.

Variety did not take Mr. Albee's high-handed tactics with good grace. *Sime* fought back. Under the headline: ASKING ALBEE A QUESTION, Variety disclosed the existence of a billboard opposite the UBO offices on the sixth floor of the Putnam Building. The billboard, Variety reported, carried an ad for the show *Are You a Crook?*

Sime Silverman waxed exceeding wroth in a March 28, 1913 editorial, well remembered by show business veterans. It also became a journalistic landmark, newspapermen comparing Variety's editor with crusaders like Dana, Pulitzer and Bennett. He wrote bitterly in part: "Were you ever blacklisted? No? Well, it's like going to a party and finding no one will dance with you. . . . This 'blacklist' against Variety by the big 'managers' has us very sore. We are really ver-y, ver-y an-gry, and that's not stealing any of George Munroe's stuff. We dislike talking about ourselves, but here we are publishing a paper many people want to advertise in, and the big time won't let them, although the big time does not suggest any other medium the intending advertisers will accept. . . .

"Within the past two weeks three bigtime managers have had to advertise in Variety without having their names in the advertisement. It's almost a shame that when a man must spend his money, he can't get a little publicity through it for his name, because a money-order collecting little grafter (who was kicked out of Chicago for being caught with the goods) is going to read Variety early Friday morning. . . .

"Anyone 'blacklisted' receives much sympathy during the siege, but it is seldom shown excepting in speech. One fellow is . . . full of sympathy, but he is always looking up and down the street to see if any of the big managers will catch him talking to you. . . . And again there comes along the fellow who says, 'I hear Albee and you are not speaking.' He's the innocent boy who wants you to call Albee names because he doesn't like him himself, but is afraid to say harsh things through fear one of the stool pigeons might be around to hear it. Or the blasé young man, who, with a yawn, remarks, 'That's funny; I heard you were talking to Beck,' and you can't make up your mind whether he thinks anyone is a fool to waste time talking to Beck. Or the facetious person who exclaims, 'How are Murdock and you getting along?'—as though anyone could get along with Murdock! . . .

"Perhaps the blacklist on Variety may account for the bad vaudeville shows in the New York theatres. If the big timers occupy so large a quantity of their wakeful moments in doping out schemes against Variety, how is it possible for them to give proper attention to the bills? . . . Not another word, though, along these lines or we would be talking about ourselves, something Martin Beck holds the patent rights for. Did you ever catch Beck asking anyone what the people thought of him? If only he knew! One day when it's raining, with no poker game in sight and nothing to do, we are going to tell some truths about Mister Beck. Better buy every issue until that one appears, for the investment will be worth it. . . ."

For, as the editor of Variety freely admitted, he was ver-y, ver-y angry. Freedom of the press is freedom of the press, on Main Street or Broadway, E. F. Albee, et cetera, notwithstanding.

origin of the white rats The present-day organization of theatre artists, Actors Equity Association, had its origin in England as far back as the last century, when actors banded together in an organization called the Water Rats of London, "Rats" being "star" spelled backwards; "water" for the chief sport of the group—excursions on the Thames. Fifteen American actors started an American counterpart called the White Rats of America.

The White Rats, like most of the actors' groups of those days, was principally a fraternal order, until working conditions under Keith-Albee became so intolerable that actors were forced to fight back with their own organizations.

The White Rats' first revolt in 1900 was a sad failure. There was little unity or courage within the group, and that little was quickly dissolved when the Rats' leaders were sent on long and distant tours. Many of the leaders, including (Dave) Montgomery & (Fred) Stone, were blackballed forever in vaudeville, to the gain of the legitimate stage. Others, like George Fuller Golden, who was the real founder of the Rats, were kept out of every Keith-Albee house until seven years after the first strike.

With the emergence of Variety, and its call for action against dictatorial managers, the White Rats were spurred into action under the leadership of Harry Mountford. Conditions were as bad as ever. "Contracts in this country today," roared Variety, "amount to no more than so much waste paper." Managers—particularly Keith-Albee managers—cancelled acts when and how they pleased.

Variety originally was not satisfied with any actors' organization that existed in 1906. The White Rats, it complained, was too much of a social "benefit order." It stuck to the Rats, however, as the best of the lot, until Sime felt that Mountford's leadership was so bad that he had to oppose the group. The Associated Artists of America was allied with a labor union. A new group calling themselves the National Vaudeville Artists, sprang up, principally to oppose the White Rats. But its origins were only too clear when $1,000 death benefits were paid to survivors of deceased actors over E. F. Albee's signature.

Two minority groups had their own actors' organizations. Negro entertainers, led by Bert Williams & George Walker, Bill Cole & J. Rosamond Johnson, and Dudley, Avery & Hart, formed an all-Negro actors' society in 1906. A Variety tally of the following year showed 270 Negro principals in show business, and a total of nearly 1,400 Negro entertainers. Variety added caustically that many theatres were barring Negro patrons with a flimsy excuse: "house full —only broken seats left."

The Yiddish-speaking actors had their Hebrew Actors Union, which limited the age of chorus "girls" to 65. Striking in 1907, they won all their demands, including recognition of the age of Jewish chorus girls as a matter of union discretion.

Variety added fuel to the flames when it reported the 1906 fight of England's Variety Artists Federation against managers who forced actors to play matinees without extra compensation. The paper also brought to light the discrepancies of musicians' pay. In 1907 musicians received $2 a performance in vaudeville, $2.50 in legitimate, because of the few shows played. Others, getting $28 for 14 shows, were asking for a raise to $36. Today pit musicians get three to four times that amount, depending on the theatre classification.

into trade unionism   In 1910 the White Rats made a clean jump from the tepid waters of fraternalism to the hot waters of trade unionism. Together with the Actors International Union, the White Rats joined the American Federation of Labor. This move later induced the AFL to sue UBO as a monopoly in restraint of free trade.

In 1911 William Gould started still another actors' society, American Vaudeville Artists, but like so many of the splinter groups, it soon disintegrated. Once again to head off Morris, who was starting a new circuit with Tim Sullivan, Albee ordered the UBO to issue contracts to actors without cancellation clauses. The following year, with a split between Morris and Sullivan, UBO re-inserted the cancellation clause.

The White Rats opened an elaborate new clubhouse on West 46th Street in 1912. It was later taken over by Albee for his company union, National Vaudeville Artists. As a big-hearted gesture, Albee paid off those White Rats holding bonds on the building—out of his treasury swollen with money paid in by actors and managers.

The clubhouse still stands today—as a Broadway hotel called the Sharon.

In 1913 the White Rats gave up its four-year-old house organ, *The Player,* and accepted Variety's offer of a few pages weekly in which to report its club news. At the same time Variety declared that it would print anything for or against the Rats, as it saw fit, while the Rats would be free to print their own opinions in their section. This sort of thing made men like Sime Silverman enigmas to men like E. F. Albee.

salary cuts   Because of the eventual slump of bigtime vaudeville in 1913, two-a-day actors were the first to suffer salary cuts. By then a general salary slash in show business followed. Legit and burlesque actors were "requested" to accept cuts. Variety criticized the arbitrary manner in which these slashes were made, declaring that if actors' organizations had not weakened themselves, they could have compelled a dignified and orderly readjustment. Variety specifically chastised them for admitting agents and lay people into their ranks, and scolded the Comedy Club for permitting even important managers to sit on its directors' board.

Variety once again espoused the cause of the White Rats, waiving aside even its own past objections in an attempt to evaluate the situation honestly. "That was the proper organization for actors to join, rejoin or become active in," *Sime* wrote with objectivity. "They knew it, but they passed it up. Neglect cost the vaude actors a million dollars in cut salaries. Slipping the agent 'standing-in' and 'being taken care of' availed nothing when the cut salary came around. It was the actors' own fault, and always will be the actors' own fault, until they get together and stay together." Equity proved the truth of this years later by making conservative but emphatic demands, and standing together tightly until those demands were won.

The small-time came to the rescue of the actor by offering him long consecutive routes on the road, with inexpensive jumps, but at a generally reduced pay scale. However, the important thing was the size of the actor's bank account at the end of the year, and for that Marcus Loew was an object of thespian affection.

12

Tin Pan Alley

★

Tin Pan Alley thrived in the melodic days when no home was respectable without an embroidered motto and a piano. A popular song hit sold between 600,000 to 1,000,000 copies as early as 1905, earning its composer and lyricist royalties of between $9,000 and $50,000. Many songwriters cut themselves in on the lion's share of the tune business by publishing their own songs. Among these were Gus Edwards, whose hits like "In My Merry Oldsmobile" are still standard favorites; Charles K. Harris, ballad king who wrote the nostalgic "After the Ball"; Harry Von Tilzer, who was first to put his picture on sheet music, and whose face peered into more homes than any man of his time; F. A. (Kerry) Mills and Vincent Bryan; Ted Snyder and Irving Berlin, Joseph W. Stern and Ed Marks.

Among the best known songwriters of the time were Theodore Morse, who sang his own songs in vaudeville; Will D. Cobb, Ed J. Madden and George M. Cohan, who received a 5¢ royalty on every copy of his songs, as did Cole & Johnson ("Under the Bamboo Tree"); M. K. Jerome and Jean Schwartz; James O'Dea and Neil Moret ("Hiawatha"); Ren Shields, Paul Dresser, Egbert Van Alstyne, Leo Edwards (Gus' brother), Ernest R. Ball and J. Keirn Brennan.

Witmark-Feist's chain of American Music Stores sold sheet music and pianola rolls throughout the country in 1907. The melody business that year hit such a high note that Rotheberg's department store on New York's 14th Street offered 20,000 copies of sheet music at one cent each, which they sold out in two hours.

Music publishers stopped at nothing to popularize their wares. Jerome H. Remick, a Detroit industrialist, paid singers to plug his numbers, others offered free song slides to nickelodeons, and many purchased scenery for acts which promised to cooperate. These practices became so corrupt that, by 1908, publishers were providing claques to applaud performers singing their numbers.

When audience "community sings" became popular, publishers began to charge for song slides. Song-fest leaders, like theatre organists of a later period, enjoyed a vogue. Variety reported in 1909 that Seattle's Edward Roesch exercised his lungs at the Sullivan & Considine theatre for 110 consecutive weeks, while male thrush Arthur Elwell led Pantages vocalizers for a record 174 weeks.

There was inspiration in the 1905 air, for that year gave birth to such lasting melodies as "Sweet Adeline," "Kiss Me Again," "Tammany," "Chinatown, My Chinatown," "In My Merry Oldsmobile," "My Gal Sal," "Sylvia" and "I Love You Truly."

Witmark came out with one novelty number, peculiarly titled "When America Is Captured by the Japs."

"Coax Me," was made famous by Lottie Gilson ("The Little Magnet") who sang it alluringly to front-row baldheads on which she reflected the spotlight with a mirror. "The Man With the Ladder and the Hose" was inspired by the first movie extolling the heroics of fire-fighting. "My Sweet Little Eskimo" was sung by every bass quartet, including the Empire City Four, who first introduced "bum-bum-bum" counterpoint.

The late Sol Bloom, veteran Congressman from New York, was a song publisher in 1905. His "Carissima," became the stock in trade of every soprano in the world. Bloom later promoted the Eltinge Theatre with Al Woods and Julian Eltinge. Another distinguished personality of 1905 was New York's future mayor, James J. Walker, who composed "Will You Love Me In December As You Did In May?"

"Everybody Works But Father," a hit song of Lew Dockstader's Minstrels, reflected the trend of the times when factories put women and children on payrolls, often in place of men, and threatened father's role as head of the family. Another family tune of 1905, "The Whole Dam Family," had these lusty lyrics: "There was Mr. Dam and Mrs. Dam, the Dam kids, two or three; with U. B. Dam and I. B. Dam and the whole Dam family!"

von tilzer, ball, cohan   Harry Von Tilzer, who wrote more than 3,000 songs in his career, scored in 1905 with "Wait Till the Sun Shines, Nellie" and "What You Goin' To Do When the Rent Comes 'Round?" George M. Cohan glorified Mary with "Mary's A Grand Old Name" and "So Long, Mary."

Imitations of successful songs started in 1906. After "Bicycle Built For Two" had proved its worth, a craze of "two" songs broke out —"Cottage Built For Two," "Picnic For Two," "Hammock Built For Two" and "In a World Built For Two." A few years later, when Jack Norworth and Al Von Tilzer cleaned up with "Take Me Out to the Ball Game," George M. Cohan, Billy Jerome and Jean Schwartz tried to steal some diamond thunder with "Take Your Girl to the Ball Game," but struck out badly.

Whistlers and violinists were made happy in 1906 by "The Mocking Birds Are Singing in the Wildwood." The waltz, still unchallenged by ragtime, was celebrated in "Waltz Me Around Again, Willie." One of the first popular cowboy songs, "Cheyenne," appeared under the Remick imprint. When Anna Held got something in her eye backstage, and winked unwittingly at Gus Edwards, she inspired "I Just Can't Make My Eyes Behave," which she afterwards suggestingly sang to fame in *A Parisian Model.*

Up-and-coming hit writer Ernest R. Ball presented "Love Me and the World Is Mine," and two famous English numbers were "Waiting At the Church" and Harry Lauder's "I Love A Lassie." Other hits of the year included "Somewhere," "Would You Leave Your Happy Home For Me?" and "Not Because Your Hair Is Curly." George M. Cohan came through with "I'm A Yankee Doodle Dandy" and "You're A Grand Old Flag," which he originally wrote as "You're A Grand Old Rag," but changed when it was attacked as irreverent.

Another cowboy song, "San Antonio," appeared in 1907, along with Cohan's "Harrigan," Gus Edwards' nostalgic "School Days" and Egbert Van Alstyne's "I'm Afraid to Go Home In the Dark," a husband's novel excuse for staying out all night. Eddie Foy sang "He Goes to Church on Sundays," a satire on weekday backsliders. Other hits of the year included "Every Little Bit Added to What You've Got Makes Just a Little Bit More," "Honey Boy," "No Wedding Bells For Me," and May Irwin's popular rendition of "The Peach That Tastes Sweetest Hangs the Highest on the Tree," to which Cab Calloway gave a novel twist years later in the scat number, "If You Don't Like My Peaches Why Do You Shake My Tree?"

negro dialect songs   The famous Negro team, Williams & Walker, who gave the era its richest Negro dialect songs, offered "Right Church But the Wrong Pew" and "Bon Bon Buddy" in 1908. Other hits were "Good Evening, Caroline," "Are You Sincere?", and "Yip-I-Addy-I-Ay," reminiscent of a 1947 hit tune with similar exuberance, "It's A Great Day." Jesse Lasky (later to become one of Hollywood's greats as a producer) contributed an Italian dialect number, "My Brudda Sylvest." A "cute" song, on the order of "Mairzy Doats," was "Bl-nd P-g Spells Blind Pig." "Don't Take Me Home" featured the plea of a drunken husband who was willing to go any place but there.

"Mary Took the Calves to the Dairy Show" was a suggestive song of 1908. Successive years brought other tongue-in-cheek tunes like "This Is No Place For A Minister's Son" (1909) and "If You Talk In Your Sleep Don't Mention My Name (1910).

President-to-be Taft's stock rose in 1909 with a political song, "Get On the Raft With Taft." Public satiety with the Salomé craze was expressed in "Sadie Salome, Go Home." A songwriter who had undoubtedly heard the English number, "Put On Your Old Green Bonnet," gave America its mellow, "Put On Your Old Gray Bonnet." And the Ten Commandments were paraphrased in a piece Bert Williams sang called, "Love Thy Neighbor As Thyself But Leave His Wife Alone."

One of the first ragtime songs to herald a new musical era was "Wild Cherrie Rag" in 1909. The year's production of *Yankee Girl* yielded "Whoop Daddy Ooden Dooden Day," a nonsense number in the vein of "Three Little Fishies." 1909 also came up with the lusty ballad, "Casey Jones," the inevitable bass song, "Bell In the Lighthouse," and a risqué number called "No One Could Do It Like My Father."

Irving Berlin co-authored a song with George Whiting that won instant popularity in 1909 among weary husbands, "My Wife's Gone to the Country (Hurray! Hurray!)." Its sequel was an equal favorite—"I Love My Wife But Oh, You Kid!" Two automobile numbers appeared, "Flipity Flop and Away She Goes" and "Give Me A Spin In Your Mitchell, Bill." Sentiment was satisfied with

"By the Light of the Silvery Moon," "Next To Your Mother, Who Do You Love?", "Beautiful Eyes" and "How Do You Do, Miss Josephine." In the heartbreak department were "I Wonder Who's Kissing Her Now," "I Wish I Had My Old Girl Back Again," and the inimitable Irene Franklin's version of "I Won't Send the Presents Back," which she sang from coast to coast on the Keith-Albee Circuit. Songs with special tempos were "Pony Boy" and "Cubanola Glide."

naughty songs   In Chicago's frenzied purge of 1910, "impure" songs were banned from its theatres. Censored tunes included " 'Tis Hard To Be A Lady In A Case Like That," "Without A Wedding Ring," "Grizzly Bear," "Her Name Was Mary Wood But Mary Wouldn't," "Gee Ain't I Glad I'm Single," and the two 1909 hits, "Casey Jones" and "I Love My Wife But Oh, You Kid." Chicago police stopped Sophie Tucker singing "Angle Worm Wiggle," and when the last of the red-hot mammas took it to court, the judge upheld the police.

Barbershop quartets revere 1910 as the year that gave them "Down By the Old Mill Stream" and "Girl Of My Dreams." Irving Berlin came out with two Jewish numbers, "Becky Do the Bombashay" and "Yiddisha Eyes," as well as a satire on woman's coyness, "Stop Stop Stop." Ernest R. Ball provided John McCormack with two of his greatest successes, "Mother Machree" and "Love Me and the World Is Mine." A hail-hail tribute to the head of the family was offered in "What's the Matter With Father?" A nation whose jaws wagged in more than song rejoiced in "Oh You Spearmint Kiddo With the Wrigley Eyes"—one of the pioneer "commercial" songs. Other 1910 hits included "I've Got Rings On My Fingers," "Steamboat Bill," "Under the Yum Yum Tree," "Great to Meet a Friend From Your Own Home Town" and "Winter."

Irving Berlin gave ragtime its biggest impetus in 1911 with "Alexander's Ragtime Band," followed jubilantly by "Everybody's Doin' It Now." Classical musicians began to protest—futilely—against ragtime as "detracting from the dignity of the musical arts."

Ernest R. Ball wrote "Till the Sands of the Deserts Grow Cold." Harry Von Tilzer and Will Dillon wrote a telephone song, "All Alone." Irving Berlin later used the same title for one of his songs. Harry Lauder burst forth with "Roamin' in the Gloamin'." 1911 saw a resurgence of old-fashioned love ballads: "Let Me Call You Sweetheart," "I Want A Girl Just Like the Girl Who Married Dear Old Dad," "Girl of My Dreams," and "Don't Wake Me Up, I'm Dreaming." In the same sentimental vein was "My Little Grey Home In the West." At the opposite pole, "Oh, You Beautiful Doll," "Look Out For Jimmy Valentine" and "When Mariola Does the Cubanola."

In 1912, Bert Williams introduced "My Landlady" and "You're On the Right Road But You're Going the Wrong Way." America heard the English song, "It's A Long Way to Tipperary," but was indifferent to it until two years later when it was cabled to the States from Europe as an "English marching song." Ball's "When Irish Eyes Are Smiling" won its greatest fame via Chauncey Olcott. There was a lugubrious prophecy of the H-bomb in "Last Night Was the End of the World." And Americans sang, "Moonlight Bay," "Waitin' For the Robert E. Lee," "When It's Apple Blossom Time In Normandy," "When You're Away," and "Daddy Has A Sweetheart, and Mother Is Her Name."

The Harry Thaw murder case produced a tuneful bit of 1913 curiosa in "Why Don't They Set Him Free?" declaring, "Just because he's a millionaire, everybody's willing to treat him unfair." Another tragic-toned melody was "The Curse Of An Aching Heart" ("You made me what I am today; I hope you're satisfied"). Ragtime was represented with "When Uncle Joe Plays A Rag On His Old Banjo." Another automobile tune, poking fun at the hardships of motorists, was "He'll Have to Get Out and Get Under."

"You Made Me Love You," a number that Al Jolson sang to fame, appeared in 1913, as did "Take Me to That Swanee Shore." An early-day "Oh, Johnny" was "On the Front Porch, Oh! Charlie!" Other top tunes of 1913 included "Trail of the Lonesome Pine," "That Old Girl of Mine," "Be My Little Baby Bumble Bee," "My Turkish Opal," "Dear Old Girl" and "You're A Great Big Blue-Eyed Baby."

The ragtime craze in 1913 provoked rag dancing contests in ballroom and vaudeville theatres. Many rag songs were a little too torrid for the temperature of B. F. Keith's in Boston, which promptly kept Bostonian ears unsullied by a time-honored ban.

A new development that year was the sudden reluctance of many vaudeville singers to use popular songs in their acts. Published songs traveled too fast, making a vaudeville singer's rendition of them often seem stale, and putting them in competition too often with other singers. Even acts which had been "payolaed" * by publishers began to realize that they were selling themselves short. Many singers began to use exclusive, tailor-made numbers. This was long before the speed of radio's make-'em-and-kill-'em-fast made overfamiliar pop songs a show business problem.

13

Critics—and 'Friendly' Reviewers

★

Actors Equity Association was organized in 1913 and quickly made its weight felt to the extent that Lee Shubert was stung into replying to their grievances with a frontal attack. "Acting is more nerve than skill," he scoffed. The actor was patently ungrateful for all the manager did for him, such as taking all the financial risks of a production. Actors were paid high salaries—and "these same people could not earn $10 per week at any other trade, working 8 hours a day."

But Mr. Shubert left unexplained the mystery of why he bothered to employ these ungrateful wearers of the buskin at all, when he had the pick of self-assured ribbon-counter salesmen at $10 a week.

The reviewers of the 1905-1913 era had little weight outside of the legitimate, but in that realm they were omnipotent. They were so greatly feared by producers of the day that the Shuberts barred regularly those critics who attacked any of their shows.

The Washington roll of honor of blacklisted critics included Willard Holcombe, Will A. (Piggy) Page, a former press agent until he began to promote himself harder than his clients, and Channing

* The *"payola"* (payment to an act, band, singer) is a continuing evil, and is detailed later.

Pollock, whom the Shuberts drove out of two-on-the-aisle into shining fame as one of America's most successful playwrights.

The critic who did the most to elevate David Belasco to uncritical heights in the theatre was William Winter, who wielded a scholarly, graceful and learned pen. His contemporary on the New York *Morning Sun*, Franklin Fyles, lacked Winter's profundity but possessed a lively style that animated his first attempt at playwriting, *The Girl He Left Behind Him*, which utilized such surefire devices as a flag rippling out from a hollow staff in a gale caused by a concealed blower.

Alan Dale of the New York *Journal* was a triton among minnows. Dale's forte was the ability to write amusing leads to his reviews. When Hammerstein produced the ballet *Marguerite*, at the Olympia Theatre, it included a circus number with four girls prancing under the guidance of a ringmaster. "If those horses had tails," Dale commented wistfully, "I could have written a great story." In his later years, after Dale had a row with the Hearst organization, he became a Variety staffer covering legit for a short time, but didn't last long. Unlike the illustrious Jack Lait, latterly editor of the New York *Daily Mirror*, and before that manager of Variety's Chicago bureau, Dale couldn't be sufficiently objective. His Hearstian builder uppered byline was too first-person and very singular for the objectiveness that goes with being a Variety mugg.

to continue, of the other new york critics Acton Davies of the *Sun* was the master of the verbal stiletto. Reviewing Otero, a heavy-footed, small-voiced Spanish dancer brought over by the Eden Musée to compete with Carmencita, he wrote blandly: "We have seen Otero sing, we have heard her dance." In summing up a play about the Spanish-American War which opened at the Grand Opera House, he reported: "The second act takes place in a castle which, like most of the women in the play, had been ruined by the Spaniards."

Louis De Foe of the New York *Morning World* had a peculiar method of satisfying both his own conscience and the advertising department. When reviewing a new play, he wrote with informed honesty, a habit deplored by both producers and the paper's business manager. But in his Sunday recapitulation of the week's offerings,

De Foe often toned down his judgments, and sometimes even reversed himself, which may have confused his readers but delighted everybody else.

Charles Darton of the New York *Evening World* was much more consistent. He seldom used hard words, and was extremely tender in his reviews of Shubert shows, causing Broadway to wonder whether Darton was not on more than one payroll. He and De Foe (on Sundays) were so "dependable" that their names were left in lights on the Shubert electric sign over the Winter Garden in the certain knowledge that they would produce favorable quotes on the new Shubert production.

Leander Richardson, editor of his own *Dramatic News* and later drama critic of the New York *Morning Telegraph,* was highly respected for both his integrity and honesty. He engaged in several fist fights with actors who resented his notices, and was entrusted with backstage confidences by Broadway producers who knew he would not betray them. Richardson also wrote for Variety.

Rennold Wolf, who followed Richardson on the *Telegraph,* was not a particularly capable critic, but he was greatly esteemed as the best toastmaster the Friars Club ever had. The Louella Parsons of her day was ex-actress Amy Leslie, who covered Chicago. The West Coast had the late Ashton Stevens who later shifted to Chicago and the *Herald Examiner.*

Three brilliant critics of the period were E. D. Price, considered Broadway's first real columnist with his "Man Behind the Scenes" featured in the *Telegraph;* Frank Butler, who succeeded him—"too lazy to do his best, his second best being very good"; and the aesthetic James G. Huneker of the *Commercial Advertiser,* whose books were eagerly read by the intelligentsia.

The impact of Variety's reviews in the pre-World War I period was chiefly on vaudeville and burly. Managers studied Variety's reviews of acts as a measuring rod for bookings or rejecting, paying particular attention to Variety's report of audience reaction. Until Variety appeared on the scene to print honest reviews and news "without regard to whose name is mentioned or the advertising columns," reviews in other trade journals were regarded by actors as "blackmail—give 'em an ad and you're great stuff—don't advertise and they pan you."

first film reviews   The first review of pictures in Variety appeared in January 1907, with the coverage of the Pathe film, *An Exacting Honeymoon,* and Edison's *Life of a Cowboy.*

In 1907 Variety also began its reviews of acts in France and Italy, noting an 18-year-old Italian girl who ably portrayed 15 characters as a quick-change artist.

Actors were extremely sensitive to Variety criticism. After a flaying of their act in 1908, the Cherry Sisters replied with a steaming-hot letter which Variety printed, as they did many actors' rebuttals of their critics.

"In your issue of March 21," the Cherry Sisters wrote, "you had an article which was one of the most malicious, violent and untruthful writings we have ever read. The person who wrote it is not deserving the name of a man, but is instead a contemptible cur. You said in your paper that we advertised ourselves 'the worst show on earth,' which makes you a liar, point blank. We have always advertised ourselves as one of the best, and we would not be far from the truth if we said the best. . . . Although we have the best act in vaudeville and are the best drawing card on the stage, we have no swelled heads, as some others have. We have had more knocking since we went into the theatrical business than any other act in the history of the world, and we have come to no other conclusion why this is done except we are not of the character of these unprincipled editors and managers who have done the knocking and slandering."

Variety's editor added a concise footnote: "The Cherry Sisters are slightly mistaken that the article said they advertise themselves as the 'worst show on earth.' It mentioned the general opinion which obtained regarding their act." Sixteen years later, when the Cherry Sisters staged a comeback, Variety sent a reviewer to Des Moines.

" 'Perfectly terrible' was never more applicable," Variety summed up. "As terribleness, their skit is perfection . . . The manager, who happens to be punished by having them placed on his bill, has only one opportunity—that of billing them as a comedy duo."

trapping a larcenous competitor   In 1908 Variety became irked and tired of being plagiarized by a would-be rival, the New York *Dramatic Mirror.* *Sime* laid a trap, after his muggs had ascertained that no *Mirror* reviewer had ever been seen in Tony Pastor's. Variety reviewed a new "surprise act" at Tony Pastor's,

"Pleasant and Newburg in a comedy skit, 'The Undertaker,'" with a detailed resumé of the act. The following week an almost identical review appeared in the *Mirror*. Whereupon Variety revealed that the act was a nonexistent hoax, and headlined the exposure: "The Thieving *Dramatic Mirror* Caught Red-Handed With the Goods." The *Mirror* has long since suspended publication.

Epes Winthrop Sargent, who wrote for Variety as *Chicot*, explained the blunt candor of Variety's reviews in this fashion: "The average actor was too dumb to appreciate niceties of language. I could not say he was a bad actor. I had to tell him he was a damned bad actor. . . . It was taking chances to tell an acrobat that his comedy would make a horse vomit, but it was part of the risk, and I only got one black eye."

Epitomizing Variety's role as reviewer, he added, "It was colloquial and ungrammatical, but so were the actors, and they loved it."

Variety was the first to review each new act as an entity, under the department "New Acts," rather than incidentally as part of a complete show. The shortest review of a New Act was written by Variety's *Jolo* (the late Joshua Lowe) who covered a trick horse act called "Napoleon."

Jolo's review, in its entirety, read, "Giddyap Napoleon. Small time bound."

Variety's unique style of criticism will be automatically touched on in ensuing chapters. Variety wasn't always right. Joe Bigelow gave Marc Connelly's Pulitzer Prize play *The Green Pastures* quick death. Jack Conway's uniquely gifted talents as a slangist, of course, got him widespread attention, including a short hitch in the Hollywood vineyards which was marred only by the fact that in all of his first six months on the lot he never saw his producer.

PART TWO

WAR COMES TO SHOW BIZ 1914 - 1918

14

'. . . Too Proud to Fight'

★

Leutnant-Kapitan Schwieger, Commander of U-boat 20, peered through the periscope. Above the wrinkling waves he could see the ship's four stacks, the proud gold letters on its bow spelling out the name, *Lusitania*. It was Friday, May 7, 1915, 2:08 P.M. Off to the starboard of the big liner were the sloping, peaceful hills of southern Ireland.

Schwieger shouted a terse command. Torpedos leaped through the sea. There was a violent, churning explosion, and billowing clouds of smoke rose into the clear sky. At a cost of 114 American lives, Germany had delivered her warning to the United States that an American passport held no privileges when used on a ship belonging to Germany's wartime enemy.

Less than a year later, *Leutnant-Kapitan* Schwieger's fellow-countrymen, interned aboard the *S.S. Vaterland* in New York, sent their band ashore to serenade Americans at a Loew theatre. Cheers, not merely applause, greeted their performance.

The cause of the Allies was not too popular in America in 1914, 1915, and even 1916. If many Americans sympathized with the Allies before 1917, the vast majority were not pro-anything European. They re-elected Woodrow Wilson in 1916 because "he kept us out of war." The moral aspects of the quarrel on the Continent were summed up by the popular sentiment, "It's our good fortune that we're not mixed up in it."

If neutrality was good enough for Wilson, it was good enough for Variety. Many Americans sincerely subscribed to neutrality as the best course because of a widespread belief that the war could not last long. In 1914 most American "experts" were predicting it would be over by three to five months. That was hardly surprising when, the following year, a poll of English opinion showed that 25 per cent of the English expected peace in 1915, while 40 per cent expected it to be over by March 31, 1916.

In 1914 and 1915 the average American flipped past the war news to read about Congress passing the bill for Mother's Day; a five-month coal strike; Billy Sunday; the growth of transcontinental and international telegraphy; Ford making his 1,000,000th auto; Gil Anderson setting a new speed record of 102.6 miles per hour; the Frank lynching in Georgia; and the electrocution of Police Lieutenant Charles Becker.

complete escapism   In show business songs were manufactured to fit the prevailing pattern of neutrality. Movies thrived and became too big for the cramped theatres. Dansants zoomed to the peak of their popularity, then crashed to a swift decline. Professional society dancers were swept out of the limelight to make room for Ziegfeld girls and "jazz" dancers. Hammerstein's closed and the Palace boomed. Over 60 per cent of some 2,500 Philadelphia students polled in 1914 chose vaudeville as the form of entertainment they liked best.

But in 1914 vaudeville, like all of show business, was flopping badly in a terrible b.o. year. This, after New York had just finished spending $8,870,000 for new theatres the year before. Los Angeles showmen groaned as worse followed bad when snow, flood and washouts ruined business in the land of eternal sunshine.

1916, a year of unrest, uncertainty and nervous tension, marked the turning point in American war sentiment. We were no longer "too proud to fight." Neither were we at war. We were following the new magic Wilsonian watchword—"Preparedness!" Washington issued stern warnings to Germany about its submarine warfare. As though in answer, munitions plants in Black Tom Island, Jersey City, blew up mysteriously. Secretary of State Robert Lansing's statement at the end of the year that America was being drawn into the war, caused frantic stock market trading.

Nervous Americans sought relief in entertainment. Show business boomed that year, aided by the boom in paychecks which followed "preparedness." Musicals and revues sold out for weeks in advance. The theatre's one nervous moment in 1916 came with an infantile paralysis scare that threatened to close theatres in many major cities.

The year that America entered the war was a breathless one, filled with confusion, hysteria and sudden change. War was declared on April 2, with the first draft act taking effect June 15.

For show business, the first half of 1917 was a drunken, joyous spree. The latter half proved a hangover. B.o. receipts dropped with a sickening thud. Ticket money went into buying Liberty Bonds. Parents stayed home to scan newspapers for reports of their sons' regiments. Close to a million men abandoned theatre attendance for close-order drill. Many more millions were busy with war plant overtime, and the Government added the finishing touch in December by forcing a blackout and curfew on Broadway.

Show business grinned feebly, led the drive for bond sales and recruiting, and hoped for the best. At the height of its troubles it still had time to enjoy a typical actors' prank like Charlie Judels' impersonation of a French sailor. Dressed for the part, he delivered a spirited address to visiting French officers of high rank, from the steps of New York's Public Library on Fifth Avenue. The officers, who didn't understand a word of it, applauded vigorously. They assumed he came from a different part of France. Judels' fractured "French" was merely some early vintage double-talk.

foreign b.o. upbeat   Although America's entry into the war seemed a death-knell to American show business, it spurted boxoffice receipts abroad, where the theatre had already passed through its dark phase and made a recovery. Canada had the best theatrical season in history. Audiences in other Allied countries indulged in a spree of entertainment. America was in the war. Ergo, the war would be shorter, and victory was assured. Let's go to a show!

The first American soldiers were killed in action in January, 1918. Wilson made his famous 14-Point speech, and in the spring 10,000 troops a day left America's shores. There was Chateau-Thierry in July, the month that America launched 100 ships. There was the Fourth Liberty Loan in October, and the 2,000,000th Yank to land overseas. November brought a false armistice, a real armistice and an end to censorship four days later. New York raised its steel antisubmarine net in December, welcomed the first troops back, and saw President Wilson off to the Peace Conference.

Unnoticed in all the excitement was the passing of the woman suffrage bill, and negation of the child labor laws of 1916 as unconstitutional. Noticed was the wild leap in the cost of living, and the nationwide flu epidemic. Noticed, too, and fiercely resented by returning troops, was the approaching end of America's right to drink, which taboo became a law in the first month of 1919.

Only one branch of show business shared that resentment, the cabarets. Other branches found that the boxoffice was actually benefited in those states where prohibition was in effect. But for cabarets, Volsteadism was synonymous with bankruptcy.

All of show business felt the flu epidemic, during which almost a quarter of the nation's population fell sick. Nineteen out of every 1,000 downed by flu died. Deaths tallied were between 400,000-500,-000. Reaching into Army camps at home, the flu killed off half as many soldiers as died overseas.

Nine out of 10 American theatres were shut down. Many cities forbade public gatherings. Of the one theatre in 10 allowed to remain open, few were able to do better than break even.

And the flu killed actors, too.

15

Show Biz's Patriotic Rally

★

"The theatre," President Woodrow Wilson said, "was one of the most potent contributing factors to American victory in the World War." But while show business did a great deal for the war effort, the war effort did very little for show business.

When cities like Bridgeport became boomtown munitions centers as early as 1915, there was general rejoicing at the boxoffice, which stayed open morning, noon and midnight. But by 1918 boomtown workers were so exhausted by overtime that they had neither energy nor time for anything but sleep. Theatre receipts flopped badly. A notable exception was the boomtown Washington, D.C. So many armchair generals jammed the theatres that producers seriously considered making the nation's Capital a rival to Broadway.

Juvenile patriotism also hit theatre managers. When public school propaganda successfully urged Los Angeles children to save their dimes for War Savings Stamps, 23 film houses closed. War Stamp purchases by small fry also caused a bad slump throughout the Midwest.

With some 2,000,000 males summoned by the Army, it was only natural that a great many theatre tickets went unsold. Perhaps hardest hit in the draft years were burlesque theatres, who couldn't hope to compensate for this loss by increased feminine patronage.

Rocketing prices and shortages plagued the theatre too. Paper, inks, scenic canvas, paints and costume materials were both scarce and expensive. Half-built theatres were left unfinished, plans for new ones scrapped, when the Government froze steel supplies in 1917. Variety was forced to raise its price to 15¢.

Between 1914 and 1918 there were often more hardships in being a trouper than being troops. When the Government took over the railroads in 1918, trains were abruptly cut out of time-tables, and actors headed for Denver frequently wound up in Dallas.

chorus boy-less musicals   The draft thinned out casts as well as audiences and single acts became more prevalent. Musical comedies eliminated chorus men entirely and backstage technicians soon became irreplaceable. Broadway suffered a 10:45 blackout late in 1917 on Government orders, to conserve fuel. In 1918 a 10 P.M. curfew was declared on all theatre performances. As a result, many legitimate shows eliminated intermissions to make the deadline.

Boxoffices reeled when all theatres were ordered closed on Tuesdays, "Garfield holidays," as they were named in honor of Wilson's fuel administrator. Shudders coursed through Broadway night spot owners upon hearing that the Government had shut every cabaret and roadhouse in New Orleans.

Film exhibitors scrambled frantically for any feature with a war title or angle. A Keith manager, Ned Hastings, won front-page headlines by announcing that, in the event we went to war, sea lions would be offered to the Government for scout duty. They would be specially trained, he explained, to spot enemy submarines and make a bee-line for home.

And in 1916 most young actors who belonged to the National Guard were discussing with enthusiasm the imminence of war duty on the Mexican border, chasing Pancho Villa.

Once Wilson had cast the die, however, show business became violently patriotic. It became the leading force in recruiting, selling Liberty Bonds, maintaining home morale, and in boosting the spirits of Americans in khaki, wherever they happened to be.

In the recent war John Golden was the chairman of the theatrical committee which gave millions of free theatre tickets to servicemen. In 1917 Golden headed the show business committee pledged to support the Liberty Loans. For the Second Loan, the Palace Theatre alone turned in $750,000. For the Third Loan, show business pledged the staggering sum of $100,000,000, with 25 per cent of the total to come from Greater New York. The quota went over the top.

Government "four minute men" teams—pledged not to speak over four minutes each—were allowed to sell bonds between acts. Lillian Russell announced that she was returning to vaudeville again for one reason only—to speak about Liberty Bonds. She neglected, however, to mention that this patriotic stirring was rewarded at the rate of $2,500 a week. A much more laudable figure was vaudeville's Corporal M. H. Plant who, after winning a Croix de Guerre with America's first raiding party, was sent back by General Pershing to aid the Liberty Loan.

Woodrow Wilson, like F.D.R., was an ardent theatre fan. It was not unusual, then, for him to appear in a box at B. F. Keith's in Washington, 10 days after he had delivered America's declaration of war, where he was cheered lustily for five minutes after it was announced that he had purchased a $1,000 Liberty Bond.

Millions were added to Red Cross coffers by benefits such as the Lloyds Neck, L.I., open-air pageant, which netted one-night proceeds of $34,000.

lauder and paderewski   Harry Lauder donated his salary for three performances every week to the Red Cross. Paderewski spearheaded the movement to raise funds for Polish war sufferers. Vaudeville houses collected $86,000 in 1917 for a soldiers' and sailors' smoke fund. The only sour note was sounded by the musicians of the show, *Seven Days Leave,* who refused to join actors and stagehands in playing a benefit performance for the Stage War Relief Fund.

The forerunner of the recent war's U.S.O. camp shows were the Liberty theatres, which were hurriedly built on 1918's army posts. The first Liberty Theatre was at Camp Sherman, Ohio, which offered *Cheating Cheaters.* House managers for Liberty theatres were designated civilian aides, given the rank and pay of second lieutenants.

Irving Berlin's smash musical hit of World War II, *This Is The Army,* with an all-soldier cast, was history repeating itself. Berlin did exactly the same thing in World War I with *Yip Yip Yaphank,* which opened at the Century Theatre with 350 soldiers from Camp Upton. Star of the show was Berlin himself, singing his own songs. In one number he appeared in K.P. costume, water-bucket in hand, to lament: "I scrub the dishes against my wishes to make this wide world safe for democracy."

Nobody was more surprised at the roof-raising ovation given *Yip* at the first night than Camp Upton's Major General J. Franklin Bell, who had taken a dim view of Berlin's request. Speaking from a box, the delighted General orated, "I have heard that Berlin is among the foremost songwriters of the world, and now I believe it. . . . Berlin is as good a soldier as he is a songwriter, and as popular in Camp Upton as he is on Broadway."

Variety dusted off its seldom-used superlatives and lavished them on *Yip.* "One of the best and most novel entertainments Broadway has ever witnessed," it stated. "There's no theatrical manager who wouldn't grab it without the uniforms."

And they tried to. Producers battled for the rights to produce the Berlin show with a professional cast, once the singing soldiers had toured it in Boston, Philadelphia and Washington. The show cleared $120,000 in two weeks run in New York alone. That proceeds were intended to build a community house, or service club, for Camp Upton did not deter Broadway ticket offices and speculators from demanding $4.50 and $5.50 a pair for tickets (robbery in those days) and getting it.

The 27th Infantry Division, intrigued by *Yip*'s success, put on its own soldier show, called *You Know Me, Al.* With 109 men of the 27th in the cast, it played at the Lexington Opera House for a successful two and a half weeks.

When the emphasis shifted from army camps at home to those overseas, a unique mass meeting of actors was called at the Palace Theatre. Chairman George M. Cohan presented the plan of E. H. Sothern and Winthrop Ames to form an Over There Theatre League. He called for those who would volunteer to entertain troops overseas to signify by standing up.

Every seat in the house clattered back.

About 350 volunteers were finally selected and their applications cleared through Washington "to ascertain that the applicant is thoroughly American and eligible to go abroad as an entertainer behind the lines." They were sent to England and France under the auspices of the Y.M.C.A., which arranged for their uniforms, transportation, a $3,500 insurance policy and a monthly salary of $125. Actors paid for their own food and lodging, toward which the Over There League chipped in $2 a day extra.

One of those who was not "thoroughly American," but to whom the Government readily granted permission, was Harry Lauder. His son had been killed in action.

slackers, too   Like all fields, show business had its quota
of reluctant patriots. Bernard Granville found that out after he had
signed up about 100 actors for a "depot brigade," assuring them their
duties would simply consist of a short drill weekly. When Granville's volunteers reported and learned that they would be required
to swear an oath of allegiance to the Army, all but 30 quickly disappeared.

Broadway was a bad hideout for draft dodgers. Government
agents frequently rounded up crowds there and demanded registration cards. Lounge lizards quickly disappeared when Rector's
and Churchill's afternoon teas were discontinued under General
Crowder's "useful occupations" order and Governor Whitman's
"Loafer's Law."

Under this bill men from 18 to 51 had to be employed at a useful
trade or profession at least 36 hours a week. Otherwise they had to
work on a farm or in a munitions plant. Failure to do so brought a
penalty of a $100 fine or three months in jail. Actors were classed
in a bracket with teachers and students, and declared entitled to a
two months' vacation "after a winter's toil."

The perplexed draft board granted a deferment.

The Four Marx Bros., all subject to the draft, turned up as a
quartet at a Chicago recruiting station to enlist in the Illinois infantry. One was rejected for defective eyesight. A second for flat
feet. A third for physical disability incurred by an operation. And
the fourth—"for general reasons."

"That's nothing," Groucho boasted to the recruiting sergeant,
"You should see the *fifth* Marx brother: two heads!"

During the years England was at war and America wasn't, the
presence of English actors in America presented a delicate question.
In London, 1,500 out of 8,000 male actors joined the British army,
and were sending home printed letters which permitted them to
check off appropriate sentiments and news.

The first time "slackers" was used was in 1915, when the British
Consulate so designated Englishmen in America who didn't return
to join the British Army. It further dismayed the Consulate when
the following year 5,000 British nationals applied for American citizenship.

On the callboards of London stages were posted lists of British
slackers who were clinging to the security of American bookings.

When even this disgrace failed to shake loose the expatriate English thespians, a British recruiting mission arrived in America in 1917 to round up 600 actors on their list.

Four months after America declared war, however, over 60 English actors presented themselves at British recruiting offices in New York for enlistment in the British Army. A great many more donned British and Canadian uniforms without bothering to sign up, and were bitterly denounced by the British War Commission in the States as "uniform fakers." Special permission was required to wear the British uniform on an American stage.

The impact of the war on show business abroad was understandably more severe than at home. From early 1914 on, actors, managers, composers, authors and technicians in Europe were enacting roles in the theatre of mud and shell-scream, rather than of greasepaint and kettle drums.

In the first year of war all English seacoast theatres were closed. Pathe, Gaumont and all of France's picture studios shut down. It was like that over most of the Continent. Some 900 acts crowded the boats from Europe to seek American bookings, causing no little havoc to employment on United States circuits.

Variety estimated that 150 American acts were stranded overseas at the sudden outbreak of war, unable to get out because of battle conditions. There were 80 such acts in Germany and Austria, 20 in France and 15 in Russia. American acts playing in London were being paid in paper money difficult to convert into dollars.

yanks in piccadilly   London theatre managers in 1914, quick to realize the drain war would place on English talent, lost no time calling upon American show business talent. In that year London presented its first all-American bill. It was the year that launched Eddie Cantor as a solo artist, after he split with his partner Sammy Kessler in London, and joined a revue at the Alhambra.

English agents and managers placed luring ads in Variety, urging acts not to be afraid of submarines or mines, and promising lush bookings. These appeals were well-timed, coinciding with a wave of salary-cutting on American circuits. Some actors were afraid to cross the Atlantic, but many saw London as the golden opportunity to win both a reputation and a fat purse. Despite the red tape wound around passports for England, many acts did make the crossing, and a good many stayed there. The trend was so well-defined that 1916 saw nine American plays in London.

Most of the actors who returned from English engagements brought back the new wristwatch fad. Few wore them publicly, however, for fear of being branded effeminate. A more widespread affectation among both ladies and gentlemen of the theatre, was the carrying of British swagger sticks.

Reaction to the American theatrical boom in England set in during 1917. With America now at war, the status of American actors in England assumed a different complexion. And also, there was a natural feeling of resentment on the part of English actors whose stars had fallen because of the invasion. The British Board of Trade barred American actors from landing, notified all steamship companies to this effect, and made it obligatory for any actor to secure a permit from the Board before he was allowed to set foot on English soil.

English ads in Variety still coaxed American actors in 1916. "England is safe for Americans," timid thespians were assured. "The air and sea are clear of danger. . . . Zeppelins have been stopped during the winter by new guns, and the cold of higher altitudes. . . . In their last raid, eight Germans froze inside a Zeppelin. . . . The seas have been freed of subs by English control."

But in 1917 German air raids compelled many theatres to suspend night performances. Those shows which defied the Zeppelins and stayed open were invariably well filled. "Artists and audiences," Variety reported, "remained calm while London is bombed."

English managers, at the outset of war, used the upset as an excuse to slash actors' salaries 30 to 50 per cent, and attempted to introduce split-week bookings, in imitation of American managers. Some managers pleaded poverty, claiming they couldn't pay full salaries, and persuaded acts to work on a percentage of the house. Although a few acts profited by this arrangement, most did not. Managers' profits meanwhile fattened.

In 1915, while slashing actors' salaries, operators of the London Music Hall declared large dividends and paid lush salaries to the directors and board chairmen. The Victoria, managed by the astute Sir Alfred Butt, wound up the year with a profit of $224,000.

In the legit, the war gave even mediocre plays long runs, due to the difficulty of getting new shows. This fact also accounted for a high percentage of revivals. Plays and musicals did a booming business, with revues the top money-makers. Oddly enough, London's first cabaret revue, Tom Ryley's "Frolic" at Ciro's, was practically hooted off the stage by both public and press because of "unnecessary extravagance in wartime."

a real 'quickie'   Revues were so popular that even Sir James M. Barrie planned one, touching off a quarrel over ethics with George Bernard Shaw. Barrie, it seems, invited prominent people to a dinner, during which they were secretly filmed. Shaw later charged that Barrie intended using the film in his revue, but had been foiled because two of the "prominent people" had behaved too amorously for the camera. "Barrie," Shaw thundered, "invited people to an 8-shilling dinner, getting a valuable picture at minimum cost."

Two revues featured fighters. Alfred Butt signed France's Georges Carpentier for the *Merry-Go-Round Revue* at the Empire, paying him $3,500 a week and billing him as "The White Champion of the World." Jack Johnson gave a boxing demonstration in a revue at the Euston Music Hall, during which two British femmes daintily mopped his brow between rounds.

The vicissitudes of show business in America and England were as nothing compared to what happened to show business in France. During the Battle of the Marne in 1914, when the Germans threatened Paris, every Parisian theatre was closed for two months. After the Marne victory only one film house opened its doors, then a few vaudeville houses. Many actors had to join the growing queues at soup kitchens.

No one cross-section of show business felt the impact of the war as much as German and Austrian actors. With the coming of war in 1914, an hysterical spy scare swept the Allies. England immediately ordered all German actors place photos on their passports, forbade them to carry arms, or travel over five hours at a time, and compelled those who had changed their names to resume their rightful identities.

Despite these stringent precautions, English managers cancelled German acts indiscriminately. Mixed nationality teams split. One German acrobatic act assumed Japanese names, and appeared in Oriental makeup.

Many Dutch comedy acts fled to Canada, where a great number became Irish comics. The spy scare was so heightened that when the Pantages Theatre in Edmonton, Alberta installed a wireless to relay war messages between acts, the Canadian Army seized it. American burlesque troupes touring Canada were compelled to remove German characters before risking performance. Canada finally· warned in 1916 that it would intern any Germans and Austrians who came to play within its borders.

The spy scare in the United States assumed gigantic proportions after an exposé in 1915 which forced the German consul to leave New York, and the Black Tom explosions of 1916 which rocked the New York-New Jersey area. Once war had been declared by Congress, Secret Service agents checked on all German actors in the country, and set June 9, 1917 as the last day on which they could travel without permission.

The special attention paid to Germans in show business was not without justification, as evidence showed that Germany was furthering its propaganda through its theatrical artists. Mata Hari, the dance queen of Holland, had been executed. It was open knowledge that German actresses in Switzerland had pried war secrets out of Allied soldiers over empty bottles and under ruffled bed linen. Variety reported that even Max Reinhardt's theatre company unwittingly contained five German spies.

16

'What Kind of an American Are You?'

★

"*Deutschland, Deutschland Über Alles*" and "*Die Wacht am Rhein*" were the songs on the lips of German soldiers as they marched lyrically to war. And it was "Fatherland, My Fatherland" that the Kaiser's troops sang as they conquered.

The British troops, with less mechanical minds, sang their unofficial war song, "It's A Long Way to Tipperary." This song had been ignored by America two years before, but in the fall of 1914, plugged by American publishers as "The Song They Sing As They March Along," at 30¢ a copy, it was whistled, sung, hummed, danced and applauded in America to the tune of over a million sales.

London's song hits in the early part of the war were anything but martial. Typical war songs included "Sister Susie's Sewing Shirts For Soldiers," "Are We Downhearted?" and "Love Me While the Loving Is Good." In the gang's-all-here spirit, Englishmen sang "You're Here and I'm Here" and "Are We All Here?" And as Zeppelins dropped their calling cards, you could hear, "The Sunshine of Your Smile," "When Irish Eyes Are Smiling," "S'nice S'mince S'pies," and "Wonderful Rose of Love."

Despite the fact that Irving Berlin wrote "I Hear the Voice of Belgium" in 1915 for the Belgian Relief Fund, the year's song crop was largely antiwar, proneutrality. Even with the sinking of the *Lusitania* and the exposure of Germany's spy network in America, we were, in President Wilson's words, "too proud to fight."

Tin Pan Alley responded with "We're All With You, Mr. Wilson," "Go Right Ahead, Mr. Wilson" and "Our Hats Off To You, Mr. Wilson." The latter song, indiscreetly sung in Canada by Trixie Friganza and other American singers, was greeted either with violent hisses or a deadly silence.

Antiwar songs laid heavy stress on "mother" sentimentality. "Don't Take My Darling Boy Away" and "I Didn't Raise My Boy To Be A Soldier" were shrewdly designed to appeal to a lucrative market—the mothers of America. But a subtle change in America's attitude during 1915 became evident when sales of the latter song suddenly dropped off in a month's time.

Very gradually America began singing songs like "I'd Be Proud To Be the Mother of a Soldier," whose chorus declared, "It would be a different story if they trampled on Old Glory—then I'd be proud to be the mother of a soldier!" Unsophisticated hearts began to beat faster to "America, I Love You" and the prophetic advice, "Save Your Kisses Till the Boys Come Home." (World War II had its counterpart in "Don't Sit Under the Apple Tree With Anyone Else But Me.")

After Wilson had been re-elected, and the national theme changed
to "Preparedness," Tin Pan Alley was not slow to read the revised
handwriting on the wall. War songs flooded the country, and singers
found them sure-fire for bringing an audience to its feet.

England's big hit of 1916 was "Keep the Home Fires Burning."
Americans sang, "My Country, I Hear You Calling Me," "Follow
the Flag You Love," and "Stand By Your Uncle Sam." Young men
sang, half-ruefully, "I Hate Like Hell to Go," "The Army Blues,"
and "Just Say Hello To the Girls We Know Back on Old Broadway."

Young women sang earnestly, "I'm Proud of You, Laddie" and
"Soldier Boy, I Kiss Before You Go." All this, incidentally, a year or
so before America's first draft act. In some cases the war sentiment,
however, didn't refer to the big league battle at all, such as "They're
On Their Way to Mexico."

the flag-wavers   As the last shreds of American neutrality
were ripped from the nation's reticence, songsmiths ground out war
songs with feverish haste and blatance. "What Kind Of An American Are You?" Americans sang to each other in 1917. One tunesmith came up with "America Needs You Like A Mother—Would
You Turn Your Mother Down?"

Among the unabashed flag-wavers were "For Your Country and
My Country," "Root For Uncle Sam," "You've Got To Be An Amer-
ican to Feel That Way" and "Liberty Bell, It's Time To Ring
Again." George M. Cohan, with an equal mixture of romance and
patriotism, gave America "There's Only One Little Girl and One
Little Flag For Me."

The mother appeal figured in "America Here's My Boy," "So
Long Mother," "That's a Mother's Liberty Loan," "There's A Vacant Chair In Every Home Tonight," "There Is a Service Flag Flying At Our House" and a revival of the Spanish-American War
tearjerker, "Break the News to Mother."

America's melting-pot population was urged "Let's All Be Americans Now" and "Don't Bite the Hand That's Feeding You." Men
who stayed behind were implored "Don't Try To Steal the Sweetheart of A Soldier." Enlistments were coaxed with "It's Time For
Everybody to Be A Soldier," "If I Were A Boy You Bet I'd Belong
to the Navy," "Dixie Volunteers," "I'm In the Army Now," and a

hillbilly song, "Long Boy" ("Goodbye Maw, Goodbye Paw, Goodbye Mule").

Outraged decency was appealed to with "For the Freedom of the World," "Joan of Arc," "Belgian Rose," "Rose of No Man's Land" and "Hang the Kaiser Under the Linden Tree." The arrival of American troops in France gave rise to "Somewhere In France Is Daddy," "When Yankee Doodle Learns to Parlez Vous Francais" and "Say A Prayer For the Boys Over There."

Ex-President Theodore Roosevelt vainly sought permission from Secretary of War Newton D. Baker to raise a Roosevelt Division under his command. His cause was assisted, however fruitlessly, by the song, "If We Had A Million More Like Teddy." War workers and farmers, chafing at all the melodic glory bestowed upon the men in uniform, were pacified with a lyrical eulogy, "The Man Behind the Hammer and the Plow."

The song of World War I, of course, was George M. Cohan's stirring "Over There," introduced in 1917 by Nora Bayes and Irving Fisher in her own show at New York's 39th Street Theatre, at Cohan's request. Feist paid $25,000 for the song, and in less than one year sold 440,000 copies at a dime each. Although almost every American knew the words of this immortal war song by heart, Cohan forgot the lyrics when he sang it at Ebling's Casino for his father's pet charity. Irving Berlin and Joe Laurie, Jr. had to run onstage and help him out.

War songs were considered so important to America's war effort that George Creel's Committee on Public Information prepared a collection in booklet form, at Government expense, for use in connection with a corps of song leaders he appointed to take charge of community singing in the nation's film houses.

Vaudeville houses featured war song contests, in which music publishers were allowed to plug one or two of their war numbers, with the audience judging the best. Each publisher, of course, sent along his own callous-palmed claques. At Keith's Fifth Avenue, the voting, in order of selection, went to "Break the News To Mother," "Joan of Arc," "Somewhere In France Is A Lily," "Send Me Away With A Smile" and "It's A Long Way to Berlin."

In the climactic year of the war, it was the rare melody that was unaccompanied by Mars-tinted lyrics. Songwriters were still thumping the drum with hats-off numbers like "Let's Keep the Glow In

Old Glory and the Free In Freedom, Too" and "America Makes the World Safe for Democracy."

the home-front A heavy battery of tunes were concentrated on home-front activities. Food shortages were reflected by "We Don't Want the Bacon, What We Want Is A Piece of the Rhine." To back up fuel conservation Americans were implored in song to "Keep Cool, the Country's Saving Fuel," and Irving Berlin attacked fuel-hoarders with "The Devil Has Bought Up All the Coal."

Liberty Loans were floated to the tune of "What Are You Going To Do To Help Our Boys?", the official song; "We'll Do Our Share While You're Over There"; and the dire imprecation on slackers, "Those Mother's Tears Will Bring A Curse On You." The ladies who fought the war with needles enjoyed "Listen to the Knocking at the Knitting Club." The Fulton Theatre posted a sign at its boxoffice: "Ladies are requested not to knit during the action of the play, as it disturbs other patrons."

After the superficial pride induced by numbers like "Giving My Son to the U.S.A." had worn thin, songwriters hastened into the breach with cheer-up numbers, the best-known of which were "Smiles" and "Cheer Up Father, Cheer Up Mother." The wave of Pagliacci philosophy in Tin Pan Alley embraced our Allies as well, with the tender advice, "Belgium, Dry Your Eyes."

At the same time tears were invited with "Just A Baby's Prayer At Twilight," "A Soldier's Rosary" and "When the Flowers Bloom In No Man's Land." Astute performers frequently chose for their repertory beginning or middle numbers which would make audiences lachrymose, and for the finish—in the approved Greek tradition of catharsis—songs which would bring down the house in a blare of optimistic or militant cacaphony.

Humorous Army camp songs enjoyed a continuous vogue with "They Were All Out of Step But Jim," "Oh, How I Hate To Get Up In the Morning," and "Would You Rather Be A Colonel With An Eagle On Your Shoulder, or A Private With a Chicken On Your Knee?" The girls left behind were reminded "Your Lips Are No Man's Land But Mine" by Guy Empey, in answer to which many sang plaintively, "A Good Man Nowadays Is Hard To Find."

Creel's Committee, corresponding to the recent war's OWI (Office of War Information), made sure there were sufficient songs glamorizing each of the service branches, such as "Give A Little Credit to the Navy" and "Tell It To the Marines." It is unfair, however, to blame them for all cheap, vapid songs which burlesque the sufferings of men at war for the sake of trick phrases. Among these were "The Russians Were Rushin', the Yanks Were Yankin'," "Trench Trench Trench the Boys Were Marching," "We're All Going Calling On the Kaiser," "Hunting The Hun" and "Bingem On the Rhine."

Local bands, playing draftees off to training camps, usually serenaded with "Auld Lang Syne" and incongruously, "Marching Thru Georgia" (in the North); while the South just as incongruously bade farewell with "Dixie" and "The Bonnie Blue Flag."

The songs sung at home were not the most popular with soldiers, who had their own decided preferences. They sang, of course, the service songs of the field artillery, the coast artillery and other pieces of military chauvinism. The songs they selected from the popular pot were generally those with an appeal that rang true in camps and trenches—"Goodby Broadway, Hello France," "Madelon," "Dearest, My Heart Is Dreaming," "Long Boy," "No Man's Land" and "Over There."

Songs with lusty humor were popular—"K-K-Katy," which gave rise to a thousand Army parodies such as "K-K-K-P" and "K-K-Cootie"; "How You Gonna Keep 'Em Down On the Farm After They've Seen Paree"; "Good Morning Mr. Zip Zip Zip, With Your Hair Cut Short As Mine"; "Hinky Dinky Parlay-Voo"; and the immortal "Mademoiselle From Armentières."

Many songs out of the sphere of Armageddon reflected changing times and trends of thought in America. A suggestive 1914 song, "Beautiful Eggs," leeringly referred to what the American male was seeing as female limbs became more and more emancipated. The growing influence of movies was indicated that year by a song called "Poor Pauline," after a film title. "Those Charlie Chaplin Feet" (1915) mirrored the sudden and fantastic Chaplin craze which swept the nation and established him as America's leading comic artist.

Al Bryan, who wrote "I Didn't Raise My Boy To Be A Soldier," came to the defense of American motherhood once more on the issue of woman suffrage with "She's Good Enough To Be Your Baby's Mother, and She's Good Enough To Vote With You."

1915, the heyday of the Ford joke, also offered "The Love Story of the Packard and the Ford." And Tin Pan Alley celebrated the opening of the New York-San Francisco telephone line with "Hello Frisco." Irving Berlin, despite his pro-Allied sympathies, accurately put his finger on the pulse of American thinking that year when he wrote nostalgically, "When I Leave the World Behind."

hawaiian craze   As all eyes were focused reluctantly on Europe in 1916, the ivory tower, never-never land of Hawaii came in for escapist serenading. There were "Yacki Hacki Wicki Wackie Woo," "My Lola Lo," "Yacka Hula Hickey Dula," "Hello, Hawaii, How Are You?" "On South Seas Isles" and "Since Mary Ann McCue Came Back From Honolulu." These coincided with a rise in popularity of the Hawaiian guitar.

A reminder of the debt President Wilson owed to California was contained in the 1916 postelection song, "Be Good To California, Mr. Wilson, California Was Good To You." There was an amusing sequel to the year's sob song, "There's A Broken Heart For Every Light On Broadway" two years later when a Broadway blackout inspired "On A Lightless Night With You."

Top of 1914's hit parade were Feist's "On the Road to Mandalay," which sold 500,000 copies, followed by Remick's "Rebecca of Sunnybrook Farm." In the year that saw the sack of Louvain, widespread unemployment and Coxey on the march, and a nationwide coal strike, tunesmiths dwelled heavily on the theme of a good time—"This Is The Life," "He's A Devil In His Own Home Town" and "If That's Your Idea of a Wonderful Time, Take Me Home."

"Ballin' the Jack," after a dance of the same name, was popular, as was Jerome Kern's "They Didn't Believe Me" from his show, *The Girl From Utah*.

The following year Ireland—possibly because of its neutrality—enjoyed Tin Pan Alley's spotlight. There was "Dancing Underneath the Irish Moon," "I'm On My Way To Dublin Bay" and "My Mother's Rosary," written by Sam Lewis and George W. Meyer, both of whom were not exactly of true Gaelic extraction.

Ragtime was still in fashion, with "Everybody Rag With Me," "Oh, What a Beautiful Baby" and "Ragging the Scale," which was bought outright from the writer for $25 to become a smash hit dance tune. Another popular dance number was "Underneath the Stars," written as a slow ballad but played by orchestras in fox-trot time.

Al Jolson gave his all to "Tennessee" and "When the Grown-Up Ladies Act Like Babies." Two well-liked love songs of 1915 were "There's A Little Spark of Love Still Burning" and "If I Were A Bee and You Were A Red, Red Rose."

The nonwar song parade of 1916 was a scattered mélange. Ireland came in for another plug with "Ireland Must Be Heaven For My Mother Came From There" (composed by that non-Hibernian, Fred Fisher). The escapists found new havens in "There's Egypt In Your Dreamy Eyes" and "Araby." The beginnings of an upheaval in morals, bedfellow of war, were hinted at in "You're A Doggone Dangerous Girl" and "Whose Pretty Baby Are You Now?"—made more pointed by the yearning songs, "All I Want Is A Cottage, Some Roses and You" and "What A Wonderful Mother You'd Be"—and scornfully emphasized by wild songs like "Down In Honky Tonky Town" and "Yacki Hacki Wicki Wacki Woo."

Other hits of the year were "The Sunshine of Your Smile" and two Mason-Dixon numbers: "She's Dixie All the Time" and "Mammy's Little Coal Black Rose."

In the last year of the war, nonmilitary songs leaned heavily on tried-and-true June-Moon themes. Lovers squeezed hands to "For Me and My Gal," "Love Is A Wonderful Thing," "When Shadows Fall," "Give Me the Moonlight, Give Me the Girl," "Just As Your Mother Was" and "Give Me the Right to Love You."

There was no Bonnie Baker to sing "Oh, Johnny" but it was the hit of 1918. Another teasing type of song, built around a play on words using the name of the era's top hallelujah-shouter, was "I Love My Billy Sunday But Oh, You Saturday Night!"

The Hawaiian craze continued with "They're Wearing Them Higher in Hawaii," and the successor to "Yaaka Hula," "Yaddie Kaddie Kiddie Kaddie Koo." The new type of jazz dancing was glorified in "Everybody Loves A Jazz Band" and the lively "Darktown Strutters Ball." A growing nostalgia for "going home" produced "Indiana" and "There's A Long, Long Trail A-Winding."

the prisoners song circuit   The urge to sing even extended through prison bars, and became part of America's parole system in 1914, when Elmira, New York allowed a quartet of prisoners to take vaudeville bookings without a guard. They gave their first show to inmates of Auburn Prison.

Even the paper shortage, which compelled music publishers to put out songs on single sheets in 1916, couldn't dampen public support of the song business. Pianola rolls with imprinted lyrics won instant favor, and Henry Waterson (Waterson, Berlin & Snyder) sold a fortune's worth of 10¢ music rolls as well as 10¢ Little Wonder records.

Irving Berlin's name became touched with such magic that his publishers boosted his songs to a retail price of 30¢ a copy, an unheard-of extortion which was cheerfully paid.

'blues are blues'   That year also saw a unique battle between music publishers Roger Graham and Leo Feist, over the alleged piracy of blues. Feist, who had published "Barnyard Blues," claimed that Graham's "Livery Stable Blues" was an infringement. To settle the issue the court called in a blues writer named Professor White as an expert. White was asked, "What are blues?"

"Blues are blues," explained the professor empirically, "that's what blues are. See?"

curbing (?) the payola   The song business achieved one major step forward during the war years to partially solve a problem which had vexed it for a decade—the payola, or payment to singers for plugging songs. When *Sime* pointed out to the music publishers that some $400,000 was being paid to singers every year for this purpose, he engineered formation of the Music Publishers Protective Association (MPPA). The music publishers agreed that this highly ruinous practice would be outlawed, and while still an intra-trade problem, it has been considerably curtailed.

The Vaudeville Managers Protective Assn. (V.M.P.A.) backed up the just formed MPPA by barring any singers from bookings who were known to be paid by publishers for services rendered. Lest publishers be drowned in their own virtuous ethics, however, Al Jolson placed a large ad in Variety warning them to stop placing his picture on song sheets of numbers he didn't intend to sing.

A different type of songplugging appeared in a 1916 issue of Variety with an ad headlined: SONG WANTED! The ad explained, "Newspapers all over the country are talking about a song that's in the air, and yet no one seems to know much about it, except that wherever sung, it is a sensation. We like sensational songs, and we admit that the title of this song, 'Are You Half the Man Your Mother Thought You'd Be' appeals to us."

The publishers urged the writer of this song, "whoever and wherever he may be," to get in touch with them quickly. "We admit it is unusual for a music publisher to advertise in this way, but this seems to us to be an unusual song and to require unusual methods. If the song is half as good as the papers say it is, we can no doubt put it over in a jiffy."

The sequel appeared with an ad in Variety two weeks later, announcing the "discovery" of the "lucky" songwriters, Leo Wood and Harry DeCosta, and trumpeting a big advance sales order. All of which was corn quite as green as the song itself.

In 1917 the Music Publishers Protective Association put teeth into their proposals to wipe out paid songplugging. The previous resolutions had proved more noble in word than deed. Singers chuckled cynically at the new gathering, until they found that this time all the publishers meant business, and there would be no defections. At least right now.

Top-rank singers were pleased. Prior to that, it had been almost impossible for a singer to select his own style of song. Publishers preferred to put up their own choices on the auction block, giving paid contracts to singers for pushing songs the publishers wanted pushed. With the payment system abolished, singers were free to do their own window-shopping for what looked best on them. And when the Music Publishers Association reached an agreement with the V.M.P.A. that only their songs could be sung in theatres, it meant that publishers who were expelled from the Association for violating the pay taboo would be in a bad way.

That was teeth. And it worked. But where there's a will, there's a loophole. Some publishers found it when they "cut in" payolas as "co-authors" and paid off in royalties!

17

From Tango to Shimmy

★

The war years brought swift changes to the night life department of show business. Dansants, at their height in 1913 and 1914, suffered an ignoble decline thereafter, and with them tumbled the heyday of the society dancer. The graceful glide of the tango and the adolescent fever of ragtime gave way to the sophisticated jazz tempo of the Shimmy. Dance orchestras found themselves challenged by the rise of a perplexing new phenomenon—the jazz band.

Cabarets thrived, expanded, introduced the Continental idea of cover charges. They aimed at and fleeced thrilled out-of-towners. Liquor flowed, headwaiters were tipped, floor shows grew lavish. Then as the bluenosed shadow of Prohibition fell across Broadway, cabarets kicked the roof off prices to grab what they could before a Federal Government cork was slammed on the bottle and business.

Even small dancehalls were grossing in the neighborhood of $2,500 a week, catering to wives who were bored staying home during the day. Part of the dansant's undoing was too much competition and too much of the same thing. But the death blow was dealt by a revolt of outraged husbands. At first men protested because their dansant-mad wives were crippling them financially by a vain attempt to compete sartorially with professional dancers.

These protests became explosions when husbands realized what sort of men patronized dansants. This species, later identified as "gigolos," were unscrupulous male butterflies who depended upon their smooth dancing and a smooth line to fascinate naive wives who were desperate for excitement. Most of the dansant men were content to settle for expensive wardrobes and pocket money in exchange for romantic services. When a few went in for blackmail, these scandals, more than any other factor, accounted for their shutting down on weekdays in 1914.

Some dancehalls charged as little as a dime admission, with a fixed charge of 5¢ per dance per person. Since the gentlemen hangers-on at places of this calibre were inclined to be a little too rough, policewomen were in frequent attendance. More than one gallant who pinched where he shouldn't was chagrined to find that he, too, had been pinched, albeit differently.

The public craze for dancing was so strong in 1914 that Cincinnati staged penny dances in its public parks—and within one month was able to buy a piano out of proceeds for Inwood Park. New York's Hotel Astor pulled apart its main dining room to lay down a large dance floor. Gimbel's department store in New York gave 4:30 tango teas, charging 75¢, and regaled dancers with a fashion show of the very latest from Paris.

In 1915 Murray's, a New York cabaret on West 42d St., put in a revolving dance floor. The Arena Skating Rink switched to dancing after 11 P.M. Leo Carrillo bought the Casino at Freeport, Long Island, to open it as a roadhouse with dancing. William Morris staged a dance contest in the New York Theatre Roof Garden, and inveigled 200 prizes from business firms, much as today's radio quiz shows play Santa Claus with gift merchandise contributed by companies in return for credit mentions.

Tired of unglamorous charity work in slums, Mrs. W. K. Vanderbilt and other society women hit upon the idea of a low-priced dansant for the poor woiking goil. So, on top of the Strand Theatre, they opened a cafeteria-lunch-dansant, without liquor, at a 50¢ admission with a 20¢ lunch feature. Thrilled stenographers jammed in, as much to see Mrs. Vanderbilt and her blue-blooded friends serve as waitresses, as to enjoy dancing and a cheap lunch.

The dances in 1914 were the Castle Walk, Maxixe, Argentine Tango, American Tango, Congo Tango, Whirlwind Waltz, Hesitation Waltz, Aeroplane Waltz and the Negro Drag. Although the Turkey Trot had largely passed from favor, a notice on the callboard of the New Amsterdam Theatre, where *The Little Cafe* was playing, read: "Any member seen Turkey Trotting in a public place will be subject to immediate dismissal."

The "neck hold" was popular in dancing. Women clasped their partners around the coat collar. Men held their hands around the base of women's necks.

cakewalk craze—and the castles   There was a Cakewalk craze, and Cakewalk contests all over the country in 1915, when Dave Genaro revived it with a 25-girl chorus doing the dance at the New York Roof Garden. The following year a new dance originated in Chicago called "Walkin' the Dog," which became a favorite with Negro dancers.

The jazz dance was first heard from in 1917. Joe Frisco, working in a tuxedo, derby and cigar, introduced it at Chicago's Green Mill Garden. When Frisco danced it at Rector's in New York that year, it had already become so famous that he was billed as "Creator of the Jazz Dance."

The Shimmy had its origins in the Barbary Coast, but was first introduced to New York in 1918. Considered a lewd outgrowth of the new jazzmania, the Police Department threatened to revoke the license of any cabaret or dancehall which permitted it. The Shimmy Shewabble, as it was properly called, seemed even more indecent when performed in the bare-legged, revealing costumes in vogue during the war's final year. Variety reported that the Shimmy attracted considerable attention on those dance floors which dared to permit it, but that it could be danced decently "only with much difficulty."

Prime exponents of the Shimmy craze were Gilda Gray and Bee Palmer, both given their Broadway showcasing by Sophie Tucker. Like Joe Frisco, both hailed from Chicago. The Shimmy eventually segued into the hula vogue and the prime exponent of that was Doraldina who, too, played at Reisenweber's.

The Castles, Irene and Vernon, were the darlings of dance-mad America. They set the style of ballroom dancing, and somehow symbolized to a nation in search of values the ideal exponents of a design for living—a continuous, romantic love affair within the marital framework, crowned with grace and success. Women copied Irene's daring clothes, her "modern" hair style, and tried to copy her style of dancing.

In 1914 the Castles were at the pinnacle of their career. A week of one-day stands rewarded them at an average of $31,000. When Madison Square Garden decided to run an amateur dancing tournament, only the Castles were important enough to sponsor it.

The war, and not a decline in their popularity, brought an abrupt end to the Castle legend. A zealous champion of England's cause,

Vernon took flying lessons in 1915. He went to England and joined
the Royal Flying Corps as a second lieutenant, winning a promotion to captain after shooting down two German planes.

He was sent back to Canada in 1917 to train pilots. When America entered the war, he was transferred to Texas where, in February
1918, he was killed in a flying accident. "Castle," Variety said by
way of obituary, "set as striking an example of dancers by enlisting
as he had previously done in dancing."

Apart from the Castles, the number of society dancers who were
prominent at the tail-end of the craze included only Mae Murray
and Clifton Webb; Joan Sawyer, who collected between $700 and
$800 a week through a percentage of cover charges; and the only
successful new dancer of the era, Doraldina. As a sign that the
lady-and-gentleman dance team was finished, Rector's introduced
comedy dancers on its floor in 1914—a boy and girl who worked in
rube costumes and bucolic makeup. By 1916 dansants were gone
forever, and matinee dancing was taboo in all but a few places of
poor repute.

gave impetus to jazz bands   The rising comet of
dancing in America had carried on its tail a new interest in dance
bands. When the dancing comet plunged, the tail stayed high in
the heavens of public affection, and flew even higher. The recent
enthusiasm for band drummers, which elevated inspired trap-
thumpers like Gene Krupa to solo stardom, was another instance
of the repetitive cycle of public fads.

In 1915, too, the public was fascinated by drums and drummers.
Earl B. Fuller, drummer with the Banjo Wallace Orchestra at Rector's, was given 64 square feet of floor space for his traps, which were
worth $1,000. Drummers argued among themselves over who had
the largest number of traps.

In the year that saw the first poison gas attack of the war, New
York's drummers held a competition at the Strand Roof. Listening
to the all-colored contestants, judges Jerome Kern (the composer)
and Max Hershfeld (another Tin Pan Alleyite) tied first place
between "Buddy," from the show, Castles In the Air, and "Battle Axe" from the Winter Garden. Bill Bailey Jones of the Reisenweber's cabaret won second place, and Pippin Reeves of the Strand,
third.

With the interest in dance bands steadily mounting, each orchestra leader strove to win public favor with innovations. In 1917 Earl Fuller added a xylophone soloist, George Hamilton Green, to his Plaza Hotel band in New York, creating a minor furor. The sudden wave of Hawaiian songs brought ukuleles and guitars to the front of the bandstand as solo instruments. And 1917 saw a strange cycle of jug bands which were wowing the hinterland and heading for New York.

But it remained for Chicago to produce the most significant dance band of all—one which had an impact not only on the entertainment world, but on the whole era of the Roaring Twenties to follow. This was the jazz, or as it was originally spelled, "jaz" band.

The usual itinerary for a Broadway rounder in 1914 began with the cocktail hour, followed by a show, an hour or so of dancing in a restaurant cafe, then a tour of the drinking spots—"to be seen." A frequent route wound through Murray's; the Claridge; the New York Roof; Rector's, Churchill's or Reisenweber's; then the 400 Club after the regular room closed, until 4:00 A.M.; breakfast at Ciro's or Jack's; and to bed about six. To vary the "monotony" there would be the downtown bohemian spots of Joel's, Joe Brown's or Walter Sweeney's, incubators of uptown entertainment.

For a while the Claridge lost its standing in this approved route when the proprietor, a man named Hill, stated, "I'll give $5 to every Jew in the place if he will leave." The word spread rapidly, and every Jewish guest did leave. So did every Christian guest, with the exception of four, in the entire 12-story hotel. Faced with ruin, Hill swallowed hard and spilled out frantic statements to the effect that "if not for Jews, hotels and restaurants wouldn't exist," *ad nauseam.* But he couldn't sell it, and the Claridge stayed empty until Hill sold out to the Hotel McAlpin, whereupon the guests returned and the Claridge thrived once again.

Widespread unemployment in the spring of 1914 left its mark on the cabaret business. It was a poor time to raise the price of champagne, which cost cabarets from $6 a case to $7 a quart; and to up the cost of beer—if the place carried it—to 15¢ a pint. Broadwayites began to be aware that a round of mixed drinks at a Broadway bar, with seltzer instead of charged water, would cost them only 80¢ or a dollar, compared to a cabaret's $2.60.

coney island   Coney Island was the poor playboy's paradise.
Although many of the cabarets were hole-in-the-wall size, there were
a good number that were spacious, provided excellent entertainment
if no big names, and cost little. Perry's was the swankiest spot, with
waiters in tuxedos, a captain on the floor, and a hatcheck man in
uniform. The show was always splendid. But customers only had to
part with a dime for beer and a quarter for cocktails.

The nearest thing to the Parisian style cabaret was to be found
in New Orleans, and there only. Chicago's cabarets were considered so blue that the city's reformers were sharpening axes again.

Gloom still encompassed cabaret owners in 1915, when the Broadway Rose Gardens folded, a flop that included $179,000 worth of
furnishings. Restaurant proprietors Lea Herrick and Percy Elkeles
decided Broadway was ripe for a "free" revue, i.e. *sans couvert,* and
offered "Keep Moving" with no admission or cover charge. The
sole male in the revue was Frank Crumit, later of Crumit & (Julia)
Sanderson fame.

To the other extreme went Flo Ziegfeld, who opened the *Midnight
Frolics* on top of the New Amsterdam Theatre. He slapped a firm
$2 cover charge on every plate. But he gave New York something
new in the cabaret line—a bevy of Ziegfeld beauties with "bare
shoulders." Bare shoulders and bald heads being opposites which
attract, the *Frolics* did a lucrative business.

Ziegfeld's success made the cover charge a cabaret standard in
1916. Broadway hotels had once tried to impose a 10¢ cover charge
on the check for bread and butter, but protests had forced hotel
managers to stop it. Now, however, the same guests paid 50¢ to a
$1 cover charge at cabarets without a squawk. A few cabaret own-
ers, worried about public reaction, made a policy of imposing it
only upon guests they didn't know, or recognized as light spenders
—a practice that obtains today.

Slowly cabaret owners began to realize the value of featuring and
promoting their own talent. Some did this by advertising, some by
circulars, and one put his star's name in lights outside the cabaret.
A few places introduced "Special Nights," whereby they okayed the
checks of the guest of honor and his party, in return for a guest star
performance. It was nice publicity for the star and an inexpensive
way to entertain his friends, while it provided cabaret owners with
a sparkling added attraction at very little cost. (They're called

"Celebrity Nights" today, although the talent guilds frown on its practice.)

lavish cabarets   Cabaret on Broadway began to subdivide into two categories in 1917. Those located in special "name" rooms of the better hotels, and in certain areas of Broadway, catered to various strata of Broadway and society, each a loyal clique. The more spectacular cabarets, as their reputations spread far and wide across the land, became showplaces for the visiting firemen.

The two best-known cabarets in the latter class were the Palais Royal and Healey's Golden Glades. Both charged couverts, which alone netted each approximately $2,500 to $3,000 a week. The Palais Royal, which slapped a $1 cover charge on its supper plates, tried vaudeville acts in its pretentious floor show. The manager expressed disappointment with the experiment, declaring that vaudeville acts didn't fit into the cabaret pattern.

Vaudeville managers, in turn, decided to take action to stop acts from appearing in cabaret. Their disgruntlement was based on the fact that too many had already been lost to musical revues. And cabaret salaries, which were rapidly growing as fantastic as vaudeville's had once been, were giving vaudeville acts lofty notions. The Knickerbocker Hotel, for example, was paying the Dolly Sisters $2,000 a week in 1917.

1918 was the most riotous year in the history of cabaret since its inception. The factors at work behind the scenes were the approaching end of the war and the tomorrow-we-die philosophy which created spree spenders. And, most important, the rapid strides made by Prohibition. Already 22 states had voted dry, and it was a penal offense to mail liquor into any one of them.

Wartime Prohibition was scheduled for July 1918, as part of the Federal Government's drive to conserve grains. Actually, it didn't go into effect until September. Even worse, from the standpoint of the cabarets, was the permanent Prohibition Amendment which had already passed Congress, and would take effect in December 1918.

Cabaret was a generic term that included hotels, restaurants, cafes, saloons and dives—every place that sold liquor, with entertainment thrown in as an attraction. All of these were worried. Some hoped vainly that the public somehow wouldn't mind paying 50¢ for a grape juice highball for the privilege of dancing and watching a good floor show. Most cabaret managers, however, were realistic cynics who understood that the whole structure of cabaret, as it was constituted in 1918, rested on a liquid foundation. Without liquor, cabaret was finished.

just as in world war ii Accordingly, they stuck the knife into customers up to the hilt in that last of the wet, go-to-hell years. Menu prices puffed fantastically. Some cabarets printed new menus—and prices—daily. Doomsday coming, boys . . . soak the suckers while you've got the chance! One hotel charged $1.30 for a portion of lamb chops—one chop to a portion. Special bargain: two chops for $2.

The $2 bill that once paid the food check was now only fit for a tip. Every item on the menu skyrocketed except two—pepper and salt. Cabaret profits soared dizzily. And with them the ability to pay top prices for talent, which would attract more customers to make profits soar even dizzier.

The Palais Royal spent $18,000 to produce its floor show, plus another $3,800 in performers' salaries. Healey's $1 cover charge bought a novel floor show production costing $10,000, with a cast worth $1,700 weekly. Rector's, the Ritz and Rockwell Terrace paid salaries ranging from $1,200 to $2,000. And then there were the roof garden cabarets.

Ziegfeld's *Midnight Frolics* on the New Amsterdam Roof gave two different shows a night with a $2 and $3 cover charge respectively. Both were lavish productions, as glittering as musical comedy, but with no dialog or book. The production cost Ziegfeld $30,000 a week, with a performers' payroll of $6,400. Principals received $700 each, with chorus girls averaging $50 and $60, the lowest-paid getting $30.

Rivaling Ziegfeld's cabaret was Morris Gest's *Midnight Whirl* which gave one show nightly on the Century Roof (now the Century Apts. on 25 Central Park West, New York City). Gest's production cost $20,000, with operating expenses of $7,000. Both cabarets were paying higher salaries than their casts could have earned in legitimate Broadway revues.

The Armistice lifted the 1 A.M. curfew and legally ended wartime prohibition. In the little time left before Volsteadian Prohibition would descend again—this time for over a decade—cabaret owners concentrated on the lucrative transient trade. "They spend more and kick less than the natives," one explained. "And an out-of-towner comes to have a riproaring time in New York. He don't figure he had one unless he's been burglarized."

No one could be served with liquor who had on a uniform. If he sat at a table with civilians, the civilians had to do without as well, on the presumption that anything else would be flagrantly discriminatory to the armed services. Some cabaret owners, however, their hearts overflowing with gratitude toward "the boys"—and never reluctant to pick up an honest dollar—waived the rules.

And while cabarets grabbed what they could before the well of liquid dollars dried up, down in Hattiesburg, Mississippi, where 30,000 soldiers were stationed, a drugstore opened a cabaret with two entertainers and a jazz band. This cabaret wasn't worried.

It was doing a whale of a business on the house specialties—soda and icecream.

18

Twinkle, Twinkle, Big Film Star

★

The war years made mighty changes in the film business. The major alteration was a pure paradox. In the era 1914-1918, movies surpassed every branch of show business, expanding to the gigantic proportions of a helium-inflated float in a Macy's Thanksgiving Day parade down Broadway. Paradoxically, the bigger the movie industry became, the unhealthier grew its financial rewards. For many companies, success and bankruptcy were synonymous.

The second most important change was the emergence, in full bloom, of the screen star. As the novelty of films wore off, fewer patrons went to the movies just to see "a picture." They went to see

Charlie Chaplin, Mary Pickford or Theda Bara. With this basic shift of emphasis went a shrewd appreciation by stars of their own worth, and the beginnings of film actors' fortunes.

The physical metamorphosis of the film house from nickelodeon to movie palace was the third great change. As the cost of films spiraled upward, the small-capacity, low-admission movie house became unprofitable. Pretentious, large "cathedrals of the cinema" blossomed, beginning a trend capped by the Radio City Music Hall in New York long years afterward.

In 1914, while the public focused its attention on new films, the picture companies focused their attentions upon one another. On the strength of one or two successful pictures, yesterday's nonentity became the next day's Famous Players, which under Adolph Zukor was celebrating its first anniversary. And today's Biograph could quickly become tomorrow's nonentity, as happened less than two years later.

Costs were the Achilles heel of production. An extravagant overhead, and the high cost of stage stars, were the principal red ink items. There was also the prohibitive price of materials such as picture carbon, which was no longer forthcoming from its prime source, Germany. The pinch came when producers tried to shoehorn cost-swollen products into cramped, cheap outlets.

There were too many theatres, few with a rewarding seating capacity. Tense theatre competition posed a sore dilemma for exhibitors. On the one hand it prevented them from raising the price of admission. On the other, it forced up the price of film rentals above what most could afford in the competitive bidding. And even the poorly directed and produced European films were no longer available to ease the dependence on the American product.

A way out of this squirrel-in-a-cage situation could only come with an expansion of the number of filmgoers who could be seated for each unit showing of a film. In 1914 a farsighted trio of exhibitors plunged $1,000,000 into opening the Strand Theatre on Broadway, seating 3,300 on two floors, with an organ and an orchestra of 30. Only films were shown, top price was 25¢.

Oscar Hammerstein opened his Lexington Avenue Opera House with pictures. Vitagraph took over the Criterion Theatre, splashing Broadway in light with a $10,000 electric sign. Marcus Loew, in search of a really capacious theatre, opened Ebbetts Field, Brooklyn, as an outdoor film and vaudeville resort.

Loew was also one of the first to appreciate the vaudeville value of screen personalities. While running a serial called *Million Dollar Mystery* at his houses, he paid two of the cliffhanger's stars $300 a week to make personal appearances, during which they obliged by playing the piano. A few years later Pearl White, of *Perils of Pauline* serial fame, talked to enthralled Loew audiences as she was whisked from one house to the other, covering six different theatres a night.

70 pix producers   There were about 70 picture companies on the West Coast whose annual production costs came to $25,000,000. Some films were ticketed with an expense exceeding $100,000, unheard-of in the annals of live-talent production. For advertising alone, the Mutual, Equitable and World companies paid $300,000 annually, Paramount running up with $250,000.

But the day of bankruptcy was also dawning. Several of the largest companies were reported on the verge of a crash. Telephone companies considered movie firms bad risks, and jerked out phones when bills weren't paid promptly within two weeks. To add to the industry's troubles, 20 large companies were told to get out of Manhattan by municipal authorities, who stated they were a public menace. Ironically, New Yorks' city fathers periodically pleaded years later for Hollywood to move the film industry back to Manhattan.

The drive for larger movie houses continued through 1915. When the Hippodrome closed, $100,000 in arrears in rent, Charles Dillingham snapped it away from the Shuberts, changed the policy to pictures, and did well. Although their days were numbered, small-time exhibitors clung grimly to their petty livelihoods. A few of them were caught "bicycling films"—hiring a print for one house, then pedaling it furiously around to each other. One movie house in Cincinnati was showing five-reel bills at an admission of 3¢.

There was, as yet, no frozen format for film lengths and types, as we know them today. Producers turned out features ranging from one to five reels, serials, film series, and special productions of any length. An exhibitor's bill could be any combination of these. His discrimination depended upon his clientele. If he operated a "time-killer," catering to salesmen waiting for trains, shoppers with some shopping time left over, or bored housewives, his tastes were generally as low as his admission price. An estimated 85 per cent of the nation's movie houses in 1916 were cheap 600-seaters or smaller.

Their demise was hastened by laws passed in New York that year setting new standards of ventilation, building, seating and sanitation for theatres. These laws were widely copied throughout the country, and led to the scrapping of nickelodeons. This was a boon to the film industry, now engaged in producing expensive special productions which hole-in-the-wall houses could not afford.

1917 brought the producers in fear of a film and coal shortage. But most worrisome was the deeper chaos into which the financial end of the business had fallen. Show business heard behind-hand hints that none of the major producers was showing a single dollar's profit. Extravagant waste, fierce competition, burdensome stars' salaries and poor organization all suggested that movie manufacturers had lost control over their own industry.

There were reorganizations. Dividends were passed in order to meet interest on loans. Shaky pix outfits tried desperately to borrow money to tide them over. Those that failed were taken over by others which tried to hold the pieces together. Some companies tried to bluff through the storm by showing paper profits to deceive investors.

The final year of World War I found the film industry in not much better shape, and with a staggering new millstone around its neck. This was the high-priced star—the Frankenstein monster the movies itself had created. The star was now indisputably the drawing card of any film. Every picture without a big name had to stand or fall on its own merits, but the magic power of a star's name drew audiences even after a succession of bad vehicles.

And the stars knew it. Just as in the lush mid-1940s movie stars became dissatisfied with Hollywood salaries, however large, and wanted to be cut in on the financial pie, so the stars of 1918 began to demand a share of profits. The average first-run rental of a film with an important star brought in $375,000, at an exhibitor's cost of between $100 to $150. A large slice of this went to pay the star.

Despite the fact that producers realized they were slowly cutting their own throats, they had no alternative but to raise stars' salaries even higher by fierce competitive bidding. Any company without its share of star talent was doomed. The stars, meanwhile, began to realize that they were hurting themselves by making as many as eight or more films a year, and cut down their appearances on the screen to three, four or five productions. This led to fewer pictures, and better ones.

The same turn from quantity to quality was mirrored in the weeding out of inefficient movie houses. Higher rentals and the competition of larger theatres forced many of the small-potato exhibitors to close. Although a 1918 census showed a reduced number of film houses, this was more than compensated for by the increased seating capacities of the large picture palaces.

The emergence of screen actors as stars was almost as much a surprise to film producers as to the stars themselves. The movies were not at first recognized as a theatrical medium which could produce great acting figures as the flesh-and-blood theatre could. This attitude was understandable because movies had only recently emerged from the nickelodeon novelty stage, and had the further limitation of speechless emoting. This was "posing," not acting.

That is why, when film producers first thought of bolstering the boxoffice attraction of their pictures with stars, they turned not to the men and women already working for them, but to the legitimate stage stars of Broadway, whose names held national glamor. In 1914 and 1915 a steady caravan of stage stars traveled west.

Ethel Barrymore was paid $10,000 by the All Star Film Corp. to "pose" in a film production of her stage hit by Clyde Fitch, *Captain Jinks of the Horse Marines*. Weber & Fields signed up for two-reel comedies. Elsie Janis, Cyril Maude and Mrs. Leslie Carter each made feature films.

The United Booking Office became alarmed. They warned high-salaried actors in vaudeville to turn deaf ears to the movie siren song, because this "would depreciate" the value of their appearances in the flesh. And they pointed to the undeniable fact that Maude, Miss Janis and Mrs. Carter had, after making films, found themselves playing in competition against their own shadows. Mrs. Carter's picture had followed her, as opposition, all over her circuit.

The trend was fought bitterly in 1915 from another source—the film actors, many of whom balked at the humiliation of being forced to play supporting roles to stage actors in their own celluloid medium. Francis X. Bushman and Lottie Briscoe quit movies in a cold fury. Much bitter comment was caused by the death of John

Bunny, one of the screen's most popular funny men, whose estate showed an accumulation of only a paltry $8,000.

bushman and bara Producers began to realize two truths. First, they were not building for the future by paying huge sums to stage personalities who would only desert the movies for their real love. Second, the sole alternative to hiring stage stars was to create their own film stars, which they felt could be done by spending the difference in salaries on advertising and exploitation. William Fox did precisely this with Theda Bara, making her the world's most famous vampire. Metro did it with Francis X. Bushman, the first movie matinee idol.

Although many stage stars, tired of making films, drifted back to Broadway footlights in 1916, many more continued to step before the cameras. George M. Cohan made *Broadway Jones* for Artcraft, and followed it with *Seven Keys to Baldpate*. Eva Tanguay made *Wild Girl* for Lewis J. Selznick, father of David O. and the late Myron Selznick, one of Hollywood's fabulous agents. Will Rogers appeared in *Laughing Bill Hyde* for Samuel Goldwyn.

Julian Eltinge, John Barrymore, Elsie Ferguson, Florence Reed, Alice Brady and Billie Burke were among the stage stars who "posed" for films. Fred Stone was paid $150,000 for 10 weeks' movie work. Al Jolson, who turned down an offer of $50,000 for one picture, finally appeared in a film for Vitagraph, which they told him was for the benefit fund of the traffic police. When Jolson learned that the picture was being released generally, with only a percentage going to the fund, he had it suppressed.

One of the first movie stars to emerge in her own right was Mary Pickford, who was signed by Famous Players in 1914 on a play-or-pay basis of $2,000 a week. This was double what she received under her last contract. In addition she was given the unique privilege of selecting her own stories, wardrobe and casts. Even though Adolph Zukor added to this a percentage of profits, bringing her earnings to $175,000 a year, Miss Pickford quit in 1915 to go with Artcraft, which promised to give her her own company under its banner. By 1917 she was earning only $50,000 under a million a year. At the end of 1918 her war tax alone amounted to $300,000, as compared to England's highest actor-taxpayer, George Robey, who gave his government $60,000.

The First National Exhibitors Circuit met in 1918 to discuss the feasibility of acquiring Mary Pickford. One director, an intimate of Adolph Zukor, said cautiously, "While we are here considering paying Mary Pickford double the amount of salary that has heretofore been paid, I wonder if all of us realize that the one man who knows what her real earning capacity value is has dropped out of the competition for her services."

Rivaling, or possibly even surpassing the meteoric rise of "America's Sweetheart," was the amazing career of Charles Chaplin, ex-vaudeville comic in a music hall turn. His two-reel comedies for the screen won uproarious laughter and appreciation in every big city and tiny whistle stop. He had arrived on the screen by the very simple process of walking unannounced into Mack Sennett's office and asking for a tryout in Keystone comedies, only a few months before his name became a smile on America's lips.

the chaplin craze   So swiftly did success come that in February 1915, a mad Chaplin craze swept the country. Every theatre, including major circuits like Loew's, held amateur contests for Chaplin imitations. The price of Chaplin films shot up sharply. In 1916 Chaplin's *Floorwalker* broke all existing picture records, its 200 prints earning $10,000 a day. Essanay made over a million dollars on its Chaplin films, and paid the comedian a salary of $125,000, with an extra $10,000 for each release. Then, turning down an offer of half a million a year, he signed with Mutual for $670,000, plus $150,000 bonus, paying $75,000 to his brother Syd Chaplin for arranging the deal.

Far from being a climax for the little man with the baggy pants and a cane, it was only a beginning. In 1918 it was reported that his salary had reached the million mark. And his latest comedy, *Shoulder Arms,* which rented for $62.50 daily, was expected to gross the equal of his annual salary—a cool million. Keystone, Chaplin's first stepping-stone to this financial heaven, had filled the enormous gap left by Roscoe (Fatty) Arbuckle.

The third famous screen star to emerge in the war years was one who was already an established success on Broadway—Douglas Fairbanks. In 1917 he demanded, and got, the largest salary in both the film and legitimate theatres—$15,000 a week. In later years he was known exclusively as a screen star, with few of his devoted admirers knowing of or remembering his brilliant stage past.

When the income tax collector came around in 1918, Variety declared that "there are good grounds to believe the stars of the films will turn over to the Government a larger sum than the manufacturers who engage them." And they did, paying a heavy war tax as high as 40 per cent for earnings which reached $100,000.

Among the top-salaried film stars disclosed by income tax payments were, in addition to Miss Pickford, Chaplin and Fairbanks, William S. Hart and Olga Petrova.

A 1917 nose-count by Variety as to who was who in films, apart from those already mentioned, included Polly Moran, playing a character known as Cactus Nell, Montagu Love, Norma Talmadge, Doris Kenyon, Creighton Hale, Madge Evans, Wallace Reid, Mae Murray, William Farnum, Buster Keaton, and Marion Davies—all of whom were destined to become well-known stars of the postwar era. Also in films of that year were four women who would become important names in other branches of show business—Texas Guinan, Julia Sanderson, Florence Reed and Ann Pennington.

Although the emergence of the star system brought fame and certainly fortune to many film actors, it was not without its penalties to those it exalted. It meant the end of privacy, on a scale whose consequences we see today in the goldfish bowl of Hollywood, where every breath drawn by a star is of immense interest to millions of people who group themselves in fan clubs. A star no longer belonged to himself, but to a mass giant who worshipped its idol, praised it, censured it, kept eyes glued incessantly upon it.

The strain proved too much for Fatty Arbuckle, whose life shattered to pieces under its weight. Ditto Wallace Reid, Barbara LaMarr and others. Even as today, Charlie Chaplin's acting was not enough—he was compelled to make public his "strange" desire to retain British citizenship.

19

A Rejection Slip for Hamlet

★

Whether by accident or intention, a plague of films about Napoleon Bonaparte fell across the nation's screens in 1914. There were *Napoleon From the Cradle to the Grave, From the Tuileries to Moscow and Back Again, Napoleon As He Really Was* and *Waterloo,* among others. Meanwhile the Napoleon of 1914, Kaiser Wilhelm of Germany, ordered German cameramen to take films of every battle of the new war, which he intended to have ready as an answer to the charges of German atrocities which he expected —and got.

Film sentiment crystallized sharply only when the European war became America's war. Then movie stars like Mary Pickford, Charlie Chaplin and Douglas Fairbanks appeared at open-air Liberty Bond rallies, drawing enormous crowds. Theatres ran slides to introduce Four Minute Men teams who would interrupt the movie bill to plug bond sales from the stage. America's 17,000 movie houses ran films for the Government announcing September 12, 1918 as registration day for the new draft of men between 18 and 45.

Four of 1918's war films were smash hits—*The Spy Menace, The Beast of Berlin, My Four Years in Germany,* and D. W. Griffith's *Hearts of the World.* But, although film audiences were willing to shudder at cinematic versions of the horrors of the Hun, they reserved their most enthusiastic patronage for war comedies on the order of Chaplin's record-breaking *Shoulder Arms.*

Filmdom's final contribution to America's first great adventure was on December 6, 1918, when President Wilson sailed for the Versailles Peace Conference. With him on the peace ship went 15 choice films of the Famous Players-Lasky Co., a gift to America's No. 1 movie fan and the American delegates.

The war films of 1914-1918 were, on the whole, without distinction. It was too soon for the understanding and artistry which later gave birth to *All Quiet On the Western Front, The Four Horsemen of the Apocalypse, The Big Parade,* and *Journey's End.* It was even too soon for *What Price Glory?* The fault lay as much with the American public which, in the early war years, was apathetic to war themes. Later, the war was too much with them—too suddenly, and for too brief a time.

The outstanding film of the era was one whose theme sprouted from the seeds of war—but a distant war. This was D. W. Griffith's masterpiece, *Birth of A Nation,* which dug out of the ruins of American history the South's dusty theme.

It was a strange work of art. It undeniably advanced the technique of film-making to its highest level of that day. But it was vicious propaganda worthy of the Kaiser's latter-day successor. It stirred up racial hatred against the Negro. It glorified the Ku Klux Klan, sowing the seeds for a revival of Klan atrocities which actually took place in the two years following the war.

Birth of A Nation opened in 1915 at the Liberty Theatre, New York, in a blaze of advertising glory that cost $12,000 in the first week. Seats sold at a mad pace for the $2 top opening. And the film made history by staying on Broadway for 44 solid weeks.

Singling out the near-rape scene as the secret of Griffith's phenomenal success, one company rushed into production with a film called *The Hypocrites.* This bright gem had nothing to distinguish it except a brief sequence which showed a naked lady. But unbridled nudity was no match for a costumed wrestling match with nasty implications. *The Hypocrites* quickly faded, while *Birth of A Nation* gestated merrily on.

In the same year, while 40,000 people paraded in Chicago as a demonstration against the closing of saloons on Sunday, one producer came out with a film called *Prohibition,* which pleaded the cause. It was joyfully boosted by several antisaloon societies.

The film hit of 1917 was Sam Goldwyn's *Polly of the Circus,* which broke b.o. records when it was released simultaneously in 80 cities. In 1918 another 80-print showing did a stunning business; at the same time it carved a future career for Johnny Weissmuller. The film was, of course, Edgar Rice Burroughs' *Tarzan of the Apes.* And at the tail end of the war, by boxoffice contrast, Producers Dis-

tribution Corp. presented Evelyn Nesbit and her son, Russell Thaw, in a dramatization of the Thaw murder case called *Her Mistake.*
  It was.

'big' script prices   The play and the novel became the thing. In 1914 Pathe daringly offered $4,000 for the screen rights to Dr. Daniel Carson Goodman's best-selling novel, *Hagar Revelly.* Dr. Goodman made them gasp by asking $5,000. Producers excitedly discussed among themselves the wisdom of paying out so much for a story—the same producers who were to scarcely bat an eyelash at paying from $500,000 to $1,000,000 for the latter-day *Life with Father* or *Harvey.*

  The run-of-the-mill scenario writer found his salary steadily climbing from $50 a reel to $100 and better. Good routine screen stories brought $500. Pix were slamming the door shut on high school graduates who would work for $10 a week. And opening it for scenario chiefs who demanded $10,000 a year. It was the beginning of the Hollywood where a writer's literary worth was measured by the salary somebody would pay him.

  The drive by producers for better scripts—and consequently better movies—moved so fast that by 1917, $25,000 was offered for an unproduced stage play, *Susan Lenox*—and $50,000, or 10 per cent of film profits, was asked. The record purchase of the era was *Within the Law,* the stage play for which producer Al Woods was paid $50,000, as Broadway gasped.

  In the last year of the war Variety reported a true tale which deserves to be Hollywood's epitaph in gold—because it could happen today, as surely as it did in 1918. An author called upon a movie company and verbally outlined the plot of a story to the scenario editor. "Make a wonderful film," declared the author.

  The plot, as he told it, concerned a king who had a brother-in-law with big ideas. This guy and his sister, the queen, frame up a deal to poison the king, which they do by pouring stuff in his ear. The king dies, but later his ghost appears to his son, who is a lovesick nut. The king's ghost spills the dirt to the son. The kid rounds up a bunch of actors and rehearses them in a play he wrote, which tells the story of the poisoning. When the play gets a rise out of the kid's mother and his uncle, he knows the ghost's story is on the level. So he kills them both, and then kills himself to wind up matters.

"What do you think of it?" the writer asked eagerly.

"Nothing doing," growled the scenario editor. "There isn't a chance of a yarn like that getting over. In the first place, that ghost stuff is all bunk. And how could a guy be poisoned by putting poison in his ear? There's no plot to it!"

It took 30 years and a British company for Sir Laurence Olivier to put Shakespeare's *Hamlet* on the screen.

documentaries and church pix   Although the film industry was primarily concerned with feature films, as early as 1914 it was turning out documentaries as well. These were the forerunners of the pure documentary films.

The current wave of Technicolor religious films being shown at churches all over the country had its origin in a colored documentary of 1914 called *Life of Our Savior*. Shown in regular theatres, it flopped.

New York Police Deputy Commissioner George S. Dougherty supervised six reels of a documentary called *The Line Up,* which was based on police records. This was released through Gus Hill. Health films were turned out for auditorium showings, with doctors or nurses delivering an accompanying talk, under the sponsorship of civic or sociological authorities. They're called sexers in the trade, albeit dealing with social relations problems on a lofty plane.

Film technicians attached to the United States Army Signal Corps turned out training films and war documentaries, much as was done in World War II. It was a great satisfaction to everyone in the film industry when permission was secured from George Creel's Committee on Public Information to show these publicly at the Apollo Theatre in New York in March 1918. Variety began its review of the event by declaring, "Dissenters, critics, malcontents and carpers against the methods of this Government got it squarely in the eyes last week when . . ."

The film industry itself closely co-operated with Creel in turning out and releasing war documentaries asked for by the propaganda committee. These included *Pershing's Crusaders, America's Answer* and *Under Four Flags*. In addition to which stills, stereoptic slides and comedy films were prepared for the entertainment and morale of troops in camps at home and overseas.

The most popular documentary of all was the newsreel, which grew enormously in stature during the war years. William Randolph Hearst, whose financial interests in the film industry were growing since 1916, bought out Universal News in 1918 for $1,000,-000, and promised exhibitors a daily service.

These were the days when not a single American had ever seen or heard of Mickey Mouse, incredible as that may seem. But there were animated cartoons as early as 1914, principally "Gertie," the film cartoon creature drawn by Winsor McKay, of the Hearst papers. There were also animated songs, hired to exhibitors for some $10 a week, which eventually led to the popular "bouncing ball" community-sing features.

Those with enough years behind them remember the expressionless pianists who accompanied the old silents in emotional mood with wonderful dexterity. Actually, the adroit switches from andante to allegro were not as impromptu as they seemed. In 1915 Metro and other companies were supplying exhibitors with special cue sheets suitable for each release. Film fans who would never wittingly subject themselves to classical music—"That highbrow stuff!" —were often surprised to find out later that they had been imbibing it for years as accompaniment to William S. Hart and Mary Pickford.

The first short subjects with an all-children cast, anticipating the Our Gang comedies, were a series of one-reelers called "Kids of the Movies." Designed exclusively for the juvenile trade, the producer didn't bother with subtitles. The first football game to be recorded for the cameras was the 1915 Yale-Harvard match.

In 1918 Variety, in a passion to see justice done, revealed the obscure fact that the great colossus which had become the motion picture industry was not the outgrowth of the labors of Thomas A. Edison at all, but of a man named Edward Muybridge. Muybridge, Variety claimed, had begun his experiments in "instantaneous photography" in 1872, to study animal movement for the use of art and science. His first experiments were backed by a California governor who wanted pictures of his race horses in action, and later by the University of Pennsylvania which granted him $40,000.

"Muybridge built a shed which was painted black, and was 120 feet long. Opposite the shed he constructed a camera house with 24 cameras, each having a lens three inches in diameter. In front of these cameras a horse galloped. The back shed was the background. The cameras, operated first by strings which were broken by the horse's progress, caught successive exposures. Later a motor operated the cameras, and thus a series of successive movement pictures was obtained. . . . Muybridge also projected them on a screen, leading directly to the exhibition of motion pictures. He lectured and presented these pictures beginning in 1880 and, at the Chicago Exposition in 1893, in a specially constructed building, showed motion pictures of birds flying and athletes wrestling. Here was the real beginning of the motion picture, later given splendid contributions by Edison, Eastman and Tourneur."

20

Keith Is Dead—Long Live the Palace!

★

The most powerful man in vaudeville, B. F. Keith, died April 1, 1914. As though in keeping with the significance of the date, not one cent of his $8,000,000-$10,000,000 fortune was bequeathed to any theatrical charity. Even in death the King of the Two-A-Day retained a mine-and-thine cynicism toward the actors who had built both his empire and his fortune.

The sceptre fell to his son, A. Paul Keith, and to his prime minister, E. F. Albee, who continued as acting head of the circuit. If few actors mourned Keith, they lost nothing of their respect for the Keith theatre which had come to symbolize the best in vaudeville—B. F. Keith's Palace in New York.

What the White House represents to a political hopeful, a Palace booking signified to an actor. It was honor, recognition and a springboard to fame. But it was also a severe test, before the most critical vaudeville audience in the nation. Actors frequently requested postponements of their bookings, in order to polish their turns to a gleaming sufficiency. The widespread practice of grooming for the Palace had a beneficial effect on the quality of vaudeville in every part of the country.

The average weekly gross of the Palace in 1914 was $21,000, of which between $6,000 and $8,000 was profit. Commensurate with its dignity and prestige, the theatre offered bills studded with headliners, and coming headliners, at a $2 top. The management, like George M. Cohan, believed in keeping the show moving at a furious and breathless pace—no dull spots, no stalling. For a time the management even attempted limiting acts to a maximum of two bows but that couldn't work.

In the same year that Keith died, lightly mourned, his contemporary and the greatest showman of the prewar years, also died —widely mourned. Willie Hammerstein passed away at the age of 42. The destinies of Hammerstein's passed into the hands of his brother Arthur, who struggled valiantly to compete against the Palace.

But the simultaneous deaths of the two outstanding figures of show business had curiously different aftermaths. Keith had built an empire, a machine, an impersonal colossus which would work for anybody who controlled the switch. Willie Hammerstein had built a great theatre out of imagination, daring and his own personality. When Willie Hammerstein died, Hammerstein's died.

With a cautious eye on the Palace, and Albee's United Booking Office, Arthur Hammerstein began to wield his new broom. First prices were cut. Then the axe was out for sensationalism. Hammerstein's had booked a sketch called "Hanged," at the climax of which the actor playing a warden protested he couldn't spring the trap because he didn't believe in capital punishment. A volunteer was then called from the audience, who would come up and pull the rope.

Arthur Hammerstein considered this too gruesome. So the act was changed to "Electrocution," in which one of the audience was asked instead to come onstage and pull the death switch. The actor in the chair would pretend to die as some sparks shot out from beneath him. But even this was too much for Hammerstein, and the act was jerked out.

Out, too, were the job applications of the wives of convicted gangsters—Mrs. Lefty Louie and Mrs. Gyp the Blood, who would have rejoiced the heart of Willie Hammerstein. But Arthur had an ear cocked toward the UBO office, where Albee had issued an edict to the effect that publicity headlines won by "criminal proceedings" would no longer be tolerated on the part of vaudeville headliners.

Arthur Hammerstein made other minor but traditional changes. He replaced Negro male ushers, who had been with the theatre for over 15 years, with Negro usherettes, and a white male head usher. To meet the threat of Palace competition, he introduced 22-act bills.

When the dancing Castles were available to Broadway, they appeared at both the Palace and Hammerstein's, with their own 12-piece Negro orchestra. The regular pitmen at Hammerstein's, exhibiting a rare case of theatrical chauvinism, refused to play in the pit with the Harlem orchestra, forcing them to go onstage with the Castles.

One of Hammerstein's interesting features of 1914 was ballet dancer Paul Swan, billed as "The Handsomest Man In the World." His graceful cavortings were done with bare arms, legs and chest. Variety's review declared, "Of Mr. Swan's three dances, the first, second and third seem to be over the heads of the audience. He died in the final dance, and it's tough to die at Hammerstein's." Gallery audiences enjoyed the choice remarks of the customers much more than the terpsichore of The Handsomest Man In the World.

The Palace, in the summer of 1914, was also making some changes. Deciding that warm weather customers were principally transient, it reversed its ruling on holdovers, and extended bookings of acts for as long as three weeks. Topliners like Ruth Roye and Sylvester Schaffer accepted these extensions at lower salaries on the theory that a long run at the Palace paid off later in prestige.

The Palace also suffered a change of heart in regard to Harry Lauder, whom Keith-Albee had refused to book for $500 a week prior to his coming to the States. Now they played his films, billing the Lauder name in large letters out front, with the words "Singing Pictures" in microscopic type beneath.

The Palace gave vaudeville something new in 1915 when it presented a "Style Show," complete with the latest fashions from abroad and from the salons of leading dressmakers at home. It made a tremendous hit, was held over, and launched a flood of fashion shows at all the New York theatres. While the Style Show packed crowds into the Palace, pugilist Jess Willard was paid $4,000 a week by Arthur Hammerstein to make competition. But it was no contest.

Arthur Hammerstein gave up in 1915. The theatre became the Rialto for film showings, and the policy exists to this day. With William Morris, Hammerstein took over the 44th Street Theatre as a vaudeville house. But Albee's UBO refused to make any acts available to them, claiming that Hammerstein's contract was only valid for the Victoria.

exit hammerstein's victoria   Only one year after the death of Willie Hammerstein, the theatre of Willie Hammerstein was no more. But ironically, though the original had died, an imitator flourished. McVicker's Theatre in Chicago was rapidly becoming known as the Hammerstein's of the Midwest. Here Barney Bertsche, convicted of swindling, performed by telling about the cops who had been partners with him in a fortune-telling racket, and received $700 a week for his true confessions. Here, too, played "Nell of the Cabarets"—Miss Nellye De Onsomme, who had married Herbert Updike, the man convicted of plotting to kill his aged parents to inherit their money. Willie Hammerstein had, indeed, gone West—spiritually and by example.

Unfettered by the last shred of vaudeville competition, the Palace grew fatter and greater. It could now afford to indulge in "stunt" acts, without seeming to steal some Hammerstein thunder. One of these in 1916 was the "12 Speed Mechanics," who amazed audiences by assembling a Ford onstage in two minutes flat. And in 1917 it was still the only logical showcase for the great Sarah Bernhardt who, 73 years old and with a leg amputated, could still hold them spellbound with a 33-minute sketch. Eventually she alternated three different playlets for her vaude flyers. As part of the showmanship, two legends cropped up: 1, that she always slept in a coffin-like bed; and 2, that with characteristic Gallic frugality and forethought she insisted on $500 being paid her, *in gold,* after every performance, or $1,000 a day for the mat and nite shows. That year was her swan song in America and at the Palace where she alternatingly did two playlets, "From the Theatre to the Field of Honor" for three days and her *Camille* excerpts the rest of the week. She died in 1923 in her native France.

When Sarah Bernhardt first essayed vaudeville, in 1913, she grossed a peak $22,000 week at the Palace, remaining three and one-half weeks. The curtailed final session was because of her boat sailing. Her leading man in one of her vehicles was Lou Tellegen, later to become an American matinee idol. In another sketch, "Phèdre," she had three ladies in waiting. At one matinee Laurette Taylor, Jane Cowl and Elsie Janis did the three bits as a gesture to the great French tragedienne—and to themselves.

Vaude in the war years was beset by a series of skirmishes and full-dress battles. Actors fought with managers, particularly over the arbitrary wage cuts imposed upon them in 1914. An unseasonable Indian summer which affected the boxoffice, and not the European war, was the excuse.

Reverberations followed in almost every branch of show business outside of vaudeville. The ease with which vaudeville managers had been able to curtail overhead inspired "requests" that legitimate actors and burlesque people accept salary slashes. About a million dollars dropped out of the pay envelopes of actors—of those who had weakened actors' organizations by supporting managers in trade struggles, as well as those who had fought consistently for an outright actors' trade union.

Bigtime vaudeville fought the small time. When the bigtime cut salaries, the small time, headed by Marcus Loew, won headliners away by offering comparable pay with a solid circuit booking. By 1917 the lines were sharply drawn between big and small time through the latter's increasing devotion to movies at the expense of vaudeville. Small time exhibitors began to pay as much as $700 for films, cutting into the budget for live talent. The bills began to show it. But the customers of the 10-15-25¢ houses were satisfied, because they were attending primarily for the movies.

sime and marcus loew   When Loew later bought the Bartholdi Inn property for the present-day GHQ of the Loew's empire, including Loew's State Theatre on the corner of Broadway and 45 Street, this automatically displaced Variety's first mid-Times Square office location. The paper's 1536 Broadway address went with the Bartholdi Inn realty parcel which gave the State sufficient depth for its nearly 3,500 seats. For several years, however, since *Sime* moved up from the St. James Building, which was then below "the line," as 42d Street was known, the Variety trademark, in green neon, blazed out over Times Square, as much an attraction to sightseers as the Hotel Astor marquee.

Never overly given to self-exploitation and decidedly not on a personal basis, *Sime's* instinctive showmanship created the characteristic green cover for the paper's earlier years. With it came the matching green stationery, to this day a company trademark.

In order to remain as close to the Square as possible, *Sime* bought the Madame Frances Building at 154 West 46 Street, then housing one of the best known *couturières* in America. Then, as now, the Variety building adjoins Loew's State Theatre's stagedoor.

One day, Loew came to *Sime* with a worry, "If I have to book any more acts to fight that s.o.b. Albee, who's going crazy with vaudeville at the Palace, would you sell me your building, *Sime?* That's the only way I see where I could put the added dressing rooms."

"What picture product do you play, Marcus?" asked *Sime.*

Loew told him he had all of the Metro pictures, of course, and half of the Paramount and United Artists franchise. *Sime* said, "I think that'll take care of your problems, Marcus, but if you ever need our place, we'll get another building, and you can spread out any way you want. But I know that if you have the pictures, no matter what type of vaudeville Albee plays, he can't compete with Hollywood." That was to have been a prophetic, albeit casual, conversation between the two showmen.

As the case progressed Variety admitted that the Government would easily prove it was "human nature not to build up an opposition to your business if that may be prevented, or not to aid a competitor." But, Sime Silverman argued, "the show business is the show business, peculiar to itself, something that the Government . . . will find it extremely hard to regulate, according to the strict lines of commercial pursuit that the Commission understands much better than it does theatricals." He was right; the suit was quashed.

Sime's w.k. penchant for roadhousing, as his surcease from the midtown newspaper whirl, led him "up the road" (Pelham roadhouses) and "down the road" (as he phrased it when hitting the trail down the Merrick Road to the Pavillon Royal and Long Beach roadhouses for dinner). As he'd motor along he'd notice new developments. Variety would come out with a story that "Marcus Loew is developing a new realty project on the Grand Concourse, and a prime focal point will be a deluxer in the Bronx." (And thus was Loew's Paradise born.) Or, when down Long Island way, the story would be, "Loew toppers Nick Schenck, Bob Rubin and prexy Marcus Loew were driving toward Long Beach when they were struck with the idea that Jamaica would be an up-and-coming residential development, and accordingly took an option on a corner site for a theatre." (Thus was Loew's Valencia, in Jamaica, spawned. While all this was news to Loew & Co., the idea was so sound that they would meander up to the Bronx or to Jamaica, and realized that this *would* make an excellent theatre site.) To this day, they are known as "the Loew theatres that *Sime* built."

the revue vogue   In addition to fighting each other and actors, vaudeville managers fought with revue producers. The revue craze started about 1915, when some producers found that, with the proper amount of glittering costumes and no worry about a book for the show, they could turn a vaudeville bill into a $2 legitimate stage "revue." The raids on vaudeville talent began, and two-a-day managers had to struggle to keep their acts from deserting. Vaudeville comedians became hard to find, and harder to hold.

But by 1918 the trend had run its course. The 1917 season had been an eye-opener. Long rehearsals and short runs, owing to both bad shows and slump conditions, found the transgressors short of pocket and repentful. The "privilege" of being connected with a $2 show, in return for a reduced salary, lost its allure. And so they straggled back to the fold.

The fourth battle vaudeville fought in the war years was a more subtle one—to hold and tighten its grip on audiences, in the face of new forms of entertainment and the exaggerated fluctuations of economic conditions. In 1914, at a loss for new novelties to offer a public which was becoming jaded by repetitious bills, managers turned to dancing acts, booking the best-known ballroom dancers at the height of the dansant craze. This spurted business at first. Then —just as the public grew weary of dansants—the dancing act began to turn away more trade than it attracted.

Vaudeville sought something different. It tried to impress audiences with a new "tone." Playlets and special productions became lavishly dressed, costumed and mounted—at considerable expense—to provide a plush atmosphere of "class." This was partly a challenge to the revues of 1916. Combined with a good business year, it kept vaudeville boxoffices busy.

vaude continues big   Despite the slump of business in the year America entered the war, vaudeville kept its head above water. In some measure this was due to the increasing number of good acts released by flopping revues, and to good acts which were kept from overseas bookings by the turn of the war. Other branches of show business, particularly movies and small time vaudeville that depended on movies, found business off about 20 per cent. The Government's economy drive, the war tax, and money diverted to Liberty Bonds, were blamed. But the bigtime, concentrating on bigger and better bills, rode through the rapids with only a few cold sprays.

The final year of the war found vaudeville holding up extremely well, despite hardships caused by theatre closings to save coal, a sharp advance in the cost of living, and a nation-wide influenza epidemic which crippled show business everywhere. Soldiers and sailors on leave in New York helped boom metropolitan vaudeville, and also gave rise to an innovation whereby many acts were given holdover engagements, making it possible for them to be booked for as long as 20 continuous weeks in Manhattan.

The war era which opened with the death of B. F. Keith came to a close with the death of his son, A. Paul Keith in 1918, a victim of the influenza epidemic. The Keith interests now rested on the shoulders of one man alone, E. F. Albee. The year also saw the demise of another great name in vaudeville—George Castle, of the western Kohl & Castle circuit, who died at the age of 70.

passing of the giants   The Keiths, Hammerstein and Castle. The giants were passing—as one day vaudeville, too, would pass.

One phase of vaudeville had already passed in 1915—the day of Union Square as the heart of show business, before the birth of the gaudy, fast-paced Broadway district. By 1915 the whole of 14th Street was considered "decadent." The Academy of Music finally gave up the ghost on the block that had once proudly claimed the old Tony Pastor's, as well as Tammany Hall. The whole 14th Street block was turned over to the Consolidated Edison Co.

Vaudeville had not only moved uptown, but it was also going to sea. Steamship companies in 1914 were offering cutrates to traveling actors in return for playing four shows during the voyage. The *Aquitania* gave one such show on the eve of her maiden voyage. In years to come this blossomed into a regular seagoing circuit, with acts being booked on ships going to Bermuda and other vacation points out of the war orbit.

Albee's inevitable enemy, William Morris, popped up again in 1916 with a new venture to worry UBO and the Keith interests. With John Cort and Oliver Morosco he began a roadshow circuit. Whether in retaliation or as an independent gesture, Albee issued orders to UBO's 106 agents that they were to scout acts only in theatres which dealt with UBO. And wary of another landslide of actors following the Morris banner, UBO began to groom and produce some of its own acts, known to the trade as "office acts."

Marcus Loew's stock continued to rise steadily through the war years. A shrewd, cautious business man, he rarely made mistakes. But when he did, as in 1914 when he bought out the Sullivan & Considine circuit, paying $1,500,000 for goodwill, the mistake was a big one. He reduced prices from 10-20-30¢ to 10-15-25¢, and inaugurated a new policy of supper shows at 6 P.M.

This was a mistake, born of an Easterner's misjudgement of Western show business. The West wasn't used to shows at 6 P.M. The usual practice was one matinee and two shows at night. The next year John W. Considine took back the circuit from Loew, with the latter out of pocket half a million dollars in nine months.

the henry ford of show biz   Loew could afford such mistakes. His prestige and fortune were increasing with every month. At a dinner tendered to him by Broadway show people in 1916, George M. Cohan bestowed upon him the accolade of "the Henry Ford of show business." It was an apt comparison. And just as Henry Ford went from Model-A's to streamlined roadsters, so the Henry Ford of show business spent $8,000,000 in 1917, building 10 new theatres in eight cities.

Loew joined almost a Who's Who of Vaudeville in 1918 as a co-defendant in a suit brought by the Federal Trade Commission, charging monopoly. The alleged monopolists besides Loew were A. Paul Keith, E. F. Albee, Sam A. Scribner, Martin Beck, B. S. Moss, the V.M.P.A. (Vaudeville Managers' Protective Association), the N.V.A. (National Vaudeville Artists), the UBO (United Booking Office) and the Vaudeville Collection Agency. And for good measure, Sime Silverman, the editor of Variety.

vaude oddments   In the odds-and-ends bureau drawer of vaudeville during the war years were a strange assortment of items which shed light on that branch of show business during the five years that men were killing each other in Europe. These were not war-influenced events—they were the normal trivia of normal times. But they are of interest here only because they *could* happen simultaneously with the wholesale slaughter of human beings.

In 1914, for example, while soldiers on the Continent dove to earth clutching their stomachs, the "Six Water Lillies" dove into a water tank on top of the New York Roof, making audiences gasp with a stunning display of bare legs.

In 1915, while French and British troops fought desperately at Ypres, and Nurse Edith Cavell was shot in Brussels, there was a sensation caused around the Palace Building when someone presented booker Dan Hennesy with monogramed golf balls—*and* a machine that put monograms on golf balls.

Charles Kenna, the original "Street Fakir," took a page ad in Variety to call sarcastic attention to the piracy of his act. He did it by giving permission to anyone who wanted to use his stuff, provided the pirate notified him by penny postcard which part of the act had been swiped. Kenna declared he would then substitute something else in his own act when booked in the same city with his imitator.

With Kenna's death, both W. C. Fields and Clyde Hager popularized the pitchman ("Get away, boys, you bother me"); and in turn, many years later, Sid Stone, doing the pitchman's routine on Milton Berle's TV program plugging Texaco, came to attention with this time-honored street fakir routine.

sawing a woman in half   Perhaps the most heated talent battle was sparked by Horace Goldin when "pirates" adapted his "Sawing a Woman in Half" illusion. Goldin's act had a hot vogue for a season or two, but pretty soon copyists were emulating his stuff on the lesser circuits. The showman, pointing to his patents on the illusion of dismembering his comely femme aide, engaged in a series of litigations, claiming heavy damages, but all he got out of it was the publicity payoff on these suits, which was the prime purpose in the first place.

A year later Variety inaugurated a "Protected Material Department," where actors, writers and producers could deposit their ideas and dramatic properties in sealed envelopes to prove the date of origin against pirates.

In 1915, show business gossip enjoyed the morsel of the mistake made by a funeral parlor which sent an urn containing the ashes of Mabel Hite (Donlin & Hite) to Murray's Restaurant. The suspicious manager of Murray's, alarmed by the recent exposé of the German spy system in America, called in Inspector Eagan of the Bureau of Combustibles. The inspector promptly soaked the packaged urn in water. Her partner and husband, the great ballplayer turned vaudevillian—Mike Donlin—promptly soaked the funeral parlor with a heavy law suit.

In 1916—Verdun, the Somme, the Irish Rebellion—American audiences were bemused by both vaudeville and films which exposed the backstage mechanics of show business. Films showed how movies were made, methods of double-exposure, and other tricks of the trade. Some Loew houses introduced public rehearsals, with actors appearing onstage tired and dirty from long trips to rehearse in front of the audience. Then they would reappear, cleaned and dressed before lowered backdrops, to give the formal performance.

nix on 'exposé' stuff Variety long frowned on exposé stuff. As proponent of show business, the paper always felt that any shattering of illusions wasn't consistent with the best showmanship. *Sime* objected to come-lately columnists who he thought were smart-alecky when they "exposed" how certain effects were done.

Eventually the syndicated Broadway and Hollywood columnists, in pace with the spread of radio and talkers, made most of America privy to much inside stuff. *Sime* then decided that Broadway had become a state of mind, every town and hamlet between Maine and California was as hep as was Broadway. In fact, he observed, because of the time differential and the retarded film bookings in the bigger key cities, the lesser towns got their radio and pix ahead of Broadway.

However, to keep personal faith with himself, for years Variety was kept off the subway stands in New York. Ward & Gow, the then big New York City news distributors, wanted to handle Variety, but *Sime* argued "it would serve no good if some layman picked up the paper and read that Al Jolson was getting $15,000 a week at the Capitol. They wouldn't understand it," he continued, "and, besides, that would be uppermost in their minds when they did pay their 50¢ to see Jolson. You can't make them understand how much it took for any headliner to get up to that coin, or even how little of it he can keep after taxes."

21

Winchell Sings a War Song

★

If the movies recognized the war as dramatic material only belatedly, vaudeville hardly recognized it at all. In 1914 comedians showed their awareness of world events by gazing down at the men in the orchestra pit and asking roguishly, "How are you boys down there in the trenches?" The war sketch came in for a brief period in 1917, but managers quickly cut it out. When the Armistice was signed, there was hardly a war sketch left in bigtime vaudeville. Signs were promptly posted backstage in all theatres: CUT OUT WAR SONGS AND GAGS.

The acts with a war motif which were allowed in vaudeville were in the nature of charity benefits. What vaudeville would not permit as an art form it cheerfully blessed as a duty. Thus in 1917 vaudeville houses played an act called "The Shrapnel Dodgers"—three Canadian veterans, one with an eye missing, another with one arm, and a third with an amputated leg—who sang and narrated their war experiences.

Lady Aberdeen, wife of the Viceroy of Ireland, appeared in vaudeville the next year in an act representing a lawn fete, with a cast of 20. The act was for the benefit of widows and children of Irish servicemen, with Lady Aberdeen delivering a short talk on the effect of the war upon children.

Another, Lady Duff Gordon, donated the salary for her 1917 fashion show to a fund for disabled soldiers. After a successful booking at the Palace, Lady Gordon toured the Keith Circuit with diminishing acclaim. Variety, in reviewing her act later at a New York neighborhood theatre, found that "Madame has lost her poise somewhere en route, since playing the Palace. Her 'Washington cocktail' story was most indelicate, to say the least . . . Holiday Harlemites did not take kindly to Madame's extreme models, and laughed at them instead of absorbing their artistic value."

winchell & green   The husband-and-wife team of Walter Winchell & Rita Green appeared at Loew's American Roof in New York in 1918. His patriotic impulses were even then in evidence. "While Miss Green is making a costume change," Variety's reviewer wrote, "Winchell handles a war song, and he gives way for the girl's eccentric solo dance. . . . A likeable act for the No. 2 position." *Ibee*—the late Jack Pulaski—reviewed the act.

In later years when *Sime* became vexed with his journalistic protégé, Winchell, the paper (September 24, 1930) printed part of some letters written by Winchell in 1920 to the late Howard Langford, vaudeville sketch player and writer, who wrote an act for Winchell at the time. The letters denoted Walter's great hunger even then to get out of "the No. 2 spot." Writing Langford on November 20, 1920, he said in part:

"My dear Howard: I am writing you again to tell you that a wonderful proposition has been made to me from the Keith Exchange to be assistant editor of the *Vaudeville News*. I have accepted, believing that the future of such a position holds remarkable things for me (if I show 'em what I am made of) and has unlimited possibilities.

"You no doubt don't blame me, because you have heard me mention that I would love to become a figure in the world, preferably the news game. I have always had an inclination toward it, and at last I have had my wish granted.

"Of course the money is not a heluva lot, and I know I cannot save, but the fact is that any day may bring more wonderful things, as the connection itself with such a wonderful organization as the B. F. Keith Exchange can give.

"I also realize that when I tire of this (if I do) I can always go back to being an ordinary actor, can't I? . . ."

Winchell went from the Keith-Albee house organ, the *Vaudeville News,* to Bernarr Macfadden's ill-fated tabloid, the New York *Graphic,* and eventually with Hearst's New York *Daily Mirror* and world-wide fame.

Winchell and Variety in recent years get along very well. There was a time when *Sime* burned up at the columnist over an incident which may have been a Variety ad solicitor's fault, but *Sime,* ever loyal to his own staffers, groused at the columnist whom he had counseled during his formative years on the *Graphic.* The same was true of boys like Mark Hellinger, but no editor did for the *Graphic's* conductor of the "Your Broadway and Mine" column what *Sime* did for Winchell. In Winchell's own words, "The best tips I had when I was first getting a reputation on the old New York *Graphic* came from Sime Silverman, the editor of Variety."

It seemed preposterous that the editor of the bible of the show world would hand out hot news to a rival covering the Broadway circuit. Winchell, grateful for the tips but puzzled, came out one day and asked *Sime* why. "Walter," he said, "I give you tips to use so I can jack up my staff for being scooped."

world war I jokes President Woodrow Wilson's second marriage, Ford's Peace Ship (which scarcely needed burlesquing), Ford jokes and the snickering subject of B.V.D.'s furnished the chief risible fodder for vaudeville comics in that pre-World War I period. To these were added sophisticated expressions like "You said it," "You said a mouthful" and "You said something!" It was no longer mirthful to refer to girls as "chickens"—the term was now "flappers."

Other surefire vaudeville material of the time included ukulele numbers, Chaplin imitations, foxtrot specialties, mother songs (with a gulp between bars), and war songs (out of the side of the mouth and with great waving of fists). Nearly every act began to use the spotlight. Middle-aged actresses preferred a yellow spot as the kindest, brunets requested green. And male singers inevitably took off their hats for the last two lines of a pop song.

Gone or going in 1916-1917 from the vaudeville stage were parodies, which were usually suggestive and considered too objectionable for a family audience; sketches with a cast of only two or three, which were being supplanted by more expensive units with casts from 10 to 12; and the professional society ballroom dancers.

Vaudevillians were resorting more and more to the "kind applause" trick in special localities by referring to local conditions, using Yiddishisms in a Jewish neighborhood, an Italian phrase (usually mildly profane) in an Italian neighborhood, and so on. [A third-of-a-century later on radio quiz shows, a contestant for the remarkable reason that he or she comes from Brooklyn, usually gets the same type of applause.]

Burlesque dramas were used by a good number of acts in 1917 who found them easy to do and productive of laughs, such as a Theda Bara-like Cleopatra calling up her "easy Mark" (Antony) on the phone. The last year of World War I brought an influx of jazz songs and dances, and solo acts of "nut" comedians and comediennes. For some reason not too clear, single turns were scoring more successfully than teams, and many partners broke up to ride the tide unencumbered.

the eternal billing battles   Old stars continued to shine, and new stars rose. The inevitable sign of the vet headliner, or the newly-arrived headliner, was a squawk about the size of billing. Any vaude manager with more than one headliner on his bill usually needed aspirin.

A newcomer named Eddie Cantor began to be heard from. He was then a stooge for Jean Bedini. In 1914 he joined Al Lee in an act called "The Master and the Man." Singing in blackface, with effeminate mannerisms, "Kid" Cantor won an ovation with songs like "Victrola" and "Snyder's Grocery Store." Before the war years were over, he was an established star in revues.

Still struggling up the ladder was George Jessel, who did impersonations in Gus Edwards' 1914 Song Revue. "Jessel's impersonations of Bert Williams, Ruth Roye, Eddie Foy and Raymond Hitchcock," reviewed Variety, "were very self-conscious. His Foy was good . . . the nearest thing to the rest was the clothes."

Harry Lauder was still Harry Lauder, concluding his seventh triumphant "farewell" tour in 1914. A few years later, opening at the Lexington Opera House, he brought $30,000 a week to the b.o. In Houston, Texas, he drew $6,000 for a single matinee and night show. At the end of the war, the Manhattan Opera House took off its top hat in awe, and booked Lauder for two weeks—the first performer ever to play there who was not from the world of the opera or dance.

The Marx Bros., advertising themselves as "the greatest comedy act in show business; barring none," were starring in an act called "Home Again," with a cast of 17. In 1914 the boys were playing under their real names, with Groucho billed as Julius, Zeppo as Milton, Chico as Leonard and Harpo as Arthur. Their surname was spelled Marks then. Their mother, Minnie Palmer, a vet vaude trouper in her own right, was mentoring her brood into the professional intricacies.

mae west—'brinkley girl'   Mae West billed herself as "The Original Brinkley Girl" in 1914 vaudeville. Two years later, her fifth fling at the two-a-day was in a singing act with her sister. For a finale she appeared in masculine evening clothes, a somewhat spectacular physical achievement for her. Variety turned thumbs down. "She'll have to clean up her style—she has a way of putting dirty meanings in innocent lyrics." Miss West couldn't imagine where the reviewer got that idea and was quite volatile about it.

Variety's frank criticism naturally was not designed to win friends from mediocre talent ranks, especially when said reviews influenced managers into sometimes cancelling bookings. By the same token, a favorable mention ofttimes meant a season's vaudeville route. It was understandable, of course, that acts who reaped what they thought was a poisonous panning would frequently descend on the editorial offices. The muscular acrobats were the toughest problem, and for their especial benefit a king-size baseball bat was kept in reach as an equalizer, if not a pacifier. The Teutonic acts, usually of the two-man-high, hand-to-hand calibre, used to be the most demonstrative in their grief over a bad notice; and when they took it too personally, and threatened mayhem and the like, somehow the

Variety muggs had a habit of being around at strategic moments to re-enact the famed flying-wedge that the waiters at the old Jack's, opposite the now extinct Hippodrome, utilized under similar stress.

There were cases, too, of wiry Italian acts, of the musico-comedy calibre, who sought to use a stiletto to accent their aggrieved attitudes, but this was as nothing as a woman scorned. Especially when the blot was on her French escutcheon. *Sime* had panned a comedienne for her "Hoboken French," and it called for all of Wilson's 14 points of diplomacy to calm her, especially since she produced her birth certificate to prove she was Canuck French (Canadian-born). She by-passed the critical captiousness about her singing talents.

Silver-voiced John McCormack made vaudeville magnates gasp at the salary he demanded for appearing in vaudeville. McCormack, who received $1,500 a concert, simply multiplied that by the 14 turns a week he would have to do in vaudeville, and asked $25,000. P.S.— he didn't get it.

another president's daughter   Another famous name of the day that refused to appear in vaudeville was Margaret Wilson, the President's daughter. Unlike Margaret Truman, Miss Wilson considered a theatrical invitation as a tribute to her father's prestige rather than to any prowess of her own.

Sophie Tucker set some sort of endurance record for both performer and audience in 1915, when she stayed onstage at the Palace in Chicago for 39 minutes, singing no less than 16 songs.

The oldest vaudeville team going in 1917 was revealed as Fox & Ward, who were celebrating their 50th year together. Albee awarded them the present of a two-year contract at $300 a week, with choice jumps and billings, in a typical gesture of patronage. The second oldest team known were McIntyre & Heath, and the third Ward & Curran. Variety turned a handspring the following year to salute Fannie Ward, who was still trouping. "With a new name this past year," Variety grinned, "she could have butted into pictures and made all the young soubrets sit up and take notice. Fannie Ward is some chicken!" Incidentally, it is show biz lore that McIntyre & Heath, for all their veteran partnership, never spoke offstage in all their 40 years as a team. Today Joe Smith and Charles Dale, of "Dr. Kronkheit" fame, are the oldest vaude team, together 52 years although technically not a two-act all those years since both started with the Avon Comedy 4. Just before them the late Willie & Eugene Howard were the oldest stage combo.

Eva Tanguay was still a sensational boxoffice attraction in 1918, getting $3,500 a week for her act in which she wore a dress made of dollar bills trimmed with the even scarcer treasures of coal and sugar, as well as other fabulous costumes.

broun's blitz on tanguay   Heywood Broun, as drama critic for the New York *Tribune,* reviewed her act under the headline: SOMETHING ABOUT WHICH EVA TANGUAY SHOULD BE MADE TO CARE. Wrote the acidulous Broun: "Ours is a democracy, so probably nothing much can be done about the singing of Eva Tanguay. But, even in a free country, there should be some moral force, or physical if need be, to keep her away from the 'Marseillaise.' She should not be allowed to sing it even on her knees, and it is monstrous that the great hymn of human liberty should be shrilled as a climax to a vulgar act by a bouncing singer in a grotesque costume begirt with little flags.

"Miss Tanguay sings in French, and I have no idea whether she is trying to be funny. I never know what she is trying to be except noisy. I think she is the parsnip of performers. The only cheerful song in her repertory yesterday was one in which she hinted that some day she would retire. Miss Tanguay is billed as a 'bombshell.' Would be to Heaven she were, for a bomb is something which is carried to a great height and then dropped."

The outraged Eva promptly took an ad in Variety. With more courage than prudence, she reprinted the withering Broun review under the scornful headline: EVA TANGUAY—THE PARSNIP OF PERFORM-ERS. And then Eva let loose her blast of indignation, in some very free and fiery verse:

"Have you ever noticed when a woman succeeds how they attack her until her character bleeds? They snap at her heels like mongrels unfed, just because she has escaped being dropped into FAILURE's big web. They don't give her credit for talent or art. They don't discount a very hard start. They don't give her credit for heartaches or pains; how she grimly held tight to the reins when the road ahead was rocky and drear; how smiling she met every discouraging sneer. AND . . .

"Now to you who have slandered, YOU are dirt 'neath my feet, for I have beaten YOUR game and it's a hard game to beat!"

longhairs—long b.o.   At the opposite pole of vaudeville actors, the longhair artists of show business found the war years remarkably kind to opera. In a 1914 Sunday night performance at the Hippodrome, with an overflow of 575 customers onstage behind him, John McCormack drew $9,000.

The Irish revolutionary movement, brewing in 1915, affected McCormack's repertory on tour. He refused to sing "It's A Long Way to Tipperary" in Kansas City, and cancelled his Toronto engagement. He didn't mind singing "God Save the King," he explained tactfully, but he didn't wish to enter into any "controversy."

A sensational leap from smalltime vaudeville to grand opera was made by Rosa Ponselle. In 1915 the Ponzella Sisters were a singing act, with Rosa at the piano and Carmela doing most of the vocalizing. But in 1918 Rosa—not Carmela—was engaged by Giulio Gatti-Casazza of the Metropolitan Opera to sing the role of Carmen, and the following year scored a tremendous success.

If the Met took a generous view toward talent blossoming on the vaudeville stage, it was quite hostile toward any which flirted with the movies. In 1917 it refused to renew the operatic contract of Geraldine Farrar, who had committed the serious misdemeanor of lowering herself by "posing" for this inferior art form.

Caruso spared the Met any such embarrassing predicament. In 1917 he had paid $60,000 in war taxes on his income. Subsequently he refused $55,000 for six concerts because, he explained, fully half this amount would be paid to the Government in taxes.

caruso's fling in par pix 'pag'   The hierarchy at the Met sighed deeply upon hearing in 1918 that Caruso had signed with Adolph Zukor for $200,000 to do two films, one of which would be *Pagliacci*. Each film would be a $250,000 investment, supported by a powerful ad campaign. With Caruso's views on taxes, there was no question of his considering any concert appearances that year, and therefore no problem for the Met. The Caruso films, incidentally, were dismal failures.

Incidentally, also, Caruso was snagged into becoming a glorified songsmith by the then struggling Tin Pan Alleyite, Earl Carroll. They collaborated on "Dreams of Long Ago," words by Carroll and tune by Caruso, which Feist published and which the great tenor ultimately recorded for Victor but that, too, like his Par pix trys, didn't click.

The Victor Talking Machine Co. gave the opera world a new great singer, Amelita Galli-Curci. After signing her for some records, they won her an opening with Campanini's Chicago Grand Opera. When the company played at New York's Lexington Opera House in 1918, she swept to fame overnight. Victor's special campaign featured her records. They were so certain of her ultimate triumph that they had prepared the ads months in advance. When Galli-Curci later that year gave a concert at the Hippodrome, speculators demanded $17.50 a pair for tickets. She, too became a member of the Met roster.

The audience for grand opera grew larger through the war years, a somewhat inexplicable development in an age that was reaching its logical culmination in jazz. Chicago, in only four days' time, subscribed $200,000 for grand opera in 1915. In the year following, a crowd of 25,000 paid $40,000 at $2.50 top prices to witness *Die Walkure* at the Yale Bowl in New Haven.

The era produced two ironical developments in the longhair division. John Philip Sousa, the bandmaster who had once arrogantly refused to play at an amusement park because of the 10¢ admission, accepted $70,000 in 1915 for nine weeks at the Panama-Pacific Exposition, where he was used as a free attraction against the Boston Symphony Orchestra. And Leopold Auer gave a concert at Carnegie Hall which tailspinned financially.

Auer was the man who taught Mischa Elman and Jascha Heifetz.

sky pilot boff b.o.   1915 saw the introduction of a unique branch of show business—evangelism. In a tradition later to be developed by Aimee Semple McPherson, an ex-baseball player named Billy Sunday sold God to audiences with a bang-up performance that was strictly b.o. A one-man, all-star show, he toured the nation on a tabernacle circuit, garnering sensational publicity.

Billy Sunday didn't like actors, and they didn't like him, which might have been professional jealousy. He flayed the theatre as the work of Satan, and succeeded in crippling business in Philadelphia when he stumped there for an 11-week run with heavy collection plates. That, of course, not only helped "God's work" but killed Sunday (no pun intended) biz in theatres. Actors labeled him a clown with a low comedy act.

A temperamental evangelist, Sunday had a way of walking out on his faithful when he was displeased. He did this in Paterson, New Jersey, when the collection plate was too light. He did it again in San Francisco, when a number of clergymen criticized both him and his methods.

By 1917 he was still going strong, getting as much as $90,436 in one day's collection at Boston. New York, however, was a bit too sophisticated to swallow Sundayism raw. His revival there in the same year failed to affect the business of Broadway theatres. And, an ironic commentary on the audiences who went to listen to him, one saloon near his tabernacle had to add four bartenders to handle the increased business. (The same thing was to happen years later when Aimee Semple McPherson's personal appearance at the Capitol sent that Broadway deluxer to its all-time low of $6,000.)

Crackpot of the sawdust trail or not, the Rev. Dr. Billy Sunday was invited to deliver a prayer in the House of Representatives in Washington, which he began by thundering, "Thou knowest, O Lord, that no nation so infamous, vile, greedy, sensuous, bloodthirsty ever disgraced the pages of history." Referring, of course, to America's new adversary at war.

And when he fulminated that the Government was forbidding him to build the "tabernacles" in which he "served God," the War Industries Board deemed it advisable to write him respectfully explaining the need for wartime priorities in construction.

But by 1918 Billy Sunday was slipping. As one sign that he himself recognized it, with a possible eye toward future theatrical bookings, he began to go out of his way in sermons to say conciliatory things about the theatre and moving pictures—institutions which he formerly had villified.

It was also discovered that his choir leader, Homer Rodeheaver, known as "Sunday's Sousa," was one of the best songpluggers in the country—head of the firm that published all Sunday's hymns and songs. At each revival Homer would deliver a sales talk on the songs, urge the brethren to join in singing (just as they did in the

movies and vaude houses), and circulate his salesmen through the
crowds to sell the song books.

Beneath the headline, BILLY SUNDAY'S CHICAGO FLOP, Variety in
March 1918, reported the decline of the self-made messiah. Although
50,000 Chicagoans gathered to hear Sunday on the opening day of
the Midwest campaign, "the intake of the stew-pan brigade was less
than $3,000."

The following day, apparently brooding over this financial in-
gratitude, Sunday didn't preach at the tabernacle. On Tuesday he
played to an afternoon attendance of 4,000, and a night crowd of
16,000. The collection dropped more than 50 per cent, with less than
$1,500 rewarding his histrionics. On Wednesday less than 10,000
people attended, and the receipts dipped to a new low.

That did it. The next day there were rumors that Sunday, instead
of completing his 10-week run in Chicago, might desert the city
with his troupe for Duluth after only three weeks, "if the people
didn't open up their purses as well as their hearts."

Or, as Variety put it, "Ecclesiastical show biz not so hey-hey."
One wag commented, "Billy's only hope is to start stripping off
more than his coat."

22

Ziegfeld Over Broadway

★

Rarely could Broadway producers recall a season as terrible for
show business as 1914. The corpses of shows that could normally
have been expected to prosper littered the Main Stem from 38th
to 50th streets. Reports from the hinterland were equally funereal.
Nothing helped—neither rave reviews, heavy advertising splurges,
nor publicity campaigns. There seldom had been a year with so
many enthusiastic newspaper notices, and so many calamitous flops.

Producers brooded over the reasons for this melancholy state of affairs. Many blamed the war and the depression of early spring. But the roots went deeper. In New York the boom in show business had brought about a plethora of theatres. In legit alone, the city had 36 top-rank houses seating about 54,000 a night. Competing with them for the New Yorker's dollar were over a dozen major vaudeville theatres, almost 50 vaudfilm houses, and a vast number of straight picture theatres.

Only about six of the three dozen legit theatres had made any money out of the 1914 season. The b.o. was so bad that many managers shut down entirely two weeks before Christmas, rather than take advantage of the customary half-salary clause which would have permitted them to continue those weeks at reduced cost.

The road was moribund for a different reason. Managers touring roadshows with third-rate casts in previous seasons had killed the goose by feeding it with glowing adjectives and tired turkeys. Now they were shopping more selectively. A wide choice of pix and vaude gave them plenty of latitude.

Business continued to lag through most of the following year, but perked up toward the fall, as the impact of America's orders for war goods made itself felt in fattening profits and paychecks. 1916 seemed more like old times, with every Broadway legit house prospering, and two dozen shows waiting for a vacant theatre. There was also a big demand for original Broadway companies on the road, which was still rejecting No. 2 and No. 3 companies. Oddly, the boom in legit found the take in film houses off some 25 per cent.

When the dollars poured in even faster and thicker during the first half of 1917, the legit settled down to a new and unprecedented era of prosperity. Many shows were doing so well that they had been held over from the previous year, and were running straight through the summer months. Actors were awarded equitable contracts. The Globe, presenting Fred Stone, and the Century, showing *Miss 1917*, raised their prices to $3 top. Nearly 50 theatres were doing well with $2 attractions. Road business was thriving.

Then suddenly, in November, there was a sharp slump—so sharp that it set a new record in poor boxoffice. Worried managers considered slashing salaries. Shows starring such names as Billie Burke, Henry Miller, William Faversham, Robert Hillard and Grace

George all opened—and quickly closed. By the end of the fall season, of the 75 productions which had been on the boards, 36 were
in Cain's warehouse, 10 were touring, and 29 remained on Broadway. Of these 29, less than a dozen were hit shows. The remainder
were hanging on.

The Winter Garden, which had joined the climb to a $3 top,
swiftly rescinded its decision and reverted to a $2.50 scale. The Globe
and the Century refused to follow suit. Fred Stone continued to
draw, but *Miss 1917* lost patronage. Arthur Hopkins, presenting
Gypsy Trail at the Plymouth, put ball bearings under his prices, retaining a $2 top weekends, but charging $1 and $1.50 for orchestra
on weekday nights. More and more roadshows pulled in to New
York from the hinterland.

The freak storm clouds rolled away in 1918, as the first heavy impact of America's entry into war eased. Business boomed again for
the legit both on Broadway and on the road. August, normally a
listless month, seemed like December. Nothing, it seemed, could
stop the upward flight of profits this time.

But in early September something did—a serious, nationwide epidemic of influenza. Theatres in almost every major city except New
York were shut down. Then just as the epidemic seemed at an
ebb, and theatres opened again to a renewed throbbing business,
a second wave of "Spanish influenza" set in. The loss in rentals
for theatres which were forced to remain dark ran into six figures.
Otto Kahn, noted financier, swore off playing angel to shows.

The era came to an end, however, with a thriving post-Armistice
business that augured well for the future. Legit producers who were
still dizzy from the roller-coaster plunges and flights of the war years
hoped for the best—and kept on good terms with their favorite
pawnbrokers.

Musical comedies and revues were the favorite money-makers
during the war years. The revues, which robbed vaudeville of approximately 100 headline acts, produced a new and undisputed
revue king—Flo Ziegfeld. His *Follies* and *Frolics* became the last
word in extravagance, glitter, feminine beauty and glamorous stage
mountings. In Broadway's unhappy year of 1914, tickets for the
Follies after the opening night soared to $5—almost as impressive in
that year as the Jazz Age price for opening night, in later years, of
$100 a pair.

Every chorine dreamed of becoming a Ziegfeld Follies girl. Even in 1914 that achievement was an open door to riches. Tommy Manville's wife-of-the-year, Florence Uber, was suing her playboy-husband for divorce and a $150,000 settlement. Where did she come from? The *Follies,* of course! And with true Ziegfeldian hauteur, Florence was disdaining to bargain with Tommy's father, who offered $100,000.

Among the stars who flocked to the Ziegfeld banner during 1914-1918 were Will Rogers, Fanny Brice, Eddie Cantor, Bert Williams, the Fairbanks Twins and W. C. Fields. Rogers, playing in the *Frolics* in 1917, was beginning to develop into the homespun political philosopher. During his act he asked the audience to mention any prominent person or event, and he'd talk about them.

After appearing in his first show, *Canary Cottage,* in 1916, Eddie Cantor was signed by Ziegfeld for the *Frolics.* Cantor wanted to make vaudeville appearances at the same time, but Ziegfeld refused permission. Graduating to the *Follies* in 1917 and 1918, Cantor sublimated his urge by running an ad in Variety declaring he would *write* vaudeville acts. Ziegfeld couldn't stop that.

W. C. Fields appeared in the 1916 *Follies,* singing two choruses of a song, and impersonating Teddy Roosevelt and Secretary of the Navy Josephus Daniels. The latter takeoff was in the nature of personal revenge. Daniels was the darling of the Prohibition forces for his order prohibiting the use of liquor in the Navy after July 1914.

Ziegfeld, in partnership with Charles Dillingham, made a sizable killing by taking over the musical, *Century Girl,* at the Century Theatre in 1916. The show cleaned up that year, and in 1917 played to gross receipts of $1,000,000, of which $360,000 was net profit.

Almost as much interest was taken in Ziegfeld's private life as in his scintillating productions and superbeauts. He married Anna Held, having managed the French star until her retirement after *Miss Innocence.* They were divorced in 1913, and Ziegfeld married Billie Burke. In 1918, at the age of 45, Anna Held died.

Irving Berlin wrote one of the few big hits of 1914, *Watch Your Step,* which opened at the New Amsterdam. Incidentally, it was his first Broadway musical. Other top musicals of the year were Jerome Kern's *Girl from Utah* with Julia Sanderson and *The Beauty Shop* with Raymond Hitchcock.

The following year George M. Cohan paid a glowing tribute to a rival songwriter when, in his revue *Hello, Broadway!*, starring himself and Willie Collier, he sang a medley of Berlin tunes. *Hip Hip Hooray* at the Hippodrome, under the management of Charles Dillingham, played to $60,000 a week. Ned Wayburn clicked at the Century with his *Town Topics* revue.

The legit season in 1916 was devoted almost exclusively to musicals, revues, comedy and farce. Only three serious dramas appeared all year. The outstanding musical and revue was *Stop! Look! Listen!* with Gaby Deslys. This year and the next saw the wholesale desertion of vaudeville stars to revues, including McIntyre & Heath, Frank Fay, Leo Carrillo, Trixie Friganza, Charlotte Greenwood, the Dolly Sisters, Billy B. Van, Louise Dresser, Carter de Haven, Al Jolson and Irene Franklin.

the shuberts at war—again The Shuberts, no less than the Allies, were waging a war on all fronts—as usual. Their first campaign was again directed against dramatic critics who panned Shubert shows. In 1914 Alan Dale rapped their production of *Miss Daisy* as poor entertainment. The Shuberts, already stung by a very poor season, put pressure on Dale's paper, Hearst's *American*, which obligingly ran favorable notices of *Miss Daisy* in later editions. Dale quit, later joining Variety as its first columnist for legit.

The Shuberts scored another triumph in 1916 when the State Court of Appeals ruled that they had a legal right to refuse admittance to their theatres to New York *Times* critic Alexander Woollcott. They didn't have to worry about *Tribune* critic Heywood Broun, as that frank gentleman was overseas reporting the war. Nor about William Winter, dean of drama critics, who died at 81 in 1917.

The war between the Shuberts and Klaw & Erlanger broke out afresh in 1914, with the tempers of both sides frazzled by the bad season. This battle had been waged, on and off, since 1902, when Klaw & Erlanger forced Nixon-Zimmerman to withdraw from partnership with Sam S. Shubert. But the axe was buried again in 1915, with Klaw & Erlanger joining hands with the Shuberts in booking plays for the new season.

The following year the Shuberts took a 6-year lease on the

Astor Theatre, paying Cohan & Harris $125,000 bonus for the deal. To pad out this dent in their treasury, the Shuberts thought of the bright idea of charging minor acts in their Winter Garden show, *Doing Our Bit,* $25 a week for putting their names in lights.

Klaw & Erlanger unburied the hatchet in 1918 by guaranteeing Cohan & Harris a 5-year profit of $1,000,000 if they would stick with them, and not go with the Shuberts. The Shuberts had further cause for mourning the ingratitude of mankind when Marilyn Miller left them for Ziegfeld.

The only two managerial units in legit who made big money in 1914 were Cohan & Harris and Charles Dillingham. The latter's two shows (the only ones he produced that season) were the top hits. Cohan & Harris were cleaning up with *On Trial* and *It Pays To Advertise.* Belasco's *Phantom Rival* was also an outstanding success, continuing its run through 1915.

The following year brought John Barrymore in an underworld melodrama, *Kick In,* Marie Dressler in *A Mix Up,* Ina Claire in *Lady Luxury,* John Drew in a revival, *Rosemary,* and a $10,000 prize play about New England, *Children of Earth,* written by Alice Brown and produced by Winthrop Ames. It was a prize flop at the b.o.

Boomerang, one of the few nonmusical attractions of 1916, was going strong after 39 weeks, the 1916 season's record sellout show. Other legits included Ethel Barrymore as *Our Mrs. McChesney,* two Shakesperian and two Shaw revivals, Otis Skinner as *Mister Antonio,* David Warfield in a revival of *The Music Master,* John Drew in Thackeray's *Major Pendennis.*

Two war plays appeared in 1917—*Lilac Time* with Jane Cowl, and *Out There* with Laurette Taylor. George Arliss appeared as *Hamilton,* Ina Claire as *Polly With a Past,* Julia Sanderson as *Rambler Rose,* John Drew as *The Gay Lord Quex.* American actors accused producer Oliver Morosco of trying to dodge local salaries when he hired an all-English cast to support Emily Stevens in *The Fugitive.*

Three serious plays with the longest runs of 1918 were, surprisingly, war plays—*Billeted, Friendly Enemies,* and *Three Faces East.* The latter two were the two biggest dramatic hits of Broadway. *Friendly Enemies* was called the "million dollar show," because it was expected to earn that much for producer Al Woods. There were other war plays as well—Marjorie Rambeau in *Where Poppies Bloom,* Effie Shannon and Shelley Hull in *Under Orders,* and *The Better 'Ole,* the Bruce Bairnsfather comic character translated in stage terms for Charles Coburn who played Old Bill.

1918 also ushered in one of the most phenomenally successful plays of all time, *Lightnin'.* It originally opened for a week in Washington, with Frank Bacon in the lead, then closed for doctoring. Opening at the Gaiety on Broadway later that year, it began its long, record-breaking run of 1,291 performances.

In later years it was eclipsed by nine other shows. The record-holder for marathon stay on Broadway remains *Life With Father,* 3,216 performances; followed by *Tobacco Road,* 3,182; *Abie's Irish Rose,* 2,327; *Oklahoma!* 2,248; *The Voice of the Turtle,* 1,557; *Harvey,* 1,775; *Arsenic and Old Lace,* 1,444; *Hellzapoppin,* 1404; and *Angel Street,* 1,295.

Incidentally, Richard Rodgers and Oscar Hammerstein 2d's *Oklahoma!* is the champ Broadway musical long-runner with *Hellzapoppin*—perhaps as much a tribute to a one-man journalistic campaign by columnist Walter Winchell, who indubitably converted mediocre notices into boffola b.o.—the No. 2 long-run marathon stayer. Irving Berlin's *Annie Get Your Gun,* with 1,147 performances, is the No. 3 musical long-runner; and still another Rodgers & Hammerstein musical, *Carousel,* gets into the Big 5 among musical boxoffice champs with 890 performances.

No. 4 top musical, *Pins and Needles,* with 1,108 performances, is in itself a phenomenon. This was the semi-professional cast show, produced by and with International Ladies Garment Workers Union personnel, but notable for its playing-down of "social significance." Incidentally, this musical brought songsmith Harold J. Rome to the fore.

As of Labor Day, 1951, long runs on Broadway for 500 or more performances include:

Plays	Number Performances	Plays	Number Performances
Life with Father	3,224	Oklahoma!	2,248
Tobacco Road	3,182	Harvey	1,775
Abie's Irish Rose	2,327	The Voice of the Turtle	1,557

Plays	Number Per-formances	Plays	Number Per-formances
Arsenic and Old Lace	1,444	Dead End	687
Hellzapoppin	1,404	Dear Ruth	683
Angel Street	1,295	Where's Charley	680
Lightnin'	1,291	East Is West	680
Annie Get Your Gun	1,147	Chauve Souris	673
Pins and Needles	1,108	The Doughgirls	671
Kiss Me Kate	1,077	Irene	670
Mister Roberts	991	Boy Meets Girl	669
Born Yesterday	979	Gentlemen Prefer Blondes	727
Anna Lucasta	957	Blithe Spirit	657
Kiss and Tell	956	The Women	657
South Pacific	983	A Trip to Chinatown	657
Carousel	890	Bloomer Girl	654
Hats Off to Ice	889	Rain	648
Follow the Girls	882	Janie	642
The Bat	867	The Green Pastures	640
My Sister Eileen	865	Is Zat So?	618
White Cargo	864	Separate Rooms	613
Song of Norway	860	Star and Garter	609
You Can't Take It With You	837	Student Prince	608
Three Men on a Horse	835	The Happy Time	606
Stars on Ice	830	Broadway	603
The Ladder	789	Adonis	603
State of the Union	765	Street Scene	601
The First Year	760	Kiki	600
Sons o' Fun	742	A Society Circus	596
The Man Who Came to Dinner	739	Blossom Time	592
Call Me Mister	734	The Two Mrs. Carrolls	585
Claudia	722	Finian's Rainbow	582
I Remember Mama	713	Brother Rat	577
Junior Miss	710	Show Boat	572
Seventh Heaven	704	The Show-Off	571
Peg o' My Heart	692	Sally	570
The Children's Hour	691	One Touch of Venus	567
		Happy Birthday	564
		The Glass Menagerie	561

[The Drunkard, *a hokum meller rated a legit show of a sort, has been running consecutively 16 years in Hollywood. Also from the Coast came Ken Murray's glorified vaude-revue,* Blackouts, *which ran seven years in Hollywood and lasted seven weeks in New York.*]

The year 1918 also presented Tommy Manville's rival, Nat C. Goodwin, in *Why Marry?* at the Astor. At the time, Goodwin, who had turned 60, had gone through six wives, including Eliza Weatherby, Maxine Elliott, Edna Goodrich and Marjorie Moreland. Before he died, he hit the jackpot with a total of eight, a couple better than Artie Shaw. The title of his 1918 vehicle apparently made very little impression upon its star.

The era was saddened by the death of some of the legit's best-loved figures. Playwrights Charles Klein and Justus Miles Forman. Producer Charles Frohman went with the *Lusitania*. A year later the final curtain rang down for Josephine Cohan, sister of George M. and wife of Fred Niblo; Dave Montgomery, Fred Stone's partner for 22 years; and Joseph Murphy, the stage's richest actor, noted for his play, *Kerry Gow*. Murphy left a personal fortune of $3,000,000.

'the road'—circa 1914-1918 The fortunes of road business during the war years were closely tuned to the ups and downs of Broadway. The road covered a multitude of sins as well as cities. There was small time, like the *Uncle Tom's Cabin* company playing two-night stands in Brooklyn, under canvas, in 1914. There was big time, like the 20 Al Woods roadshows of 1915, which paid out $200,000 in train fares alone. And there was old time, too, such as minstrel shows which celebrated their 31st year, in 1917, under the aegis of Al G. Fields.

Not all the successful shows of the era opened on Broadway, however desirable that might have been for prestige. In 1916 a show called *Experience* opened in Chicago. The demand for tickets was so great that it became the first legitimate show in American history to give daily matinee performances, and a Sunday show. The weekly gross ran to $20,000.

In the same year David Belasco produced a show written by George Scarborough which opened in Boston. It was called *Oklahoma*. Many years later another show called *Oklahoma!* was to open in Boston, run five years on Broadway and seven years on the road, and then return to Broadway in 1951 for a sock repeat.

The South made 1917 a banner road season, as a result of 26¢ cotton and the opening of many Army camps. Flushed Southerners flocked to boxoffices—but chose their b.o. carefully. If they were goin' to pay out top money, by Gad, then they wanted top shows and original casts. And that's what they got. Business boomed, and producers set a $2.50 scale for road musicals. Lush times largely prevailed until the demoralization of one-nighters' booking dates by the transportation troubles of 1918.

Stock companies—the poor man's Broadway—persisted in the face of giant competition by road companies, as well as by local picture and vaudeville houses. Stock blossomed when the regular theatre faded—in the summer. Many film houses, finding their summer patronage off, turned to stock as a stopgap. And when roadshows folded for the summer, stock had a wide selection of available talent. Stock was also winning a reputation as the showcase for new talent, plays and ideas. Managers watched this hothouse for fresh blooms which might thrive on Broadway.

Although stock in cities like New York, Chicago and Boston sprang up and disappeared like spring rains, a 1918 film field development gave them a sporting chance. The high cost of film production raised film rentals. Exhibitors in turn had to raise prices. In many cases these prices were above what theatregoers would have had to pay to see a live stock show.

The East was the favorite stamping ground of traveling stocks in the last year of the war. Some would play towns for as long as a week, offering a different repertory show every night. In New York City, because of the stiff competition, no stock company was able to put down roots for a full season. That is, except in Brooklyn, where one stock company did exactly that, showing a handsome profit. But then, as any Dodger fan will scornfully explain, "Brooklyn ain't New York!"

23

Burly Is Hurly

★

Despite the fact that a huge hunk of burlesque's traditional audience marched off to war in 1917 and 1918, the years of wrath yielded very luscious grapes to this unique division of show business. Socko was the word for boxoffice, even when floppo was the word for the b.o. in most branches of the theatre.

In 1914 the two principal burly circuits were the Columbia, known as the Eastern Wheel, which had 28 shows working, and the Progressive, which operated 30. The first all-Negro burly show, "Darktown Follies," appeared on the Progressive circuit that year, opposed by Columbia's "Smart Set."

The big companies on the Eastern Wheel apparently winced under the $13,500 weekly—$450,000 a season—they were forced to pay in railway fares for their traveling companies. The Interstate Commerce Law (I.C.L.) prohibited kickbacks from the railroads, but Eastern Wheel executives hit upon a happy subterfuge . . . "accepting" heavy advertising in their programs from railroads they patronized.

It was a happy idea, that is, until the Government found this to be a distinct evasion of the I.C.L., in the specific instance of the Central Railroad. Columbia pleaded guilty and was fined $7,500.

Burlesque was being cleaned up so well that in 1915 it was even staging cake-walk contests, and won admission into the city of Los Angeles for the very first time. With lowered prices and clean shows, burlesque boomed all through 1916. One circuit, the Independent, went bankrupt because it refused to scrap its blue policy. The new trend was amazing to old-time managers, who believed burly couldn't make a dime without cooch dancers or blue stuff. The whitewashed burly show was also attracting the attention of newspaper critics with new talent and a higher brand of comedy.

The fall season of 1917 revealed some amazing—for burlesque—boxoffice figures. The Columbia in New York, at $1 top, was playing to as high as $10,000 a week, including Sunday shows. And even this was dwarfed by a record-breaking 1918, during which a show that only played to $3,200 a week was considered a lemon. In former burly times, that would have been a fine week.

But in 1918 it was considered normal for a good burly show to average $8,500 a week, an astonishing phenomenon to the producers of $2 legitimate shows. There were more incredible whistles on Broadway when it was learned that one burlesque house, despite the flu epidemic, would wind up the year with a net of $175,000.

With very little ostentation or publicity, burlesque theatres also pitched in on the theatrical war effort, raising hundreds of thousands of dollars. The curtain of the war years fell upon a burlesque —pure, patriotic and prosperous—which was hardly recognized by those who knew it when.

circuses nsg   The circus, in 1914, was on its heels. There was no chance to go abroad for new sensations, and what novelties were available were playing for more money at the Pacific Panama Exposition. The circuses were so desperate for new attractions that one big top near Chicago featured a Tango Dance, with "Mr. and Mrs. Cristle." Amusement parks cut into circus business, and there were too many circuses abroad for so poor a year. Some of the biggest shows folded tents in the middle of the season, including the big Sig Sawtelle Show.

A circus needs a lot of people backstage and in the rings to keep it going. The growing shortage of manpower in 1916 hit the big tops hard, forcing many to cancel bookings. At New Castle, Ohio, one circus had to close down when its razorbacks walked out to take better-paying jobs in the town's munition plant.

Despite a bad start, circuses did well in 1917, which was a banner year for most of show business. Jess Willard proved a strong drawing card for one white tent outfit. The Richards Show set a circus precedent by being the first to use motor trucks in making overland jumps.

In 1918, the Miller Bros.' 101 Ranch Wild Wester confessed making more money than it had ever made before in the big circus business—by selling horses to the Government for the cavalry. The Hagenback-Wallace Circus added another tragedy to its strange history of disasters—being almost destroyed by fire in its early years, and badly damaged by flood in 1913. And now (1918), its circus train crashed into an empty troop train, resulting in 69 dead and nearly 100 injured, with many of the dead burned beyond recognition.

Four notable circus figures died during the war era. Hassan Ben Ali, who died in 1914, was the greatest owner of Arab circus troupes in the world. Alf Ringling, oldest of the famous circus brothers, died in 1916. A year later, Lieutenant Frank Cody was killed in action while flying for the R.A.F. over London. He was followed to the grave in a few months by his father, Colonel William F. Cody, better-known as Buffalo Bill.

If the circuses were having a rough time, so were the amusement parks. Bad weather in 1914, added to bad times, equaled a bad hole in the parks' bankrolls. Many managers blamed the spread of movies as largely responsible, satisfying a summer urge for entertainment which otherwise might have lured thousands to the parks. Even the roller skating rinks no longer drew crowds, despite increased offers of prizes. And to make things blacker, operating expenses were up, with parks compelled to add between four and five men to their dance hall orchestras.

Coney Island was offering "The Wreck of the *Titanic*," and "The Castles' Summer House," a concession without the Castles. Dreamland had a circus and freak show at 10¢ a throw. Jap rolling ball games replaced the French plate-dropping gyp, and baby dolls were the big gift stand prizes to lure flushed swains. But even with a Mardi Gras thrown in, Coney Island, like the rest, stared at a large eight-ball.

And in 1915, when a new law ordered women's bathing suits to be equipped with at least a two-inch sleeve, as police trudged the sands with tape measures. Coney Island—along with the other amusement parks—continued to enjoy the customary bad season.

The trials and tribulations of circuses and amusement parks, however, did not daunt many cities, which were entering show business as municipal producers. In 1914 St. Louis presented a pageant on the biggest stage ever built, in the natural amphitheatre of Forest Park, with its lagoon on three sides. Over 7,000 citizens of St. Louis took part onstage.

In 1915 San Francisco staged its highly-publicized Exposition, at which Lincoln Beachy, one of America's earliest aviators, was killed in a spectacular stunt flight. The Exposition flopped badly. Outside its gates an entrepreneur with a street wagon, featuring "Alaskan Gray Fox—Penny A Peep," did a whale of a business.

New York put on war expositions in 1917. The first was a quasi-exposition at the Grand Central Palace, an Army and Navy Field Equipment Bazaar, ostensibly to furnish regiments with equipment that the Government didn't provide. Receipts were $71,475, with net profits for the regiments of—$754. The exposition had been conceived and operated for profit by private promoters.

A genuine war exposition replaced it a few weeks later—"Heroland," with 105 war charities participating in a 16-day bazaar to raise $1,000,000. The following year Chicago opened a United States War Exposition, charging 25¢ admission, and clocking over 100,000 people past the gate in the first day.

ice-skating vogue As the roller skating fad died, a new skating craze rose to take its place—on ice. The craze began at the St. Nicholas Rink on New York's West 66th Street in 1915. It spread to the Biltmore and Waldorf-Astoria hotels, which put in ice-skating floors. Costume tailors began to advertise special ice-skating costumes for women.

From New York the craze did a figure-eight around the nation, chiefly through Charlotte, the toe-skipping ice skater who was "solid" at the Hippodrome. Gradually society began to pick up ice skating—and rink attendants began to pick up society. Ice rinks spread rapidly, but suffered a setback when the Fuel Administration closed them because too much fuel was used to keep their ice plants operating.

The paths of prizefighters and show business continued to cross as usual during the war era. In 1914 Bob Fitzsimmons, with his son who was billed as "The White Hope," was in vaudeville. The hope never came true. The following year Jess Willard signed with Miller's 101 Ranch at $1,000 a day. "The Masked Marvel," a wrestler who many claimed was Frank Gotch, drew great crowds to the Manhattan Opera House where he was booked. The wrestling tournament staged there by Continental showman Sam Rachman ran for six weeks, netting $5,000 a week profit.

The big fight of the era was the Willard-Johnson fracas of 1915, which had two showmen as backers, L. Lawrence Weber and Harry H. Frazee. The fight took place in Havana, with the Cuban government stationing soldiers around the racetrack fight grounds to police any possible racial disorders. Jack Johnson was counted out in the 23d round, as newsreel cameras recorded the event for movie fans; and was lost to the public eye until he turned up in 1933 as conductor of his own jazz orchestra. Jess Willard wound up operating a Hollywood market.

24

Taboo

★

Even without the war to spur it, America was on its way to a new era of freedom in 1914—an era that reached its climax in the Roaring Twenties. But the impact of war undeniably speeded up the process. At first, when the war had not yet become our concern, America's preparedness program drew women into factories and offices. Women found themselves with a new economic freedom, and on a basis of equality with men. This was the first breach in the dam.

Later the hysteria of bond drives, boom towns and "doing one's bit" for the soldier boys, swept women into an emotional maelstrom in which the old moral values were splintered. As 2,000,000 men prepared to sail to an unknown destiny overseas, "eat, drink and be merry, for tomorrow . . ." was the most quoted line in the nation. And when the boys were gone, women grew lonely. Some resented the stories floating back from "gay Paree," and determined to make some hey-hey themselves.

The forces of morality had their hands full. As always, in times when moral delinquency rises, the brunt of official suspicion fell upon show business. Ignoring the obvious fact that any major transformation in public morality could only stem from the times and economic conditions themselves, public sachems chose to regard the phenomenon as the fruits of immoral examples on stage and screen. Puritans exorcised the whips of taboo.

Burlesque, which was cleaning itself up swiftly and efficiently, was an obvious target. In 1915 New York's Commissioner Bell revoked the licenses of the Olympia and Garrick theatres. Their shows, the Commissioner deplored, "reveal instances of indecency almost unbelievable." The Olympia had "indecent ads" in the lobby. The Garrick was closed in the middle of a performance because of nudity and "wrestling" with undraped femmes.

The Columbia Amusement Co. sent out letters to all its managers ordering them to eliminate cooch and "Oriental dancers," bare legs, smutty dialog, vulgar jokes and skits. Tab shows on the road were ordered to clean up or get out.

The bluenoses of America rose in their wrath in every state and every city. In 1916 the demon rum was scourged in seven states—Colorado, Washington, Oregon, Arkansas, Iowa, Idaho and South Carolina. A year later the number had swelled to 22.

In Denver, music was prohibited from hotel dining rooms. In Cincinnati, the Hamilton County Federation of Catholic Societies, with 10,000 members, began to boycott shows. *Family Cupboard,* one of their targets, was as bare (of audiences) as Mother Hubbard's (of food). The Gertrude Hoffman show was on the Societies' list, so she very prudently skipped Cincinnati on tour.

Atlantic City barred Sophie Tucker from singing "Who Paid the Rent for Mrs. Rip Van Winkle, When Rip Van Winkle Was Away?" Soph quit in disgust. Boston banned bare legs on the stage.

Scottish kilts were tolerated provided actresses wore tights or long stockings. Cincinnati's mayor, worried about that 10,000 vote, joined hands with Boston in censoring nude limbs behind footlights.

Eva Tanguay's pious Christian Science philosophy, expressed in her Variety ads with "Naught can disturb—God is Peace," didn't prevent her from falling afoul of Syracuse authorities, who banned posters picturing Eva in action. The management where she was playing was inundated with requests for the posters as souvenirs.

Anthony Comstock led his righteous lads, and the police, into Hammerstein's in 1915. Hammerstein, J. Edward Crapo and Mlle. Gomez were arrested for their act, "Garden of Passion," which was depassionized considerably for the evening performance and the rest of the week.

cabaret taboos Cabarets were on the list, too. In 1917 vice cleanup committees swung into action. The Strand Roof was raided, the charge being that women were soliciting men via the waiters. The Strand lost its dance license, but the place was packed for the next few days by thrilled sightseers. Salt Lake City went a step further, when the Mormon fathers barred all female entertainers from the city's cabarets. In Chicago, the tango, hesitation, and other "extreme" dances had already been placed under ban by the General Federation of Women's Clubs in an annual convention.

Chicago closed a show, *Our Betters* (not the Somerset Maugham play of that title), which had enjoyed a good run in New York. And as part of its general cleanup, it gave a group of gamblers—which included some vaudevillians—12 hours to get out of the city.

In the film field, Variety set the pace as early as 1914 by refusing advertising for "vice films," on grounds that these were injurious to both the trade and the public. Chaplin's first film for Essanay, *A Night Out,* was barred by the Department of Licenses. And in 1916, New York City banned five movies—*Sex Lure, It May Be Your Daughter, War's Women, Protect Your Daughter* and *Twilight Sleep*—all of them "vice films" which Variety had castigated.

The war brought censorship to Tin Pan Alley, with the axe being wielded by the Government. When the draft loomed, two songs were censored on the Orpheum Circuit—"I Don't Want To Get Well (I'm In Love With a Beautiful Nurse)" and "There'll Be A Hot Time For the Old Men When the Young Men Go To War."

Considering these tunes "opposed to the best interests of the draft," Federal officers forbade them to be sung, and compelled Feist to destroy all copies of the sheet music. The year following, all songs with the theme of "peace" were barred, under suspicion of being German propaganda.

first world war's firsts   The era which gave show business its first world war also introduced a number of other "firsts" of major and minor importance. The first radio broadcast in America took place on May 13, 1914, when phonograph music was relayed from Wanamaker's department store in New York to the Wanamaker's store in Philadelphia.

The first icecream parlor and dancehall, with the first license for such an establishment, opened in Los Angeles in 1915. Called the "Broadway Winter Garden," it was the forerunner of California's future Pig 'N' Whistle chain. The owner's name, Violinsky, appeared in electric lights three feet high out front. Explanation: he was the former vaudeville actor and songwriter. Rag dancing was permitted, and encouraged, between banana splits, making it the only establishment in Los Angeles which did not ban ragtime.

Sylvester Schaffer, opening at the 44th Street Theatre, New York, in 1914, was the first man to be a complete vaudeville bill. Performing alone for 80 minutes, he entertained audiences with sharpshooting, trained horses, Japanese juggling, card and coin palming, magic, rapid sketching in oils, a tumbling turn with five dogs, a violin solo, heavyweight juggling, and quick changes of costume.

May La Var, of the Dancing La Vars, was the first girl in vaudeville to wear a diamond kneelet containing a tiny watch, which started a fad that fortunately was short-lived. Earl Carroll was the first man to build a penthouse in New York, in 1916, when he had a star-swept bungalow constructed on top of the office building at 7th Avenue and 49th Street.

William Jennings Bryan became the first American Secretary of State to appear on a bill with acrobats, jugglers, female impersonators and Swiss yodelers. Bryan's poor investments compelled him to accept lecture bookings at Chautauquas, at which he shared the spotlight with vaudevillians.

The era saw many innovations in the methods whereby theatre managers sought to lure indifferent customers to the boxoffices. Most of these were developed in the abysmal year of 1914, when a customer was worth his weight in premiums.

The first Country Store night in the Times Square district appeared at the American Theatre, with hams, cheese and meats added to the entertainment stores onstage. Proctor's Fifth Avenue, New York, wooed attendance by introducing foyer dancing, with refreshments served to dancers, at the height of the dansant craze. The Fire Department stopped it—not enough lobby exits.

Poli's, in Bridgeport, Connecticut, introduced an "afterpiece," the first time in 10 years it had been seen. The afterpiece was an impromptu finale of old vaudeville bills, with all the acts ad libbing. Boston's Hippodrome became the first theatre to seduce customers with free parking space.

One film house in Ogdensburg, New York, gave away diamond rings and offered the holder of a lucky ticket a free trip to Bermuda. Moss & Brill's McKinley Square Theatre, New York, introduced the first theatrical commutation tickets—six matinee admissions for a quarter, or seven night admissions for $1.

Cutrate admissions gradually developed into a big business of its own. In 1915 the largest handler of cutrate theatre tickets—at that time called "Moe Levys" in show business—was Joe Leblang, who also sold tickets for hits at speculators' prices. He was paying $5,000 a week for eight weeks for all tickets to Al Woods' *Song of Songs*. Woods kept the show, but Leblang took all profits over the $5,000 a week guarantee.

'went over with a leblang'   To compete with Leblang, many managers issued their own cutrate tickets at half-price, under subterfuges like "People's League Ticket" and "Special Playgoers Voucher." But Leblang was unchallenged king of cutrate (or "cut-throat," as some embittered managers declared). In 1916 Leblang admitted in a courtroom that he earned $320,000 a year on cutrate tickets alone. Variety in later years observed that many a Broadway weakie "went over with a Leblang" for he kept many a legit show running.

Among the speculators, who made their money by charging above-boxoffice prices for hit shows, the leader in 1916 was Tyson & Co., followed by the McBride and George Bascom agencies.

Even the mighty Palace, in 1914, was forced to condescend to a premium gesture by giving out lemonade at matinees. Not to be outdone, Hammerstein's distributed mint-flavored chewing gum, promoted from the manufacturer who offered 2,000 packages for every performance, in return for credit on a screen slide at the finish of the show.

Cabarets, feeling the pinch as well as the theatre, cluttered up their shows incongruously with country-store nights. The Academy of Music, New York, lured customers in with amateur nights, at which the audience was permitted to express its disapproval by throwing eggs. And the height of desperation was reached by a legitimate show in Seattle, called *Today*. A coupon clipped from the local paper, plus one penny, admitted audiences to a "1¢ matinee."

Last of the White Rats

★

In April of 1917 the Rats gloomily admitted defeat—and bankruptcy. They sold out their new clubhouse to Albee, who purchased it for his National Vaudeville Artists. Jubilant managers of the V.M.P.A. cheerfully assumed all costs of the strike, such as it was, paying off every member who had suffered "for the cause of all." Acts that had struck or picketed were put on a blacklist which was observed for some while.

It was all over but the shouting. In June 1918, the A.F.L. discussed revoking the White Rats' charter, during which it was revealed that the organization membership was 3,000. "The reported attitude of the Executive Committee," Variety said, "was that as the Rats was a dying organization, it was useless to waste the time of the delegates by submitting a resolution for the revocation of the charter."

The sinking ship had deserted the White Rats.

the nva—company union   The National Vaudeville Artists, as a well-behaved company union that asked, instead of demanded, was highly regarded in managerial circles, which actually had given birth to it. In 1916 the managers used it to help thrust the knife deeper into the White Rats by announcing that they, the managers, would award the N.V.A. everything the White Rats were fighting for, except a closed shop.

In 1917 Albee helped boost the stock of N.V.A. by having the United Booking Office award noncancellable contracts, once the White Rats were crushed.

It was a successful technique. Actors flocked into the N.V.A., and its membership swelled. N.V.A., to prove that it had no intention of turning into a militant union rather than a chummy club, voted to admit lay members. Variety admitted its numerical strength by issuing its first N.V.A. Anniversary Number. By 1918 there were over 12,000 N.V.A. members.

A new era of sweetness and light set in. The managers, realizing that they had much to gain by supporting N.V.A. and keeping its members pacified, cooperated to the extent of helping N.V.A. minimize grievances. If an actor had a complaint against a manager, a joint committee of both the N.V.A. and V.M.P.A. would investigate. If the charges were found to be true, the V.M.P.A. which, of course had the real power, actually did penalize managers. In fact, managers and agents were more often penalized than actors. The N.V.A. also made its members happy by taking disciplinary action against act pirates, an action long overdue.

And to prove that they were really the friends of the actors, managers decided to pay a full week's salary, in spite of the Tuesday layoffs occasioned by the Government's fuel conservation program.

If the trade union movement languished in vaudeville, it thrived in other branches of show business. Equity, headed by Francis Wilson, was really doing a job for legitimate stage actors. Although the White Rats held the only A.F.L. charter in 1916, Equity members voted to join the A.F.L. and later were awarded this charter. Equity won recognition and a legitimate-wide contract with the managers in 1917. And it set a precedent in actors' organizations by electing three women to Equity's council board in 1918, Florence Reed, Helen Ware and Katherine Emmett.

The Authors' Assurance Association sprang up in 1914, when

Jack London, Rex Beach, Steve Reynolds, Rupert Hughes and 50 other top writers drew together to stop film companies from plagiarizing their magazine work. A Hollywood practice was to lift a magazine story, re-name the characters, change a few minor details, and presto—a shooting script.

A year later Jake Wilk, then publicity manager for World Film Corp., and latterly a Warner Bros. executive, acknowledged, "The scenario writers' day is rapidly approaching. Picture stars were the first to receive recognition. High-salaried directors were next to be appreciated. The time is coming soon when authors will receive commensurate financial emolument." Prevailing scenario prices were an average $500 to a top of $1,000.

The mighty organization of today has its traditions in the firm, we-mean-business tactics of the American Society of Composers, Authors and Publishers of 1914. Then the Society compelled 60,000 cabarets, hotels and restaurants which used its copyrighted music to pay royalties. In 1917 ASCAP started its drive to collect for the music played in film theatres, and that year began to "license" cabarets and hotels.

The stagehands' union succeeded in keeping its ranks firm through the war years, and won signal advances in salary. Stagehands were hit by the closing of many small movie houses in 1914, but their position was strengthened somewhat by the stricter enforcement of fire laws, which involved hiring more stagehands.

The growing union sentiment in the theatrical field received an oblique testament from Variety in 1916 when it printed this announcement: "Variety is requested by the White Rats Actors' Union to state that this paper is printed in a union shop, C. J. O'Brien's at 227 William Street, New York City, carrying label No. 4, Typographical Union No. 6."

And an echo of this sentiment came from across the Atlantic in 1918 with news that the Actors Association of England had pulled off its kid gloves and become an out-and-out trade union.

more theatrical clubs   It was a standing gag of the era that whenever three actors got together for a talk, they wound up forming a club. Gregarious by nature, actors felt the need to congregate in groups where a common language was spoken—the language of the theatre. New clubs sprang up constantly, but few survived.

The Comedy Club was typical. Beginning as an actors' group to protect actors against pirates, it wound up as a social club which admitted managers, agents, and nonprofessionals. So heterogeneous a collection was bound to produce dissension and disinterest. The Comedy Club closed its doors after eight years. Some of the older members tried to resurrect its spirit in a new group called the Jesters, but this failed, too.

Undeterred, two new clubs blithely formed the same year. One was the Gamut Club, "for professional women," with Mary Shaw as its president, and Lillian Russell as vice-president. Negro musicians banded together in their own Clef Club, designated as a "social and protective association."

In 1915 actors in Freeport, Long Island, organized the Long Island Good Hearted Thespian Society, whose initials spelled LIGHTS. "Angel" (president) of the Lights Club was Victor Moore, with Fred Stone, Will Rogers and Harry Bulger as directors.

Songsmith Bert Kalmar gave the Lights an odd idea. Actors, he said, were always working or traveling at Christmas and New Year's, and almost all other holiday times. Why not hold holiday festivities for them in the traditional summer layoff time at the Lights' clubhouse? And so they did. Each Wednesday night in July and August, the Lights lit up a Christmas tree, and arranged unseasonal get-togethers for hot-weather "Christmas," "New Year's" and "Thanksgiving" celebrations.

The Lights lasted many years, but finally split up, like all the others, when vaudeville died out, and lay members who were admitted took over, crowding out the performers.

The Friars, whose "Abbott" was George M. Cohan, opened their Monastery (clubhouse) on New York's West 48th Street in 1916. They, too, suffered from "laymanitis."

In 1917 another organization, the Actors Social Club, bit the dust when it was suspected of being an undercover branch of the White Rats. Disbanding, it donated its treasury and furniture to the Actors Fund.

The war years produced bountiful benefits for actors under the category of "good and welfare." In 1914 plans were made for the

New American Hospital in Chicago, dedicated to the theatrical profession, under the supervision of Dr. Max Thorek and a prominent board of directors from show business.

Actors' training was advanced in the universities. Carnegie Tech introduced a course, modeled after the Columbia School of Journalism, which would train actors, managers and stage technicians in its own theatre. Graduates would be awarded a B.D.—Bachelor of the Drama. Harvard began to build its own theatre, to be used in conjunction with Professor George Pierce Baker's dramatic course which soon boasted some distinguished show biz alumni.

sime's technique with gyps   In the heyday of the 1920s, when floating crap games got a big play in peripatetic gambling joints over a garage, in a mortuary, and places like that, there were a bunch of sharpshooters in the neighborhood of New York's Somerset Hotel, hard by the Palace Theatre stage door on West 47th St., which got to be known as the Grouchbaggers. Acts coming off of an extended Pan, WVMA or Orpheum route—even those playing the "death trail" houses for Ackerman & Harris, Gus Sun and the T. & D. Junior Orpheum time—invariably had their ready cash in the traditional actor's "grouchbag." This was a form of suspended money-belt worn underneath the man's shirt. (The more prudent femme half of a mixed team had her own "first national bank" stash-away system, but more often the male half of an act was custodian of the coin.)

The 47th St. sharpies knew that, and many a tragedy occurred with educated dice when a glad-to-be-back vaudevillian indulged in the cameraderie so typical of the itinerant trouper. The dice cheaters knew their timing well; the Variety route lists always cued who was "due to come off the route," and naturally the first stop was in the Palace Theatre orbit. It was against these that *Sime* trained his guns, and only the threat of publication of names kayoed this mob.

No other profession or business in the world looked after its indigents as well as show business. The N.V.A. Fund became an important factor in theatrical charities. Theatres like the Palace and the Hippodrome were donated free for the N.V.A.'s annual benefits, at which 35 to 40 acts would give gratis performances. Each benefit would swell the Fund by as much as $50,000. The V.M.P.A. added to the Fund fines imposed upon acts for missing trains, backstage fights, and other misdemeanors.

The Actors' Fund was the frequent beneficiary of special shows like *Julius Caesar,* which played with an all-star cast and 5,000 extras at the Hollywood Amphitheatre. Witnessed by 40,000 people, the show turned over $10,000 to the Fund. Charlie Chaplin, appearing at the New York Hippodrome to lead Sousa's Band, gave half his percentage to the Fund, and half to England's Variety Artists Federation.

The key to all this philanthropic activity was the simple fact that there are few people as sentimental as show people.

The credo of "Merrily" Rogers, a manager of his day, was one accepted by most of show business. In its unashamed sentimentality, as published in Variety, it was: "I shall pass through this world but once. Any good thing, therefore, that I can do, or any kindness that I can show to any human being, let me do it now. Let me not defer it nor neglect it, for I shall not pass this way again."

PART THREE

BIG BOOM

1919 - 1929

26

Jazz Age

★

The difference between the American and Russian peoples is a topic which intrigues the world today. It was never clearer than in 1919, when a wave of disillusionment and unrest swept through nation after nation. It produced its logical extremes in the U.S.S.R. and the United States.

Russians took arms physically against their discredited and rejected regime. Americans rebelled against the old order by launching a wild campaign against the moral standards for which it stood. Russians grimly set about reconstructing their lives by harsh, hard work. Americans gaily set about kicking hell out of their lives by frantic, hysterical play.

The whole pattern of the Roaring Twenties in America was that of a gigantic playground, reaching its ecstatic peak in 1929. Spurred on by Prohibition—the last gasp of the dying old order—Americans went on a glorious 10-year bat. Sex was rediscovered, and the nation reacted to the rhythms of the Charleston and the Black Bottom. In between bouts with bottles and blondes, it staggered to the window to cheer Al Capone, Charles A. Lindbergh, Peaches Browning, Gertrude Ederle, Herbert Hoover and Aimee Semple McPherson.

Show business, usually in the vanguard of the march of public mores, now had a tough time keeping up. Once Americans had been too busy earning a living to invent fads and foibles. Now that they had suddenly switched from work to play, it was show business that became the mirror, rather than the mirrored.

In the process, tremendous changes took place in the fabric of public entertainment. Seeking a more intimate, noisy and wild degree of pleasure, Americans surged into the cabarets. From there they quickly found their way into speakeasies, joints and dives.

King Vaudeville, once omnipotent, watched the crowds go by in doddering bewilderment. Too rigid to change, too incredulous to believe that its day was over, it stood by helplessly as its empire was first absorbed, then destroyed.

Legit did not share the fate of the theatrical giant which had once dethroned it, because it was more flexible. Sensitive to prevailing winds, it sexed up its plays for a public that wanted to be shocked and titillated. Spice was the accent in revues and musicals.

The movies soon devoured vaudeville. It was impossible for vaudeville to buck "Cast of 1000!" spectacles at popular prices. The new champion of popular entertainment rose to a swift peak of triumph, only mildly alarmed at the new threat presented by an up-and-coming, brand-new type of entertainment which promised "something for nothing"—radio. The skyrocket growth of radio during the Twenties might have succeeded in thrusting Hollywood off its summit of public favor, except for the sudden catastrophe which shook the film industry late in the decade. Talking pictures, at first viewed with dismay and alarm by the celluloid colony, became Hollywood's guarantee of survival. In that era, radio's best hour was between 10 and 11 P.M., as one radio man of the day admitted, "because by that time the people are back from the picture houses."

Because of the paper prosperity which flushed the nation's cheeks in a facsimile of economic health, b.o. totals reached fabulous amounts. As never before, show biz became big business. And as it did, Wall Street "bought in." The big butter-and-egg men of the Twenties were not only out in front, but were frequently the secret men "behind." The diamond-studded elastic garters that adorned showgirls' legs were often made of ticker tape, offstage as well as on.

The era began, grimly enough, with a nation-wide wave of steel and coal strikes that almost paralyzed industry. Bankers were seriously worried, eyeing what was going on in Russia, where the First Communist Internationale was already being organized. Fox Films led a movie industry campaign against Red Bolshevism by preparing a film in which they asked members of America's "400" to appear, showing their happy, quiet family lives. The idea was apparently to sell the Russkys the comfortable notion that J. P. Morgan and his coterie were "just folks," and should be spared liquidation.

those red bolshy blues   Attorney General A. Mitchell Palmer rounded up 6,000 suspects in a Red scare. The Thomas Committee of the 80th Congress must have seemed like Old Home Week to Charlie Chaplin, who also had to defend himself against cries of "Red!" back in 1919. At that time he was accused of backing Max Eastman's pro-Bolshevist magazine, *The Masses*.

Labor was given its martyrs in the 1920 Sacco and Vanzetti case when two Italian radicals were arrested for murder, tried and convicted for being radicals. In the fall of that year a bomb was thrown at the House of Morgan in Wall Street. After that the fireworks faded and the Red scare subsided.

Uncle Sam's postwar activities, and international standing, seem to vary little from war to war. In 1919, 21 cities held charity showings of a war film, *Ravished Armenia,* at a $10 top. Paderewski, then premier of Poland, appeared in a film whose proceeds were donated to the Polish Red Cross. Herbert Hoover's official propaganda film was *Starvation,* eight reels of hunger in 20 countries, including Russia and the Balkans.

hot cars—rolls royce vintage   Other familiar postwar phenomena were the affluent war profiteers, and the smaller boys who had managed to latch on to a good thing. Claude Graham-White had bought gas-stranded Rolls Royces during the war for between $4,000 and $11,000 each, and was now getting rich disposing of them with prices ranging up to $30,000 apiece.

Welcome-home parades, the Red scares, and 800 per cent Americanism heightened nationalistic intolerance. In the New York City of 1919, there were 7,000 musicians in the union's local, of whom 2,000 were not citizens. Government verdict: all non-citizen musicians must take out citizenship papers, or prepare to be deported.

Antagonism ran high against artists who had fought on the losing side (as in 1946). Fritz Kreisler had to be placed under guard in Rochester, because the American Legion took a dim view of his service in the Austrian army. He nevertheless opened with the Philadelphia Orchestra to a packed audience. Despite threats against him, there was no disturbance.

Germany had recovered sufficiently by 1921 to slap a 5-year boycott on English acts in Berlin, as reprisal, while welcoming American acts. Three years later, England reluctantly scrapped its ban, in exchange for lifting the Berlin blockade on the English.

Prices galloped up the first postwar era exactly as they did in the second. Taxes continued stiff as the tabs got stiffer. Coney Island in 1919 was selling 20¢ icecream sodas (war tax extra) as well as rotgut hooch at tophat prices. New Yorkers paid a 3¢ tax on a 30¢ soda fountain check, a 4¢ check on a 30¢ movie ticket. On 1919 salaries, it was a slight case of murder.

Variety reflected the upward spiral of prices by raising its price to 20¢ an issue, and then adding on another nickel. Still later it cut back to 15¢ "in order to make it possible for every chorus girl to have her own copy." (Variety has a rather extraordinary multireadership per copy, but upped costs forced back the 25¢ weekly price during World War II.)

due-bills on the b.o.   By 1921, with prices above the clouds, and the threat of depression looming, theatres again began to feel the pinch. In nine states of the Middle West, and part of the South, managers began selling movie tickets on credit. Patrons gave I.O.U.'s, and redeemed them when in funds.

The threat of depression brought prices down slightly for a while, but there was no stopping the upward sweep of prices, wages and

profits that marked the period of the Big Boom. Between 1922 and
1927, the nation's purchasing power increased over 2 per cent annually.

The fluctuating fortunes of Broadway were emphasized in 1922
by producer William A. Brady's admission that he had been broke
10 times in the previous 20 years. Said Variety, "That carries
no real news to Broadway, which knows that the line between sol-
vency and stringency among Broadway producers is proverbially
thin at most times. Being Broadway broke is a condition that has
no equivalent in any other business save that, perhaps, of the race
course. The purseless producer of today may be the prospective
bonanza king of tomorrow."

Many Broadway figures that year were beginning to get their feet
wet in stocks and bonds as one way out of being "Broadway broke."
On top of its editorial page, Variety carried a warning to them to
read an article in the Saturday Evening Post called, "Bucket Shops
and How to Avoid Them" by Richard D. Wyckoff.

But the brakes were off, and nobody wanted to listen to the
prophets of gloom. Between 1924 and 1927, Americans were daz-
zled by the news that the crop of millionaires had increased from
a paltry 75 to 283.

Show business of 1924 was bulging at the seams. There were
21,897 theatres, museums and concert halls; 190 circuses, and 8,836
other types of exhibitions.

A 1925 issue of the Saturday Evening Post, circulation 2,750,000,
carried 240 pages of ads that cost $1,300,000. This was the year of
the big Florida real estate boom, when the promoter of Coral Gables
brought William Jennings Bryan down to lecture in a lagoon on
Florida sunshine. Following this divertissement, there was shimmy
dancing by Gilda Gray.

Buying and selling Florida acreage became a national disease.
Even such unmortgaged figures as Jack Dempsey and Gene Tunney were meeting all comers in Miami, "Fair White Goddess of
Cities," selling hunks of the goddess to the eager. The bubble began
to burst in 1926, and collapsed with a wail in September of that year
when a particularly vicious hurricane swamped the Miami boom area.

March 24, 1928 marked the beginning of the bull market on Wall
Street which swirled the nation to the pinnacle of its financial raz-
zle-dazzle. Everybody from bootblack to steeplejack plunged into

the market for a bite of the golden apple. By the end of the year Variety reported sadly: "It is claimed that through universal interest in the stock market, no theatrical office anywhere is securing over 50 per cent efficient service daily from its staff. The other half of the time is spent looking at tickers, phoning or talking over stocks." (In a later era, when the race-track bug bit Hollywood, bookies had priority phone service to many top film studio executives, producers, directors and writers.)

the big fawdown   Then, at the height of the speculation, Variety ran its now-historic, Oct. 30, 1929, headline: WALL STREET LAYS AN EGG. It followed this with a wry report of the new Broadway slogan: "Got change for a match?" And the obituary columns were heavy with names of celebrities last seen departing from a 10-story window.

Claude Binyon, now the Hollywood writer-director, authored the oft-quoted WALL STREET LAYS AN EGG headline. Variety's present editor was headquartered in Paris during that 1929-1930 period and only saw the debacle vicariously. He saw showmen like Al Woods, Winnie Sheehan, Benny Fields, Jack Osterman, Ricardo Cortez, Borrah Minevitch, the Duncan Sisters, and Lee Shubert, among others, haunt the brokerage offices of H. Hentz & Co. on the Rue Cambon, opposite the Ritz, or the Banque de Saint-Phalle, on the Champs Elysées, which was correspondent for many Wall Street houses.

The ashen-gray aspect of people frustrated by time and distance is an indelible memory. This was not the era yet of the fast plane across the Atlantic. Phones and cables to New York were clogged. Some managed to get to London and effected communication with New York that way. The common objective was to cover margins. Paper profits shrank fast. The late Al Woods, who had $1,000,000 in cash put away for emergency, managed (unfortunately) to get to his wife in New York with the information where to find the box and cover his margins. He would have been that much ahead had time and space defeated him at the time.

sime out of the red   This was the era of great affluence. Even Variety, for the first time in its quarter-of-a-century, was out of the red. *Sime* said so in a memorable editorial. He accented that, if as and when Variety ever saw black ink importantly enough he'd be the first to record it. Variety had reaped the economic benefits of a series of "special numbers" dedicated to Adolph Zukor, RKO, Paramount, Balaban & Katz, Fanchon & Marco, and others in show biz.

Sime foresaw the talkies as a possible key to a multi-lingual edition of Variety, linked to the possible trend of making films in four or five basic languages; shoot the original in English and have French, German, Spanish and Italian casts re-enact the same script in its native language.

It was for this reason that the paper sent Abel Green abroad. Prime purpose was to organize a foreign news service to keep pace with the obvious extension of the international markets for pix and other talents; and, secondly, explore the possibility of a Continental edition of Variety, with condensed news in French, German, Spanish and Italian. It was soon obvious, of course, that the Europeans have their own language plus at least one other, usually English. *Sime's* vision for a subpublication, for more localized influence, culminated in 1933 with the founding, in Hollywood, of Daily Variety. The late Arthur Ungar was its editor until his death in 1950. Joe Schoenfeld succeeded him.

The financial bankruptcy of 1929 was the logical culmination of an era which began in 1919 with spiritual bankruptcy. At the close of the war, American soldiers watched President Wilson knifed at the peace conference, and buried by the Senate. In place of the good world promised, they saw a frenzied scramble for profits.

Bitter, the younger generation decided to go to hell and enjoy it, because there was no place else to go. Along with them went a revolution in morals and dress. Consciously or unconsciously they may have counted on all this to shock the older generation which presumably had betrayed them. They ended up with a crying jag, feeling sorry for themselves. Sans revenge, too, since the older generation merely followed the path they blazed—and had a high old time.

The fireworks were set off in April 1920, with the appearance of F. Scott Fitzgerald's novel, *This Side of Paradise*. As a report of the younger generation, amatory division, it raised hair on parental scalps from Hoboken to San Diego. It spoke of hip-flasks, petting and necking in parked cars, and a lot of dirty stuff spread around by a guy named Freud. Freud's stock zoomed, and sex began to climb out of the parked cars into the living room.

s. a. on the loose   Short hair on a woman became a sure sign that she was either a radical or practitioner of free love, probably both. Rouge and lipstick were the clinchers, and enjoyed a sudden vogue. Men and women broke the 18th Amendment together at bars, and a few others elsewhere.

Dresses started to climb as a 1921 bill introduced in the Utah legislature called for fines and imprisonment for women who trod the pavements in "skirts higher than three inches above the ankle." Skirts were then about seven inches off the ground. By 1927 they had risen another 25 per cent, a highwater mark at which they remained until the ebb of late 1929.

Oddly, the sexual mores of the day called for styles which were brutally mannish. The flapper's bobbed hair, flat breasts, straight hips and concealed buttocks were supposed to be the last word in what it takes to make a man's temperature rise. In one Chicago eating house a restaurateur compelled his waitresses to dress in knickerbockers, apparently on the theory that he had hit upon the ultimate in sex appeal.

Electric Park in Kansas City smashed attendance records by holding a Flapper Contest Parade. "Flapper" became a speedy addition to the American slanguage. Chorus girls without too much upstairs were glorified as "Dumb Doras," and in Negro circles as "clucks." College campuses provided "flamper," for a flapper who vamps, and "swinging" for the time-honored tradition of necking.

With an increased tempo in the shedding of inhibitions, men began shedding hats in 1925, to the consternation of night club coatrooms. Three years later, women shed stockings, as hosiery manufacturers shed tears. Ladies of the evening began wearing slave bracelets in 1925, which they shed the following year for slave anklets. Ladies of the evening (amateur division) set the vogue in exclusive 1926 night spots by viewing males and merriment through monocles.

In 1929, the year of frenzy, Hollywood came through with a fitting climax to the fashions of the Twenties for men. Males were seen adorned in black shirts, berets, riding breeches for all activities, camel-hair coats and fancy sports shoes for semi-formal evening wear. Tieless shirts were open at the collar, polo coats tightly belted, shoulders padded and trousers pleated. Men also wore suspenders over sweaters, turquoise blue knickers, and slave bracelets.

Since it was obvious that you couldn't go to hell properly on drink alone, smoking was also considered a properly sophisticated vice. The first wedge was driven in 1919, when picture houses permitted smoking in the gallery to encourage male patronage. That year there was a wave of excitement in London's music halls, created by the spectacle of women smoking. Some distraught managers sent ushers into the breach to stand beside the offenders and frown forbiddingly.

The first theatrical smoking room for ladies was opened in 1920 at the Woods Theatre in Chicago, which also offered them a well-known brand of cigarette. At first, most hesitated, simply carrying out the cigarettes to their escorts. But by September of the following year, Variety ran a story headlined: WOMEN SMOKING IN THEATRE LOBBIES. "And on the sidewalks, during intermissions," the paper reported. "The habit was formerly confined to the ladies' room in the theatres, but appears to have received its open air impetus through the wife of a New York daily dramatic reviewer who, early in this new season, had her smoke on the sidewalk."

One year later Loew's State, on Broadway, opened the gates of hell by permitting women to smoke in the balcony and loges. And in 1925, Parajon Park in Massachusetts installed the first public smoking benches for women, with the legend: RESERVED FOR LADIES— SMOKING PERMITTED.

Extra! Extra! Read All About It!

★

Show business had its toughest competition from the newspaper headlines of the 1920s. There was enough excitement and scandal wrapped up in 2¢ and 3¢ packages to offer second-hand thrills to patrons who hesitated to pay for them first hand. And there was no mistaking the kind of scandal they wanted to read about.

The Teapot Dome exposé was a big explosion, but small potatoes compared to the black headlines awarded the star sex and murder scandals. These were the sensations that paid off in jazzed-up circulation and national attention. The era started off neatly with the Stillman and Fatty Arbuckle cases in 1921, followed by the Hall-Mills murder case in 1922, and the Leopold-Loeb shocker in 1924 (recently unearthed as the basis for the Patrick Hamilton stage play, *Rope's End,* and the Alfred Hitchcock film, *Rope*).

But the Twenties really went to town with the advent to glory of Peaches and "Daddy" Browning. Peaches was the shape that launched a thousand quips, few of them clean. The unlamented New York *Graphic* scooped the world with a "composite" photograph showing "Daddy" chasing his half-naked wife around the room, yelling at her, "Woof! Woof! Don't be a goof!"

Peaches' suit for separation from her bacchanalian husband was celebrated by tunesmith Lon Mooney in a song called "I'm All Alone in a Palace of Stone."

The little bird in Daddy Browning's gilded cage did all right for herself, however, when she appeared the following year in vaudeville on the Pantages circuit, where the boxoffice rejoiced.

Peaches slid off the front pages when Joyce Hawley chalked up another historic high for the era by stepping nude into a wine bath for Earl Carroll and his guests. Both items were choice morsels of popular and stage humor, rivaled only by more gruesome laughs at the expense of the decade's choice murderers.

So important was the exotic Hall-Mills murder case considered—with its "pig woman" and bodies under De Russey's Lane crab apple trees—that writers of the stature of Theodore Dreiser were sent to report it for New York *Journal-American* readers. Other reporters included Heaven's press-agent, Billy Sunday, and that other pounder of the drums of hell, the Reverend John Roach Straton.

The cast of commentators was widened to include David Wark Griffith and Will Durant, when the Snyder-Gray murder case came along a few months later with a neat assortment of sex, corsets, sash weights and mayhem. In the face of such competition, the appearance of Harry K. Thaw's book, *The Traitor,* aroused only superficial interest in the now relatively tame and antique Harry Thaw-Stanford White-Evelyn Nesbit triangle.

Even the sex-mad, gore-thirsty public of the Twenties was slightly sickened by the parade of filth trotted before them with such juicy relish by the drooling tabloids. This revulsion turned to wry amusement, and finally open kidding. "The tabloids," sighed F. P. A., "are making it more difficult to burlesque them."

lindbergh crowds off sex   Newspaper editors, trapped in the cesspool of their own making, looked desperately for a way out. It came in the shape of Lindbergh, whose feat was startling enough to switch any headlines his way. Editors promptly swung over to the new sport of hero worship and deification. The sex artists and murderers were given a well-deserved period of privacy.

The odds and ends that went into the grinders of city editor desks, 1919-1929, formed a richly-colored kaleidoscope of the era. In 1920, woman suffrage went into effect without creating a ripple. Radio broadcasting, starting in November, became a tremendous force in the American way of life within 12 months.

This was also the era when the ex-singing waiter from Nigger Mike's, Irving Berlin, married socialite Clarence H. Mackay's daughter Ellin; of Dr. Coueisms ("every day in every way I'm getting better and better"); the Florida boom; the Scopes evolution trial; Daddy Browning and Peaches; Gloria Swanson's marriage to a marquis; the discovery of King Tut's tomb; Michael Arlen's *The Green Hat,* Noel Coward's *The Vortex,* and Samson Raphaelson's *The Jazz Singer* starring George Jessel, which was later to give such impetus to talkies under the Warner Bros.-Al Jolson aegis; The Teapot Dome scandal; Notre Dame's immortal Four Horsemen; the Black Bottom; the John Held, Jr. prototype of Joe College with his "Oxford bags"; and the birth of crossword puzzle books as best sellers.

1927 found Al Capone at his height, and floods in the Mississippi Valley, with millions of dollars' worth of relief raised by show business benefits.

In 1928, headlines were made by the over-rated sinking of the *Vestris,* the first all-talking picture (*The Lights of Broadway*), the gang murder of Broadway gambler, Arnold Rothstein, and the birth of two "eugenic" babies—one to Mrs. Grace Mailhouse-Burnhams (sired by actor Roscoe Ails), and one to his former vaudeville partner, Kate Pullman, who offered credit to a 6-foot, 190-pound Viking named William Diner.

In 1929 the St. Valentine's Day Massacre shocked a calloused public, but not nearly so much as what happened in Wall Street.

ouija boards, put 'n' take, crossword puzzles

The fads of the Twenties were a neat indictment of the national IQ, if any such indictment were needed. In 1920 there was a ouija board craze, and a less reprehensible enthusiasm of actors for a fashionable game called golf, which became a national sport by 1925. Number rackets began in 1921, with guesses on the three middle numbers appearing daily in the Clearing House Exchange.

"Toddle Tops" made their appearance in 1922, giving rise to gambling sessions of "put-and-take," until the sale of these spinning dice was prohibited. In 1923 mah-jong fell upon suburban housewives like canasta. The following year, the nation bent its mental energies over crossword puzzles which, with radio, constituted the intellectual exercise of 1925.

Contract bridge popped up in 1926, the year of the Charleston, and rubber cigars as instruments of sophisticated merriment. And in 1927 wits went around playing the retort game known as "Ask Me Another." Harlem had the best idea of private entertainment with "rent parties" in apartments, which offered gambling, refreshments and dancing to "lowdown" tunes, under the guise of raising funds to pay the rent. 1928 crowned them all with the ingenious contribution of "indoor golf."

The era also saw a steady growth of vicarious sports participation— the great American sport of sitting in a grandstand and cheering. In 1925 the cheers were for Gertrude Ederle and "Red" Grange. In 1926 for Dempsey and Tunney. In 1927, for Lindbergh and Alvin "Shipwreck" Kelly's siesta atop a pole. In 1928 for Bobby Jones, Babe Ruth, and the "Bunion Derby." In 1929 four women and 14 men treated Chicago to a rocking-chair marathon, and Los Angeles staged the first night football game at the Rose Bowl, Occidental versus Arizona.

And in this same period, Sinclair Lewis hurled *Main Street* and *Babbitt* at the nation; Mencken and Nathan threw acid in the new

American Mercury; and the sophisticated *New Yorker* made its bow, breaking even with a 30,000 circulation.

the tabloids   The New York *Daily News* and later the *Mirror* (Hearst's tabloid) were cradled and eventually prospered. Apparently they were the answer to the subway reader's prayer. Born of the Jazz Age, the condensation of news, angled in certain departments along certain freak, frank or baldly s.a. lines, found ready response. Like radio and television to come, these evolutions didn't supplant but merely augmented the traditional values. Most New York families now buy their favorite morning or evening paper for unexpurgated or detailed news, plus the tabs for special columns and features; just as the advertisers found supplementary dollars to expend for radio and TV without cutting-back on press, mags or billboards. Bernarr Macfadden's New York *Graphic* brought tabloid "journalism" to its ultimate in degradation—and eventually its own extinction. But it spawned personalities like Walter Winchell, Jerry Wald (radio editor now a Hollywood producer), Ed Sullivan and Louis Sobol.

Popular landmarks of the day were Milt Gross' "Gross Exaggerations," in which he made Jewish humor nationally popular with his burlesque Jewish dialect ("Nize baby, eat hup all the spinach!"), and the ribbon light sign put up on the New York *Times* Building in 1928, just in time to report the end of the era.

the no. 1 triple-a hero   The return of the air hero Charles A. Lindbergh to the United States in 1927 was the signal for one of the most astounding demonstrations ever given to a citizen in American history, not matched until the General MacArthur welcome in 1951. Fifth Avenue was jammed to the rooftops for a welcome-home cavalcade. Crowds even refused to let Gertrude Ederle, erstwhile heroine of a few years before, squeeze through for a glimpse of their new wonder boy. Fox Movietone News brought the Lindburgh face and voice to palpitating millions.

Lindbergh received 3,500,000 letters, 100,000 telegrams, and 7,000 job offers. One film company offered him $1,000,000 if he would marry a girl of his choice, and give them exclusive rights to film the marriage. He was swamped with thousands of proposals of marriage, three invitations to go to the moon via skyrocket, 14,000 gifts, and requests from 500 "close" relatives for financial assistance. The letters he received contained over $100,000 in stamps for return postage.

A rash of Lindbergh songs swept the country. "Lucky Lindy," "Lindbergh, Eagle of the U.S.A.," "When Lindy Comes Home" (by George M. Cohan), and "Hello, Yankee Doodle" (by Eddie Dowling and Jimmy Hanley) were a few of the lyrical tributes. A number called "Plucky Lindy" was used in Lindbergh's Washington broadcast over 52 stations.

As the best exploited individual of the century, Lindbergh was offered $100,000 for a 28-day, two-a-day vaudeville tour; $25,000 for a week at the Roxy; $10,000 for a week at a Fox-West Coast theatre; and $500,000 for a year in pictures. But Variety ran a mournful headline: LINDY LOST TO SHOW BIZ. "Showmen know he can't be had," the paper reported. "President Coolidge ruined the last chance by placing the Colonel among the immortals. He's acknowledged to be the greatest b.o. attraction ever known." As showmen plucked their hair, Lindbergh signed with the Guggenheim Foundation for five years at the not inconsiderable sum of $2,500 a week.

When immaculate New York Police Commissioner Grover Whalen greeted the next Atlantic fliers, Chamberlin and Levine, there were more songs—"Levine and His Flying Machine" and "Levine, You're the Greatest Hebrew Ace." Another Atlantic hopper, dentist's assistant Ruth Elder, also received an ovation and an offer of $6,500 a week at Loew's State. She prudently signed a contract for 25 weeks at $5,000 per. After that the flights came so thick and fast that it was hard to keep track of them.

The air heroes provided commercial aviation with a tremendous boom. In 1927, the first United States airmail was flown under contract, instead of by the post office—38 hours from Chicago to San Francisco. And coast-to-coast flying service later that year was shaved to a new low of 30 hours. The honor of being the first personality in show business to fly the now famous Variety route—"N.Y. to L.A."—went to Billy Rose.

In the air, it was the age of pioneers; but on the ground, Americans did their own getting around via automobile. Henry Ford's contribution to progress not only took Americans out of their homes, but also—if early critics were correct—took the home life out of Americans. In 1920 sedans were being assailed by outraged religious and civic forces as constituting "houses of prostitution on wheels." But by 1923, there were millions of families who proudly owned cars—if not bathtubs.

great names a-borning   Through the uproar and ballyhoo of the decade, Variety astutely caught fascinating glimpses of young showmen on the way up the ladder—men and women who were to emerge as headliners of the 1930s and 1940s. In 1920 Walter Winchell is seen joining the staff of the *Vaudeville News* as assistant editor; leaving in 1924 to write a column for Bernard Macfadden's *Graphic,* first called "Broadway Hearsay," then "Your Broadway and Mine."

Mark Hellinger, in 1925, begins a Broadway column for the New York *Daily News,* leaving three years later for the *Mirror.* His successor is Sidney Skolsky, formerly a press agent for Earl Carroll's *Vanities.*

In 1925, Mary Hay is doing a dancing act with a partner named Clifton Webb. *The Puzzles of 1925* features a baritone named Walter Pidgeon. For stage entertainment, picture houses offer a singer named Morton Downey. The name of the piano player in Ben Bernie's orchestra at the Rialto Theatre, N. Y., is Oscar Levant. The revue called *Red Hot* has an act named "Harmony Syncopation," featuring Paul Ash with assistance on the piano and ukulele by Charles Correll and Freeman Gosden, two men better known later as Amos 'n' Andy.

An ex-scholastic swimming champ turned hoofer wins his first talking part in the show, *Outside Looking In.* His name is James Cagney. The following year he teams with his wife, June Vernon, on Loew's American Roof, New York, to do an act called, "A Broadway Romeo," and in 1927 becomes an understudy for Lee Tracy in *Broadway.*

A 1925 Variety ad calls attention to "The fastest Charleston dancer and surely the most sensational. In *City Chap* . . . also Parody Club, Del Fey Club, and now at the Rivoli Theatre." The signature is George Raft. A very flip young fellow holds down the No. 2 spot at Loew's State with three songs, an imitation of Eddie Cantor, and a hoofing finish. Milton Berle.

That same year, at a Boston elocution and oratory school, lessons are given to a vacationist named Fred Allen, who returns to vaudeville after a four-year absence for a big click. In 1927 Allen is glimpsed as a master of ceremonies at the Palace. He's part of Allen & York, who address each other onstage as Mr. Fink and Mr. Smith.

The Broadway of 1926 is crawling with youthful genius: George Gershwin, Ira Gershwin, Vincent Youmans, Richard Rodgers, Larry Hart, Leo Robin, Herbert and Dorothy Fields. Variety reviews another youngster on February 10 of that year under "New Acts," predicting she will go places—Kate Smith.

Ruby Stevens, a Ziegfeld chorus girl and cabaret dancer, changes her name to Barbara Stanwyck and wins a featured role in the Broadway play, *The Noose.* Joan Crawford, another chorine from the Winter Garden, is now out in far-away Hollywood and starting to climb in pictures. The company manager of the show, *Broadway,* produced by Jed Harris, is Herman Shumlin, later a top director and producer. Its press agent is Sam N. Behrman, later a name dramatist. Arthur Kober, successor p.a., also made his mark since.

In 1927 a chorus girl named Billie Beck who had been with Will Seabury's act, and then stranded in Los Angeles, is working for Cecil B. DeMille under the name of Sally Rand. An actor named Edgar Bergen is on tour in England, France and Sweden. Emcee of the Little Club, off Broadway, and also appearing at Loew's, is a fiddling comedian named Jack Benny, formerly known as Ben K. Benny.

In 1928, appearing in a "New Faces" week at Keith's Palace, are Milton Berle and the Three Rhythm Boys; one of the trio is named Bing Crosby. With the Paramount Theatre stage show is a good-looking number named Ginger Rogers. The emcee at Pittsburgh's Stanley Theatre is Dick Powell.

And in 1929, Proctor's 86th Street Theatre, New York, offers a new comedian reviewed under "New Acts" by Variety. "He sings 'True Blue Love' for laughs, and 'Pagan Love Song' straight—both very good," nods Variety's reviewer. Bob Hope.

28

Making Whoopee

★

In Texas Guinan's night club one a.m. in the Twenties, the illegally stimulated patrons watched a nude dancer do an exotic version of Leda and the Swan with a sleepy, 8-foot boa constrictor. In a night spot across the street, a bank clerk who had turned embezzler paid $100 to a singer, who meant nothing to him, to warble "Mother Machree."

The 18th Amendment did not become law until January 16, 1920. Six months before that, Wartime Prohibition went into effect, not without some protest on Broadway. On the last night before the ban fell, angry patrons at Rector's demanded more liquor at closing time. Refused, they wrecked the place before the police could get there. Groups of soldiers and sailors roamed around the Main Stem, taking over Broadway saloons on the cuff.

A few days later Nellie Revell, press-agenting for the show, *Listen Lester,* filled a Borden truck with cans of butter and milk, and the cast of the show, beneath a banner reading: 'LISTEN LESTER' BUTTERMILK BABIES TAKING BUTTERMILK TO THE MARINES. Broadway guffawed as they unloaded at a Marine recruiting station on 23d Street.

Following Wartime Prohibition, people began to be careful of drinking in places where they weren't known, as cases of liquor poisoning began to be reported. The price of liquor began to rise, slowly at first, then like a skyrocket. Dewar's Scotch sold in Montreal for $27 a case, brought $25 a bottle on Broadway. Nicholson's London Gin sold for $15 a bottle.

Dealers began to be afraid to handle job lots of liquor, for fear the bottles had been tampered with. Creosote was found in Scotch; 90- and 100-proof whiskies were adulterated to the extent that one bottle of pure stuff yielded half a dozen of the cut. Job lot prices were also extravagant—$130 a case for champagne, $175 for Jameson's Whiskey, $140 for Otard Brandy.

In anticipation of a permanent 18th Amendment, restaurants and hotels began to bury their best liquor, serving the worst, on the theory that Prohibition would boost the price of the good stuff to a record high. Early in 1919 bars had sold decent whiskey at 15¢, two for 25¢; brandy 50¢ a drink. Now they served up inferior stuff to unprotesting customers for $1, while restaurants upped the ante to $1.50 and $2.

Before the year was over, retired liquor dealers were buying up movie theatres, rivaling the investments in other forms of show biz by war profiteers. Both knew that, deprived of places to drink, John Doe would seek relaxation at shows instead. States already dry provided evidence that amusement revenues rose 50 to 100 per cent following the ban on liquor. It was also obvious that the less money the public drank away, the more it would have for theatre tickets. Consequently, even the most bluenosed theatre managers in the country recognized the black-ink virtues of Prohibition.

Before 1920, however, the subject was highly controversial. The Orpheum vaudeville circuit forbade acts to make any reference to Prohibition, straight or comic. And then the Volstead Act became law on January 16, 1920, with little opposition from a public which had not the slightest idea of the wild forces of anti-law and disorder it had unleashed upon itself.

By 1921 Canada was the busy center of a new industry—supplying liquor to ingenious border smugglers. The shrewdest of these operators was a gang who dressed as nuns and priests, who were never molested until they suffered the misfortune of a blowout right at the border. The customs man offered to help, but the priest driving the car declined. Struggling with the tire, he exclaimed in exasperation, "God damn this son-of-a-bitch!" The astounded customs inspector this time took a really good look.

In July 1924, another slick idea came to light. It was quite common for ice blocks to be shipped from Ontario to the United States. Then one day the weather turned scorchingly hot, and unlabeled bottles of gin and alcohol began to clunk and smash in the sudden thaw.

wide-open canada   With things wide open in Canada, cabaret business there boomed in 1921. Performers received twice as much for Montreal and Toronto engagements as they did in New York.

In the early part of the decade, entertainers had to be wary of using any material which might intimate humorously to the audience that the Volstead Act was less law than polite hope. In 1922 Belle Baker introduced a new song at the Palace, "I'm a Mother of a Case of Scotch." The anxious management told her to cut the song out. She first refused, then yielded. Five years later manufacturers were openly advertising bars and beer taps for the well-accoutred home.

Broadway cabarets and restaurants took a dim view in 1919 of the coming of legal Prohibition. Their only hope, they felt, was a clientele wildly anxious to dance sober. And who, sober, would be chump enough to pay the prices they were charging for food and soft drinks?

Sullenly, these entrepreneurs threatened to raise a fund to test the constitutionality of the Volstead Act. But instead they concentrated on throwing their price lists away, and squeezing their patrons while there was still time to squeeze.

By 1921 a great many of them were out of business. Only about two dozen really worthwhile ones remained in New York, including Reisenweber's, Healey's, Shanley's, the Cafe de Paris, Little Club, Palais Royal, and Folies Bergere. Even in these renowned spots, patronage was slack. Prohibition was confining New Yorkers to their homes or clubs to indulge in "locker spirits."

The situation was somewhat different in other parts of the country, where police were not so vigilantly patroling the night haunts. Business was fairly good in such cities as Baltimore, Boston, Philadelphia, Pittsburgh, Chicago, St. Louis and New Orleans, where patrons still discussed Prohibition over rye highballs.

The year 1922 saw great changes. Cabarets fought desperately to hold their clientele from slipping away to restaurants and dance-halls, which offered everything the cabarets could—at subdued prices. (They weren't called nite clubs yet.) Some cabarets had already become *ipso facto* dance palaces, like Shanley's (dancing at $1.50) and Rector's, now called the Cafe de Paris. Churchill's had turned into a chop suey restaurant.

'yellow peril' over broadway   In an effort to stem
the tide, cabarets like the Monte Carlo offered the Dolly Sisters, at
$2,000 a week, and flopped dismally. The Palais Royal presented
Evan Burrows Fontaine, who danced almost nude as customers
continued eating and drinking. The Palais Royal then spent $30,000
to produce a lavish floor show, with a salary payroll of $4,500 a week
—and still the customers drifted away. (Eventually the Palais Royal
was to become the Palais d'Or which, despite its golden French
billing, was the keystone in what Variety at the time called "the yellow peril of Broadway." The chowmeineries were to take over, with
their bargain $1.25 table d'hotes, including the fast-tempoed B. A.
Rolfe orchestra—later to set the standard for George Washington
Hill's Lucky Strike style of accelerated dansapation, a buildup via a
WEAF radio wire, and a pretty good floor show. All this and moo-
goo-guy-pan too! Incidentally, in those uninhibited days, Variety
thought nothing of calling them chink joints and using terms like
"yellow peril," whereas today, if reference to Irving Berlin's origin
as a catch-penny singing waiter in Nigger Mike's place on the Bowery (Chatham Square) comes up, the joint is just referred to as
Mike's. Hebe comedians, tad comics and Yonny Yonson-type jokes,
were terms devoid of any politico connotations, as they are now.)

Before the Palais Royal succumbed to the "yellow peril," a happy
formula was discovered when it signed Paul Whiteman and his
Band—with no floor show. Whiteman was so solid a draw by 1922
that he was able to form a corporation farming out combinations of
musicians, in any size band required, to be shipped where requested.
"Paul Whiteman's Orchestra" looked almost as good outside a
cabaret, on ocean liners and cruise boats, as the more significant announcement, "Paul Whiteman *and* His Orchestra."

For the most part, cabarets were discovering that their attraction
for the public was largely liquid entertainment. Cabarets split into
two classes, the "popular price" and the "exclusive." The former
were those charging a *couvert* of less than $2; the latter more, with
a strong suggestion that you were naked in anything less than evening dress.

The great bulk of cabaret customers, however, were lost to brand-
new competitors, night clubs and speakeasies. Night clubs started in
the summer of 1921, with the Club Deauville on East 59th Street,
New York City. Chief charm of the night club was that it was

highly informal—staying open as long as its "members" cared to throw around their folding money. Its numbers increased rapidly.

But the most astounding growth of all was shown by the speakeasy, an openly illicit establishment. By 1922 Manhattan held over 5,000 of them, over 1,000 in an area circumscribed by 5th to 9th avenues, 38th to 59th streets. Replacing the old corner saloon, they were located in back rooms, "tea rooms," cold-water flats, apartments and "novelty shops." All you had to do to win admittance most of the time was to knock twice and murmur, "Joe sent me."

One little "tea room" in the 40s, whose walls would have bulged if 30 customers had congregated inside its all-important back room at one time, took in between $200 and $250 a day. Profits among the successful night clubs (and some cabarets) were enormous. They sold champagne (cost: $80 a case) at $25 a quart; Scotch ($50 a case) at $20 a quart; mineral water (12¢ a bottle) at $1 to $1.50; and cocktails (11¢ per) at $1 a throw. With a capacity of less than 125, one night club reported a weekly profit of $2,500.

The cabarets that did well did *very* well. A few on Broadway reported $8,000 a week profits, representing food sold at 100 to 250 per cent profit, plus stiff cover charges, plus charges for every accessory item— especially cracked ice.

Three years later, by 1925, the thrill of thumbing a nose at Prohibition was no longer sufficient inducement for patrons of night haunts. There were so many night clubs, speakeasies, joints, cabarets, and just plain dives, that it became mostly a matter of not *where* to get a drink, but *which* place.

booze no longer a draw   Entertainment came back into its own with a bang. Biggest business was done by places that offered Ziegfeld-type revues, in the grand manner. Top-hat Broadway spots like the Lido, Flamingo (ex-Trocadero) and Mirador presented ace dance teams. The Club (Harry) Richman and the Casa (Vincent) Lopez appealed to the pop trade with dansapation and frothier *divertissement*. Tiny, out-of-the-way spots that didn't advertise offered sophisticated entertainment for "the wise mob." The Tiffany trade also went uptown for thrills to Harlem's Nest, Small's Paradise, Connie's Inn and the Cotton Club, the latter the cream of the "mob joints" in Harlem.

Nitery singers began to have special lyrics written for their "intimate" songs. The emcee began to enjoy his biggest vogue. His value was the economic one of hypnotizing the patrons nicked by fancy *couverts* and tariffs that the lightweight talent was well worth squirming for on an uncomfortable chair, at a small table, in foul air, with the privilege of dancing on a postage-stamp floor.

Biggest nitery sensation, of course, was Texas Guinan. "Galli-Curci would flop in a nite club," Variety mused, "and yet Tex knocks out three grand for her bit, all through the knack of hammering a socially prominent matron on the cranium with a kleeter-klatter clapper. The others flock to her museum of unnatural hysterics to see 'em take that treatment on the 'nut' religiously, and apparently relish it." Tex helloed the suckers and they loved it.

When District Attorney Buckner, prodded into a gesture of law enforcement, swept down in 1925 to padlock no less than 30 Broadway night spots, the Tex Guinan Club was one of those forced to turn lights out. Whereupon, with racketeer-taxicab tycoon Larry Fay, who was later shot to death in a fight with the doorman of one of his own clubs, the Napoleon, now known as the Place Elegante, Texas promptly opened the El Fey Club, taking with her the whole staff of the tabooed nitery. On opening night she wore a necklace of gold padlocks.

During 1926 her profits soared to $30,000 a month. When in 1927 Tex was carted off to jail, laughing and waving, for continued Prohibition violations, the orchestra played "The Prisoner's Song."

The era also spawned Clayton, Jackson & Durante, who announced their opening at the Dover Club, New York, on Variety's pages with a burst of lyricism:—

> *Don't tell nobody you saw us,*
> *Don't tell nobody we're here;*
> *But to those who know, we'll tell 'em—*
> *We are on 51st Street and 6th Avenue near,*
>
> Jennie dear.

The following year they moved—with their enthusiastic following—to the Parody Club on West 48th Street. Their ad announced the opening as "formal and informal . . . featuring two brand-new dinner suits—Guess who's using the old one?"

Variety reported that Eddie Jackson had refused a $1,000 bill as salary payment, because no big salary should be paid in such a small way. "He wanted all fives—in a bundle," Variety explained.

Cabarets lost ground steadily during 1925-1926. A sign on the door of Joel's, a longtime 41st Street landmark, read: "Closed without great financial success, but I trust with many good friends . . . Joel Rinaldo." Two Times Square cabarets, of which one was owned by a gentleman who never wore anything but a sweater, lost $115,000 by barring admission to any save those in evening clothes. The Twin Oaks Cafe, opened by 48 investors in the basement of 1560 Broadway, closed with a loss of $2,500 each for the hopefuls. Billy Rose nevertheless chose 1926 to open the Fifth Avenue Club, presenting "Billy Rose's Sins of 1926."

As the cabarets waned, speakeasies waxed. There was a hopeful moment when Frank Hale was made chief of the Division of Prohibition Enforcement. He was a Broadway graduate—Hale & Paterson, a dance act. But the raids continued as before, doggedly and futilely. Shortly after a speak or night club was padlocked, it would reopen—usually with two new neighbors.

Night clubs felt the reaction from having overplayed their hand by a slump in 1927. Ethel Waters took over the 300 Club, formerly Texas Guinan's human museum, and had to close. Reopened as the Club Hitchy with Raymond Hitchcock, it flopped again in a dismal five days. Even the great Guinan dived as a drawing card, because her "Hello, Sucker!" had been so overpublicized that tourists really became afraid of the prices that went with her.

the gyp 'n' take   Variety took a caustic look at the reasons niteries were taking a financial shellacking. "With the surreptitious drinking," it noted, "surreptitious romancing was a natural, short and quick step. The 'hostesses' soon looked down on $20 tips for the privilege of lending their frames for purposes of wrestling to music in the name of Terpsichore, and foiling for and fooling with the money guys. The chump, in order to have money, must be 'somebody.' Simple psychology. Being 'somebody,' anything he was taken for accordingly was part of the racket. . . . From the gals to the keepers (bosses), the racket is worked for all it could stand.

Sex was still the fundamental of New York night life. Hideaways for mistresses were the fashionable thing for butter-and-egg men.

Routine for the evening's entertainment was a polite dinner at a conservative hotel, restaurant, or speakeasy; then touring the rounds of night spots; ending at dawn in hot-and-lowdown saloons, joints or bars.

The better niteries and cabarets, less inclined to hit and run, fared better than the swindle joints. The Durante ménage was a persistent favorite with the after-theatre crowd. George Olsen drew Park Avenue trade at the Club Richman. Van & Schenck were doing well at the Silver Slipper.

Trade was brisk for Helen Morgan at The House of Morgan; Vincent Lopez and Jack Osterman at Casa Lopez; the Dan Healy revue at the Cotton Club, featuring the Berry Brothers and Duke Ellington; Benny Davis and Fuzzy Knight at the 54th Street Club; Will Oakland at Oakland's Terrace, and a number of others. The good hotels in town were enjoying a mild boom, as a result of the patronage of customers who simply wanted good food and music at a reasonable tariff. They also received a lift from a 3 A.M. curfew slapped on cabarets and night clubs.

'a joint is a joint'   The principal distinction Variety found in the night spots of 1928 was between "those that sell, and those that don't." Any place that sold, whether a $100,000 investment or a back room, whether supper club, drinking club, night club, speakeasy, dancehall or dive, was a "joint." Explained the paper, "A joint is a joint. Even the operators of the joints admit it."

The dance joints that sold were mostly back-room, ground floor, or one-flight-up affairs. The dives, Parisian-style cabarets, with hostesses, were for those who didn't want to go home after the other places closed. Dinner clubs were on side streets, in four-or-five-story former residences, sometimes closing as early as 11 P.M., for fear of neighbors' "blowing the whistle."

Supper clubs, the then new variation of the present-day night spots, drew well. In the persistent drive for novelty, places off the beaten Broadway path attracted a sizable number of customers. These included Harlem clubs, Germantown beer halls, Hungarian and East European restaurants on the East Side, and most of the "dialect eateries"—Italian, Japanese, Indo-Chinese, Turkish, Swedish, French, Russian and Chinese restaurants.

"Non-selling" night clubs depended on their floor shows and band attractions, with a minimum $4 *couvert*. A typical bigtime 1928 opening was the "Versailles Varieties" in C. Morton Bellak's nightclub in East 6oth Street. The room cost $175,000; the weekly vaudeville show had a talent nut of $5,000; capacity was 400, at a $5 tag per plate. To let Broadway know about it, Bellak hired no less than five press agents simultaneously. It was a flop then, and later as the Villa Vallee (Rudy), but today is one of the best money-making niteries in America as the Copacabana.

In the better clubs—or joints—that "sold," less poison hooch was being served. Club owners had long since learned that swindling on liquor was the quick route to bankruptcy. Places with bars also had an arrangement with bartenders, whereby the latter received a one-third split of the take. "Selling" joints in Chicago were reported in trouble, because 16,000 "beer flats" in that city were luring customers out of the joints.

Despite heavy competition, money continued to pour into the night-club racket until early that black October in 1929. The monocled places still held a $4 and $5 *couvert,* while those struggling for business either abolished or cut them down. The real late-hour center shifted to Harlem, whose joints were more numerous, hot and lavish. The only late spot to remain open on Broadway after the 3 A.M. curfew was a Negro club, protected by the hotel clause.

dance styles: shimmy, etc.

Dance styles of the Twenties began, appropriately, with the advent of the Shimmy— "a vulgar cooch dance, at its best," derided Variety in 1919. The first and best to bring it to New York were Bee Palmer and May (later Gilda) Gray. The Shimmy vibrated to fame in the company of the jazz number, "Indianola."

It was enthusiastically introduced into musical comedies, and danced by both sexes of the cast, thus giving it the added s.a. overtones audiences relished. Vaudeville, more inhibited, kept a wary eye on the percentage of steam generated by Shimmy practitioners on its stages. In London that year, English audiences sat through their introduction to the Shimmy with cold, hostile eyes. Oddly enough, the branch of show business in America that barred it was burlesque.

Mae West, never loath to experiment, brought down the house with her very wiggly Shimmy in the 1921 show, *Mimic World*. But it was Gilda Gray who cooched to fame and fortune on the dance, taking double-page ads in Variety to proclaim her superlative artistry. (In later years, Gilda Gray, suing under her private life name of Maryanna Michalski, claimed that Columbia Pictures' *Gilda* invaded her privacy and felt that only $1,000,000 balm would assuage said intrusion. The Shimmy virtuoso contended that *Gilda* is a name only linked with her identity. It is much the same as Tallulah Bankhead's suit against the Prell Shampoo people because of a Tallulah commercial jingle.)

Viewed with horror by the sedate, along with the Shimmy dancer, was the jazz—or jazzing—dancer. There was little doubt in anyone's mind, including the minds of its practitioners, what the jazz dance was intended to interpret. The word "jazz," in fact, rapidly became an opprobrious synonym.

The Shimmy and jazz dances were, of course, primarily exhibition dances. The public itself danced to saxophone-shrill foxtrots, in cheek-to-cheek, body-to-body clutches. The distinction between popular dances to watch, and popular dances to dance, was wiped out in 1925 with the coming of the Charleston.

the charleston   First introduced in the cabarets, the Charleston craze quickly spread beyond the ranks of the entertainers. As no dance before it, it flashed around the country, and none was immune. Kids danced it on side streets, and in front of theatres during intermission, for "throw money."

In Boston's Pickwick Club, a tenderloin dancehall, the vibrations of Charleston dancers caused the place to collapse, killing 50. The following year saw a Charleston marathon at Roseland Ballroom on Broadway, which lasted 22½ exhausting hours. The winner was John Giola, 23 and the father of two children. His reward was a week's engagement at the Rivoli Theatre, New York.

The Charleston was ousted out of favor, after brief but violent glory, by the Black Bottom of 1926. Alberta Hunter, the first woman to present the dance, had it copyrighted. Harlem's Billy Pearce and Buddy Bradley taught it to many white dancers. Almost as swiftly as the Charleston, it swept into vaudeville, burlesque, musical comedies, night clubs, songs and verse.

The name was supposedly derived from the muddy black bottom of the Swanee River, and the movements suggested the dragging of feet through the mud. London took to the dance, but balked at the name, which had a different significance in England. They presented it as the Black Base, or Black Bed. Actually, no one in America either believed that the "Bottom" of the name referred to anything but the spot slapped by its dancer.

In 1927, Billy Pearce attempted to rival the success of the Black Bottom with a new dance called the Sugar Foot Strut, but it was too complicated for popular dancing. So were any number of other attempts such as the New Low Down and the Varsity Drag.

The public, surfeited by freak dances anyhow, let the pendulum swing back to slow, smooth and lazy foxtrots. Rudy Vallee, one of the earlier radio-made names, influenced the pattern for smoother dansapation and croony vocalizing. The pioneering radio personalities like Vaughn de Leath, the Happiness Boys, the A&P Gypsies (Harry Horlick's band), the Clicquot Club Eskimos (Harry Reser's), had yet to make their impact, as did Vallee later. And thereafter came Russ Columbo, who pioneered the Bing Crosby school—although Benny Fields, when vaude-touring with Blossom Seeley, now his wife, rates the credit for that style of vocalization.

Crosby was to become the "Gentile cantor" refinement of that throaty, minor-key modulation which fell to Jolson, Fields, Harry Richman, Sid Gary and others as a racial heritage.

As a sidelight, when Jolson fought shy of radio, his protegé, Richman, was then playing the piano for Mae West at a 7th Avenue honkytonk in New York. It was during the Prohibition era that Richman was prevailed upon by Nils T. Granlund (NTG) to go on WHN, the Loew's, Inc. station (now known as WMGM). Richman started to sing his ballads and when Jolson, a year later, finally succumbed to radio, people wanted to know, "Who was this guy stealing Richman's style?" How were they to know that Jolson had been grooming Richman as his successor? And such was the power of radio that many, apparently, never heard of Jolson, whereas the people who came into their homes, over their loudspeakers, were somebodies close to their hearts. Eventually America was to set its time by Amos 'n' Andy, at 7 P.M. Jack Pearl's "Voss you dere Sharlie?", the late Joe Penner's "Wanna buy a duck?", Ed Wynn's "Texaco Fire Chief", Eddie Cantor and his Ida and their five daughters, Major Bowes and his amateurs, Jack Benny and his stinginess, Fred Allen's drolleries, Winchell's staccato newscasting, and Drew Pearson's predictions of things to come were to become as part of the American scene as ham 'n' eggs. And the same will be true with Television.

the dancehall craze   By 1928, Broadway was going in for Tango Teas and adagio teams. A good percentage of the sex-and-liquor male patronage that drifted away from the cabarets with the coming of Prohibition, found its way to newly-mushrooming marts of amusement, the dancehalls. Hip-flask-toters paid 10¢ a dance to hostesses of their choice.

When the first dancehalls had originated on the West Coast, colloquially known as "creep joints," the gimmick was the "instructress" charging 10¢ a "lesson" to legalize the enterprise. Dancehalls springing up around the country in 1919 offered a choice of as many as 40 to 50 hostesses apiece. Dancing an average of 60 times nightly apiece, they worked up a very profitable thirst for the halls' soft drink bars. The girls usually worked on a 40 per cent commission, or a 4¢ kickback out of every dime.

One 7th Avenue (New York) dancehall of 1919 admitted averaging $1,500 a week. San Francisco reported a six-story dancehall, with dancing on every floor. By 1921 there were 1,000 new "dance palaces" in the East, and New York had applications for 1,800 more licenses.

Chicago led the way in 1922 for glorifying the dancehall to heights never dreamed of in the "creep joint" days. The Trianon Ballroom opened at a cost of $1,000,000, with $5,000 paid an orchestra for a six-day engagement. The dancing craze that swept the country the following year found dancehalls installing two orchestras each, with a boom at the b.o. that cut heavily into the patronage of picture houses and the balcony trade of the legitimate theatre.

The dance business climbed another step higher on the ladder of respectability in 1925, when dancehalls made way for "modern ballrooms." These were more properly theatres of popular dancing than dancehalls, attracting a family-type trade which was content to sit at ringside seats, and in balconies, to watch exhibition dancing, novelty bands and other entertainment. Even fashion shows found their way to the ballrooms. Prices were scaled at 50¢ to $1.25, with extra revenue from soft drink concessions.

By 1927 dancehalls and ballrooms were doing an amazing business from coast to coast. Some were affluent enough to pay top orchestras a percentage of the gross. And in 1928, with the advent of

Tango Teas, a brand-new class of business showed up to the joy of hall owners—frustrated housewives. And their number was legion, as in the days of the wartime dansants.

Radio—'Something for Nothing'

★

Radio—the something-for-nothing entertainment that all show business boxoffices dreaded—began in the spring of 1920. In East Pittsburgh, Dr. Frank Conrad of the Westinghouse Electric Co. began broadcasting phonograph music and baseball scores from his barn, as a research hobby.

So many amateur wireless operators were found to be listening-in that a Pittsburgh newspaper hit on the notion of advertising equipment which would allow Smoky City residents to tune in to Dr. Conrad's programs. This ad spurred Westinghouse officials to open the first broadcasting station in the world, as a means of increasing sales.

This was East Pittsburgh's Station KDKA, which opened November 2, 1920, in time to broadcast the Harding-Cox election returns. The new idea was slow in spreading at first, because of technical difficulties and the sparsity of receiving sets. But by the next year other stations were on the air, and the ether was disturbed by experimental church services, political talks and concerts. In July 1921, the first boxing match—Dempsey vs. Carpentier—was broadcast to 80 wireless outlets by three ringside announcers.

The transformation of "wireless telephony" into radio came about with a rush during the winter of 1921.

The "passing novelty," by late 1922, saw over 3,000,000 radio sets in operation, listening to over 200 stations. Most sets, costing from $50 to $150, were tuned to the "wireless concerts" which were all the vogue. Westinghouse maintained four "canned concert" stations, and from its Newark outlet that year aired the first radio opera, Mozart's *The Impresario*.

Kansas City concerts won listeners over a 2,000-mile span of ether. Wearers of earphones heard the stage show of the Ashland Theatre; a 10-day broadcast of a Chautauqua; and the first musical comedy written for radio—"Jazz Versus the Classics" by D. Kemper and Duke Yellman—with a cast of 11.

Both Kansas City papers, the *Star* and the *Post,* waged a fierce fight for control of Middle West radio, with theatre managers caught in between. The *Post* announced it would present Trixie Friganza, playing at the Orpheum Theatre, on one of its radio concerts. The *Star* promptly notified the manager of the Orpheum that if she broadcasted for the *Post,* the *Star* would throw out Orpheum advertising. The *Post* threatened that if Trixie were switched to the *Star's* radio concert, the *Post* would kick out Orpheum ads. P.S. Miss Friganza did not broadcast.

Theatres and show people began to experiment with new uses of radio. In Chicago, the lure of the *Ziegfeld Follies* at the Colonial Theatre was enhanced by offering patrons a radio concert in the rotunda. Actress Aileen Stanley advertised that she was the first to appear onstage with a radio outfit and amplifier. At Oakland, California, McCormack & Winchell (not Walter) did part of their act at Loew's State, then rushed to the Oakland Hotel and completed the act at the local broadcasting station, from which it was piped into onstage amplifiers at the theatre.

radio hypnotism   Vishnu, a hypnotist appearing at Kansas City's Empire Theatre, put a girl to sleep on the stage by broadcasting his mesmerism from a radio studio several blocks away. She was then placed in a store window for 24 hours, after which she was taken back to the theatre and snapped out of it. More than a quarter of a century later, in 1950, a hypnotizing act was still "big stuff" over a network program. Ralph Slater by name.

Exhibitors began to discuss radio as a genuine boxoffice menace just as with television many years later. Even magazine publishers were becoming alarmed—circulation had fallen off 30 per cent, and radio was the only explanation. [Again TV got the same blame in 1949.] Apparently nothing was going to stop the new "fad"—not even whispering campaigns that listening was bad for the ears, and that electric storms started fires in homes with radios. Not even the genuine warning by the New York Board of Fire Underwriters that the careless use of radio apparatus represented a threat to life and property. (Again, with TV, this was repeated in relation to eyestrain and other maladies.)

Performers of 1922 hailed with both joy and incredulity a Westinghouse announcement that the company intended to spend $5,000,000 for radio talent. Incredulity because there was very little "electric money"—actors' terminology for radio emolument—around those days. Most actors who appeared were paid off in "publicity." Writers solicited to turn out comedy for radio asked (as they asked television years later) "How much?" A very pertinent question, Variety agreed.

Early overtones of Petrillo were heard in August 1922, when music publishers and writers forced a showdown with representatives of the radio stations, insisting upon royalties for broadcasts of their songs. They claimed and proved that radio music was cutting into sales of sheet music, player-piano rolls and phonograph records.

Rooms with television were considered a shrewd notion in 1947 when hotels introduced the attraction. It was also shrewd in March 1922, when the hotels rushed to equip their rooms with radio sets. Other business also caught the bug. Silsbe's, on 72d Street, was the first New York restaurant to install radio music—in place of its orchestra. The Central Theatre, showing *The Storm,* drew crowds to its lobby by channeling the Leonard-Tendler fight via radio. The performance was a sellout. (Closed circuit sports events, on an exclusive basis, were to prove similarly beneficial to theatres with big-screen TV projection, dating from the summer of 1951.)

'24 for underwood'   The big radio event of 1924 was the broadcast of the Democratic National Convention held in New York. "24 for Underwood" became a catchphrase from coast to coast. That was in July. In October, Variety introduced a new department called "Radio," beginning with coverage of a Radio World's Fair in New York. And by December, Variety was pounding a fist on the roundtable of show business: "Radio now is the biggest thing the amusement business ever has had to encounter as 'opposition.' And show business is helpless against it. About all the theatre can do is keep quiet and wait!" The theatre waited, and the following week Variety brought them the dismal news that there was a "radio traffic air jam"—with 35 new stations scheduled to open in the next 60 days.

That radio was stern competition was evident by reports from the nation's boxoffices. Over 3,000 music-lovers had bought seats for a Fritz Kreisler concert in Boston, when it was suddenly announced that the concert would be broadcast. More than 1,500 tickets were returned for refund, as showmen brooded over the lesson of trying to sell something at the same time you gave it away free.

Record sales fell off 85 to 90 per cent—why buy records when the radio gave you music for nothing? Keith's, feeling that songs plugged on the air had lost their entertainment value, barred them on the circuit. Fight receipts fell off as fans seemingly preferred to stay home in comfort and listen. Tex Rickard blazed the way for television bans of today by refusing to allow the Berlenbach-Delaney fight to be broadcast.

Radio station managers were still trying to avoid saying it with $$$. They cajoled talent by pointing to such success stories as Vincent Lopez and his band. The management of the Pennsylvania Hotel, N. Y., had insisted that Lopez broadcast as publicity for the hotel. His broadcasts not only zoomed the Pennsylvania's business, but also made him a tremendous drawing card in vaudeville.

Equity argued that the publicity wasn't worth working for on the cuff. Chicago's Station KYW made radio history by being the first station to have a strike. James C. Petrillo, then president of the Chicago local, ordered union musicians out when the manager hired two non-union pianists. KYW wasn't too worried, because they were getting almost all the music they wanted "for publicity" from cafe and hotel orchestras.

no more publicity payoffs   The adaptation of radio by other businesses continued. Gimbel's department store in New York built a broadcasting studio on its premises as an exploitation stunt. Loew's WHN charged $50 a week to cabarets for running wires in to allow the cabarets to broadcast from their home grounds. First to sign up was the Hotel Alamac, featuring Paul Specht's Band. When the Chicago management of *We Moderns*, a legit, paid for radio advertising that upped the b.o. $4,000 on the week, that was the turning point in the raging argument that radio could be made a boon, not a bane, at the boxoffice. "It depended," Variety argued. If the want-to-see was sufficiently great, radio people could prove big draws in the flesh.

The year came to a smashing climax in November when Variety ran a three-bank black headline: FIRST RADIO ADVERTISING EVER PUBLISHED FOR TALENT WITH SALARY TO BE PAID. The lead paragraph said breathlessly, "Variety last week carried the first advertisement of its kind ever published anywhere—an announcement soliciting talent for radio and to be paid for."

A Variety reporter was sent out to track down the story behind the ad, wound his way through a maze of interlocking booking agencies and companies, and finally knocked on the door of the Packard Theatrical Exchange. "Mr. Packard became quite petulant, said he had nothing to give out, that they wanted to learn first what the result of the ad might be, and if Variety printed anything about the ad, the American Broadcasting Corp. (the company behind the ad) would not advertise again in Variety."

By 1925, there were 563 stations in operation—37 had folded, but 34 new ones had applied for licenses. Radio manufacturers were chortling over a $44,000,000 gross—five times the sales volume of 1921. Radio exports had increased by 400 per cent. Variety's radio reviews, first national, became international.

The year was studded with milestones. The first arrest for operating a radio station without a Federal license took place in Los Angeles, and the fellow's name was George W. Fellows. More Federal action was anticipated when President Hoover asked Congress for a $125,000 radio police force to provide mobile sleuths for checking on broadcasters who "sneaked" over allotted wavelengths, or were guilty of radio interference.

Station WOR's sound-effects man was the first to amplify dance steps by putting a marble slab under Ned Wayburn pupils. WHN aired the first Broadway legit reviews via (Miss) Bland Johanneson, then critic of the New York *Mirror*. The first direct air opposition to a Broadway play came with the broadcast by WGY of a radio version of Ibsen's *The Wild Duck,* while *The Wild Duck* with Blanche Yurka was asking orchestra prices at the 48th Street Theatre, New York.

a.m. calisthenics and amateur nites   1925 was also the historic year that introduced the first 6:45 morning exercises, cajoling all to snap vertebras by remote control. It was also the year that introduced televised motion pictures. Secretary of the Navy Wilbur watched a movie transmitted via radio by C. Francis Jenkins, who had broadcast still pictures as early as two years before.

Radio stations broke out in a rash of amateur nights, billed as Radio Nights. WRNY was the first to set up the listening public as a board of judges, urging dialers to write in their choice for a $25 First Prize, a $10 Second Prize, and a fountain pen Third Prize. Some stations obtained vaudeville engagements at $60 to $75 a week for winners. Vaudeville houses spotted them on dull nights, advertising: "Your Favorite Radio Star Will Appear Here In Person."

The first fighter to utter those bromidic pearls, "It's all right, mom, I won," over a microphone was Dave Shade, when he defeated Jimmy Slatterly at the Polo Grounds, where N.T.G. (Nils T. Granlund) of Station WHN introduced radio interviews of ringside spectators and fighters. That same year WHN pulled a transcribed broadcast of the Dundee-Terris fight at Coney Island Stadium. Getting returns from the Brooklyn *Daily Eagle,* the station broadcast a round-by-round description (taking one minute each, instead of three) and simulated whistle, gong and crowd voices. Piano solos and ads were rendered in between the rounds.

The battle still raged in 1925 as to whether radio helped or hurt actors at the boxoffice. On the credit side, broadcasts of Harry Richman and his floor show resulted in a booking at the Palace as "A Night At Club Richman." In Cleveland, songwriters Tommy Malie and Sammy Stept, heard on all Cleveland's stations, were booked at the State and shattered all house records with a $24,000 gross. On the debit side, John McCormack withdrew from radio when Victor dealers and concert managers both reported radio had hurt his drawing power and record sales.

Radio, an $800,000,000-a-year business in 1925, was still pleading poverty to entertainers who demanded payment. Station WEEI in Boston grudgingly gave $500 to the Duncan Sisters for a half-hour show, and Sears Roebuck's WLS in Chicago gave the Keller Sisters & Lynch a two-week contract for 10 pieces of mike work. The general reluctance of station managers to talk turkey led a group in

Chicago to form the Radio Broadcasting Artists Association (to-day's union is the powerful American Federation of Radio Artists), whose specific purpose was to put radio art on a sordid cash basis.

With national sponsors grabbing air time, dignity was becoming a necessity. Radio announcers with bland, cultured voices began to find themselves in demand. Gimbel's WGBS invited a public vote for its favorite mike spieler. The talk boys found easy spots for themselves announcing such big-sponsor shows as "Touring In A Packard 8," "Eagle Neutrodyne Trio," "Atwater-Kent Entertainers," "Silvertown Cord Orchestra," and "A & P Gypsies." Sponsors' checks averaged $400 an hour, or $100 for 10 minutes. WHN received $750 a week for two half-hour shows alone. Yet these stations still "didn't have a dime" for talent.

As radio grew, so did its enemies. There were squawks about the increasing commercialism of the air—squawks which swelled steadily even to the present day. The first recorded protest of a listener, made to the police, dealt with the public nuisance and annoyance WHN constituted by broadcasting jazz music far into the night, as well as its immoral advocacy of certain "dives" of dubious character. WHN dismissed the squawk as one inspired by other "dives" which were not getting equal publicity, and the matter died in a pigeon-hole.

In Memphis, the city council classified radio, and other musical instruments, as a public nuisance when used in stores to attract the passing public. Listeners themselves banded together under W. Howard Johnson, who organized the National Radio Service League; objective to keep tabs on radio legislation.

superheterodyne nuptials   1926 as a radio year began at 8 P.M. on January 1 in an aura of sweetness and light. Station KQW's director, Dr. Clarence Herold, married his assistant, Mrs. Belle Chapman, over that San Francisco station—radio's first wedding.

Deeper cuts into the show business pie were made by radio in the year of floods and hurricanes. Before a three-act play called *Beau Nash* reached the stage, it had been broadcast in toto. Radio replaced bands on steamships from Boston to New York. Music sales of "Mandalay" and "Mighty Lak' a Rose" were murdered by radio's hammering of the tunes. There was irony in the show given at the Mecca Temple by WEAF radio actors. The attendance was practically zero, which the philosophic mikesters attributed to radio's having taught the public to pay nothing for anything connected with radio. In later years, of course, radio-made "names" fetched fancy fees when making "personal appearances."

Associated First National Pictures went out on a limb by giving radio permission to broadcast an outline of one of its forthcoming films, with a dramatization of its climax. Variety shook its head disapprovingly, calling the move a first-class error of judgment. Again, in later years, the Lux Theatre of the Air gave contradiction to this. And still later Hollywood was fighting off the television monster although, all the while, admitting it was only a matter of time when the wedding of the two would come to pass.

Picture houses' fear of the new medium was only too evident. Chicago's Senate Theatre management encouraged its organist, in a solo with slides, to razz radio to the scornful theme, "You're a nut if you listen to radio programs!" Among the deficits of radio as entertainment were singled out dull lectures, boring songpluggers and squeaking noises.

In the latter six months of the year alone, 127 new stations started broadcasting. With so many small independents in the field, it was only a matter of time before most of them would be gathered up in one or two financial bosoms. The gathering began in 1926, with the formation of the National Broadcasting Co. (NBC), whose key stations were WEAF and WJZ in New York. The most significant change this brought about was the possibility of offering network time—tremendous radio coverage for important sponsors, with a consequent big dollar sign placed on every branch of radio. Going national with NBC meant equivalent, or better, advertising coverage than magazines, newspapers or billboards could offer the big companies.

Small-town, independent stations were at a distinct disadvantage against the chain station, which could now offer the cream of entertainment, and which reaped a neat share of the big advertising pie the network took out of the oven. Radio stations' values increased so markedly that WTAS in Chicago was sold for $600,000.

pioneer name announcers   With radio going big time, the stock of name announcers also shot up. Star spielers of that year were Norman Brokenshire (who was to make a remarkable comeback in the late 1940s, following an admitted tussle with too much of "the cup that cheers"), NTG, Graham McNamee, Major J. Andrew White, Phillips Carlin, Milton Cross and Edward B. (Ted) Husing. Husing was the first radio announcer to run an ad in Variety, while he was head wordmonger at Washington's WRC.

NBC's national debut was the outstanding radio event of the year, from both an historic and audience viewpoint.

Merlin H. Aylesworth, head of NBC, introduced an inaugural program from the Grand Ballroom of the Waldorf at 8 P.M. attended by 1,000 newspapermen, radio stars and celebrities. It ran until midnight—the biggest single all-star show in radio history. It went out to 23 stations as far west as St. Paul and Minneapolis. Mary Garden and Will Rogers were picked up from Chicago and Kansas City respectively, at a fee of $2,500 each. Eddie Cantor received $1,500; Weber & Fields, $1,000 for eight minutes. Included in the $25,000 talent cost were the George Olsen, Vincent Lopez, Ben Bernie and B. A. Rolfe orchestras; the New York Philharmonic Orchestra with Walter Damrosch; Edwin Franko Goldman's Band; the Gilbert & Sullivan Light Opera Co., and Titta Ruffo, the famed Metropolitan Opera baritone.

Small wonder that over 4,000 daily newspapers cut out free radio advertising. If radio was now NBC size, it was big enough to pay for newspaper space. And since radio depended on newspapers to publicize its events and attractions, radio stations had no choice but to begin paying for its program advertising.

"Radio," said Will Rogers that year, "is too big a thing to be out of." That was beginning to be the general idea in show business, especially with key NBC stations like WJZ out after name talent. WJZ had come around to the very novel notion that radio needed sustaining as well as commercial shows, and that it was the function of the radio station to pay for talent on sustaining shows. Even commercials were being revamped in new style, with plugs being woven by scripters into skits or dialog, rather than merely thrown straight at wincing listeners.

Music was still 90 per cent of radio in 1926. Paul Whiteman, key baton-waver of the land, received $5,000 for an hour broadcast. Many of the lesser fry, however, were willing to pay for time on WEAF, acknowledging that the advertising was worth it.

The Royal Typewriter Co. became the first sponsor of fight broadcasting, coming up from an offer of $15,000 as Tex Rickard came down from $40,000 to settle at $20,000.

While Sears Roebuck's WLS in Chicago was paying a $5 top for guest appearances, NBC was paying Eddie Cantor $1,500 for 15 minutes—or $100 a minute—on the Eveready Hour, which also permitted him to plug his picture, *Kid Boots*. Radio critics panned the show, but Cantor received 20,000 requests for his photograph, bearing out his contention that he was "giving the public what it liked."

tv on the horizon, back in '26   How fast radio was going, technically as well as in the financial and entertainment ends, can be judged by a General Electric announcement of 1926. RADIO ARTISTS MAY BE SEEN AND HEARD IN TELEVISION was Variety's prophetic headline of the news that General Electric was developing a new device which would enable dialers to see as well as hear radio performers.

NBC was too powerful by 1927 to remain unchallenged, so radio war broke out with the organization of Paramount and Columbia as rival networks to NBC. Despite the big money flowing into radio coffers, surprisingly only 10 out of 694 stations in the United States were breaking even. But parallel to the case of today's television stations—also in the red at the start—it was obvious that pots of gold lay just beyond the horizon.

National advertisers were channeling more and more of their huckster money into the airwaves, as radio proved its ability to plug brand names for companies like American Tobacco and General Motors. When concerns with programs on a few local stations would go on the air in new territories, an immediate upsurge in sales of those added areas would win believers among the checkbook set.

With 20,000,000 families, 20,000,000 radio sets and an estimated listening audience of 50,000,000, radio could no longer afford the smalltime approach. Half-baked entertainers who exchanged their services for "publicity" had to make way for paid talent. After the Eveready-Cantor deal had broken the ice, Socony signed Van & Schenck for a 13-week, quarter-hour daily show at $2,000 a week. Then all the big companies started plunging.

General Motors signed up for 52 weeks on a 28-station hookup, footing a bill for $624,000 that included such talent as Weber & Fields, Leo Carrillo, and William Collier. The Palmolive Hour grabbed Gene Tunney and the Duncan Sisters, Tunney getting $500 a minute for a five-minute turn.

Radio also began to discover its own talent, and build it to box-office proportions. Fancy salaries were paid by picture houses to stars who had made their reputations on radio such as Vincent Lopez, the Happiness Boys (Billy Jones & Ernie Hare), the Ipana Troubadours (Harry Reser), the A & P Gypsies, Harry Richman and Whispering Jack Smith, who had risen from $75 a week as a songplugger for Waterson, Berlin & Snyder to a radio stylist at $1,250.

The year previous, when Amos 'n' Andy (formerly Sam 'n' Henry, né Charles Correll and Freeman Gosden) had opened at McVicker's in Chicago they had received $250 for the week. In 1927, riding to the top of radio, they played the Balaban & Katz picture theatres at $2,000 a week, and in 1928 at $5,000 per. Radio was proving it could make stars. (Some 20 years later CBS was to "buy" Correll and Gosden for over $2,000,000 on a "capital gains" deal.)

Radio, as competition to show biz, was intensely effective—at first. In the concert field, which had lost 25 per cent of its usual trade, 130 concert managers went out of business in 1927. In later years, radio-popularized and film-ballyhooed longhair personalities like Jeanette MacDonald, Nelson Eddy, José Iturbi, Lauritz Melchior, Gladys Swarthout, Lily Pons, André Kostelanetz, Artur Rubinstein, Mario Lanza, Dorothy Kirsten, Risë Stevens, Robert Merrill, Jan Peerce and others were to prove bigger than ever as concert attractions.

On the night that Dempsey fought Tunney, radio broadcasts kept theatres all over the country empty. Tex Rickard, who had first frowned on fight broadcasts, now came to the conclusion that they were a wonderful stimulus to boxing interest. He promptly built Station WMSG on top of Madison Square Garden.

first of the 'feuds'   1927 saw the first use of the insult routine between two star performers, as a gag for running laughs, when a mock feud was inaugurated between N.T.G. and Harry Richman. The Ben Bernie-Walter Winchell and Jack Benny-Fred

Allen "feuds" took their pattern from this. It also saw the first broad-casting from airplanes over Broadway. Jolson went on the air for the first time to sing and appeal for funds for flood sufferers.

The first radio censorship came into effect with the song, "Little Red Riding Hood." Station WFAA, mulling over the line, "How Could Red Riding Hood Have Been So Very Good, and Still Keep the Wolf From the Door?" decided that the song was improper and suggestive, so it was given the heave-ho. And Minneapolis intro-duced the first local radio regulations—no two stations permitted on the air at the same time; none to operate over 500 watts, or for more than 12 hours weekly.

Radio in 1928 was the year of the Dodge Brothers. Their first venture into air exploitation came in late March, with a highly-touted hour of United Artists movie stars. This NBC network show added up to the glittering cost of $1,000 a minute. Because of the precious net value of the talent, the broadcast was made from a locked studio, with no one admitted.

Among the stars who studded up the microphone were Norma Talmadge, Dolores Del Rio, Douglas Fairbanks, Charlie Chaplin, John Barrymore, D. W. Griffith and Paul Whiteman. Fairbanks was master of ceremonies. The extremes in attitude by the cast were represented by Chaplin and Barrymore—the former almost perish-ing with mike fright (he hadn't talked on the screen up until then), the latter in a well-oiled, what-monstrous-claptrap-this-is! mood.

Encouraged by the tremendous publicity which greeted this star festival, Dodge took another full hour to introduce its Victory Six model, and spent $22,500 on talent, including Will Rogers—who garnered top money at $7,500—Whiteman, Al Jolson and Fred Stone.

scripts versus gags   NBC's   spectacular   successes brought the Columbia Broadcasting System into the field as chief challenger. Columbia went after sponsors with strong script mate-rial, reasoning that while sporadic extravaganzas might dazzle dial-ers into tuning in, it wouldn't hold them week after week the way a good story continuity would. Hence, at CBS, script writers be-came the stars—a pattern that later became radio's white hope when dialers became nauseated by their crucifixion on the 12-year-old IQ fixation of networks and sponsors.

Smalltime radio—the independents—found themselves crowded away from the table and forced to pick up crumbs. Consequently, anyone with a pitch and a fee was welcome. Local stations turned over air time to phony stock salesmen, furniture and household commodity peddlers, and even bootleggers. This latter fact was discovered when broadcasts giving price quotations for the "white stuff" (gin), plus a telephone number, were spotted after midnight.

In its coverage of the Smith-Hoover campaign, radio began to feel its way toward developing its facilities as a "newspaper of the air." It also began to pacify critics by rendering other "public service" features—educational talks, weather reports, market conditions, food quotations, time signals, health programs, and sundry other items stirred well with music.

It also began to keep a weather eye peeled for stars with a proclivity for going off the deep end, as a result of the tempests stirred up by Al Jolson and Will Rogers.

Jolson gagged about Clara Bow's "sleeping catercornered in bed" —and listener outrage was so intense that NBC started censors poring over all scripts. Rogers did an imitation of Coolidge, without announcing it as such. It had almost the reverberations of Orson Welles at a later date and his invasion from Mars. Many chuckled, as Rogers had meant them to do—but President Coolidge was not among the amused.

More and more eyes were turned to the future. Fans, tired of building radios, were now going in for constructing television sets. Cortlandt Street (New York's radio row) shops did a rush business in gadgets. NBC demonstrated a process developed by Dr. Alexanderson, by which a photo of Jimmy Walker was broadcast to another station 25 miles away in 90 seconds.

In the year of the big crash, radio had climbed to the nation's fourth major industry. It began to go international, with American programs beamed over CKGW in Toronto, and Dominion stations in turn broadcasting over NBC. Radio exports were 100 per cent higher than in 1928, with Chile leading a list of customers including Argentina, Brazil, Spain, Italy, the Union of South Africa and China. There were 594 United States stations, a climb of 261 over 1927, and fully 16,629 licensed amateur stations.

Radio's first theme song made its appearance with "The Voice of RKO," written by Tom Kennedy for the RKO Radio Hour. The soap-opera circuit reached out for juvenile trade—"Momma, buy me a package of Oatmush so I kin get a boxtop to send for a Secret Seven badge!"—with continued serial shows, based on the plots of old movie serials.

Winchell went on the air for the first time on January 18, 1929, over a 42-station hookup, billed as "New York by a Representative New Yorker." Harry Lauder was paid $15,000 for three songs by Enna Jettick Shoes. He not only broke his no-work-Sunday rule, but threw in a hymn for free. When Station KFI in Los Angeles announced that he would sing, cancellations flooded into the Los Angeles theatre where he was booked. Again—"something for nothing."

Maurice Chevalier made his radio debut for Coty Perfume over WABC, at a $5,000 payoff. Willie and Eugene Howard appeared on the NBC Majestic Radio Hour for $2,500 worth of Grisby-Grunow Radio Co. stock, a unique emolument for radio. And 1929 was the year that Pepsodent latched on to Amos 'n' Andy with a 52-week NBC contract, six days a week.

The era in radio came to a prophetic close with the announcement by Trade Commissioner S. H. Day at Johannesburg, South Africa, that television was already being given public demonstrations in that country by the Baird Telephone Co. and the African Broadcasting Co.

"Radio is here to stay," Variety confidently summarized at the close of the Twenties, "as much a part of contemporary interest as baseball, the weather and prognostications on where is this jazz age leading us to?"

30

Pix Biz Boff B.O.

★

If movies had become "the opiate of the people," as intellectuals scoffed, they were also the opiate of its First Citizen by 1920. To console himself in his illness, President Woodrow Wilson secretly had movies screened for him in the White House two and three times a week. An enthusiastic movie fan, he dubbed his projectionist—manager of a local Washington theatre—"my movie doctor."

In 1919 movies were leaving every other form of amusement far behind. Early in the year Variety predicted that war-made millionaires were contemplating throwing "as much as $1,000,000" into the movie industry, after a thorough investigation of films as an investment risk. The prediction was much too conservative.

Marcus Loew garnered millions alone to help expand his empire. Samuel Goldwyn, Adolph Zukor, William Fox and other moguls received equally gigantic sums from Wall Street.

By 1920, over 35,000,000 Americans went to the movies at least once a week—a vastly more infinite total than attended baseball. Producers began to carp at the nation's newspapers, which were devoting 10 times as much space to the diamond than they gave the screen.

There was a sudden and drastic retrenchment in the film business in 1921. The factors were complex, but they had to do with fear of an impending depression; the high cost of living being felt at the boxoffice; a plot to discipline movie exhibitors; and a stern attempt to wipe out the graft and corruption which Wall Street had inspired in its wake.

Financial chicanery was so flagrant in Hollywood that Variety ran a slashing attack under the headline: GRAFT IN PICTURES.

The paper pointed out that the sticky fingers of everybody from prop boy to producer and president were bleeding film companies into the boneyard.

No single transaction in the production of a film, it charged, was free of rakeoff or kickback. Promoters signed stars at $1,500 a week, who kicked back gladly with $500 a week because they would have been happy to sign at $750. Stars always knew of "the perfect story," managing to get a rakeoff from the author's agents, who also paid off the promoters and directors. Thus a $10,000 story sale wound up costing some $30,000 or more.

The director got his by signing with an agent for exclusive casting, and by kickbacks from the continuity writer he hired. Actors loved signing up for a graft-ridden production, because they knew shooting would be protracted to allow everybody to squeeze as much loot out of it as possible.

As a consequence, a number of companies went bankrupt, and others were reorganized. Producers trying to raise money from banks were turned down firmly. A standard Hollywood gag had a producer asking a banker for a loan on a picture, to be met with the reply, "Oil painting, yes. Movie, no."

An interesting sidelight of the "recession" came from Portland, Oregon, where a theatre increased receipts by allowing patrons to pay as they left—a psychological come-on. But the manager was forced to get back into line by the Northern Film Board of Trade under penalty of suspension of service.

With the boom that began in 1922, a chastened Hollywood began to boom again with the times. Its influence strengthened so rapidly that by 1924 the Federal Government itself was paying Hollywood a million dollars to make educational films, as Congressional solons protested that this was lining the pockets of private business by extolling oil and other companies in the guise of "education." Private enterprise was also thumping its own drum with commercial films it paid exhibitors to present as "entertainment" shorts.

Film company grosses in 1925 made Variety begin to brush up its superlatives. For its first 40 films, Famous Players collected $21,000,000. Metro grossed $16,000,000, and First National $11,000-000. A year later Variety predicted that films would put vaudeville out of business.

hollywood's 'know-how'   The film industry showed a "know-how" vastly superior to its hoary and tottering rival, vaudeville. Keith-Albee had spent $6,000,000 on one theatre, but hadn't thought of a cooling system. Movie theatres not only installed cooling systems, but gave out with that "Roxy service," such as free checking, and prospered fabulously.

By 1927 Hollywood was beginning to take itself seriously as an "art" form. The Academy of Motion Picture Arts & Sciences was formed, Douglas Fairbanks, its first president. Hollywood gag men were retitled "comedy constructors." Comedians no longer threw pies, but instead "lent comedy relief." Heavies and villains were now properly dignified as "the menace," offering "dramatic suspense."

Wall Street influence began to make itself felt strongly again in 1927, with a gigantic merger of RKO, Pathe and F.B.O., engineered by Wall Streeter Mike Meehan and industrialist Joseph P. Kennedy, later United States Ambassador to Great Britain. The Warner Bros. merged WB with the Stanley Company of America and First National Pictures.

Pictures with vaudeville became the prevailing trend, with Marcus Loew in the lead as the nation's No. 1 vaudfilm chain operator. It was the most successful year Hollywood had ever had, and no one could deny that it was the picture end of pic-vaude that did the b.o.

There were more financial quakes on the West Coast in 1928, with Wall Street arranging deals over the heads of film and theatre magnates. William Fox began to worry major producers by becoming the biggest independent factor in the industry. More aspirins were required for the Senator Brookhart hearings in Congress on the practice of block-bookings of films; and for a Wall Street-dictated economy wave which compelled centralized purchasing of all studio properties.

With movies and audiences becoming more sophisticated, the Westerns—or oaters, giddyappers, mesa mellers, thatawayers, as Variety called them—lost ground for a spell. Formerly surefire boxoffice, they were now almost completely junked. Variety, going by the theory of "cycles," predicted that it would be another seven years, or 1935, before actors began calling each other "pardner" again on the screen. (How prophetic this crystal-ballgazing may be, fact is that twice seven years later, circa 1949-1950 saw (1) the big spec West-

ern making a decided comeback in Hollywood, and (2), the upsurge of Hopalong Cassidy on the telescreens. The kids, particularly,
brought the old Hoppys, Lone Rangers, Hoot Gibsons, Roy Rogers
and others on the comeback trail, and especially fancy coin since
TV sponsors underwrote the old and new giddyappers. The kids
ate up both the Westerns and the breakfast foods which usually
sponsored them, although for a time when mama sought to induce Junior to partake of food, and lure him away from the video,
he'd demur, "I ain't hankerin' for no chaw, ma!")

accent on articulation   After a wild moment of panic,
when the talkie established itself as the new future of films, Hollywood devoted most of 1929 to mastering the intricacies of speech.
Threatened by radio, it rode out the storm of its crisis to triumph,
in a traditional Hollywood fadeout, to live happily ever after.

Movies killed vaudeville, but gently—a little at a time. First pictures
annexed vaudeville as an aging and ailing, but still valuable partner.

Marcus Loew was the moving spirit behind this drama. He
sounded the tocsin in 1919 by buying up the realty adjacent to and
including the Bartholdi Inn, on the corner of Broadway and 45th
Street, once a favorite haunt of such names as Pearl White, Mack
Sennett, Charlie Chaplin, Conway Tearle, D. W. Griffith and Eva
Tanguay. The Bartholdi Inn came down, and in August of 1921,
Loew's State Theatre opened its doors.

In 1920, Loew bought out Metro for $3,000,000, and his name went
on the lead title frames of Metro films. A roar of protest rose from
rival theatre exhibitors, first in New York, then across the nation,
who demanded that the Loew name be erased from Metro films.
No manager wanted to be compelled to advertise on his own screen
the name above the marquee of the theatre next door.

Just before the war period slipped away, Americans were going to
the movies to thrill at Doug Fairbanks as *The Knickerbocker Buck-
aroo;* sigh over Mary Pickford in *Daddy Long Legs;* scream at
Charlie Chaplin in *Shoulder Arms;* weep at D. W. Griffith's *Broken
Blossoms;* leer at Theda Bara and cheer Pearl White from chapter
to chapter.

In 1919 Hollywood was turning out "special" pictures, with an eye
toward capturing boxoffice interest with timely topics. *The Red
Viper* was the film colony's contribution to help explain the Soviet

revolution to Americans. First National came out with *The Fighting Roosevelts.* Charles A. Schwab put $150,000 into *Deliverance,* the film starring blind Helen Keller.

Uncertain about story values for the changing generation, producers played it safe by bidding for screen rights to Broadway plays. Demand sent prices up. Doris Keane asked $200,000 for her hit play, *Romance,* including her own services as star. *Bird of Paradise* was sold for $100,000, the tariff also paid for *Way Down East.* A show called *Turn to the Right* brought $80,000, and *East Is West* met where the twain earned $60,000.

As in later years, the trend brought a flock of new producers to Broadway, putting on turkeys that opened and closed swiftly, for the sole purpose of selling rights to Hollywood. Standards of literary value in 1919 were, for Hollywood producers and the public in general, decidedly uncertain. One Chicago manager of a film house advertised on his screen: TOMORROW—IBSEN'S "DOLL'S HOUSE"—BRING THE KIDDIES. And they did.

Costume films and spectacles began to enjoy a wide vogue in 1922 with Douglas Fairbanks in *Robin Hood* and Marion Davies in *When Knighthood Was In Flower.* They were still going strong in 1924, when *Scaramouche* with Ramon Navarro chalked up a record for the Capitol Theatre on Broadway with $67,958. Encouraged, Hollywood sank $6,000,000 into *Ben Hur* the following year, winning plaudits for it as "the greatest picture ever made."

Hal Roach made his bid in 1925 for the spectacle trade with a curiosity called *Black Cyclone,* showing wild horses running, fighting, making love, being rescued from quicksand, and attacked by wolf packs. It thrilled Capitol audiences, none of whom realized that the horses and wolves were magnified, clever German toys— as was a previously exhibited horse star, Rex.

more of that 7-year cycle   1926 saw the advent of the first war films, seven years after the close of World War I. (Variety's seven-year cycle of the coming and going of theatrical trends.) *The Big Parade,* starring John Gilbert, Reneé Adoree, Karl Dane and George K. Arthur, was first on the screen. A hoked-up pocus of sentiment, thrills and comedy, it set a new world record for films by grossing $1,000,000 in its first year.

In a tougher vein, and presenting the first Quirt-Flagg ("Sez you!"—"Yeah! Sez me!") opus, *What Price Glory?*, starring Victor McLaglen and Edmund Lowe, opened in December of 1926 at the Harris Theatre, New York. War was still something to laugh about, in retrospect, until 1930, when the truly great war film of all time was produced—the unforgettable *All Quiet On the Western Front*, with its magnificent portrayal by the late Louis Wolheim. This film—still a classic in movie revival houses today—proved Hollywood's right to be considered a serious art form.

In 1927, the cycle of underworld films—reflection of the gang wars of the Prohibition age—began with the filming of Ben Hecht's *Underworld*. It was also the year of the terrific blunder of Universal in sinking $2,500,000 into a film version of *Uncle Tom's Cabin*, with Uncle Tom going into the red for half that sum. And the year saw the first financial plunge into Hollywood of a wealthy, 27-year-old, who backed *Two Arabian Knights* for John W. Considine at United Artists. The relatively young man declared he was ready to back up with big cash his own judgment of what pictures should be made. He did it again in a big way 21 years later, when Howard Hughes bought out RKO in 1948 for nearly $10,000,000.

It was Marcus Loew who found that when his film attraction was a turkey, the boxoffice line could still be held by stage presentations to bolster the bill. So it was that the man who gradually killed vaudeville became the inheritor of many of vaudeville's biggest acts. By 1927, still operating on the principle of movies-plus, Loew's Capitol was offering big-name bands as well as vaude.

On September 28, 1927, Variety published a special Marcus Loew memorial issue, in which the astute showman was characterized as a "gentle, tender, endearing soul . . . a just Solomon, a wise Moses, a patient Job and a kind David in judgment and in counsel." The occasion was the death of Marcus Loew, at the age of 57.

Loew was genuinely mourned by all show business. He had been a friend and defender of the actor. "Every wrong, crooked scheme had to stop when it reached the borders of Marcus Loew's domain," praised Variety. "He was a square dealer to those inside and outside his domain."

His closest friend had warned Loew, when the latter first considered the giant financing problems involved in financing Loew's Enterprises into Loew's, Inc., that it would take 10 years off his life. Loew replied that if it would help him justify the trust others had placed in him, he would willingly give the 10 years. Variety concluded sombrely, "And he did."

A challenging rival to Loew in pic-vaude was William Fox, who in 1920 was already adding 40 theatres to the 30 he owned. The trend continued, with a climax in 1925 when Famous Players bought out the Balaban & Katz circuit, Hollywood's biggest plunge into the theatre-owning end by that date.

Theatres were counted in 1926, showing a total of 21,000, of which only 500 belonged to the field of the legitimate. This was the year the New York Paramount in Times Square opened, dazzling the Main Stem with a world's record boxoffice gross for the week—$80,000. So frantic was the excitement to see this new milestone in movie palaces that police had to be called out regularly. In its first year of operation, the Paramount netted $1,000,000.

The following year saw a spectacular opening on the Coast—Grauman's Chinese Theatre in Hollywood, which cost $1,000,000 to build, and seated 2,200. Chosen as a suitable spectacle to premiere the theatre, Cecil B. De Mille's *King of Kings* played to a $2 top.

the roxy   But the biggest news of 1927 was the New York Roxy, whose 6,250-seat capacity required a weekly overhead of $50,000. Cost of the Roxy itself was $8,000,000. Opening night tickets went for the staggering sum of $11 an orchestra ticket, to see an obscure film called *Wolf's Clothing* with Monte Blue and Patsy Ruth Miller. Premiere alone played to a $30,000 house. The first week's gross smashed the Paramount's record with $110,000.

Obviously, it was not the film alone which was the attraction of the movie palace. As Roxy refined the trend, it was a show business package tied with a blue silk bow. Audiences wound around the block, waiting to get in, for a combination of luxurious pleasures including a comfortable seat in super-gorgeous surroundings; a thunderous symphony orchestra directed by the late Erno Rapee; a lavish and spectacular stage show; a master of ceremonies; and a film which, with a little luck, might turn out to be passably good.

The Roxy celebrated its first anniversary with a birthday cake of $5,500,000 in gross receipts. During the year it had had one peak week of $144,267, and its lowest week was $83,000.

The public had long since forgotten that it had once paid 5¢ a ticket to see the best movies available.

the pix crix Conscious of the ever-growing influence of film critics on the b.o., Sam Goldwyn gave 30 of the tribe an all-expenses-paid train trip from New York to Hollywood in 1929 for a special preview of *Bulldog Drummond*. Not to be outdone, Mary Pickford followed suit soon afterward. Handling critics with velvet gloves rapidly became a Hollywood custom.

Producers did everything for the reviewers except the one thing Archer Winsten of the New York *Post* was still complaining about, in a column late in 1948. A review could contain 900 words about a film, all of them uncomplimentary, including the phrase: "The most extraordinary bunch of claptrap ever filmed!" The next day movie ads would inevitably scream: "EXTRAORDINARY . . . says Archer Winsten in the *Post*."

According to a German competitor of Variety's, *Die Lichtbild-bühne,* there were 47,000 picture theatres in the world of 1921. The United States had 18,000; Germany, 3,731; Great Britain, 3,000; Russia, 3,500; France, 2,400; Italy, 2,200; South America, 1,200; and Central America, 500.

The spread of international movies gave Hollywood some qualms in 1922, for fear the foreign film companies might invade the United States with product superior to the home-grown brand. Variety soothed the industry with these words: "There will be the occasional foreign picture brought over that may make a hit with the public and the exhibitors, but any thought that pix produced in England, France and Germany, or any part of Europe, will ever make a dent in the American market, is poppycock."

Variety and Hollywood were both to see the day when French, Italian and Russian films were to nip off sizable segments of film-goers, to be followed by assaults on the popular trade by England's Alfred Hitchcock, J. Arthur Rank and Sir Laurence Olivier.

England of 1925 wasn't too well pleased with the Hollywood product. G. A. Atkinson, radio critic for the BBC and termed by Variety "the most powerful and influential newspaper and radio critic the world has ever seen," lashed out at American films to 7,000,000 BBC listeners.

"A torrent of sophisticated barbarism," were his biting words. If Americans were truly reflected by their screen, he challenged, they were "non-moral," weakening marriage ideals, scoffing at parenthood, despising decency, and worshipping no god but the dollar.

To Variety, Atkinson wrote: "I find that the mentality behind the average American social photoplay is diabolically cynical."

Variety's editor privately commented, "Well, the films we send over there are at least as pure as the Scotch they send over here."

By 1927, at least 40 per cent of Hollywood's "barbaric torrent" was in demand by foreign countries. It was a reluctant demand, because overseas nationalism and desire to exploit their own boxoffice resources made other nations anxious to encourage their own film industries. The British slapped a quota bill on exhibitors, compelling them to show a fixed percentage of films labeled "Made in England." But no foreign film companies of that date could hope to equal the technical perfection, and cash resources, of Hollywood.

filmland scandals The honor of being the nation's leading city of sin has changed hands four or five times. Up until the 1920s, it was often a tossup among San Francisco, Chicago, New Orleans and New York City. But by 1919 Hollywood was crowding them all out. It was, of course, no better or worse than any other fairly sophisticated community. But Hollywood paid the special penalty of being both the nation's leading influence, and its most publicized acreage.

Not that the business end of Hollywood itself didn't often ask for it. One film producer advertised in 1919: "Brilliant men, beautiful jazz babies, champagne baths, midnight revels, petting parties in the purple dawn, all ending in one terrific smashing climax that makes you gasp." Churches, already clench-fisted over Sunday films, called forth God's lightning.

Film actors and key figures felt the steam generated by so much hellfire. They complained to the Los Angeles Chamber of Commerce that the city was prejudiced against them. Landlords refused to rent to them, classifying them with babies, dogs and other "undesirables." Whatever they bought cost them 5 to 10 per cent higher than other customers were charged. And they were bitter about the fact that murders were committed every day, but when film people became involved in any kind of trouble, they were always front-page fodder for the nation's breakfast tables.

In 1921 two terrific scandals broke out that stood Hollywood—and the rest of the nation—on its head. The Fatty Arbuckle mess gave the feeling that not only the comedian, but all of Hollywood was going on trial.

The second scandal rushed right on the heels of the Arbuckle case. William Desmond Taylor, an important director for Famous Players-Lasky, was mysteriously murdered in early 1922. Mabel Normand and Mary Miles Minter, both prominently mentioned in connection with the case, collapsed at the funeral. The case was never solved, but the headlines forced an important change in the movie industry—the appointment of a "czar" of movie morals.

He was Will H. Hays, Postmaster General in the Harding Cabinet, who resigned to head the Motion Picture Producers & Distributors Association of America, Inc., better-known simply as the Hays Office. Just as he was wading in to put Hollywood's house in order, a third scandal broke out to plague him—Wallace Reid's drug addiction. Reid died the following year.

The advent of "Czar" Hays, which Variety heralded as "the biggest thing that has happened in the screen world since the closeup was first evolved," was a blessing to Hollywood financiers and a catastrophe for the proponents of film artistry. "Novels and plays, which dealt honestly with life, found themselves banned from the screen," they argued, "while claptrap received a benediction provided it had a blatantly moral ending and served up its sex appeal with hypocritical disapproval."

The scandals subsided, and Arbuckle was freed when his jury disagreed. The Hays Office, considering this a vindication, announced it would allow him to return to films. Whereupon a storm of protest broke out anew, with violent threats of boxoffice reprisals against Hollywood by women's clubs, church organizations and other antivice guardians.

Hays and Adolph Zukor hastily conferred with Joe Schenck, advising him to withdraw all Arbuckle films, which were doing badly anyhow. The Hays Office issued a front-line communiqué, stating that Arbuckle was retiring as an actor, and would only serve films as a director. Meanwhile, Arbuckle took his talents to the cabarets, and in 1924 accepted a vaudeville circuit tour. At the Pantages in San Francisco, he received a two-minute ovation—tribute to the underdog making a comeback from the audience that had made him an underdog. In 1927 Arbuckle returned to directing films—but under his mother's name of Goodrich.

Exhibitors were going to town on sexy film ballyhoo. The ads promised a great deal more than the pictures could fulfill. "Tell no one what you see through *The Bedroom Window*," was one gem. Another, "Betty Compson in *Woman To Woman*—it bares the soul of an unmarried mother." Pola Negri, in *Men,* was offered as "the woman who pays and makes men pay, too!"

phony talent schools   In 1926 the District Attorney's office pushed aside the Hays Office to investigate 75 California movie schools charged with fleecing pupils and giving them "casting couch" screen tests. That year Hays warned producers not to allow films to ridicule Prohibition. In 1927 he shook a finger at them about sex again, and placated pool parlor and manufacturing interests who were violently upset because the favorite haunts of the gangsters in Hollywood underworld sagas were always pool halls.

He maintained a dignified silence that year under the attack against himself and Hollywood by Canon Chase, a professional reformer, busying himself instead by seeing to it that Hollywood's 23 marriages of 1926 received due notice (not, of course, their 14 divorces and 3 separations). It didn't disturb him unduly that Mexico was barring films which showed Mexicans as villains.

Hollywood naturally sought every method of winning favorable publicity for itself as an institution, as well as for its products. In 1922 Warner Bros. decided to spread the word about three of its releases—*Rags To Riches, Main Street* and *Dangerous Adventure* —into the nooks and crannies of the country. So it sent a truck with radio and amplifier across the nation to stop at every Main Street and talk up the films.

The top publicity stunt of 1923 was in behalf of the film, *Down to the Sea in Ships*. Pressagent Milton Crandall planted a whale on top of Pike's Peak one night. Tipping off the papers that a whale had been sighted there, he raced up to the Peak and lay on his back shooting occasional sprays of seltzer into the air as excited Denver citizens pointed and yelled, "Thar she blows!"

Hollywood's home state went in for some publicity of its own. Worried about an 11,000-acre tract of land being offered to film companies by promoter Felix Isman for a movie city in Florida, during the boom, California decided to spend $1,000,000 for national publicity to beat down the upstart sunshine mecca.

A bit of free publicity came the way of Hollywood through the Los Angeles Plumbers Convention of 1926, where the gathered men of iron agreed that the bigger and better bathrooms displayed in films helped the plumbing business. And as a fitting close to movie publicity of the 1920s, Hollywoodians were treated to a living 24-sheet—16 semi-clad beauts shaping letters to spell out *Hollywood Revue of 1929.*

hollywood gold and dross   Life on the West Coast in the 1920s was fabulous for those who had climbed into the golden circle—precarious for the thousands who battered vainly at its shiny circumference, hoping daily for the "break" that never came. In the slump of 1921, Variety headlined: EXTRAS STARVING AS SLUMP GOES ON, WITH BANKS DEMANDING WORK IN EAST.

With Wall Street demanding that production be shifted to New York and Florida, Variety reported: "Actors are talking of the East and the chances there, and trying all sorts of means to flit to New York. Some have gone so far as to register their names with local undertakers as willing to accompany dead bodies back East, thus obtaining free transportation."

Stars' salaries dropped from $1,000 and $2,000 a week to $300 and $500, many taking any roles offered to them. Extras jostled for jobs in stores and hash-houses.

Yet the film industry a few years later paid Cecil B. De Mille a 16-week royalty of $310,514 on *The Ten Commandments.* For the convenience of Marion Davies, Metro built a $25,000 bungalow on a studio lot. The fortunate within the golden circle of 1926 had accumulated $10,210,000 worth of personal real estate, including some 109 film colony homes.

Extras of that year earned an average of $8.64 daily, which dropped to $8.18, then $7.10, in the wave of salary-cutting that hit the 24 studios in 1927. Of the 9,973 employees on Hollywood payrolls, 1,800 were girl extras. One male extra, whose casting value was a long beard, was slashed from $7.50 to $5, whereupon he trod before the cameras with half of his beard tucked in his vest.

A star of that year was tied up by a $500-a-week contract, and his bosses refused to raise the ante despite the fact that he had become boxoffice material. He blandly took up flying as a hobby, pointing out to the frantic studio officials that there was nothing in his contract to prevent him. He won a new contract at $2,500 a week—with a no-flying proviso.

Top stars of 1927 balked when producers stalked their paychecks with long knives, but lost an aggregate of $350,000. They protested bitterly, pointing to the high tariffs that continued to flow to those on the other side of the camera. George Marion, Jr., a title writer for Famous Players-Lasky, was drawing $2,500 a week. M.G.M.'s director Clarence Brown was clicking a weekly $5,000, and scenario writer Ben Glazer collected $3,000.

By 1928 the boom was on again, with a nose-count showing 235,000 people employed in all branches of film work. Stars were receiving 32,500,000 fan letters a year, and Hollywood shelled out $2,000,000 to the post-office in answers.

united artists formed   The only concern of top stars in the golden circle of the Twenties was getting enough canvas bags in which to haul away their gold. In 1919, William Gibbs McAdoo was hired as counsel at $100,000 a year by the Big Five—Mary Pickford, William S. Hart, Douglas Fairbanks, D. W. Griffith and Charlie Chaplin. A prudent investment, since the income taxes of the top stars amounted to over $3,000,000. It took a total of 10 lawyers to draw up ironclad contracts among Chaplin, Pickford, Hart, Fairbanks and Griffith, organizing as United Artists with veteran film distributor Hiram Abrams as their president.

In 1919 even blasé Hollywood gasped when Adolph Zukor signed Mary Miles Minter to a three-year contract at $1,300,000. New stars cracked the ice at a usually much slower pace, as Norma Shearer did in 1925, when she signed a 5-year contract at $150 a week, becoming a star two years later with a raise to $2,500.

When Clara Bow was billed in 1926 as the "Hottest Jazz Baby in Films" in *The Plastic Age,* each studio had one kingpin star which represented its biggest asset, as well as salary expense. Famous Players had Gloria Swanson; First National, Colleen Moore; M.G.M., Lillian Gish; Fox, Tom Mix; United Artists, Chaplin; Warners, Monte Blue; Universal, Reginald Denny; Pathe, Harold Lloyd; F.B.O., Fred Thompson; and Chadwick Pictures, Lionel Barrymore.

The highest-paid star of 1928, however, was John Gilbert, who received $10,000 a week as result of his romantic success in *The Big Parade.* And in the last year of the decade Variety risked an estimate of film and stage fortunes, showing the wealthiest actor of all to be David Warfield, with ten to twelve millions.

Eddie Cantor came next with five to six millions, closely trailed by Hollywood's top money figure, Marion Davies, at $5,000,000. Al Jolson was next with three to four millions, and bringing up the rear with a paltry $3,000,000 apiece were Pickford, Chaplin and George M. Cohan.

l. b. mayer kayos charlie chaplin   Charlie Chaplin, storm center of the film industry through two wars, started the decade characteristically by being knocked out in a hotel fight by Louis B. Mayer, who took his glasses off to do it. The following year, when Chaplin visited London, British troops were called out in his honor with the pomp and circumstance reserved for visiting monarchs. The Palace, in New York, honored him further by admitting its first five-reel film, Chaplin's *The Kid,* which ran one hour and 10 minutes, cutting two of the usual nine acts off the bill.

The next year, Chaplin's *Pay Day* struck pay dirt, and *The Champion* opened Boston's Loew's State, with speculators hawking pasteboards at $5 apiece.

In 1925 Chaplin went to court to stop an actor named Charles Amader from billing himself as Charlie Aplin. The following year New York's 5th Avenue Playhouse screened *The Pilgrim,* with a foreword by the management that declared: "This picture was made when Charlie Chaplin had but one motor car—and no baby carriages—and his mind was on his work." Chaplin's amatory troubles were national legend even then.

In 1928 a full page in Variety was taken by Al Jolson for one of his enthusiastic outbreaks over the work of a fellow artist. The film that had excited Jolson was *The Circus,* which he described as "the greatest comedy picture ever made. If a greater one is ever made, Charlie Chaplin will make it. Dem's my sentiments. Oh, Boy, wait till you see it! (signed) Al Jolson."

'ideal' couple   The biggest Hollywood event of 1920 was the "ideal" marriage of Douglas Fairbanks and Mary Pickford. The public was delighted, and jammed theatres to see their pictures. When the couple went to London, they were given a royal reception that rivaled a British coronation. It took seven years before screen fans were thrilled by another big star union, when Rod La

Rocque and Vilma Banky were married in a ceremony that had all the aspects of an opening night at Grauman's Chinese.

Harold Lloyd, who lost a finger and thumb in the explosion of a trick bomb in 1919, and consequently always wore gloves in his films, moved up from two-reelers to the bigtime comedy class with *Grandma's Boy* in 1922. His star rose so rapidly that, following *The Freshman* in 1925, his pictures began to earn more money than even those of the great Chaplin. In the comedy field Lloyd was always far ahead of Buster Keaton, who was acclaimed the find of 1920, and of Harry Langdon, who scored a big hit with his first film, *Tramp Tramp Tramp* in 1926.

There was a steady drift of stage comedians from Broadway to Hollywood, as legit figures realized their in-the-flesh drawing power became immeasurably enhanced by film appearances. Will Rogers, after two and a half years in films, returned to Shubert vaudeville in 1921 at $3,000 a week.

In 1925 W. C. Fields made his first film, *Sally of the Circus,* which led to his eventual establishment as one of Hollywood's top funny men. In 1926 Eddie Cantor left for the Coast to screen his Ziegfeld musical comedy *Kid Boots,* and George Jessel for *Private Izzy Cohen.* Ed Wynn's first film was *Rubber Heels* in 1927, and Joe E. Brown scored so heavily with his film debut, *Hit of the Show,* that he belonged to Hollywood from then on.

glamorpusses of the silents   In the *femme fatale* sweepstakes of 1920, Theda Bara outdistanced the field. Earning $4,000 a week in films, she went to Boston to star in a play called *The Blue Flame.* The flame proved a bonfire on an opening night that took in $2,600, with Boston police hard put to it to hold the crowds in check. Theda's reward for vamping in the flesh was $6,000 a week.

She was eclipsed by a new star who out-Baraed Theda, besides resembling her—Pola Negri. With *The Red Peacock* in 1922, Pola raced up the ladder of acclaim as the lady whom John Doe would most like to be shipwrecked with, until in 1924 she rivaled Gloria Swanson as Hollywood's ace money card. Both stars were nudged aside by a magnificent bosom, followed by Mae Murray, who in 1925 could spurn a $5,000-a-week vaudeville offer because her screen salary was $7,500.

In 1926 the chief talent for making male jaws droop belonged to Greta Garbo, who also had that effect on Louis B. Mayer when she refused to expend her sultry charms for M.G.M.'s cameras under her $750-a-week contract. Five thousand a week, said Garbo, or Ay tank Ay go home. Mayer threatened her with loss of her permit to work in the United States, but settled for a hike of $2,500 a week. Wondering if he had made a mistake, because already the pendulum was swinging to a new brand of sexual charm—"It," as personified by Clara Bow, who was smashing records.

Among the *hommes fatals,* top honors went to the Rudolph Valentino, born Rudolph Alfonzo Raffaele Piere Filibert Guglielmi di Valentina d'Antonguolla. As star of the *Four Horsemen of the Apocalypse* in 1921, he brought opening night tickets to a tariff of $10 apiece. The following year, opening at the New York Rivoli in *Beyond the Rocks,* an Elinor Glyn story, with Gloria Swanson opposite him, he accounted for a $30,000 gross. When his *Blood and Sand* hit Broadway, it was held over for four weeks, then unusual.

In 1926 he died at the age of 31, heavily in debt. His manager skillfully arranged for his body to lie in state at a Broadway funeral parlor, and arranged a cortege with top Hollywood mourners. The crowd stretched for 11 blocks, and emotional riots broke out with some spectators leaving in ambulances. The publicity was so luscious that a prompt reissue of Valentino films put his estate hundreds of thousands of dollars in the black.

After Valentino, the trend in male leads grew steadily softer, with boyishness and sweetness most in demand, perhaps to compensate for the hard sexiness of females, on-screen and off. In 1923 the Dream Boy was Richard Barthelmess, who starred in *Fury* opposite Dorothy Gish. In 1928 he had become Charles "Buddy" Rogers, who rose to stardom in *Fascinating Youth,* and the following year was billed as "The Love Rouser" in the film, *Halfway to Heaven.* He reached his ultimate in 1929 as Rudy Vallee, for whose film, *The Vagabond Lover,* the trailer announced: "Men hate him—women love him!"

the theywentthatawayers   At the beginning of the decade, Westerns were riding high. Fred Thompson, a former minister and athletic champ, had ridden the celluloid trail, in the wake of William S. Hart and William Farnum, to snag $7,000 a week with his blank cartridges. By 1926 three companies were fighting to get him, one waving a check for fully $15,000 a week.

On the Paramount lot of 1927, Gary Cooper was bringing varmints to justice with signal b.o. success. But the era was rapidly becoming too sophisticated to thrill to the old hoofbeats and scheming cattle rustlers.

In the recession that hit the Coast that year, Westerns were axed by the dozen. Tom Mix, stung and troubled, denounced Hollywood producers in Variety, charging that if other businesses were run as extravagantly and wastefully as the film colony, they couldn't avoid failure and bankruptcy. "Remember the Romans!" he warned grimly. In 1928 Fox didn't bother to renew his contract, so Mix huffily removed his equine talents to South America.

The first celebrated name from outside the theatrical field to go into films during the decade was Jesse James, Jr., who signed a three-year contract with the Mecca Corp. at $100,000 a year, in 1920. He was then a criminal lawyer in Kansas City, where the local paper, the *Journal,* commented: "The stage seems to hold an irresistible lure for the James family. The father held them up, and now the son proposes to hold them down." James also made personal appearances in vaudeville, selling the idea that his father had been driven into being an outlaw by political persecution. Variety reported that James in the flesh drew more cash than in the can.

Another celebrity went to the Coast that year—Babe Ruth, who starred in *Headin' Home* for the diamond trade. Gilda Gray signed for a film in 1925 at $6,000 for the picture, plus 20 per cent of the gross over $250,000. Jack Dempsey got into the act with his wife, Estelle Taylor, in a screening of *Manhattan Madness*. In 1926 Gene Tunney was featured in *The Fighting Marine* as "Pathe Serial Contender for Dempsey's Crown." And in 1928 *Take It Big* featured ball players Jim Thorpe, Bob Meusel, Irish Meusel, Ernie Orsatti, Wheezer Dell, Tillie Schaefer, Mike Donlin and Chet Thomas.

Among the up-and-coming film stars of 1927 Variety singled out Lupe Velez, Nancy Carroll, Lina Basquette, Mary Nolan, Louis Wolheim, Bill Boyd, Jimmy Gleason, Gilbert Roland, Gene Morgan, Richard Arlen and Gary Cooper, who survived the Western debacle to emerge as a straight lead.

Fox's top stars of that year were Madge Bellamy, Tom Mix and Buck Jones. The star stable at Warners was led by Rin-Tin-Tin (voted the most popular film performer of 1926) and included Dolores Costello, Monte Blue, John Barrymore, Al Jolson, Syd Chaplin, Irene Rich and George Jessel. At Universal the headliners were Laura La Plante, Reginald Denny, Jean Hersholt, Conrad Veidt, Mary Philbin, Norman Kerry and Glenn Tryon.

First National, later absorbed by Warners, had Colleen Moore, Billie Dove, Norma Talmadge, Richard Barthelmess, Corinne Griffith, Harry Langdon, Milton Sills, Constance Talmadge, Johnny Hines, Ken Maynard and Will Rogers.

Clara Bow was the sensation of Paramount, which also had under lock and key Pola Negri, Harold Lloyd, Thomas Meighan, Esther Ralston, Florence Vidor, Raymond Griffith, Douglas MacLean, Eddie Cantor, W. C. Fields, Jack Holt, Adolphe Menjou, Emil Jannings, Bebe Daniels and Ed Wynn.

al jolson's 'jazz singer'   The two biggest thunderbolts to hit Hollywood during the decade were Al Jolson and the talkies—simultaneously. Jolson's first visit to the Coast in 1923, under oral contract to D. W. Griffith for a film, was a fiasco. The film was to be *Mammy's Boy,* which called for Jolson in both blackface and whiteface. Jolson was in his element under burnt cork, but he couldn't go through the whiteface love scenes without clowning them. When he saw a few of the rushes, he walked out.

Whereupon Griffith sued for $500,000, and three years later was awarded a $2,627 judgment. That would probably have been the end of Jolson's relationship with Hollywood if the Warner Bros., fighting hard to establish talking pictures in the summer of 1927, had not bought talking (and singing) rights to *The Jazz Singer,* a play by Samson Raphaelson starring Georgie Jessel. When the latter refused to do the film version, the Warners urged Jolson to be seen (and heard) in the title role of the filmization.

Jolson, intrigued by the idea of movies that would allow him to sing, agreed. The film was shot silent, except for Jolson's singing sequences. However, the applause of the film extra "cafe audience," after Jolson finished singing "Dirty Hands, Dirty Face," was so enthusiastic that Jolson declared: "Wait a minute! Wait a minute! You ain't heard nothin' yet!"

The Warners decided to leave that in the film, and later added a scene of dialog between Jolson and the actress playing his mother.

The rest of the film was given a musical score. Opening on October 6, 1927, those bits of dialog entranced the audience. *The Jazz Singer* convinced moviegoers that talking films were more than a novelty, and built fires under exhibitors to get their theatres wired for sound. The film earned over $3,000,0000 for the Warners.

Jolson followed that triumph with *The Singing Fool,* which opened at the Winter Garden, the first film ever to play that theatre. It was also the first $3 top movie Hollywood had ever known. The Winter Garden didn't need the running ribbon light sign they erected to announce the attraction. Variety predicted it would probably gross over $8,000,000 before its run was finished.

Musing over the two films which had "placed him at the head of all show business as the greatest drawing card in grosses the theatre knows," Variety drew a dramatic parallel between Jolson on the Sullivan-Considine Circuit of 1905, doing three-a-day at $175 a week, and the $75,000 he received to sing five songs—the Jolson who would sing as many as 20 songs at a single stage performance.

"Maybe that's the best record of the show business—Al Jolson," *Sime* pondered. "It demonstrates the mechanical era the business has gone into. For Al Jolson without a talking picture wouldn't mean a thing on the screen." But a talking picture without Al Jolson could mean plenty—as long as it was about him, and had his voice —as *The Jolson Story* and its sequel, *Jolson Sings Again,* proved almost 20 years later. Where *The Jazz Singer* earned $3,000,000 for the Warners, and put them into the big league, the two "Jolson" pictures, via Columbia—Jack L. Warner had nixed the first one— grossed $15,000,000, and over $5,000,000 of that has accrued to Jolson as his net. Thus, already a legend within his own time, did Jolie complete the cycle from vaudeville to minstrelsy, to star at the Winter Garden, to the historic impetus that gave soundpix their start, and finally to glorification in celluloid as the subject, twice-over, of two biopix.

It might be added that at one point, before *The Jolson Story* was conceived, "the king," as Bing Crosby ofttimes called him thereafter, when they paired on their multi-radio programs, couldn't get himself booked on a benefit. It is now Hollywood lore that Jolson got a sort of brushoff okay to *close* a Sunday night benefit at Hillcrest Country Club, in Beverly Hills, but despite the 1 A.M. hour, on the heels of a dream benefit bill that included almost everybody of any stature in Coast film and radio circles, Jolson came on and held them glued for over an hour with a memorable one-man cavalcade. That was the convincer to prexy Harry Cohn of Columbia Pictures, and *The Jolson Story* went into production.

lee de forest's phonofilms   Hollywood was shown that it could become articulate, if it chose, by Dr. Lee de Forest on April 15, 1923. Variety carried an ad on De Forest Phonofilms— "films that actually talk and reproduce music without the use of phonographs." The first sound-on-film feature was inaugurated at the Rivoli in New York. De Forest's pioneer stars included Weber & Fields, Sissle & Blake, Phil Baker, Eddie Cantor, Eva Puck & Sammy White, and Conchita Piquir.

Experiments kept perfecting the new technique, until it was ready for commercial adoption by Hollywood in 1925. But Hollywood didn't want it—for the same reason that radio was at first reluctant about becoming godfather to television. (And, as at this writing, the motion picture industry is ignoring Phonevision, or any other proposal to telecast topflight new film product into the home —for a fee—for fear of going into competition with their old customers, some 18,000 exhibitors.)

Inarticulate Hollywood, and silent film exhibitors, were all prosperous. Why rock the boat? What would happen to millions of dollars worth of silent equipment in the studios? What about the tremendous investments required to wire theatres for sound? What would happen to the class theatres with expensive orchestras and stage shows, if any jerk-water movie joint was to be able to give its patrons gorgeous feasts of music via the screen?

The major studios refused to touch the newfangled contraption for fear of bringing down the entire industry in chaotic ruins. But Samuel L. Warner was intrigued by the possibilities of the talkie. Here, he knew, was a magnificent risk—one which, if successful, could put the tiny Warner Bros. company on the very top of the movie heap.

He convinced his brothers, Harry, Albert and Jack, and Warner money was thrown into experimental work. By April 1926, the iron was hot, and the Warners formed the Vitaphone Corp., entering into a license agreement with Western Electric. Then on August 6, 1926, the Warners took the wraps off with the premiere of John

Barrymore in *Don Juan,* with synchronized music, and a program of Vitaphone shorts, demonstrating talkies, with a speech by Will Hays; music by the New York Philharmonic Orchestra, Mischa Elman, Efrem Zimbalist and Harry Bauer; and songs by the Metropolitan's Giovanni Martinelli, Marion Talley and Anna Case.

The *Don Juan* program, apart from the 127 kisses bestowed in the film by Barrymore, created a furore of excitement throughout show business, as well as among the public. Many regarded the new development as absolute magic. "No closer approach to resurrection," declared Professor Michael I. Pupin of Columbia University, "has ever been made by science."

Alarmed enemies of the talkies rushed to the attack. "I don't think," scoffed William Fox, "that there will ever be the much-dreamed-of talking pictures on a large scale. To have conversation would strain the eyesight and the sense of hearing at once, taking away the restfulness one gets from viewing pictures alone." Another film tycoon predicted extinction for the talkers "because sound will keep movie fans awake—they come in to relax and, maybe, catch a nap!"

warners force exhibs into wiring   But nothing could stop the jubilant Warners—not even the reluctance of theatre owners to wire their houses for sound at a cost of $16,000 to $25,000 apiece. The Warners simply dug down into their own pockets and footed the wiring bill in key cities such as Chicago, Boston, St. Louis, Philadelphia, Hollywood and Detroit on the theory that these would be enough to whip up a popular demand to force theatres into wiring.

Keeping three Vitaphone shows running in New York during 1926, the Warners then started dickering with Jolson for their next smash hit. Meanwhile, in January 1927, Fox did a hasty flip-flop and came up with a new process called Movietone, which he showcased in talking shorts billed with *What Price Glory.* In March 1927, Variety began reviewing Vitaphone and Movietone as complete shows.

Fox, now an eager-beaver and believer, offered the first sound Movietone News at the Roxy in April 1927, showing West Point cadets parading. By June, Roxy audiences heard President Coolidge greet Lindbergh in Washington. While on the Vitaphone end, a

milestone was chalked up with the first case of talkie censorship—
rubbing out some words in songs by Winnie Lightner. In September
Fox scored another scoop by taking three days to "shoot" Mussolini, who declared in English via Movietone that "this can bring the
world together and end war!" (*Sic.*)

During this historic year of re-birth for films, death came at the
age of 40 to the man who had made the future of Hollywood possible—Sam Warner.

The confusion of the movie industry during 1928 was almost in-
describable. It was now conceded that the die was cast—everything
had to go vocal or go under. Wall Street flooded the West Coast
with $300,000,000 in new capital to finance the sound revolution that
nothing could stop. It was found to cost $7,500 to vocalize shorts;
from $15,000 to $25,000 apiece for features.

Financial mergers took place with breathtaking speed. Fox swallowed the Poli circuit. RCA took over the Keith-Albee-Orpheum
theatres, and FBO as its studio. It also introduced a third talkie
process—RCA Photophone, which it demonstrated in October with
the FBO feature, *The Perfect Crime.*

Everyone in Hollywood was busy scrambling to learn how to go
vocal to save his or her job. As *Variety's* iconoclastic reporter observed under a headline: THE GREAT HOLLYWOOD PANIC—"They're all
trying to chisel an angle that will save that pink swimming pool
and Hispano-Suiza. Actors . . . are ruining all the house parties reciting 'The Blue Velvet Band' or 'Gungha Din.' Writers who
couldn't write a prolog for an acrobat are cracking about the stuff
they used to write for the speaking stage, and directors who couldn't
find their way around backstage without a guide are screaming
about 'When I was putting on stuff for the Theatre Guild' and 'I'll
never forget that summer of stock I produced at the Pratt Falls opera
house . . .' "

early talkies   Film studios began a frantic hunt for legitimate stage stars to replace at least a third of their stars whose voices
left much to be desired. An electric sign could have lighted on the
voltage generated between East and West Coast stars.

With the studios busily reconverting, talking shorts constituted
the bulk of soundfilms of 1928, during which only 1,000 out of 18,000
movie houses were able to wire for sound. Warner Bros. and Fox

turned out the bulk of the shorts, signing up for one and two week salaries what name stars from vaudeville they could enlist, including Chic Sale and Clark & McCullough. Vaudevillians quickly realized, however, that they were hurting themselves by doing their regular acts for Vitaphone, so they refused to appear except with special, substitute material. Norma Talmadge utilized Vitaphone to substitute for a personal appearance scheduled at the opening of Stanley-Fabian Theatre in Jersey City.

Air Circus, with Louise Dresser, David Rollins, Arthur Lake and Sue Carol (now Mrs. Alan Ladd), was the first full-length Fox Film (September 1928) to contain dialog sequences—a solid 15 minutes of talk; the rest with sound synchronization.

The first 100 per cent all-talker opened at the Broadway Strand in July—Warner Bros.' *Lights of New York,* produced by Bryan Foy for under $100,000, in seven reels, with Dolores Costello and Cullen Landis. It garnered over $2,000,000 profit. That month Variety ran a full-page ad urging all show people to advertise themselves, or what they had, in Variety, because "IT'S ALL-TALKING PICTURES NOW—throughout the entire show business of this country!"

By 1929 Hollywood had made the switchover. In January, Fox came out with its first all-talkie, *In Old Arizona,* with Warner Baxter. M.G.M. launched the first musical comedy in sound, *The Broadway Melody,* a smash hit which cost $250,000. Paramount had another scream musical, *The Cocoanuts,* featuring the first movie appearance of the Marx Bros. Tiffany-Stahl made the musical grade with George Jessel in *Lucky Boy,* singing "My Mother's Eyes."

Music was in the air—and on the soundtrack. Studios began backing Broadway musicals as the cheapest way to secure screen rights. Warners went through the back door and bought up the Harms, Remick and Witmark music publishing interests, not stopping until it had $10,000,000 worth of music in their laps.

New stars were born, old ones passed into oblivion. Harold Lloyd, now a multimillionaire, shrugged, retired and installed sound equipment in the projection room of his home for his personal enjoyment. Hollywood wondered, "What about Chaplin?"—and Chaplin wasn't talking. Lon Chaney refused to appear in talkies because he claimed he couldn't change his voice with every make-up. John Gilbert, whose voice was a horrible letdown from the romantic figure he presented, was finished.

But Will Rogers made his first talkie for Fox—*They Had to See Paris*. It was a hit. Paul Muni went vocal for Columbia with *Song of Love*. Muni was a hit. Gloria Swanson spoke and sang in *The Trespasser*. Not such a hit, and Gloria strolled slowly toward the studio exit. (Not until 1950 was she to reimpress cinematically with her comeback film, *Sunset Boulevard,* from which she segued into renewed prominence in a legit revival of *20th Century,* her own radio and TV shows, a fashion line, and a 1951 legit starring vehicle.)

Hollywood had heeded the voice of the future.

31

Here Lies Vaudeville

★

Vaudeville in 1919 had resolved itself into a tug-of-war between big time and small time. Big time was the Keith-Orpheum Circuit, reorganized with $50,000,000 capital, charging $1 top and higher. In the case of the star showplace in its diadem, the Palace in New York, the scale was a challenging $2 top on weekdays.

Small time was the Marcus Loew Circuit, recapitalized with $100,000,000, at a 50¢ top. At first the two circuits were not precisely opposition to one another. Keith vaudeville was aimed at a class audience—the kind that went to Broadway plays. Loew vaudeville was machine-built for a mass audience—the kind that wanted their money's worth with a movie *and* "some acts." Marcus Loew's credo was "a low price so the entire family could go."

Keith vaudeville, now led by E. F. Albee, was still undisputed kingpin in 1919, with the Palace the nation's leading vaudeville money-maker. The United Booking Office, first organized in 1908, was changed to the B. F. Keith Vaudeville Exchange, as both a commemorative gesture and claim of supremacy.

Two theatre openings in 1919 announced a completely new trend which was to dominate all of the 1920s—theatre show places as dazzling as anything they could hope to put on the stage. The State-Lake Theatre in Chicago was the first, opening with popular-priced vaudeville and grossing better than $20,000 a week for months afterward.

New York's reply was the Capitol Theatre—5,300 seats making it the world's largest theatre of 1919, at a cost of $3,000,000. It opened with the film, *His Majesty the American,* starring Douglas Fairbanks, and a stage show that included Arthur Pryor's 70-man band and a glittering Ned Wayburn stage production with a cast of 50.

By the following year the rush to build showplaces was so pronounced that there was a public outcry against it. Organizations demanded that theatre building be banned, along with all other kind of building, except that of homes. There was, it seems, a postwar housing shortage with which a later generation was to become similarly familiar.

Toward the end of 1920, grosses at straight vaudeville houses began to sag badly. Some managers blamed the high cost of living and fear of depression. Others said it was movie and popular-priced competition. Still others said it was a surfeit of revue bills—silk curtains and gowns, and sow's-ear material. Even the houses that played both pictures and vaudeville were beginning to complain.

By 1921 many theatres that had previously played both dropped vaudeville, offering films alone, or with only one feature act. Whatever their previous policy, fully 25 per cent of all theatres changed it to something else, at the expense of vaudeville. A Variety survey showed 12,000 vaudeville acts idle.

As antidote to the bad business, the showmanship-minded manager of Loew's State, Oakland, California, distributed blue medicine bottles labeled "State Remedy" to the public. He prescribed visits to the State "twice weekly—every week faithfully—for men, women and children who need a pleasant tonic."

birth of the 'state-lake policy'   The Orpheum Circuit, its frock coat a trifle threadbare, introduced the four-a-day, or "State-Lake policy," into many of its aristocratic two-a-day strongholds, at reduced prices. The new vaude policy was definitely headed for larger audience capacity, popular prices, and several shows daily.

To augment the new decision, Keith's opened the Palace in Cleveland, dubbing it "the finest theatre in the world." Special trains brought the press to the opening from other cities. Not long afterward came the Albee in Brooklyn, and the New York Hippodrome and Keith's Memorial, Boston.

By 1924, the State-Lake, Chicago, showed an annual profit of $600,-000 to $700,000, earned from 18,000,000 tickets sold during its five-year existence. The Hipp in New York was clicking $50,000 a week, the biggest vaudeville boxoffice up to that date, and never sinking below a $35,000 week.

Steam shovels went into action in 1925 for new super-theatres in which the emphasis would be definitely and emphatically films, with support from elaborate stage shows. Arthur Sawyer and Herbert Lubin, promoters with Chicago capital, paid $2,000,000 for a car-barn at 51st Street and 7th Avenue, New York City. From the ashes of the carbarn was to rise the spectacular Roxy Theatre. Destruction was begun on the famous Shanley's in the Putnam Building—to make way for the equally palace-like Paramount. "Roxy service," "cathedrals of the cinema," "picture palaces" became catchphrases in and out of the trade.

By 1925 straight vaudeville was tottering, shoved on one side by the great new show houses, on the other by the popular-priced movie theatres, many of which were now being swamped by acts deserting the sinking ship of the Orpheum Circuit. As more and more vaudeville houses went pix, vaudevillians were reduced to bookings in only about 100 independent theatres. These theatres booked acts through agents for so little money that they were known as C. & C. —the Coffee and Cake circuit. The curtain was falling fast on vaudeville.

1926 was the two-a-day's big year of disaster. By December, 97 per cent of all theatres were film houses, with only 100 of these charging above an 85¢ scale. The other 3 per cent were legit, burlesque and vaudeville theatres. The day of bigtime vaudeville was definitely over. In the whole nation of 70,000,000 Americans, there were only six bigtime vaudeville theatres in the East, and another six scattered throughout the country. What was left of vaudeville was now in tattered circumstances. The two-a-day had become "continuous performance"—which was the status vaudeville had reached fully 30 years before.

'variety' makes pix the no. 1 dept.   The signs of what was happening were unmistakable. Variety moved its film news to the front of the paper on April 28, 1926, as vaudeville news was moved into the balcony section and curtailed. Big-name vaudeville acts were now giving first call to the film houses, 100 of which used vaude "as support" in New York. Marcus Loew, who now paid more for his acts than the bigtime vaudeville houses were able to offer, stated flatly, "It's the film that draws 'em, and the vaudeville that fills in."

Wherever the film theatre met the vaudeville house in open competition, Hollywood's celluloid scored a solid victory. Even the haughty Palace took an unmerciful drubbing, and was forced to cut salaries of all employees and lay off a number of them. It also fired the sidewalk patrol it had used to keep an eye on speculators hawking Palace tickets, because speculators no longer bothered about the Palace.

None of the Palace guard would admit it, of course, but all of show business knew that the film theatre men—headed by Marcus Loew and his magic formula of popular-priced films-plus-vaude— had signed the death warrant of the bigtime theatre men by surpassing them in value, entertainment, theatres and showmanship.

Violent upheavals took place backstage of the big time. Keith-Albee and Orpheum merged to become the Keith-Albee-Orpheum Circuit. Now watching every move made by Loew, who had bought up Metro to unify his growing empire, K-A-O grabbed Pathe and F.B.O., forming Radio Pictures. E. F. Albee, now old and tired, withdrew from the organization. Confusion reigned as banking syndicates took over. When the smoke cleared away, K-A-O and Radio Pictures found themselves inexplicably in the hands of the electrics, which had slipped into show business through back-door control of radio and talkie patents. The following year, Keith-Albee-Orpheum issued stock for $35,000,000, with Albee holding $5,000,000 and Mrs. Caroline Kohl (& Castle, Chi theatre interests) holding half that amount.

beginning of the end   But no amount of backstage reshuffling could save the big time. In 1927 the comparison between what straight vaudeville houses had to offer, compared to the film theatres, was ludicrous, if not pathetic. The two-a-day gave only 14 shows a week—and poor ones—at prices of $1.25 to $3.30. The film houses gave 30 shows a week—and excellent ones, by standards of those days—at prices of 50¢–60¢–75¢–99¢.

The two-a-day was openly desperate. The Capitol announced it was beginning stage shows—the Palace put an electric piano in its lobby. The Cleveland Palace put a Ford car on the bill as a head-liner, offering it for the best essay of 500 words to explain why the new Ford and Keith-Albee vaudeville were "great achievements." And with the Riverside going into "continuous performance," the end of 1927 saw the Palace the only bigtime, two-a-day vaudeville theatre left in New York City.

What vaudeville remained on Keith-Albee-Orpheum in 1928 was merely window dressing to bolster a last hopeless attempt at pres-tige, or at least face-saving. The flood of talking short subjects, which were really screened vaudeville acts, narrowed the field for vaudevillians still further, particularly on the Loew Circuit. There was, nevertheless, a surprising resistance to this trend by movie house audiences, which suddenly began to feel cheated when man-agers failed to back films with stage talent. The film-stage show combination did the best business of all.

The entrance of radio interests into Keith-Orpheum pumped new blood into an almost-dead organization. Now tied into one complex bundle, renamed Radio-Keith-Orpheum, or RKO, were the Radio Corp. of America, the Keith-Orpheum Circuit, F.B.O. Pictures, RCA Photophone (talkie equipment), Victor Records, and the Na-tional Broadcasting Co.

The old Keith-Albee sign was lowered from the Palace, signalizing that the king was dead—long live the new king, RKO. Ironically, for the first time there was room on the Palace sign for the names of stars which had made it the hall of vaudeville fame it once had been. The first names ever to go up in lights at the Palace were those of Fanny Brice, Al Trahan and Fowler & Tamara.

The end came with bitter speed in 1928, despite RKO's purchase of the six Pantages theatres on the West Coast for $3,750,000, and the 12 Proctor houses in the East for $8,000,000. There were only four theatres left in the whole nation offering vaudeville without films—New York's Palace, Keith's Philadelphia, Chicago's Palace and Los Angeles' Orpheum. Alabama won the distinction of being the first state to be without a single theatre showing vaudeville.

National Vaudeville Artists (N.V.A.), the once-powerful company union Ed Albee had created to break the White Rats, now passed into the hands of film interests, in a move sponsored by William Fox. Symbolically, the new president of the N.V.A. was an actor who had been a great vaudeville star and was now rising to new fame in Hollywood—Eddie Cantor.

On March 10, 1929, the greatest and prominent exponent of the big time, the two-a-day—the New York Palace—quietly began three-a-day Sunday performances.

the shubert vaudeville debacle   The most sensational vaudeville clash of the 1920s came in the early part of the decade, as the unexpected renewal of an ancient feud that had slumbered for a decade. In 1921 the 10-year agreement signed between Keith on one hand, and Klaw & Erlanger and the Shuberts on the other, expired. This agreement had pledged that the Klaw & Erlanger and Shubert interests, which had inspired "Advanced Vaudeville" in 1911, would keep out of vaudeville for 10 years.

Now Lee Shubert rubbed his chin thoughtfully. Why not pull the same stunt that had worked so well before? He told his brother J. J. that if they started Shubert Vaudeville, they should be able to sell out to the exasperated Keith circuit for $2,000,000—at the very least, $1,000,000. Jake Shubert, whom Variety described as knowing "more about vaudeville than Lee has ever found out," refused to have anything to do with the scheme.

Lee Shubert went ahead on his own. Utilizing Shubert-owned theatres, he introduced the "Shubert Advanced Vaudeville Circuit" and started a wholesale raid on the Keith star stable, offering heavier salaries and hints that the new circuit was a golden route into Shubert musical comedies.

At first Shubert started with straight bigtime vaudeville, in imitation of Keith's. Later in the year, he changed his presentations to "unit shows," or abridged musicals and revues. These made a serious dent at Keith box offices. Despite an increasing number of acts deserting to Shubert, Albee not only refused to meet Shubert salary offers, but actually slashed Keith salaries. Albee believed that the postwar inflation, and imminent depression, called for retrenchment, not further inflation.

More and more acts flocked to Shubert in retaliation. The Shubert shows, growing more elaborate, were costing from $15,000 to $20,000 a unit to produce. Shrewdly, Lee Shubert hedged on his venture by booking the unit shows to play the American and Columbia burlesque circuits, at weekly guarantees.

Meanwhile Albee, in an effort to stem the landslide of acts jumping on the Shubert bandwagon, offered long-term contracts with clauses guaranteeing special publicity and exploitation. He also began to develop his own acts, under ironclad contracts, to replace defections in his ranks.

No offer to buy out the raider issued from grim-lipped Keith officials, to the chagrin of Lee Shubert. Albee sat tight, waiting for that to materialize which was obvious to him. The Shubert unit shows, weighed down by extravagant salary and production costs, were bound to operate in the red. And they did, to the dismay of the American Burlesque Association, which found that it had jumped on the saddle of a white elephant and couldn't get off. Lee Shubert smiled dryly and shrugged—the burlesque houses were having b.o. trouble but he was sure of his weekly guarantees.

In the wake of the flop of Shubert's vaudeville policy, producers went broke, "some into bankruptcy and some into their graves," Variety charged. Hundreds of aggrieved actors were left stranded, cursing the Shubert misadventure and casting piteous glances in the direction of old man Albee.

Chuckling, officials of the Keith and Orpheum circuits agreed to take back their black sheep—on one condition. Each would have to insert an ad in Variety, stating his or her experiences with Shubert vaudeville, apologizing for playing the circuit, and advising other acts not to make the same mistake. Outraged and furious, Lee Shubert demanded that Variety reject these ads.

Variety refused. Shubert hesitated, then sent word that if Variety would reject the ads, and tell him each time it refused one, he would pay Variety the cost of each ad. *Sime* refused again. Shubert barred Variety from all its offices and theatres—exactly as Keith-Albee had done not too many years before.

By 1923, the Shubert Advanced Vaudeville Circuit was abandoned —unloved and unmourned—with the loss of $1,500,000, borne mostly by burlesque producers. Many acts had to sue for their salaries. A good many came back to the Keith and Orpheum circuits via the public apology route, while others had to sign up with smalltime independent circuits at bread-and-butter salaries.

In August 1923, Variety read the funeral oration of Shubert Vaudeville in a biting open letter to Lee Shubert from the editor: "They are asking us, Lee, where Shubert Vaudeville is, and Lee, we don't know. . . . You said there would be Shubert vaudeville while you had a dollar left. It's a horrible thought, Lee, that you might be broke, but don't you remember, Lee, you gave your word of honor on it. So you either haven't any money or any honor left. . . ."

albee's ban on niteries and radio   Although Albee scored a signal triumph over Lee Shubert's abortive opposition vaudeville try, he had his hands full for the rest of the era against genuine opposition to bigtime vaudeville. At first Albee felt reasonably secure against Marcus Loew since he felt their two circuits were appealing to different levels of audiences. When Loew's State opened in 1921, Albee generously sent the Keith Boys Band to the front of the theatre to serenade the occasion.

But one year later this musical good-neighbor policy developed a few sour notes. Keith actors were forbidden to play in movie houses, which were now declared "opposition." Any actor who disobeyed the edict was considered guilty of violating his contract. And as part of Albee's new get-tough policy, Keith artists were also forbidden to appear on any radio program.

The next blacklist issued against opposition was imposed on any acts of 1925 which played for Earl Carroll on Sundays. The following year cabaret acts were barred from the Keith Circuit, but the edict had to be rescinded as the inroads made by Loew made it tough to get headliners. Keith also, reluctantly, lifted the ban on radio, since almost every star in show business was getting his or her feet wet in the new medium.

Albee felt helpless against the new threat of super-vaudeville presented on Vitaphone's second program at the Colony Theatre. The $40,000 bill included shorts with Al Jolson, Elsie Janis, George Jessel, Willie and Eugene Howard, and the New York Philharmonic Orchestra—*plus* a full-length film, *The Better 'Ole*. That was opposition, plus!

two who never played the palace   About the only two famous actors who never played the Palace were Al Jolson and George M. Cohan. The reason they never did was because preparing for the Palace took too much energy, and if an an actor flopped—well, it took everybody in show business a long time to forget a flop at the Palace. Not that Jolson or Cohan need have worried on that score.

But stars were the lifeblood of the old Palace bills. Once, in 1922, someone in the management got the bright idea of running a show without a single headliner, featuring nobody. It was an outstanding flop. Vaudeville without stars was like Amos without Andy.

Although this was the last, and dying, decade of vaudeville, there were still plenty of stars shining on the bigtime. Fred Allen was on the Pantages Circuit in 1919, albeit as a juggler. Three years later he was playing a Sunday performance at the Winter Garden. When he couldn't be heard beyond the fifth row, the audience started clapping in rhythm. Allen walked off the stage. When the audience forced him to come back by yelling for him, Allen told them, "Sorry you didn't like me this time." And he promptly walked off again.

An actor named Ben K. Benny was disturbed in 1920 because his name was too similar to that of bandleader Ben Bernie. So he advertised in Variety that henceforth he would be known as Jack Benny. The new nomenclature seemed fortunate, because by 1927 Jack Benny was master of ceremonies at the Palace, and was held over for three weeks in that capacity at the Los Angeles Orpheum.

The first theatrical ad to break into the select *Christian Science Monitor* was placed by William Morris, to advertise the Harry Lauder show. Lauder was as great in the twenties as he was during the two preceding decades. In 1923 he smashed all records at the Boston Opera House with a $38,000 gross. His name was still such magic in 1926 that Keith, in one of its Western houses, billed "Harry Lauder"—and in smaller type beneath, "Namesake and nephew of FAVORITE SCOTS COMEDIAN."

Among the brightest lights of 1921 were the team of Gallagher & Shean ("Absolutely, Mr. Gallagher? Positively, Mr. Shean!") Their imitators became so numerous that the Keith office was compelled to issue orders limiting bills to only one Gallagher & Shean imitation. By 1923 the vogue was so widespread that it was a stock bit with all jazz bands, rendering the imitation with two instruments. In 1925, as so often happens to teams made uncomfortable in double-harness by success, Ed Gallagher and Al Shean went separate ways.

In its drive for headliners, vaudeville made actors out of those who made headlines. In 1921 Babe Ruth was booked with Wellington Cross in a vaudeville act, striking out at the boxoffice, unlike the filmed story of his life 27 years later. Swimmers of the English Channel commanded a good salary until vaudeville was flooded with them. Loew offered Gertrude Ederle $100,000 for 20 weeks, then withdrew the offer when Mlle. Gade and Ernest Vierkotte repeated the stunt and minimized its value. Miss Ederle nevertheless appeared at the Philadelphia Sesqui-Centennial in 1926, earning $10,000 on a percentage basis.

Gus Sun, the No. 1 smalltime impresario, broke in the acts of Jack Dempsey and Gene Tunney in 1926. Tunney's cold personality made him poor b.o., compared to the grinning and earthy Manassa Mauler.

Mae West turned up at the Colonial, New York, in 1922, and was reviewed by *Sime* who reported, "No dancing in the present act. It's clean as a whistle and good. It can play anywhere and will entertain anywhere. Harry Richman at the piano. The years Mae West wasted!" This, a few short years before Miss West's sex shows involved her with the law.

Eva Tanguay, the I-Don't-Care girl, broke Loew's State (New York) record in 1922 with a $29,000 take at 50¢ top. This landed her at the Palace later that season at a $3 top.

In 1923 the Jefferson Theatre on 14th Street, New York, offered Pilcer & Douglas, a vaudeville act assisted by a tango dancer who dressed à la Valentino—George Raft. The following year Chester Morris appeared at the Palace in a family skit, "All the Horrors of Home." The year was also notable for the introduction of Robert Benchley at the Palace, delivering his famous "Treasurer's Report."

Other stars were ringing up records at the new movie palaces. Julian Eltinge set a record for all picture theatres in 1924 by grossing $40,000 for Grauman's Metropolitan in Los Angeles. This was topped the following year there by Gilda Gray, who shimmied the customers out of $45,000 (her share over $14,000)—during Holy Week.

In the East, in 1925, Loew's Capitol on Broadway was offering Roxy's Gang onstage, later to become Major Bowes' Gang. Edward

J. Bowes succeeded S. L. Rothafel (Roxy) as managing director of that theatre. Roxy subsequently lent his name to the famed showplace on 50th Street and 7th Avenue, renowned for its "Roxy ushers" and "Roxy service," and of course in later years he opened the Radio City Music Hall and the Center Theatre, both with rather tragic results.

The Palace had an all-English bill, and then an almost all-femme bill that included Marie Dressler, Cissie Loftus, Marie Cahill, May Irwin and Yvette Rugel. Dressler & Loftus teamed for good measure as a sister act, wowing them with such "fast" material as: "She never married, did she?" . . . "No, her children wouldn't let her."

One bill also was to have included Weber & Fields, but for the first time in their careers the team failed to appear, pleading illness. The real reason was that Weber & Fields had been billed second to Marie Dressler, once a member of their own troupe.

The Palace of 1926 offered Ethel Barrymore in Sir James Barrie's *Twelve Pound Look*. Variety's Jack Lait described the act as "Sir James Barrie moralizing and our first actress Barrymorealizing." In that year Borrah Minevitch organized 32 small fry (contest winners in various theatres) into the first professional harmonica troupe, asking $3,000 a week for the Minevitch Harmonica Rascals from the picture theatres.

In 1927 the movie palaces were definitely first choice with the stars. Gertrude Lawrence, doing five-a-day at the Paramount, collected $3,500 a week. Another Paramount draw was Ruth Etting, quondam Ziegfeld chirper, backed by the Paul Whiteman band. (Miss Etting made an abortive "comeback" 20 years later via a radio buildup and some sporadic nitery engagements.) Elinor Glyn packed them in at Loew's State, New York, even if she didn't stay "Three Weeks."

Jolson, of course, towered above them all, earning $17,000 a week at the Los Angeles Metropolitan, on a percentage split. In St. Louis, his personal appearance brought him $16,500. San Francisco's Warfield Theatre, two years later, reported that Jolson had smashed house records with a $57,000 gross.

In 1927 the desperate Palace threw in its first Mistress of Ceremonies to hold the line, Florence Moore. They gave Clayton, Jackson & Durante their first booking—but only after the boys had made their vaude debut at Loew's State, a block away. And in 1928 the

Palace booked Sally Rand, with a company of nine. Her specialty then was toe dancing, no fans. Variety commented, "Too much legs on the gal."

That year the picture theatres showed how things stood by shelling out $7,500 a week, plus a 50-50 split over $24,000, for the Duncan Sisters, Rosetta and Vivian, alias "Topsy and Eva."

Two new stars were making their way in 1929. Kate Smith, already on Velvet Tone Records and Vitaphone shorts, was playing the Loew's movie palaces. Rudy Vallee and His Connecticut Yankees were showcasing their talents at Keith's 81st Street, New York City.

Although all of show business knew that the days of the Palace were numbered, it was still a source of pride to Al Trahan, a piano-playing comedian, that he was booked there. He paid $1,500 to announce the fact by having it sky-written over Broadway.

As picture palace magnates smiled and shook their heads.

band craze   The styles and trends of vaudeville in the 1920s changed with ever-increasing tempo. In 1919, acts tended to be pretentious, carrying their own sets, curtains, drops and, of course, wardrobes. By the following year even the acrobats were wearing evening clothes. There was a general feeling among vaudevillians that if your act had "class," it would rate more money as well as better position on the bill. So they "dressed" their acts.

The effect of this sartorial vaudeville was so stultifying that managers were grateful to singers who livened it up with offcolor songs, despite the dangerous effect this had on the family trade, backbone of vaudeville.

One of the earliest intimations of the band craze that was to hit vaudeville so hard came in 1920 with a band composed, oddly, of House of David musicians organized by Ernie Young, a Chicago agent. Variety ran Young's ad which reprinted the paper's nose-holding reviews, and added: "For two consecutive weeks 'my pal *Sime*' has seen fit to pan my act. All I can say in reply is that I will wager a doughnut to a safety pin he doesn't know music when he hears it. If, after a week's rehearsal, *Sime* is able to sing the chorus of 'Dardenella,' I will give $50 to charity. P.S.—What's the difference between a critic and an old egg? None! They're both rotten!"

The band craze swept through vaudeville in 1921, replacing the

Shimmy and jazz dancing which had held sway. Henry Santry started the vogue by coming east with his band of "jazz musicians." Paul Whiteman and his band was next onstage, at the Palace, for a run of several weeks. Soon bigtime, smalltime and neighborhood houses were flooded with band acts. At least 17 vaudeville acts replaced their piano players with their own bands as accompaniment. Proctor's Fifth Avenue began Amateur Jazz Band Contests.

The trend was still going strong in 1922, but the widespread sale of jazz records soon hurt the appeal of live bands at the boxoffice. Bands were their own worst enemies, as well, through their lack of originality. Audiences quickly tired of hearing the same music played the same way by bands with different faces. The bands which survived 1923 as headliners were those with distinctive styles, special arrangements, and band specialties.

Waring's Pennsylvanians made their New York debut at the Strand Theatre in 1924, when there were 60 bands in vaudeville. No band, however, could achieve the lofty status of Paul Whiteman's organization, which was paid $7,500 for a week at the Hippodrome, a new high in vaudeville up to that time. Whiteman turned down a guarantee of $1,000,000 for a three-year contract to play the picture houses, stating he feared this would hurt his concert road tours. He was getting $9,000 a week in picture houses by the end of 1925. Two years later he was still playing the movie theatres for $12,000 a week, with all transportation paid for himself and his 33 melodians. Waring, who with Ted Lewis and Vincent Lopez, and of course Whiteman, have outlasted many of their earlier contemporaries, is now payrolled at $20,000 a week on television.

A new idea in vaude was introduced in 1921, when Phil Baker and Aileen Stanley, single acts on the same bill, joined to do a double act later in the bill. This idea was copied by many singles, and was highly popular with managers for obvious economic reasons.

Throughout the decade, copyists were as great a plague to original artists as ever. Let one act click with a fresh approach, and it was mirrored by 100 other acts before the week was out. Any act which left vaudeville for musical comedy was certain to be replaced by a carbon copy within 24 hours.

gag-lifters—again   In later years, with the widespread impetus of radio, plus the syndicated Broadway columns going in for quips "credited" to this or that comedian—but, at the same time, dissipating freshness of the *bon mots*—this became a truly grave problem. Radio's lush salaries, however, permitted fun factories to be kept richly boiling. But in the relatively parlous vaude days, bits and comedy were jealously guarded.

The Vaudeville Managers Protective Assn. officiated as arbiter ofttimes over "lifted" material. Both the NVA and Variety's Protected Material Dept. were repositories of original scripts. But the best "insurance" in those days were the stagehands whose sense of fair play frequently assumed vigilante proportions. An act coming to the 105th St., Cleveland, for example with a bit of a routine previously done by another was told to "lay off." If the copyist persisted, scenery would suddenly get in his way. For the convincer, backstage sandbags might suddenly drop too close for comfort until the act "got the idea" that even the stage crews didn't like a poacher.

The dress-up trend of "tony" vaudeville died dismally about 1924, when oversized shoes began to outnumber tuxedos. The change became pronounced as admission prices (in the movie theatres) dropped the cost of vaudeville, attracting a less class-conscious audience. The acoustics of the movie palaces also called for a broader type of comedy, with emphasis on visual slapstick.

In 1926, possibly as a reaction to an overdose of the Roaring Twenties, the old-fashioned virtues of Americana came in for a brief play. New England theatres witnessed a wholesale revival of oldtimers onstage in spelling bees, amateur nights, country store nights, woodchopping contests, marble-shooting, jackknife flipping, pie-eating, and fireman's balls—red shirts and all. Even the lofty Palace featured a Country Store, with hams and groceries to lucky ticket-holders. Henry Ford's favorite, Mellie (Dunham) the Fiddler, started a craze for old-time fiddlers. And there was a revival of old-time song slides in many neighborhood theatres, as well as by organists in the movie palaces. All this nice, gentle nostalgia in the year of the Halls-Mills murder case, the Charleston and the hysterical funeral of Rudolph Valentino.

bluenose stuff   Keith's led the blue-pencil brigade of vaudeville for most of the Twenties. In 1921 songs with the expressions, "hot dog," "that's the cat's meow," "the cat's pyjamas" and "hot cat" were axed out of acts as too vulgar. In 1922, by special request from the new czar of Hollywood, no cracks were allowed to be made about Will Hays. Prohibition was another forbidden word on vaudeville stages that year.

The clammy hand of Federal censorship reached into vaudeville in 1922, stopping an act called "The Sailor and Yeoman," featuring Fields & Harrington. "Discouraged recruiting," the Government complained. The act was forced to cancel in Buffalo.

In 1924 the Palace barred bare legs, and more than two curtain bows or speeches. The following year the scissors snipped hells, damns, Gods, references to red neckties, Kip Rhinelander, cops and the Klu Klux Klan. Jack Benny was forced to slash the line, "I took my girl to see *Ladies of the Evening,* so now we can speak freely." Loew's Circuit contented itself with rejecting Maurice Costello in a skit called "The Battle," because it dealt with dope.

Blackouts came into vogue in 1926, to punctuate sexy punchlines or suggestive stage business, and allow audiences to blush in the dark. That year the Palace added to its taboos by barring drum rolls and spotlights because, Albee explained, there was already too much noise and glare in vaudeville theatres.

By 1929, with vaude coasting speedily downhill, the reins became lax and "blue stuff" was given its head. Beatrice Lillie sang a Noel Coward song, "World Weary," at the Palace which finished, "I see the same goddam faces!"

Nobody slapped Lady Peel's wrist.

The times were never too Elysian for vaudeville actors, even at their best in the early years of the decade. By 1924, the band craze and the film theatres were causing a layoff of 1,000 acts a week. A recession of film production on the Coast threw more headline and feature acts into the Eastern vaudeville hopper.

the borscht belt   There was slight consolation in the opening of a new field for actors—summer camps, called the "Borscht Circuit" because of the popularity of this Russian dish among guests. Actors were paid $200 to $500 a season, with board, for putting on amateur shows, concerts, readings, debates and minstrels. The Borscht Circuit was to serve as a springboard for many distinguished Broadway, Hollywood and radio talents.

Distinguished alumni of the Borscht Belt include MGM production chief Dore Schary, Van Johnson, Danny Kaye, John Garfield; producers Don Hartman, Max Liebman, Vincent Sherman, Robert Gordon, Herb Polesie, Jerome Robbins; playwrights Moss Hart, Clifford Odets; librettists Morrie Ryskind and E. Y. (Yip) Harburg; comedians Sid Caesar, Phil Silvers, Jackie Miles, Red Buttons; songsmith Sylvia Fine (Mrs. Danny Kaye), actors George Macready, Pat Duggan, agent Harold Hecht (producer-partner now of Burt Lancaster), Anita Alvarez, Mati & Hari, and others.

In 1925 vaude actors were looking for employment on new types of stages, and found it. The Edison Lamp Works at Newark and Harrison, New Jersey, each booked acts for 20 minutes of vaudeville every other day, to entertain employees at noon hours. On alternate days they had bands for dancing. This idea for big factory morale found its echo 17 years later in another wartime America.

Things looked up in 1926, when the expanding vaudeville departments of the picture theatres, plus cabarets and night clubs, absorbed many of the vaudevillians crowded out by the dwindling vaude circuits. But far from the majority of them. An N.V.A. census of 1927 showed only 300 of 2,000 standard acts receiving regular bookings; 500 always laying off; another 500 acts abandoned. Yet this was the year that the Palace, unable to get headliners, was holding attractions over and going in for repeat bookings. Those actors who were booked in vaudeville played with their eyes on radio and their hearts in Hollywood. Worried Keith-Albee-Orpheum interests were handing out three-year contracts, with slight raises each year, to keep K-A-O acts from leaping off to greener pastures.

By 1929 less than 1,500 out of 6,000 vaudeville acts were working. "No longer can a couple of hoofers expect $400 for the No. 2 spot," Variety reported, "nor the bunk and punk flash act ask $1,200." And just ahead, beyond the double brace of chickens in every pot, and the dwindling glory that was vaudeville, lay the breadlines of the early 1930s.

32

Mae West, Young Man, Mae West

★

Boff b.o. was the word for legit in 1919. Eighteen musical comedies and revues were on the boards. Owners of theatres demanded and got guarantees, even from w.k. producers, of between $8,000 and $10,000 a week for musicals. Producers shot ticket prices to an all-time high of $5 top.

Despite the upheaval of a bitter Equity strike, the year was a red-letter occasion in black figures. Release from the tension of war sent the public massing to relax at musicals. The musicals led the field in kicking the roof off prices. Pioneer of this movement was the *Ziegfeld Follies,* with a $3.50 top that soared to $5 on special occasions.

Producers continued drinking champagne through 1920, but woke up with a hangover in 1921. The national skyrocket of prices had provided new headaches as well as higher-priced tickets. Overhead expenses were suddenly some 300 per cent taller than in 1919. Settling the Equity strike had boosted actors' pay about 200 per cent. Musicians and stagehands had to be paid more; rail charges were leaping; Government taxes were heavy. And moving pictures were slashing off balcony trade in heavy slices.

Of 100 new plays and six revivals which hit Broadway during 1921, only one out of five made the grade. The ratio was about the same on the road. A movement began to grow to scale down box-office admissions. Most dramas settled at a $2.50 top, musicals at $3. Smash hits set their own scales.

Outstanding event of the season was the opening of Irving Berlin's new Music Box Theatre, promptly acclaimed as one of Broadway's finest; and with its first *Music Box Revue* was dubbed "America's greatest show," to quote Variety's Jack Lait. Cast included Sam Bernard, William Collier, Florence Moore, Joseph Santley, Ivy Sawyer, Emma Haig, Wilda Bennett, the Brox Sisters and Chester Hale; staged by Hassard Short.

The accent was still on gaiety in 1922, with the opening of the Earl Carroll Theater. But the gaiety had a slightly hollow ring, with 31 out of 49 shows being offered at cutrates. Cain's Warehouse was jammed to overflowing with the wreckage of the bulk of the season's 196 tries.

As Broadway legit flopped heavily, fewer shows took to the road that year. A "little theatre" craze suddenly sprang up, spreading throughout the country. Fifty appeared in New York, and almost an equal number in Chicago. Over 400 little theatre groups in all were counted. New York's Drama League, started 12 years before, now proudly exhibited a subscriber list of 12,000. Smalltime thesping clicked so solidly that by 1926 there were no less than 5,000 little theatres selling tickets.

Variety's boxscore of 1925 showed a 72 per cent failure ratio for the season, which introduced 192 shows—138 flops, 54 successes. Producers took new heart at Hollywood's interest in buying rights to Broadway shows for the screen. But the record showed that only 14 out of 107 dramas and comedies had been sold. The following year was little better—only 13 out of 151. And the same pattern of failure persisted—136 closings out of 193 new offerings.

Six shows, nevertheless, pushed their price scales over a $5.50 top in 1926. It was becoming fairly firmly established that, good season or bad, the smash hits could be as bold with their prices as they dared.

The 1927 season was gloomy, with many theatres dark in the fall. The main reason, producers pointed out to each other, was that not a single legitimate attraction was featured on the nine best blocks on Broadway, which were all crowded with film theatres. Legitimate balconies grew emptier in 1928, as the movies and Vitaphone theatres grew more crowded.

The smash hits of 1928, as usual, went their unperturbed way, with no fewer than 10 musicals at a $6.60 top. Variety reported a distinct social trend in connection with the "better" attractions. Society considered a playgoer's seat location an index of his social standing. Tuxedos and evening dress were expected of opening nighters occupying any row in front of "L." Behind that, dress was admittedly "informal." Sole exception, of course—the critics, because it was notorious that "critics never dress."

Variety also pointed out, under the caption: 'IGH 'ATS IN GAL-
LERY, that these curiosities were to be seen in the balcony and gallery
of the Maxine Elliott, where Helen Hayes was starring in *Coquette,*
because orchestra seats were so difficult to get. Sidewalk speculators
accounted for part of the shortage, hawking $2.50 upstairs tickets
for $10 apiece.

1929 ushered in what Variety termed "the worst legitimate season
in a 9-year period." Blamed were the talkies and the Wall Street
fiasco. Both factors were equally ruinous to roadshows, even forcing
two of Broadway's top musicals on tour to call it quits. Critics wondered if legit might suffer the same fate as vaudeville.

Variety urged legitimate producers to start drumming up some
goodwill for themselves. "Legit managers," it pointed out, "read or
hear what the dailies are saying, from New York to all over, and
they are doing nothing. Not one thing to counteract the impression
that the legit is through—that the shows are no good—that prices
are too high—that the specs have killed the business—that legits
never treated the public properly and are now reaping their reward."

Producers with empty pockets nodded sadly. Producers of the
smash hits smirked and poured themselves another drink.

bawdy era of legit   In addition to a trend toward lavish
productions, the legitimate theatre of the 1920s showed a marked
disposition toward bawdiness. Avant garde audiences of the Jazz
Age were bawdy—and legit felt it had to keep one step ahead to
shock and titillate the sophisticates.

The New York *Times* sounded the keynote of the era by refusing
to print ads for a 1919 production of *Good Morning, Judge.* The
art work of the ads was considered highly improper for *Times'*
readers, who were allowed to read these only *sans* illustration.

Tone of the drama in 1921 was established by its three outstanding
successes—Andre Picard's *Kiki* (Lenore Ulric-Sam B. Hardy-
Thomas Mitchell), Somerset Maugham's *The Circle* (Estelle Win-
wood, Ernest Lawford and Robert Randel; John Drew and Mrs.
Leslie Carter headed the Chicago company); and Clemence Dane's
A Bill of Divorcement, with Allan Pollack, Janet Beecher and Pol-
lack's just-discovered Katherine Cornell, who that year had married
Guthrie McClintic.

William Anthony McGuire's *Six Cylinder Love,* with Ernest Truex, June Walker and Hedda Hopper in the cast, was in high favor; and another Al Woods bedroom farce, *The Demi-Virgin,* with Hazel Dawn and Charles Ruggles, was a sellout owing to some shrewd publicity which dragged it into the courts as "immoral."

By 1922 the farces were so Rabelaisian, and straight plays so "outspoken," that agitation was heard for censorship by the New York License Commissioner. When the Commissioner did revoke a license, Al Woods fought the case to the higher courts, which agreed such powers were too great to be vested in any one individual. Hastily, managers, playwrights and actors combined with various civic associations into a voluntary censorship jury, with a panel of 300 jurors. This "Citizens' Jury," at it was called, was obviously designed to forestall any official stage censorship.

That it functioned largely on paper was shown by the 1923 "living curtains" which were offered by George White's *Scandals* and Shuberts' *Passing Show*—nude showgirls draped on curtains. The following year *Broadway Brevities* and *Cat's Meow* were called on the carpet by the authorities for lewdness and profanity.

The uproar against blue shows had spread to other cities by 1925. Letters began to shower down on Congressmen demanding some kind of action. The Citizens' Jury hastily pushed to the fore with a great show of indignation to "try" four shows. Changes were ordered in *Ladies of the Evening,* a play by Milton Herbert Gropper, which had Beth Merrill, Edna Hibbard and James Kirkwood among the cast prominents, and in Edwin Justus Mayer's *The Firebrand,* with Joseph Schildkraut, Frank Morgan, Nana Bryant and Eden Gray.

The other two plays were cleared. They were Sidney Howard's *They Knew What They Wanted* (Richard Bennett-Glenn Anders-Pauline Lord) and *Desire Under the Elms* by Eugene O'Neill, with Walter Huston, Walter Abel, Mary Morris and Macklin Marrow. (*They Knew What They Wanted* won the Pulitzer Prize of 1925 as the best American play of the year.) Out in Cleveland, the cops made the Shuberts dress up their "Artists and Models."

Finger-shaking had little effect on the shows of 1926, so the Citizens' Jury was forced to take drastic action against two hopelessly dirty shows—*Bunk of 1926* and *Great Temptations,* which were compelled to close. Two others—*The Shanghai Gesture* (with

Florence Reed-Mary Duncan-McKay Morris) and Mae West's *Sex* were given one week to clean up. For some reason *The Harem* and *A Good Bad Woman* were overlooked.

The year also introduced a new note in illicit thrills with shows emphasizing miscegenation. The most notable "mixed" show was *Lulu Belle,* with 19 white and 93 Negro members of the cast. These were followed by other "Negro-and-white" shows like *Deep River, Spring Magic, The Creole* and *Black Boy.*

The Citizens' Jury also tried *The Captive* that year, and found the show not guilty. Produced by Gilbert Miller and starring Helen Menken, the New York city fathers looked askance at the lesbian angle in the Edouard Bourdet play, which Arthur Hornblow, Jr., now the MGM film producer, had skillfully adapted for America. The accent the play placed on violets as a symbol of the third sex for some time kayoed the violet business at florists.

mae west's duo   *The Captive* quit voluntarily in 1927—a year that belonged properly to Mae West and *Sex,* the show she had written to star herself, under the pen name "Jane Mast." Here was *Variety's* opinion of that remarkable vehicle, via its then reviewer (now M-G-M producer) Bob Sisk: "Never had disgrace fallen so heavily upon the 63d Street Theatre as it did Monday night, when a nasty red-light district show—which would be tolerated in but few of the stock burlesque houses in America—opened and called itself *Sex.* . . . Many people walked out on it before its first act was over . . . The second act saw more withdrawals, and the third act played to lots of empty seats . . . Mae West plays the rough gal, and in the first act does it well. But she goes to pieces after that, because she doesn't change when the play calls for it . . . The script has her speaking the lines of a good gal, when she's still slouching and showing the figure just as if she were drumming up business as a bad one . . . Best that can be said for the rest of this cast of unknowns is that they must have been obliged to accept parts in a show so vile and strongly resembling the dramatic garbage of the year."

Three of the daily reviewers who covered the opening, realizing that the sole salvation of the play lay in publicity on its lasciviousness and a possible police arrest, agreed not to mention how dirty it was, kidding it as a dud instead. But this technique failed; the play was raided. Mae West was sentenced to 10 days in the workhouse, and *Sex* was put back in its box.

Unperturbed, the archpriestess of Eros turned up in 1928 with another dual stint as writer-actress—*Pleasure Man*. Variety, mindful of Mae's fatal attraction for the law, hastened to catch the tryout at the Bronx Opera House. The late great Jack Conway (*Con*), Variety's reviewer, was intrigued.

"It's the queerest show you've ever seen," Con marveled. "All of the Queens are in it . . . If that Mae West can't think of the oddest things . . . The party scene is the payoff. If you see those hussies (actors playing homosexuals) being introduced to do their specialties, you'd pass out . . . The host sang a couple of parodies, one going 'When I Go Out and Look For the Moon.' Now I ask you. Another guest very appropriately sang, 'Balls, Parties and Banquets,' and I ask you again . . . Go early, for some of the lines can't last."

Neither did *Pleaure Man,* when it opened on Broadway. Raided on opening night, it closed its doors two days later. Mae considered that a bit rough, since *The Captive* which had used homosexuality as a theme, had been exonerated by the Citizens' Jury two years before.

dirt no legit b.o. hypo   Surprisingly, the experiences of three "blue" plays of 1927 showed that newspaper publicity about raiding could not stampede the box office. The plays of that year were so lowdown that they led to a Wales "Padlock Bill," calling for shutting down any show that really let rip. *The Captive* had been doing $22,000 a week until it was raided. Newspaper stories about the raid scared off the "class" clientele, and the show folded.

Sex started slipping on the day the arrests were made. It dragged along until the trial, then took another b.o. nosedive, and the cast had to take salary cuts. *Virgin Man* had been about to close when the gendarmes swooped down. "Presented" by Times Square Productions, Inc., authored by William F. Dugan and H. F. Maltby, the latter achieved a dubious double-indistinction by also staging it. A no-name, nondescript play, it erred chiefly in that the composite whole was dull rather than dirty, but the impressarios hopefully kept it open, pending trial, and only went deeper into the red. Other flops among the below-the-belt entries that year were *Pearl of Great Price, Red Blinds, Galloping Sheik* and *Seed of the Brute.*

Once again there was a clamor by reformers for legislation which would close any theatre for one year if its manager was found guilty of harboring a salacious play. But Governor Al Smith did not sign a padlock bill offered to him by New York State's Legislature. Because, once again, there was a voluntary "Committee of Nine"—managers, authors and actors—which sprang up to clean house from within. It lasted a few months, then vanished.

Lee Shubert caused a howl of laughter to sweep through Broadway in 1928 by complaining through his attorney to District Attorney Banton that O'Neill's *Strange Interlude* was a dirty play. This charge came from the 99 44/100 per cent pure producer who had presented *Red Blinds* (stopped by the police in Newark); *Pearl of Great Price* (locale: a whorehouse); *New York Exchange* (hero: a homosexual); *Great Temptations* (a revue which offered nudes revealing their posteriors to the audience); *Maya* (ordered closed by the District Attorney); and *Artists and Models* (show's first-night chorus waved nude breasts at the first row, starting a wave of censorship.) No one on Broadway was coarse enough to suspect Lee Shubert of spite work against the Theatre Guild because that organization preferred to book with Erlanger rather than Shubert. Purely a matter of Lee's aesthetic sensibilities.

With sex at a premium in the legitimate—despite the fact that audiences were intelligent enough to reject plays which had nothing but smut to offer—it was to be expected that some of the headliners in the tabloid scandals would be wrapped in a few acts and hurled at Broadway. Evelyn Nesbit was the first, in 1920, opening out of town in a play called *Open Book*. The critics hurled the book at *Open Book,* and Evelyn closed it.

Peggy Hopkins Joyce bowed in and out of Broadway in a play that lasted two weeks. Peaches Browning lent her talents to *The Squealer*—which lasted two weeks. Texas Guinan, who slayed them at fabulous sums in the niteries, couldn't make the grade in Broadway legit at $4.40. Variety succinctly wrapped up the explanation, "The public wouldn't buy a 2¢ tabloid rep at $3."

holdover hits   Broadway in 1919 rolled in strong carry-over attractions from the war years. *Friendly Enemies* (Louis Mann-Sam

Bernard), *Three Faces East* (Violet Heming and Emmett Corrigan), *The Better 'Ole* (Mr. and Mrs. Charles Coburn), *Listen, Lester* (Johnny Dooley, Clifton Webb, Ada Mae Weeks, Ada Lewis, Gertrude Vanderbilt), *Dear Brutus* (William Gillette, Hilda Spong and Helen Hayes), *Tiger! Tiger!* (Frances Starr, O. P. Heggie and Lionel Atwill), *Up In Mabel's Room,* an Al Woods farce which had Adele Rowland, Hazel Dawn and Enid Markey topping the cast; the marathon *Lightnin',* by and with Frank Bacon (whose son, Lloyd Bacon, was to become a distinguished Hollywood scripter and director), and *East Is West* which starred Fay Bainter supported by George Nash and Hassard Short.

The new hits were *The Jest,* with John and Lionel Barrymore; and St. John Ervine's *John Ferguson,* a surprise click which put the Theatre Guild into the bigtime among legit producers. The Guild had started with less than a $1,000 bank roll, actors being paid a token $25 a week, but *John Ferguson* swelled the newly founded organization's exchequer to $40,000.

It was a year of elaborate and costly spectacles as well. *Aphrodite* had a $200,000 advance sale. Opening night seats, scaled up to $10, were hawked by the specs at $75 a pair. George White produced his first *Scandals* in 1919, and Ziegfeld's 1919 edition of the *Follies* cost $100,000, with a weekly overhead of $20,000. His first *Follies* had cost only $19,000 to mount.

Variety also observed that year that Eugene O'Neill, son of well-known actor James O'Neill, who had already won some attention with one-act plays, had completed a three-act play called *Beyond the Horizon.*

Lightnin' rolled into its third year in 1920 and other smashes were Ina Claire in *The Gold Diggers* and Edith Day starring in *Irene.* But the year's biggest legit stage news—as in almost all other branches of show biz during the decade—was again Jolson, who received $2,000 for two Sunday shows at the Century and Winter Garden theatres.

the perennial jolson   The Jolson name was such magic by 1921 that the Shuberts built a theatre at 7th Avenue and 59th Street and named it the Jolson when he opened there with *Bombo,* introducing the song, "April Showers." Always a man to give audiences more than their money's worth, he held a Chicago audience at

Bombo after the show to hear him rehearse a new song with the orchestra—George Gershwin's "Who Cares?"

In *Artists and Models* of 1926, Jolson was only supposed to do a 15-minute turn. The opening night audience, however, refused to allow him to leave, keeping Jolson onstage until 11:45. The final scene of the show had to be omitted. Playing the show in Chicago, he was credited with establishing the biggest gross ever taken in by a musical production in the history of the stage—$60,400. New Year's Eve gross was $17,000, at $11 top for the evening performance and a $5 top for the midnight show.

In 1927 Jolson earned $350,000 for the season, and the following year was paid $50,000 for four weeks to appear with *Night In Spain* at Chicago. When the era drew to a close, he was undisputed holder of the top salary ribbon in both film and stage fields.

Coming up fast behind Jolson was Eddie Cantor, who left Ziegfeld in 1920 to sign with the Shuberts at $1,400 a week. His first starring tour was with the *Midnight Rounders* on the road, which played to S.R.O. throughout the country. By 1929, when Cantor was drafted to M.C. the opening of the Ziegfeld Roof ($500 and $1,000 a table), he was such top-drawer material that Old Golds, which had paid Al Jolson $2,500 to endorse their smokes, put $7,500 on the line for Cantor's signature.

The biggest musical of 1921 was *Sally* (Marilyn Miller-Leon Erroll-Walter Catlett) which earned over $1,800,000 that year—with weekly averages of about $30,000. *The Music Box Revue,* at a $5 top, was expected to net its owners $500,000 for the theatre's first year. Other musicals that were holding the fort nicely were *Good Morning, Dearie, Tangerine, The Perfect Fool* (Ed Wynn) and *The O'Brien Girl.*

Blossom Time, an operetta, scored heavily, along with such stand-out straight plays as *The Green Goddess, Liliom, Just Married, The Bat* and *The First Year.* By the end of the year the miracle play, *Lightnin',* which had opened at a $2.50 top, then jumped its price to $3 (Saturday, $4) wound up with a gross of $2,000,000. The following year Marilyn Miller drove *Sally* past that record for the new boxoffice championship.

1922 was a big year for Eugene O'Neill. Charles Gilpin, the only Negro star touring the South, was starring in *The Emperor Jones*— to superb notices and excellent business. On Broadway, Louis Wolheim—later the sensation of the film, *All Quiet on the Western Front*—was starring in *The Hairy Ape* at the Plymouth.

GET "THE HAIRY APE"—BEST CURSING ON STAGE was *Variety's* headline on its review by the effervescent Jack Conway. "Get a load of the *Hairy Ape* before they back in and take the joint. . . . Coming out of the theatre, all the peasants had a different version of what it was all about . . . A tossup whether O'Neill is taking a backhanded slap at the caveman propaganda, or whether he was fitting Wolheim with a vehicle that would scare Dempsey out of his title."

Jack Dempsey, incidentally, was also onstage in vaudeville in 1922, featured with Doc Kearns and Larry Williams in "Get Together" at the Hippodrome. Working on salary and percentage, his take was $7,000 a week.

David Warfield, the Old Music Master, returned to Broadway with *The Merchant of Venice.* The revival aroused controversy among Jewish circles, because of the character of Shylock. The Baltimore *Jewish Times* assailed the revival, while Rabbi Wessel delivered a sermon extolling it. Two years later, when Warfield returned from a season on the road with the show, it had rung up an $80,000 loss. Warfield disappeared from the theatre, retiring a multimillionaire. He was one of the biggest stockholders in Loew's, Inc. (Metro) and about 10 years ago reportedly was offered $1,000,000 to make a film, which he refused.

In 1944, when he was 77, Warfield explained, "I had done what I wanted to do, and that was *The Merchant of Venice,* and I quit. What was the use of continuing? I didn't need any more money and I saw no sense in making any more. I had been ambitious to do other Shakespearian roles, but I didn't want to go on. Why go on for more applause? . . . When I quit on tour in *The Merchant,* I knew that was my swan song. I didn't want any farewells. Not a word. I just sneaked out of the theatre as I had sneaked in. I'd had more than 40 years of it, and that was enough." He died in 1951.

not forgetting 'abie's irish rose'   The miracle show of 1922 was *Abie's Irish Rose,* of which *Variety* said skeptically, "It may waver while the public decides whether it is to bloom or wilt." Dramatic reviewer Robert Benchley lamented the new depths to which the legitimate theatre had sunk, and spent the next five years thinking of ingenious ways to ignore the existence of the play.

By 1924 Ann Nichols was holding down the number of road companies of *Abie* deliberately, to keep her profits under a million for income tax purposes. By 1925 it had broken every record for long runs in the American theatre, including London's long-distance show, *Charley's Aunt*. There were six *Abie* companies, and Variety signalized the show's accomplishment by turning over a special edition to it, making it the first show ever so honored. In 1926 there was an Australian company, and in 1927 a London company. *Abie* finally called it a day—until revivals popped up—with the all-time record run of five years, five months, or exactly 2,327 performances. For the annals, the original *Abie* cast comprised Marie Carroll, Bernard Gorcey, Alfred Weisman, John Cope, Mathilda Cottrelly and Robert Williams. Only *Life With Father* (3,228 performances) and *Tobacco Road* (3,182 performances) have eclipsed it in American theatre annals.

great ladies of the theatre   1923 on Broadway belonged to the Great Ladies of the Theatre. Jane Cowl and Ethel Barrymore were dueling each other with rival Juliets. The decision of the critics went unanimously to Miss Cowl, who also triumphed at the box office with a record run, for Shakespeare, of 20 weeks. This inflicted defeat upon another Barrymore—John—whose *Hamlet* had set the previous Bard notch at 12 weeks.

Eva LeGalliene rose to stardom in Molnar's *The Swan*, as direct result of extraordinary critical acclaim. Eleanora Duse, after a flop b.o. tour in Gabriele d'Annunzio repertory, whammed 'em in a single farewell at the Metropolitan Opera House. Dorothy Stone was introduced to Broadway in *Stepping Stones*, with her famous father, Fred Stone.

Opposing the distaffers in the 1923 season were Raymond Hitchcock in his first legit role as *The Old Soak;* W. C. Fields with Madge Kennedy, Jimmy Barry and Luella Gear in *Poppy;* and Willie & Eugene Howard, Francis Renault and Fred Allen in *The Passing Show*. Joe Cook co-starred with Peggy Hopkins Joyce in Earl Carroll's first *Vanities*.

The year's top smashes were *Rain,* based on Somerset Maugham's *Miss Thompson,* which catapulted Jeanne Eagels to the top under Sam H. Harris' aegis; Austin Strong's *Seventh Heaven,* with Helen Menken, Frank Morgan and George Gaul; Channing Pollock's

The Fool, with a cast headed by Lowell Sherman, Henry Stephenson, James Kirkwood, Frank Sylvester and Arthur Elliott; and Anne Nichols' unpredictable *Abie's Irish Rose.* A little theatre, Greenwich Village's Cherry Lane Playhouse, set the season's low with a murky item called *Mud* which grossed $7.

Critic Ashton Stevens, the dean of Chicago drama oracles, made Broadway buzz in 1924 by issuing his listing of the greatest actors of the day. The honored artists were Ethel and John Barrymore, Irene Bordoni, Ina Claire, George M. Cohan, Willie Collier, Leo Dietrichstein, Mrs. Minnie Maddern Fiske, Al Jolson, Pauline Lord, McIntyre & Heath, Bruce McRae, Julia Marlowe, Will Rogers, H. Reeves-Smith, Laurette Taylor and David Warfield. Mr. Stevens diplomatically always listed his selections alphabetically.

His nomination for the "ideal" show was the first *Cohan Revue,* with Cohan and an added cast including Willie Collier, Ina Claire, Sam Bernard, Frank Tinney, the Duncan Sisters, Fanny Brice and Martha Lorber. Needless to say critic Stevens was suddenly unpopular in many neglected quarters.

In 1924 Morris Gest, in association with F. Ray Comstock, imported Max Reinhardt's *The Miracle,* a $400,000 production which entailed Norman Bel Geddes metamorphosing the Century Theatre into a cathedral-like auditorium. Lady Diana Manners, Rosamond Pinchot, Werner Krauss and Rudolph Schildkraut were in the cast, but the prime appeal was the pageantry and lavishness of the Gest-Reinhardt spectacle.

The critics got into David Belasco's hair that year by panning his offering of *The Harem.* The impresario took ads in all the dailies to express this sarcastic greeting: "Gentlemen of the Press, I Thank You!"

More mellow—and hence better remembered because of its courtesy and humbleness—was the ad which Fredric March and his wife, Florence Eldridge, inserted in the New York papers, following the pannings their play, *Yr. Obedient Husband,* had received from the critics in 1938. It was a replica of a cartoon from the *New Yorker,* which showed the man on the flying trapeze missing his partner, who exclaimed, "Oops! Sorry!" The Marches—aided by their press agent, Dick Maney—borrowed the cartoon and caption as their method of expressing regrets.

In contrast to the Belasco fiasco, a new comedy star cradled in the same burlesque and vaudeville traditions which spawned Fanny Brice, Al Jolson, Eddie Cantor and Bobby Clark, and was later to graduate Phil Silvers and Joey Faye, came to the fore. He was Bert Lahr, whom the Shuberts presented in one of their musicals. Fay Bainter surprised *Dream Girl* audiences by letting her hair fall down on her shoulders in the play—a completely unfashionable gesture in the era of the Jazz Age bob.

Earl Carroll's third edition of his *Vanities* in 1925 introduced a night club note into legit. He had hostesses dancing with patrons, and a row of eight tables for $11 customers who were rewarded by having showgirls sit with them. Ushers in short skirts and sheer stockings introduced patrons and hostesses to each other, a chore shared by emcee Julius Tannen.

This, too, was a burlesque evolution, started years ago when the customers would come onstage to terp with the choristers. Under existing regulations in New York, "mixing" by the chorus with patrons is taboo, particularly in the niteries, as a defense against the clipjoints, which is why Carroll had to engage special "hostesses" for the out-front stuff. In the heyday of burleycue, "Beef Trust" Billy Watson first introduced the chorister-customer terping.

The year also saw Noel Coward's debut in his own play, *The Vortex;* Will Rogers cleaning up $10,000 and $12,000 a week on his concert tour; and the first completely non-Equity show in five years, *Bringing Up Father In Ireland,* which had no lucky shamrocks at the b.o. It was a dismal flop.

The year 1926 marked the first setback for Flo Ziegfeld. The Ziegfeld Follies, Inc., dissolved, with a loss to the producer of $187,000. The following year the new Ziegfeld Theatre opened with a hit, *Rio Rita,* and in 1928 there was *Show Boat* with its memorable cast including Helen Morgan, Norma Terris, Charles Winninger, Edna May Oliver and Jules Bledsoe, the first to sing the durable "Old Man River" by Jerome Kern and Oscar Hammerstein 2d. (Paul Robeson did the role in a later revival).

But in 1929 the Ziegfeld Roof was shuttered, $75,000 in the red, and *Show Girl* was the first Ziegfeld production in Broadway history to go begging at the cutrate counters.

Show Girl had all the elements of top artificers and ultra production, with people like Clayton, Jackson & Durante, Eddie Foy, Jr., Frank McHugh, Harriet Hoctor and Ruby Keeler in the cast.

It had a Gershwin score; a J. P. McEvoy book; dances by Bobby Connelly and Albertina Rasch. And, above all, it had an unofficial, unpaid star who never worked for Ziegfeld for money but who, almost nightly, would accidentally-on-purpose stroll down the aisle singing "Liza" while his wife, Ruby Keeler (Mrs. Al Jolson), was tapping her tootsies. And even that couldn't keep *Show Girl* running beyond 111 performances.

those $55 openings   Raquel Meller, the Spanish star, opened on Broadway in 1926 to a $27.50 first night top, and grossed $27,000 weekly. Not to be outdone, George White offered the first 10 rows of his new *Scandals* at $55 a seat opening night, claiming that, if Raquel Meller was worth $27.50, his show was worth twice that.

In actuality these ridiculously high tariffs were for publicity and ballyhoo purposes although in that era of wonderful nonsense there were not a few butter-and-egg men and other well-heeled chumps who went for the idea of $55 and $110 a pair.

This recalls Harry Hershfield's favorite gag about a 7th Avenue sales executive wanting to impress an important out-of-town buyer. He paid a fabulous price to a scalper for a third-row-on-the-aisle pair for the *Ziegfeld Follies,* and then made the strange request of the boxoffice man at the New Amsterdam Theatre would he "please punch holes in my tickets; I wanna make an impression on that tough buyer from the Brandeis store in Omaha that Ziggy and I are 'that way' and show him the punched tickets which will prove that Ziggy even won't let me pay for tickets to the *Follies,* and the holes will prove they're Annie Oakleys." The boxoffice man thought he'd humor the big man from south of 42d Street, but unfortunately for the garment sector salesman the night of the performance saw Eddie Cantor ill and the performance had to be cancelled. Which, of course, left the shallow garment sales executive in a tough spot since, looking like real "skulls" (passes), he couldn't return them or exchange them.

Death stalked Broadway legit in 1926. *Lulu Belle* finaled with a stranglehold. *The Great Gatsby* was shot, along with Sessue Hayakawa in *Love City.* The two lead characters in Michael Arlen's *The Green Hat* (Katharine Cornell, who had Leslie Howard and

Margalo Gillmore as cast prominents) and John Colton's *The Shanghai Gesture* (Mary Duncan, foiled by Florence Reed's 'Mother Goddam' and McKay Morris) expired before the final curtain. And *The Dybbuk* and *Great God Brown* rang down with a call for the undertaker. Stark drama called for stark death.

Top shows of the 1926-1927 semester were *Broadway,* by Philip Dunning and George Abbott, with Lee Tracy, Tommy Jackson and Robert Gleckler; *Criss Cross,* a Jerome Kern musical starring Fred Stone with his daughter, Dorothy, and his wife, Allene Crater; Kenyon Nicholson's vehicle for Walter Huston, *The Barker;* and Robert E. Sherwood's *The Road to Rome* (Jane Cowl-Philip Mcrivale).

Also *Burlesque* (Hal Skelly and Barbara Stanwyck, which also included Oscar Levant in the cast); Fred and Adele Astaire in the Gershwins' *Funny Face* (Victor Moore, Allen Kearns and Billy Kent in support); *Connecticut Yankee,* a Rodgers & Hart musical with William Gaxton; Eddie Dowling in *Honeymoon Lane,* which also introduced Kate Smith; *Good News,* with Zelma O'Neal, Gus Shy, John Price Jones and George Olsen's Band; and Vincent Youmans' *Hit the Deck,* which had Charlie King, Louise Groody, Madeleine Cameron and Stella Mayhew topping the cast.

Lemon of the year was *That Smith Boy,* with tennis star Bill Tilden, which averaged $26 a performance at Leblang's cutratery.

$750,000 fiasco   An amazingly bad show that made theatre history was launched in 1926 at the Mansfield—*The Ladder*. The backer was Texas oil tycoon Edgar B. Davis, and the author J. Frank Davis—no relation, which kayoed the one possible explanation. Before the season was finished, *The Ladder* was $200,000 in the red. The producer then calmly rented the Waldorf Theatre at $5,000 a week, and gave everybody Christmas presents. The cast got a 10-week further guarantee, and the public got seats free for the holidays. But still few came.

By the end of 1927, *The Ladder* was still going, albeit not strong —with all seats free at every performance to the public—and the show in hock for $750,000. It closed in New York finally after a run of one year and five months. The whole thing had simply been the whim—or hobby—of the fabulously wealthy Edgar Davis, who made $10,000 a day out of his oil wells. In 1928, the money apparently gushing in faster than he could dispose of it, Davis reopened *The Ladder* in amazed Boston.

Just as amazed was the boxoffice man at the theatre housing *The Ladder* when *Sime,* wanting to know a bit about the metaphysical theme which inspired oilman Davis to go for such a large bankroll, asked the present editor of Variety to accompany him and "catch the first act anyway." Admission was for the asking, and as is axiomatic when anything is "for free," few came. You could arrest the ticket-taker and the boxoffice man for vagrancy and so when *Sime* stuck a bill to pay for the seats we had a pleasant row with the man in the cage who didn't know the legend that *Sime* "always insists on paying." We were in an audience comprising 10 other people, all sur-le-cuff.

A latterday Edgar Davis, of course, has been Anthony Brady (Tony) Farrell, whose Albany chain factory profits produced a chain-reaction in only one commodity—beaucoup red ink ever since he invaded Broadway. But even he couldn't take it and finally closed *All for Love,* a 1949 musical with Grace and Paul Hartman and Bert Wheeler, which had a theoretical long run but cost Farrell plenty, including refurbishing a theatre. He bought the old Hollywood Theatre from Warner Bros. and renamed it the Mark Hellinger. Between that and the ensuing year's *Hold It,* Farrell donated beaucoup bullion on Broadway although future investments augured possible recouping of some of the losses.

from broadway to hollywood   Film personalities of a later decade were much in evidence on Broadway in 1927. Brian Donlevy was in *Hit the Deck.* Gregory Ratoff and Frank McHugh were in *10th Avenue.* Barbara Stanwyck won plaudits from fellow legiters by refusing a Metro screen test, stating she'd rather devote her talents to the dramatic stage—at least right now. As Ruby Stevens, a nitery hoofer, Miss Stanwyck had catapulted to attention first in *The Noose,* and more resoundingly as the Bonnie to Hal Skelly's Bozo, the errant low comic in the Arthur Hopkins-George Manker Watters play, *Burlesque,* the ensuing season.

Flop record of the year—and possibly for the decade— was achieved by *He Loves the Ladies* at the Frolic, atop the New Amsterdam Theatre. At one Thursday matinee the curtain rose with every seat in the house, without exception, empty. And Mrs. Henry B. Harris struck back at Walter Winchell for his bad review of her show, *Blood Money,* by barring him from the Hudson Theatre.

the specs—again!   Throughout the decade, while Capone was making a good thing out of Prohibition, ticket scalpers had fastened to show business for an equally plush racket. In 1919, one Chicago scalper cornered that city's legitimate ticket market for a weekly profit of $5,000.

Earl Carroll tried to give audiences a break in 1922 by numbering the rows in his theatre, instead of lettering them. Loud squawks from the ticket-hawking department made him retreat. Lettered rows were nicely confusing. Customers sometimes couldn't figure out quickly enough whether tickets marked "M" were really 12th row back, as glibly represented. Not to mention the AA and BB and CC front rows in some theatres.

Variety, noting the influx of classical plays on Broadway in 1922, dryly observed that this was the first time Shakespeare had had a chance to get acquainted with ticket speculators.

The Shuberts came forth with an ingenious plan in 1923—a Central Ticket Office where all theatre tickets would be sold at a 25 per cent premium. Stock in the company would be apportioned most "democratically"—according to the number of theatres owned. Considering that the Shuberts owned so many theatres, and obviously could control the company, caused other managers to blandly turn thumbs-down.

When the Shuberts initiated a "pass tax" on courtesy tickets, the tax represented 10 per cent of the face value of the tickets. In 1924 Variety estimated this had earned no less than $250,000 for the Shuberts. It pointed out caustically that, whereas burlesque's Columbia wheel had contributed $10,571 from its pass tax to the Actors' Fund, not one penny of the Shuberts' $250,000 had trickled in that direction.

Most theatre tickets of 1925 were being handled by the agencies, which were legally allowed to charge 50¢ over boxoffice price. To get in on the gravy train, hit dramas raised their top scales from $2.75 to $3.30. So many speculators were getting far above the legal 50¢ surtax allowed that a number were brought up on charges.

The ticket agencies were first jubilant, then dismayed, by legal and Government action in 1927. They cheered when the New York

State law limiting the ticket premium of brokers to 50¢ was declared unconstitutional by a Supreme Court vote of 5 to 4, which declared that such a law amounted to price-fixing by legislation.

That kayoed the 50¢ premium, and the roof went off prices at all ticket agencies. But in May, Federal investigators collected incriminating information on the ticket agencies for failing to pay the Government one-half of all excess premiums charged over 50¢ per ticket. The hawkers were tried in alphabetical order; Alexander Agency was first in the dock.

The Agency's two partners were fined $5,000 each; the Agency itself another $5,000; and the partners sentenced to eight months in jail. When the United States Circuit Court of Appeals affirmed the decision, another 23 brokers pleaded guilty. Further investigation by the Government revealed that the brokers were not the sole culprits. They had been forced to split with certain theatre managers and boxoffice men, as well as compelled to accept tickets for flop shows in order to get the hits. Testimony showed that the ticket agencies had had to shell out $55,000 to one management which had also cut in on half the under-table money slipped to certain boxoffice treasurers. (That's called "ice" in trade. Treasurers of lucky hit shows periodically sport a "so and so hit" car, meaning that's how they were able to purchase that year's new model.) To settle the mess, the Government offered to drop charges against the agencies, if the latter would agree to pay the taxes they owed the Government, and promise to stop charging outrageous premiums on tickets.

Joe Leblang, the cutrate king, popped up again with the Central Ticket Agency idea. A number of managers were now for it, but A. L. Erlanger, Flo Ziegfeld and Charlie Dillingham wanted no part of a Shubert-dominated agency. The plan fell through a second time. And in 1928, Congress quietly slipped a rider into a bill on theatre admissions that provided a raise of ticket brokers' premiums from 50¢ to 75¢ a ticket.

Apparently nobody has ever thought of a bill being passed that would allow a legit patron to walk up to the boxoffice, as he does at the Roxy or Radio City Music Hall, and buy a ticket for the price stamped on the pasteboard.

33

Low Gags and High Divas

★

Amazingly, while the legit of 1919 were throwing away the book and presenting everything on the stage this side of French postcards, burlesque was presenting shows which would hardly bring a blush to your maiden aunts.

The Columbia Theatre, Broadway showhouse for the Columbia wheel, refused to allow a single Shimmy on its stage. Blue dialog and indigo stage "business" were strictly taboo. It wasn't merely that burlesque had gone high-hat, raising its prices to a $1.50 top, with elaborate productions; the sentiment of the Columbia people was simply that the time was long overdue for burlesque to win new audiences, and new respect, by being free of the taint so persistently associated with burlesque.

As part of the cleanup, the Columbia wheel ordered advertising curtains and candy butchers eliminated from its theatres. Smoking was ruled out of the orchestra, and productions were kept onstage and out of the laps of the audience. The other half of the nation's burlesque empire, the American Burlesque Association, was also trotting out its brooms as a postscript to its election of a new president, I. H. (Izzy) Herk.

The Columbia advanced its price scale to $2 top in 1920, and business continued on the upbeat. Burlesque, dressed in its Sunday best, actually did attract new customers—even women who, a few years before, would have worn a veil if forced to pass a burlesque house. Now on its best behavior, the Columbia wheel even forbade any references to Prohibition or woman suffrage on its stages.

Burlesque discouraged its comedians that year from using Irish dialects, because of Sinn Fein activities; and "Dutch" dialects, because of the anti-Teutonic feeling of postwar audiences. Comedians switched to Jewish dialect instead. In 1921, burlesque's most sensational attraction was "Sawing A Lady In Half," which was also in vogue in vaudeville, carnivals and circuses. Horace Goldin brought suit against copyists, claiming originality—only to have it proved in court that a Professor Hegler was on record as having performed some lady-slicing in the early 1880s. A New Orleans burlesque house was offering the act with a Negro woman as the victim, under the title, "Black Magic."

Both wheels of burlesque made a tactical mistake in 1921, plunging both treasuries into disaster. Worried by the boxoffice decline that was hitting all branches of show business, and the rising costs of productions, burlesque managers of the Columbia and American circuits joined hands in declaring an open shop for stagehands and musicians.

Managers promptly found their scenery burned with acids. Trucks loaded with props and scenery started out for certain theatres, but never arrived, or were switched to different towns. To make matters worse, stagehands and musicians took their case to burlesque's own audiences, who in many towns were largely workingmen and naturally sympathetic. This tactic cost both "wheels" (burlesque circuits) heavily in goodwill, as well as some $200,000 in hard cash. The managers threw in the towel, and arguments broke out between Columbia and American wheel executives which embittered relations between the two formerly friendly allies.

Hard times dogged both circuits in 1922. Only six of the American wheel's 34 shows operated in the black; and only 10 of Columbia's 38. The Columbia wheel found itself on the horns of a dilemma. The Shubert unit shows were shaping up as serious opposition to Columbia burlesque, with some ex-Columbia producers going over to Lee Shubert. To meet the threat of this de-luxe competition, Columbia ordered another rigid housecleaning. Over a dozen shows were ruled off the wheel's stages, and forced to replace costumes, bits, numbers, principals and anything else considered substandard or indecent.

minsky on the horizon But tugging in the opposite direction were the Columbia's oldline customers, who were demanding low comedy and the accompanying s.a. paraphernalia. A new threat also appeared on the horizon in Billy Minsky. Worried, the

Columbia execs relaxed on bare legs in the chorus, and looked the other way when Columbia comics gagged below the belt.

They tightened up again in 1923, when business showed a 25 per cent improvement. The Columbia wheel's St. Louis house, the Gaiety, took in $192,813 in 15 weeks, a new record for burlesque. Columbia executives were even more delighted when all of New York's first-line critics showed up for the Saturday night premiere of a Columbia show, *Let's Go*. Encouraged by these new exalted heights of respectability, Columbia executives threw three off-color shows off the circuit, and waved a bluenosed stick at the others to keep them in line.

But Columbia burlesque managers were resentful. The American wheel, now re-named Mutual Burlesque, had swung its shows over into the low-and-dirty ranks. Minsky's and the small Western wheel were hurting with cooch dancers and smut. Minsky's Apollo on New York's 42d Street had enhanced its reputation by getting raided. Against this enticing swing to the sewer, Columbia comics —sanitized by executive order—were failing to amuse, rendered eunuch by material which lacked properly potent burlesque risibility.

The conflict became more pronounced during 1925. Columbia producers were unable to clean up their shows and keep them entertaining. Mutual producers were allowed to take the lid off, and business boomed. Clean burlesque was doomed once again, as soon as Columbia executives realized their downward trend of profits was not a temporary dip. When the *Powder Puff Review* played the Columbia in New York, legs and breasts were presented in the Minsky manner.

But the following year Columbia found itself too far behind the others to catch up. Stock burlesque had almost cornered the market in dirty shows—Minsky in New York, Fox & Krause in the Northwest, and Oscar Dane in St. Louis. The Mutual wheel was giving customers what they wanted—low gags and tall gals. Columbia knew drastic action was called for when, for the first time in history, a Columbia show, *Not Tonight, Josephine,* was forced to close without notice in Philadelphia, stranding the company which was paid off in I.O.U.'s.

legit tabs nsg for burly Columbia decided on a new policy. Holding only 15 burlesque shows, the wheel signed up for a series of pop revivals of former Broadway successes—*The Gorilla, The Bat, Cat and the Canary, White Cargo,* and *What Price Glory?* among others. These were sent out on the circuit at $1.50 top, and at first did well in towns which had played the original productions on tour at higher legitimate prices. To these shows Columbia added a number of black-and-tan revues.

Two significant developments of 1927 brought about an end to the feud between the Columbia and Mutual wheels. The first was the eventual failure of Columbia's experiment with pop priced legit, which flopped badly after a promising start. Columbia's aping of Broadway shows and musicals, with less expensive casts, could not compete either with legitimate shows on the road, or the regular burlesque competition.

The second development was the rising wrath of authorities against the extent to which stock burlesque producers were prodding the tolerance of "decent citizens." A sample was Billy Minsky's show, *Irish Justice,* at the lower East Side's National Winter Garden (not to be confused with the Winter Garden on Broadway). The show was raided, then performed in court before a Magistrate Simpson to judge the extent of its indecency. During the command performance, one lame-brained showgirl lifted her skirt, waved a neat limb at Magistrate Simpson, and simpered, "How about meeting me at 7:30, Judgie?"

The Mutual wheel, which had held its shows somewhat in check because of its prominence as a target for civil knuckle-rapping, nevertheless found itself smeared by the same brush that tarred Minsky & Co. It was burlesque, and burlesque was salacious, and that was that. To make matters worse, although Mutual had the name, it didn't have the game—its reasonably decent shows could not compete with the lurid sex offered by the stock burlesque outfits.

So both Columbia and Mutual found it to their combined advantage to join hands once again. For Columbia it meant strong help on the road back to regular burlesque. For Mutual it meant solidified wheel burlesque against stock burlesque. The merger had a happy effect throughout both empires, convincing performers and house managers alike that burlesque was here to stay, and eliminating the petty jealousies that were part of wheel rivalry. So jubilant was the atmosphere in both camps, in fact, that Variety reported, "Even the girls on the runway are grinding more vigorously."

City police authorities, considering banning burlesque altogether because of the sins of stock burlesque, were won over by the merged wheels' promise of good behavior. Mike Joyce for Columbia and Emmett Calahan for Mutual formed a censorship committee of two to keep a watchful eye on both wheels' attractions.

The jubilation was short-lived. "As a money-maker," Variety reported in 1928, "burlesque is practically washed up. The top salary paid is never over $75. In stock burly, the necessity to fix the cops takes away any profits. Picture theatres usually have a girl act, and that hurts burly plenty. The dirt show cannot live . . . and burly today is a dirt show."

Columbia-Mutual, now combined under the banner of the Mutual wheel, controlled only 40 shows and theatres—or just equal in opposition strength to the stock burlesque troupes. Over 500 people were employed weekly by stock burlesque in Chicago alone. Mutual troupes, containing about 30 people each, averaged $55 apiece (including top principals), while Mutual managers received about $200 weekly profit. And to get that, managers had to skimp on production costs, resulting in poorer shows.

By 1928 there was no longer any pretense at "refined" burlesque. It was all straight Minsky—in both the Mutual and stock burlesque houses. In those cities where the police could be properly added to the expense account, managers bid desperately for the male trade with shows that went the limit. "And the limit in burly," Variety grimaced, "is about the most disgusting stage show ever publicly presented."

cooch stuff The star appeal of 1928 burlesque was the chorus line. With bare epidermis in abundance at musicals and revues, burlesque sought gingerbread trimming, and found it in the "cooch dance," re-named "the shake." Sure that they had something there, Mutual managers made all the principals and chorus "shake" in unison, as well as singly, which gave the customers a tremendous amount of mammary vibration to stare at.

Then came the beginnings of the striptease—"little tricks of dressing and undressing," as Variety explained it then. To make sure that none of this art escaped notice, theatres put in runways which took soubrets and chorus into the audience at a suitably titillating elevation. Despite all this, Variety warned, "The problem of Mutual is to hold a fast-waning patronage . . . an audience that is getting tired of the same legs and gags week after week."

The fate of vaudeville threatened burlesque at the windup of the decade. "This year," Variety declared in 1929, "proved that burly is shot. Even the morons are getting fed up with the dirt. Mutual Circuit, survivor of the wheels, started out promising 50 houses and 50 shows, and now has 43 houses and 48 shows, giving all shows a 5-week layoff for the season. . . . As soon as a 'blue' gag is new, all the comedians cop it—and all shows have the same gags. Many shows have been pulled up on dirt, leaving a hole in their perform-ance, as that is all they depend on. What's left of the clientele wants rough-house, and gets it when the gendarmes don't interfere. Stocks are dirtier than wheel shows. They top 'em for filth and get away with it . . . also with most of the business."

And the pig got up and slowly walked away.

from striptease to longhair   At the opposite pole of show business, the Metropolitan Opera House was having its head-aches as the decade opened. In 1919 the Chicago Opera Company's booking of New York's Lexington Opera House for a 5-week season was a distinct thorn in the august side of the Met, whose 23-week season cost about $1,000,000.

The feeling was made more bitter by the fact that Campinini, who had been Oscar Hammerstein's foremost conductor, had be-come director of the Chicago Opera when the Met had bought out Hammerstein to have a clear field in New York opera. Campinini had made the grade because Toscanini refused to be tempted to come to the United States for less than $75,000 a season.

"In no other country," Variety noted that year, "is the operatic field so limited to newcomers as in America." Despite the excep-tional case, which permitted Rosa Ponselle to leap from vaudeville into the Met, and Dorothy Jardon from vaudeville to the Chicago Opera Co., the opera of that year was a closed door to artists with less than 5-syllable names. (Not so, of course, in later years under Edward Johnson, and still later under Rudolf Bing.)

Lions of the longhair were understandably jolted by an upstart named Al Jolson who gave a one-man concert in May of 1919 at the Boston Opera House. Singing 17 songs, accompanied by a 50-

piece orchestra, the upstart played to a $4,100 house at $2 top—with 2,000 disappointed concert-goers turned away.

Opera that year was also improved, or hurt, depending upon your point of view, by the anti-German animus which led to the downfall of German opera in the German tongue at the Lexington Opera House. The all-German Star Opera Co. packed and made ready to go home.

That the Met was the home of opera-lovers, and not merely social snobs, was evident in 1919 by the fact that many New Yorkers paid $200 for a single seat, and $5,000 for a box, for one of the Met's sterling performances. By an odd coincidence, it happened to be the night chosen for a visit to the opera by Albert Edward Windsor, Prince of Wales.

Whatever the appeal of the Met, the institution astounded itself in 1920 with a one-week visit to Atlanta, Georgia. Gross for the week was $140,000, and that's certainly marching 'em to the Georgia b.o. In New York that season, the Met was further delighted by being rewarded for its 23 weeks with a gross of $1,800,000, the largest in its history.

In its longhair division of 1920, Variety reported that singer John McCormack was running into trouble Down Under. His concert in Adelaide had been broken up with cries of "Sinn Feiner!", because McCormack had omitted opening the Australian concert with the British national anthem. The singer explained he thought "God Save the King" only had to be sung when the State's Governor was present. Prudently, McCormack cancelled all concerts in Adelaide and moved on back to America.

caruso sock b.o.   Caruso set a world's record that year by garnering $23,864 at the Atheneum, New Orleans, with tickets scaled to a $11 top. Caruso was guaranteed $10,000 for the night, another world's record. Counting up, and checking his income tax records, the great tenor announced he was through singing for the season.

When Caruso died in 1921, his body was scarcely cold before Tin Pan Alley had provided a musical tribute—"They Needed A Song Bird in Heaven, So God Took Caruso Away." It is highly probable that if Caruso had not died before this gem appeared, he would have shortly afterward.

Among Variety's longhair notes of 1924 could be found mention of Sousa's $120,000 profit on a 33-week season; the debut of Negro tenor Roland Hayes at Aeolian Hall; and the subsequent debut there of another Negro, ex-vaudevillian Jules Bledsoe, who was to rise to fame as Joe in *Show Boat* three years later.

Otherwise, opera as usual, with very little of note to report until Billy Rose decided to slip the Met a hotfoot in 1948.

34

Songs of Our Time

★

There was no doubt, back in 1919, that Americans were getting set to blow off steam. The motto, as promulgated by Tin Pan Alley, was "Take Me to the Land of Jazz!" The pleas, "Let's Help the Irish Now" and "Take Care of the Man in the Uniform," had received scant attention, as did the sober farewell upon the occasion of the death of a great President of the United States, "Goodbye, Teddy Roosevelt, You Were A Real American."

Much more to the point, as inspired by postwar problems, was the taunting query, "How You Gonna Keep 'Em Down On the Farm, After They've Seen Paree?" A nostalgic echo of wartime Europe was heard in "He'd Say Oo-La-La Wee Wee!"

For throats parched by Prohibition, there were the liquid melodies of "Alcoholic Blues," "America Never Took Water—And America Never Will," "I'm Going to Settle Down Outside of London Town (When I'm Dry, Dry, Dry)" "I'll See You In C-U-B-A," "What'll We Do On Saturday Night When the Town Goes Dry?," "The Prohibition Ball" and "Smart Little Feller Who Stocked Up His Cellar (That's Getting the Beautiful Girls)," which was refuted by "You Don't Need the Wine to Have a Wonderful Time (While They're Still Making the Beautiful Girls)." Those who needed their engines oiled before going into high gear on the dance floor sang mournfully, "You Cannot Make Your Shimmy Shake On Tea," which was the great comedian Bert Williams' classic in the *Ziegfeld Follies of 1919.*

In the wistful, tear-in-your-eye division, there were "Oh, What A Pal Was Mary," "Smiles," "Broadway Rose," "My Isle of Golden Dreams," "Nobody Knows and Nobody Seems to Care," "Daddy, You've Been a Mother to Me," "Love Sends a Little Gift of Roses" and "Dear Old Pal of Mine." The ivory tower clique was entranced by "Let the Rest of the World Go By," "I'm Forever Blowing Bubbles," "I'm Always Chasing Rainbows," "April Showers" and "Look For the Silver Lining." Those who couldn't afford to blow bubbles or chase rainbows because of the rent sang "Oh! Oh! Those Landlords!"

Songs archly hinting at newly-acquired arts of Jazz Age lovers were "You'd Be Surprised," "Ma! (He's Making Eyes At Me)," "I'll Say She Does" and "The Blues My Naughty Sweetie Gives To Me."

The regional sweepstakes were won by "Beautiful Ohio," "Tuck Me to Sleep In My Old Tucky Home," "Carolina In the Morning," "Chicago," "On the Gin-Gin-Gin Ginny Shore," "O-HI-O," "Way Down Yonder in New Orleans" and "Rockabye Your Baby With a Dixie Melody," the latter a Jolson special. And there was a strong Oriental vogue teed off by the smash hit, "Dardanella," including "Hindustan," "Japanese Sandman" and "There's Egypt In Your Dreamy Eyes." No publisher had wanted to touch "Dardanella" under its original title, "Turkish Tom Toms"; renamed, it was the "Nature Boy" of its day.

With all attention focused on the new moral liberation of women evident in 1920, songs of that year were woven around their names —"Margie" (the same song revived so enthusiastically only recently), "Ida (Sweet As Apple Cider)," "Broadway Rose," "Second Hand Rose," "Rose of Washington Square," "Peggy," "Peggy O'Neil," "Sally" and "If You Knew Susie."

Sunday blue laws led one tunesmith to lament, "If They Ever Take the Sun Out of Sunday." In the novelty slot the era yielded "Barney Google," "Runnin' Wild," "Yes, We Have No Bananas," "You Gotta See Mama Every Night," "Oh By Jingo," "Hot Lips," "China Boy," "Wabash Blues" and "Wang Wang Blues." A backward glance at some rapidly diminishing American mores was contained in "My Home Town Is A One Horse Town" and "Early to Bed and Early to Rise."

Hot love in the early 1920s was represented by "Dapper Dan," "I'm Nobody's Baby," "Annabelle Lee," "I Never Knew (I could love anybody, honey, like I'm lovin' you)," and some practical advice, "Say It With Liquor." The lukewarm love spigot poured "Do You Ever Think of Me?," "I've Got the Blues," "Forgive Me," "Bright Eyes," "Love Bird," "A Kiss In the Dark," "Three O'Clock In the Morning," "Song of Love" (from Romberg's *Blossom Time*), "My Man" (from the French "Mon Homme"), "Over The Hill" and "I'm Coming Back to You—Maybe," which Ted Lewis sang over the phone from San Francisco to an interested New York publisher.

More novelties were produced such as "Lena (She's the Queen of Palestina)," "Ain't We Got Fun?," "Hello, Hello, Hello (Cherabubkeh! Cherabubkeh)," which was Lewis & Dody's vaudeville comedy specialty.

A prize bit of corn was produced by Ballard Macdonald and Bryan Foy, who wrote the lyrics to celebrate the arrival in the United States in November 1921 of the Unknown Soldier. It was called "My Boy Joe."

In 1922 there was a wave of revivals, spurred by blues recordings of old songs. Some liberties were taken with the originals, as "Just A Song At Twilight" ("Tell Her At Twilight"), "Break The News To Mother" ("Take the Blues From Mother"), and "When You and I Were Young Maggie Blues." A new blues song was added— "Blue Danube Blues." Tin Pan Alley variations of this technique appear with each musical vogue or trend, such as rhumba, samba, polka, and bebop arrangements of standards.

Signs of the times were reflected in "Hello Prosperity," intended to reassure the worried; "Lovin' Sam, the Sheik of Alabam'," a satirical reference to the sheik mania set by Rudolph Valentino; "Over the Radiophone" ("Please let me talk to my mammy"), the first popular song to take note of radio.

Later regional contributions were "Beautiful California," "Dear Old Southland" and "Kentucky Home on the Swanee Shore"—the latter a gem of geographical wizardry. Eddie Cantor lent a hand to tunesmiths Gerber and Schwartz to concoct "My Yiddisha Mammy" —foreshadowing Sophie Tucker's later "Yiddisha Mama." Ragtime

was represented by "Aggravatin' Papa (Don't You Two-Time Me!)."
The nut song of the year was "Oogie-Oogie Wa Wa," represented
as an Eskimo love call.

nut songs   The biggest smash hit of 1923 was a nut number,
"Yes, We Have No Bananas," which displaced the previous record
made by "Oh By Jingo" (2,000,000 copies). "Bananas" swept the country, even to the most remote one-horse towns (via radio). In vaudeville Harry Holbrook, "The Singing Marine," copyrighted an "operatic version" he originated.

Other hopeful nut numbers of the year were "Nutsey Fagan,"
Olsen & Johnson's "Oh Gee, Oh Gosh, Oh Golly I'm In Love," Billy
Rose's "Barney Google," "In Hotsy Totsy Town" and "Old King
Tut," who had just been dug up in Egypt. The sorrowful songs
were "That Old Gang of Mine," "Who's Sorry Now?," "You Know
You Belong To Somebody Else," "Mother In Ireland," "My Sweetie
Went Away (and she didn't say where)" and "Who Cares?" Ragtime
offered "Raggin' the Scale," "Runnin' Wild'," "Bambalina" and
"Charleston."

In 1924, the year that Variety paid increasing recognition to Tin
Pan Alley by beginning a chatter column called "Abel's Comment"
(by Abel Green) to cover songwriters and the business, there was
le jazz hot with "Limehouse Blues," "Mama Loves Papa" and
"Hula Lou (Oh, how she could shake her sea-weed-dees!)." Timely
numbers were "Mr. Radio Man, Tell My Mammy To Come Back
Home" and "Ray and His Little Chevrolet." The months came in
for adulation with "May Time" and "June Night." For crying in
your beer there were "The Pal That I Loved (stole the gal that I
loved)," "All Alone" (Berlin), "Memory Lane" and "Rock-A-Bye
Baby Days" and the regional rage, "California, Here I Come."

1925 brought "The Prisoner's Song," "Let Me Call You Sweet-
heart," "Collegiate," "Dinah," "Rose-Marie" (Friml), "Who?"
(Kern), "Valencia," "I'll See You In My Dreams" and "When the One
You Love Loves You." For the boys who liked it fast, there were
Cantor's "If You Knew Susie" and "Dinah." The weepers had "Pal
Of My Cradle Days," and the soft-and-sweet addicts, "Midnight
Waltz."

A wave of wistful sentiment swept over Tin Pan Alley in 1926,
when songsmiths wrapped gentle sighs in "After I Say I'm Sorry,"

"Always," "Remember" (the latter two by Irving Berlin), "Tonight You Belong To Me," "I Wish I Had My Old Girl Back Again," "Somebody's Lonely," "In A Little Spanish Town" and "Love Found You For Me."

There was also the lilting "Pretty Little Baby," and signs of the times—"Everybody's Charleston Crazy," "The Black Bottom" and "Death of Floyd Collins." Otto Harbach, the lyricist whose boxoffice royalties from the legit musical, *No No Nanette,* were only $14,700 earned almost $500,000 from the record and sheet music sales from his *Rose Marie, Sunny, Song of the Flame* and *Wildflower.*

"My Blue Heaven" in 1927 sold so many Victor records that it made its recording artist, Gene Austin, rich and famous. In the same love-is-all vein that year were "At Sundown," "Thinking of You," "Among My Souvenirs," "Girl of My Dreams," "Without You Sweetheart" and "Chloe." Built for the guitars were "Rio Rita" and "An Old Guitar and An Old Refrain." Moon song of the year was "Honolulu Moon." Hot and lowdown were "Shake That Thing," which made Ethel Waters on discs, and "Dixie Stomp." In tune with the times was "Lucky Lindy." Two of the year's real musical standouts were "Old Man River" (from Jerome Kern's score for *Show Boat*) and "Hallelujah" (from Vincent Youmans' *Hit the Deck*).

those theme songs   The 1927-1928 season also saw the first soundfilm theme songs: "Charmaine," "Jeannine (I Dream of Lilac Time)," "Diane," "Sonny Boy" and "Ramona." "Charmaine" was from *What Price Glory?*, "Jeannine" from *Lilac Time,* "Diane" from the Janet Gaynor-Charles Farrell classic *Seventh Heaven,* and "Sonny Boy" and "Ramona" both from the pictures of the same name. The trend caught on, with Hollywood bottling extra sales appeal by writing in theme songs which carried film titles, such as the slightly impossible, "Woman Disputed, I Love You." The straw that broke this camel's back was a theme song for a George Bancroft he-man film, *Dynamite Man,* which offered songsters the opportunity to warble, "Dynamite Man, I Love You." This classic so ridiculed Tin Pan Alley that it ended theme songs for a while.

With radio and night clubs riding songs to death in 1928, producers began to be wary about allowing extra-curricular airing of musical comedy hit numbers. Jerome Kern withheld "Who (. . . stole my heart away?)" from the Marilyn Miller show *Sunny,* and

Max and Louis Dreyfus, heads of Chappell-Harms, kept strict reins on the smash numbers from Flo Ziegfeld's *Show Boat*. "Laugh, Clown, Laugh" inspired parodies by the dozens and Henry Ford was distressed when a Jewish songwriter turned out a hit called, "Since Henry Ford Apologized To Me."

Variety reported, on the eve of 1929, that songwriting in America had come a long way during the decade. "It wasn't so long ago when the conventional moon-June-spoon-croon and the blue-you-two-true doggerel was still the accepted standard in production and popular song lyrics. Along came some new thoughts, new rhythms, and new rhymes and new constructions by such expert lyricists as Irving Berlin, Irving Caesar, Lorenz Hart, Oscar Hammerstein 2d, Howard Dietz, Otto Harbach, Buddy DeSylva and Ira Gershwin and put the pop writers to shame. Not that the pop songsmiths do not gross as much, and more, as their highfalutin' contemporaries, because, after all is said and done, a simple idea simply retailed clicks biggest with the great American Babbittry."

The hits of 1929 were apparently all simple ideas simply retailed. There were the no-place-like-home eulogies such as "A Little Town Called Home Sweet Home" and "My Castle In Spain Is a Shack In the Lane." In the bargain basement of love were "My Tonia," "Cradle Of Love" and the jazzier "Kansas City Kitty." And for the baby-talk special, "I Faw Down and Go Boom." It took wits of the day very little time to discover the association between the latter song and what happened in Wall Street.

irving berlin   The biggest single figure behind the scenes of music of the 1920s was unquestionably still Irving Berlin. In 1919 Berlin left the firm of (Henry) Waterson, Berlin & (Ted) Snyder, severing the 12-year relationship to go into business for himself with Max Winslow, the man who "discovered" Berlin, and Saul H. Bornstein, now head of Bourne Music Corp. All show business signalzed the event with an Irving Berlin Week all over the country that year. Music stores had special displays, and Loew's Circuit had two current Berlin songs on every program in their theatres. Berlin observed the occasion by appearing for the week in New York vaudeville. Despite the year's excitement, he still found time to launch with E. Ray Goetz, whose sister he married, the Song Writers Protective Association, to provide care for sick and disabled songsmiths.

Berlin's decision to go into business for himself in 1919 was the making of his fortune. In 1921, after only 18 months as his own entrepreneur, Berlin had earned $195,000 in disk and sheet music royalties from Berlin, Inc. He made the front-page in black head-lines in 1926, when, some years after the death of his first wife, he married Ellin Mackay, daughter of Postal Telegraph's Clarence H. Mackay, against the latter's thundering opposition. So important and controversial was the match between Catholic Ellin and Jewish Irving (born Israel Baline), that special dispensation was granted by Pope Pius XI for the marriage.

It had been during the courtship, when Mackay had sent his daughter to Europe to break up the romance, that Berlin had writ-ten "What'll I Do? (. . . when you are far away?)." Ellin turned the tables on her father by getting an audience with the Pontiff at the Vatican, thus procuring papal dispensation. Mackay angrily warned Berlin that he would cut his daughter off without a cent. The songwriter shrugged and stated he would give Ellin $2,000,000 as a wedding present. When circumstances kept Berlin and his Ellin apart he composed the famous "All Alone (by the telephone)." "Always" capped the climax of their romance.

The marriage of the boy who rose from East Side rags to Tin Pan Alley riches to the daughter of one of the 400 called forth an outpouring of Cinderella articles in newspapers and magazines. Al Dubin and Jimmy McHugh attempted to musically immortalize the event by composing:

> *When a kid from the East Side*
> *Found a sweet society rose,*
> *He sang a sweet little love song*
> *That his lonely heart composed,*
> *He said, "You forgot to 'Remember,'*
> *But she did 'Remember,' he knows,*
> *'Cause the kid who came from the East Side*
> *Got that sweet society rose.*

When the Berlins married, with Mackay still thumbs-down, Harry Hershfield sent a wire, via Western Union, CONGRATULATIONS. HERE IS THIRTYFIVE CENTS 'POSTAL TELEGRAPH' WON'T GET. As is generally known, Berlin and Mackay eventually reconciled.

disk boom   The first song hit ever to be made exclusively through the medium of records was George Stoddard's "Mary" (not to be confused with George M. Cohan's) in 1919. It was never sung on any stage. Stoddard offered it to several publishers for $100 outright, but found no takers. Victor put it on a record, and in three months it sold 300,000 platters, earning Stoddard $15,000 in royalties.

Records were hitting the very big time by 1920. Brunswick signed Eddie Cantor to a five-year recording contract at a staggering pay-off of $220,000, putting him in the top record brackets along with Caruso, Galli-Curci and McCormack.

In that year a surprising new source of competition was spring-ing up in the music business—the Woolworth five-and-tens. With 1,200 stores in the United States, and many more abroad, Woolworth's was found to be selling over 200,000,000 copies of songs a year. Wool-worth's turned publisher that year with the song "Afghanistan." Plugged at their piano counters, it sold 400,000 copies in four weeks, at 10¢ a copy. Tin Pan Alley blinked and viewed with alarm. It was Record Alley's turn to gulp in 1927 when Woolworth began to mer-chandise 10¢ disks with a hit song on one side, and a non-royalty number on the other.

Variety turned the spotlight on the graft in music publishing of 1921, which was supposed to be free of payoff to orchestra leaders for plugging a company's numbers. It was business as usual, Variety charged, with publishers putting baton-wavers on their payrolls as "staff writers" at $10,000 a year, also paying them $100 bonuses for "special arrangements"—which were hardly more than changing a few notes.

Manufacturers of musical instruments that year were also a little tired of their own form of extortion. Some companies had gone to the extent of outfitting bands completely with instruments, uniforms and equipment, in exchange for publicity photos which allowed them to exploit the fact that Joe Blow and his Band all tootled on Hotnoise instruments. Now they balked, weary of the demands by bands, de-ciding, no more equipment on the cuff or at special discounts.

The American Society of Composers, Authors and Publishers also was snapping its suspenders in 1921 and going after everything that threatened to rob writers and publishers of the benefits of their mu-sic. One big achievement was a contract with 800 film houses, guaranteeing a payoff of 10¢ per seat per year to ASCAP. This amounted to $1,000,000 a year that first annum.

In San Francisco, the musicians' union did a burn when private dances and parties made use of the "wireless telephone" for their music. If this radio thing was allowed to continue, musicians cried, who would want to hire live bands and orchestras any more? (Shades of James Caesar Petrillo to come.)

ASCAP began to feel the same way about its own members the following year, deciding that radio concerts would have to pay royalties for any songs they used. Huddling with radio station executives, ASCAP won an agreement with broadcasters that music would be prefaced with, "Permission was granted to play . . . ," and that royalty terms would be worked out.

a lady out of jazz   Paul Whiteman, who introduced soft-toned dansapation when New York was swamped by brassy jazz bands, already had a $1,000,000 income by 1922. He controlled 11 bands in New York, 17 on the road, and received royalties from 40 more bands playing Whiteman arrangements. Recognition as more than just a popular bandleader came in 1924, when he and his Palais Royal Orchestra gave a concert at Aeolian Hall, New York, assisted by George Gershwin, to present "symphonic syncopation." This event made a lady out of Jazz.

The program included Ferde Grofe's "Russian Rose," Gershwin's "Rhapsody In Blue," and a rendition of "Yes, We Have No Bananas" which showed the debt this number owed to Handel's "Messiah." From that time on, it became fashionable to regard both Whiteman and jazz as serious exponents of modern music.

The slow decline of vaudeville in 1924 was felt in the world of music. Of Local 802's 12,000 union musicians in New York, only 5,000 were working. To get jobs, musicians were taking bookings below union scale, under cover.

Radio, at first suspected as a menace by the music world, proved a boon by 1925. Radio's plugging of songs sent new millions to the music counters. By the time these numbers were on the pianos, radio was plugging new songs, and back came the customers again. Radio's biggest feature was music, and music was in the air—so much so that there was a very definite music craze that year. A Variety count showed 60,000 bands in the United States, both amateur and professional. An harmonica craze, plugged by radio, brought astonished mouth organ manufacturers orders for 20,000,000 of the instruments in 1925.

The highest-priced four-piece jazz band in history played the Palace in Chicago that year. When Herb Wiedoeft (brother of the great saxophonist, Rudy Wiedoeft, from whom Yaleman-saxer Hubert Prior Vallee took his professional first name) was booked there with his trumpet, he was joined onstage as a tribute for one show by Paul Whiteman and his violin, Abe Lyman at the drums, and Paul Ash at the piano. And out in Omaha, where the music craze had developed contests of endurance, piano player J. N. Waterbury dropped from exhaustion after banging the ivories for 57 hours.

If 1925 was radio's year in music, 1926 belonged to the record companies. Chagrined at the dent made in their sales by radio, Victor, Brunswick and other companies came out with new, improved phonographs. Victor showed a net profit of $5,000,000 in only nine months of 1926.

The year also saw the re-election of James Caesar Petrillo as president of the Chicago Federation of Musicians, with a pay hike from $200 to $250 a week. Music critics began to call jazz lovers "musical illiterates." And music publishers ignored vaudeville as they went after song plugs to the musical illiterates who were flocking into the picture theatres.

In 1927 Variety again sounded the tocsin on graft by music publishers, pointing out that now it was being shelled out to the stage personnel of the picture palaces—dance bands, masters of ceremonies and featured house singers. Variety warned film theatre managers to keep their eyes peeled, or risk having lemons hurled at their audiences by bribed talent.

Radio, which had started buying talent by 1927, signed George Olsen's Band at $2,500 a week. He gave up his hotel stand for it, although his radio contract permitted him to play anywhere. Less cheerful about radio's relationship to the music world was Petrillo, who signaled the fight against "canned" music by pulling musicians out of the Marigold Gardens in Chicago, where they were being alternated with radio music.

The big deal of 1928 was once again theme songs for Hollywood. With every studio rushing talking musicals into production, Tin Pan Alley suddenly found itself metamorphosized into a plush boulevard. Producers fought each other to make deals with the big music houses. Warner Bros. grabbed Harms, Remick and Witmark while Metro bought control of Robbins, and later Feist and Miller Music. The idea was not only to latch on to the affirmative for use of each publisher's catalogs, but also to get special themes written by star tunesmiths of each house.

"Diane," "Jeannine," "Charmaine," "Pagan Love Song," "Ramona" and a gilt-edged piece of corn by DeSylva, Brown & Henderson called "Sonny Boy," which Al Jolson made his own, were the result among many others.

hollywood gold rush   With music riding a new gravy train, the boys who wrote it began to give considerable thought to riding in the engine seat. Many tunesmiths began to go into publishing for themselves. DeSylva, Brown & Henderson hung out a shingle. (Larry) Spier & (Sam) Coslow, who had turned out, "Was It A Dream? (. . . or are you really mine?)" was another new firm. Tunesmiths (Bud) Green & (Sammy) Stept, on the strength of "That's My Weakness Now," which Helen Kane boop-a-dooped to hitdom, also joined the ranks of new entrepreneurs, along with Vincent Youmans. George Gershwin and Jerome Kern already were in business for themselves under the benevolent guidance of Max Dreyfus. And, of course, so was Irving Berlin.

Songwriters were seduced to the Coast by $350 to $1,500 a week salaries. Annual guarantees of $25,000 income were offered to amazed tune carpenters who once had begged from music publisher to music publisher, unwanted songs rolled under their arms.

The talkies influenced not only the publishing houses, but also the record companies, which had also been recording all the theme songs. In 1929, however, Victor, Brunswick and Columbia announced they were going to disk only those themes which were tied up with films more likely for the boxoffice.

Petrillo, however, speaking for the non-Hollywood enriched musicians, lashed out at the talkies with a $5,000-a-week radio show in Chicago. He announced his intention of fighting the sound screen, and swore he would prove to the public that canned music was an anemic substitute for real, live music.

Variety's opinion of a certain segment of the music branch of show business, as it was constituted in 1928, was not exactly complimentary. "It is doubtful," declared the paper, "whether in any other field there is so much chicanery, double-crossing, double-dealing, duplicity and hooey, a condition that comes about not so much because of economic jealousy, but because of the petty business of 'landing a plug.' "

Variety also heralded the future of the bandleading-masters of ceremonies of 1928. The paper pointed out that the day of the non-musical m.c. had gone, and that only those who had been smart enough to jump in front of a band—doubling in brass—had survived.

Warner Bros. proved, in 1929, to be the most important Hollywood factor in the music business. Controlling a majority of the governing board of ASCAP, it was able to set its own standards of financial arrangements between Hollywood and Tin Pan Alley. ASCAP didn't mind, because Warners' notions of musical rewards were suitably heart-warming.

The curtain fell approximately on the music world of the Jazz Age when the critics hurled a fresh onslaught of slings and arrows at the outrageous fortunes which had brought jazz to America. "Unbuttoned music," they sneered at it. "Youth set to music . . . symphonic rickets of musical malnutrition!"

Yes, they were not having any bananas, thank you.

Harlem to Broadway and Moscow

★

Circuses, which had had a bad time during World War I, found themselves in top position when the shooting stopped. In 1919, the leading combine, Barnum & Bailey-Ringling Bros., stepped into a good thing in Chicago by offering to donate 10 per cent of the gross on a special date to the Soldiers and Sailors Memorial Fund.

Chicago city fathers allowed them to pitch tents in Grant Park, a million-dollar site, where the Big Top played to capacity.

The following year the combined circus broke all records for Madison Square Garden in New York with a five-and-one-half week engagement that took in $700,000. The show featured the first German act to be admitted to the United States since the end of World War I—an acrobat team called the Sandwinis.

The Sells-Floto Circus was having trouble in the minor league slot, and sold out in 1920 to Ed Ballard and Jerry Mugivan. Two years later, Variety noted sharp rivalry between the Sells and Ringling shows at San Francisco. Ringling's erected a spite fence to cut off the Market Street entrance to the Sells-Floto site. Nothing daunted, the Floto management trotted out one of its elephants to tear a sizable hole in the fence.

Variety also called attention that year to an unusual branch of circus business—the Canadian lumber camp route. It was the monopoly of Leo De Facto, a traveling clown for 40 years, and his family. The De Factos swung around the lumber camps of lower Quebec, offering acrobatics, magic, tight-rope walking, and general circus fare. They traveled by dogsled, no mean feat for De Facto, who was over 60.

By 1925 circus business was sizzling. Grosses of $30,000 a day were not uncommon. Frank Buck was kept busy making three trips a year to India to satisfy the demand for wild animals. And the three-ring circus was well on its way toward becoming "smalltime." The Ringling-Barnum & Bailey combine offered no less than five rings, kept whirling with 350 performers.

It was the year the old Madison Square Garden on 26th St. was torn down, to be replaced with the new Garden on 8th Avenue at 50th St. As a farewell gesture to the old showplace, Ringling threw a party for nostalgic newspapermen, and presented an old-fashioned, one-ring circus.

The new Garden was opened in such haste—to cash in on the booming trend of special-events show business—that it was discovered too late that the architect had neglected to provide dressing rooms! In 1926 the first Rodeo—Fred Beebe's World Series Rodeo—opened at the new Garden at a $3 top, and was a smash hit. A less fortunate venture that year was a chorus of 110 Russian Cossacks, which cost the Garden management $35,000 for a total reward of $5,000.

In 1926, the year of the Black Bottom, horses and elephants delighted circus fans with four-legged versions of the dance. Overseas, circus thrill of the year was Capt. Alfield, performing with 70 lions at the Crystal Palace in London. Alfield held raw meat in his mouth while his pets bit off portions.

The death of Charles Ringling in 1926 brought to light the fact that he was the sixth of seven Ringling brothers to go. Born in McGregor, Iowa, the seven sons of a harness-maker had started in show business with the Classic Concert Co., which became the Ringling Bros. Comedy Co. The sons' great love for horses, derived from their father, eventually turned the company into a circus in 1882.

Another circus figure of note died that year, Darius Adner Alden, better known as General Tom Thumb. For 50 of his 84 years, Alden had been a glass blower and star circus attraction.

One year later, Colonel Joe C. Miller, impresario of the Miller's 101 Ranch, was overcome by carbon monoxide fumes in his garage. The Ponca Indians, many of whom had appeared in his Wild West shows, held a 10-day mourning ceremony. Another circus death of 1927 was Marceline, the famous clown, who became despondent over his unemployment and killed himself.

Variety unearthed a strange story in 1928 concerning one George Miller, 78, who had been with Barnum & Bailey as a tightrope performer since the age of 18. Miller had also held intermittent jobs as railroad night watchman, farmhand, and section hand on the Great Western. Variety's story was that George Miller's correct name was Mary Miller, and that she had posed as a man for 60 years because "men have an easier time than women, and get all the breaks."

Ringling was the kingpin outfit of 1929, having bought out the opposition shows of Mugivan, Ballard & Bowers for $2,000,000. The Miller 101 Ranch made news that year by winning a playdate in New York's Van Cortlandt Park, a feat made possible by Mrs. William Randolph Hearst for her Milk Fund benefit.

If circuses thrived in the 1920s, the opposite was true of the traveling carnival shows. The carnival business of 1921 was rough, tough stuff, with many of them working the "Number Three" racket. This consisted of luring likely prospects into three tents—Tent No. 1, where he met a very amiable young lady; Tent No. 2, where he was sold a supply of rotgut for an anticipated lively evening; and Tent No. 3, where his pants pockets were picked without his knowledge (because he wasn't in them). Tent No. 3 was also sometimes used as the scene of the old badger game.

So many towns had been fleeced by "Number Three" carnivals, that county after county went up in arms against all carnivals, refusing permits and chasing troupes out of town. This led some carnivals to masquerade as circuses in order to win licenses. A meeting of carnival men was held in 1922, with the objective of cleaning up the profession, but the reform was purely on paper.

There was a brief boom for carnivals in 1926, when there were 70 gypsy outfits on the road, each with five to seven cars. But the following year, with the number increasing to over double—150 carnivals—only 10 were reported to be making money. And in 1928 carny was definitely shot, with no hope except for the better shows at county and state fairs.

In the single year of 1929, about 100 towns blacklisted carnivals from coming in. Variety estimated that only six carny outfits in the nation had a clean bill of health, depending on honest rides and amusements for their receipts. And that was even before Wall Street got around to slapping what was left of carnival business to the canvas.

sports headliners on tour In the sports division, Babe Ruth led off the decade as the athlete most likely to get the nod from show business. When the Babe clouted 29 homers in 1919, the New York Yankees bought him for $125,000. In short order he was the home-run idol of baseball fans and kids. Oddly, when the Babe appeared in vaudeville, he was a "frost" compared to the immense b.o. of another sports figure—Jack Dempsey. Showmen put it down to the fact that folks could always see the Babe for 50¢, but had to shell out from $20 to $50 to watch Dempsey in action.

Whatever the reason, Dempsey was undoubtedly a star attraction, whether on canvas or the boards. After knocking out Jess Willard in 1919, Dempsey headed a show with 25 wrestlers and boxers, taking in $90,000 in three weeks, half of that to Dempsey.

Another boxer invaded show business the following year, Georges Carpentier, who signed with Sells-Floto at $12,000 a week, plus private Pullman car and auto, making him the biggest deal the circus had ever known. Six years later Carpentier still preferred footlights to Klieg lights, touring the Pantages Circuit.

Carpentier and Dempsey staged the first $1,000,000 scrap of the era in 1921. The gate was actually $1,650,000, paid by 75,000 boxing fans who cheered Dempsey as he flattened the French fighter in the fourth. Dempsey's stock rose still higher. In 1924 he pulled in $41,000 at Loew's State, New York, the following year appearing for a month in Berlin's Luna Park at a salary of $8,000 a week. That year bricklayers laid down their hods, demanding a $2 a day raise from Tex Rickard for building the new Garden. If Rickard could pay Dempsey $1,000,000 for 12 minutes' work, they felt he could well afford to pay bricklayers $2 more per day.

Other fighters were shadowboxing on the glamor circuit in 1925. Jim Corbett was doing well on a lecture tour, talking on "Memories of An Active Life," and offering advice on how to keep young. Benny Leonard was at the Palace on Broadway, the unfortunate recipient of the first rotten eggs ever hurled in that hallowed auditorium. His personal enemies were held suspect. Leonard was equally unfortunate in 1927, when he appeared with "Battling Butler," as a tab show on the Columbia wheel, and closed for lack of business.

In 1925 Variety carried an ad for Jeanne LaMar, who billed herself as the "Champ bantamweight and featherweight lady boxer of the world—never defeated." She claimed to be the first professional female boxer in history, as well as a prima donna, dramatic star and feature attraction.

a crooning pug   One year later another boxing showman was heard from—Joop Liet, a Dutchman who won a vaudeville engagement on the strength of flattening his ring opponent. Joop led with his chin, singing a large hunk of grand opera which was greeted by jeering laughter at the Alhambra Theatre in New York. Never a man to throw in the towel, Joop kept right on singing. "I don't care," he explained, grinning. "I like for to sing."

Jim Jeffries and Tom Sharkey toured the Pantages Circuit in 1926, the year boxing fever swelled to a new pitch with the Dempsey-Tunney match in Philadelphia. This event, which brought $1,723,394 from 145,000 fans, was also listened to by 40,000,000 Americans over the air. Tunney was promptly booked at Loew's State on

Broadway at $7,000 a week. As a final note on boxing and show
business, Variety observed in 1929 that Jack Johnson, the great
Negro boxer, was leading a jazz band "for ballrooms." Johnson
finally wound up as an attraction at Hubert's Museum on New
York's West 42d Street, best known for its flea circus.

harlemania   Negro showfolks came into their own during
the decade. The popularity of jazz, dances like the Black Bottom,
the trend toward mixed casts on Broadway, and the development
of Harlem as the uptown entertainment for "smart people"—all
these were factors. Negro troupes put on, for a while, by the Columbia burlesque wheel drew far better business than the white
companies.

Doe Green came into prominence, hailed in adjectives usually
reserved for Bert Williams and Charles Gilpin, through a show
called *Appearances* which opened in 1925 on top of the New Amsterdam Theatre, New York. The play was the work of Garland Anderson, a West Coast bellhop who wrote it between calls, and
launched it on Broadway with the help of Al Jolson.

Cabarets had all-colored revues, starring Florence Mills, Johnny
Hudgins, Eddie Green (later of "Duffy's Tavern"), Miller & Lyles,
Buck & Bubbles, Eddie Rector, Ethel Waters, Maude Russell and
Bill Robinson. Bessie Smith, who never played a "white" house, was
earning $800 a week, besides $1,000 a recording. Another Smith—
Mamie—made equally good money, but had to share the take with
her band.

Two all-Negro theatres were doing a lush business—the Lafayette
in Harlem and the Orpheum in Newark. The Theatre Owners
Booking Association, booking only colored troupes, sent Negro minstrel tab shows through the country. That conditions outside of New
York were not too rosy for the sepia-skinned was made evident by
a convention of Negro actors held in Washington, D.C. (still the
storm-center of theatrical Jim Crow 20 years later) to improve "conditions" of the colored circuit. Negro thespians also banded together
in an organization called The Frogs, a Negro version of The Friars.

Harlem of 1928 was going places in a hurry. "In a remarkably
short time," Variety observed, "Harlem has been made one of the
best-known spots in the entire world. Among the reasons have been
the commercial progress of the New York Negro; the international

fame of its theatrical celebrities; the popularity of books having the section as its locale; and stage pieces that included its atmosphere and characters."

Harlem was also busy sorting out its white friends and enemies. The Democrats suffered a defeat by Harlemites through a whispering campaign—nailed too late as a lie—that Jimmy Walker had walked out of a Rome (Italy) cabaret because there were Negroes at the table. John D. Rockefeller, Jr., was hailed as a friend because of his construction of Rockefeller Gardens for Negroes, and his hiring of a Negro, Roscoe Bruce, as supervisor. Famed attorneys Clarence Darrow and Louis Marshall were also solid Harlem favorites.

Many Harlem shows, contrary to popular belief, were all-white. Entertainers—particularly dancers—considered Harlem bookings an honor, since tradition had it that whites went to the Negroes for lessons. "The acid test of any kind of hoofing," Variety stated, "is an appearance at either the Lincoln or Lafayette." Both theatres, catering to an almost exclusively all-Negro audience, were owned by a white woman, Mrs. Maria C. Downs. Top favorite with Lincoln audiences was a dancer named Ginger Burke—a white entertainer—who was hailed with such enthusiastic applause that he was booked at the theatre seven or eight times a year.

The 1920s brought stature to Harlem, but decay to the white center of the entertainment world, Broadway, which celebrated the 100th birthday of 42d Street with an exposition at the Hotel Commodore in 1925. Omitted from the exposition was any mention of the dozen shyster auction stores which sprang up within the vicinity of Times Square.

That Times Square grew brighter and gaudier during the 1920s was undeniable. In 1927 over $10,000,000 worth of electric and billboard ads flared their staccato messages at bustling Main Stem pedestrians. But beneath them thrived what Variety acidly described as "Racketeer's Paradise."

"Every gimmick imaginable goes on the Big Street, from fake auction rooms to shell game; dame-baited speakeasies operating openly; creepers and badger workers with improved methods; undercover rendezvous of intermediate sex luring Freudian students, and everything else the former vice belts ever had."

Broadway, the paper pointed out sadly, was more like the Bowery in 1928 than the Bowery in its heyday. "Hubert's freak show on 42d Street . . . Traffic worse than ever, and no solution . . . The Garment Exchange with its models . . . arguing business men settling deals on the curb while holding up pedestrian traffic . . . Street fakers offering their wares and watching for cops . . . handbook men, three-card monte boys, touts, tipsters and steerers for speaks . . . The speaks are the main industry of the Square after dark. Few offer entertainment of any sort save the usual prop conversation of the take-'em gals who have the same routine their predecessors used to pull on grandpa when the Bowery was the Bowery."

That from the leading spokesman for show business and Broadway was enough for many leading clerics—subscribers to Variety, like Cardinal Spellman (who incidentally, once told the editor, "I read *your* Bible, too, Mr. Green") to spread the word throughout the country that New York is the city of sin. And Broadway, the symbol of show business, is no place for your daughter. So why not send her to church on Sunday instead?

the church offensive   The church, imperiled by the let's-go-to-hell-and-have-fun atmosphere of the 1920s, at first fought show business as the spearhead of that movement. It was clear to the clerics that if Americans were going to amuse themselves on Sunday, the church was going to suffer a severe slump—both spiritually and in the collection plate.

In 1919 the Methodist Church had three vices on their banned list—card playing, theatre-going and dancing. When the Dancing Masters Association protested, their vice was erased from the blacklist at the Methodist National Convention. The Producing Managers Association promptly demanded that theatre-going be likewise absolved of sin, since the stage was "art, amusement and education."

But if the Methodists kept thumbs down on theatricals, they were hardly averse to using theatricals themselves that year. At their Centenary Celebration in Columbus, Ohio, they spent $500,000 on a spectacle that included a chorus of 4,000, with an orchestra of 1,000 in which 125 trombones were used. Sleeping tents were erected for the 70,000 attending the celebration. Nothing like it had ever been seen since 1872, when 10 cannons had been used for the bass notes of a tremendous orchestra.

In Jersey City that year, citizens of the mosquito state had their choice of not one, but two Passion Plays—an American version called *Veronica's Veil* at St. Joseph's Auditorium, and the *Oberammergau* at the Columbia Auditorium, four blocks away. Both did excellent business; and so did the bars under each auditorium which offered both liquor and refreshments.

1919 was also the first year that the Vatican Singers ever left the papal grounds. Giving 56 concerts on tour, they played to a gross of $500,000. Some 30 years later they essayed an American tour to poor boxoffice.

The Protestant sects were mainly worried about the competition of Hollywood—despite the fulminations of the Rev. Dr. John Roach Straton against Broadway and Broadway actors. They decided to show films in their churches, and in 1921, over 4,000 churches were reported to be operating their own movie machines.

The Methodist Episcopal Church opened its own studio in Chicago that year, planning to produce films for missionary and Sunday-school work. The Methodists also drew up an approved list of Hollywood films, banning those which featured violence or scantily-clad ladies. Church agitation in New York State resulted in a censorship law passed by the State Legislature. Similar bills began to pop up in other parts of the country.

Worried, the National Association of the Motion Picture Industry produced a film called *Non-Sense of Censorship,* which starred Rupert Hughes, Samuel Mervin, Montague Glass and Douglas Fairbanks.

At least one church of 1921 had no serious scruples about the theatre. The Union Church, on 49th St. between Broadway and 8th Avenue, used a large electric sign facing the Main Stem to advertise the availability of its hall for rehearsals. Many managers used it because of its convenient location.

The Methodists began to suffer a change of heart in 1924, when protests came from within the ranks of the church. One group at Springfield termed the Church's laws against attending amusements were "embarrassing." Even bishops agreed that the laws should be amended, recommending that the church warn against "evil amusements," but leave the decision up to "individual conscience." After that, church forces, which found that they could not beat down the thirst of their parishes for the stage and screen, decided "if we can't lick 'em, we'll jine 'em."

In 1925 Cantor Josef Rosenblatt, the first cantor to appear in vaudeville, opened at Philadelphia's Fox Theatre. He proved an exceptional boxoffice hit, and won thundering applause for his rendition of—of all things—"Mother Machree."

That year the first priest also appeared in vaudeville. The Rev. Goodwin of the American Catholic Church opened in a vaudeville act called "The Double Cross" at Loew's American Theatre, New York. He was a non-Papal Catholic, like the Greek Orthodox Catholics, and claimed to have special dispensation for his act from Archbishop Gregory Lines, head of the Pacific Church Province. Later on the Rev. Goodwin ran into some trouble when it was revealed that he was as phony as his dispensation.

Religion really got into show business with Aimee Semple McPherson, who made Billy Sunday look like an amateur. In 1926 Sister Aimee was collecting $12,000 for single Sunday performances in Los Angeles, serving sinners in wholesale lots of 25,000 at a clip. The following year she came to New York for a three-day stand at the Glad Tidings Tabernacle, playing to 3,500. And in 1928 she branched out into the cemetery business, offering 2,500 lots at from $40 to $250 apiece in Blessed Hope Memorial Park, Los Angeles. No tombstones were permitted except one for Sister Aimee. "On the appointed day," the brochure promised, "those who sleep together will rise together under the direction of Mrs. McPherson's own spirit."

Billy Sunday, still raising hellfire but completely dwarfed by the radiant Aimee, was attacked in 1927 by the Rev. D. A. McGregor of Chicago as "an eccentric comedian" preaching "vaudeville religion." But evangelism was the sweeping spirit of the Twenties. In 1928, Judge Rutherford, a Missouri lawyer turned evangelist, established one Sunday broadcast, under the auspices of the International Bible Students Association.

It was show business that gripped the American imagination in the 1920s. To re-grip it, religion had to "make its pitch" through the popular channels of show business . . . the very institution it so often professed to damn as sinful.

european echoes   Overseas, London enjoyed a postwar entertainment boom, just like its cousin city of New York. The big problem was a shortage of theatres—with attractions sitting tight in available theatres at capacity business, while no new shows were able to get space. Producers actually sent to New York for building materials for two theatres to be shipped to London on freighters. Later in the decade, wealthy Americans abroad put an ironic twist on this request by buying English castles and shipping them in pieces to the United States.

One of the big 1919 London hits was the American musical, *Chu Chin Chow*, in its third year and still playing to $25,000 weekly. Its principal actor and author, Oscar Asche, admitted that it had boosted him into the millionaires' rank. Asche, as representative of American showmen coming over to London in American plays, irked the London *Express*, which complained, "American plays and managers, and American specialists, are elbowing British acts out of British theatres and music halls."

The *Express* conveniently neglected to mention that in the same year English artists were appearing on American stages. Wilkie Bard was the first that year at the Palace, flopping badly at his Broadway opening, but coming back during the middle of the week to restore his reputation. Wish Wynne, an English actress of some note, played next at the Riverside, New York, with unhappy results. The third British import of 1919 was Alice Lloyd, also at the Palace, after an absence of three years. Following an all-star bill, next to closing, she drew more applause than any act that had preceded her, and was held over. The fourth foreign artist was the French clown, Grock, who opened with little ballyhoo at the Riverside, but was forced to take 16 curtain calls on his second night.

Variety's report on Czechoslovakia in 1920 showed that the newly-created democracy had gone "amusement-mad." Audiences showered their stage favorites not with flowers, but with food. One gratified and hungry actor was presented across the footlights with a live and squealing pig, and did not draw the wrong conclusion.

A less cheerful report came from Vienna. "Something more than a population, something finer than a political conception, something more wonderful than an empire, is facing death on the Danube," ran the dispatch. "This something is a conception of life—charming, fastidious, entrancing. All the world is in debt to it. The American theatrical world in particular owes it a great deal. Plays, music, a great actor and several very lovely women have come to Broadway from Vienna, but, more than this, has come (for Viennese standards have shaped our white-lighted street) a sense of the values that make life interesting."

Variety's mugg in Austria urged Broadway to beat the drums for admitting Viennese theatre people to the United States—"if we don't get them, the German will. He knows their value."

The slump that upset Broadway in 1921 also had its reverberations in London, where 2,000 chorus girls were reported to be out of work and hungry. In 1922 Variety reported an interesting innovation in the London legitimate, where Godfrey Tearle, tired of his stupidly-written role in *The Way of the Eagle* at the Adelphi, began to kid it and play it for laughs. Audiences relished the idea, and the show—teetering to a close—became a hit. Bobby Clark used the same idea in 1948 when he appeared in a revival of Victor Herbert's *Sweethearts.*

News from London in 1924 revealed that Fred and Adele Astaire were scoring heavily at the Strand in a show called *Stop Flirting.* Another interesting London attraction of that year was "Doctor" Brodie, who lectured in vaudeville against capital punishment. One of his stunts had been sitting in an electric chair onstage and taking voltage. Now he was demonstrating a "death ray" which could stop a motor, halt an airplane in midair and blow it up.

By 1925 the predominating trend in entertainment all through the world was films. Germany led all nations in the attempt to produce films that would rival the glamorous productions of Hollywood—less in glamor than in quality. South Africa depended almost exclusively on films for its theatre, because of the long hop to that end of the world for live entertainers. Radio was unimpressive to South Africans, as it was to Australians, who were giving long runs to American films. Radio was as popular in England, however, as it was in America. All of Europe—with the exception of lyrical Italy—was united on one thing . . . total opposition to American jazz. But, ultimately, to no avail.

The spread of the little theatre craze in America extended to England in 1926, which had over 9,000 dramatic groups (1,000 in London alone) with a membership of 400,000 amateurs. Increasing resentment against American acts coming over led that year to a ban on American bands, like Ben Bernie and Paul Specht, who found it tough to get labor permits. But Will Rogers was welcomed, and tied up the show at London's Pavilion in a 40-minute spot.

Sophie Tucker, even then, was a London rage, and bands like Paul Whiteman's and Ted Lewis' panicked them.

In the Paris of 1926 the toast of the city was Maurice Chevalier, with his partner Yvonne Vallee, who were delighting Parisians in their slightly naughty show at the Casino de Paris. And from France that year came the first decoration awarded by the French government to an American showman—the Legion of Honor presented to Marcus Loew.

1928 saw two British innovations. In London, the Palladium rocked the Empire by passing out icewater to patrons . . . the first time in British history a theatre gave out anything free, and especially *iced*! And up in Glasgow, Harry Lauder had a cold . . . missing his first show in 25 years.

the russians   By 1925 Soviet Russia, still viewed askance by American business interests as a nation of property dynamiters, was nevertheless shaping up as a lucrative foreign market. Warner Bros. won control of all films going into Russia from the United States, maintaining an office in Moscow. Russia that year became the first foreign nation to maintain its own actors' booking agency, hiring American actors and paying off in American dollars.

Variety took a dim view of the Soviet's methods of rewarding its own top entertainers in 1926. The government awarded Paul Orlieniff, on the occasion of the Russian actor's 40th stage anniversary, with the honorary title of "Artist of the People." All very well, Variety muttered, but what about paying Artists of the People decent salaries, as they were doing in Germany?

Like Germany, Russia was jumping into film production with both feet. In 1926 their studios turned out about 250 pictures—"better stuff, too," Variety admitted. The following year the Soviet declared that films were a necessity, not a luxury, to explain their preoccupation with celluloid. They cut down on film imports, as they strengthened their own industry, making their own equipment, and propagandizing Europe to promote the artistic supremacy of the made-in-Moscow product.

A first-hand look at Russian show business came in 1927 through a report by Trade Commissioner George Canty to the United States Department of Commerce. He found that the Russians liked their films straight—serious or comic—but without musical froufrou. The theatres usually gave two performances a day. A six-to-eight show was reserved for labor union members, and the evening performance for the general public.

Canty quoted Lunatscharsky, the Soviet commisar for public instruction and films, as stating, "The realistic and truth-bearing character of the Russian film alone would not have called the attention of the whole world to our motion pictures. It is because we choose the truths ourselves, and also because we do not picture the 'dreadful sides of life' without motive. Our best films are propaganda films in the highest artistic sense of the word."

36

More of the Golden Twenties

★

In the good and welfare division of show business, the decade produced some violent ups and downs, as well as sharp changes in the direction from which the good and welfare emanated. In April 1919, actors looked to E. F. Albee as their patron saint. When the new National Vaudeville Artists' (N.V.A.) clubhouse was opened that month, the keys to the former home of the White Rats were officially turned over to N.V.A. by Albee.

More than 1,500 show business figures gathered to listen to his dedication address. Enthusiastic applause, and the sentiment of the occasion, moved Albee to unexpected generosity. He told actors to take engagements wherever they could get work—on any circuit— and they would not be blacklisted on the Keith Circuit for playing the opposition. He also urged them to take up all complaints with N.V.A. officials—and if they couldn't get satisfaction, to see him personally.

This uncharacteristic paternalism was almost too much for the actors who heard him. It was the final nail in the coffin of the White Rats, who were declared insolvent by a court.

Labor lightning struck next that same year at the legitimate end of show business. When Actors Equity blew the whistle, Variety lined up on their side. "The strike should never have started," it declared. "The managers brought it upon themselves, and through that left the actor, represented by the Actors' Equity Association, with the best basis there can be for a strike—a just cause."

The "just cause" was a rebellion against long rehearsals without pay, contracts broken at will, dismissal without redress in the midst of rehearsals, dismissal after the opening either to cut-price, if too costly, or to cut-price, if the role could be portrayed by somebody of lesser stature, especially if the play got good notices. Paying for wardrobe, abuse of choristers through long, indefinite and nonremunerative rehearsals and other accumulative complaints had been piling up.

The strike also embraced the grievances of chorus girls, who used to contribute gratis rehearsals for from 6-12 weeks. One show had actually rehearsed its chorus for 14 weeks "with no payment for rehearsals, and no guarantee of the show being a success." With chorus footgear costing a chorine as much as $60, Marie Dressler became indignant and offered her services as president of the Chorus Girls' Union. Every striking chorine in the nation rallied behind her, as "Tugboat Annie" led the fight for a square deal in the high-kick department.

In the one month—August 7, 1919 until after Labor Day—that the strike lasted, it cost over $500,000 per week. The theatres lost $250,000, the actors, $100,000, stage crews and musicians, $40,000. Over 60 shows were stopped in rehearsal, causing uncounted losses. The closing of 35 theatres added up to $140,000 weekly in overhead. Even speculators were squawking that it was costing them some $30,000.

George M. Cohan, whose sympathies should normally have been with the actors, became embittered during the strike. The first flint of his opposition was struck when he moved the Cohan & Harris show, *Seven Keys to Baldpate,* from the Astor to the Gaiety. Stagehands forced Cohan to put on a road crew of three men for the rest of the run, claiming the attraction had become a roadshow by moving.

actors and boilermakers During the strike, Cohan re-signed from the Managers Association, because the organization had agreed in private council to concede a closed shop. Cohan in 1922 took a full-page ad in Variety to announce his diehard opposition to the closed shop, stating that the average actor was against it but afraid to say so. He objected to labor organizers "who look and talk like boiler-makers. What have they to do with the theatrical profession? Acting is highly specialized—therefore should not be run like a labor union."

Cohan's fight against the closed shop angered actors and working show people, all of whom were solidly behind the gains won for them by Equity, which incidentally inherited the American Federation of Labor charter of the old White Rats. Some—old friends—refused to speak to him. One staunch friend, John O'Connor, then a Variety staffer, personally took space in the paper to lash out at Cohan's detractors.

"George M. Cohan," he charged in a page ad, "until this strike broke, was on a pedestal, theatrically, that ran second to none, and that includes the pedestals occupied by the Pope and the King of England. The old-timers loved him. The newcomers admired him because the old-timers educated them. Cohan couldn't be wrong. Cohan was a square guy.

"Three weeks ago, if someone put Cohan on the pan to the aver-age showman, he either went away with a good bawling out or a busted face. If some of the regulars were in a financial jam, Cohan's phone number was easy to find and Cohan never ducked a phone call. Touches came so often he used to go home with a lame arm—lame from digging into the bankroll.

"But—the strike came along. Cohan, retired as an actor, was a manager. The very fellows whom he had helped, the very fellows who called him 'Georgie' and bragged about knowing him when he was a chump kid, the very fellows who often had only Cohan be-tween them and the morning pork chops, started to yell 'scab' at the top of their voices. (Cohan had stepped into the role of an actor in in his play who had quit during the strike.)

"They panned George at The Lambs, and George resigned. The Friars, the club that fairly breathed Cohan's nature, cursed him, and Cohan resigned . . . Tell the whole world what you think of managers, but remember, George M. Cohan was always a square guy, is a square guy now, and all the panning you birds slip along won't change a square guy's makeup."

The actors for a long time had turned from him because they felt he had manifested more managerial instinct than the partisanship that comes from the player's viewpoint. They felt that Jere and Helen, his parents, and Josephine, his sister, had all been raised as actors, and that as one of the time-honored Four Cohans his sympathies belonged with them.

With the managers not particularly sympathetic, and his own thespic colleagues refuting him, Cohan never forgot or forgave the Equity strike. Were it not for this backsliding, Cohan today would still be the patron saint of all actors because he was the most versatile man on the American stage—actor, manager, songwriter, song-and-dance man and playwright. He was a "right" guy, a fast man with a buck, and it was said that he and Variety's *Sime* for a time "had the longest pension lists on Broadway." Cohan, however, in time did come back into the Lambs and Friars fold.

The strike was effective in Chicago, Boston and other major cities. Despite the fact that many theatres were ordinarily dark during the summer season, the strike was regarded as a serious blow to the boxoffice because the summer of 1919 happened to be a record-breaker for legit. With Broadway shuttered tight, the jubilant and determined actors decided to give New Yorkers a taste of their own brand of entertainment. They produced a benefit performance (for the strike fund) at the Lexington Avenue Opera House—acknowledged to be the greatest benefit show ever played, with a cast of just about every great name on Broadway.

The benefit had an odd by-product in that it lifted a previously obscure comedian and dancer, James Barton, into overnight fame. Allowed to show his stuff on a stage overrun with million-dollar talent, Barton clowned and hoofed his way to a tremendous ovation and repeated curtain calls. Acknowledging this acclaim of fellow artists, which he knew had stamped him that night as bigtime caliber, Barton further panicked the customers by reprising that all-time show biz bon mot when he stated, "Thanks for the use of the hall." (Arthur Rigby, an old minstrel man, first ad libbed this many years before.)

Producers were still confident the strike would crash of its own weight by Labor Day, when actors would be anxious to get back on the boards in time for the fall season. But the morale and the ranks of the strikers remained undaunted and undented beyond Labor Day. Whereupon the alarmed managers pulled in their horns and settled. The strike was a smashing victory for Equity, which since has been the undisputed spokesman for the legitimate player.

However, actor-managers like George M. Cohan and Louis Mann, had sparkplugged the shortlived Actors Fidelity League, a group espousing the idea that legit stars were above unionism.

Partisan thespians, ever reverent of the Cohan tradition, sidestepped too much captious criticism, but Mann and others were singled out for intra-trade barbs as only gifted showfolk are capable of uncorking. It was at this time that the wheeze was cradled, "An empty taxi drew up in front of the Friars Club and Louis Mann got out."

The aftermath of the strike brought an understandable amount of confusion. About 90 per cent of the shows were able to reopen without boxoffice difficulties, but road routes were hopelessly tangled. While the big attractions had been held off the road for the duration of the strike, smalltime "turkeys" had stolen into many towns with noncancellable contracts. Where the turkeys didn't slip in, feature films did. There was further confusion in the holdover of shows that had been scheduled to leave New York for the road. This, in turn, kept shows out of New York that were slated to come in.

george m. cohan's burn   Echoes of the strike were still being heard in 1920, when the Producers and Managers Association revealed they had been forced to pay $89,000 for lawyers' fees during the clash, and had also had to dig down for some $121,000 in miscellaneous costs. George M. Cohan was so bitter against what he considered was a "raw deal" handed to him by Equity, that he dissolved his 17-year-old partnership with Sam H. Harris and announced his intention of retiring from the theatre.

Cohan was caught between a double grouch, both at the Managers Association and also against Equity. The Managers Association situation was the basis for his split with Harris. There are sundry legends as to what was at the bottom of the time-honored Cohan & Harris business and personal alliance. The schism was a shock to Broadway because it was truly a Damon & Pythias association. But Cohan was a bitter man at that time and he vowed that "if Equity won I'd run an elevator," to which Ed Wynn rebuttled, "I'd sell peanuts if Equity lost." Cohan never became an indoor aviator and Wynn never got anywhere near the peanut concession at the circus or the zoo.

Cohan vowed he would return only when and if Equity "closed shop" was beaten. Actually, he returned a year or so later with the Equity shop in full bloom. He had announced he was going to England to produce shows—and didn't.

Although Equity had risen to a new power and stature that it had never before known, it was still far from wielding the powers of a Petrillo. In 1922 it had little to say about Broadway shows that cut salaries 25 per cent. It had to stand by in 1924 when actors began taking "notes" in lieu of outright salary cuts in the legitimate. By 1929 it had prospered to an extent that allowed it to demand union contracts for actors from Hollywood, as Equity shifted its attention west with the new migration of stage stars to the new Hollywood gold rush that was the talkies.

In the general strike upheaval of 1919, the film operators also asserted themselves, and won a six-day work week instead of their regular seven-day grind.

In 1924 Equity rolled up its sleeves again, and demanded that theatre managers sign an agreement with an 80-20 clause . . . providing that all shows must have at least 80 per cent Equity members. They won their demand, after initiating strike action to back it up. By the following year, when things were purring smoothly on all sides of the theatrical fence, Equity rescinded its ban on Variety, which had criticized the way the union had been run.

Despite the lush year, 1925 was still full of hard months for unlucky members of the lower rungs of show business. Actors were found chiseling the Automats with a concoction called "the tin roof," because it was on the house. They took large glasses provided with pieces of lemon, which were supposed to be taken to pay faucets and filled with tea, and used them to add sugar and ice water instead. Variety also reported a wave of discouraged chorus girls attempting suicide with iodine and veronal.

Equally unlucky that year was the hypnotist, J. Robert Pauline, who threw a waiter out of a window of the Flanders Hotel ("The Friendly Hotel") and received a sentence of six months to three years for this unfriendly gesture.

sweetness and light dept.   The new deal in vaudeville ushered in by Albee's N.V.A. seemed to be working out well for actors, whose complaints against managers dropped from a high of 360 a month to a new low of about 20. The N.V.A. clubhouse, refurbished at a cost to Keith's of $500,000, so impressed actors that one wag declared "acrobats were walking in on their hands." And Keith's, for the first time in vaudeville history, was issuing "play or pay" contracts.

Albee explained the transformation in 1920. He had been wrong for 20 years, he admitted, and wanted to rectify mistakes of the past. The private opinion of show business was that he was the richest man in the theatre, making more money than he knew what to do with. Tired of fighting, tired of being pictured with horns because he had been the front man used to protect Keith's and vaudeville producers as a whole, Albee had apparently decided to call it a day and wind up his career by winning the goodwill of those who had once regarded him as their worst enemy . . . the actors. Albee was the brains behind the idea of the annual N.V.A. Benefit, with 400 theatres donating matinee proceeds of approximately $200,000, part of which went for actors' insurance.

the lighter side   Meantime, the social columns of Variety paraded the romance between American comedian Frank Van Hoven and British comedienne Lily Lena. When she came to the United States, while Van Hoven was in London, he placed an ad in Variety urging all his friends to swamp her with good-luck wires . . . "as it is her first week in the country after an absence of seven years, and she went over on the boat all alone and is very, very lonely . . . It will be one little way of being good to her for all the wonderful things she had done for Americans in her own little England." When "sweet little Lily Lena" opened at the Brooklyn Bushwick, she was practically battered down by squads of messenger boys.

A 1921 social event of note was The Friars' "Insult Night," at $5 a seat, for the benefit of the Relief Fund. The Friars later that year packed the Manhattan Opera House for their annual Frolic, at a $10 top, and grossing $13,000. Among the attractions was a minstrel show featuring Jim Corbett and George M. Cohan as interlocutors, and end men Pat Rooney, Eddie Cantor, Harry Kelly, Richard Carle, Willie Collier and Lew Fields. The show also offered George

White and Lou Holtz; Alice Brady and her father, William A. Brady, who did the wharf scene from *After Dark* during which they leaped into a stage tank and emerged dripping; and a double barber-shop quartette made up of genuine cops.

A Friars event that made newspaper headlines in 1923 was the suspension of 11 members—including Max Winslow, Jack Lait, Sime Silverman, George W. Meyer and Benny Davis. Their sin was in refusing to stop a card-game at the Friars' curfew of 3 A.M. The day after the fired Friars had been sentenced, three sandwich men showed up to picket the Friars' clubhouse. Their banners read:—

WE WANT LONGER HOURS AND UNION WAGES—
BY ORDER OF THE FIRED FRIARS.
FORGIVE US, AND GIVE US OUR FOUR ACES.
CLOSE THE LIBRARY, OPEN THE CARD ROOM TO THE FIRED FRIARS.
LISTEN: WE WON'T BE BAD BOYS NO MORE—
TAKE BACK THE FIRED FRIARS.

Friars in the billiard room dashed out of the building and rushed the unfortunate sandwich men. Keeping straight faces, the House Committee held a "hearing" and reinstated the rebels.

nellie revell   In 1924 the Friars gave a dinner to Nellie Revell, to celebrate her return to health after four years' confinement. The event was broadcast over WHN, and guests who turned up to honor the indomitable woman press agent who had fought her way back from tragic illness were George M. Cohan, Willie Collier, Irvin S. Cobb, Will Rogers, Jimmy Walker, Marcus Loew, Daniel Frohman and Eddie Cantor.

Nellie Revell had won the sympathy of all show business because she had spent her ailing years in a plaster cast, unable to move, yet never giving up the fight. She had become such a symbol to show business that it was traditional to advise anyone with a grouch to "drop down at St. Vincent's Hospital (New York) and see Nellie." The theory behind that was "you haven't a kick in the world after seeing Nellie Revell." During her confinement Nellie wrote a regular column for Variety—another sample of *Sime's* practical philanthropy.

Among the curiosa of 1922 noted by Variety was the "actress" who made the rounds of the agents and producers' offices. "She" turned out to be a female impersonator, using this method of demonstrating his talents. Another oddity was the curious discovery made by actor Johnny Scott, who played a show at Matawan Asylum . . . and found that among the audience was his ex-partner of 10 years before, William McGovern, who had used the stage name of Bissett.

Two items of the year reflected trends in good and welfare. At Proctor's 5th Avenue there was an act called "The Unseen Hand," which dealt with the child of two performers who fell sick and were cancelled at Christmas time. The act, an obvious propaganda pitch to win a pat on the head from Albee, had these sugar-candy lines about N.V.A.:—

CHILD: I think Mr. N.V.A., who helped my mom, is the biggest man in the world.
MGR.: Bigger than Chaplin?
CHILD: Yes.
MGR.: Bigger than God?
CHILD: Well, Mr. N.V.A. is young yet.

"The Unseen Hand" was mercifully chopped off at Proctor's.

That year another welfare outfit for actors made its debut the National Stage Women's Exchange at 43 West 47th Street in New York, founded by Hilda Spong. A co-operative, it featured meals served by stage girls as waitresses, with the understanding that hungry Bernhardts could fill the inner woman on the cuff.

In 1923 Percy Williams, one of the first vaudeville showmen to be absorbed by Keith, died and left his Central Islip, Long Island, estate as a home for aged actors. Proving once again that perhaps no other business or profession in the world looks after its own as well as show business . . . an example of practical philanthropy.

A cause célèbre arose that year, involving the question of the social acceptability of the acting profession. The cause was an invitation extended to Ula Sharon, 17-year-old premier danseuse of the Greenwich Village Follies, to attend the Yale Junior Prom. New Haven social circles lifted noses and voices in sharp protest. The Yale boy, Hale Ellicot Cullum of Tennessee, refused to withdraw the invitation and was backed up by his father.

A showdown on whether actresses were persona grata was averted by the revelation that Miss Sharon "happened to be the daughter of a prominent Kansas City civil engineer, and has been accompanied during her stage career by her own mother." Her credentials in order, the young actress received a special invitation from the Yale Prom Committee. Said she, "I'll be there, and I'll show the New Haven subdebs something about the fine art of dancing!"

another fight with albee   In 1926 Variety, long suspicious of Albee's beneficence, opened a broadside at the management of N.V.A., which it described as meaning, "Never Vex Albee." The paper advised actors—and N.V.A. president, Fred Stone—to take matters into their own hands and find out what was going on in the club's treasury department. "There should be about $2,000,000 in the N.V.A. treasury by this time. Maybe more; who can tell? Never, since the N.V.A. was organized, has it issued a financial statement. Never since the N.V.A. was organized, has there been an election of officers by the full membership of the club."

Pointing out that dues were enormous, benefits slight or nonexistent when needed, Variety urged actors, "Demand a full meeting. Elect your own officers. Run your own organization. See where the money is going. Take full charge. It's a gag, this N.V.A.; has been a gag since the day the N.V.A. was started as a gag."

Two months later, hot on the trail of Albee's pet hobby, Variety revealed that Thomas Kane, a tubercular actor with a wife and three young children, was living in two rooms at $14 a month rent—yet had been refused assistance or investigation by N.V.A. (which had a Charity Fund surplus of $2,000,000.) In addition, Variety charged, Kane had been threatened with having his children taken away from him.

That year Albee's right-hand man, J. J. Murdock (who died in 1948) made a 315-minute phone call from New York to San Francisco that cost $2,157.80. The 5½-hour call was for the purpose of averting a strike of Frisco stagehands and musicians. In typical Murdock fashion, the bill was offered for payment to both the labor and management interests involved.

Murdock, told that he had cancer, spent $800,000 in subsidizing cancer experiments to find a cure. Despite his worries he outlived all his doctors, to die at the age of 87. Incidentally, like several other pro-Albeeites he wound up one of *Sime's* closest friends.

Taking stock of the union situation in 1926, Variety found that

Equity had 14,000 members; IATSE, the stagehands' union, 28,000; the billposters, 6,000; and the various musicians' unions, some 125,-000. Despite the growing strength of show people through unionization, the dollar was still hard to come by for thousands of them.

One aged dancer created his own circuit in 1926 by performing in the subways of New York. Each train being operated then by only one man, he had little interference. He wore tap-dancing shoes to be sure of being heard above the noise of the wheels. Acrobats of that year were picking up extra change by teaching acrobatic dancing to chorus girls. A few years later, when clashes between Arabs and Jews in the Far East made Arabs unpopular in the United States, six acrobats who called themselves "The Flying Arabians" hastily changed their billing to "The Flying Demons."

Japan also came to the attention of actors in 1926 through that nation's subtle flooding of the American market with made-in-Japan goods bearing pseudo-American trademarks. There was Jackie Coogan Face Powder, Pierce Arrow Dye Soap, Nash Lead Paint, and Chevrolet Grease Paint. This was later followed by Japan's naming a town "Usa," so it could stamp goods, "Made in USA."

The heart of show business was again revealed in 1927 by Variety, which reported that 500 crippled war veterans at the Walter Reed Hospital were being entertained once a week by all performers in Washington. And in 1929 the N.V.A., prodded by Variety's clawing, opened a sanitarium for actors at Saranac Lake, later called the Variety Clubs-Will Rogers Memorial Hospital.

some real showmanship   Although Willie Hammerstein was dead, the spirit of his showmanship and ingenuity still prevailed through the Twenties. In 1919 when a flu epidemic hit Wisconsin, managers prevailed upon city authorities to let the theatres remain open. Their solution: patrons would be allowed to sit only in every other row.

Lecturers were proving top showmen that year. Eddie Rickenbacker packed them in at the Metropolitan Opera House with a one-hour talk, and one-hour of films and slides on the war. Lowell Thomas was in London with a travelog talk. His manager, Perry Burton, refused to let him go to Balmoral Castle to lecture before King George and Queen Mary because "he's already making too much money—playing to $15,000 a week."

Unidentified showmen of 1920 astonished Broadway with a 25¢ museum on Broadway between 46th and 47th streets . . . the first Broadway museum in 30 years. Attractions included freaks, knife-throwers and the usual "clutter and jungle of the old-time museum." The following year there was a new gimmick on Broadway—pretty girl shills used by sightseeing busses to lure tired business men and out-of-town Main Streeters into a trip to Coney Island or around New York at a buck a throw. Girls were left sitting on the rear seats of empty busses, as bait, but disembarked as soon as the rubberneck wagons took off.

A minor explosion in show business was set off in 1921 by a Loew manager named Fair, for Nashville's Vendome Theatre. Fair had the bright idea of teaming up with a local store for a special publicity stunt called "A Trip to Spotlight Land." The plan was to promote an offer to all patrons of the store to go backstage at Loew's and watch performers from the wings. Actors at the Vendome set up a howl of protest, echoed by actors all over the country, who argued this would set a dangerous precedent that would destroy much of the illusion of the theatre. Manager Fair grieved for the unpopularity of his idea, which he knew was based on perfect audience psychology—as the movie fan magazines of a future date, giving the "inside" stuff of the studios, proved to great profit.

That same year the manager of New York's 14th Street Olympic, once Tony Pastor's, decided to revive amateur nights, with all the old-time paraphernalia, except the hook. To make sure of results, he used professional amateurs, who submitted to some terrible onstage shenanigans to get a $5 payoff.

The third laurel for 1921 showmanship went to the Newton (Kansas) Opera House, where a Durock-Jersey sow was sold from the stage by a livestock improvement association for $115, as hogs squealed and clowned all over the stage.

One of the most unusual pieces of show biz strategy took place in Rochester, New York, in 1922. The Fennyvesseys of that city, who operated a group of smalltime and stock burlesque houses, offered to call for and deliver patrons to their theatres. They chartered special trolleys on lines which passed their showplaces, placarding the cars with notices that passengers were bound for the Strand, Rialto and Family theatres. The same cars were used to take patrons home. All trolleys were timed to reach the theatres at the start of performances, and riders were serenaded by musicians sent along in each car.

cheesecake   Top showmanship was displayed in late 1921, when Atlantic City held its first Beauty Pageant. They offered girls in bare knees and skin-tight bathing suits, which launched the one-piece bathing costume—and also Atlantic City. It also served as a boom, through publicity, for swimming pools in amusement parks.

In 1925, when the automobile was making itself felt as theatre opposition, a Shubert press agent, Henry Myers—later to become a stage and screen writer—got the idea of a Broadway block party, the first in history. Called the "Gay Paree" block party, after the Shubert musical whose principals acted as hosts, it turned into a riotous affair. Held in the private thoroughfare between the Shubert and Booth theatres—now known as Shubert Alley—it was jammed by thousands who were served refreshments, and watched Charleston contests judged by Al Jolson and Winnie Lightner. Phil Baker and Eddie Conrad did a "sister act," and a scantily-draped chorus man won roars of laughter by burlesquing "The Perfect Venus" number of the *Gay Paree* show. The party didn't break up until 1:30 A.M., and only then because of squawks by Hotel Astor guests.

That same year Loew showed his shrewdness by booking the Siamese Twins—Daisy and Violet Hilton—who had been rejected by the Keith Circuit. Booking them in Newark, Loew had the satisfaction of watching them break all records with a $36,000 house. The twins' share of the take was $2,500.

The manager of the Rivoli, New York, showed how to get and hold summer business by installing a new cooling system, made by Germany's Krupp and installed by the Carrier Engineering Co. The idea spread rapidly, and four years later was copied by Macy's at a cost of $800,000 for icing up two floors.

A final showmanship note of 1925 was added by Charles Lick, of Lick's Pier, Ocean Park, California, who introduced the first Applauseograph, which registered audience applause for acts while eliminating the contributions of whistles, yells and stamped feet.

The low in showmanship of 1926 was recorded by the Philadelphia Sesqui-Centennial Exposition, which was a first-class flop. The high was reached by Edna Wallace Hopper at Pittsburgh, who took a bath onstage in front of a special matinee audience of women. Miss Hopper won herself some extra publicity when four college students were apprehended in the audience, dressed as women.

Variety noted the passing of a 115-year-old showman in 1926 who had seen the Boston Tea Party. His name was David Kinnison, a theatre manager who had delivered the spiel in his own museum at Chicago when he was 111. Kinnison had fought in the War of 1812, and was the first recorded variety manager.

In St. Louis, outdoor opera led the showmanship parade by breaking records, with $357,772 taken in for 12 weeks of open-air arias. The penny arcades were making their pitch with machine flickers that bore such tempting titles as: "What Girls Do Before Bedtime," "What Girls Do When Alone," "The Bride's Celebration," "The Naughty French Girl" and "Foiling the White Slavers."

The relatively tame entertainment of Al G. Fields' Minstrels, a perennial item for 40 years, melted into oblivion.

Showmanship went slightly mad in 1929, with the work of some unknown genius who perfected a method of pickling whales. The mammoths were trotted around the country—"Pickled Whales . . . 25¢ a Look"—with no stink to arouse local wrath.

It was also the year that ballyhoo reached its ultimate, with special exploitation services offered from a dollar an hour to $100 a day. Showmen had their choice of music on trucks, parachute-jumpers, stilt-walkers, fat men, clowns, captive balloons, walking dolls propelled ahead of autos, mechanical animals and horses, mechanical men, blindfolded car-drivers, rube impersonators, men-who-never-smile, auto trucks built like zeppelins, human flys and flying humans. The flying humans were also on display at the first aviation show, held at Grand Central Palace in New York, which took in $170,000 a week, 10 per cent of which was donated to the American Legion.

The strangest bit of show biz ingenuity of the decade occurred in 1929 at the Gayety, a Washington, D.C., burlesque house. The Gayety was the scene of a special benefit on behalf of four gamblers, sentenced to long terms, who pleased the underworld by refusing to unbutton to the police. The audience consisted of rum runners, racketeers, and gamblers, who paid $5,000 at the boxoffice and more for a souvenir 32-page program. Actors, stagehands and musicians "volunteered" their services—after strong hints from certain circles that it might be healthy to do so. Jimmy Lake, an old burlesque comic, was emcee.

It could only have happened in the Twenties.

rough stuff in theatres   Very little was *verboten* on the wide-open stages of the decade. "Once we went to the gin-mills to see it," a cynical citizen of the period declared. "Now we go to the theatre." The average show served up portions of cuticle display, saloon stories, ribald gags, sex-studded songs, suggestive situations, racy dialog, the old cooch dance under its new label of Shimmy, and a style of jazz dancing behind the footlights that was truly bizarre. While many patrons walked out and wrote angry letters of protest, managers' receipts belied everything. The public—protests or no protests—liked dirt shows most, if not all of the time. They knew that fathers and mothers didn't want children to like them. Swains didn't want their sweethearts to like them. But the cold facts were that all too many dirt shows thrived—and they wouldn't have thrived without public patronage.

Boston, as usual, took the lead in clamping taboos on the theatre. In 1920 censor Casey decreed, "Acrobatic jazz music with contortions will be tabooed. Wearing of one-piece bathing suits by women, simply to display their figures as in living pictures, will not be permitted." No dope addicts were allowed to be portrayed, either on the stage or in films. And in 1922, Boston absolutely banned any display of bare thighs as "disgusting."

That year, in Washington, D.C., a snowfall caused the collapse of the roof of the Knickerbocker Theatre. Some 95 patrons were killed, and many others injured. More concerned with their souls than their bodies, however, Boston authorities pressed for legislation that would give the state power to censor all of show business within its domain. The referendum was defeated by Massachusetts voters, to the delight of Broadway and Hollywood. But the joy of show business was short-lived, because by 1927 there was an epidemic of legislation calling for censorship in states throughout the country.

Detroit that year instituted its own inner sanctum censorship, with managers posting "don'ts" for actors appearing in their theatres. Among the taboos were the use of language "that will hurt the feelings of the audience"; addressing remarks to people in the audience, or otherwise embarrassing them; appearing in bare legs;

use of suggestive language or actions; and ordering the spotlight to be thrown on bald heads.

taboos of 1929   The Keith Circuit of 1929 had a list of no less than 73 taboos for its performers. Strictly forbidden were red-necktie pansy bits; references to Commissioner Grover Whalen, Arabs, Mayor Walker, Fiorello LaGuardia, Daddy Browning and Peaches, "Lord Epsom, Secretary of the Interior," Pantages, Aimee McPherson, Kip Rhinelander (who had married a Negro girl), and Herbert Hoover with his two chickens in every pot.

Verboten were suggestive lines like: "I'm not going to show everything at these prices"; "She was taking a tramp through the woods"; "I bet her folks had Siamese intentions"; "What do you think I am—a pushover?"; "I slept with the twins, but might as well have gone home in the rain"; "She had dimples on her hips"; "Going to the livery stable for doughnuts"; "Mother is home sick in bed with the doctor"; "Didn't I meet you under the bed at the Astor?"; "He's the father of a baby boy, but his wife doesn't know it yet"; "If I could go on the stage, I could be made"; "Summer is ending—winter draws on"; "That thing is sticking out again—flute player"; "Hurry . . . you're a little behind, Fanny"; "I said relax, not Ex-Lax"; "She calls her dog 'broker' because he does all his business on the curb"; and "He's in the automobile business—last night he gave me an auto, and tonight he's going to give me the business."

Banned bits were girls raising their skirts and announcing, "I'm a Show Girl"; girls, kicked in the rear, clutching their ends and exclaiming, "Oh, my nerves!"; looking skyward, then brushing off their hats; thumbing noses; business of tearing off women's trunks; hints to audience for applause; girls lifting skirts to show vaccinations; giving the "bird"; girls hurting their fingers—men kissing the digits—then girls taking prattfalls; rubbing violin bows across the rear of trousers; picking up spit for a dime; girls walking on carrying oars and announcing, "I just made the crew."

The Keith taboo list gave acts some excellent new material to use when playing opposition circuits.

Variety, ever sympathetic with the plight of actors at the mercy of critics, started a column in 1920 called "Comebacks," to allow criticized actors a chance to reply to Variety's critics. Managers approved, and began to complain to newspapers that *their* critics—

who disagreed among themselves—had no moral right to ruin plays and actors with one-man opinions.

Adolph Ochs, publisher of the New York *Times,* saw some justice in this viewpoint. In 1922 he let it be known that he was considering ending "personal reviews," substituting instead Sunday criticism by a group of editorial desk workers. Nothing came of the idea, however.

add: the critics   Some 20 years later, when gripes against harsh dramatic criticism were heard anew, the *Times'* Brooks Atkinson informally proposed a possible antidote to the exhibitionistic firstnighters with their yoohooing and other meretricious japeries. That was to "premiere" shows at matinees. This might serve both as a cooler-offer to the opening night fol-de-rol and give the critics that many additional hours for mature appraisal of the offerings. Some managements meantime inaugurated an 8 P.M. opening night curtain, chiefly in deference to the A.M. daily critics. It seemed also to have achieved another thing—curtailment of the dining-too-well proclivities of certain firstnighters, thus curbing some of the nonsense.

Variety laid it on the line to dramatic critics in 1924, protesting cruel criticism of a foreign-born actress who was attempting a comeback after a nervous breakdown. The criticism, Variety accused, had crushed her, bringing on a return of her ailment.

The critics yawned and buffed their fingernails, with the exception of Robert Benchley. He rarely wrote a harsh word against an actor. Without compromising his own high standards, he was nevertheless skillful enough to get his opinions over without hurting feelings or spearing reputations. Kelcey Allen, of *Women's Wear Daily,* was another kindly critic.

Less merciful, if generous men in their own way, were such topflight critics as the *World's* Heywood Broun and the *Times'* Alexander Woollcott. Almost as much the show at openings as onstage productions, Broun and Woollcott were never loath to call attention to their presence. Broun started it by turning up at an opening in his usual sloppy attire—and top hat. Not to be outdone, Woollcott bought a pair of enormous galoshes, and at the next opening sloshed up and down the aisle with them, taking care to leave them unbuckled.

Variety was the clearing house of show biz trivia and chitchat long before the syndicated Broadway columns reached the broader "lay" circulation. A "Mayor of Broadway" contest saw Eddie Cantor the winnah with 19,441 votes. Nils T. Granlund, then Loew Theatres' general p.a. and the NTG of radio station WHN (now Loew-Metro's WMGM) was runner-up. Walter Winchell clocked 4,825 for fourth place.

Incidentally, after Winchell got rolling on the New York *Graphic* he also wrote a column on Variety, purporting to be the "Diary of Joe Zilch," a slang series in which Winchell narrated the adventures of the smalltime vaude team of Zilch & Zilch.

In 1927 Variety introduced the First Film Critics Box Score, á la the Drama Critics Box Score, which was incepted in 1923. The Pix Crix tabulations were dropped some years later by Sid Silverman, successor publisher of Variety, when he and the present editor of Variety concluded that all any critic had to do was say "yes" to any and every film to get a high rating, since pix, unlike legits, more consistently were surefire b.o.

show biz millionaires   It was in 1924 that *Sime* published the financial standings of show biz personalities as indicated by the amounts of their income taxes. Douglas Fairbanks, Sr., topped with a $225,000 tax tab. Ed Albee paid $95,000 taxes; Jack Dempsey 90G; Dempsey's manager, Jack Kearns, $71,000; and George M. Cohan, $87,565.

In the "medium" brackets were Al Jolson, $45,000; Martin Beck, 39G; Richard Barthelmess, $29,995; William S. Hart, 22G; and Rube Goldberg, $20,000. Show people were intrigued by Variety's revelation that a top taxpayer of previous—and subsequent—years had slipped to the comparatively low bracket of $14,000—Louis B. Mayer.

In 1927 Variety also presented its estimate of the 20 wealthiest showmen. In terms of millions of dollars, John Ringling was credited with 60; Henry W. Savage, 40; Adolph Zukor, 40; Marcus Loew, 35; Lee Shubert, 30; William Fox, 30; E. F. Albee, 25; Jesse L. Lasky, 20; Joe Leblang, 15; Harold Lloyd, 15; Joe Schenck, 12; A. L. Erlanger, 12; J. J. Murdock, 12; Carl Laemmle, 10; Nicholas M. Schenck, 10; Marc Klaw, 10; and J. J. Shubert, 10.

sime's credo Concluding the era with a look at other show papers, as well as itself, *Sime* confessed, "Variety probably remains a mixed sheet trying to cover all of the show business, with the chances it is making a bum of itself trying. Its hookup is heavy, and though selling at 25¢ on the stands, this paper is far less prosperous than it looks.

"Variety's sloppy way of writing and printing is likely a laugh to those who know, but no way has been discovered to rectify its faults. . . . So this paper continues as the same terrible exhibit of newspaper work it always has been."

And Mencken chuckled.

Wall Street Lays an Egg

★

"Conditions are fundamentally sound," President Hoover soothed the panic-stricken country in December of 1929. The 6,000,000 unemployed by that date were puzzled but hopeful. In March Secretary of Commerce Robert P. Lamont promised that business would be back to normal in another two months. In May the Federal Reserve Board tentatively observed that the nation was in "what appears to be a business depression."

Banks crashed, along with stocks, bonds, prices, businesses, stores and jobs. In October a small handful of unemployed men were seen selling apples on the streets of New York. Three weeks later Variety reported the number of apple salesmen at 4,500, who were disposing of some 4,000,000 rosy specimens. The competition hurting, one Broadway vendor was offering *two* apples for 5¢.

Seventy per cent of Broadway hotels were reported both empty and broke, with actors owing bills of about $500,000. To protect themselves, the hotels were presenting bills to their guests every three days. In 1931, still empty and broke, the hotels began to issue "due bills" good for 40 per cent off rates. Broadway itself had a mournful appearance. There were 54 vacant stores that year on the Main Stem between 42d and 59th streets.

To help actors get jobs, and swap things they needed, Variety ran free classified want ads for show people. Its own count showed over 25,000 actors idle. As a further service, it opened an "advice to the troubled" department, with Nellie Revell in charge. In February 1921, Variety cut its price from 25¢ to 15¢.

Hearst, a past master on publicity out of public "benefactions," organized and operated two breadlines on Times Square. Broadway managers raised a howl of protest—the spectacle was certain to depress theatregoers and cut into Broadway business. Off Broadway went the breadlines.

Selena Royle and Elizabeth Beatty founded the Actors Free Dinner Club in W. 48th Street's Union Church. Stars came to eat, as well as wait on tables, so that no one knew who was there on the cuff. To cheer the dispirited thesps, the star-waiters would clown up their service, on the theory that a sandwich with a laugh meant more for morale than a steak with a scowl.

Even the greats of the concert world were touched by the depression—fees being cut for such celebrated names as Paderewski, Kreisler and Hoffman. On Broadway of 1932, about the only night life doing profitable business were those chowmeineries offering a floor show and dinner for 90¢. Penny-a-dance ballrooms opened, charging an 85¢ admission that included a 25¢ wardrobe check and 50 dance tickets.

The Broadway Association appointed a "secret committee of five" to clean up Broadway. The committee's biggest headaches were child and teen-age panhandlers, kids who played footman for cars and taxis, car "watchers" who pierced tires with ice picks if their services were rejected, and young girls who trod the Main Stem swinging handbags jauntily.

But even the depression couldn't stop the growth of golf in the United States, with theatre-owners complaining of the competition. There were 5,800 country clubs in 1930, with some 20,000,000 golfers. Miniature golf had hurt the b.o. in 1930, but died dismally in 1931.

theatre giveaways Dipping patronage in the first year of depression inspired managers to woo and hold the goodwill of their patrons. One Detroit theatre served free coffee and chewing gum to standees in the lobby holdouts. In another, an artist in the lobby free-sketched patrons, while piano acts like Tracy & Duncan entertained. Models from a nearby dress shop showed the latest styles, while in other corners "mit-" and tea-readers told fortunes for free. Instruction in bridge and checkers was also sur-le-cuff. The wonder was that any of the patrons cared about getting past the lobby. A less unctuous Chicago theatre settled for installing a chess and checker player in the lobby to take on all comers.

Radio audiences were easy bait for any gimmicks that promised temporary surcease from economic worries. "Special limited-time" offer of the Wonder Dream Book, Dr. Hormone's Sex Secrets or the True Success Horoscope lured listeners at $1 a throw. Most of the gullibles were women. The 3¢-each tracts lured a sucker list that was sold for 5¢ a name to mail-order houses.

The appearance of Austins during 1930 appealed to the American sense of irony, which saw in this pocket-size car a symbol of what had happened to the prosperity of the Twenties. A trend of the year, which suggested the disillusionment of the average American with life in the crippled industrial cities, and an inarticulate yearning for the simple security of mountain life, was the sudden craze for hillbilly songs and music.

In the groping of Americans for answers—spritual as well as physical—Clarence Darrow suddenly came to the fore again, delivering 73 talks in 1930 on religion, tolerance and other topics for musing. He offered to take on all comers in debates, arguing either side of a problem, and his antagonists were usually clergy of all faiths.

Americans, wondering why God could sanction so many millions of unemployed, flocked to hear Darrow lash out at organized religion. At one New York debate, the audience paid $10,000 to hear what he had to say. In Dallas, where Darrow argued against a triumvirate representing the three leading religions found the religious attempting to lead a walkout from the hall when Darrow's turn came. But so eloquent and persuasive was the great criminal lawyer that the audience—which had paid $5,000 to hear him— refused to follow the godly out of the hall.

Variety, of 1930, becoming more international in its outlook, featured chatter columns headed Broadway, London, Boston, Paris,

The Loop, Miami, Toronto, Nice, New Orleans, Sydney, Buenos Aires, and Berlin. It also took growing cognizance of the new talkie industry by publishing a four-page Hollywood Bulletin which it inserted gratis when Variety was distributed on the Coast. This was the forerunner of Daily Variety, its Hollywood subsidiary, now locally published.

The New York Roxy, staggered under the impact of 1930, went into receivership. Roxy (S. L. Rothafel) left Fox Film management and signed on as impresario of the newly proposed Radio City Music Hall, a Rockefeller project. During 1931, while Radio City was being built, Nelson Rockefeller was schooled in the principles of showmanship by Roxy himself. When the Music Hall opened during the Christmas holidays of 1931, the opening show began at 9 P.M. and lasted until 1 A.M. It was a fiasco in showmanship but despite bad notices the new showplace grossed $100,000 in its first week, patrons coming to see the theatre rather than the show. [Now the No. 1 cinema of America, the Music Hall is still a natural attraction on its own as a must-see tourists' lure.]

not so simple aimee   Aimee Semple McPherson, finding it tougher to get 1931 congregations to dig down, hit upon the ingenious idea of sending her ushers through the hall with clotheslines between them. Aimee urged the faithful to pin their contributions to the line . . . and it was quite clear you couldn't pin up anything but folding money.

Sister Aimee was one of the phenomena of the era, both from a sky pilot's boxoffice pull (although a dismal flop in theatres) and for her romantic escapades. Her al fresco barnstorming, for the cause of the Lord, included a radio appurtenance that went with her Four-Square Temple in downtown Los Angeles. For a time she was inclined to have her local station operate on one wavelength and for some reason, when it was found reception would be better a little further up the dial, her radio gospel spiels would turn up in that groove, and somehow the faithful seemed to know just when and at what time. The Federal Communications Commission, for obvious reasons, stepped in with the complaint that no Sabbath license was ever issued for this haphazard manner of operation. Variety reported that, to this, Aimee replied, squaring her shoulders, "God needs no license to operate."

Loew's booked her for a $5,000-a-week personal at its Broadway flagship, the Capitol, and she was as lonely as the accompanying film, portentously titled *Solitaire Man*. She sent the Capitol from a previous week's gross of $44,000 down to $17,500. When Aimee exited, the house bounced back to a $40,000 take. Variety reported that pulpits of many congregations beseeched parishioners to stay away; that "the place for preaching was the temple, not a theatre at $5,000 per." Besides the 5G, Loew's covenanted a split over $50,000 and it was anticipated she would hit 90G. Curiously enough, her then current husband, Dave Hutton, was also personaling at the Palace Theater, Washington, D.C. and pulled an above-average gross. Variety stated Loew's paid off Mrs. McPherson not to play its Capitol in Washington.

not-so-wonderful nonsense   The nation, hard hit to survive the depression, found a curious fascination in freak endurance contests. They flocked to watch who could sit on ice longer, who could hurl rolling pins further, and other such nonsense, finding a masochistic satisfaction in identifying themselves with the suffering exhibitionists. This was truly the era of not-so-wonderful nonsense, with marathon dancers, goldfish-swallowers and flagpole sitters.

While men worried where the rent was coming from, women took to wearing Princess Eugenie hats, a brave albeit somewhat ridiculous front to indicate that their heads were still above water.

The old New York *World,* decidedly under the water, passed into the hands of the Scripps-Howard chain, as a group of old *World* alumni held a wake in Hollywood. Percy Crosby, the creator of the cartoon "Skippy," published his own book assailing Prohibition, and spent more money on large newspaper ads proclaiming the bankruptcy of the Volstead Act.

Public sentiment was rising steadily against the dry law. In May of 1932 an anti-Volstead, "we want beer" parade marched down Fifth Avenue. Less than 10 months later, with F.D.R. in the White House, 3.2 beer was restored to thirsty Americans.

1932 was the year of the Lindbergh kidnapping case; the suicide of Kreuger, the Swedish match king; and the resignation of Mayor Jimmy Walker under fire. On Election Eve, film theatres lost approximately $50,000,000 worth of patronage as most Americans stayed home to listen hopefully to the news that was to shape the new American destiny for the next 13 years.

Mrs. Roosevelt, then an editor of the Macfadden publication, *Babies,* had a contract with the publisher calling for a substantial raise when and if her husband became President. Eleanor Roosevelt, however, found that she had a much more important job in Washington beginning in 1933.

Odd reactions to the presidential candidates were registered in the nation's film houses. During the campaign, newsreels of Hoover were booed and hissed, while F.D.R. won enthusiastic applause. Following the Roosevelt victory, Hoover in newsreels won the heaviest hand-clapping—sympathy for his all-around bad luck.

musso and adolf gags in '32   Mussolini entered show business in 1932 with the production of his play, *100 Days,* a Napoleonic epic, in London. It enjoyed mild business. His comrade-in-spirit, Adolf Hitler, came to the attention of American theatre patrons in humorous gags. The first Hitler joke appears to have been: "A Hitler herring! What's that?" . . . "A Bismarck without brains."

A blessing of the depression was the disappearance of the 1920s' worst scandal sheet, the New York *Graphic.* It went out of business in July 1932, trailing in its ignominious wake $7,000,000 worth of libel suits.

The wonder-boy branch of show business in the 1920s—radio—shuddered and shook on its foundations. Radio common stocks, which had soared spectacularly from 1927 through most of 1929, fell far below pre-1927 quotations.

The first change in radio was the dive in prices paid big name entertainers for mike appearances. Bankrollers, now counting their pennies, decided that one-night splurges meant little in terms of steady sales compared to a steady, season-round program that would build up a faithful following. Transcriptions, or recordings, became popular as an economy measure. Most stations used them in such a manner as to give listeners the impression they were listening to live talent.

Radio's biggest names of 1930 were Amos 'n' Andy. From coast to coast, betweeen 7 and 7:15 P.M. every weekday night, phones fell silent, and people stopped eating, as the troubles of the pair with the Kingfish and Madame Queen engrossed national attention. The nation literally set its time by Amos 'n' Andy. Runnerup standouts of 1930 were Rudy Vallee, the crooner, and the warm and human soap opera, "The Rise of the Goldbergs."

Although NBC and CBS divided the only top shows of the year between them, there were various regional favorites as well. The West Coast had Captain Dobbsie and the Reverend Bob Schuler. The Midwest had Little Jack Little. The power of local radio was demonstrated by the Beverly Hills Hillbillies, who asked for gifts while broadcasting, and received enough to open a mail-order house.

floyd gibbons, et al   Biggest radio single of the year was Floyd Gibbons, whose machine-gun chatter (217 words a minute) earned him $100,000 a year, setting the pace for the breathless announcers who followed him. Other top announcers were Norman Brokenshire, who later slid to the bottom and made a comeback post-World War II after an Alcoholics Anonymous cure; Alois Havrilla; Milton Cross of the distinguished accent; Leslie Joy; and Phillips Carlin. The latter two eventually became recording and radio executives.

Newspaper celebrities began to find their way on the airwaves. Alexander Woollcott reviewed books over WABC and a 33-station hookup on a program called "The Early Bookworm." The Brooklyn Eagle's H. V. Kaltenborn became CBS' news analyst with "We Look At the World," later known as "Kaltenborn Edits the News." Louis Nizer, attorney for the New York Film Board of Trade, turned up weekly on Manhattan's WMCA in a 15-minute, one-man debate—first talking on the affirmative side of thorny questions, then speaking up for the negative.

Despite the depression, radio advertisers—although more choosey about their programs—decided to spend heavily in the field to keep their inventories moving. Prices for choice hours on the air ranged between $10,500 and $11,380. Major advertisers allocated annual radio budgets ranging from $450,000 to $1,000,000 apiece.

Entertainers were gradually finding out what type of material was successful on radio, and what type flopped. It became quickly apparent that the airwaves had no room for sophistication. The poorest material was found to be fast gags, smart wisecracks, *double-entendres,* and anything requiring listeners to do more than lend their ears. The idea, as one radio actor explained it in 1930, was to "be simple and be funny—or if you can't be simple, be funny and lousy."

The other side of the coin was to be sad and lousy. This formula was found to be clicko on the daytime wavelengths, with housewives lapping up the lugubrious serials that soon developed into smoothly-tailored soap operas.

The idea of kidding radio commericals seems of fairly recent origin, and tied to such names as Henry Morgan, Fred Allen and Jack Benny at their height. But commercials were clowned as early as 1930 on the Quaker Oil program, as a deliberate attempt to give the program informality and make the medicine easier to take.

The movies, still chary of radio as a competitor—as they are today of television—decided to play it safe and buy in. Warners led off the trend in 1930 by acquiring KFWB, Hollywood, subsequently selling out in 1950. Paramount countered by buying a piece of CBS (and later sold out; and still later bought in on DuMont Television, and may have to sell out, in part, under Governmental taboo for "monopolistic" reasons). Metro didn't buy, believing it was protected on the radio end by its Hearst and Fox radio interests (but also later developed its WHN, New York station, into a powerful independent now known at WMGM).

Hollywood made sure to use the names of its films as part of the titles of its theme songs, so radio—like it or not—would automatically plug its pix when announcing the song titles and recordings played.

By 1931 radio had become the American Telephone & Telegraph Co.'s biggest customer, paying a 1930 bill amounting to $3,500,000. Newspapers, like film companies, had also bought in, with 99 of them owning radio affiliation (as later to be with FM and television affiliates). Despite this liaison with the fourth estate, newspapers began to ban all commercial credits in daily radio program listings. Instead of "The Fleischmann Hour," they listed "Rudy Vallee." In place of "The Lucky Strike Program" . . . "Rolfe's Orchestra." In other words—no free rides for the advertisers. But there again, program and advertiser titles sometimes were so closely tied in that sponsor identification became inevitable and automatic.

The switch of advertising revenues from newspapers to radio hurt especially small-town papers in 1930. That year 235 weeklies folded, victims of both the depression and radio opposition. Not until two years later did the first ad by a radio station appear in a newspaper. And even then, Baltimore's WCAO beamed its newspaper message to the paper's advertisers, urging them to get their slice of WCAO air time early.

Madison Square Garden, in 1931—as was the case with sports events and television—was in a dilemma over the question of yielding rights to broadcast its fights. Would radio help or hurt the b.o.? The Garden decided to find out, and accepted $5,000 from NBC for broadcast rights to the Schmeling-Stribling fight.

Cowboy entertainers surged to the fore in 1931 as popular listening fare, while comics who ad-libbed were being wiped off the air by the dozen by advertising agencies. The hucksters were afraid that a thoughtless ad lib, uncontrolled by the agencies, might wreck or ruin the bankroller's product . . . and hence lose the account for the agencies. Radio networks began to tighten up themselves, afraid of public reaction, by barring from the air any advertising of unmentionables like toilet paper, Kotex and laxatives, as well as patent medicines, liquor brands and stocks. One announcer was allowed to offer listeners an opportunity to get 7 per cent for their investment . . . but he was talking about beer.

A radio columnist of 1931 turned thespian at $100 a week, appearing as the only act on the bill at the Brooklyn Avalon Theatre. His name was Jerry Wald, now a top Hollywood producer.

Wald now likes to tell the Tinkers-to-Evers-to-Chance technique that he borrowed from *Sime*-to-Winchell-to-Wald. When the founder of Variety tutored Winchell to fear nobody and "the bigger they are the better it is to fight them," Wald conceived the idea of picking on Rudy Vallee. The crooner was then the combined Sinatra-Columbo-Crosby of his day, and by deliberately heckling him, Wald attracted immediate attention to his New York *Graphic* column.

The Church began to discover the new medium that year. Pope Pius X delivered the first Papal benediction heard simultaneously all over the world, at the inauguration of the powerful new Vatican station. NBC and CBS carried the address over both their networks, including a special talk by the man who had made the whole industry possible, Guglielmo Marconi.

There was less applause for another clerical broadcaster, Father Coughlin of Detroit. His Sunday radio talks evoked complaints from all corners of the nation, but his powerful following kept him on the air by swamping the networks with letters of praise and defense.

radio's self-regulation   The networks, mindful of the constant clamor for censorship of stage and screen, and realizing that they were now part and parcel of the average American home, organized their own system of internal censorship. They had something of a struggle in 1932 with comics from other fields who could not be persuaded to leave ad-libbing blue material outside the studio.

The studio "warmup" permitted the comedians more elasticity on the indigo gags, which was all right with the networks, the ad agencies and sponsors, so long as it achieved the primary purpose —warming up the studio audience for a readier acceptance of the actual broadcast script material. Frequently comics indulged in "sight" gags and business which, while producing audience yoks, left the abstract radio listeners wondering what was so hilarious.

The first studio glass curtain made its appearance in 1931 when NBC used the New Amsterdam Roof for broadcasts. And that year radio script writers made their first demand for recognition, insisting that they be given name credits along with the stars, announcers and products. Their demands were heeded—in 1947.

During 1932, when the advertising agencies secured firm domination of radio through the sponsorship end, the networks found that they were rapidly losing control of what would or would not go out over the air. Both networks surrendered to the agencies by lifting their ban on the broadcasting of product prices. Agencies began to shun the networks' artist bureaus, shopping for talent in the open market. Shows were being developed by the agencies themselves, with the networks serving no other function than selling the desired time slots.

Independent broadcasting stations were having their biggest battle with ASCAP over music license fees, pleading they were being unfairly penalized because they were forced to rely on transcriptions for the bulk of their entertainment. Radio at large was girding for battle with the newspapers, and rejoiced when it scored a scoop by beating the press with news of the Lindbergh kidnapping.

The big name in 1932 radio was Merlin Hall Aylesworth, who had been selected to head both RKO and NBC, making the tie between those interests clear and prominent. With Aylesworth in the driver's seat, NBC withdrew from the band-developing and booking business. One of Aylesworth's headaches, as it was for CBS, was how to protect American channels from interference by Mexican transmitters. The question was raised at the International Radio Conference held in Madrid, but no solution was found.

pioneer radio stars   The radio stars of 1932 were either the few headliners radio had already developed in its infancy, or borrowed from other branches of show business, chiefly vaudeville and musical comedy. Among the radio names who were already established strongly were Amos 'n' Andy, Rudy Vallee, the Mills Bros., Myrt & Marge, Stoopnagle & Budd, the Goldbergs, Bing Crosby, Ben Bernie, Ed Wynn, Eddie Cantor, Jack Pearl, Morton Downey and the Street Singer (Arthur Tracy), Jack Benny, Burns & Allen, Willie and Eugene Howard and Al Jolson. It was too early in the 1930s for the appearance of the Marx Bros. and Fred Allen.

The first hour-long program, arranged as a variety show, was the Fleischmann Hour, with Rudy Vallee at the helm. Burns & Allen made radio history in 1932 by being the first team to click with a routine of crossfire wisecracks. Gracie Allen's "dumb" character saved the act from being too high overhead.

The Maxwell House Showboat introduced the first hour show with the same actors playing the same characters week after week, using a continuous narrative. Further progress in kidding the commercials was made by efforts along those lines by Ed Wynn, Ben Bernie and Jack Benny, who proved to sponsors that the plugs were more effective—even if kidded—by being woven into the show.

This technique of kidding the commercials eventually segued into the phoney "feuds" between Winchell and Bernie and the later Benny versus Allen cross-heckling. It achieved the two-ply purposes of reaffirming public interest in one another's programs, and spotlighting perhaps new-found listeners (potential customers) on another show's product.

Ed Wynn—the "Texaco Fire Chief"—rose to immediate favor with radio listeners, his "Perfect Fool" routines registering close to that of Amos 'n' Andy. The latter—Charles Correll and Freeman Gosden—in pushing Pepsodent sales up 98 per cent, still clung to first place on the radio ladder despite the increasingly tougher opposition. The secret of their success was a deliberate packaging of comedy with generous portions of sentimentality—or, as we say in our set, solid hokum. They did not forget that as Sam & Henry, playing straight comedy, they had got nowhere fast for many years. And they saw what happened on radio to the "bright" comics who attempted to wow audiences with fast patter.

top chirpers   Although the public was fast tiring of crooners—with burlesques of crooning becoming popular in the theatres—Vallee, Downey and the Street Singer still held their radio following. Also singing to new heights on radio were Kate Smith, Ruth Etting and the Boswell Sisters.

Ben Bernie's informal microphone personality kept his band on top of radio's heap for 1932. Paul Whiteman and Guy Lombardo led the field with strictly dance orchestras, while Wayne King was building in the Midwest.

On the soap opera level, "The Goldbergs" finished 1932 still the top serial, trailed by Phillips Lord's "Country Doctor," which had great rural appeal; "Myrt & Marge," which clicked in the West but meant little to the East; and the then new "Easy Aces."

Rumblings of television continued to be heard through the depression years. In 1930 stills were televised from a radio studio in New York's Gramercy Park to Proctor's 58th Street Theatre, with poor results. That year Hearst tied up with Jersey City's W2XCR, when the Jenkins Television Corp. televised stills to a screen less than a foot square. Newspapermen, gathered in a Riverside Drive apartment to watch the event, held their noses.

Chicago was a big center of television development. In 1930 the first commercial telecast was sponsored by Libby, McNeill & Libby, with Ken Murray doing the pitch. Tele fans as far east as Pittsburgh reported dialing in the event.

pioneer television   Chicago had 1,000 television sets in operation by 1931. The Western Television Corp. offered two to three hours entertainment each day over W9XAO. "Dumb" acts—fire-eaters, acrobats, circus clowns and jugglers—proved the best fare. The station once offered a televised boxing match, but the fighters got out of range of the camera so often that the idea was considered impractical. The Chicago *Daily News* also operated a tele station, W9XAP, into which they sank some $4,000 a year for operation and talent. There was no opportunity for tele operators to earn money through the stations, since the Federal Radio Commission banned television as an advertising medium.

In 1932 predictions were being made that television "was only a few years away," as popular entertainment. The delay, experts explained, was not the depression, but the fact that it was still not technically perfect, nor had the commercial angles been clearly worked out. This despite rosy predictions by Owen D. Young that television (like prosperity) was just around the corner.

The television audience of 1932 numbered, unofficially, some 30,000 dialers. There were twelve 50-kilowatt television transmitting stations, each a hundred times more powerful than the transmitters of a decade previous, and capable of beaming over 10,000 miles. The big question on the inside of television was not when, but how. Would tele be broadcast over wires, as the A. T. & T. fondly hoped, or simply through the air?

The only thing certain about television in those days was that it was coming—and when it did, sets would cost a lot more than radio. Both predictions came true—but a lot later than those inside television believed.

PART FOUR

BIG BUST

1930 - 1932

38

'Stay Out of Hollywood!'

★

Film business slumped so badly in 1930 that one theatre offered 2-for-1 tickets and coupons entitling patrons to free marcel waves. Fox Theatres were in double trouble, indicated by the numerous suits filed by the divers Fox companies against William Fox, alleging malfeasance in office, manipulations of assets and misappropriation of funds.

Fox was ousted from the company he had built, although managing to retain the title of "consultant" at a $500,000 annual salary. The reorganization took 22 lawyers, at a cost of millions, with

Samuel Untermyer's bill alone coming to $1,000,000. Harley L. Clarke was made president of the new Fox company, now called the Fox Film Corp. The name of William Fox was ordered off all billing, film credits and ads.

Hearst Metrotone News scored a scoop in 1930 by getting John D. Rockefeller before their cameras, at the age of 93. The excuse was the 60th anniversary of Standard Oil. The following year, newsreel favorites were President Herbert Hoover, Benito Mussolini, Prime Minister Ramsay MacDonald, Mayor Jimmy Walker and Governor Franklin D. Roosevelt.

Theatres ran contests to discover patrons who looked most like Greta Garbo. The Hays Office ordered the use of Mexicans as movie heavies stopped, because of the sizable market below the Rio Grande. To compensate, Hays gave the nod for Russian villains because Soviet restrictions were keeping out American films.

And from far-off Jerusalem Variety reported that the talkies were being called "hearies" there . . . a term derived from the Hebrew word, *hashmonua* (meaning "hearies").

If 1930 was bad for Hollywood, 1931 was terrible. The boxoffice, crippled by the depression, was hit equally hard by public charges that the films being made were lemons, and the stars grossly overpaid. Film attendance dropped 40 per cent, forcing cuts in studio and theatre overhead. Bankers, previously lenient with the industry, began to demand more concrete collateral for loans—and the only collateral producers could offer was the diminishing interest of the public in films.

Some theatres, desperate for business, experimented with vaudeville. Most hit upon the double-feature bill, plus dishes, bank nights and other come-ons. One Broadway theatre tried television, and quickly scrapped it. Variety ironically noted February 17 as the 18th anniversary of the first showing of talking films—Thomas A. Edison's screening of a scene from *Julius Caesar* at the Colonial Theatre, New York.

k.o. to the silents   Depression or not, the talkers definitely signed the death warrant of the old silents. By 1931 only 1,500 out of 22,000 film theatres were without sound—the 1,500 being mostly of barn and store proportions. Warner Bros., who had brought all this about, went deeply into the red with about $30,000,000 in operating losses between 1930 and 1934. But so well had the organization been built that Warners survived the depression without "going through the wringer" of bankruptcy or reorganization, as others did.

There was little doubt but that the film industry still led all wings of show business in popularity even in the business debacle. A Chicago poll taken in 1931 showed the greatest familiarity with names in the following fields: (1) film actors, (2) gangsters, (3) athletes, (4) politicians, (5) musicians, (6) big business executives, (7) legitimate actors, (8) radio talent, (9) journalists and (10) film directors.

The talkers hit heavily at the ranks of the old silent stars. By 1931 there were only three stars remaining from the old silent days of 1921, and 26 new talkie stars. Among the fallen were John Gilbert, William Haines and Ramon Navarro, who retired to a monastery for a time. Even Douglas Fairbanks and Mary Pickford were slipping, whereupon she announced her imminent retirement. Billie Dove, Norma Talmadge and Marion Davies already had slid in public favor, despite the heavy Hearst publicity behind the latter.

Bert Wheeler and Robert Woolsey, Lew Ayres, Conrad Nagel, Buster Keaton, Bebe Daniels, Charles Farrell and Edmund Lowe continued to get top billing—but dwindling fan mail. Charles Bickford and Adolphe Menjou, starting the year as major stars, finished up working for independent companies. Even the great John Barrymore was let out by Warner Bros. Jack Oakie and Buddy Rogers slipped down the ladder from "starring" to "featuring." Clara Bow, after some bad publicity, faded and was counted out—only to surprise her detractors by a 1932 comeback with *Call Her Savage*.

Lionel Barrymore, who held a director-actor contract with Metro, was confined to acting only because he was considered too slow and too long on shooting schedules. The top film names of 1931 were almost exclusively those with strong voice personalities—Constance Bennett, Joan Crawford, Marlene Dietrich, Greta Garbo, Marie Dressler, Janet Gaynor, Norma Shearer, George Arliss, Ronald Colman, Wallace Beery, Maurice Chevalier, Clark Gable, Edward G. Robinson and Will Rogers. Tallulah Bankhead also made her first talkie—a film called *Tarnished*. Mickey Mouse in sound made the grade, although one of the cows in a Disney film had its udder removed by the finicky Hays Office.

Gangster films, which enjoyed a strong vogue in 1930 and 1931, began to taper off with Paul Muni in *Scarface* in 1932. Travelogs, representing colorful escapist fare, were highly popular. Not so popular was the habit of many small theatres to show commercial films —because they received these without cost, or were even paid to screen them—as supporting shorts for features. Protests forced many of the theatres to discontinue the practice.

A growing chiseling practice was the theatre owner who rented a film for one house, then "bicycled" it to his other houses in town, or perhaps to the next town. This is a violation of the Copyright Act and the industry soon took drastic means to curb the practice.

Variety noted in 1931, with something like awe, that pioneer theatre showman A. J. Balaban—formerly of Balaban & Katz— threw up his $75,000-a-year career to enter the Christian Science Church. He later returned as managing director of the Roxy.

The price of film tickets was widely considered too high for a depression year. Theatres which lowered prices did the best business of 1931. Many more followed suit in early 1932, when a 10 per cent Government tax was imposed on all tickets over 40¢. Those which refused to shave prices were forced to pass the 10 per cent levy on to patrons, hurting their b.o. still further.

cuts   As bad as 1931 was for Hollywood—with West Coast sages predicting that things could not possibly get worse—1932 set an all-time low for the film industry. United Artists cut the salaries of their executives 40 per cent, while Metro-Loew salaries went under the meat-chopper for a 35 per cent trimming.

Studios paid settlements to get out of crippling contracts with actors and directors, engaging stars on a day-to-day shooting basis. Publix Theatres warned its personnel against overuse of postage stamps, phones and telegrams. Paramount issued a salary cut—its third—of 5 per cent of all salaries up to $150, while Fox put through a second slice of 5 to 35 per cent, and Warners did likewise with a flat downbeat of 10.

Story prices slumped to an all-time low, and film operators as well as stagehands throughout the country were handed trimmed paychecks. Will Hays took a 60 per cent salary slice, and reduced his budget from $600,000 a year to $240,000. All with the same groaning and head-shaking that accompanied exactly the same financial shakeup that hit Hollywood after World War II.

National theatre advertising for and by film chains fell off 50 per cent. Practically all theatre-building ceased, and the Roxy—harried by terrible business and a staggering overhead—closed for several weeks. With labor being promised a New Deal from the White House, film theatre unions began to war against each other with jurisdictional strikes . . . the clashes driving away patrons in some cities to the extent of a 40 per cent boxoffice dip.

Alarmed at the ugly temper of unemployed America, film stars began to take out kidnap insurance policies from Lloyds of London, agreeing to Lloyds' provision that the policies would become void if the stars let the fact be known for publicity. The stars reasoned that if Lindbergh's baby wasn't safe, neither were they.

The economy move that pared Hollywood's expenses by $18,000-000 a year brought a new idea into film production—loanouts of stars, supporting players and directors. Film companies agreed the plan would work to everyone's benefit—helping the company which had highly-paid personnel under contract and idle, and also the company which needed them for special productions. This led to a growing realization by stars that they might serve their own interests better as independents, rather than under contract to a single studio.

The loanout system, essentially a sound idea, ran into difficulties later when stars began to balk at being "sold on the block" to other studios for film roles which they did not want to play. They also objected to producers renting them out to other producers for huge sums, cleaning up on the loanout deal, while the stars themselves were being paid relatively modest salaries. Some stars refused to accept loanout assignments, resulting in studio suspensions and lawsuits.

A few feeble attempts were made to bolster film business during the depression. Some film companies tried exclusive one-theatre release of first-run films. Some theatres tried not double, but triple features. Film companies refused to rent product to any theatre which did not keep admissions above a dime. The theatres promised. . . . then flooded their neighborhoods with half-price admission coupons.

Paramount tried to woo the critics by inviting them from all cities to New York previews. Warners inaugurated "trade showings" in key areas for exhibitors. But nothing could help the b.o. except the man who bought the tickets—and he just didn't have the cash in his pockets.

Jolson's $5,000,000 gross   The top money-maker in soundpix up to the end of 1932 was Al Jolson's *The Singing Fool,* which had grossed $5,000,000. Runnerup was Charles Chaplin's *City Lights,* for the most part silent save for a synchronized score and other sound effects, with over $4,000,000. (It was revived in 1950 and, in face of exhibitor fear in some quarters that Chaplin's political ideologies might militate against his b.o., it did smash biz.) The third top grosser of the period was Warner Bros.' *Golddiggers of Broadway,* also in the $4,000,000 bracket. Hollywood eyed those figures, thought of the $10,000,000 grosses each earned by *The Big Parade, Ben Hur* and *Birth of a Nation,* and sighed. (It has since been estimated that *Birth of a Nation* probably grossed nearer $40,000,000 for its sundry states rights' owners.)

"One more 'improvement' in films," said one diehard silent film producer, "and we're sunk." Sound, of course, was to prove the salvation of Hollywood.

After the beating it took in the 1920s, vaudeville was in no condition to weather a brutal depression. Variety described its plight succinctly by reporting, "Vaudeville in 1930 stood motionless on a treadmill that moved backward." The Loew Circuit dropped vaudeville as a useless expense which would drag Loew operations into the red. Independent circuits practically disappeared.

What was left of vaudeville "time" was patched together under the tattered banner of RKO, which reduced all bills to four acts, sliced the package price of each bill from $5,000 to $3,000, and shipped them out as units on a 50-week route. This reorganization meant a reasonable break for good acts, but the death knell for fair or poor acts, which were crowded out of show business. Some 1,500 acts fled vaudeville in 1930. Another 3,500 "flash" acts found their expenses too heavy for vaudeville's rewards.

The Palace, once the proud pillar of vaudeville, was now cracking at the seams. During 1930 it was losing $4,000 a week. The great showplace found itself caught in a web of its own contradictions. It had helped wreck vaudeville by raising salaries to astronomical heights. Now it sought headliners in vain. The headliners had largely deserted to other fields, since the rest of vaudeville had crumpled. The headliner shortage compelled the Palace to hold acts for two and four weeks, and to repeat them frequently . . . but that didn't add up to a year's salary.

In desperation the Palace began to entice headliners from other fields—radio, Hollywood, musicals and night clubs. It hopefully featured top-name masters of ceremonies, and encouraged ad-libbing. It even copied a page out of the old Winter Garden Sunday night shows, and had the emcees call on celebrities in the audience to stand up for bows, or to go onstage for guest shots. It tried to send audiences away tingling by using headliners to close the show.

To little avail. Bills that cost between $10,000 to $13,000 a week did well if they grossed $20,000 or $25,000. In the old days, Palace bills had cost about $8,000 a week, and had paid off an average $800,000 a year net profit. To make the 1930 picture blacker, Keith's was paying off $120,000 to acts they couldn't use—mostly "production" turns and adagio acts, which audiences were walking out on.

It was during the emcee era of the Palace that Al Jolson made his first, and last, "appearance" there because, actually, neither he nor George M. Cohan, of all the contemporary greats, ever played the Palace officially. Jolson obliged from the audience when Dave Apollon, as conferencier, called on him, and he got up and sang one number ad lib.

In later years, more of the desperation "policy" was essayed with super-vaude shows emceed by Lou Holtz, the Eddie Cantor-George Jessel bill, another sparked by Frank Fay, wherein headliners worked in and out of the supporting bill. This was not vaudeville in the real sense; it was more like a makeshift revue with neo-nite club overtones.

The Palace tried to snare Amos 'n' Andy, but the radio team refused. Their reason was that their act didn't register with actors, and the Palace catered to the footlight trade. They accepted an RKO circuit booking for all theatres except the greatest vaudeville showhouse of them all. And when they did, Variety ran an ad by McIntyre & Heath, oldest and most famous minstrel team, which claimed that Amos 'n' Andy were a "pale copy" of McIntyre & Heath, so "book the original!"

the end of the palace   In April 1930, all of Broadway was shocked and saddened by the news that their beloved Palace had undergone the final ignominy. It had been wired for sound.

There were other tokens of the evil days vaudeville had fallen upon. Loew's declared it was through booking top names because of the expense. The Vaudeville Managers Protective Association, once-powerful combine formed by E. F. Albee, folded up with no money in its treasury and no interest among managers. NVA dropped its payments of insurance and weekly gratuities to ailing vaudevillians. The White Rats officially admitted their finish, explaining there just weren't enough vaudeville actors to pay dues, and handed over their A.F. of L. charter to the new "Four A's"— the Associated Actors & Artistes of America.

By an ironic quirk, even the official name of vaudeville was changed in 1930 to "RKO Varieties"—which was the original name of vaudeville when Keith first tucked the ball under his arm and ran down the field of show business.

Eva Tanguay was typical of one-time great vaudeville stars who felt the pinch that first year of depression. Once the highest-priced single act in vaudeville—$3,500 a week—she was asked in 1930 to "show" her act. At first she indignantly refused, then thought better of her refusal. RKO gave her a "showing" date of three days at the Bushwick Theatre in Brooklyn, for $150.

RKO, trying to get away from the routine vaudeville act which made audiences yawn, booked stunt acts like Francille, who milked cows via radio, and operated miniature battleships and autos by remote control. Mae West was rejected (also by Loew's) because, as RKO's new president Hiram S. Brown explained, "Spice is all right, but dirt is out." Mae shrugged and signed with Fox, who let her do anything she wanted except cooch.

RKO went so far as to appoint a Mrs. Beatrice Mindlin as "fashion counselor" for the circuit. Her job was to tell actresses what they could and could not wear, and to impress upon male thespians the wisdom of keeping their pants pressed. She also kept a watchful eye open for any violations of the newly-restored RKO ruling—no bare legs.

Sentiment among theatre managers helped vaudeville in 1930, but sentiment died in 1931 along with most of business. RKO baldly announced that it wouldn't "bother" with vaudeville at all, if it could get enough decent films. The films were so bad that year, RKO found, that they made the four-act vaudeville bills look good by comparison. This acid view of vaude from the circuit that booked 70 per cent of the 102 weeks of vaudeville "time."

The second largest user of vaudeville acts in 1931 was the Publix Theatres 14 weeks. Warners offered 14 weeks as well, and Loew's dropped to about only 6 weeks of "time." All in all, only some 675 vaudeville acts were working a full week at any time during 1931.

The N.V.A. Club was abandoned, although it announced it would continue to maintain its sanitarium. The New York *Star*, merged with *Vaudeville News*, which was begun by Albee "to put Variety out of business," passed quietly out of the picture after 20 years. Variety discontinued its 25-year-old Correspondence Department from all towns, which were now mostly "film" towns, and in its place just reported the live stuff in key cities.

Already the name "Albee" was becoming unfamiliar to American theatregoers, who went to "RKO" theatres instead. RKO whetted the axe once again and sliced headliners' salaries, frequently more than half, and shrank its 23-week route to include cut salaries for six weeks. Now contemptuous of tradition, RKO cut actors' first names off their billing, explaining they could get the last names in bigger type by this device.

Many standard acts quit show business in despair. Even those who clung to the sinking ship felt hopeless about their future. The four- or five-a-day grind most were forced to work killed what spark their performances originally may have had. And most were working with old, hackneyed material. Vaudeville writers had fled to the Hollywood hills. To make matters worse, old vaude routines were turning up in talking film shorts, as well as on radio, hurting the original live acts in vaudeville.

The Palace continued to sink deeper into the red, and found it increasingly tougher to get headliners. To foster the illusion that vaudeville was still Broadway's favorite entertainment, the manager put a blackboard in the lobby, listing the names of celebrities attending each performance

RKO still pretended to offer "clean" shows, ruling off "pansy" bits and actors who indulged in Bronx cheers for humor. Small acts didn't dare talk or sing off-hue—bookings were too tough—but the headliners were allowed to get as blue as they preferred.

The Midwest raised some wry smiles in show business by featuring acts as "Gloryfied Vaudeville."

There was a faint glimmer of hope for vaude as 1931 slipped into 1932. David Sarnoff, speaking for RKO, declared that the circuit's four-act bills had kept RKO theatres from diving heavily into the red. They had served as insurance against the extremely bad RKO films of that year.

Bad films generally forced bigtime film theatres like the Paramount and the Capitol to strengthen their bills with name acts on the stage. They went into competition with the Palace for headliners, and star salaries enjoyed a brief spurt upward. The Palace offered a $16,500 bill. The Paramount countered with a $17,000 stage attraction, and the Capitol upped the ante to $20,000.

radio's hypo to talent   Good acts—in the midst of depression—were bewildered to find themselves being offered up to 50 per cent over their accustomed salaries. Radio acts, which had not yet even proved themselves on the air, were startled to find themselves in front of microphones on theatre stages. The most important drawing cards were rated as film personalities, musical comedy stars, radio stars and vaudeville headliners, in that order.

Jolson was paid his highest price—$15,000 straight salary, plus a percentage of the gross. Jack Pearl and Burns & Allen, from radio, were sought after. Warners gambled with Lou Holtz, on a straight vaudeville policy, and lost. The boom died as quickly as it had risen, with warring theatre interests getting together to control salaries. The issue quickly lost importance as Hollywood, having found its way through the maze of vocal problems, began to turn out better films. Before 1933 was over, vaudeville, which had drawn business for bad pictures, was considered to be keeping business away from good pictures.

RKO gave up the New York Hippodrome to Cooper & Carroll, 10¢ film operators, who made a pitch for the depression trade by offering vaudfilm shows at 15¢-25¢. The stage bills cost $150 a day, and films were scraped from the bottom of the barrel. The price lure won business at first, but the bad shows eventually K.O.'d Cooper & Carroll.

By the end of the year vaudeville found itself in a deeper hole than ever. Loew's, which had produced some of its own unit shows, closed its production department. Warners, which had 11 theatres offering stage presentations, dropped them gradually until their theatres offered films only. The Publix bookings disappeared. Vaudeville time dwindled from 102 weeks at the beginning of the year to only 25 weeks at its close. The 800 acts working a full week at first fell off to only 200 at the finish.

Only 200 in the entire United States! Vaudeville, which had ample room for 20,000 full-week acts in 1916!

One of the showmen who hearkened mournfully back to the good old days was Lee Lash, who originated and controlled the sale of advertising space on theatre backdrops. In his heyday, Lash had earned over a quarter of a million dollars a year with his idea, holding contracts with 1,700 theatres. 1932 found him with a bare handful of theatres left. And these took one-third of the $80 revenue from each 10-ad curtain.

The career of the Palace plunged further downhill—if that was possible. From its haughty two-a-day policy it had gone into straight grind vaudeville. Then it threw in films with its vaudeville, in the fall of 1932. Nothing helped. Losing $2,000 and $3,000 a week, the Palace finally announced in November 1932 that it was turning into a straight picture house, booking as its first film under that policy Eddie Cantor in *The Kid From Spain*.

That was the official kiss of death. The desertion of the Palace left only one week of RKO vaudeville in the nation—the last holdout, the Chicago Palace. Broadway, and most of the nation, were stunned by the news that live acts would no longer tread the famous boards of the Palace. As nothing else, the news sharply pointed up the passing of an era.

"Vaude never knew what the Palace meant to it," observed Variety soberly, "until the Palace passed and the newspapers all over the country wrote farewell tributes." Seventeen years later, in the spring of 1949, a form of vaudfilm was to come back to the Palace. The nation's press again sentimentally, almost lachrymosely, heralded "the return of vaudeville" to the famed flagship of the bigtime. This was fallacious enthusiasm because eight acts, at $3,000-$4,000 gross cost for the entire bill, doing four shows a day, plus a first-run film, at 95¢ top, was but a lukewarm, considerably watered-down variation of the theme.

39

The Shuberts Go Boom

★

Broadway applauded Robert Benchley when he wrote, toward the end of 1930, "I am now definitely ready to announce that Sex, as a theatrical property, is as tiresome as the Old Mortgage, and that I don't want to hear it mentioned ever again." He added, "I am sick of rebellious youth and I am sick of Victorian parents and I don't care if all the little girls in all sections of the United States get ruined or want to get ruined or keep from getting ruined. All I ask is: don't write plays about it and ask me to sit through them."

Although legit produced few notable attractions during the depression years, it did, by and large, heed Benchley. Not only was the public sick and tired of the trite themes of the Twenties, but it had no pennies to spend on them even if it had continued to like them.

The depression, which checked the sudden expansion of the new talkies, caught a lot of stage people in Hollywood short. All through 1930 they came trickling back to Broadway—to find that there was a depression on the Main Stem, too.

Some producers tried to shake some life into the legitimate by arranging to have their shows raided. Earl Carroll and 10 of his *Vanities* girls were given a ride in a police sedan, but the grand jury failed to indict. Another jury disagreed on the salacious qualities of Mae West's *Pleasure Man,* and the case was finally tossed out by the prosecutor himself.

The Shuberts made the legitimate's most depressing depression headlines. During 1930, with actors growing daily more desperate for work, the Shuberts announced they were bringing in 20 plays from abroad—complete with casts. It was small consolation to embittered American actors that most of the Shubert importations flopped.

Although Broadway hadn't fully realized it, the stock market crash had shaken the Shubert corporation severely. Lee Shubert suddenly made his corporation investors quake for their $8,000,000 by applying in 1931 for equity receivership. The Irving Trust Co. and Lee Shubert were appointed co-receivers by the court, under the peculiar arrangement that permitted the Shuberts to continue in business "for the expected benefit of the creditors." The court twice extended the period of receivership. In the spring of 1932, had Shubert theatres been sold at the prevailing low price of real estate, creditors would have received 4¢ on the dollar. The only chance the corporation had to pay off was by producing successful shows. This it failed to do. By the end of 1932, Variety reported that it was doubtful if Shubert creditors could hope to realize even 1¢ on the dollar.

Legit found 1931 its most dismal year in almost two decades. Through most of the year, Broadway was about 45 per cent dark. During the summer there were only 12 plays on the boards. Musicals lost $2,000,000 on the season. Productions closed faster than new ones could take their place.

An idea of the mortality rate is that Jessie Royce Landis in Booth Tarkington's *Colonel Satan* only lasted 17 performances; Lynn Riggs' *Green Grow the Lilacs,* which was to bloom into *Oklahoma!,* when musicalized by Rodgers & Hammerstein in later years, only flourished for 64 performances despite the cast presence of Franchot Tone, Helen Westley and June Walker. *Rock Me, Julie,* with Paul Muni, Jean Adair and Helen Menken, only kept rocking for seven performances; and Paul Kelly in *Hobo* only lasted five shows.

Even Jolson's *Wonder Bar* could only last 76 performances but on the more definite hit side there were Earl Carroll's *Vanities* (with Jack Benny), *Fine and Dandy* (Joe Cook), Moss Hart and George S. Kaufman's *Once In a Lifetime, The Greeks Had a Word for It, You Said It* (Lou Holtz and Lyda Roberti), and Katharine Cornell in *The Barretts of Wimpole Street.* Ziegfeld's *Hot-Cha!,* with Bert Lahr, Buddy Rogers, Lupe Velez, Marjorie White, June Knight and Lynne Overman heading the cast finished in the red.

In addition to the Shuberts, A. H. Woods went into bankruptcy. So did Arthur Hammerstein, who had made over $2,500,000 on *Rose Marie,* but sunk it into building a theatre to perpetuate his father's name (it's now a CBS Radio Playhouse at 53d and Broadway, New York). Other managers, caught with their plans down by the market crash, crowded the 77-B corner along with them.

For the first year in a long while, no *Uncle Tom's Cabin* troupe took to the road. Equity, with almost half its members unemployed, barred new members by raising initiation fees. Employed actors accepted salary cuts, glad to be working. Equity, which frowned on Sunday shows, waived the rules to allow three Sunday legitimate shows to play benefits for the unemployed.

Incongruously, 1931 was the year chosen by Earl Carroll to open the new Earl Carroll Theatre, which cost—including the show— $4,500,000. And Flo Ziegfeld put on his first *Follies* (with Helen Morgan, Harry Richman and Jack Pearl) since 1927. Somebody forgot to tell them what year it was.

1932 found 152 plays offered by producers, considerably less than the number introduced in previous seasons. The number of flops was high—fully 121. Only 16 shows were rated as hits, and another 15 as moderate successes. During late August, there were only six plays open on Broadway.

more banks than managers   The banks moved in as theatre operators. Shubert had tossed many theatres into their hands by defaulting on mortgages. A. L. Erlanger did the same. The banks foreclosed on Charles Dillingham and took over the Globe Theatre on Broadway. By the end of 1932, there were more banks in show business than there were Shubert and Erlanger theatres combined.

Taxes had a sobering effect on ticket prices. Most musicals were limited to a $4.40 top, with no show exceeding a $5.50 top. Some straight dramas charged $3 top, and out of this paid the 27¢ tax themselves.

There was no depression for one playwright—George S. Kaufman, who was earning about $7,000 a week. He owned 25 per cent of *Dinner At Eight,* besides his royalties as co-author and 35 per cent of the hit musical satire, *Of Thee I Sing,* which he also co-authored and which had two companies on the road.

In 1930 Al Jolson appeared at the Capitol for $15,000 a week, plus 50 per cent of the take above $100,000. Most of Broadway bet the gross would go over the top, but Jolie actually hit only $80,000, despite his five and six appearances a day. The reason was not the failure of Jolson to draw—but his refusal to sing the same songs at every show. People stayed to hear his new songs . . . and the turn-over suffered.

Later that year Jolson gave a concert at the New Orleans Auditorium, joking and singing for two hours before a packed house of 12,000. In 1931 he went into the musical, *Wonder Bar,* for the Shuberts. And in 1932 he was topping all salaries with $17,500 a week, plus a percentage of the gross.

Eddie Cantor, playing the Palace in 1930, received $7,700 a week. Booked again at the Palace the following year with George Jessel, his salary went to $8,000, with another $8,000 going to Jessel and the rest of the bill. The show, breaking all Palace records, was the first in Palace history to run for eight weeks.

winchell reverts to greasepaint Walter Winchell put on greasepaint in 1930 by making a Vitaphone short called "The Bard Of Broadway," with Madge Evans. Winchell's take was $1,750. That year, with his New York *Mirror* contract at $500 a week still good for three more years, it was torn up and replaced with another at $1,000 a week . . . plus syndicate money. But the ubiquitous Winchell could not be confined to print, even at $1,000 a week. He was signed for a radio show by WABC, offering a guest star with each broadcast.

In 1931 he accepted his first professional stage booking in 10 years —a $3,500 a week engagement at the Palace, following vaudeville appearances by fellow journalists Heywood Broun, Floyd Gibbons, Mark Hellinger and Harry Hershfield.

Winchell turned in his own review of his act to *Variety.* "Another freak attraction on the current Palace bill," he wrote, "is Walter Winchell. . . . This sort of headliner is too anemic for the best-known music hall. His appearance is oke—he has a natty tone about him. He can be heard in the last rows, too. But he is hardly bigtime material. He simply won't do. . . . Winchell should have known better and should stick to columning."

But Winchell didn't take his own advice. That year he signed with not one, but two radio sponsors—Lucky Strike on NBC, and Geraldine Hair Tonic via CBS. He also branched out into Tin Pan Alley, doing the lyrics for a song published by Bibo-Lang called "Things I Never Knew Till Now," with music by Al Van.

Since 1927 Lee Shubert and Walter Winchell had rarely seen eye to eye. Winchell as a dramatic critic was barred from all Shubert theatres. The columnist's favorite comment on the feud was, "I can't go to Shubert openings. So I wait three nights and go to their closings." When he wrote in his column, "The Shuberts lousy? Why, they are the best producers in show business," Lee Shubert sued him for libel—and lost.

In 1931 the dam broke, and Shubert invited Winchell to the opening of Al Jolson in *Wonder Bar*. The producer had decided to end the four-year ban, not out of any love for Winchell, but because Winchell's "opposition" had proved too costly. He covered the Jolson show. The Shuberts were to enjoy even greater boxoffice benevolence from the columnist in later years when, almost single-handedly, in face of a set of mediocre to downright bad notices, Winchell's plugging did a lot to put over Olsen & Johnson's *Hellzapoppin*. The Winchellian "orchids" for pix, plays, books, et cetera became a one-man boxoffice Oscar of no small potency. As far back as 1931 song-smiths Abner Silver and L. Wolfe Gilbert paid tribute to the grip he held on the popular imagination with a ditty titled "Mrs. Winchell's Boy." It was a very confidential hit.

guinan, vallee & benny   Variety glimpsed other stars cutting their way through the depression years. In 1930, Texas Guinan was writing a brief daily column in the ill-fated New York *Graphic;* Weber & Fields were on WOR every Monday night touting Webster Cigars; Will Osborne was crooning at the Brooklyn Fox, billed as originator of the style, while the "copy," Vallee, was soothing feminine hearts at the Paramount on Broadway. Copy or no copy act, Vallee had jumped in two and a half years from $3,000 to $4,500 weekly salary. And in late 1931 Variety revealed that the only new actor millionaires created since the market crash were Vallee, Maurice Chevalier and Amos 'n' Andy. Chevalier received $12,000 a week from the Chicago Theatre, which lost $15,000 on the deal, as Chevalier explained he had been the victim of sharing the bill with a bad film.

Jack Benny spent 1930 in Earl Carroll's *Vanities*. That year Fanny Brice went on tour with a big electric sign spelling out her name, for use at all theatres where she appeared. Primo Carnera entered vaudeville. Bob Burns was glimpsed coming up the ladder, as half of the team of Burns & (John) Swor, whom Fox was trying—unsuccessfully—to build up as another Moran & Mack. Mary Margaret McBride, housewife's companion of the 1940s, was noted as a cub reporter on the Cleveland *Press,* doing occasional lecture turns at women's clubs.

Harry Lauder, before returning to Europe after an American tour, broke Scottish precedent by throwing a party for 28 guests at a New York hotel. He amazed William Morris with the gift of a traveling clock, and a diamond wristwatch for Mrs. Morris. Lauder warned the guests they could only stay two hours until the maitre d'hotel assured him there would be no extra charge if the guests stayed later, whereupon Sir Harry magnanimously invited them to stay as long as they liked. "I'd also invite you all to the theatre," he added, "but I'm not playing this week, and I've spent so damn much money on this food that I haven't any left for theatre tickets."

From France came the belated report that Gaby Deslys, once the toast of Broadway and the *grands boulevards,* had been a distinguished World War I spy for the French Government. She had impersonated an Hungarian woman named Hedwige Navratil, whom she resembled, and had taken the Germans for all the secrets in their pants pockets.

Kate Smith's first radio commercial in 1931, when she hoisted her moon over the mountain for La Palina Cigars, scored a big hit. She played 11 consecutive weeks at the Palace, just missing the previous marks set by dancers Adelaide & Hughes, for 12 weeks, and song stress-comedienne Ruth Roye whose three months' stock run holds the record.

Bing Crosby hit stardom in 1931 when Paramount billed his name above the film. CBS, however, stopped him from whistling with his songs over the air because another CBS chirper, Morton Downey, had been first with the technique. Downey was broadcasting from the Club Delmonico, New York, on Friday and Saturday afternoons.

Will Rogers was on a three-week tour for the Red Cross, along with Frank Hawks, the flier, and The Revelers. Not only did Rogers work on the cuff, but paid his own expenses as well. His generosity netted the Red Cross as high as $8,900 a night, with Texas alone kicking in $50,000.

schnoz goes single   The famed Clayton, Jackson & Durante combo broke up in 1931, after consulting with *Sime.* The boys had started together at the Durante Club in 1923. The cold facts were that Lou Clayton and Eddie Jackson would anchor the talented Schnozzola, who would undoubtedly soar much higher solo. So did Variety's editor-founder counsel them. The boys were all for the change; Lou Clayton became Durante's manager, and Jimmy took good care of Eddie Jackson as well, as he did drummer Jack Roth and piano accompanist Harry Donnelly.

Eva Tanguay was still going in 1931, but at a limping pace. She opened in Brooklyn's Rockwell Terrace, a small cabaret, and later joined a Fancho & Marco unit, doing four and five a day. Babe Ruth opened a Broadway haberdashery, and closed it after five months. Ethel Barrymore, whose dressing room at the Barrymore Theatre was never used by anyone save herself, showed how she felt about Billie Burke by giving her the key, when Miss Burke appeared there in *The Truth Game.*

Lou Holtz headed an eight-week vaude show at Warners' Hollywood Theatre, New York, at $2 top, but the policy flopped. Ed Wynn, knocking them dead in *The Laugh Parade,* closed that legit musical every Tuesday to broadcast his Texaco "Fire Chief" program. Later in the year he decided to broadcast from the stage, charging admission, the proceeds to charity. He was the first to do this, and the practice became standard with many radio shows Vaudeville's highest-priced act of 1932 was the Four Marx Bros. at $10,000 a week.

Show business was further depressed during the depression by the passing of many of its favorite figures. One of the first to go was James Churchill, at 66, whose restaurant had been one of Broadway's favorite haunts before it succumbed to the Chinese restaurant invasion. Less mourned was E. F. Albee, who left only $250,000 out of his $25,000,000 to actors' charities. Bulk of that went to the Actors' Fund of America and not to the pet National Vaudeville Artists, the NVA Club which he had subsidized. Albee died a broken-hearted man; his own vaudevillians had turned on him.

A. L. Erlanger, who also died in 1930, did much worse—not one cent of his $12,000,000 going to any charity. The estate was thrown into protracted, expensive litigation on a "common law wife" suit. Although the estate had claims against it of some $7,000,000 with only $124 available as cash on hand, the Erlanger firm continued in business under the aegis of Judge Mitchell Erlanger, Abe Erlanger's brother.

Broadway grief was more readily expressed in 1931 for two of its great and respected showmen—David Belasco, who died at 78, and Joe Leblang, the cut-rate ticket broker, at 57. The same year also saw the passing of Lon Chaney, author Frank Harris, and Charles E. Manchez, inventor of the ice cream cone which symbolized Coney Island.

Flo Ziegfeld died in July 1932. His career, full of spectacular ups and downs, ended on a depressing note. He had lost two fortunes made in show business and Wall Street, the market collapse taking him for over $2,000,000. His last production, *Hot-Cha!* finished in the red, and only his final show, a revival of *Show Boat,* saved him from bankruptcy before his death.

Even more deeply mourned by all of show business was William Morris, who died at the age of 59, two years after the death of his lifelong enemy, E. F. Albee. Variety, which had so often cheered Morris in his courageous battles against the monopolies of show business, termed him "one of the greatest, if not the greatest, of agents and managers in show business."

Other deaths of 1932 included those of Mrs. (Minnie Maddern) Fiske, at 67; Chauncey Olcott at 71; Billy Minsky at 41; John Philip Sousa at 77; George Eastman, founder of Eastman Kodak, at 77; and novelist Edgar Wallace, who had turned out 200 novels and 23 plays during his lifetime, at 56.

Albee, Erlanger, Belasco, Ziegfeld and Morris—the greats were passing, and with them the chapters of theatrical history that had made the first three decades of the 20th century a fabulous tale of Scheherazade to intrigue students of the growth of American show business.

PART FIVE

NEW DEAL

1933 - 1940

The FDR Years

★

The era began, sternly and grimly, with the three harsh years of the depression, then sank to an all-time low in 1933.

In 1934 the nation was so sobered that even Hollywood reported only 60 divorces. Ironically, the depresh proved a boon to family life, drawn closer together in the common fight against the economic wolf. A 1933 survey of favorite American recreations gave first place to reading, radio second. Films, the ranking mass entertainment of the 1920s, placed third.

America's serious mood proved a boon to the apostles of viewpoint and opinion. The lecture circuit of show biz climbed out of the depths for richer dividends. Usual rates for the platform pundits were $100 a night, with $250 for outstanding personalities and $500 for the real big names. Above that level, only Eleanor Roosevelt and Admiral Byrd commanded between $700-$1,000 a night.

The national hunger for enlightenment also boomed the stocks of columnists, who were respected as repositories of encyclopedic wisdom. Top salaries and top syndication went to Walter Winchell, Walter Lippmann, Westbrook Pegler, Heywood Broun, Mark Sullivan, F.P.A., Arthur Krock and Mrs. Roosevelt among others. The same thing, of course, was to see itself repeated with World War II, and with the Korean crisis the political commentators and columnists once again got the spotlight.

Federal relief began in May of 1933, and ended at the close of 1935. During that period the economic tide began to change rapidly. "Prosperity's return to Broadway" was keynoted by the Parmalee (Yellow Cab) Co. report that its 2,000 hackies on the streets of New York showed an average uppage in tips of 25¢ per fare.

In 1933, Broadway legit sold an average of $228,000 worth of tickets per week. By the end of 1934, the weekly average had tilted to $381,000.

Niteries and hotels were equally enthusiastic about recovery under the New Deal, if not about New Deal taxes. Average checks rose from $2.80 to $3.40. Leon & Eddie's, a standard tourist spot, reported once-a-week 1933 patrons were dropping in three times a week during 1934. Broadway was an accurate barometer of what was going on in general business throughout the country.

Curves on office charts rose steadily upward. In 1936, show business divided $24,000,000 in bonuses and dividends among its employees. The number of dice, card and wheel games rose to its greatest height since the 1920s. The following year football pools were reported to be grossing more than $1,500,000 weekly, with an equal bonanza for numbers racketeers. Steamship companies reported 1,-000,000 passengers booked annually for ocean cruises, and theatres began to raise their prices.

jukeboxes and repeal   Jukeboxes reflected the rising tide of national joy, sweeping into every crossroads town by 1939. Adolescents jitterbugged to the hot licks of the nation's top bands—

for a nickel a dance. In 1940 there were 400,000 jukeboxes flashing colored lights and making music to celebrate a $65,000,000 new industry. Bars began to install "Talk-A-Vision" machines which offered musical movies at the insertion of a coin.

In the first months of 1933, when repeal seemed likely, if not an absolute certainty, radio jumped the gun by inviting liquor advertising. CBS' St. Louis outlet, KMOX, had one announcer telling the radio audience, "Put in your orders now for Blank's Whiskey. If the repeal of the Volstead Act does not materialize as expected, your money will be cheerfully refunded."

Legalization of 3.2 beer in March evoked a wave of repeal celebrations all over the country. In New York, film theatres found that business perked as film fans went for 3.2 and a film. The more sophisticated legit trade, however, turned up its nose at the plebeian offering and sought its usual refreshment in its usual speakeasies.

When full repeal was established, New York speakeasies quickly realized that their main attraction had vanished—the little peephole in the door through which patrons whispered, "Benny sent me." With liquor flowing copiously anywhere, there was no need of Benny to send anybody any place. The speaks rapidly converted into night clubs, and there was a huge demand for talent to lure trade. Some clubs tried to make patrons as anxious to get in as they had been in Prohibition days by deliberately making it tough—"reservations," a mythical "membership," and the rest of the "exclusive" paraphernalia. There are still remnants of that to this day.

The outstanding event of 1934, outside of the world-shaking events abroad, was the arrest of Bruno Richard Hauptmann for the kidnaping and murder of the Lindbergh baby in May 1932. Tried in Flemington, New Jersey, Hauptmann brought a $50,000 weekly boom to that obscure town as curiosity-seekers flocked in by car, bus and train. The trial was given the biggest newspaper and radio coverage of any trial in American history.

murder, inc.   There were further thrills in 1934 for readers and dialers in the capture and slaying of John Dillinger. The following year headline writers had a holiday with the long delayed extermination of Dutch Schultz. The era in crime closed with the sensational expose of Murder, Incorporated, a phrase coined by the New York *World-Telegram*.

England dominated the world's news in 1936, with the death of King George V; the ascension of Edward VIII to the throne; and the historic romantic abdication before the end of the year to marry "the woman I love." Edward and his American-born wife continued to win headlines all through the decade, despite the crowning of George VI and Elizabeth in 1937. The coronation was overshadowed that year by the marriage of the newly-styled Duke of Windsor to Mrs. Simpson in France. To mend England's fences in the United States, King George and Queen Elizabeth paid a 1939 visit to the Roosevelts in Washington and Hyde Park. The following year they exiled the embarrassing ex-King to the Bahamas as "Governor and Commander-in-Chief." United States show business, showing rare consideration for our English cousins, banned all Wally Simpson gags on radio, and passed up thinly-disguised "royal romance" themes for pictures as "too hot to handle."

Apart from floods and strikes, newsreels enjoyed a boom in disaster during 1937 with the explosion of the *Hindenburg* at Lakehurst, New Jersey, fortuitously filmed at the exact moment it happened by a surprised cameraman; and the disappearance into thin air of round-the-world flier Amelia Earhart. England's Coronation ceremony also won heavy newsreel footage.

The following year more air news was made by Douglas ("Wrong Way") Corrigan, who flew from Brooklyn to Dublin with neither permit nor permission. Corrigan received offers totaling $200,000 from show business, but refused them all. The rest of 1938 was taken up by war news from abroad; the arrest of ex-President Whitney of the New York Stock Exchange; the tearing down of New York's 6th Avenue Elevated after 60 years of operation; and Mexico's appropriation of foreign-held land, including 17,980 acres belonging to William Randolph Hearst—who didn't like the idea.

The news event of 1939 was, of course, the outbreak of World War II in September of that year. Slightly more than one year later America had a new Selective Service Act—the first "peacetime" compulsory military service in its history.

fdr—no. 1 showman   Unquestionably the biggest figure in all show business of 1940 was Franklin Delano Roosevelt, whose radio rating hit a new high, with a Crossley grade of 38.7. His election for a third time demonstrated, as nothing else could, the power of

American radio. More than a political contest, the 1940 election was a battle between newspapers and radio to test which medium exercised the greatest influence on the American public. When the newspapers lined up about 90 per cent solidly against a third term, Roosevelt took his case to the people via the airwaves. Newspapers denied that the victory had been a clear-cut one, claiming that the Roosevelt voice and personality were as much of a factor in the victory as the medium of radio.

On the lighter side of the ledger for the 1930s were the usual fads and foibles that always fascinated the American public come war, peace or atom bombs. A new era in publishing history began in 1933 with the appearance of *Esquire,* a magazine frankly aimed at being lusty in a slick way, offering juicy Petty and Varga pin-up girls for bachelor quarters. With the perversity of the sex—as though the publishers didn't know—women also flocked to buy it.

The Chicago *Tribune* made all of the Windy City fragrant in 1939 by running a rose-scented ad for the Allied Florists Association of Illinois. Sixty pounds of perfume were mixed with the regular ink for this aromatic scoop. The last footnote on the history of journalism of the 1930s was the appearance of New York's liberal newspaper, *P.M.,* the first big-city journal to line up openly on labor's side. Chicago millionaire Marshall Field III bankrolled it—but even he ran out of money some 10 years later.

The first of the 1930s fads was long fingernails, introduced in 1933 by Marlene Dietrich. It was also the year of the jigsaw puzzle craze, which enjoyed a long—depression-nurtured—vogue until 1936, when "knock-knock-who's-there?" games and gags, along with a candid camera craze, occupied the idle time and minds of the nation. Bars increased their take that year by installing skee-ball alleys. In 1939 and 1940, the top divertissements were gambling—pinball machines, which graduated out of the penny arcade class; and the newly-improved game of gin rummy, a Hollywood favorite.

The pace of the 1930s saw many changes, besides those in economic and political spheres. Show business rejoiced in 1933 when increasing bus competition forced the railroads to restore old party rates. Niagara Falls hotel men claimed that no honeymooners were arriving —by train, bus or car—because show business comics had ruined the town's reputation with corny gags about it.

Variety noted in 1936 that the old aspiration of youngsters to see their names in lights on Broadway had practically vanished, replaced by a determined migration to Hollywood, the new mecca. Broadway was further depressed that year by the disappearance of the old Criterion Theatre, replaced by a large and gaudy Woolworth's.

The same year, Max Schmeling made Teutonic hearts rejoice by knocking out Joe Louis. Two years later Louis made American hearts rejoice by knocking out Max Schmeling.

a couple of exes   A further token of change was noted in 1936 when Churchill met Paderewski at England's Denham Film Studios, where Paderewski was making a picture. "The last time I met you," the great Pole said sadly, "you were at the War Office." Churchill replied, "The last time I met you, you were a president."

Perhaps the most startling change of all took place in 1939, when sedate Philadelphia agreed to permit Sunday dancing but stood firm on no Sunday drinking.

When the era drew to a close, Variety revealed its usual list of the year's top salaries—implying, thereby, Americans considered most indispensable. Top of the list was Claudette Colbert, with $301,944. Next, surprisingly, came Warner Baxter, with $279,907. In the third slot was Bing Crosby's take of $260,000. Runners-up were Jack Benny ($250,000), Joseph Pulitzer ($180,000), William S. Paley ($171,849), Bob Burns ($155,900), Robert L. Ripley ($145,000), and W. R. Hearst ($100,000).

The curtain rose on 1933 to Wagnerian music offstage. On January 30, Adolf Hitler was named Chancellor of Germany—32 days before Franklin Delano Roosevelt was named President of the United States, and 27 days before the famous hoax of the Reichstag fire which Hitler used as a pretext for liquidating his opposition.

While Hitler was busy paving the way for mastery of the world, Roosevelt was busy pumping new life into our end of it. Two days after he took the oath of office, F.D.R. shut the nation's banks, stock and commodity exchanges. Six days after this moratorium he delivered his first fireside chat, to tell the nation what he was going to do.

Show business, along with the rest of the nation, hung onto every word. Something was radically wrong when stagehands were being paid more than actors, and janitors earned more money than the managers of film theatres.

nra theme song   On June 13 the New Deal became law, with the passing of the N.R.A. Act by Congress. Tin Pan Alley immediately celebrated with a song called "Nira"—after National Industrial Recovery Act; and N.R.A. quickly became the three most-frequently used initials in the alphabet of all show business comics.

Under the N.R.A.'s vaudeville code, the legal minimum wage for actors became $7.50 a day—$40 for the full week. Many independent theatre managers wailed that they couldn't afford to pay those salaries. Actors retorted that any theatres which couldn't, shouldn't be allowed to employ actors.

In November big things were rumored to be under way for show business. The Blue Eagle was reported to be hatching a blueprint to save the legitimate theatre. A theatre "recovery" movement was sparked by Gustav Blum, an indie producer, with the enthusiastic endorsement of Frank Gillmore, president of Actors Equity.

Blum's plan was for a Federal-subsidized stock theatre, with everyone connected working for nominal wages, to produce "the best plays" for 25¢ and 50¢. Meanwhile, Eva LeGallienne won the ear of Mrs. Roosevelt for her own scheme—a national theatre patterned after her Civic Repertory, with a 25¢-$1 admission.

The Blum plan won out early in 1944. On January 15, several thousand actors stormed Equity's offices for jobs in the free shows which had begun playing in school auditoriums and institutions under the Civil Works Administration. The Government's first grant was $28,000, budgeted to give 150 unemployed actors work for 32 days, each player getting $25 to $30 a week.

Angry that there weren't enough jobs to go around, 100 vaude actors marched with picket signs to New York's City Hall to demand that Mayor Fiorello H. LaGuardia shake more jobs out of Washington's pockets. Their signs read, WE DON'T WANT A DOLE—WE WANT WORK! and WE ALWAYS GIVE WHEN ASKED FOR ANY BENEFITS, FOR ANY EMERGENCY—WHAT ABOUT GIVING US A NEW DEAL?

Appropriations were increased, and the movement extended month after month, until it was taken over by New York's Public Works Division of the Emergency Relief Administration.

Early in the fall of 1934, the Government appropriated another $300,000 for W.P.A. shows to be sent into the C.C.C. camps—another New Deal innovation. These burgeoned into 20 units—four vaudeville, employing a total of 300, and the rest New York City units. These actors received $24 weekly, plus bed and board.

The W.P.A. also set up stages in the city's parks during the summer, using trucks for transportation and amplifying equipment for acoustics. At one Staten Island park performance, the audience tallied 20,000, which led some neighborhood theatres to complain that this was too much "opposition."

1935 brought a $4,880,000,000 Works Relief Bill in April. New York State revealed that it was helping to keep 2,000 actors alive. Elmer Rice was appointed regional director of a new theatre scheme for New York, which planned to try out new plays in the Bronx, Queens and Brooklyn—omitting Manhattan because of the obvious high rental cost of theatres. The question of the Government running in direct opposition with the commercial theatres soon arose.

Out of the giant fund for relief, the W.P.A. came into existence with an allotment of $27,315,000. Of this sum $10,000,000 was earmarked for the wages of actors, writers, and other unemployed but willing digits of show business.

rise and fall of the ftp   In 1936 Washington appropriated $7,000,000 for W.P.A. shows. Over 9,000 show people worked in the Federal Theatre Project in 20 states, entertaining a national audience of 350,000 nightly. In New York alone, 4,700, or over half the Federal Theatre's personnel, were employed.

The Federal Theatre saw itself maligned in some newspaper headlines and by the same papers' dramatic critics. It was not, certain writers stressed, a boondoggling project, but "one of the greatest stimulants of the American theatre had ever known." It produced great things; introduced millions of Americans who had never seen a stage performance to the legitimate theatre; and gave hundreds of talented actors, writers, composers and directors a chance to show what they had. Orson Welles, for example, was a simonpure W.P.A. product.

A memorable division of the Federal Theatre was the *Living Newspaper* troupe, which introduced a new note to Broadway—documentary plays. Among the themes tackled by the *Living Newspaper* were the power trusts, the problem of erosion, and monopolies. The staging, writing, direction and lighting were sometimes brilliant.

No troupe of the Federal Theatre Project aroused the bitter enmity of the Roosevelt-haters as did the *Living Newspaper,* which was effective propaganda for the New Deal and against the Old Guard. It was the basis for the charge that the Federal Theatre "was shot through with Communism"—because the *Living Newspaper* was pro-New Deal—and wasn't the New Deal communistic?

In 1937 all of show business, including theatre managers and show business executives, helped the agitation for a five-day week for all industry. A five-day week meant two full days of leisure—an obvious boom for the nation's boxoffices.

social security theme song   Social legislation was still pouring out of the Washington mills. To celebrate Social Security and job insurance, songsmiths Hillie Bell and Willard Egloff wrote, "I'm In Love With 234-0-567"—a number which was never assigned to anyone because the song beat Washington to it.

Show biz unionization gathered momentum. SAG (Screen Actors Guild) invaded the East, signing up all New York local studios except March of Time. In Hollywood, the Screen Publicists Guild was born. In Philadelphia, 28 Jewish cantors (not to be confused with rabbis) applied for an AFL charter—and it wasn't a gag.

Negro Actors Guild came into being. The Dramatists Guild won their first deal—a contract involving film rights to the hit legiter, *The Women*. The IATSE (International Alliance of Theatrical Stage Employees), which embraces stagehands and film theatre projectionists, announced plans "to organize the entire amusement industry 100 per cent." This proved a spurious pitch for the racketeering Browne & Bioff regime, of which more anon.

AFRA (American Federation of Radio Artists) also was formed. As late as 1936 there were cases of factory scripting methods on certain radio soap operas, grinding out several scripts a week for $25, while some radio sponsors were accused of paying off their lesser show talent with merchandise. AFRA did not win its decisive victory, however, until 1939.

The American Theatre Council, representing all theatre groups and unions, held its first convention in May of 1937. Speakers stressed the point that the biggest trouble with show business was Hollywood, which had withdrawn financial backing from Broadway shows because of differences with the Dramatists Guild over contract terms.

1938 shifted the emphasis in show business unionization. The fever suddenly infected "the front of the house." There were managers' unions, agents' unions, treasurers' unions, and press agents' unions. The Ringling Bros. Circus was also hit by a strike of laborers, which lasted two days before Ringling-Barnum & Bailey capitulated.

In 1939, Equity flexed its muscles again and proposed raising its minimum pay for actors from $40 to $50. There was an outcry from the membership, who feared they would be pricing themselves out of the market, and the matter had to be shelved until the following season.

in the red, both ways   The Federal Theatre Project collapsed early in the summer of 1939. Angry solons in Washington denied it funds, charging waste and extravagance. The real complaint, whispered in the cloakrooms, was radicalism. The House voted the Project out of existence. The Senate, more faithful to the New Deal, attempted to save it, but the House refused to compromise. President Roosevelt was forced to sign its death warrant on pain of being forced to reject the entire relief appropriations bill. Unwittingly, show business comics had played into the hands of the reactionary House by popularizing W.P.A. gags like "termites ate through his shovel handle," giving the lower body of Congress apparent justification for slashing W.P.A. funds.

41

Sticks Nix Hick Pix

★

Morale in Hollywood sank to an all-time low in 1933 because of salary cuts, dropped options, firings and the Damocles' sword that hung over the entire industry as it waited to see what the New Deal could do to put spending money in the nation's pockets. Actors wrote letters of protest to Washington over the influx of some 12,000 European actors into the United States during the depression. Broadway actors blamed Hollywood producers for encouraging the immigration. William Fox privately explained that his reason for enticing foreign stars was the hope of increasing the foreign b.o. of Fox pix.

Producers felt uneasy about the first British films coming into the country. They were good—too good. Critics had a field day, lambasting Hollywood for turning out "puerile tripe" compared to England's masterpiece, *The Private Life of Henry VIII* (Charles Laughton). *Rome Express,* with Esther Ralston, Conrad Veidt and Frank Vosper, who also did part of the dialoging job on this one, was called by Variety "probably the best British film shown over here to date and will get easy booking in the United States."

Theatre grosses declined all through the spring and summer of 1933, showing little improvement over the practically zero business of the bank holidays. Bankruptcy and receiverships were the order of the day for Paramount-Publix, RKO, and the West Coast division of Fox. Only Warner Bros. and Loew's, Inc. weathered the financial storms.

Financial fireworks on the West Coast, four years after Wall Street laid its famous egg, resulted in a general reorganization for greater efficiency. Bankers still clung to their mortgages, but were shrewd enough to turn over production, distribution and theatre management to the men who knew how. Many theatres were allowed to return to their original owners. The end of the depression found showmen once more in the saddle.

The pix biz rode into the black during 1934. Bankruptcies and receiverships were cleared up, and studios began turning out better films. It was the first year of Volsteadian repeal, and Americans were coming out of their homes again—to the benefit of film theatre boxoffices.

The year was not without its setbacks for Hollywood. The summer crop of films was extremely lightweight, and some of these began to provoke agitation from church circles for extreme film censorship. A drought in the Midwest crippled theatre attendance, resulting in film houses offering giveaways—everything except the managers' children—to lure patronage.

Exhibitors yielded to ASCAP's demands for a new music tax schedule—10¢ a seat for theatres seating up to 800; 15¢ a seat for those with a 1,600 capacity, and 20¢ for larger houses. Exhibitors were also battered by union troubles and the usual tiffs with distributors over block-booking which allegedly forced lemons onto theatre bills.

Hollywood came to their rescue—and headed off the church crusade—by releasing its top films, usually held for the favorable box-office weather of the fall, in the middle of August. This strategy succeeded in all aspects, and helped speed the return of patronage to film theatres.

1935 found the film industry the second most important in California, ranking after oil production. Government census figures showed 39 studios in operation, employing 9,022, and valued at the new all-time high for Hollywood of $97,748,377. At its World War II peak, the pix biz was estimated to be a $2,000,000,000 industry.

The optimism engendered by the New Deal, spreading into all the formerly gloomy cracks on the map of America, found a shining mirror that year in Hollywood. Industry was recovering, employment was up, and both unions and relief spending were putting more money in the pockets of more people. Film receipts climbed.

Even conservative producers began to dig deep for expensive advertising campaigns. Warner Bros., which was courageous enough to believe it could sell Shakespeare to Americans of the 1930s, splurged heavily to promote *Midsummer Night's Dream* with James Cagney. They were wrong, but only because they were premature. Not until 1948, with J. Arthur Rank's Oscar-winning production of *Hamlet,* starring Sir Laurence Olivier, did Americans really flock to see Shakespeare on the screen. "The Bard boff at the b.o.," as Variety put it.

The upbeat of 1935 could be detected by a new surge of theatre building activity; higher prices paid to Broadway for screen rights to legitimate hits; and an increasing number of film companies and stars becoming angels for Broadway plays.

The reason for a new interest in Broadway was the realization by Hollywood that the movie tripe of the 1920s was obsolete in the realistic 1930s. With the New Deal "fireside chats," social legislation and other far-reaching stimuli, the "silo belt" was rapidly becoming too sophisticated to be entertained by corn as green as their summer crops. Variety summed up the situation in its famous headline:

STICKS NIX HICK PIX. So it was to Broadway that Hollywood turned for mature story material.

That Hollywood couldn't get it fast enough—and in large enough quantities—was evident by the rapid growth of the giveaway fever in movie houses. Since most films were too inconsequential to draw heavy trade, managers vied with each other by turning performances into lotteries. In Denver, theatres were even giving automobiles away.

Urged by the film industry, the N.R.A. stepped in and forbade the practice of movie house giveaways. But—as happened when radio interests tried to stop giveaways on 1948's "Stop the Music" program—the public wouldn't permit it. It *liked* giveaways—even with the individual odds heavily stacked against the ticket-buyer. He still had a chance, didn't he? *Somebody* had to win! So managers were forced to continue with extra-legal forms of giveaways, like "bank night." Even Loew's was compelled to join the indies with screeno. Washington and Hollywood sighed and gave up.

43,945 cinemas wired for sound   A roundup of 1936 showed 18,508 theatres in the United States. Of these, 15,989 were wired for sound. Some 13,130 theatres, which the depression had shut down, still had cobwebs on the cashier's glass. The tally also showed that there were 27,956 theatres wired for sound in all of Europe, including Russia.

Business began to boom for Hollywood in 1936, when it helped the New Deal out to the extent of $100,000,000 in taxes—which it could well afford. The good films made were so good that they made the bad ones on the double feature programs look terrible by contrast—and a demand grew up for abolition of double features. Public polls were held but, like Prohibition, when they voted dry and everybody drank, so did the public actually favor two-for-one film programs.

That films were becoming better was attested to by the recognition they won in Washington, where the National Archives announced that 1936 films would be preserved for exhibition to our descendants in the year 2,436. Even that news, however, was not sufficient to impress exhibitors into killing banko and screeno, which continued even when threatened on grounds of violating lottery laws.

Fords and big jackpot cash prizes were among the inducements

offered filmgoers. One exhibitor tried offering films accompanied
by basketball and badminton games on the stage. Others went along
with the policy of Hollywood, and spent their surplus funds in the
orthodox channels of advertising.

During 1936 and 1937 there was so much foreign talent—actors,
directors and writers—streaming into the United States that actors
again pressured Washington for action. Bills were prepared in Congress to protect home talent, but they died in pigeonholes. Across the
Atlantic, English actors began to protest to Parliament that too many
Americans were invading the British Isles and keeping English
talent unemployed.

Theatres began tilting admission prices about a nickel, estimating
that the traffic would bear the increase—and it did. Film-going was
once again getting to be a regular habit of Americans, who came
and came again, despite their squawks against double features, and
the dull similarity of many films. The demand for a constantly better product even inspired a sudden craze for some of the finer old
silents, but distributors were reluctant to release them, fearful of
a drop in their regular meal-tickets.

Hollywood decided to pull the cork out in 1938, and announced
35 films budgeted at $1,000,000, or more, apiece. This was decided
upon, along with a hoopla campaign to plug the slogan, "Movies
Are Your Best Entertainment," at an industry-wide conference. Producers hoped by this concerted action to sweep aside criticism of
their less admirable efforts, and to buck the trend in giveaways. The
Hollywood ballyhooists had a field day with the idea, even playing
it for laughs by billposting a maternity ward with the slogan, "Movies Are Your Best Entertainment." The catchphrase, however, suffered a costly deflationary reflex when some captious critic discovered
that the key letters of the campaign slogan spelled out MAYBE.

Giveaways were too firmly entrenched by 1938. Borrowing from
radio, house managers staged quiz shows and spelling bees for prizes.
Cutrate exchange tickets and "twofers" (two-for-one) weren't
enough. In the Midwest some exhibitors installed "magic eyes"
which snapshotted patrons entering the theatre. The quizzes, spelling
contests and other stunts were palpably designed to circumvent the
lottery (game of chance) angle by putting the accent on "skill."
But with a frankness that hurt, one Fox theatre manager, Roy Hanson by name, heralded on the marquee: WIN $80 AND SEE A LOUSY

SHOW. Some years later, with the boom of double features, another Southern manager, with equal frankness, put up on his marquee, ONE PRETTY GOOD PICTURE AND ONE STINKER.

beginning of gov't suits   Hollywood's biggest headache of the year was the sudden attack by New Deal trust-busters on the close interlocking controls in the movie industry of production, distribution and theatre ownership. The five major studios affected were Paramount, 20th Century-Fox, Loew's, RKO and Warners. All, the Government charged, were guilty of violating the Sherman Anti-Trust Act. It filed suits against the companies, insisting upon a complete divorce between the production and distribution ends, and the theatres. Alarmed, the five companies pooled to fight the suit but the Government won out eventually, although it took them 10 years to do so.

This was the latest and most aggravating of the moves by Washington against Hollywood that had begun in 1933, when the Government had deflated the movie colony's boast to be the fifth largest American industry. It was not, chided Washington, which then revealed that Hollywood ranked somewhere between 20th and 30th.

Hollywood was one of the targets in Washington's heavy tax legislation, levied on top-bracket incomes. In 1938, Hollywood lobbied for a reduction in these taxes, but was ignored. Two years later Hollywood was suddenly hit over the head by Martin Dies, who yelled to the country in black headlines that Communists "dominated" the movie colony. Hollywood's frantic demand for a fair hearing was again ignored. History was to repeat itself a decade later when Congressman J. Parnell Thomas—who himself was found guilty of malfeasance in office—probed Hollywood for Communism and fellow-travelers. The "Unfriendly 10" were eventually found guilty and given fines and jail sentences, including among them notable scripters and directors.

1940 also brought another first-class headache in the shape of New York's Mayor LaGuardia, who had been lighting fires under Hollywood producers to move some of their studios to New York City, in recognition of the enormous income Hollywood derived from Gotham.

"You can tell the film executives for me," the Little Flower exploded in Variety's ear, "that they don't fool me one bit with their

empty gestures of 'we will co-operate,' then giving us the go-by. . . .
If necessary we'll make them recognize our claim. As a matter
of fact, that smug half-dozen or so movie producers already have
stirred up plenty for themselves with the Government because
of their habits. Maybe that will be the medium through which the
City of New York can achieve its just claims. They can't kid me
with their phony sympathies, and as a matter of fact even if we
could blast them out of their self-satisfied strongholds in California,
I'm not so sure that we want them!"

The Little Flower never lived to see Hollywood in New York.
If the studios didn't actually move East, they did come to the
conclusion, in the late 1940s, that it would be a lot less expensive
to shoot films in the actual New York locales. Their look of authen-
ticity, at least, was a plus production value.

During the 1930s, Hollywood's profit was derived—as it was
through most of the 1940s—from the foreign market. Films were
expected to earn their expenses in the United States, then bring
in the gravy from abroad. In 1933 American films were still supreme, despite the fact that Japan led the world in film footage
produced, and Germany was creeping up to the United States as
a competitor.

The tables were suddenly turned in 1934, when Charles Laugh-
ton's *Henry VIII* suddenly made not only the foreign market, but
American as well, aware that England could make remarkably
fine films. Abroad that year, the outstanding foreign boxoffice
records were made by—in the order named—Eddie Cantor, Greta
Garbo, Marlene Dietrich, Norma Shearer, Janet Gaynor, George
Arliss, Paul Muni, Clark Gable, Claudette Colbert and Ronald
Colman.

Two years later the lineup of foreign nation favorites had altered
drastically—with only three of the old 10 holding on. First was
Shirley Temple, followed by Gary Cooper, Clark Gable, the Fred
Astaire-Ginger Rogers team, Charlie Chaplin, Greta Garbo, Marlene Dietrich, Grace Moore, Laurel & Hardy, and Robert Taylor.

One foreign film made the headlines in 1936—*Ecstasy* with Hedy
Lamarr *au naturel*. The outcry against admitting it led to a Supreme
Court decision that, even though the United States Customs Office
admitted a film, any state had the right to ban it if its Board of
Censors saw fit. And most did.

broadway's hollywood invasion   Still in the swaddling clothes of the talkie stage in 1933, Hollywood felt a desperate need for romantic leading men who could both mug and talk expertly. By September of that year it had signed 315 actors from legit. The only new film names of any consequence that year, however, were Mae West and Katharine Hepburn, who scored in *Bill of Divorcement* with John Barrymore. Mae West clicked heavily in her first starring film, *She Done Him Wrong,* which was barred from Australia, where censors considered her "vulgar." It was pointed out that Aussie's headquarters, England, loved Mae West to the extent of smashing boxoffice records to watch her do him wrong.

Kate Smith's first film, *Hello Everybody,* proved so embarrassing to the New York Paramount that the theatre pulled it after six days, a fact which puzzled show business because Kate Smith in person was a powerful drawing card.

In the same year a bit player got her start on the Fox lot when George White, during a film version of his *Scandals,* had a row with the star, Lilian Harvey, who walked out. White promptly summoned a girl who had one song with Rudy Vallee's band, and made her the lead. For her work in the film, Alice Faye won a contract and later stardom.

Top movie personality of 1933, however, was conceded to be Franklin D. Roosevelt in the newsreels . . . termed by a Hollywood wit, "the Barrymore of the White House." Lionel Barrymore, an enemy of the New Deal from the start, did not appreciate the comparison. Of course they meant his "Great Profile" brother, John.

The prevailing trend on the lots that year was the filmusical, in an attempt to jump on the bandwagon of Warner Bros.' *42d Street.* One outstanding short was produced which was constantly repeated by request throughout the era—Walt Disney's *Three Little Pigs,* whose big bad wolf became a symbol for the depression that nobody was afraid of any longer.

1933 was also the year in which Hollywood first took official cognizance of Hitler in a film called *Rafter Romance.* One scene showed actor George Sidney apprehending his son in the act of drawing swastikas on doors and walls. In the words of one entranced Jewish lady who enjoyed the film, "And does he give it to the kid—*mm mm!*"

A survey of 1934 showed that the year had produced a crop of 35 new stars—22 of them in films. Some were European importations, while others were Broadway personalities who scored in their first talkies. Katharine Hepburn won the Academy Award as the year's best actress for her work in *Morning Glory* for RKO. Charles Laughton won the male Oscar for *Henry VIII*, and Frank Lloyd's *Cavalcade*, a film version of the Noel Coward stage success, took best director and film awards for Fox. Incidentally, writing later on *Cavalcade, Goodbye, Mr. Chips, Mrs. Miniver, et al.*, Variety observed, "the best British pix are still the ones made in Hollywood."

1935 was a relatively undistinguished year, offering a cycle of gangster films of which Cagney's *Public Enemy*, based on Dillinger's career, was outstanding. Cagney demonstrated a new "treat-'em-rough" technique, somewhat similar to the caveman style of the old silents' Valentino, by pushing a grapefruit into his screen girl-friend's (Mae Clarke) face. His stock soared 100 per cent as a heart palpitator among femme fans, much as James Mason's did years later with an English brand of sexual sadism. The other notable film event of 1936 was the debut of the March of Time, first documentary-type newsreel.

more new faces   New stars continued to pop up during 1935 and 1936—no less than 27 in films—as studio talent scouts scoured Broadway and college campuses for fresh faces. Among the new stars recruited from vaudeville, radio and night clubs by Darryl Zanuck at 20th Century-Fox were the Ritz Bros., Tony Martin, Don Ameche, Dixie Dunbar and Jack Haley. Musicals were still in top favor because, as Joe Schenck reported, they lent themselves easily to plugging and promotion via radio, which had proved that it could publicize any musical into top boxoffice. The craze for musicals accounted for the presence of no less than 63 of the nation's top tunesmiths on Hollywood payrolls.

The five directors of 1936 who were found turning out the most consistent b.o. successes were W. S. Van Dyke, Clarence Brown, David Butler, William Wyler and Norman Taurog. The Academy recognized *Mutiny On the Bounty* (Laughton again) as the year's best film; and gave its acting laurels to Victor McLaglen for a magnificent performance in *The Informer* and Bette Davis for her fine work with Leslie Howard in *Of Human Bondage*.

With *The Informer,* Hollywood proved to its scoffing critics that it was capable of genuine film artistry as fine as any emanating from a foreign source. So enthusiastic was the response of American intellectuals to the film—despite the unfortunate maudlin ending to the O'Flaherty classic tacked on in an effort to meet Hays code requirements—that it is still being revived as an outstanding film.

Much praise—as well as wonder—was poured out at the scene during which McLaglen, as the Informer, appears before the Irish underground court for judgment. His bewilderment and confusion were considered a classic in screen acting. Inside Hollywood gossip awarded the laurels to director John Ford, who, it claimed, had encouraged McLaglen to imbibe freely at a party, under the illusion that there would be no shooting the following day. Then, the story went, Ford had ordered McLaglen awakened roughly after only one hour of sleep, and thrust suddenly in front of the cameras, which had started grinding.

From the b.o. viewpoint, the best pix in 1936 were Chaplin's *Modern Times, San Francisco* (Gable-Spencer Tracy-Jeanette MacDonald), *Swing Time* (Astaire-Rogers). *The Great Ziegfeld* (William Powell-Myrna Loy-Frank Morgan-Luise Rainer, the latter also an Academy winner with *Good Earth* but destined not to continue Hollywood prominence despite a double-win of the coveted Oscar), *The Littlest Rebel* (Shirley Temple), *Rose Marie* (MacDonald-Nelson Eddy), *A Tale of Two Cities* (Ronald Colman) and *The Story of Louis Pasteur* (Paul Muni).

The New York film critics, taking exception to the usual pattern of Academy awards, formed their own Film Critics Circle, à la the legit Critics Circle, and now annually select their own "best" films and performances of the year.

That year was fertile indeed with solid film entertainment, because in addition to the above it produced *Mutiny On the Bounty* (Laughton-Gable-Tone), *Mr. Deeds Goes To Town* (Gary Cooper), *Dodsworth* (Walter Huston-Ruth Chatterton-Mary Astor-Paul Lukas-David Niven) and *Anthony Adverse* (Fredric March).

Sam Goldwyn made Broadway rejoice by paying the top price of 1936 for a stage hit. Sidney Kingsley's *Dead End*—$165,000. David O. Selznick acquired screen rights to the best-selling novel *Gone With the Wind* for $52,000, and turned down another producer's offer of $150,000 for a re-sale.

As a postscript to 1936, Variety revealed that the Louis-Schmeling fight films were "tops in gross for all time," and that a joint attack by the Hearst and Paul Block papers on Mae West's film, *Klondike Annie,* had resulted in a remarkably satisfying burst of business for La West at the b.o.

Hollywood still strove to freshen audience interest in 1937 with new and—it hoped—beguiling faces. Among the "starlets" it unveiled that year were Rochelle Hudson and Judith Barrett, for whom it predicted big things. Ten years later Louis Sobol got around to asking, "Whatever became of their careers?"

A new and startling trend developed in the production of Westerns. Gene Autry had the crackpot idea that Western fans would like their cowboy stars to warble as they rode—and he did. Instead of walking out, audiences lapped it up—even the small fry trade. Overnight every studio began to test its horse opera aspirants for vocal qualifications. Meantime the studios were splurging more and more with Technicolor. Sam Goldwyn announced he would toss the screen's new paintpot over every new film he made—a pronunciamento more enthusiastic than accurate.

The lush market for musicals continued. Many studios showed a sudden interest in opera divas (such as Grace Moore, Gladys Swarthout, Lily Pons and Marta Eggerth), to the consternation of the Met. The death of Jean Harlow, and its attendant publicity, was cashed in on by reissues of her films. Audiences watched the glamorous Harlow move, speak and exude s.a., with something like mingled fascination and horror.

RKO set a new high for film rights to stage hits by paying $255,000 for *Room Service* as a vehicle for the Marx Bros. The previous record was held by *Broadway,* which collected $20,000 less in 1929. Runner-up was the price for *You Can't Take It With You* —a $200,000 buy by Columbia. Highest paid writer of Hollywood in 1937 was Ben Hecht, whose annual take from Goldwyn was $260,000 a year.

The Radio City Music Hall enjoyed its biggest week, a $123,700 gross, with *The Prisoner of Zenda.* The Roxy's top for 1937 was $78,000, with *One In A Million.* The New York Paramount hit its high at $62,000, with *Double Or Nothing.*

Better "B's" was the war-cry of 1938, as moviegoers protested against the lower ends of double bills. Thomas E. Dewey's gang-busting in New York inspired a wave of gangster films that rode the tide of the headlines, along with racing and fight pictures. There was also a cycle of newspaper reporter films, portraying the Fourth Estate in the usual Hollywood manner. Top musicals enjoyed the usual good business.

Top film of the year was Walt Disney's *Snow White and the Seven Dwarfs*. Mickey Rooney scored as main prop of the new *Andy Hardy* series, MGM's bid for the family trade.

still more escapism   The trend in 1939 was for frothier screen fare, as a deliberate reaction to the grim newspaper headlines of the day. The emphasis on escapism was so strong that many war stories, particularly those anti-Nazi and anti-neutrality, were chopped from shooting schedules.

There were the usual screwball comedies, gangster, prison and G-Man films, seasoned by straight whodunits and family-trade "B's." American history was dusted off and presented in Errol Flynn in *Dodge City,* Cecil B. DeMille's *Union Pacific* and Henry Fonda in the title role of *Young Mr. Lincoln,* all of which were given special premieres in appropriate cites. Producers footed the bill for getting critics there and back by train.

As though the imminence of war had destroyed any illusions Americans of the 1930s may have had, Hollywood began to deglamorize its oomph girls. In *Hollywood Cavalcade* it showed Alice Faye being hit in the face with a pie. In other films, Marlene Dietrich was allowed to mix with barflies, and Clark Gable dragged Joan Crawford through a very muddy bed of mud.

The big deal of 1940, highly touted in the industry's most successful and expensive campaign, was *Gone With the Wind.* Among the other five top-grossing films—*Boom Town, Northwest Mounted Police, Rebecca, The Fighting 69th,* and *Strike Up the Band*— not one was an accurate or vital reflection of the world then in flames. The fact that these six were the top-grossing films lent weight to Hollywood's claim that Americans wanted escapist entertainment, not realism.

The year's six top stars were Gable, Mickey Rooney, Spencer Tracy, Errol Flynn, Bette Davis and Gary Cooper. Abroad, the best-rated stars were Gable and Garbo, followed by Deanna Durbin, Flynn and Cooper.

During the era, Hollywood ran the emotional gamut in its attitude toward radio. Suspicion of radio as a boxoffice competitor was gradually replaced by co-operation and actual participation. In 1933 many exhibs were demanding that producers prohibit stars under contract from appearing on the air between noon and midnight, so as to stifle their microphonic "opposition."

But it wasn't long before Hollywood convinced exhibitors that radio was helping to sell pix, rather than hurt the b.o. Since commercial radio depended heavily on film stars, more and more broadcasts began to originate from the Coast. In 1937 fully 95 per cent of the top radio shows originated in Hollywood. Metro went one step further—the studio went on the air under a $25,000 package deal. Certainly filmusicals, having their scores radio-exploited, were being benefited at the b.o. And with the years there were instances where even a theme- or title-song of a picture could add as much as $1,000,000 onto a film's gross.

A decade later history was to repeat itself with TV. The picture business, at first scared of the medium, realized that trailers over the iconoscopes into television homes were one way to prove to the video viewers that there was better film product available at their theatres than the 10-or-more-year old crop of pix being videocast at them.

42

'Flash! We Interrupt This Program to . . .'

★

A CBS survey in 1933 counted over 60,000,000 listeners, and over 16,000,000 sets in operation, throughout the country. In addition, 300,000 drivers were tuning in on auto sets. Network balance sheets for the following year showed a revenue of $42,900,000, up 37 per cent over 1933. Of this sum $25,000,000 represented talent costs.

The money in radio continued to climb fantastically throughout the era. The gross shot to $86,000,000 in 1935. A 1937 survey showed that the public was shelling out $900,000,000 for radio equipment, spare parts and service. In 1939, radio reported a net profit of fully $19,000,000. And the following year, with 35,000,000 radio sets tuned in, weekly air shows cost $490,000 a week in talent.

At the beginning of the era, radio was still fumbling the ball in entertainment. Most programs were dull, despite an influx of headliners from other branches of show business. The tendency of imitation was so strong that Variety in 1933 introduced a "Protective Material Department" for radio, as it had done years before for vaudeville. Little came of it, however, because, for all practical purposes, Variety always counselled idea creators that the best common-law protection—lacking a copyright on unpublished literary material—was mailing one's self a registered letter, with the idea intact, and not unsealing the envelope until some court issue arose. It's preferred that it be mailed across a state line, and of course the Post Office mark is the barometer for priority. In the heyday of vaudeville, the Vaudeville Managers Protective Assn. working closely with the N.V.A. and Variety's Protective Material Dept., was better able to police any infringements. Then, too, there were always the friendly stagehands in every key city who could psychologically "control" a copy act when the plagiarism was flagrant. In later years, however, with the speed-up of communications, such as radio, plus the Broadway columnists' habit of "crediting" this or that comedian with "the newest gag," in short order that "newest gag" was quickly "adopted" by callous, hinterland comics as their own.

Amos 'n' Andy were still the top stars of the year, radio having developed no new personalities. They did smash b.o. everywhere on their 1933 personal appearance tour, and animated cartoons using their voices mopped up.

Ed Wynn, rising to the top of radio as Texaco's "Fire Chief," decided to give the two major webs some competition in 1933. Throwing in almost $250,000, he organized a new broadcasting network—the Amalgamated Broadcasting System—with 6 stations and 27 sponsors in his pocket. Lack of advertising revenue killed it in a few months.

The big event of the year was the debut of the Kraft Hour with

Al Jolson, Paul Whiteman and Deems Taylor. "Good as any show's Broadway premiere," Variety reported. Jolson had signed at $5,000 a week for 40 weeks; Whiteman, $4,500 a week.

The audience—"strictly Woolworth people"—was separated from the performers by a thick glass curtain, with audience mikes picking up their cued applause as desired. Jolson's big hit of the opening night show was the theme song of the depression, "Brother, Can You Spare A Dime?"

Other big hit shows of the year were Rudy Vallee on the Fleischmann Yeast variety show, and Jack Pearl as Baron Munchausen on Lucky Strike. Pearl's rise in radio was meteoric—going from $3,500 to $8,500 a week in the short space of five months.

Major Bowes, managing director of the Capitol Theatre in New York, introduced amateur nights to radio in 1934. Some branches of show business, nostalgic for the lost proving grounds of vaudeville, were enthusiastic about the trend. It offered possibilities for discovery of new talent. Show biz gamblers figured the odds against an amateur clicking on Broadway at 200,000 to 3.

By 1935, Bowes was the heaviest earner in show business, grossing $1,000,000 a year for his radio show, amateur units, film shorts, and management of the Capitol. His amateur units toured the nation, supposedly arousing new interest in vaudeville among hinterland theatregoers. As many as 20 Bowes units were traveling at one time, until they dwindled to only five in number by 1937. Vaudeville was too dead for even Major Bowes to bring it back to life.

Among the curious attractions of 1933 was the broadcast of radio's first millionaire "canary"—Harold F. McCormick, of the International Harvester Co.—who came to the mike to unveil an unsuspected talent as a whistler. Negro circles applauded a Chicago station for hiring 15-year-old James Mitchell, radio's *only* Negro actor of that date. The cheers were short-lived; a companion stabbed Master James, who was carted off to the Cook County Hospital for repairs.

those catch-phrases   By 1934 it was axiomatic in radio that if you wanted to stamp your personality unforgettably into the consciousness of listeners, you had to develop a trademark—just like soap or coffee—and hammer it over the airwaves mercilessly. It was the rare star or show of that year which didn't have its aural mark of identification.

For Amos 'n' Andy it was their famous theme song, "The Perfect Song," and Andy's catchline, "I'se regusted." Joe Penner popularized, "Wanna buy a duck?" and "You nasty man, doncha ever *doo-ooo* that!" Wendell Hall's hallmark was "It Ain't Gonna Rain No Mo'." Then there were the "moon" theme songsters: Ruth Etting's "Shine On, Harvest Moon"; Morton Downey's "Carolina Moon"; and Kate Smith's "When the Moon Comes Over the Mountain."

Ben Bernie greeted his fans with "Yowza" and signed off with "Pleasant Dreams." Crosby came on with "boo-boo-boo," Rudy Vallee with "heigh-ho, everybody" and Ed Wynn with "so-o-o-o." Norman Brokenshire caught ears with "How *DO* you do, everybody, how *DO* you do." Tony Wons made "are you listenin'?" famous. Phil Baker's trademark was the yell of his stooges, Beetle and Bottle—"Get off the air!" Gracie Allen's tagline for George Burns was, "Oh, George! I bet you say that to all the girls!"

Paul Whiteman made Gershwin's "Rhapsody In Blue" his own. Jack Pearl's famed "Vos you dere, Sharlie?" was varied with mentions of his "Cousin Hoogo." Jimmy Durante became famous to radio fans with "colloseal!" and "I got a million of 'em!" Jack Benny's "Jello again" was as standard a Sunday night greeting as Winchell's "flash!" and "Good evening Mr. and Mrs. America." Jolson always had his "mammy" and "you ain't heard nothin' yet!" Almost all of these catchlines found their way into the conversational slang of the day. However, in time, they wore out their welcome for reasons of corn or monotony and only an occasional upcoming sportscaster like Mel Allen ("how do you like *that*?"), or Clem McCarthy's hoarsely exciting "They're off!", or Winchell's trademarked excitement and staccato style of news flashes, have survived.

Entertainment highlight of 1934 was the dramatic re-emergence of Broadway's one-time great star, Maude Adams (the original *Peter Pan*), who spent 44 hours rehearsing for a broadcast of Sir James M. Barrie's *The Little Minister* for Pond's Cold Cream. NBC presented a rebroadcast from BBC—a program called, "What the Fairies Know," which NBC lost no time in changing to "Fantasy for Midsummer Eve." Joe Penner was the outstanding comic to climb up that year, taking only six months to go from $950 to $8,000 a week.

By 1935 it was generally accepted that radio's policy of over-lapping all other branches of show business was permanent. Stars from films, opera, the concert, vaudeville and the legitimate theatre all gravitated toward the airwaves—most for the publicity of guest appearances; many to stay, with programs of their own. Only one star of Hollywood could not be tempted, even with an offer of $25,000 for one show—Greta Garbo. Eddie Cantor's radio appeal shot up so remarkably that he won the first unique bonus contract in radio history. Bristol-Meyers agreed to pay him a $200 bonus for every point over 20 he scored on the Crossley tabulation of radio listeners.

a bad commercial   And the first belch to be released over a national network, to amused and shocked listeners, was broadcast in 1935 by Melvin H. Purvis, ex-head of the G-Men, when he put in a guest appearance for Fleischmann's Yeast. The association of Purvis' ad-lib performance with the product understandably made the J. Walter Thompson executives highly sensitive.

The Chicago Cubs became the first baseball club to buy radio time, when they took an hour in 1936 to re-enact the games played on the days of the broadcasts.

Although radio was still developing no new stars of its own during 1937, it did take two mildly well-known personalities from outside and build them into headliners. The two were Edgar Bergen, whose showcasing on the Vallee show jumped him from $300 a week in 1935 to $10,000 a week in 1937, at the Los Angeles Paramount; and Red Skelton, whom the Vallee program boomed from $400 a week to a $2,000-a-week contract from RKO. The "Vallee Varieties" also cradled Bob Burns, the bazooka man.

The distinctive contribution of 1937 radio to American mores was the emergence of a new phenomenon—the disk jockey. The term was coined by Variety to describe announcers who held down dull midnight-to-dawn time by spinning (or "riding") records (or "disks"). Listeners, mostly women, sent in requests for their favorite numbers.

The stunt spread rapidly, and a sizable Lonely Hearts bureau was soon in operation. The ladies' requests were played—along

with their names and addresses. The songs they chose were a cue
to interested male listeners, many of whom picked up phone books—
"I'm Lonely," "Melancholy Baby," "I Ain't Got Nobody," "Lover,
Come Back To Me," and "All Alone Blues." In some localities it
was a cue for vice cops too.

Another development that year was the appearance of experimental Mr. & Mrs. "breakfast" shows in radio time slots that were
once tossed to religious services and calisthenics. These proved an
effective medium for plugging sponsors' products more heavily
than any show dared to do during the evening hours. From then
on America's habit of breakfasting in private became a lost cause.
Prior to this, the predawn platter-chatterers and later the calisthenics
cheer-up boys (usually under insurance company auspices) filled
the A.M. kilocycle void. Ed and Pegeen Fitzgerald are trade-credited
for creating the Mr. & Mrs. pattern.

In the cautious but constant search for novelties in program
material, radio tried freak celebrities in 1937, of the kind which
once rejoiced the heart of the great Willie Hammerstein. Brought
to the microphone were the white wife of the Rajah of Borneo;
the wife of the vanished Judge Crater (on Ripley's "Believe It
Or Not"); and the lone survivor of a Greek ship that sank (on
"Radio Newsreel.") Station KGFF in Oklahoma topped them all
by broadcasting a World War I shell victim, whose head ticked like
a clock.

l'affaire mae west   Mae West gave radio officials heart-
burn toward the close of 1937 when she appeared on the Chase
& Sanborn program. She delivered a Biblical story—West style
—of the fall from grace of Adam and Eve. Clergymen all over
the country shrieked protests. Newspaper editorials were headlined, "Mae West Pollutes Homes." Other newspapers rushed to
her defense, and the general defense of radio. The controversy
bubbled for months, hastening NBC's closing of a deal with Toscanini to win back some of its tarnished prestige.

While it helped her pix b.o., understandably there were no sponsors risking further Maewestian versions of "Adam and Eve"
or anything else. [*Sime* once observed in a review of Miss West
that "she has a way of making clean lyrics sound dirty."]

Gracie Fields arrived in America that year and promptly was

offered $5,000 for a guester on the Jack Benny show, which she turned down. That same weekend, at Palm Springs, she sang at a barbecue for an hour—for free. Eventually, of course, Miss Fields did plenty of United States commercial radio.

In 1938, Bob Hope's radio star shone brightly, along with Edgar Bergen and Charlie McCarthy. The Rudy Vallee show, showcase of so much new talent, started to slip, however, because of its familiar pattern. Other radio faves of the year were the usual old faces— Amos 'n' Andy, Benny, Cantor, Whiteman, Burns & Allen, Easy Aces, Fred Allen, Penner, Crosby, Spitalny, Bernie, Lombardo and Jolson. A surprisingly large quota of these was still going strong at the half-century mark.

Following NBC's Toscanini scoop—at $4,000 a performance—the year's second cultural triumph was the radio debut of Paderewski.

A new twist in quiz shows made its debut—"Information, Please!"—which pleased its sponsor as a low-cost, high-prestige, and influential package. The success of the Fadiman-Kieran-Levant-Adams quizzer caused a rash of quiz shows, ultimately leading to the type of programs inaugurated by "Stop the Music" 10 years later. The original idea, of course, was nothing more exciting than the old-fashioned spelling bee; or a step further, classroom examinations.

awesome orson   Along with Clifton Fadiman, only two other names emerged in 1938 radio to cause Variety to pause and note. One was Frank Morgan, who became the first radio actor ever to take his pants off for a laugh before a studio audience. The other was the *enfant terrible* of show business—Orson Welles —who introduced some of his Mercury Theatre ingenuity into the airwaves. Welles finished by scaring the United States out of its wits when he staged the unforgettable radio "Invasion from Mars."

Ex-Mayor of New York Jimmy Walker suddenly showed up as a radio entertainer in 1939, broadcasting off the cuff each Sunday for 12 weeks over WMCA. The Modern Industrial Bank paid for the time. With his other hand, Walker wrote his second song in 25 years, collaborating with Jimmy Hanley on a tolerance number called "In Our Little Part Of Town." Walker sang it with George Jessel at Madison Square Garden's "Night of Stars" benefit. To make this conversion to show business complete, Jimmy Walker became prez of the National Assn. of Performing Artists, a group sparked by Fred Waring. The bandleader's then manager got Walker in as "front" man in a move to collect from jukeboxes and radio disk jockeys every time a certain artist's waxing is performed for profit. The courts ruled that since this constitutes a supplementary property right, the organization is without redress under the existing Copyright Act of 1909. (It's an open secret that this now obsolete statute, in view of the advances of the electronic forms of show business, will have to be considerably revised in time.)

After a hitch as the impartial arbiter of the ladies' garment industry, acting as umpire in management-labor relations, Walker resigned that $20,000-a-year post to become president of the ill-fated Majestic Records, Inc. He had a stock interest in the disk subsid of the Chicago parent firm, Majestic Radio & Television Corp., and as he often told us at Toots Shor's, later to become his favorite New York eatery, "At least this deal (the Majestic stock) should give some protection to my children." (This never came to pass, of course, with the bankruptcy sale of Majestic Records assets.)

the hucksters   In 1940, with America tense and poised on the brink of war, radio took the lid off slightly. The election brought forth a flock of Republican jokes—"Are you a Republican?" "No, I'm just naturally thin"—and cracks with international overtones. Sex was also allowed to rear its head, at least up to the eyebrows, with gags like, "When that girl jockey was racing, one of her shoulder straps broke, and the horse finished wearing a camasole."

There was little doubt in anyone's mind—at least, those behind the scenes—as to who controlled radio in 1933. That year, food products, cosmetics, drugs and tobacco provided 70 per cent of the networks' revenue.

One NBC announcer that year received a remembrance gift from his grateful sponsor—a 60¢ jar of cold cream. This generous gesture was rivaled by a network efficiency expert, who placed half-dollars under studio radiators to test (1) whether the janitor was thorough and (2) honest.

The men who made ulcers famous later in Frederic Wakeman's *The Hucksters* were getting set for their milk diets in 1933. Sponsors switched their accounts from one ad agency to another with a fairly monotonous regularity. The old school tie equation and nepotism (such as a favorite nephew just out of college) usually figured in these ad agency maneuvers. It was considered a good batting average to hang on to a sponsor as long as 18 months.

Sponsors were protesting that year against unfair competition by "one-lung" stations which would spin platters offering stars like Ben Bernie, while Bernie in the flesh would be holding down the next wavelength on a fancy paycheck from Blue Ribbon Malt.

The late Jack Kapp, founder-president of Decca Records, however, had a visionary theory about this. He even encouraged broadcastings of Bing Crosby records, arguing that that was another step in making the singer "the best known voice in America," which he set out to do and achieved. Many years later, talents like Crosby, Guy Lombardo, Arthur Godfrey, Leopold Stokowski, Tommy Dorsey, Deems Taylor, Walt Disney, Igor Cassini (Cholly Knickerbocker), Vallee were to become glorified disk jockeys with their own shows, plugging not only their own pop and longhair platters, but those of contemporary artists, while merchandising this or that product.

The leading ad agency of 1934 was Blackett-Sample-Hummert, Inc., which bought $4,104,000 worth of air shows that year for Bayer's Aspirin, Ovaltine, College Inn Food Products, and others. Tailing B-S-H was J. Walter Thompson, with radio accounts like Chase & Sanborn, Fleischmann, Cutex, Carter's Ink, Eastman Kodak and Kraft-Phenix. In the third slot was Lord & Thomas, which boasted the Lucky Strike program. Nine other agencies each spent over $1,000,000 in 1934 radio.

The Government was prodded into action during 1935 by the below-the-belt promises, menacing and offensive huckstering that cluttered the airways. It indicated too careful an interest in radio advertising copy for both sponsor and network comfort. As a result, while NBC stood pat, if apprehensive, CBS dropped the other shoe. It booted out medical accounts and medical copy, publicized a long list of must-nots for advertisers, and pledged to cleanse the air of the medicine show aura. Listeners cheered, and CBS prestige zoomed.

A sponsor craze—more for reasons of prestige than entertainment —put big names on a radio pedestal. General Mills was the leader in the drive to dazzle dialers by packing shows with celebrity appearances. The move led to the origination of more and more shows from the Coast, where the names were more easily gathered around the mike. By 1937, radio won social recognition at Hollywood, with sweatshirts absolutely taboo at radio show premieres. Admen moved to the Coast with their shows, found the social routine and sunshine quite heady, and did everything they could to anchor radio in Hollywood.

United Fruit was the first commercial shortwave sponsor in 1939, picking up the check for a musical show with Spanish dialog beamed to South America over NBC. That year radio won another unique sponsor, also in the fruit division, with the Oregon apple growers, whose usual English market was cut off by war. Faced with apple-dumping to hold up prices, the Oregonians drummed up a war chest, sank it into radio, and kept doctors away from coast to coast.

Radio cracked a particularly satisfying nut in 1940 with the addition of department stores as sponsors. For years the stores had put all their eggs into the one basket of newspapers, refusing to entertain any notion that radio could do a better or cheaper selling job for them. In 1940, suddenly, department stores opened the door to radio, and newspaper executives from coast to coast snarled in unison.

press-radio feud The battle between radio and the press was waged hotly on every front throughout the decade. In 1933, newspapers curtailed radio publicity to an absolute minimum, in some instances banning any mention of radio whatever. CBS poured fuel on the fire by organizing its own newsgathering bureau along newspaper lines. NBC followed suit.

Hotheads on both sides of the fence were brought together for a conference. A compromise was reached whereby both networks agreed to disband their own news services, in return for which the wire services agreed to feed the nets with news. Meanwhile, newspapers were secretly jubilant over the return of many radio advertisers to the printed medium, on the theory that they were dealing with many less tangible factors in newspaper ads.

The following year, radio ran into more opposition when stations in Denver and Omaha put microphones in police courts and broadcast proceedings. The New York Bar Association voiced a protest, stating it considered the move prejudicial to justice. The organization moved into action when New York's WMCA broadcast a three-week hearing of the Morro Castle disaster. The Bar Association succeeded in getting WMCA banned for the balance of the hearings. Insiders stated the real reason the ban had been allowed was that the broadcasts had resulted in heavy criticism of the Government's steamship inspection methods, and also of the Ward Line for incompetence. In 1951, television's spotlight on crime (the Kefauver investigation) and kindred telecasts of other Congressional committee probes cued the new order of things under this medium.

The clash between press and radio that year was highlighted by the law suit filed by two radio writers of the New York *Daily News* against Eddie Cantor. Cantor had declared, during an interview, that in his opinion radio editors were dishonest. The suit was later dropped for lack of grounds, because Cantor hadn't mentioned any names.

Variety inspired its own uproar by coming out in 1934 with its "Showmanship Ratings." Everyone in radio who placed lower than No. 1 squawked, and for a while in radio circles Variety was less friend than "another network."

The press-radio feud broke out afresh in 1936, when Gabriel Heatter's 35-minute ad-lib broadcast of the Hauptmann execution far overshadowed anything the papers were able to come up with. To heighten color to the event, the newscaster's marathon gabbing was made necessary by the fact that something went awry with the electricity that circuited into the Lindbergh baby killer's death chair, and it was quite a feat of emergency radio showmanship and savvy. The broadcast lifted Heatter to the top, which didn't endear either him or radio the more to the press.

As the decade drew to a close, newscasts became radio's most important achievement. They were so highly regarded for attention value that one cigar manufacturer of 1937 offered extra pay for one-minute spot commercials between newscasts of flood rescues. To the credit of radio that year, he didn't get it.

The press, realizing that it couldn't stop the competition of radio, moved by indirection in 1937. By the end of the year newspaper interests owned 25 per cent of the radio industry.

Radio's contribution was recognized by the Government in 1938 with the setting up of a United States radio studio at the Department of Interior. It was the occasion of America's first attempt at official broadcasting, designed especially to strengthen ties between North and South America. Eventually shortwave radio propaganda to our World War II allies and enemies, via the BBC (British Broadcasting Corporation), the AFN (Armed Forces Network), and the "Voice of America" programs, were to become important in the world struggle against totalitarianism.

The press, which had been licking its wounds and biding its time, jumped on radio hard when the occasion presented itself in 1938. That occasion was the Orson Welles "War Of the Worlds" broadcast. The background of the broadcast, of course, was the war abroad —and the war-jittery nerves of Americans. It was an hour show, and many who tuned in after the opening announcement were under the illusion that they were actually listening to on-the-spot news reports—cleverly handled, even to ad-lib asides, awkward pauses and offstage noises—of an invasion from Mars.

The show undoubtedly alarmed or baffled millions of listeners who heard it. And many did rush into the streets, or into the attic for rifles. But the newspapers joyfully pounced on the story and made it seem as though every American in the land had gone crazy. By exaggerating to the hilt, the press was able to bring down severe reproach on the heads of CBS executives—and all of radio—including crippling restrictions as to the use of news-type techniques in dramatic programs. No single broadcast in radio's history received more press publicity and general notoriety than this one. It, of course, catapulted Welles to stardom—and Hollywood.

Most newspapers that year took another punch at radio by cutting down space devoted to radio to a minimum. But the war eventually swept radio to such a pinnacle of American interest that the pin-prick was hardly felt. As Variety summed it up in 1939, "Radio has capacities possessed by no other channel of communication. Its place in the lives of everyone becomes more intimate."

Radio not only had to slug it out with the press, but with opposition from many other sources as well. In 1933 the networks were waging internecine warfare over the question of spot broadcasting by individual stations of the nets. The Federal Radio Commission —now the Federal Communications Commission—was gunning after radio scalps for unethical advertising. And all of radio was fighting the music unions.

In 1934 the Tugwell bill hit out at radio advertising, and Mayor

LaGuardia contemplated junking New York's municipal-owned WNYC. In 1935 there was national revulsion and Government action against offensive air advertising. In 1936 name orchestra leaders tried to stop the broadcasting of platters, on grounds that this cut into their disk royalties; and the F.R.C. handed down adverse decisions against a number of stations for code violations.

Lawsuits against radio comics, who ad-libbed unfortunately, and their sponsors, were more of the headaches that dogged radio. In 1939 the Preferred Accident Insurance Co. helped out by offering to insure both against the consequences of these nuisance suits.

radio vs. ascap—again   In 1940 radio was once more battling vigorously with ASCAP over music fees; RCA-NBC television was in hot water with the F.R.C.; the two major nets were busy fighting off a Government investigation of monopoly charges inspired by the Mutual Broadcasting System; the Federal Radio Commission was pressing the case for F.M.—a new system of Frequency Modulation broadcasting, as distinguished from AM (Amplitude Modulation).

Radio was in trouble up in Canada during 1934, when an actor named Art Joseph aired his criticism of the Governor-General, the Earl of Bessbrough, for an alleged slight to Mary Pickford. Joseph and radio both were scored off for their temerity. There was no official censorship in Cuba that year, either, but soldiers stood on guard in all radio stations as a hint to anybody with ideas about criticizing the regime.

In 1936 the first Jerusalem radio station began transmitting, inaugurating with the words, "This is Jerusalem calling," and broadcasting in English, Arabic and Hebrew. Free radios were distributed in small towns to make the broadcasts effective. This inspired Milton Berle's crack, "Star of stage, screen, and Tel Aviv."

And that year, in France, radio won a signal distinction when Cardinal Verdier designated a patron saint for radio—Saint Genisius.

The first television note of the New Deal was made by the Don Lee Television Station on the West Coast, which televised a Paramount film, Pathe News and a trailer. In 1935, A.T. & T. asked for an experimental license for "voice and picture transmission," and was scored off by the F.R.C. for attempting to monopolize the new coaxial cable field.

The German Olympics of 1936 were televised, but with blurred and general unsatisfactory results. Television boomed that year in London, however, when films were telecast in the summer. At the end of the year, tele was demonstrated on an 8 feet high, 6 foot 6 screen (1949 American home tele screens were still only 10 by 8 *inches*) at the Dominion Theatre, London. Inventor John Baird, from a studio in the building, talked to newspapermen seated in the theatre audience.

Philadelphia had a Philco tele demonstration in 1937, which Variety chalked down as bad. When the New York World's Fair was televised that summer by NBC-RCA, Variety complained, "It was an exposé, rather than a demonstration—pics flickered much too much." The Federal Radio Commission thumbs-downed television schools beginning to spring up, promising to train recruits for "highly-paid" tele jobs.

RCA-NBC produced the first televised drama in May 1938—"The Mummy Case," starring Tom Terriss. Terriss had been on the King Tut expedition. For several months that year RCA-NBC ran regular five-hour weekly tele shows, beamed from studios in the Empire State Building, booming a sale of television sets at eight New York department stores. RCA-NBC finally decided to call it quits—the venture had been experimental—until later in the year. Set owners in New York were stranded with nothing to look at but the mahogany on the expensive sets they had bought from the eight stores.

The same year, the British Broadcasting Corp. in London televised a full-length play directly from the St. Martin's Theatre—J. B. Priestley's *When We Are Married*. It was the longest single-stretch video show of that date, running two hours and 25 minutes. Set-owners reported the mechanical end had been perfect, but the eye-strain for so long a period had been too great.

some video firsts   Variety began to review television shows on June 14, 1939. It also carefuly compiled a list of television firsts, in its capacity as historian of show business. The first President to be televised was F.D.R. The first governor, Herbert H. Lehman of New York. The first mayor, LaGuardia. The first name band, Fred Waring. The first jugglers, the Three Swifts. The first film cartoon, "Donald's Cousin Gus." The first take from a Broadway show, "Mexicana." The first fencer, Nadi. The first midgets, Paul Remos

& His Toy Boys. The first magician, Robert Reinhart. The first tap dancer, Ann Miller. The first harpist, Margaret Brill. The first Negro team, Buck & Bubbles. The first ventriloquist, Bob Neelor. The first comic drunks, Frank (Fritz) and Jean Huber. The first skaters and skiers, the Sun Valley Show. The first hillbilly act, Judy Canova. The first composer, Richard Rodgers. And the first King and Queen, George and Elizabeth.

The outbreak of war in Europe set television back sharply. In 1939, England called all bets off. In New York City, there were no scheduled broadcasts, and less than 500 purchasers of television sets, at $600 apiece, plus a $50 installation charge. The main progress made during the year by television was in publicity, with the magazines painting rosy pictures of things to come—things that no longer sounded like Buck Rogers copy.

Set-owners were jubilant at the televising of the Max Baer-Lou Nova fight at the Yankee Stadium on June 7, 1939. There had been an earlier attempt to televise a sporting event—the Columbia-Princeton baseball game at Baker's Field in New York in May—but the fixed camera and blurred image were heavily disappointing. The only tele transmitter licensed in Chicago in 1939 was the Zenith station, W9XZU, which operated daily. But if Zenith was ready, television was not, and their sets had to be loaned out instead of sold to viewers.

Singers from the Metropolitan were telecast from Radio City in 1940, but the results were not inspiring. The big news of the year was a private preview by CBS, for trade and press, of something new —color television, invented by Dr. Peter Goldmark. It was kept carefully under wraps, for fear of upsetting black-and-white television. Rumor had it that there was inner warfare in tele circles between color enthusiasts, and the black-and-white men who opposed it because it would mean scrapping millions of dollars worth of expensive equipment as junk. RCA opened experimental TV in 1928, and for the next 20 years poured $50,000,000 into television. At the opening of the N. Y. World's Fair in April 1939, David Sarnoff made the first commercial telecast with, "Now, at last, we add sight to sound."

43

Legit Bounces Back—Ditto Longhair

★

For the first time in theatrical history, 1933 saw every Broadway legitimate show in the cut-rates. Post-rumblings of the great crash of 1929 were still being heard. The New Amsterdam Theatre, once the fortress of Klaw & Erlanger and Flo Ziegfeld, was surrendered to the Dry Dock Savings Bank. Three years later the Gaiety and Fulton passed to the banks also, and the last of the Erlanger houses vanished from Broadway.

The bank holidays of 1933 crippled Broadway. Theatre managers implored actors to accept salary cuts. Equity reluctantly okayed the cuts, then changed its mind when stagehands and musicians refused to go along. The stagehands finally agreed to reduce the number of men backstage at each show—rotating the work among union members—but would not allow a slash of union scale.

Many theatregoers offered checks at the boxoffice, during the bank holidays, and these were accepted. Incidentally, very few bounced. Some managers did the noble thing and maintained salaries and full staff, operating at a loss, until the banks once more opened.

For the Shuberts, 1933 was a remarkably fine year. They bought back out of receivership all their properties, worth some $16,000,000, for $400,000. Playing their cards closer to the chest, they gradually eased out of the producing field, concentrating on being theatre-owners, and only occasionally investing in shows.

Many stage actors were entraining back to Broadway from Hollywood, in 1933, as it became apparent that Broadway was slated for a boom via Hollywood money. Film producers were bidding for Broadway hits, and trying to buy a winning ticket by backing dark horses for win, place or show. In 1934, Hollywood dished out $800,-000 to Broadway for screen rights to hits. By 1936, the ante had risen to $1,000,000, and Hollywood was the acknowledged backer of at least one out of every four Broadway openings.

In 1929 there had been over 200 stock companies in the United States. Then, when *The Jazz Singer* introduced talkies to the road, the stocks fell by the wayside. By 1939 there were only five Equity stock groups left in the United States. Film theatre chains which shuttered some of their theatres kept these shut, rather than rent them to stock outfits. Hollywood believed in boosting legit on Broadway—for their own purposes—but not on the road, where legitimate shows represented competition to films. In 1940, Hollywood paid Broadway $1,200,000 for screen rights, two-thirds of that going for plays produced during the 1940 season alone.

Something new in legit was introduced in 1934 with the debut of the Center Theatre, a Rockefeller Center-RKO-RCA project. The vast showplace opened with *The Great Waltz,* which played to capacity throughout a year which boasted only 13 clean-cut hits. The explanation was a mammoth publicity campaign which had as its links radio (via NBC), film trailers (via RKO), and outdoor billboards at Standard Oil gas stations. Despite the average weekly take of $43,000, the production never got all its money back.

As Thousands Cheer, a top-grade Irving Berlin-Moss Hart musical, with Marilyn Miller, Helen Broderick and Clifton Webb, before he turned baby-sitter for Hollywood, finished a 49-week run in 1934 with a total gross of $1,200,000, at $4.40 top. George S. Kaufman-Moss Hart's play "Merrily We Roll Along" (with Jessie Royce Landis and Walter Abel) was also current. The road, ostensibly dead, came through nobly for Katharine Cornell who played 75 towns in 29 weeks, doing *The Barretts of Wimpole Street* and *Candida* for a total gross of $650,000. Lillian Hellman, a $35-a-week script reader for Metro, scored on Broadway with her first play, *The Children's Hour*—and promptly demanded $1,000 a week from Metro to go back on the lot.

Faces were bright on the Broadway of 1935. The number of chorines working in legitimate were counted as 390—the highest since the crash. With the general recovery of the nation, New York recovered; and when New York recovered, legitimate producers rejoiced. The year provided the comedy, *Sailor, Beware,* which so shocked a visiting lawyer from Minneapolis that he sued the management for $4 and expenses. And from Boston came word that the critic of the Boston *American,* George Holland, had hit upon a novel idea to keep himself from being barred from theatres whose plays he rapped. He had himself appointed Deputy Fire Commissioner, and as such could not be denied admittance to any theatre.

The boom of W.P.A. shows in 1936, Broadway estimated, had kept hundreds of actors off the street. Managers didn't fear the competition of the W.P.A. shows, because their content and prices appealed to a different type of clientele than the legitimate's regular trade. But they were worried about the possibility of a permanent Federal Theatre, which might raise new problems.

Back in 1932, when *The Green Pastures* had played in Washington, special Sunday performances were given for Negroes—who were not allowed, in the capital of the United States, to attend the regular performances to watch a cast of their own race perform. The Washington atmosphere, under the New Deal, was vastly different. For the first time in 100 years, racial barriers were dropped for the 1936 Washington run of *Porgy and Bess* at the National, and Negroes were accorded their Constitutional rights as both theatregoers and citizens. The National, in the next decade, again became the stormy center of the race question, the management again refusing to admit unsegregated audiences stating it was compelled to comply with local customs regardless of its own personal feelings on such an issue. Eventually the capital, where the Constitution's principles are administered and interpreted, was to be without a legit house because of Equity's edict not to permit its members to participate in a policy which was so discriminatory. Some strange things have happened at D.C. boxoffices, among them the necessity of colored Americans to simulate foreign accents or demand *deux billets, s'il vous plait,* and thus gain admission in white houses which, adhering to the principle of diplomatic courtesies to foreign nationals of maduro tincture, felt it was OK for them, but not OK for native colored Americans.

With the boxoffice in a flowering condition in 1936, productions became more lavish and spectacular. Three Broadway shows alone used a total of 169 stagehands. These were *The Eternal Road, White Horse Inn* and *The Show Is On*—incidentally all costly flops.

the bard—and george m. cohan   Shakespeare came into his own with a 1936 duel of Hamlets. The rival Melancholy

Danes were Leslie Howard and John Gielgud, and the two Hamlets over Broadway were regarded as an histrionic joust between Broadway and Hollywood. Broadway won. Gielgud stayed, and Howard suffered the slings and arrows of the road.

As though there weren't enough Hamlet to go around, Eva Le Gallienne did it again the following year, in stock at Dennis, Massachusetts. On Broadway, Maurice Evans scored with *King Richard II,* grossing $21,000 a week. *Anthony and Cleopatra* (Tallulah Bankhead-Conway Tearle) was less successful Shakespeare, losing $100-000 for its backers. But the Bard was boffola b.o. with Orson Welles' surprise version of *Julius Caesar* in modern dress at the new Mercury Theatre, where Welles was attempting also to give Broadway a lesson in lighting effects.

George M. Cohan, after knocking them dead as an actor in the 1933 presentation of *Ah, Wilderness,* turned up again in 1937 with songs and dances in *I'd Rather Be Right.* Highlight of the Gershwin musical was Cohan's impersonation of F.D.R., which the President enjoyed heartily. *Ah, Wilderness* was Cohan's first thesping under a management not his own, and so was *Right* which also set a precedent for the Theatre Guild in billing a star above the production.

Pulitzer prizewinner of the year was Moss Hart and George S. Kaufman's *You Can't Take It With You* (Josephine Hull and Henry Travers), which scored a long run with 103 weeks, although the Critics' Circle award went to Maxwell Anderson's *High Tor* (Burgess Meredith). Incidentally, Anderson's personal choice for the season's "best" play was *Johnny Johnson,* by Paul Green and Kurt Weill, which ran a meagre nine weeks with Russell Collins and Morris Carnovsky in the cast. The distinction of the critics' scallions as "the worst play of a decade" went to something called *Bet Your Life* which ran briefly at the John Golden Theatre. There was also a revival of *Abie's Irish Rose,* for those who cared.

Thornton Wilder's *Our Town,* with Frank Craven and Martha Scott, took the Pulitzer for 1938, although the New York critics again dissented by giving John Steinbeck's *Of Mice and Men* (with Broderick Crawford and Wallace Ford) the nod. It was about to folderoo when the award gave it an unexpected lease of life.

Another 1938 theatre note was provided by the newly-founded Mercury Theatre, Orson Welles' repertory established in the old and almost-forgotten Comedy Theatre on West 39th St. Welles' staging, direction and lighting, as well as his new conception of old classics, won him applause as an "uplifting" force in the theatre. Welles followed *Julius Caesar* with Dekker's Restoration classic, *Shoemaker's Holiday,* also a click.

Looking forward to the highly-touted New York World's Fair of the coming year, Broadway got out its brooms in 1938. Cooling systems were installed in almost all theatres that didn't have them, to catch the overflow summer crowds from Flushing Meadows. The opening of the Fair was a crippling event for the legit during the first month. But by June Broadway's expectations were being realized, and the Main Stem enjoyed a wonderful and unusual summer boom.

Olsen & Johnson's *Hellzapoppin,* with a strong hypo from Winchell, shook the 1939 World's Fair visitors for $31,000 a week. *The Philadelphia Story* (Katharine Hepburn), *Streets of Paris* (Carmen Miranda, Bobby Clark, Abbott & Costello), and *No Time For Comedy* (Katharine Cornell) were also socko b.o.

The most costly production of the year was Max Gordon's patriotic spectacle *The American Way* by Kaufman and Hart at the Center Theatre in Radio City which, despite the cast presence of Fredric March and his wife, Florence Eldridge, was too heavily budgeted to pay out. It just about broke even when Hollywood bought the screen rights, but never filmed it because, by then, the subject matter had become cliche. If legit patrons wouldn't buy propaganda, certainly film fans wouldn't.

Howard Lindsay and Russel Crouse's *Life With Father* settled down at the Empire Theatre to a run that was to make theatrical history, and the bellicose *Man Who Came to Dinner,* Kaufman & Hart's opus, launched Monty Woolley to stardom and a new Hollywood career. The critics were unable to agree on the best show of the season, so no Critics Circle award was made.

garment workers over broadway Big surprise of the year, however, was furnished by the International Ladies Garment Workers Union. This union, which had thrived and grown under the kindly aegis of the New Deal, decided to introduce a realistic note into the theatre by staging a labor union musical.

The show was *Pins and Needles,* presented at the Princess Theatre, off Broadway, which promptly became the "Labor Stage." The show began as a weekend affair, then went daily when critics threw their hats up in the air. It clicked so solidly that the very people it mocked and ridiculed—the carriage trade—came in droves.

In 1940 the critics were able to make up their minds—and were slightly embarrassed to find themselves in agreement, for the first time, with the Pulitzer Prize Committee. The unanimous choice was the unpredictable William Saroyan's *Time Of Your Life,* with Eddie Dowling, Julie Haydon, Gene Kelly, Celeste Holm and William Bendix. Saroyan promptly threw the Pulitzer Committee into confusion by rejecting the prize, becoming the first to do so since Sinclair Lewis handed back his Pulitzer award for the novel *Arrowsmith.*

The road was reportedly prosperous in 1940, as a result of the steady increase of the national income through the union-active years of the New Deal. That year Variety found that it was offering 735 playing weeks, and accounted for an annual legitimate gross of $9,000,000. The era came to a close with the return to Broadway, after an 18-year absence, of John Barrymore. When the great Barrymore had played last in New York, it was as Hamlet at the Harris Theatre, which had since become a movie grind house. Barrymore's return vehicle was *My Dear Children,* a light comedy which sat heavily on critics' stomachs. To some of the old-timers on the aisle, it was painful to see one of the world's formerly great artists destroy memories with a performance that all but caricatured himself. The play staggered along on the Barrymore reputation, and round-the-town gossip that Barrymore's ad-libbing could be expected to provide unexpected entertainment.

longhairs' upbeat too   The New Deal, with its tremendous changes in the national fabric, also stirred new life into the opera and concert field.

The first sign of this New Deal in longhair was the emergence during 1934 of, not one, but three native American operas—a record for show business. The first was the world premiere of Howard Hanson's *Merry Mount* at the Metropolitan. The second was Gertrude Stein's baffling but intriguing *Four Saints In Three Acts.* The third was *Helen Retires* by John Erskine and George Antheil. Of the three, the Stein opus received wide national attention, and opera was suddenly amazed to find itself in the popular limelight.

Opera stars could be seen rubbing elbows in Lindy's with radio comics. Stokowski was an enthusiastic audience for Benny Goodman's swing sextet. "Minnie the Moocher," sung in tights, was presented on a concert stage. Baritones sang traditional Wagner at the Met and 24 hours later were swinging pops with a radio or disk fave on a coast-to-coast hookup.

New York's Town Hall pulled a Hammerstein and offered an armless pianist. The Philharmonic Symphony chamber group suddenly went berserk and played "hotcha" music at one session. Salmaggi offered Wagner at the Hippodrome for 99¢, complete with an advance apology. Radio tenors went into concert. If not highbrow, America's musical tastes certainly were getting more middlebrow.

a male striptease   The Met's standout hit of 1936 was Col. Wassily De Basil's Ballet Russe de Monte Carlo which overfilled its 3,500 seats and played to standees, grossing the Met $8,500. Star piece of the ballet was "L'Apres Midi d'Un Faun," presented for the first time in the United States in 20 years. "A male striptease done in six minutes," according to Variety.

The big news in the longhair field of 1938 was Yehudi Menuhin, who at the age of 21 was the year's top concert draw. With 38 playdates, Menuhin played to a gross of $500,000, of which half was his personal share.

Variety noted in 1940 that "the opera and the concert are doing quite nicely in the United States, without national, municipal or other official subsidy." During the year, over 20 opera companies toured the nation. There were between 500 and 600 performances given in some 100 large cities, at prices ranging from 25¢ to $7 a seat. The total annual gross was estimated at $5,000,000, with the Met alone grossing almost half that amount in New York and on tour.

This accounted for Variety's headline that year: NAME SINGERS FIND GRAVY TRAIL IN HINTERLAND—STIX, NOT OPERA, PAYS INCOME TAX.

Lawrence Tibbett was the best-paid among concert singers, at $2,500 per performance, although Grace Moore got between $2,500 and $3,000 in some spots. Richard Crooks, John Charles Thomas and Kirsten Flagstad all averaged around $2,000 a night. Gladys

Swarthout commanded between $1,500 and $2,000, while Nino Martini slumped to about $1,500.

Among violinists, top billing was shared by Jascha Heifetz and Fritz Kreisler, each receiving about $2,000 to $3,000 a performance. Yehudi Menuhin, who used to average that in his prime, slipped to about $1,750 a performance in his hoary dotage of 23. Serge Rachmaninoff and Vladimir Horowitz led the pianists, with the pianist-composer drawing $3,000 and Horowitz slightly less. Josef Hofmann held down third place with an average fee of $1,750.

Tickets were also quickly sold out whenever Benny Goodman decided to appear as a concert clarinetist, and Alec Templeton as an exponent of classic and jazz.

1940 also found the face of opera vastly changed. The change was wrought by the gradual disintegration of its old audiences, the box-holders, whose coffers had been cut into by the New Deal; and who regarded with contempt the singers offered by the opera to replace the golden voices of the Carusos, Gadskis, Galli-Curcis, Pattis and De Reszkes. The greats no longer were being supplied by Europe, where opera patrons had largely been decimated by two wars, and sponsors of new operatic personalities were now few and far between.

With the passing of the old guard, the Met decided on a fresh approach. Its herald was Edward Johnson, Canadian-born tenor, ex-musicomedy chirper who had to Romanize his name into Eduardo Giovanni in order to impress the Met with his singing prowess. New York would now have an opera house, Johnson declared, which would get support from the general public. He tied up with a radio network for a kilocycle subsidy, to which many of the die-hards mumbled deprecations, hollered "communism," and cursed That Man In the White House. Years later Billy Rose was to catechize the Met and Johnson for the outmoded methods, and eventually Rudolf Bing was brought in as impressario with even more advanced production methods and "modern" ideas.

44

Vaude: *Corpus Delicti*

★

In the deepest year of the economic drought, the odds were heavily against vaudeville surviving even in tatters. Films and radio were the cheap popular entertainment of 1933. These media had hardened the theatregoers to the corn which was too often the stock in trade of vaudeville. Some circuit theatres still offered vaude acts, but only—as usual—to bolster bad films, or because competition made a plus value necessary. Most stage shows were dropped to cut expenses.

Vaude's booking time fell to a new low in 1933. From 179 weeks at the start of 1932, it slipped to 46 weeks of scattered playdates. To play them all, an act would have had to make a grand tour of the United States and Canada, with the vast bulk of its time spent in traveling. Loew's offered 15 weeks of playing-time; RKO 13, Fancho & Marco 10, Paramount 5, and Warners 2. As the exception that proves the rule, the Winter Garden was offering Sunday night vaudeville concerts at $2.50 top, and doing well.

Most of vaude of 1933 was cast in the shape of unit shows, featuring scenery and costumes above the bands and talent. Many were tabloid versions of old legit musicals and revues, with props out of the warehouse. Some played theatres on percentages and guarantees ranging from $5,000 to $8,000 a week.

The year's outstanding vaude presentation was Mary Garden, who appeared for the first time at popular prices at the Capitol in New York. She shared top billing with the Mills Bros. Grace Moore, scheduled to play the Capitol later, was vastly disturbed at this "humiliation" to ofay artists. She insisted upon a "no-colored-act" clause being written into her contract. The Loew management called the deal off rather than agree.

Miss Moore's attitude had its counterpart in the early 1900s when Walter C. Kelly, the Philadelphia-born "Virginia Judge," refused to play a Hammerstein's vaude bill with Williams & Walker. It caused much excitement at the time, and resulted in a big gross for Kelly, and ditto on the week when the great colored comedy team played there. It was subsequently suspected that the showmanly Willie Hammerstein engineered this one too.

The trade in 1934 indulged in lachrymose recriminations about the demise of vaude—"Did it fall, or was it pushed?"

Hollywood took most of the blame, but the profilm fans pointed to the fact that vaudeville thrived—and still does—in Great Britain, and the English are just as ardent pix patrons as the Yanks.

In 1934 vaudeville's principal excuse for being was as a peg on which stars from other fields could hang their hats for brief personal appearances. Earl Carroll's Casino Theatre, on Broadway, made a vain attempt to hypo vaude by presenting *Casino Varieties,* at a 75¢-$1.50 scale, with George Jessel and Walter O'Keefe as twin M.C.'s. It died in three weeks. The United States Patriotic Society— which hadn't been told vaude was dead—backed "Flashes," a hodge-podge at the 42d Street Lyric. This, too, was quickly draped with crêpe.

columnists' 'benefits'   The only innovation of the year was the appearance on vaude stages of Broadway columnists. The bookings were awarded on the basis of a curious kind of boxoffice draw—the ability to entice top talent on stage as "guest stars" at no cost to the management. Influential, syndicated columnists naturally have a way with talent which depends on year-round publicity.

Although the rest of show business made a comeback in 1935, vaude stayed put or slipped further. Variety noted that the hands which had once been outstretched to it, out of sentiment, were now conspicuously absent. "The dollar sign still speaks louder to theatre operators," it pointed out. Films came in convenient cans, while vaudeville meant booking problems, stagehand and musician worries.

All that was left of vaude was 24 weeks in the hinterland. In New York there was only Loew's State and Capitol, RKO's Tilyou Music Hall stage shows. The Palace was playing straight films— (Coney Island) and the 14th St. Jefferson; besides the Roxy and double features. Most of the vaude acts playing the one- and two-night stands of the road made the jumps by car. In unit shows, $75 was tops for comedians, $20 to $27 for chorus girls.

Vaude had fallen on such evil days that when an English booking agent came to New York to look over American acts, there was no place for acts to "show" for him. William Morris arranged for a special showing of 20 acts at the Biltmore, a Broadway legit theatre.

Headliners were scarce. The few theatres that still played vaude turned to radio mostly for their talent. Major Bowes took his amateur units onstage, and Jack Benny was another radio figure whose name went on marquees. Small towns which couldn't afford Bowes units staged their own amateur nights—giving their theatres a "stage show" at practically no cost. And with no Willie Hammerstein to give him a stage, Jafsie Condon, the celebrated Lindbergh case witness, accepted a booking at the Capitol, Lynn, Massachusetts, where he also appeared for an hour in the store window of the Kane Furniture Co. to demonstrate—aptly—ladder models, nails and chisels.

Vaudeville, sinking fast with amateurs and units as its last props, found that its props were termite-ridden. The am shows began to pall, turning more and more audiences against stage entertainment. And the unit shows became tawdry, with nudity entering the ranks of vaudeville for the first time.

Unit show producers with short bankrolls and shorter ideas went in for burlesque types of production. It was vaude on a shoestring—and dressed about the same—with units playing for about $150 a day. The bubble dances, fan dances, veil dances and flame dances all had one motive—epidermis display. With this descent into strip-tease, vaude lost its last vestige of respect, its last distinction as "family entertainment."

The lone bright spot of 1936 vaudeville was the success of the New York Paramount with a new pit band and stage show policy. Otherwise the downbeat trend continued to be emphasized. Even the stubborn Chicago Palace threw in its chips and joined its New York namesake in a straight pix policy. The Cleveland Palace deserted vaudeville for five weeks, but business fell off so badly that the management was forced to return to it. Eventually New York's Jefferson and Tilyou Theatres closed, leaving no RKO vaudeville in Gotham for the first time in history.

Vaudeville, no longer in the theatres, went underground, and emerged chiefly in the more hospitable fields of hotel and nitery entertainment. Variety recognized this fact by merging the vaudeville and night club departments.

Eddie Cantor, proving once again that top talent did not have to worry about prevailing conditions, chose 1936 to set a new vaudeville record by getting $25,000 for a six-day week at the RKO Boston, with only a payroll of six in his act. This topped the record of Ed Wynn and Al Jolson at the New York Capitol.

But despite this, vaude was so dead that Edith Maxwell, the Virginia farm girl who was twice convicted for killing her father, couldn't win an engagement while out on bail, though every vaudeville booker in New York was approached. Vaudeville was dead, and Willie Hammerstein was dead. Appropriately, Variety reported that Baltimore burial ground salesmen were booking acts for "the cemetery time."

In the hands of the burly operators, vaude took another lacing during 1937. Vaude-burly was nothing more than burlesque with its face washed. And, as Variety caustically noted, dirty burly was bad enough, but dull, albeit clean burly was worse.

Many units were thrown together in an attempt to imitate the success of the Broadway Paramount and its bandshow policy. These tabloid musical shows, some costing between $3,500 and $5,000 weekly to mount, failed to find enough playing time to pay off costumes and transportation. The few theatres offering stage shows couldn't even win headliners from Hollywood for a few brief weeks, because the stars were eschewing personals to hold down their income taxes.

And while vaudeville cried in its beer, from overseas came the report that a headliner who had once flopped with a two-week engagement at the Palace in 1930—Gracie Fields—had grossed $760,000 that year. If vaudeville was dead, England hadn't heard about it.

Vaude didn't sink much further in 1938—because it couldn't. For the first time in several years, there wasn't a single tab show—boiled-down version of an old Broadway musical—available. Nor was there one night club troupe, such as the French Casino flash revue, which had played the major circuits a few years back. The heavy losses of unit producers had frightened off new tries. And theatres were refusing to play unit shows on anything but a straight percentage basis, with no guarantee of any minimum.

B. A. Rolfe and Jack Horn tried to give vaude a boost via a shoestring device called "Vaude-Vision." This dispensed with sets, scenery and live music, projecting the scenery via film with a musical soundtrack, to which acts synchronized their turns. It was introduced at the RKO Hamilton, but was stopped in its tracks by a firm thumbs-down from musicians, stagehands and film operators' unions.

Boston was entirely without a single stage show until the end of the year. In Cleveland, RKO tried a few feeble weeks of vaudfilm at the start of the season, quickly reverted to straight films, and swung back again to vaudfilm in November, after four solid weeks of film flops. Minneapolis, Pittsburgh, Detroit and Indianapolis continued to offer stage shows in support of films—because most films needed support.

jitterbug craze   The jitterbug craze in 1938 helped vaude by making bands big headliners for the year. Although the average band commanded $7,500 a week, it was a cheap stage buy for many theatres offering stags shows, which otherwise would have had to pay between $3,500 and $7,500 for a name act, plus the cost and trouble of booking four or five other acts. In most cases, the bands provided the entire stage show.

On Broadway, the Paramount was making its name band policy pay heavy dividends. The Strand, setting its band on the apron instead of in the pit, as the Paramount did, likewise found a gold-mine in "hep" audiences. The Roxy and Loew's State also went in heavily for the bandstand policy.

A form of vaudeville received another chance—and a big one—when Billy Rose opened his lavish theatre-cabaret, the Casa Mañana. Actually it was nitery entertainment. For a while it flourished, arousing speculation over a possible vaude revival via the Rose technique. Henny Youngman cracked that he could remember "all the way back" when a vaudeville career meant 40 weeks of work a year instead of a Sunday night at Billy Rose's Casa. But when 1939 rolled around, there wasn't even that Sunday night.

1939 dipped United States vaudeville to a total of 11½ weeks playing time. A wave of bad films gave vaude a temporary lifeline, with nine New York theatres adding acts two or three days a week for a brief period. RKO put one-a-day vaude bills in some of its neighborhood theatres. The Brandts tried to revive straight vaude at the New York Audubon and Carlton, Jamaica, L. I., quickly giving it up.

The downbeat of vaudeville was best summed up by a Variety reviewer's summation, "In place of variety entertainment is the bandshow. In place of humor as the backbone of a stage layout is the percussion acrobatics of a drummer, or a trumpeter's hot licks. . . . What little soul vaudeville had left has passed out." Musicians had become comics, hoofers and chirpers.

Some succor for talent came with the hot weather on the Borscht Circuit, as the Catskill Mountain and Poconos (Pennsylvania) resorts got to be known. The "Sour Cream Belt" was spending $75,-000 to $100,000 a year for talent. The resort inns had grown up; it was no longer a case of "we had to dance with the customers," as in the pioneer life-of-the-party era in the Borscht Belt. Actors, in short, were doing a lot better at the 20 to 25 class and middle-grade hostelries in the Catskills than in all the other theatres east of the Alleghenies.

Even the splendid surroundings of Radio City's Music Hall couldn't sell straight vaudeville in 1933. The Music Hall tried it for two weeks, but was quickly forced to feature films plus stage show. The old Roxy won a court decision which made Radio City take Roxy's name down from its marquee. Roxy himself stepped down from his $50,000-a-year job as managing director of Radio City Music Hall the following year, after a dispute with the Rockefellers over high costs. To beat the $78,000 a week overhead, Roxy wanted to hold films over for runs of longer than a week. Rockefellers refused . . . but later came to see it Roxy's way, after Roxy had left.

To rival Radio City's Center Theatre, which had turned to legit in a big way with *The Great Waltz* in 1934, the Hippodrome introduced another spectacle in 1935. It was *Jumbo* and cost Billy Rose's backers—John Hay (Jock) Whitney and friends—some $300,000. Even with Jimmy Durante, Paul Whiteman, a Rodgers & Hart score and elephants it flopped. It grossed $18,000 opening night but nose-dived thereafter, causing a Broadway crack, "You just can't mix silk and fertilizer." The Hipp, a white elephant, was still trying to find a place in show biz when, in 1938, it converted into a fronton for jai-alai. In the Hipp tradition that soon flopped too.

The Center's career was checkered, mostly in red ink. A musical, *Virginia,* spelled a $250,000 loss, in 1938. This was preceded by one of the most costly failures in show biz history—the pageant, *The Eternal Road,* at the Manhattan Opera House in 1937, which wound up over $500,000 in the red. And the year before that saw an American version of *White Horse Inn,* with a strong cast including William Gaxton, Kitty Carlisle, Carol Stone, Robert Halliday, Buster West and Billy House, go for a quick $160,000 loss. Size and spectacle were not boxoffice insurance quite obviously. *The Eternal Road,* a religioso theme, was not expected to turn a profit, having been heavily underwritten as a morality play.

The Center Theatre eventually was to become a fairly paying proposition in the heyday of the Sonja Henie-Arthur M. Wirtz ice shows, but eventually succumbed to television and became an NBC-TV house.

45

Blue Blood Blues Singers and Cuffo Society

★

The quickest pickup of New Deal show business was in the night life branch, particularly for the large places. The hotels, emerging from receivership, began to compete with the niteries for an increasingly lusty Broadway trade, using name bands and acts as bait. The average tariff was $2.50 to $3 for a table d'hote dinner, which rose to $4 on Saturdays.

The big clubs were going in for mass business. They offered seminude shows, sans cover charge, at a $1.50 to $3 minimum check, which included dinner. Their shows cost as much as $9,000 a week, but their average 1,000-seat capacity meant weekly gross receipts of $20,000 and upwards.

The old speakeasies with small capacities were forced to hike prices to stay in business—and had little to offer for the increase in tariff. The mobster element of the speaks largely disappeared, to be replaced by suave front men who represented the change of the speak from a fleeting racket to an established and courteous business.

Billy Rose, with a generous bankroll from "the boys," set the pace for the new style in night club entertainment with the Casino de Paree, formerly the Gallo, and later the New Yorker Theatre on West 54th St. The entertainment was along music hall lines, patrons afterward mounting the stage to dance to the music of two bands in stage boxes. The raised dance floor-cum-stage gave exhibitionistic patrons a vicarious feeling of being spotlighted. The Manhattan Casino, formerly Hammerstein's Theatre, followed suit, and Ben Marden renovated the Palais Royal along the same lines. Clifford C. Fischer's French Casino, on the site of Earl Carroll's Theatre, was the most successful operation of this type later.

Repeal gave the hotels their opportunity to swing from the conservative patronage of their residents to the more lucrative trade of the transients. In 1934 they offered "cocktail hours" as a means of dramatizing themselves as centers of social life. The end of Prohibition definitely proved the salvation of the Waldorf-Astoria, where the management had formerly shut off several floors at a time to trim overhead. By 1934, the Waldorf was 85 per cent rented, and bolstered its income with revenue from its various bars, cocktail lounges and other social rooms.

The various hotel "rooms" quickly became an integral part of upper-class night life. Women liked the respectable and pleasant atmosphere; men had more confidence in the food and drinks. The hotels were quick to respond by adding suitably appealing talent and name bands, as well as by decorating their social rooms in what was considered the latest and smartest manner, à la Joseph Urban. Some even went so far as to install cabaret floor shows and ice revues to the horror of a few more fossilized guests—but OK b.o. for the bonifaces.

The Rockefellers, who had already made show business sit up and take notice with Radio City Music Hall and the Center Theatre, also stole the night club show in 1934 by opening the Rainbow Room on the 65th floor of the RCA Building. "A night club in the clouds," Variety called it, "in a natural setting of beauty and magic which not even the Rockefeller financing could conjure up were it not for the gratis aid of Nature."

Among the remarkable features of the new club, as Variety noted them, were glass walls; the first super-organ ever installed in a nitery; a revolving dance floor; every seat a ringside seat; and imported talent. "The nut for the Rainbow Room really doesn't matter, as the Rockefellers couldn't break even if they turned 'em away every night. Which places the oil tycoons in the category of show biz philanthropists rather than show biz investors."

The cover charge was $1.50 and $2 on Saturdays. Reservations had to be made in advance, and formal dress was a must at first, but later relaxed. For those who just wanted to see the view and relax on top of Radio City, a 40¢ cocktail paid the way in the afternoon via the more informal Patio cocktail lounge. During the day both the Rainbow Room and Rainbow Grill merged into a membership luncheon club, still operating, for the convenience of Rockefeller Center tenants.

Business was generally lush for most of the night spots in 1934. Popular prices, no cover charge, and an elaborate floor show were the magnets—drawing mass patronage which had never been possible in the days of the Club Lido's $5 couvert and Texas Guinan's $20-$25 "champagne." Now customers were attracted by the advertised $1.50 dinners; came to find that $2 bought a better dinner, and a $2.50 minimum check assured ringside tables. The longer the floor show, the longer they sat, the more they ordered and drank. Drinks at 75¢ a throw gave most clubs a very neat margin of profit.

Billy Rose's Music Hall offered $1 dinners, and employed 100 hostesses and 100 singing waiters. Rose, who was only the front man for the Hall and Casino de Paree, was soon ousted by the shoulder-holster boys who controlled them when he had the temerity to ask for a bigger share of pie.

Among the reformed speakeasies which made the grade by dressing for dinner were El Morocco; Leon & Eddie's, which took in between $11,000 and $12,000 a week in 1934; "21"; Joe Zelli's; and Hector's Club New Yorker. The Stork Club debuted at its present 53d St. site. Several have become Gotham institutions.

On Broadway, Morton Downey and Dan Healey were pulling them into the Palais Royal. Rudy Vallee was the attraction at the Hollywood Restaurant. The Paradise was baited with Sally Rand and an N.T.G. revue. The Broadway segment did well, but kept an anxious eye on the east-of-Fifth Avenue clubs and hotels which were shaping up as sharp competition.

the debs go hildegarde   1934 was the year which saw the first influx of society debutantes into show business via the night clubs. The first to start the vogue was Eve Symington, daughter of Senator Wadsworth, who earned $1,000 a week for warbling at the Place Pigalle on 52d St. off Broadway. Her salary went to charity at first, then it became a career. Lois Ellman, daughter of a wealthy realtor, sang for the Club New Yorker. The Embassy Club had blueblooded Adelaide Moffatt, who later took to the air via CBS.

The trend was inspired by the Social Register aura given night clubs with the bow of the fashionable Rainbow Room. Cafe managers encouraged it, considering a Blue Book background more valuable than top professional talent in drawing the trade from which the socialite songbirds stemmed. And it was good newspaper publicity.

Sally Rand, who had started at the Chicago Fair in a sideshow called "Streets of Paris" for $125 a week, was drawing a $6,000 weekly paycheck from the Paradise in 1934. To discourage competition, she copyrighted her bubble dance. And did the dance behind a specially-constructed screen, to keep her modesty intact by preventing any playful contact of patron's cigarets with her big balloon.

With the revival of east- and west-side night life in New York, the vogue of Harlem went into decline. The Ubangi Club, formerly Connie's Inn, made its principal bid to a specialized trade of jazz addicts. The Cotton Club, which called itself in ads "The Aristocrat of Harlem," dropped its aristocratic $2.50 cover charge and ballyhooed the absence of same. The following year, however, Harlem was exerting its old lure of the 1920s again, although Connie's Inn decided to move downtown into the stand of the old Palais Royal.

1936 and 1937 were such boom years for Harlem hotspots like the Cotton Club, the Kit Kat, the Harlem Uproar House, Ubangi, Small's Paradise, Plantation, Black Cat, Dicky Wells and others, that there was a shortage of sepian talent for the Negro theatres, which had to hire ofay actors to round out their bills.

america's montmartre   The French accent came into vogue in 1935. Variety observed, "New York today is more Frenchy than the Paris boulevards." There were about 25 niteries of all types, prices and ranges congested within one block on West 52d, between 5th and 6th avenues, reminiscent of the bistros, bars and boites of Paris' hilltop, Montmartre. Patrons were demanding vintage wines. Even Schrafft's served Scotch with whipped cream, while the Paramount Theatre Bldg. Childs' restaurant installed an emcee and swing band.

The fan dancers of 52d St. were a little more restrained, if not any more clad, than the Montmartre brand. One near New York gambling casino-roadhouse, à la the Riviera version and as part of the French lure, had the double-zero removed from roulette wheels for two hours each day to give players a better chance. Broadway's French Casino (Clifford C. Fischer's elaborate theatre-restaurant) was in the chips, grossing $50,000 weekly.

The hotels, with one eye on the Rainbow Room, wanted to achieve the same stratosphere by insisting upon formal dress but they found business slipping. A compromise of a split policy—formal dress only if on the ringside—also flivved.

The 25th cafe opened on 52d St. in 1936, when the sector became known as "Swing Street." Variety reported that the top night club city in the nation was not New York, as most supposed, but San Francisco, which had the largest number—1,252.

The revival of night life, and the glittering social tone lent by the evening wrap trade, brought about a resurgence in popularity of the dance team—always a pet with society. In 1936 the top teams were Tony & Renee De Marco, Veloz & Yolanda, Ramon & Renita, Rosita & Fontana, Dario & Diane, Lydia & Jeresco, Fowler & Tamara, Minor & Root, Gomez & Winona, Stone & Collins and David & Hilda Murray.

Nobody was quite sure why, but in 1937 night clubs were badly dented. Most fingers were pointed at the new International Casino, a vast and spacious nitery which opened at popular prices and catered to mass patronage. There was no denying that the International sent the Hollywood into bankruptcy by practically kidnapping all of the latter's trade. The International was strategically situated in the heart of Times Square, directly opposite the Hotel Astor, on the site now occupied by the new Criterion Theatre and the giant Bond clothing store. The Hollywood, further up Broadway, at 48th Street, was a cleanup with its mass-capacity, super-floorshow to a "no cover" policy that started at a theoretical $3 minimum tariff.

Meantime the French Casino, which enjoyed a brief revival, went into the discard and was picked up by Billy Rose who relabeled it the Casa Mañana.

Some of the class spots, wondering what had hit them that year, decided to revert to a Prohibition technique—make it tough for the customers to get in. One or two found that it worked, as customers damned the owners, headwaiters and captains . . . and *demanded* admission. The Stork and "21" still employ that technique for unknown or "undesirable" patronage.

To prop sagging business, some niteries began to throw in free dishes, much as the movies were doing. They also offered bingo, lucky number contests and rhumba contests. Even the Rainbow Room, along with El Morocco and the Versailles, smeared honey on the boxoffice via "champagne dance contests." The Stork Club tied up with 20th Century-Fox in a film-talent contest.

Leon & Eddie's tried five acts, with a $1 table d'hote lunch. The Paradise threw in Rudy Vallee. But the trend was downward, and a number of 52d St. clubs folded. The summer slump made some clubs desperate. These ordered their girls to mix with the customers. A few even descended to straight honkytonk tactics, and some had arrangements for a 25 to 50 per cent split with female "steerers." The cops came.

As the b.o. dropped, so did the clothes of some nitery performers. Strippers didn't mind the ogling, but many strongly resented the sudden candid camera fad. The issue was solved when the New York License Commissioner stepped in with a stern ban on all nitery stripping.

An old escapist theme, the hula vogue, entered night life in 1937, resulting in the Lexington Hotel's Hawaiian Room, and Leon & Eddie's $15,000 Pago Pago Room, with windstorm and rain effects. There was also a new dance craze—"The Big Apple"—which made its debut in the Rainbow Room. Originated by Gullah Negroes around Charleston, South Carolina, who danced it barefoot, it was described by Variety as "requiring a lot of floating power and fannying."

The year saw America once again dance-crazy . . . or in Variety's terminology, "hoof nutty." The trend was more toward audience-participation. Besides swing and the jitterbug vogue, the Lambeth

Walk craze started. There were also the Little Pear and Little Peach.

In 1937 ice-skaters and saucy songsters both suddenly found themselves in demand by night clubs. Dwight Fiske, whose risqué entertainment had been barred from London, found delighted fans at the Savoy-Plaza, in New York. Sheila Barrett was another 1937 favorite, while Hildegarde—still to make her giant success of the 1940s—sailed for Europe. With the irony of which only show business was capable, Charles King—only a few years before a top-priced film star—was discovered to be one of a trio singing at tables in the Victoria Hotel, New York. He also did a stint at Bill's Gay Nineties spot, that New York haven for old-time troupers.

Society was still in the spotlight in 1937 with "Junior League Follies" and similar amateur theatricals.

The Savoy-Plaza introduced what it thought was a smart new note by inviting audience-participation, via a mike, which recorded the conversation for an immediate playback. Russell Swan, the magician, asked the guests to recite some toasts. Some debs promptly gave out with strictly stag toasts. Swan hastily found some excuse for not playing the record back.

The drought on Broadway continued in 1938. Among the clubs that "parlayed themselves into 77B," or went bankrupt, were the Paradise, Hollywood, International and La Conga, which had enjoyed a brief boom on the wave of the still then new Latin American cycle.

Variety noted a letdown in tone of some clubs on the "Park Avenue circuit." The St. Regis' Maisonette Russe booked a Negro band; and the Waldorf let its august walls shake to Benny Goodman, installing a milk bar for the jitterbug trade.

But the debs were still in there pitching. Cobina Wright, Jr. went into the Waldorf's Sert Room. Sally Clark, a Roosevelt in-law, tried out at the New York Plaza, then decided to get married, with popular approval. Eleanor French and Lois Ellman were doing vocals with bands. A socialite amateur contest won a regular job at Le Coq Rouge for Annee Francine. And Adelaide Moffatt shocked her sister debs by announcing, at Harry Richman's Road to Mandalay, that she was making show business her career.

Billy Rose opened his Diamond Horseshoe in the basement of the Paramount Hotel. Jack Dempsey opened his new Broadway Bar, flashing films of his early ring triumphs for the customers to ogle, eventually foregoing the Dempsey's Restaurant on 8th Ave. and 50th Street, directly opposite Madison Square Garden, which he never quite put over. Another nitery venture in that socially conscious era was Cabaret TAC (for Theatre Arts Committee)—the first American night club which appealed to the politically-minded trade. European capitals like Paris and Berlin, particularly the German capital, in the 1930s spawned the political nitery where the conferencier spoofed the mores of nations.

cuffo society Variety spilled the beans that year on the why-and-wherefore of the heavy socialite attendance at niteries. It pointed out that most of this was strictly on the cuff, with the management taking a beating in order to staff his club with the proper "tone," to win society and gossip columnist mentions and photos, and to lure the subway trade which liked to go where it was "smart to be seen." When the chips were down, it was plain Joe Doakes who paid for the bluebloods' entertainment— including their choice seat locations and special catering.

The type of night club represented by the International Casino, and Midnight Frolic (the erstwhile Paradise) went heavily into decline in 1939. The International, $250,000 in the red, went on the auction block. But business boomed for the hotel rooms, and most clubs switched from lavish to nostalgic entertainment. The leaders in this field were Bill Hardy's Gay Nineties, Billy Rose's Diamond Horseshoe, the Sawdust Trail, the Brown Derby, and Joe Howard's Gold Room in the Hotel Ambassador.

The bar of the Sherry-Netherland went in for old Chaplin films, along with beer and pretzels. Other spots featured old-time silent newsreels, along with current news clips. The season's most interesting personality was Alec Templeton, the blind pianist who rose from a $350-a-week turn in the night clubs to a concert personality commanding $1,000 a night.

1940 proved a generally desultory year, tolling the Midnight Frolic and Jack Dempsey's Restaurant (the one on 8th Ave. and 50th St., not the Dempsey Broadway Bar) among the principal foldees. With business off, a return to clip-joint practices was noted.

46

'Don't Take Off Your Panties'

★

Burlesque started the 1930 season with 37 shows and 37 theatres. It ended ignominiously with 27 shows and 24 theatres. Burlesque—and not the depression—was to blame. While the Columbia Circuit had operated, it was possible for burlesque to defend itself against accusations that it was unclean. When Mutual took over, burly was roughed up to give the public "what it wanted" . . . or what Mutual considered would turn a fast buck.

Nudity and outright crudity have little fascination . . . at least for any protracted length of time. Dirt dished wholesale tends to bore and that means chasing 'em. Lana Turner in a sweater, shapely gams, a chantoosey with a slightly tilted eyebrow can pique the male trade more than a chorus of nudes.

That was burlesque's big mistake. Having gone the limit in dirty dialog, Mutual frantically tossed in strippers. But the strips were all alike.

The more lowdown burlesque was forced to get, the more, too, it invited trouble. Civic authorities won convictions in city after city. Burlesque was caught between two fires. If it cleaned up, it was too late; if it didn't, patronage slipped anyhow, and the cops came besides.

Some shows tried to grasp at straws by adding vaudeville acts, but vaudevillians couldn't stand the degrading atmosphere. The competition of cleaner and better entertainment made burly's $1 and $1.50 top prices impossible. In 1930, the name "burlesque," once so enticing to the male trade, was enough to murder the boxoffice of any theatre which flaunted it.

Mutual Burlesque died in 1931, to be replaced by another try of the Columbia Wheel under I. H. Herk, who collected $500 apiece from producers wanting to tie in. Stock burlesque settled down to a dreary routine which emphasized strippers on runways, comics filling in between strips with bawdy jokes long enough for the strippers to change costume. "They can't get any hotter," Variety noted wearily, "or the police would interfere, and they can't cool off because the customers would drop off. No cleverness—men just go to see nakedness, and that's all they get. Save to the degenerate and moron, there is little to attract in burlesque but mere nakedness."

In a desperate effort to drum up business for the burly show at the Gaiety, the manager opened the front doors facing Broadway, so that passersby could get an eyeful of the strippers on the runways. The stunt attracted crowds—outside. Minsky's stock burleycue on 42d Street advertised "Fannie Fortson From France—dances at all shows." The Minsky diet included "strippers, tossers, hip-heavers and breast-bouncers."

the old no. 3 routine Road burlesque developed a carnival twist in 1931 with one burly traveling in its own train. At towns where it gave shows, the girls would be "auctioned" to the audience—highest bidders winning the privilege of after-show dinners and dates. The suckers, anticipating a delicious evening, were delighted when the girls suggested that—since there was usually no place to go in the small towns—they go aboard their special train. Once aboard, the suckers were further delighted by being taken to the "privilege car," where they could order drinks and play cards. At midnight, when the suckers began to have ideas, a fake raid would be pulled by some of the men in the show, claiming to be railroad detectives, and ordering "strangers" off the train. The suckers went home, and the girls went wearily to bed.

When New York authorities sternly said, "Clean up—or else!" in 1932, burlesque actually didn't know how to go about obeying orders. Especially the Minsky shows, which had become infamous even outside New York as the dirtiest theatre in the big city. But the Minskys realized the city authorities meant business—it was either clean up or get out.

They thought of Sam S. Scribner, who had represented everything that was clean about burlesque—he was one of the founders of the original Columbia Burlesque Wheel—and who had quit when it turned dirty. Scribner agreed to become the censor or czar of burleycue, and was influential in getting City Hall to OK re-opening Minsky's Republic, with the explicit understanding Scribner would bluepencil all shows. Instead of strips, the Minskys turned to such sensational marquee items as Kiki Roberts, sweetheart of the notorious gangster, Legs Diamond. She got $1,500 a week.

The bits and routines of the average burly show were as inflexible as sewage drains. Comedy scene; strip; comedy scene; strip; intermission curtain and the aisle hawkers. Most customers yawned and read their newspapers between strip numbers.

There was practically no competition in 1934 burly, with the exception of a brief show of fight by a new eastern wheel. The two principal wheels of that year, Supreme and Independent, together served a total of about 15 cities. Only in one city did they play in opposition—Philadelphia. Variety summed up the situation, "The conflict is over who is going to get those six customers in Philly."

The same set of boxoffice conditions prevailed in 1934 as in most years. In cities where the authorities could be persuaded to look the other way, and stripping went the limit, the company didn't starve. Where the lid was on, the show echoed over empty orchestras. Yet burly executives kept mouthing the sentiment—as though they believed it—that it was time to cut down on stripping and emphasize comedy.

The New York police made their usual number of raids in 1934, with the Irving Place Theatre making the wagon again. Convictions were rare, however, which encouraged burly managers to believe their lawyers who told them there was no urgent need to mend their ways.

ann corio and gypsy rose lee   The top personality to emerge from 1934 burly was stripper Ann Corio, who had scored such a personal success that she was about the only name in burlesque known to other branches of show business, with the exception of producer Allan Gilbert, who won attention by staging some novel "flash girl numbers" at the Apollo and Irving Place theatres.

"I don't like to be called a stripper," Miss Corio told Variety's Cecelia Ager. "In fact it absolutely galls me. But as long as they give me the money, that's all I look forward to. . . . Why should I give up my percentage of the gross for $100 a week and glory? . . . Where are all the Broadway beauties now? When I finish I'll have a bankroll."

She explained the secret of her success. "Make yourself as feminine-looking as you can. Go in for a lot of frills, furs, ruffles and parasols. Always put everything you have into your work to put it over. . . . Don't take off your panties; it makes a girl's figure look prettier to have those little gadgets on."

The road, said Miss Corio, was lovely territory for strippers. Apart from the 15 to 25 per cent of the gross she was paid, compared to the $750 a week straight salary she drew in New York. "I love the road. They don't expect so much from you. New York audiences just want to see how much you'll take off . . . I love New England best of all. It's so easy to please. You don't have to do much in New England because they haven't had it."

She was also conscious of the "better" type of audiences. "I love the two-a-day houses best, where the audience is such a different class. In the four-a-day lots of the customers sit through two shows, and by the time the second show rolls around they're exhausted. That doesn't inspire a girl to do her best work . . . They're too tired to care what you're hiding."

In 1940, Miss Corio apparently had enough in the bank to take a flier in less remunerative fields. She appeared in strawhat versions of *The Barker* and *White Cargo*. A newspaper reporter asked whether she considered what she was doing art. "Art?" replied the indignant stripper. "I should say so! Why, I've been to the bank twice to draw money to eat on!"

Another Irving Place graduate, who soon eclipsed Miss Corio in the national spotlight, was Gypsy Rose Lee. Her first break came in 1936, when she jumped into the Shuberts' *Ziegfeld Follies* at the Winter Garden . . . still as a stripper. Her debut in legit rated more newspaper space in two months than all of burlesque had received in the previous two years. Miss Corio also received legitimate offers that year, as in other years, but until 1940 persisted in doing her undressing in burlesque, where she took top money as burly's No. 1 stripteuse.

Gypsy Rose Lee was unique because she put the accent on her IQ as well as s.a., later demonstrating her versatility by turning novelist. She was also clever enough to show far less than almost all the other strippers, and yet get the boys out front applauding wildly. She proved that strippers could draw for burlesque without stripping down to their skeletons.

london finally falls for strips Other top strippers of that year, who carried what was left of burlesque on their G-strings, were Evelyn Meyers, Margie Hart, Carrie Finnell (an ample-sized performer whose stock in trade was her mammary St. Vitus), Countess Nadja, Hinda Wassau, Georgia Sothern (a redhead who practically tore down the curtains with the violence of her grinds), Jeanne Carroll, Betty Howland, Toots Brawner, Maxine De Shon and Gladys Clark. The following year stripper Diane Ray left for London, to export the new American art into the British Isles. It must have taken a while to register, because not until 1940 did Variety report, "London Goes For Strip-Tease."

The Minskys, who dominated three of the five burlesque stands in the Times Square area, were primarily responsible for bringing down on burly's neck the fiery breath of Mayor Fiorello H. La-Guardia. After outlawing of the word "burlesque" in 1937, the burly operators did everything but promise that it would be as pure as Shirley Temple. The mayor relented to the extent of permitting them to reopen as "Follies" shows—no filth, no strippers.

Burly—or "Follies"—in New York dropped from 40 weeks of playing time at the start of 1938 to 12 by the year's finish, with only two summer weeks in New York. The rest of burly was handled by 10 stock companies operating throughout the country. One burlesque operator conceived an idea for defeating the La-Guardia ban, in the manner of the floating speakeasies, via a burly show offshore. He chartered the *S. S. Yankee,* a Hudson River showboat. License Commissioner Paul Moss got wind of the plan, and New York's finest were at the pier before the *S. S. Yankee* could get up steam. The sailing was held up on a docking technicality, with intimation that the technicality would last indefinitely, and that kayoed that idea.

All that could be said for burly in 1938 was that it was the last spawning ground of new talent since vaudeville had died. Burly, desperate for any kind of entertainment, often opened its arms to genuine, if untried, talent, which soon left it for greener pastures.

great cradle of talent "Peanuts" Bohn jumped from burly to English music halls. Abbott & Costello left to go with Kate Smith on the radio and subsequently their own radio and Hollywood stardom. Joey Faye went into legit with *Sing Out the*

News, and of course subsequent television stardom, as did Sid Stone into *The Fabulous Invalid,* legiter, before clicking on the Milton Berle video show. Rags Ragland and Phil Silvers joined Rudy Vallee. Sid Kent graduated to Eddie Cantor's writing staff, and Joe Yule went to Hollywood to appear in a film with his son—Mickey Rooney. The upsurge, through the years, from such cradled-in-burlesque talents as Bert Lahr, Fanny Brice, (Bobby) Clark & (Paul) McCullough, Leon Errol, Jim Barton, and Jack Pearl has given rise to periodic grievance among showmen that that great school of the future funny men and women—among the greats on the American stage—is no more.

While the State Street (Chicago) honkytonks are still running, and there are still 35 burlesque shows in the United States at this writing, the twilight of burlesque was a combination of spurious economics and no talent.

When Izzy Herk conceived the Mutual Wheel idea of a stationary line, with the principals only traveling from city to city, as a measure to cut down traveling expenses, the choristers in short order became local favorites, but soon thereafter palled on the steady clientele.

Meantime Herk had acquired a fresh bankroll via a Toledo concessionaire who urged more turnovers and intermissions as a bolsterer for his candy butchers and comic-book salesmen. The 4- and 5-a-day burlesque thus came into being, plus midnight shows, Sunday shows, and the like.

Variety was still scratching its head over the fact that burlesque was still around in 1940. "Burlesque's survival—in fact, its prosperity," it confessed, "can only be based on the greatly underestimated lunatic fringe in this country. Though a family-type entertainment, such as vaudeville, can barely keep what head it has above water, the dirty slapstick and sloppy G-stringers manage to keep going, and very profitably in most instances, without the buying public first asking what picture is playing."

Getting down to cases, Variety attributed burly's resurgence in 1940 to the industrial boom under way, which created greater defense spending, and also gathered together burly-ripe audiences at Army and Navy reservations.

Vaudeville acts of 1940 had tough sledding to book 20 weeks a year. But burlesque had two new, and separate circuits routing shows for a total of 25 weeks' playing time. One was the Midwest Circuit, a co-operative group, and the other was the Izzy Hirst Wheel.

Asked Variety, almost plaintively, "And how many legit road companies get 25 weeks outside of New York?"

Hep to the Jive

★

During 1933, Americans in the depths of the depression mournfully sang "Stormy Weather," "Are You Makin' Any Money?," "I'll String Along With You" and "Who's Afraid of the Big Bad Wolf?" Lachrymose romance was in vogue with "It's The Talk of the Town," "Sophisticated Lady," "Smoke Rings," "Don't Blame Me," "It Might Have Been A Different Story" and "Trouble in Paradise."

As counterpoint, swing was struggling to set a to-hell-with-it note by offering "Jive Stomp," via Duke Ellington, and "New Basin Street Blues." The natural setting was featured in "In the Valley of the Moon," "Under A Blanket of Blue," "Shadows On the Swanee," "My Moonlight Madonna" and "Down the Old Ox Road."

Love, pure and very simple, was offered in "Sweetheart, Darlin'," "My Love," "Love Is the Sweetest Thing," "Don't Blame Me," "Here You Come, Love," "Close Your Eyes," and "Ah, But It's Love." Top novelty number of the year was "Lazy Bones," and Bing Crosby crooned "Learn to Croon" to fame.

A key song of the year, "The Old Spinning Wheel," touched off a nostalgic series of songs about old things in 1934—"By the Old Wheel Pump," "The Old Covered Bridge," "The Old-Fashioned Girl," "The Old-Fashioned World," "The Old Trunk in the Attic" and "The Old Grandfather's Clock."

Billy Hill, composer of "Spinning Wheel," sparked still another 1934 cycle with "The Last Round-Up," which provoked a score of Western numbers on the order of "Wagon Wheels" and "Night In the Desert." Hill was awarded a special $1,200 prize by ASCAP for "Spinning Wheel," and publishers fought for numbers which he had sold at $25 apiece before clicking with "Round-Up."

The year also brought an eye cycle, with "I Only Have Eyes For You," "With My Eyes Wide Open," "I'll Close My Eyes," and "It Happened When Your Eyes Met Mine." Some smash hits came via the filmusicals of the year, which offered "Love In Bloom," "Beat of My Heart," "Cocktails For Two," "A Thousand Goodnights," "Did You Ever See A Dream Walking?" "Love Thy Neighbor," "The Very Thought Of You" and "I Never Had A Chance." An ineffectual attempt to revitalize the waltz tempo was made by the legit musical *Great Waltz*.

The hit song of 1935 was "Isle of Capri." That year a number of old tunes were protested as derogatory to Negroes by the Society for the Advancement of Colored People. Among these were "That's Why Darkies Are Born," "My Old Kentucky Home," "Swanee River," "Muddy Waters," "Carry Me Back To Old Virginny," "River, Stay Away From My Door," "Without A Song" and "Underneath the Harlem Moon."

Indicative of the new festive feeling of the nation, and heralding the swift advance of swing by 1936, was the comedy number, "The Music Goes 'Round and 'Round." Its earnings exceeded those of the fabulous "Yes, We Have No Bananas," and launched a new cycle of "Round" numbers, including "The Merry-Go-Round Broke Down," which inspired a subcycle of its own with "Love Is Like A Merry-Go-Round" and "The Girl That I Met On the Merry-Go-Round."

The South Seas vogue of 1937 was reflected in music by a revival of Hawaiian numbers, and new popularity for the ukulele. The vogue prompted O. O. McIntyre—for whom Meredith Willson had written "The O. O. McIntyre Suite"—to remark that, "Those Hawaiians always say goodbye—but never go."

"Blue songs are the rage among bluebloods," *Variety* noted that year—a spectacular year for swank night clubs. "Songs have dirty lyrics, framed in semi-polite language, and are put across in the fashionable cafes by beautifully-gowned chanteuses or immaculately-groomed gents who conduct themselves like members of a London regiment. Swells delight in the indigo, and the later the hour becomes, the more outspoken the lyrics."

Less sophisticated, but with the same basic appeal, were the records offered to wayside rests which couldn't afford live talent. Known as "operator's specials," these disks included such titles as "Pool Table Papa," "Four or Five Times" and "Give It To Me, Daddy." They were infinitely more popular than the poor crop of 1937 numbers turned out for the standard field.

The floods of 1937 inspired a Mills number called "Flood Waters," while a number exalting the gloved victory of Joe Louis called "Joe the Bomber" was composed, arranged, rehearsed and recorded in 24 hours. The recording artist was "Billy Hicks and His Sizzling Six." Other timely numbers were songs woven around radio catch-lines of the day—"Vass You Dere, Sharlie?" "Today I Am A Man," "Oh, You Nasty Man"—all of which rated zero in popular favor.

The biggest hits of 1938 were the songs from *Snow White*. With the advent of swing, songstresses began to use the tempo on Scottish classics, and then on nursery rhymes. The vogue inspired swing versions of "Tisket-A-Tasket," and "All Around the Mulberry Bush." Other top tunes were "Ti-Pi-Tin," "Thanks For the Memory," and "Bei Mir Bist Du Schoen," adapted from a Yiddish song, a surprise hit. Orders for the latter number poured in to baffled music dealers as "That new French song, 'Buy A Beer, Monsieur Shane,'" "My Mere Bits of Shame," and "Mr. Barney McShane."

musical echoes of the war drums   America was too prosperous and happy in 1938 to want to be reminded of war in the outside world. But they were glad to sing Irving Berlin's "God Bless America," an old number he wrote and discarded in 1917 as puerile until Kate Smith rediscovered it. Another topical number was "Wrong Way Corrigan," celebrating the insouciant flier who took off from Brooklyn without permit or passport and landed in Dublin.

Songwriters in Europe, however, were very much aware of the war. Hermann Leopoldi wrote an Austrian "youth song" called "We Are On the Dolfuss Road To Better Times." Then came Anschluss, and Leopoldi landed in a Nazi concentration camp for writing the wrong song. Austrian composers quickly took the hint, and one of the first songs turned out after Hitler's Austrian putsch was "Soldier From Berlin, Girl of Vienna."

England gave America its best songs of 1939—despite the war— with "Penny Serenade," "South of the Border," "My Prayer," "The Beer Barrel Polka" and "Boomps-A-Daisy." Broadway replaced Hollywood as the feeder of hits that year with "South American Way," "Comes Love," "Are You Having Any Fun?," "Get Out of Town," "I Didn't Know What Time It Was" and "Do I Love You—Do I?"

More and more tunesmiths were discovering wonderful melodies —in the tunes of previous centuries. As Variety dryly reported, "Refugees coming over observe, 'My, what a wonderfully musical nation America is! They even whistle Mozart, Tschaikowsky, Debussy and Chopin in the street!'"

Among the numbers which owed more than inspiration to the classics were "Our Love" and "My Reverie" (Debussy and Larry Clinton); "Moon Love" (Tschaikowsky and Andre Kostelanetz) and "How Strange" (M.G.M. and Prozorovsky).

Escapism via juvenile songs came with "Little Sir Echo," to be followed by "Little Mischief Maker," "Little Skipper," "Little Genius" and "Little Lad." This in turn touched off a "cute" cycle—"Oh Johnny," "Chatterbox," "Baby Me," "Goody-Goodbye" and "Three Little Fishes."

Swing was represented by "Hold Tight," "Well, All Right," "T'aint What You Do, It's the Way Thatcha Do It," "I Want the Waiter With the Water." Benny Goodman introduced "Sonata to ASCAP," "Opus Local 802" and "AC-DC Current." Woody Herman offered "Woodchoppers Ball," "Neurotic Goldfish," "A Deb's Diary" and "Weekend of A Private Secretary."

By 1940 "God Bless America" had risen to the status of a new national anthem, and there was a strong movement on foot to replace "The Star-Spangled Banner" with it. Some newspapers criticized Berlin for "making money" out of patriotic feeling, apparently unaware that a committee comprising Col. Theodore Roosevelt, Gene Tunney and Herbert Bayard Swope, at Berlin's own request, were administering all the song's profits and royalties, divided equally between the Boy and Girl Scouts of America. Whereupon Bucknell University awarded Berlin a Doctorate of

Music. Berlin purposely placed a high royalty on the song in order to swell the fund which has realized over $130,000.

With England fighting for existence, and the rise of anti-Fascist feeling in America, war songs began to make their appearance in 1940. There were "Thanks America," "Let Freedom Ring," "What Will I Do If I Marry A Soldier," "Your Homeland and My Homeland," "Liberty Bell, It's Time To Ring Again," "What Are You Doing For Your Uncle Sam?" "Is It Love—Or Is It Conscription?," "Who'll Take the Place of Mademoiselle From Armentieres?," "Give the Stars and Stripes A Permanent Wave" and "He's A Typical American Boy."

How can you have a war without war songs?

dance vogues   For its dances of the 1930s America turned at first to foreign and pseudo-foreign styles—notably the rhumba, the Carioca and the Continental, the latter two made popular by Fred Astaire and Ginger Rogers via their filmusicals, *Flying Down To Rio* and *Gay Divorcee* respectively. In 1934 Gene Edwards introduced a new idea at Sherry's Park Avenue—a dance orchestra composed of half Negro, half white musicians—"to blend natural Negro syncopation with the more restrained white dance rhythms." Bing Crosby was the top creator of song hits, with Rudy Vallee leading on the air, and Dick Powell first warbler of the films via Warner Bros. musicals. Tin Pan Alley was enthusiastic about two English music maestros—Ray Noble and Jack Hylton.

Swing began to develop on two levels in 1935. On the top level was "musician's music"—or bands whose most enthusiastic audience consisted of other musicians. In this bracket were Benny Goodman, Louis Armstrong, Fats Waller, Louis Prima, Wingy Manone, Farley-Reilly, Red Norvo, Red McKenzie and Adrian Rollini. On the lower level were the popular swing bands, whose popularity was based on less complex renditions of swing for dancing and listening.

Among the up-and-comers were Hal Kemp, the Dorseys, Kay Kyser, Eddy Duchin, Dick Haymes and Ted Fio Rito.

Guy Lombardo still held his tremendous following, explaining that the secret of his success was, as a radio band, playing for listening rather than dancing. "He believes," Variety reported, "that despite the misguided conceptions of some ad agencies that folks in the sticks roll up their carpets and dance to the radio, what most of 'em really do is just listen. Hence Lombardo's smooth, reedy music is 99 per cent patterned for ear-appeal. Most listeners either just recline, some lie down, others play bridge or read with the radio going."

birth of swing   The first swing contest took place in 1936 at the Imperial Theatre, New York, with 17 orchestras swinging it for three hours. Variety, sidestepping any "best" label, handed out adjective awards. Glen Gray was "most elegant"; Stuff Smith, "most personable"; Bunny Berigan, "most jam"; Paul Whiteman, "most finished"; Louis Armstrong, "most penetrating"; Artie Shaw, "most arresting soloist and clarinet." Mildred Bailey won the laurel of "most compelling chanteuse."

Variety's editor asked top swing musicians for their definition of the new brand of music. "It's jam," said Mike Farley, "but arranged." Wingy Manone declared, "It's a livelier tempo, you know —swingy-like." Red McKenzie was more explicit: "It's an evolution of 'The Dixie Style,' that is, the Original Nick La Rocca's Dixieland Jazz Band's style. It's the difference between the old and the new music. It's definitely the music of the future. Swing dates from 1914, with the 'Livery Stable Blues' and the 'Original Dixieland Jazz Band Blues.' That's only 20 years or so ago. Swing is carefully conceived improvisation. . . ."

According to Red Norvo, "It's a desire to achieve a definite, livelier rhythm, and only advanced musicians can do that. It's a tempo that inspires the listener to accelerate in rhythm with an ultramodern swing. You know, they *swing* with you."

The contest between swing and sweet music for American favor was still going strong by 1938. To establish swing's right to be considered as serious American music, Benny Goodman gave a recital at Carnegie Hall, where, as Variety noted, "the longhair crix didn't savvy his jive." Paul Whiteman also appeared at Carnegie Hall and found the welcome warmer—as official spokesman for jazz who had made it respectable at Carnegie Hall and Town Hall 15 years before.

Swing influenced dancing among the younger generation, which found its expression in jitterbugging. The vogue at first amused, then dismayed older generations which found themselves literally kicked off the dance floors of the nation. The adolescents of 1938, thanks to swing and jitterbugging, were vastly different specimens from the serious, depression-conscious youths of the early 1930s who had taken their revolt against their elders out by joining unions, and various "progressive" movements. These youths, now in their late twenties, regarded their adolescent successors with undisguised contempt.

Even in 1938 swing was having its moral repercussions, through the association of "muggles" or "reefers," as marijuana cigarets were called, with "cats," "alligators" and "ickeys." The use of drugs by swing musicians—a vice which later spread to juvenile swing addicts—was a private but not yet public scandal in 1938.

Swing made the nation so band-conscious that in 1940 bands were the top stage entertainment. Some high-rating bands playing film houses even were able to get away with specifying the type of "A" films to accompany their engagements, a function "old-fashioned" acts usually left to theatre managers. The latter also strongly resented the stiff price tags on name bands. The average good orchestra rated only $1,400 weekly in night clubs and hotels —because of radio hookups which made these engagements profitable—but rarely asked below $6,500 from the theatres.

Vaude's oldtimers further resented the bands because of "lazy stage habits." Musicians frequently refused to wear makeup, and band singers thought nothing of doing their solos in street attire . . . sometimes in sweaters. As Variety pictured the bands in vaudeville, "Nearly all of them have jamming, jaw-grinding trapmen; wide-stanced, wooden-faced singers; pale-faced and blue-jowled musicians (all without makeup); and an always-smiling leader, to whom none of the musicians pay any apparent attention. That's now the core of what was once vaudeville."

one of ascap's major fights The musical world of the 1930s was stirred behind the scenes by a running battle between ASCAP—undisputed spokesman for America's composers, lyricists and publishers—and the National Association of Broadcasters. The battle actually dated from a first skirmish in 1925, when the American Society of Composers, Authors and Publishers won a court verdict against Station WLW of Cincinnati which set the precedent that radio stations would have to obtain licenses from

ASCAP, and pay fees, if they wished to broadcast ASCAP-controlled music.

ASCAP, not fully appreciating the extent to which radio was destined to grow, was content to collect only nominal fees from radio under this arrangement until 1932. Then, realizing that radio was the biggest and most important consumer of music in the nation, the Society demanded in addition to its fee a share of radio station revenue. Its argument was that since ASCAP music was largely responsible for radio entertainment—and hence the money paid in by sponsors—it should be rewarded accordingly.

Independent radio stations protested vehemently, but the networks signed a contract giving ASCAP 2 per cent of sponsor revenue for 1932, 3 per cent for 1933 and 4 per cent for 1934. Independent station owners continued to denounce "the oppression of the music front" at each annual convention of the National Association of Broadcasters.

In 1934 NAB was prevailed upon to get the United States Department of Justice to haul ASCAP into court on charges of violating the anti-trust law. The case wes suddenly shelved after a few weeks of trial because the Government's special counsel, Andrew Bennett, found that he did not have enough evidence to go ahead.

Frustrated, NAB then instructed its managing director, Jimmy Baldwin, to insist upon a special clause in its next contract with ASCAP. That clause would compel the Society to collect its fees directly from the networks, on network commercials. But while Baldwin cooled his heels in a suite at the Hotel St. Regis, New York, waiting to hear from ASCAP's president, Gene Buck, the networks shrewdly worked fast and signed a five-year contract with Buck that raised the payoff of ASCAP to 5 per cent annually. The first that the astonished Baldwin heard about this was when the networks sent out wires to their affiliates announcing that all, because of the new contract, would have to be licensed by ASCAP.

Furious, NAB hired Andrew Bennett away from his Government job to become the spearhead and strategist of a campaign of harrassment against ASCAP. The campaign resulted in lawsuits in eight state courts; hostile legislation in every state where it was possible to get it; and three tussles before the United States Supreme Court. The fight cost ASCAP almost a million dollars, not including the loss of revenues from the states of Washington, Montana, Nebraska and Florida, where NAB had won out. Despite these headaches, ASCAP cleared $6,950,000 in 1939, of which $4,300,000 represented radio revenue. By 1951 *ASCAP's* music license fees from all sources, including television, was nearer the $14,000,000 mark.

Neville Miller succeeded Baldwin as managing director of the NAB. After examining the fruits of the organization's struggle with ASCAP, he then let it be known that he was prepared to sit down with the Society and discuss a new contract. But misunderstanding of the arrangement for such a conference led to no conference—and mutual recriminations. ASCAP let it be known that its next contract would include a direct fee derived from all network revenues, rather than just sponsor income.

bmi vs. ascap   CBS decided to pitch its lot in with the predominantly independent-run National Association of Broadcasters. It suggested to the NAB that the only way to lick ASCAP was by building a musical reservoir of its own, which radio could draw upon. And it lent one of its lawyers, Sidney M. Kaye, for the purpose of forming a rival to ASCAP called Broadcast Music, Inc., yclept BMI. The first step in this maneuver was the leasing by BMI of the Edward B. Marks Music Publishing Co. catalog for $1,250,000.

ASCAP watched with amused contempt, confident that BMI would prove a flop. ASCAP had the nation's top tune writers, publishers and songs in its pocket. BMI had nothing but third-string songs and talent, and classics like "Jeannie With the Light Brown Hair," which was played several million times during 1940. But NBC, after hesitating, joined CBS and the NAB in boycotting ASCAP tunes from sustaining shows.

Variety stayed neutral, running battle stories in which both sides were given equal space to tell their stories, to make and answer accusations. Among the accusations made by ASCAP prexy Gene Buck was his charge that NAB had, out of spite, engineered his arrest as a fugitive of justice from the state of Arizona—"a state I had never visited in my whole life"—an example of the legal persecution and skullduggery being carried on against ASCAP. The outcome of the battle was still undecided when the curtain rang down on 1940.

payolas—again   Songplugging with bribes, the bane of the industry since Variety had come on the scene in 1905, was still a headache throughout the 1930s. Pluggers themselves realized, in 1934, that if publishers could get their songs plugged merely by sending along a $10 bill to orchestra leaders or singers, there would be no need to employ songpluggers for the same work.

So the music "contact men"—fancy for pluggers—themselves set fines of between $1,000 and $2,000 for any plugger or publisher found guilty of bribery to obtain plugs. Lou Diamond, head of Famous Music, Inc., a Paramount subsidiary, used the raw knuckles approach, threatening that if any competitor tried bribery, he would subsidize a bribery campaign of his own to the extent of $100,000.

Variety presented a composite picture of the songplugger at work in 1937. "Every new song becomes 'the greatest ballad we ever had,' or the 'greatest score Berlin ever wrote.' . . . That's where the personality comes in. That's where nights of carousing, days of golfing, sessions at a beach club, great manifestation of care and worry about this or that radio act or band's welfare, stand the personality song contact men in good stead."

Plugging also called for "gigoloing on the side." As Variety explained, "The gal warblers may cotton to this or that contact man who knows how to buy them an interesting lunch or dinner, and manages to step a nifty dance set as a coincidental social grace . . ."

That payoffs were still very much in evidence by 1938 was indicated by the sudden interest of the Federal Trade Commission in the problem. The FTC advised ASCAP that bribery for plugs was definitely an unethical business practice, and that the close ties between Tin Pan Alley and Hollywood entailed "subsidies" which were in effect paid for plugs. FTC pointed out another subtle method of bribery—the appearance of bandleaders' names on music as "co-authors." This obviously gave bandleaders a financial interest in the success of certain songs. ASCAP promised to check up on name-singer or bandleader "co-authors" to ascertain whether the collaboration was genuine, or just a cut-in.

The growth of the American Society of Composers, Authors & Publishers was a reflection of the boom in music through post-1933. In 1934 Decca of London invaded the American market with Jack Kapp, former general manager of Brunswick, as its president. The music business began to move uptown into Radio City. First Tin Pan Alley resident on Rockefeller soil was Marty Bloom, who became the first music publisher in the business without a piano. The Rockefellers wanted no disturbing noises on their dignified premises. But as more and more of Tin Pan Alley moved in, the ban was broken, and pianos banged merrily from Remick and Witmark, Marks, Chappell, Fox and Harms.

ASCAP, the Music Publishers Protective Assn. and the Post Office joined hands to war against mail-order racketeers who were swindling some $2,000,000 annually from would-be songwriters. ASCAP's guns were also trained on the peddlers of 5¢ song sheets containing unauthorized reprints of song lyrics. The situation became confused when the M.P.P.A. made a separate deal for "authorized" lyric sheets.

Variety reported the musical favorites of Japan that year, finding Beethoven on top of the list, followed by geisha songs and Japanese jazz. But two years later Variety was gratified to note that the best-selling record in Tokyo was "St. Louis Blues," trailed by "Sweet Sue." Japan was getting more "American-minded."

Something new entered the American music world in 1935 with "Muzak"—or wired radio. The process was developed as early as 1922 by a Belgian engineer. By the time it was introduced into America, it was already serving 66 per cent of the populations in Belgium and Holland by home subscription. The foreign service fee was high—$20 a year.

Muzak agreed to pay ASCAP a 4 per cent split of profits, and began to rent out its "wired music" to restaurants, niteries and hotels, which paid for the service on a basis of customer capacity. For home set owners, the tariff was set at between $1.50 and $4.50 a month, depending on the type of channel desired. Its big attraction was that it would offer continuous music, with no advertising and only the briefest of announcements.

During 1935, piano sales shot up 40 per cent—prosperity was returning—and sheet music sales zoomed accordingly. Royalties for the performance of music were estimated at $4,000,000 for the year. From then on until the close of the decade, music was a seller's market, with a climax reached in 1938 through the *Snow White* songs. The Disney numbers sold over 1,500,000 disks and 1,000,000 copies of sheet music.

In the next decade the music business was to experience more new trends. For one thing, ASCAP suffered a second Consent Decree, this time at the hands of a group of New York exhibitors known as the ITOA (Independent Theatre Owners Assn.) They balked at paying a double music tax, i.e. for the film synchronization and a seat tax for their theatres, and the Government upheld them.

Meantime, however, new horizons via television asserted themselves and by midcentury ASCAP had exceeded the $10,000,000 gross annual revenue, and AA writers saw $18,000-$20,000 annual dividends. For a topnotch songsmith this was tantamount to a $1,000,000 annuity at a 2 per cent yield. As Billy Rose once told the editor of Variety, "Of all the worldly goods I have and can leave Eleanor (Eleanor Holm; Mrs. Rose) is my ASCAP income. It pays out like a gold mine."

With the second Consent Decree there were new mathematical hurdles for the songsmith in that the "current usage" of a work became an important method for calculating income. Thus the "country club set" within ASCAP, as some of the old-timers were labeled, could not rest on their laurels but had to return to creating or reactivating their old and new songs, because their compensation was so closely tied to a payoff predicated on a continuing current usage of their songs. In turn, the new "payoff on performances" system skyrocketed the dividends of Irving Berlin, Cole Porter, the Gershwin Estate, Richard Rodgers and Oscar Hammerstein, 2d, to $35,000-$45,000 a year.

Meantime BMI moved forward and in the post-World War II era, where nostalgia and a yen for the folksy music asserted itself, many an obscure BMI publisher enjoyed the top hits, and both the big league ASCAP writers and publishers found themselves eclipsed.

Dance band styles, too, reverted to the smooth and sweet; bebop died aborning; balladeers like Bing Crosby, Vic Damone, Frank Sinatra, Perry Como, Frankie Laine, Gordon MacRae, and smooth songstresses like Dinah Shore, Doris Day, Jo Stafford and Margaret Whiting sold records into the millions.

48

World's Fair—and Overture to War

★

Chicago opened its Century of Progress Exposition in May of 1933. Costing $38,000,000, it ran for two years, with an interruption between November and May of 1934. Chicago show business enjoyed a boom, with night clubs and beer gardens spending $150,000 weekly for talent. The 16,000,000 visitors enabled the Exposition to pay off all of its bondholders.

Top gravy of the Exposition went to the Greyhound Bus Co., which took in $1,647,000 with its sightseeing "yap wagons." The Union News Co. earned $1,301,000 with souvenir postcards. And the rest-room concession, with the fee set at a nickel—to the outrage of out-of-towners—earned $862,000 in five months.

There was a spree of expositions in 1936, with an estimated $200,000,000 being spent by Dallas, Fort Worth, San Francisco and New York. Overseas the following year, the International Paris Exposition was the outstanding tourist draw of Europe.

In 1939 San Francisco beat New York to the punch and opened the Golden Gate International Exposition in February. But the big expo event of the decade took place two months later on the 1,216 acres of Flushing Meadows—the New York World's Fair, which opened to a first day's business of 600,000 payees.

New York hotels and theatres, which expected a tremendous boom in business as result of the Fair, were dismayed by results of the first few months. Tourists weren't arriving in the expected numbers. Most came with thin wallets, staying at the Fair all day, and returning to their hotels too tired to do anything but rest their feet or sleep. The few who had enough reserve energy to patronize night clubs were quickly voted by waiters as the "two bit" trade.

Broadway night life was further hurt by the flocking of its usual patronage to the fancy restaurants in the foreign "pavilions" at the Fair for dinner. This trend didn't last long, when New Yorkers discovered that the French, Belgian, Italian, Brazilian and other pavilions charged exorbitant prices for inferior meals. They were further antagonized by poor, and frequently insolent service.

Not until June did Broadway feel any of the promised benefits of the Fair. Then the New York *Daily News* editorialized, "The Fair, which at first almost knocked the props out from under the New York theatre and night club business, is now pulling in enough customers from outside to furnish encouraging gate receipts to both the Fair and Broadway. We're more than glad to note this justification of the confidence of those who always said the Fair, for all its $150,000,000 investment, would be a paying proposition for New York City in the long run . . . It was admittedly one of the greatest shows ever put on in the world."

The most successful attraction at the Fair was Billy Rose's Aquacade, which earned $1,000,000 net profit during the Fair's first year. The aquamarine amphitheatre seated 10,000 at a price scale of 40¢-83¢-$1.10. Variety called the show, which starred Johnny Weissmuller, Eleanor Holm, Morton Downey and Gertrude Ederle, with a cast of over 500, "the greatest spectacle in the history of show business."

The biggest show of the San Francisco Exposition was Sally Rand's "Nude Ranch," which did $40,000 a week, top-grossing attraction of the Fair midway.

growth of outdoor show biz   When the nation began to have some money in its pocket, and moved outdoors again in 1934, the outdoor show business rejoiced. State and county fairs showed increased grosses of between 50 and 85 per cent, while circus receipts rose 33 per cent over 1933. The growing boom revived hundreds of carnivals, and pitchmen were once again barking their way into three squares a day. Small truck and wagon shows began to roll through the countryside.

The Tom Mix-Sam B. Dill show, moving in General Motors trucks, grossed handsomely. Al G. Barnes brought his show back to California with $150,000 in profits. Ringling's show had one of their best years, contributing heavily to the $75,000,000 record chalked up in 1934 by all of outdoor show business. Even the fake

Cardiff Giant, which had earned $200,000 before being exposed as a hoax made of gypsum rather than an exhumed ancient giant, returned after 20 years to tap the cash customers.

Two new notes were introduced in 1936. "Auditorium circuses" gained a four-months' winter route—playing special organization dates for the Shriners, American Legions and others. And at Dobbs Ferry, New York, an outdoor showman borrowed a rodeo stunt: baseball played on donkeys.

In 1937, a banner year for circuses, the Ringlings paid off the Manufacturers Trust Co. to regain control of the Big Top. There were 350 carnivals in action, scooping an annual $100,000,000 at beaches, parks and fairs. Madison Square Garden, however, guessed wrong that year with a Carnival of Champs, offering four fights for the price of one. The loss tallied $30,000.

The Garden was soothed the following year when Sonja Henie opened her ice revue, clicking profitably with an opening night audience of 16,000. When she returned there in 1940, the advance sale was $200,000, with the Garden jammed every night. In 1939 the Garden offered something new in Rodeo—cowgirls, most of whom were the daughters of well-known ranchers. And in 1940 the Ringling-Barnum & Bailey circus racked up the record boxoffice of $52,000 in a single day.

more commercials   Show business found a strong new route opening during the 1930s—the private enterprise circuit. More and more, business firms found that by utilizing the glamor of show business, they were able to attract crowds to their goods and services.

In 1934 Macy's opened a talent booking bureau for parties. Hearn's department store booked a Fancho & Marco unit. Standard Oil of New Jersey paid Guy Lombardo and his band $10,000 a week for a tour of big city auditoriums. The price of admission was simply a driver's license—Standard Oil charging the stunt off to select-group advertising. Theatrical pressure forced Standard Oil to call it off. The theatres feared that it would set a precedent for other big corporations to offer free shows as part of their advertising budgets.

In 1935 Philip Morris Cigarettes hired Marshall Montgomery, a vaudeville ventriloquist, to tour the better hotels and cafes as an innocent-looking guest, while putting "Call for Philip Morris" into the air. The new Liggett drugstore on Broadway and 42d Street turned its opening into an all-star show, with Benny Leonard as emcee.

Almost every United States department store today goes in for Christmas showmanship; in fact merchandising is another name for showmanship. Today there is more cheesecake in intimate apparel and depilatory advertising than would be countenanced in connection with out-and-out show biz attractions. The brassiere industry is a good example. But in that era Gimbel's was pioneering when it toured a reproduction of Barnum's Museum, freaks, animals and all. Macy's annual parade is now a New York civic institution.

In 1936 a Los Angeles brewery presented a vaudeville show, charging bottle caps for admission. And in 1950 the latest 20th-century style medicine show booked was the $350,000 one toured by Louisiana Senator Dudley J. LeBlanc, headed by Mickey Rooney and Connee Boswell, admission, one Hadacol boxtop which nostrum the Senator manufactures at Lafayette, Louisiana. For more limited spots, where Hadacol invades a new potential market, Senator LeBlanc has booked such "extra added attractions" as Jimmy Durante.

The depression years gave industrial (or commercial) films their biggest hypo. Automotive, oil, tobacco, harvester and kindred industries paid film exhibitors on a basis of per-1,000 seating capacity, per performance, for exposing their audiences to pix plugging certain products. Sometimes these films were one-minute celluloid commercials, and sometimes they were well-made industrial shorts so sugarcoating the trademark or the commodity being exploited as to be downright educational and entertaining. Lucky Strike made 1937 a big year for commercial shorts by producing some that were good enough to be shown in some of the country's best theatres. By 1938, industrial films had 6,000 playdates, and were a $20,000,000-a-year business.

A grocery chain in Hollywood started using vaudeville acts in 1937, offering "two-a-day" with stars. Variety pondered this phenomenon as the possible beginnings of a new "carrot circuit." Wholesale grocers and food distributors, in time, borrowed this idea with real name acts to glamorize their conventions. One New England food distrib paid Amos 'n' Andy $12,000 and Edgar Bergen $10,000.

THE CHURCH AND SHOW BIZ

This same grocery wholesaler was eventually to go in for a glorified banknite or giveaway, with automobiles as door prizes, in lieu of the talent lure.

Among the other oddities of show business noted was the first rooftop skating rink on Broadway, opened in 1933 by Philadelphia Jack O'Brien above Roseland. In San Francisco that year, the Tai Chug Wah Theatre on Jackson Street was still going strong after 66 years, dramatizing current events in China at $2.50 top. The Walnut Street Theatre in Philadelphia, America's oldest legitimate playhouse, was reopened in 1937 for Yiddish films. The Morro Castle wreck in 1934 was turned into a performance by Asbury Park, which sold postcards, peanuts and popcorn to visitors who came to gaze at the hulk.

the church and show biz Church figures played their usual active role in show business of the 1930s. Aimee Semple McPherson started the ball rolling with a personal at the Capitol Theatre, New York, for which she received $5,000 the week of Sept. 26, 1933. Covering the event, Variety remarked, "She wears a white satin creation—sexy but Episcopalian." Despite the gown, the Capitol dropped $20,000 on the week's business.

The church's heavy hand made itself felt that year through the act of the New York censors in clipping the Fox short, "Pirates of the Deep." The scene objected to was the love life of the clam —and the film had to be released with its romance scissored.

The church, which had been fulminating against the immorality of films for several years, blew up in 1934 and went into action. "Undesirable" films were placed on blacklists, and pledges solicited all over the country for membership in the newly-organized Legion of Decency. In Philadelphia, the Catholic Church slapped a boycott on all film theatres, regardless of their attractions. Alarmed, Hollywood producers began to scrap or re-shoot films. The Motion Picture Producers & Distributors Association took stock of the situation, and decided that no film would be released unless it had been certified 99 44/100 per cent pure by Joe Breen, the industry's censor.

But the church refused to call off its watchdogs. Throughout the decade there was constant friction between the theatre and church over what was art—and what was smut. In 1936, Oklahoma

City, which had never banned or blue-penciled a play or film in its history, balked at the touring *Tobacco Road* company.

The following year the church, needling the New York legislature, succeeded in sneaking through the Dunnigan Bill, which would have given one man the power to decide what New Yorkers should or should not see. All of show business became suddenly aroused and united behind the cause of defeating the bill. Every New York newspaper editorialized against it, influencing Governor Herbert H. Lehman finally to veto and kill it. The only organization fighting hard for the bill was the Knights of Columbus.

The church had its axe out in 1938 for the Mae West burlesque of the Adam and Eve legend over NBC. The red-faced network made meek apologies, although the skit was actually the brainchild of the J. Walter Thompson ad agency. But when the church shot arrows at Eugene O'Neill's *Beyond the Horizon,* so many respected names in literature and the drama came angrily to its defense that the church discreetly dropped the hot potato.

In 1939 the church joined parents in attacking radio's programs for children, taking a sideswipe at the same time at films—both for exciting youngsters with crime stories. A decade later this campaign took an encore with television.

Radio's biggest headache with the church was centered in the figure of one cleric—Father Coughlin. Radio found itself caught on the horns of a dilemma—how to shut up Coughlin without being accused of denying him freedom of speech, and without alienating a large, if lunatic fringe, following. In 1939 Coughlin was finally banned by the National Association of Broadcasters, which cited his word-for-word parroting of Nazi propaganda.

sime dies in 1933   The era was marked by the passing of some truly show business greats. When the founder of Variety, possibly the most influential and best-loved man in the amusement industry, died in 1933, the nation's press eulogized Sime Silverman.

A relatively unknown great, because he so shunned the limelight, the dailies ran laudatory editorials on his integrity, courage—and the unique living monument that he left as a perennial reminder of his special journalistic genius.

That same year saw the passing of that unique product of the Prohibition era, Texas Guinan; scenic artist Joseph Urban (who designed most of the opulent Ziegfeld musicals), Fatty Arbuckle and at age 73 the great matinee idol of an earlier era, E. H. Sothern. Death also took author Ring Lardner, and from the sports world, Jim Corbett, William Muldoon and Jockey Tod Sloan.

In 1934 show business lost producer Charles B. Dillingham and Otto Kahn, who had angeled many Broadway productions. The year also saw the passing of Rockefeller's top publicity consultant, Ivy Lee, who originated the idea of John D.'s dime giveaways. At the age of 77 death took Maggie Cline, once known as "The Irish Queen" and "Brunnhilde of the Bowery," whose most famous song was "Throw 'Em Down, McCloskey."

Will Rogers was killed in 1935 while flying with Wiley Post in Alaska, his death mourned deeply and personally by all of show business. De Wolfe Hopper also died that year, at 77, the same span of years which claimed the New York *Times'* Adolph S. Ochs.

The movies led the obituary list of 1936, with the deaths of Metro's production genius, Irving Thalberg, at 37, and its one-time great star, John Gilbert, at 38. The great showman Roxy passed on at 53, and Alexander Pantages at 65. Marilyn Miller died at the age of 38, Madame Schumann-Heink at 75. (The great opera star was accorded a military funeral.) Other deaths of the year included John Ringling, last of the seven famous brothers, and Alexander Glazounoff, composer of "The Volga Boatman."

gershwin and ravel   Music lost George Gershwin, at 38, in 1937, and Maurice Ravel, composer of the "Bolero," at 62. The theatre lost playwrights Samuel Shipman, John Drinkwater and Sir James Barrie; stage stars William Gillette and Mrs. Leslie Carter, and producer Winthrop Ames. The films lost actress Jean Harlow and oldtimer Joseph Jefferson (J. J.) McCarthy, who started film road-shows by touring *Birth Of A Nation* at a $2 top. Vaudeville lost S. Z. Poli, pioneer New England vaudeville man, and James McIntyre, of McIntyre & Heath, most famous of all oldtime blackface acts. Tom Heath died one year later, at the age of 85. Other deaths of 1938 included the widely syndicated columnist O. O. McIntyre, at 54, and Ben Harney, pioneer of ragtime music, at 66.

In 1939 the films lost Douglas Fairbanks, who died in his sleep at the age of 55, Alice Brady at 47, Carl Laemmle at 72 and Ford Sterling, an original Keystone cop, at 56. The Fourth Estate lost

Heywood Broun at 51, and Floyd Gibbons at 52. The stage lost Fay Templeton at 74 and noted Jewish actor Boris Thomashefsky, whose death at 71 was the occasion for wide East Side mourning. Ernie Hare died at 55, evoking memories of 1921 when, as "The Happiness Boys," Billy Jones and Ernie Hare, were radio bywords. The year also saw the passing of noted magician Horace Goldin, at 65, novelist Zane Grey, at 74, and musician Hugo Riesenfeld at 60.

The opera was the greatest sufferer through deaths of 1940. Gone were Giulio Gatti-Casazza, impresario of the Metropolitan for 27 years, who died at 71; opera star Luisa Tetrazzini, at 65; Italian tenor Alessandro Bonci, at 70; and violinist Jan Kubelik at 60. The films lost Tom Mix, who died in an auto accident at 69, leaving an estate of less than $115,000; and film pioneers Dick Turpin and Flora Finch, both at 71. Vaudeville lost a pioneer, Martin Beck, at 73, and the stage its "grand old man of show business," Daniel Frohman, at 89. Other deaths of the year included Dr. Paul Nipkow, television inventor who conceived the idea over 50 years before, at 80; and Ernest Thayer, author of the famous "Casey At the Bat," at the age of 77.

the roll of drums   Throughout the 1930s, the muffled overtone of war could be heard "offstage." The noises grew more disturbing each year, but America, enjoying a resurgence of prosperity and new security under the New Deal, preferred to concentrate its attention on the home front—until the bombs of the Fascist nations were too loud to hear the strains of "God Bless America" in comfort.

In 1933 Hitler, then the new Chancellor of Germany, was a curse at the American boxoffice. An anti-Hitler film made in Belgium was offered to New York exhibitors for three months, but nobody wanted to touch it. *Kultur,* a play ridiculing the German aversion to culture, laid a quick egg on Broadway. *Germany In Flames,* a Jewish production with a star cast, fo'ded in five days. In that year of depression, the American people had too much trouble with the wolf at the door to worry about the wolf at other peoples' doors.

Nevertheless, the first Hitler gags began to sneak into vaude and night club turns. A typical bit of business called for one actor to put his hand on his hip effeminately, while the other cracked, "Ah, a Hitlerite!," a reference to the notorious homosexuality rife in top Nazi ranks.

In 1934, Variety reported that night life in Nazi Berlin was at a standstill. Drinks at $1 and cigarettes at $3 a pack spelled no tourists—and no tourists spelled no night life. Ben Beyer, an American comedy cyclist, booked a month's stay at the Scala, Berlin, in 1936, explaining that he expected the Hitler regime to be defunct by that time.

In 1936 Mussolini, who had appeared three years earlier in a Columbia release called *Mussolini Speaks,* appropriated several million dollars for films that glorified war. The following year, with the Japanese end of the Axis alienating Americans by slicing into China, Hollywood stopped using Chinese villains—or at least used Chinese actors, but labeled them Japanese.

1938 was radio's big year—the year of the Anschluss in March, and Munich in September. The growing significance of political events in Europe began to dawn upon most Americans, who turned to their radios for enlightenment. Radio, sensing what was expected of them, turned from straight newscasts to political analysis. Commentators such as Fred Bate in London for NBC, and Ed Murrow for CBS were rapidly catapulted to fame.

War scares and excitement speeded the tempo of radio's growth from an entertainment medium to the nation's watch-tower. H. V. Kaltenborn, at the mike all day and all night, sleeping on a cot at CBS, became a household name. Max Jordan, Maurice Hindus, William Shirer and others sent their voices 3,000 miles across the Atlantic to inform an anxious American public.

Hitler's Nuremberg address of September 14, 1938 broadcast and translated over the networks, caused a nation-wide sensation. Radio's first-hand reports helped inspire the resolution of leading theatrical organizations and stars calling for a boycott of all trade with Germany. Concessionaires cashed in on the rising tide of anti-Fascism by putting Hitler's face on the old African Dodger game, and did a huge business with Americans who itched to bean Der Fuehrer with a speed ball.

Because of America's jumpy state of nerves—for which radio was unwittingly responsible—the Orson Welles radio scare succeeded much more brilliantly than radio executives expected. It also pointed up sharply the trust and reliance the American public had grown to place on radio, which made it now a kind of quasi-public service.

radio's new stars   The outbreak of war in 1939 placed
newscasters and commentators in the category of show business stars.
Each had a tremendous following, which tuned in faithfully for its
own favorite. Undoubtedly much of the commentary was flash stuff,
and even misleading, but on the whole the American public was
well informed. Aid to England would have been a dubious American possibility if the nation's sympathies and horror had not been
aroused by overseas broadcasts.

War news came so fast that year, one station's announcer actually
said, "We interrupt this flash to bring you another flash!" Shortwave listening increased vastly, with newspapermen among the more
eager dialers. The increasing excitement of the night hours also attracted new sponsors to late time slots which once had been impossible to sell.

It came as something of a shock to the American public in 1939
to hear over their radio some of the distortions and lies being aired
from Fascist European capitals. It made United States dialers appreciate their own radio—with all its commercial shortcomings—more
than ever before. It also convinced set owners that radio had an ob-
ligation to keep off the American airwaves United States counter-
parts of the poison peddlers rampant in Europe.

The movies joined the anti-Fascist crusade in 1939. Warner Bros.
produced *Confessions Of A Nazi Spy*. Fritz Kuhn, head of the German American Bund, fruitlessly sued for $5,000,000 libel, claiming,
"We are loyal Americans organized to uphold the Constitution of
the United States."

Interest in world events catapulted lecturers into top pay brackets.
Mrs. Nicholas Longworth received $1,200 a talk; Eve Curie, $1,000;
and Dorothy Thompson was too busy to accept $3,000 for a night's
engagement. Hitler had a depressing effect on the business of Arizona Indians, who blamed him for a sudden drop in the sales of
Navajo blankets, which bore old Indian designs that too closely resembled the Nazi swastika.

In the London of 1939, the Cocoanut Grove Night Club issued
handbills announcing, "Open as usual. Approved air raid shelters.
Refreshments and dancing from 10 P.M. by special request. Special
arrangements for officers in uniform of H.M. Forces. P.S.—The
safest niterie in London."

Radio was the show business standout through all of 1940—the crucial year of the Battle of Britain. It was radio, rather than newspapers, which kept a tense American public informed—almost at the moment of happening—of the collapse of Holland, Belgium, France; of the fall of Neville Chamberlain and the rise of Winston Churchill.

Radio contributed memorable on-the-spot descriptions of historic happenings—an achievement which later gave CBS the idea for its "You Are There" radio series, projecting listeners backward in time as it covered famous events in history, just as radio had covered them in 1940.

The British Broadcasting Corp. recorded a shot-by-shot description of the air battle over the Strait of Dover, the climax of the Battle of Britain. Radio covered the evacuation of Dunkirk, the bombing of Coventry, the scuttling of the *Graf See*. And it stimulated American recruiting by the shortwaved sounds of gunfire and explosions over London.

Commentators found their jobs growing increasingly perilous. Fred Bate, of NBC's Victoria Embankment offices, was wounded by a bomb fragment. Ed Murrow of CBS was twice blasted out of his London offices. Max Jordan was forced to do more of his broadcasting from Switzerland and less from Germany. William L. Shirer, Eric Severeid, Quentin Reynolds, Bill Downs and W. L. White were among the other commentators running the war gauntlet with a mike in one hand.

On this side of the ocean, commentators took the fragments of news pouring in and shaped them into meaningful designs for their listeners. Among the analysts whose names grew more famous daily were Elmer Davis, Raymond Gram Swing, John B. Kennedy, Paul Sullivan, H. V. Kaltenborn, Edwin C. Hill, Gabriel Heatter, and Boake Carter.

The drama of war via radio inspired American film stars to donate ambulances which raced through London bearing the names of their donors. Generosity of a somewhat less admirable calibre was demonstrated by audiences of the film theatres in the German Yorkville section of New York City who responded when the hat was passed for the Nazi Winter War Relief Fund.

And then the overture was finished, and the curtain was set to go up on the Big Show—once again.

PART SIX

BIG SHOW
1941 - 1945

Soldiers in Greasepaint

★

War work created a vast audience of Americans with a yen for entertainment and the means to pay for it. Booming defense industries made every night a Saturday night for show biz.

The nation buzzed with the noise of workers shedding white collars, and housewives shedding aprons, to pick up blowtorches and fat pay envelopes. To stop the traffic congestion on 6th Avenue, New York City ordered all employment agencies to list their job offerings inside, rather than on boards facing the sidewalk.

Actors on the road found it increasingly tough to get hotel accommodations. They were competing on one hand with defense workers moving into big cities, and on the other with the ever-increasing trade conventions. New floods of profits made their way principally to Miami, which had clothed itself in the garb of the French Riviera. Government funds, disguised as defense contract profits, oiled the gambling casinos, niteries, fashion salons.

While the Japs were mopping up in the Pacific—including American bases—newspaper readers devoured such tidbits that Mae West had won a divorce from Frank Wallace, whose 1911 marriage to her had lasted two weeks; and that Al Jolson's brother Harry lost a suit for $25,000 against Al, presumably representing the $150 a week Harry claimed Al had promised him for staying off the stage. Jolson again made news by marrying Erle Chennault Galbraith, niece of General Chennault, and 40 years his junior. She was an X-ray technician in the hospital where the star convalesced following his serious illness incurred in North Africa where he entertained our troops. It almost cost Jolson his life and cost him his left lung. This was an episode in *The Jolson Story* and *Jolson Sings Again,* both unusual in the rich history-making career of the great American star in that (1), it set a new pattern for filmusicals where a great star's voice was matched to a younger personation of the stellar subject, in this instance Larry Parks, of course; and (2), it was the first time that a pix biog had a sequel. Jolson was to repeat history for the third time by becoming the first big name to fly to Korea to sing for the United Nations troops in the fall of 1950. He died shortly after his return from the battlefront, "as much a war casualty as any GI," said the War Department which awarded him the Medal of Merit posthumously. Jolson's will was a dramatic, democratic document wherein he split his more than $4,000,000 estate equally to Jewish, Protestant, and Catholic charities, after setting up scholarships for needy undergraduates, a $1,000,000 trust fund for his widow, and $500,000 trusts for his two adopted children.

In 1943, the year the Allied forces invaded Italy and knocked Mussolini out of the war, Charles Chaplin's marriage to playwright Eugene O'Neill's daughter Oona also made news.

In 1945, the Allied year of victory, these tidbits further leavened the news: Peggy Hopkins Joyce's fifth marriage and Gloria Swanson's fifth divorce. The latter, five years later, was to make a signal comeback in Paramount's *Sunset Boulevard* film. Shirley Temple's marriage to John Agar made readers suddenly feel their age, although their subsequent divorce three years later was to spell box-office downbeat. George Jessel, who was accumulatively to earn the soubriquet of Toastmaster General of the United States for his yeoman after-dinner speechmaking through the length and breadth of the country, formally notified radio networks that he was "not amused" at the avalanche of radio comedians' gags about his private life and child brides. The only exception, he noted, was that anything Eddie Cantor or Fred Allen quipped about him was OK with him.

winchell vs. isolationists   Meanwhile, Jessel's and Cantor's fellow-alumnus of a Gus Edwards "School Days" act, yclept Walter Winchell, was slugging the isolationists on his broadcasts. Three Montana stations dropped his program, for which Winchell blamed isolationist Senator Burton K. Wheeler. In 1943, the Andrew Jergens Co. ("with lotions of love"), worried about their $5,000-a-week hot potato, tried to tone Winchell down, but he refused. The following year he tore into Martin Dies of the Un-American Activities Committee, then confounded that gent by letting him go on the Winchell program for a 15-minute rebuttal of Winchell accusations.

The power that one man on radio could wield was demonstrated in 1945 when Winchell advised listeners to sell stocks and not get stuck when the crash came. The market promptly broke. Winchell didn't quite mean it that strongly, and thereafter was more cautious about his prognostications. More affirmatively he sparked the Damon Runyan Cancer Fund, collecting $5,000,000 for cancer research, which is still going strong. In turn, fellow columnist Ed Sullivan became active in promoting the Heart Fund, while the Alfred J. McCosker-Harry Hershfield Cardiac Home was a continuing charity, as spark-plugged by the former WOR-Mutual Network board chairman and the veteran newspaper columnist-cartoonist. Incidentally, Jergens' caution about Winchell notwithstanding, it upped his $5,000 fee to $7,500, and successive sponsors, Kaiser-Frazer and Richard Hudnut, with their $12,500 fees made Winchell's $1,000-a-minute the record high compensation on the radio, considering that his 15-minute Sunday night newscast reduces to 12½ minutes net, after opening, middle and end commercials.

The dime-dance-and-romance philosophy, an outcropping of

America's defense program, suddenly froze on the day of December 7, 1941. The news was so stunning that theatre managers and night club owners forgot, for a while, to notice that the boxoffice was dead. It stayed dead for several weeks, while the nation strove to get its bearings. The impact was too strong and overwhelming to escape via entertainment—that would come later.

Top showmen offered their services to the Government as dollar-a-year men. Others, notably Elmer Davis and Robert E. Sherwood, went to Washington to take part in hemispheric defense work. Billy Rose staged a giant benefit at Madison Square Garden to help the United Services Organization (USO) raise $10,000,000. A check for $100,000 went to the USO for troop entertainment, signed by Edward G. Robinson.

Actors readily agreed to managers' plans for paying off 25 per cent of their salaries in Government bonds. Philadelphia film houses charged aluminum pots and pans as the price of admission. Broadway opened the first Stage Door Canteen, a tremendous hit with GI's, and provided free theatre tickets which earned New York the reputation as the nation's "friendliest city" in Army circles.

uso-camp shows USO-Camp Shows received a $500,000 appropriation, later raised to $800,000, which started nine out of 24 proposed Army shows rolling. Each camp show unit was paid between $2,500 and $3,000 a week for its 28 to 30 members. The first two-hour touring unit opened at Camp Upton, New York, on a percentage basis, with 20 per cent of the gross going to the post exchange fund. This show offered a 10-girl orchestra plus an 8-girl dance chorus. The first legitimate unit for the camps was *My Sister Eileen*. The first Army show produced by soldiers was a satire called "The Wizard of Ord" by soldiers at Fort Ord, California.

England's equivalent to the USO—E.N.S.A.—was supported by Government funds, rather than public subscription. Top salaries paid actors were $80 a week, with the minimum set at $16, plus transportation and board. Prime Minister Churchill drafted Gracie Fields for an American fund-raising tour. In 10 weeks of one-nighters in the United States and Canada, she raised $302,000 for British War Relief. In London during the same year, Bebe Daniels and Ben Lyon introduced a song called, "Thanks Mr. Roosevelt," to convey British appreciation of the President's aid to Britain. *ENSA* stood for the Entertainments National Service Association.

Variety's editor summed up what show biz was doing for the war in 1942 with some unabashed sentiment: " 'Morale,' it is called, from the front line to the home front. Morale means entertainment; entertainment means making a heavy heart lighter—a strained day of work or warfare just a shade brighter. The man at the front is sustained by a song on his lips; the men and women on the home front, ceaselessly twisting bolts and riveting steel, are bolstered by a laugh. To dwell on 'morale' may be something akin to corning a cliché, but whatever its label, it's entertainment—and entertainment is Show Business."

Glum news from the fighting fronts dented the Broadway b.o. during spring and summer, making New York "a weekend town." But the weekends were big, Saturday night crowds reminiscent of New Year's Eve. The war made Sunday performances permanent on Broadway, which helped ease the blow suffered by the blackout of all New York marquees.

Getting around the Main Stem became increasingly difficult. All Broadway traffic lights were hooded in dimout covers, showing only slits of light. Tire restrictions, anti-parking regulations, air raid and blackout precautions, gas rationing all helped to scare away the out-of-town trade. Thursdays were particularly glum because of the blackout tests from 9:00 P.M. to 9:30 P.M. MAIN STEM A GHOST ALLEY, headlined Variety. MAZDA LANE HAS SHOT ITS WATTS.

With war plants going on a 24-hour basis, midnight shows became popular throughout the country. The road, despite all the crippling restrictions and delays in travel, began to enjoy a huge revival.

topical stuff   The gagsters began to reap a harvest of new corn. Old jokes were refurbished with new topics—impudent waiters, gas rationing, the omnipotent butcher, priceless nylons, the vanishing servant, rationed tires, rubber salvage and meatless Tuesdays. Broadway knew it was at war when it saw femme cabdrivers.

Show business continued to furnish a heavy share of the nation's top taxpayers. Out of 3,000 Americans who paid taxes on over $25,000 a year, 800 came from show business. The $25,000-a-year ceiling for earnings caused a minor panic in Hollywood, where some stars conceived the idea to finance their own units to get out from under via a "capital gain."

On the patriotic side of the ledger, Equity announced in 1942 that 25 per cent of its membership was already in uniform. Equity bestowed on each of its soldiers and sailors a subscription-for-the-duration to Variety, which furnished a special rate.

The Stage Door Canteen, set up by the American Theatre Wing in the basement of the 44th Street Theatre (the old Little Club), which the Shuberts donated rent free, became famous in 1942 as the mecca for any man in a uniform. Buttons popped along the White Way when Mrs. Roosevelt declared it was the finest of all contributions toward war morale. Branches popped up in Washington and Philadelphia, and finally the Hollywood Canteen opened in a blaze of klieg lights. Stars came not only to entertain but also to wash dishes.

Theatres helped in the junk salvage campaign, collecting scrap iron, copper, brass, zinc, aluminum, lead, rubber, rags, manila rope and burlap. The United Theatrical War Activities Committee enlisted disaster units of singers, dancers and comics, prepared to rush into any bombed zone of New York to help victims. The Criterion Theatre, on Broadway, turned its lobby over to selling "Crack-A-Jap" cocktails for a dime apiece—the cocktails being glasses of water plus a 10¢ defense stamp.

Abe Lastfogel, Marvin Schenck and Howard Dietz took up an idea started by Winchell, and staged a Navy benefit show at Madison Square Garden. Boxes went for $1,000 apiece, seats at $16.50 top. Sales of a 55-page souvenir program netted $35,000 alone. The one performance earned $142,000, an all-time record for any one-shot theatrical performance. Show business also united in the Army-Navy drive for relief collections, and helped garner the lion's share of over $2,000,000 raised.

this is the army   The show business sensation of 1942 was Irving Berlin's soldier show—*This Is The Army*—sequel to his World War I *Yip Yip Yaphank*. It opened on the Fourth of July for a 4-week date, but the demand for tickets was so overwhelming that it stayed on Broadway for 12 weeks, averaging $47,000 a week.

Yaphank in World War I had grossed $83,000 in its 4 weeks' stay in New York at $2.20 top. It was primed to build a barracks for actors visiting Camp Upton's Liberty Theatre, and didn't go on any road tour. *This Is The Army,* in its three years on tour, plus revenues from the Warner Bros. movie version, turned over to the Army Emergency Relief Fund almost $10,000,000—the most fabulous fortune earned by one show, and easily the biggest private gift ever turned over to the United States Government. In time Uncle Sam honored Berlin with the Legion of Merit.

Canadian Navy Relief had its own service show; the British staged theirs abroad also, although its E.N.S.A. units in Australia and other South Pacific outposts contributed most of the morale entertainment. Moss Hart staged the ambitious *Winged Victory* for the Army Air Force; there was a Coast Guard special musical revue, and others.

uso camp shows—the new big time   The USO Camp Shows circuit of 1943 was the new bigtime—bigger than even vaudeville in its heyday. The combined USO tour offered an act seven years of playing time—if it were possible to play the whole circuit. With a $14,000,000 budget, the USO was spending $100,000 a month for soldier entertainment. Bert Lytell, on a civilian committee advising the organization, drew only $8,000 in expenses for the full-time job. It was largely through his counsel that soldiers at Fort Meade, Maryland, were given a chance to see *Macbeth*—and to the amazement of the camp's top brass, asked for "more of that Shakespeare stuff." Subsequently, Major Maurice Evans' streamlined version of *Hamlet* proved a big hit with the GIs in the Pacific areas.

Kay Kyser was one of the camp circuits' most energetic adherents, giving a record 1,700 shows in service bases. When commended for this patriotic duty beyond call, he cracked, "It's not only fun, but where else can I get meat?"

Mayor LaGuardia unveiled the service flag of show business in Times Square during 1943. It showed 135 gold stars, and 78,808 members in the armed services. President Roosevelt paid further tribute to the patriotism of show business at a Madison Square Garden benefit for the Red Cross.

Show people put on a testimonial show called "Theatre People's Dedication To A Cause" at the Winter Garden, paying tribute to actors entertaining soldiers at home and at the fronts, and to the USO-Camp Shows' victims of that plane tragedy at Lisbon.

During 1943 actors began to perform in factories during lunch hours as a morale stimulant to war production. In San Francisco, film theatres ran help-wanted trailers and slides for shipbuilders; and the Frisco Stage Door Canteen made its debut, as host to over 9,000 service men. The nation's writers sent their scripts to the Writers War Board, and gags, skits and blackouts were made available to soldiers for their own entertainment.

In the 1943 bond-selling ranks, Kate Smith led all the others with a total of $37,000,000 worth to her credit—a good share of which was paid for the privilege of listening to "God Bless America." Ralph Edwards was the next strongest bond salesman, with a radio record of $34,000,000. To help raise $17,000,000 for Camp Shows and foreign war relief, Ben Hecht packed them into Madison Square Garden to see "Tribute to Gallantry," a pageant with 300 in the cast, depicting the struggle of the world's little people against barbarism.

zoot-suiters   There was also a liquor shortage, which led to a 10:30 P.M. curfew of saloons and liquor stores. Harlem had some riots over the early shutdowns. The general dimout of New York itself stimulated crime. Teen-agers, left to shift for themselves by overtime fathers and factory-working mothers. turned to zoot suits, flagrantly loud and overlong costumes introduced by Mexicans in Los Angeles, as a method of winning the attention they were being denied in their homes. Zoot suits soon became associated with juvenile delinquency. Zoot-suiters, aided by "zooterinas," plagued theatre managers by slashing seats and defacing restrooms.

The teen-age crime wave was not limited to New York or Los Angeles. A spree of pyromania broke out in theatres all over the country, almost all of it traced to youthful vandals, who were particularly active in Pittsburgh. So many juveniles were stealing into theatres via side doors and fire escapes that managers were forced to put up signs outside these exits warning that breaking in was a Federal offense, because of the failure to pay the Federal amusement tax.

The boxoffice was so big in 1943 that it completely disregarded the usual seasonal limitations. Grosses for Holy Week, instead of taking its traditional drop, actually exceeded normal biz. There was a slight letdown at matinee performances, but this was attributed to the effects of victory gardens and women going into factories.

The star branch of 1944 show business was legit. The American Theatre Wing, at the request of Army heads, prepared and financed an Army production of *The Barretts of Wimpole Street* (with Katharine Cornell) and turned it over to USO Camp Shows. This was followed by Ruth Gordon's *Over 21,* and 22 other legitimate shows. They were designed to play both the United States camps and the foxhole circuit overseas. Show business won new applause when famous stars donned the USO uniform and went to the Pacific and the E.T.O. to entertain troops near the fighting fronts.

cantor's 'purple heart circuit'   That year Eddie Cantor created the "Purple Heart Circuit." Actors toured hospitals to perform at the bedsides of sick and wounded soldiers. There were also a large number of "Lunchtime Follies" troupes, which provided noon entertainment in factories for factory workers. Kate Smith stuck to her bond sales division, a year after her 1943 record of $37,000,000, making Washington dizzy by selling $108,000,000 worth in just 18½ hours of singing and plugging. Eddie Cantor's bond drive turned in a total of $40,000,000 sales in 24 straight hours.

Al Jolson, knocking himself out playing bond rallies and hospitals, felt a little bitter about some of his colleagues who continued to "fight the Battle of the Brown Derby" in Hollywood. He felt strongly, as Harry Lauder did that year, when the great Scots entertainer refused a fat offer for his film biography by explaining tersely, "This is no time for private gain."

The O.P.A. travel ban of 1944 hit show business where it hurt. New York theatres were silent, but the city's hotels squawked when Mayor LaGuardia asked vacationists to stay away from New York. The year was one of stringencies—paper shortages for newspapers or theatre programs (many New York dailies had to turn down many columns of advertising); cigarette shortages; and few of the other things Americans had learned to do without since Pearl Harbor. Liquor began to reappear in stores, but a bottle of Scotch was still coin of the realm in buying favors or scarce goods.

Show business, almost to a man, backed Roosevelt for a fourth term, and showed it at a New York rally to urge his re-election. Some show business figures decided to run along with him. In California movie actor Albert Dekker, radio commentator Hal Styles, and Melvyn Douglas' wife, Helen Gahagan Douglas, ran on the Democratic ticket and won state and Federal offices.

Show business was still helping to write American history in 1945, the year of victory. Comedian Joe E. Brown, whose son had been killed in the war, was presented with the Bronze Star for his tireless work in entertaining front-line troops in the Pacific. Abe Lastfogel, head of USO-Camp Shows, received the Medal of Freedom for outstanding service.

Show business put its shock troops once again into the job of putting the 7th War Bond drive over. *Here's Your Infantry,* a pageant put on at the Yankee Stadium, sold over $10,000,000 in bonds. Broadway legitimate theatres—16 of them—arranged special matinees for purchasers of war bonds. The best seats were awarded according to the scale of the bond . . . from $25,000 to $25. The unions contributed their services for the matinee gratis. In New York, 23 department stores took page ads in the New York papers to plug the shows, which chalked up 19,100 individual sales. All of show business that year joined, in honor of the late President Roosevelt, to put over the March of Dimes. Some 13,000 theatres helped raise over $5,000,000 for paralysis sufferers.

With their jobs done, the Broadway and Hollywood Stage Canteens closed their doors, to great applause. Show business also revealed that during three years of war, over 9,000,000 free tickets to shows had been given to servicemen—only 35 per cent of whom had ever seen live entertainment before. Although the gesture was intended generously, there was no doubt but that it had also served as a sampling campaign, whetting the appetite of a new young audience for the legitimate theatre.

V-J Day on Broadway, with all motor traffic stopped by the police, provided a colorful spectacle which even show business at its most ingenious couldn't equal. Four years of worry, waiting and inhibitions exploded in wild jubilation. While in New York harbor the first boats from the Pacific were bringing home troops.

Almost overnight the cry rose all over the land, "Bring 'em all home!" Politicians made hasty promises, but the Army, which knew better, called on show business again to help keep things in hand. It wanted all the second-hand saxophones, trumpets and trombones it could get for use overseas—anything that would blare or bleat.

In one week it garnered 700. If GI Joe had to lay in his foreign bunk, sweating out transportation, he could at least blow his brains out dreaming of a white Christmas.

50

Radio Goes to War

★

During 1940 and 1941, prior to Pearl Harbor, radio found itself exalted to new heights as the nation's forum for important discussions of our foreign policy. With as many as 30 or 40 million listeners tuned in simultaneously, the spoken word gathered a tremendous new importance. While the world at war waited anxiously for America to make up its mind, Americans turned to their radios to have their minds made up for them.

The networks had to be careful to maintain an unbiased position —that of the owner of a great hall who rents it out for a debate. Hollywood could and did take the initiative in making anti-Fascist and pro-British films. Radio could not—without raising a storm of protest from isolationist listeners. Radio had no legal right to propagandize on the air, which belonged to the American people, and was only allotted to them by the F.C.C. It did the next best thing and offered freedom of speech for all viewpoints—reasoning correctly that the Fascist line was bound to lose out in free competition with the pro-Allied cause.

The events of December 7, 1941 automatically ended "the great debate." But before they did, Charles A. Lindbergh had made the mistake of unpolitic remarks in Des Moines, Iowa, in 1941. Almost immediately, Station WOR refused to give him any time unless he dropped his pro-Berlin accent, an example followed by many other stations. Hard-hitting radio commentators sarcastically asked Lindbergh to prove his disaffection for Hitler by melting down the medal the Nazis had awarded to him in 1938.

The Lindbergh issue, and heated debates over forum programs, led one Massachusetts state senator to introduce a bill dealing with radio slander. It was killed because, explained Senator Blanchard, "slander never hurt anybody."

Radio was the vehicle of many historic broadcasts throughout 1941, up to and including December. In May listeners heard Stephen Vincent Benet's classic, "Nightmare of Noon," and Carleton Morse's "The Case of Robert." In August there was the star-studded "Treasury Hour." On December 2, there was Archibald MacLeish's "Introduction of Murrow." On the 7th, the unforgettable news broadcasts. On the 9th, President Roosevelt speaking on Pearl Harbor. On the 15th, Norman Corwin's "Bill of Rights." And on the 26th, Winston Churchill's address to the United States Senate. This was radio—a new, adult radio—in 1941.

Station WMCA, New York, won commendation that year with its program, "Listen America Now," designed to foster the spirit of fraternity and tolerance among youngsters. The show contained one blue-ribbon line, spoken by a boy: "If you don't like another kid, don't call him dirty names because of his race. Just shout, 'You're a stinker'!" That pretty well summed up the case for democracy.

With radio's new maturity came a growing appreciation by sponsors of the worth of its advertising time. The industry net rose staggeringly from $44,296,000 in 1940 to $107,500,000 in 1941. This despite the cancellations by some advertisers, especially in the cosmetic line, who could not get essential ingredients for their products. Jack Benny's 10th year on radio was celebrated by his friends with a special congratulatory section in Variety.

Major Bowes, after nearly 1,000 weeks on the air starting in 1922, finally bowed out.

All of radio chipped in to plug United States bonds, and were credited with much of the $707,000,000 sales record chalked up by June of 1941.

The war made a number of changes in radio the following year. All request song numbers were dropped by programs, Army brass fearing that the titles might contain enemy codes. Sirens were eliminated on all programs, to prevent any listener's confusion, à la the famous Orson Welles broadcast. Weather reports were eliminated for fear of giving vital information to enemy air forces.

603 radio war shows A count showed 603 war shows on the networks—202 newscasts, 173 war commentaries, and 54 others with a martial overtone. One program, beamed abroad in collaboration with the Office of War Information (O.W.I.) overseas branch, gave "News From Home"—keeping a small-town flavor, talking about minor league baseball, rural politics, and hot music. It was radio's way of making the small-town boy feel closer to home, wherever he was.

Radio's boxoffice bulged in 1943 with the four networks earning $150,000,000 in billings—an all-time high. The prevailing trend, despite the war—or rather, because of it—was humor. Top comedy scripters, once hat-in-hand as ad agency executives spelled out terms, now dickered like full-fledged stars. Quiz shows came back, with announcers who played them heavily for laughs—Ralph Edwards, Phil Baker, John Reed King, Bob Hawk, Bill Slater, Paul Douglas, Kay Kyser, Parks Johnson, Bill Cullen, Warren Hull and Garry Moore.

The church was not slow to cash in, via radio, on the resurge of religious feeling in the nation, as a result of parental worry over boys in the service. Variety estimated the church collection, via appeals over the airwaves, at $200,000,000 a year, and noted the program listings of local stations as top-heavy with religious shows. "The church," it concluded, "has become big biz in radio." Gospel broadcasting paid the Mutual network its biggest individual revenue —$1,566,130—with programs like "The Pilgrim Hour," and "Old Fashioned Revival Hour" beamed to 211 stations.

Variety itself went radio in 1943, when Philco sponsored its "Hall of Fame," a one-hour show. Variety selected the cream entertainment, a kind of Hit Parade of all show business, with the top names appearing before its mike. Show biz grinned as it turned to the radio reviews in the paper, and while Variety liked its own first show very much indeed, some of the later ones came in for considerable panning. Variety's editor, Abel Green, was co-producer and co-author of the weekly Philco-"Hall of Fame" presentations.

Other radio notes of 1943 included the appointment of Paul Whiteman as musical director of the Blue Network; the bowout of the kiddies' Uncle Don from WOR after 18 years; and Pepsi-Cola's anguished demand of all radio comics to stop using its product as a target for radio tomfoolery.

For its war record that year, radio contributed $6,500,000 worth of free time to plug the Second War Loan. The following year radio shelved millions of dollars' worth of revenue to go all-out for coverage of D-Day, radio's biggest story in its history. This didn't prevent another record-smashing year—$383,900,000 in 1944, of which the $250,000 spent by Republicans and Democrats for vote-snaring was merely pin-money.

Censorship reared its head in 1944 when Eddie Cantor was cut off the air while singing "We're Having a Baby (My Baby and Me)," excerpt from his legit musical, *Banjo Eyes*. The "objectionable" lyrics ran:

GIRL: *Thanks to you, life is bright, you brought me joy beyond measure.*
CANTOR: *Don't thank me, quite all right, honestly it was a pleasure.*
GIRL: *Just think—it's my first one.*
CANTOR: *The next one is on me.*

Sponsors were summarily off the air left and right during 1945, when history claimed their air time. Within several weeks there was news of the atomic bomb, the Russian declaration of war against Japan, and V-J Day. When the Japanese surrender was official at 7 P.M., Aug. 14, 1945, radio was prepared. All of its programs and facilities were turned over to complete and full coverage of the significance of events.

Prior to V-J Day, world news also crowded out paid radio time. There was the death of President Roosevelt in April, with a three-day mourning period. The month also produced the San Francisco Conference, demanding radio coverage, and in May—V-E Day. Commercial radio was blitzed out of its time slots to the tune of $500,000 network loss.

The most important dramatic broadcast of the year was Norman Corwin's V-E Day "On a Note of Triumph," a beautifully-written summation of the war and its significance, and a jewel in the diadem of radio's 25th anniversary.

Variety noted that year the progress made in radio by women entertainers, either solo or in double harness. The lack of male talent, increasingly serious as the war progressed, found the women taking on the burden of network shows, and carrying them successfully. Among the outstanding radio women of 1945 were Kate Smith, Joan Davis, Dinah Shore, Ginny Simms, Gracie Fields, Arlene Francis, Judy Canova, the Andrews Sisters, Fanny Brice, Charlotte Greenwood, Hildegarde, Mary Small and Beatrice Kay. They accounted for much of the $46,864,000 talent cost for 1945, which was $7,000,000 higher than for 1944.

There were no new exciting personality discoveries, although ex-Mayor LaGuardia proved a radio find at $3,000 a week, after first clicking over the municipal-owned WNYC Sunday morning broadcasts by reading the funnies. Ex-Police Commissioner Valentine of New York also took to the airwaves. One wag suggested that before any candidate for New York City office was seriously considered, he would first pass an NBC audition.

video's 1941 brushoff   The progress made in television that year was mostly in the words department. "Make every theatre a pari-mutuel outpost," suggested Thomas F. Joyce, vice-president of RCA. "Houses can be connected with racetracks by television so that patrons can see better than if they were in the grandstand. They can open a pari-mutuel window to accept bets, just as is done at the track. It would provide the Government with added sources of taxation."

The New Yorker Theatre, at a cost of $30,000, rented tele equipment, including a 15 x 20 screen to televise the fight between Billy Soose and Ken Overlin at the Madison Square Garden, which used a pink canvas for the event. An audience of 1,200 watched, complained of eye-strain, declared the pictures were not as clear as the newsreels.

The first rate card was issued to sponsors for television in 1945. Charges included $120 for a weekday evening hour, $60 for a weekday afternoon hour, $90 for an hour Sunday afternoon. News, weather and time spots called for $8 a minute evenings, $4 a minute during the day. There was also a production charge of $150 an hour for the use of large studios, $75 an hour for smaller ones. Five years later a TV network hour came to $20,000-$25,000, depending on the number of outlets.

First sponsors (for NBC) were Sun Oil, Proctor & Gamble and

Lever Bros., who put their plugs on video baseball games that emerged in a blurry and indecisive manner.

In 1943, Dumont's W2XWV televised entertainment from night clubs under the title: "Wednesday Night Session." The first live show in 16 months for NBC's New York outlet, WNBT, was a video version of the Madison Square Garden rodeo. With only one camera riding with the broncos, the camera work was unimaginative. Reception was clear when there was little movement in the arena—but when the cowboys were letting 'er rip, the result was a series of blurred shadows.

NBC, which had been granted the first commercial tele license by the FCC in 1931, maintained a limited schedule of weekly broadcasts of films, sporting events and modest studio stuff during 1944. Chicago's WBKB that year televised the first video show produced, written and directed by service personnel—a Navy show, to sell war bonds. Variety, seeing the handwriting on the wall—even if it was just the back wall—inaugurated a television department in its format.

The largest audience to view a tele show up to 1945 was on hand for NBC's preview of long distance video hookups. The Curtis Publishing Co. picked up the bill for a telecast of the Army-Navy game in Philadelphia, which went out to viewers in Philly, New York and Schenectady.

But the end result of this phase of the kilocycle era was evidence in plenty that radio had come of age. It did a terrific job for morale, and proved just as vividly successful in projecting direct contact between Government and the people, whether it was President Roosevelt's "fireside chats" or directives and other "messages" integrated into the more popular radio scripts. It set the pattern for information not only within our own borders but around the world whenever a crisis called for beaming direct to the masses. Thought control by totalitarian ideologies can never be wholly regimented under such auspices.

51

New Stars Are Born

★

The first impact of the war on Hollywood was newsreel censorship. The Navy cracked down on shots of naval vessels under construction, forcing their deletion despite newsreel executives' protest that no secrets were revealed.

Senator Nye opened up on Hollywood from Washington, charging —before Pearl Harbor—that the movie moguls were "guilty" of "warmongering." December 7 provided a belated and ironic vindication of Hollywood's allegedly "premature" anti-Fascist stand. Senator Nye had no harsh words for Germany, whose Nazi propaganda film *Lowland Blitzkrieg,* was playing at Yorkville's 86th Street Theatre. While anti-Nazi German-Americans picketed the theatre, anyone showing a membership card in one of the "approved" organizations was offered free admission.

The new high war taxes made stars less ambitious. Many, instead of working for dollars they couldn't cling to, cut their schedules and divided their time between loafing and playing benefits. The new taxes were estimated to be costing Hollywood an extra $55,000,000 a year. Despite this, Hollywood helped raise $2,000,000 for various war charities—20 per cent of the quota for the whole Los Angeles area.

Principal trend of the 1941 films, to relieve the grimness of newspaper headlines, was comedy—low comedy, of which Abbott & Costello were undisputed top dogs. Close behind them as boxoffice favorites were Bob Hope and Mickey Rooney, with Bette Davis clicking in the drama division. One of the year's top grossers was a Technicolor outdoor yarn, *Northwest Mounted Police.*

The year's most unusual film was Orson Welles' *Citizen Kane,* which outraged William Randolph Hearst, who took it personally and forced as many theatres as he could to boycott it. Hearst's rancor against the film was so great that Hollywood feared Hearst would blast the entire movie colony because of it.

Academy laurels that year went to Joan Fontaine for her role in *Suspicion,* and to Gary Cooper for *Sergeant York.* The Academy film award went to *How Green Was My Valley* and its director, John Ford. Other credits were divided among *Here Comes Mr. Jordan* (Robert Montgomery), *Citizen Kane* and Walt Disney's *Dumbo.*

The National Archives in Washington that year received 53,840 cubic feet of historical records—everything from film shots of the Coolidge and Hoover administrations and World War I activities to sound recordings of 60 Indian tribe dialects and sign languages, Amos 'n' Andy and the Columbia Workshop.

During 1942 stars were coaxed out of their "why-should-I-work?" attitude by some sage producer arguments. In the first place, said the producers, stars owed it to their public—were they going to be dollar patriots? In the second place, if the stars refused to go before the cameras often enough, they risked having the public forget them. The stars saw the light, $25,000 salary limitation or not.

peak pix attendance   Film audiences had never been so large as they were in 1942—an estimated 90,000,000 a week, all prosperous on defense paychecks. Hollywood was feeling prosperous, too. The total film gross for 1941 had tallied $1,100,000,000—or just $100,000,000 better than for the preceding year. Calamity howlers among the executives who mournfully predicted that the new 60-hour work week would prove disastrous to the pix biz shut up.

Benefits proved booby-traps to many Hollywood stars. A star who had played perhaps a dozen in one week, and who begged off a 13th, was frequently threatened with stigmatization as "unpatriotic." To ease the situation, a special bureau was formed to "assign" benefits to actors, and all requests had to clear through this bureau.

One of the amusing transformations made by the war in Hollywood was the sprucing up of Russian characters in films. Until 1942, movie Russians were either wild comic characters, evil menaces, or hopelessly inept stooges. With Russia our ally, the Russians shown by Hollywood were quickly shaved, washed, sober, good to the folks, 100 per cent family men, Rotarians, Elks, and 33° wowsers.

Leading the boxoffice parade of 1942 were Gary Cooper, Abbott &

Costello, Betty Grable, Mickey Rooney, Bob Hope, Dorothy Lamour, Spencer Tracy, Jack Benny and Bing Crosby. Greer Garson won acting honors for *Mrs Miniver,* while James Cagney carried off the male Oscar for impersonating George M. Cohan in *Yankee Doodle Dandy*—the first film biography of a then still-living show biz prominent. Jerome Kern also lived to see Metro's *Till the Clouds Roll By,* a more or less loose biopic of his career; and another Metro filmusical, *Words and Music,* was based on the careers of the late Lorenz (Larry) Hart and the very much alive Richard Rodgers (now so successfully teamed with Oscar Hammerstein 2d.) Topping all, of course, was Columbia Pictures' *The Jolson Story.* That, with its sequel, *Jolson Sings Again,* again gave the fabulous Al Jolson the edge on any show biz cycle.

Nostalgia and sentiment about famous or distinguished show business figures inspired a host of filmusical biographicals. Irving Berlin says he'll never have his biopic made during his lifetime since he counts upon that as an important heritage for his family when he passes, although the 20th Century-Fox filmization, *Alexander's Ragtime Band* in 1938, was misconstrued by many to be a loose version of his career. There have been and will be biopix based on the life and times of Paul Dresser, Dan Emmett, Oscar Hammerstein I, Will Rogers, the late Bert Kalmar & Harry Ruby, Eddie Cantor, Marilyn Miller, Sime Silverman (*Mr. Broadway,* written by Abel Green, for Warner Bros.), Nora Bayes & Jack Norworth, Fred Fisher, Texas Guinan, Gus Kahn and Joe E. Howard.

Others winning cinematurgical distinction were Van Heflin for his work in *Johnny Eager,* Irving Berlin for his song, "White Christmas" (part of the *Holiday Inn* score); and Walt Disney for his short, "Der Fuehrer's Face."

By 1943 Hollywood began to feel the pinch of the loss of male talent—stars as well as the men behind the cameras. But to its own amazement the loss did not seem too important. Second-rate films, with second-rate stars, cleaned up. First-rate films continued to set new records. Films without any stars wound up with over $2,000,000 rentals. One of the major companies found it had grossed $16,000,000 on just six fair films.

flock of indie producers   The Hollywood gold mine brought independent producers into action by the dozens. Many reasoned, correctly, that with the $25,000 salary limitation, stars could be coaxed away from major studios by percentage deals and shares in film proceeds, which could be spread out over a longer period. But early in 1943, Congress tossed out the salary ceiling, and the inducement of the independents lost its punch. They went ahead nevertheless, with or without stars.

Hollywood lost 29,000 men to the armed services. Of these, only a handful were important b.o. names, but those few stars represented hundreds of millions of potential ticket sales. To offset their loss, major studios began to pay higher prices for plays and books, as well as studio scripts, to give weaker star names strong support at the boxoffice. Older film stars, whose lustre had faded, were dusted off and thrust before the cameras again. Simultaneously, all studios engaged in a vigorous talent hunt. "God makes stars," said Samuel Goldwyn. "It's up to the producers to find them."

Among the new stars to emerge were a dog, Lassie; a horse, Flicka; and an elderly actor, Charles Coburn, who was to win an Academy Oscar for best support in *The More The Merrier.* The year also produced Jennifer Jones in *Song of Bernadette,* Paul Lukas in *Watch On the Rhine,* and Katina Paxinou in *For Whom the Bell Tolls* (Ingrid Bergman-Gary Cooper), all of whom won Academy awards. William Saroyan's *The Human Comedy* (Mickey Rooney-Frank Morgan), Norman Krasna's *Princess O'Rourke,* Irving Berlin's *This Is the Army* and Frank Sinatra's RKO short, *This Land Is Mine* also got nods from the Academy.

Female stars enjoyed a tremendous war worker and soldier vogue, with their cheesecake photos in high demand. Pin-ups of Betty Grable, Dorothy Lamour, Lana Turner, Jinx Falkenburg, Hedy Lamarr and Donna Drake headed the list of stills, many sold for 50¢ apiece. And their male following packed their films, even when admission prices were boosted an average of 28¢ during the year.

Hollywood's policy of building skyrocket stardom for newcomers, to replace the missing old faces, paid off handsome dividends in 1944. Older stars, who had stuck to their guns about laying off after one or two films a year, because of taxes, began to regard their laurels anxiously as the public demonstrated its enthusiasm for new faces.

Metro's Van Johnson and Frank Sinatra; 20th-Fox's Jennifer Jones; Sam Goldwyn's Danny Kaye; Warners' Lauren Bacall, were the new hot stuff.

Among the new ingenues were 20th Century-Fox's June Haver; Paramount's Diana Lynn and Louise Allbritton.

RKO gave its all to Sinatra (on a split contract with Metro), build-him with *Higher and Higher* and *Step Lively,* and lending him out to Metro for *Anchors Aweigh.* Metro also came up swimmingly with Esther Williams.

Academy honors, however, were reserved for the established stars that year. Crosby walked off with the Oscar for his blithe priest in *Going My Way,* and Ingrid Bergman for her slow torture in *Gaslight.* Ethel Barrymore won recognition for her moving supporting role in *None But the Lonely Heart,* and Barry Fitzgerald for his support of Crosby in *Going My Way.*

hollywood's morale job   With the West Coast the important staging area that it was for the GIs going to the Pacific fronts, Hollywood and San Francisco had an important function in the war entertainment formula, particularly the glamor-loaded Hollywood. The Hollywood Victory Committee did a particularly laudable job in rotating top names to Veterans' Hospitals as well as training camps. Shows ran from the portable jeep variety—a mobile stage on a jeep, with portable mike, an emcee, guitar player, comic and/or singer, and the like. Sometimes a harmonica player substituted for the guitar. Writers mobilized by making plays and playlets, comedy skits and joke files available to one and all—the touring professionals and for self-entertainment by GI talents in the camps.

Hollywood was also winning recognition that year for its morale service in supplying films for the fighting fronts. Many a GI was tickled to reflect, as he sat on an oil can in a coconut grove in the Pacific, that he was watching a film premiere before it had even reached Broadway. GIs sent home amusing stories of the reactions of island natives who watched the first films they had ever seen with a mixture of awe, terror and fascination.

In recognition of Hollywood's service, the Government issued a special postage stamp, honoring the 50th anniversary of the industry. The design showed GIs and WACs looking at an open-air screen on a South Pacific island.

Films played an historic role throughout the war in helping train raw recruits in record time through Government shorts, which were an integral part of training camp curriculum. At the close of the war they served another Government purpose—evidence at trials of Nazi criminals. Atrocity films were also released for general distribution in the United States, inspiring renewed demands for a tough peace.

Hollywood turned out two fine pieces of work that year, for which the movie colony won handsome recognition. The first was a 10-minute reel called *The House I Live In,* in which Sinatra punched home the lessons of democracy and anti-discrimination to his teen-age following. The second was *The Lost Weekend,* which won the Academy Award, and inspired a new approach toward chronic drinking as an illness, rather than a matter of moral turpitude.

The major studios revealed that they were spending $3,000,000 a year in salaries to employees in the service—including the ubiquitous Mickey Rooney, whom Uncle Sam tapped in 1945.

new film czar   Eric Johnston was appointed the new head of the Motion Picture Producers & Distributors Association, succeeding the original film "czar," Will H. Hays, and Jean Hersholt succeeded Walter Wanger as head of the Academy of Motion Picture Arts & Sciences. Oscars for 1945 went to Joan Crawford as *Mildred Pierce,* and Ray Milland for *Lost Weekend.* Supporting Oscars were won by Anne Revere in *National Velvet* and James Dunn in *A Tree Grows in Brooklyn.*

Hollywood ended the war in its best financial shape. Films were grossing $480,000,000 a year, of which the domestic take was $310,-000,000, with film rentals bringing in $6,250,000 a week. Oddly, despite this sensational showing, and the top money being earned by film theatres, no showplace of World War II could top the record of the old Roxy, back in August of 1929, which garnered $164,600 with the Edmund Lowe-Vic McLaglen film, *The Cockeyed World.*

But Hollywood, at the close of the war, was jubilant at its overall record—with few prophets predicting the downbeat to which the industry would be plunged in a few brief years.

52

Legit and Nitery Boom

★

Defense spending brought a boom to "the road"—the market for the living theatre outside of New York City. Legit's most distinguished ladies lost no time in making tracks through a hinterland newly paved with gold. Helen Hayes, touring in *Victoria Regina,* grossed some $2,000,000, topping the record for the decade past. Katharine Cornell, however, held the record for the most frequent road engagements over the same 10-year period.

The third femme fave of 1941 was Katharine Hepburn, whose tour with *The Philadelphia Story* garnered $753,183 in 32 weeks on the road. This compared impressively with the $961,665 the show had earned during its 52-week Broadway engagement.

Tallulah Bankhead hit the road with *The Little Foxes,* playing 121 stands, of which 104 were one-nighters. For this grueling engagement, the plum was $649,820, or about $25,000 higher than the show's earnings during its hit Broadway run.

Lynn Fontanne and her husband Alfred Lunt took the Pulitzer Prize play, Robert E. Sherwood's *There Shall Be No Night,* on the road for a 40-week cleanup of $800,000. Only the outbreak of the war stopped them short of the $1,000,000 mark. Paradoxically, the play was woven around a pity-poor-Finland theme, with Russia the heavy of the piece. Everybody concerned wanted to forget it hastily when Russia was suddenly our ally, and the Pulitzer Prize choice for 1941 became a national embarrassment.

That phenomenal play, *Tobacco Road,* which confounded the critics to run for seven and one half years on Broadway, finally closed May 31, 1941. During its historic run, it had had about 70 weeks in the red, and 42 during which it broke even. Hitting the road, the show took in three to four times its New York receipts.

George M. Cohan took *I'd Rather Be Right* on the road, after a Broadway grab of $986,904, and rolled up another $691,512 on a limited tour, smashing his own records for the road engagements of *Ah, Wilderness.*

Loose cash was so plentiful in the hinterland that the summer stocks and the strawhats cleaned up some $3,000,000 in 1941. Chicago's Auditorium, formerly the home of the Chicago Civic Opera Co., took in the Olsen & Johnson madhouse, *Hellzapoppin,* and found that uproar paid off much more handsomely than arias.

Although Hollywood was being cautious about putting money into Broadway productions, the pix biz shelled out $2,290,000 in 1941 for screen rights to current and previous season's hits.

Governor Lehman struck a blow at the Shuberts that year by signing a bill forbidding theatre managers to refuse admission to any critics or columnists who bought tickets. New York *Post* columnist Leonard Lyons, himself an ex-lawyer, engineered the statute as retaliation against an old Shubert custom of barring out too captious critics. Alec Woollcott, Heywood Broun, Winchell, Lyons and others have variously been targets of Shubertian spleen.

The New York *Daily News,* for no particular reason in 1941, ran a poll to select the greatest actresses of all time. The poll was taken among 49 leading actors and actresses, and the honored actress was Eleanora Duse. Sarah Bernhardt won five votes, Mrs. (Minnie Maddern) Fiske four, Mrs. Sarah Siddons three, and Ethel Barrymore, two.

Three years later six New York critics were asked to name the First Lady of the Stage. Three of the six, Robert Coleman, Burton Rascoe and Ward Morehouse, nominated Ethel Barrymore. Said Coleman: "Her name is synonymous with the stage." Said Rascoe: "She is the epitome of the theatre at its best." Said Morehouse: "Years of active stardom." He tossed in an illegal, nostalgic vote for Maude Adams as well. Burns Mantle and John Chapman gave the nod to Helen Hayes. Howard Barnes split his vote three ways— Barrymore for voice, Cornell for personality, Hayes for technique.

Perhaps as a result of the war, 1942 was an off-year on Broadway, with 54 flops and only six genuine hits. Hollywood cut down its purchases of screen rights to $1,200,000. Straight plays were given the edge over musicals. The Pulitzer Committee passed up giving any award, but the critics voted Judith Anderson in *Macbeth* and Burgess

Meredith in *Candida* as the season's best performances.

Although Sunday performances on the road were big boxoffice events through 1942 and 1943, the road began to feel the pinch of war in 1943 because of gasoline shortages and travel restrictions. The gasoline ban ruined the one-nighters, as well as stock and strawhats. Cars stayed in garages, and ticket money in pants pockets.

'oklahoma!' & co. But Broadway legit went into high in 1942-1943 with the unveiling of *Oklahoma!* which was to be the musicomedy high mark until Richard Rodgers and Oscar Hammerstein 2d were to top themselves eight years later with the phenominal *South Pacific* (Mary Martin-Ezio Pinza). *Oklahoma!* didn't depend on its players as much, although it did project Celeste Holm and Alfred Drake, who went on to new heights in Hollywood and on Broadway with the successive seasons, the latter proving particularly scintillating in *Kiss Me, Kate*.

Other leading 1943 shows were the *Ziegfeld Follies* (Milton Berle-Ilona Massey-Arthur Treacher), Mike Todd's Cole Porter musical, *Something for the Boys* (Ethel Merman-Allen Jenkins-Betty Garrett-Bill Callahan-Murvyn Vye); the anti-Nazi play, *Tomorrow the World,* by James Gow and Arnaud d'Usseau, starring Ralph Bellamy, Shirley Booth and Skippy Homeier as the hateful Nazi youth.

Two revivals in the heavy money class were *Othello* (Paul Robeson-Uta Hagen-Jose Ferrer), and *The Merry Widow* (Jan Kiepura-Marta Eggerth).

The season also saw the dream of every legit manager—a single-set show with a three-person cast, and a smash hit—*The Voice of the Turtle*. John van Druten's comedy had the proper amount of spice for the matinee trade, and Margaret Sullivan, Elliott Nugent, and Audrey Christie made the most of their script opportunities. Moss Hart was represented on Broadway also that year with his war show, *Winged Victory,* the Air Force's answer to *This Is the Army*. Among the GI cast were Lee J. Cobb, Edmond O'Brien, Danny Scholl, Barry Nelson, Marc Daniels, Zeke Manners and Peter Lind Hayes who were to become more prominent in later civilian pursuits in Hollywood, legit, radio and niteries.

The Critics' Circle and the Pulitzer Prize committee were again at odds over the season's best. The former favored Sidney Kingsley's *The Patriots* (Madge Evans was featured in her playwright-husband's play along with Raymond E. Johnson, House Jameson and Juano Hernandez), but the Pulitzer trophy went to Thornton Wilder's *The Skin Of Our Teeth,* which boasted a cast including Tallulah Bankhead, Fredric March, Florence Eldridge, Florence Reed and Montgomery Clift. *Teeth* had a long Broadway run but was a dismal flop on the road; lasted a week only in Boston and folded.

A freak long run was reported from the Coast where an ancient morality meller on the evils of intemperate tippling, *The Drunkard,* was cleaning up by playing for ten-twent'-thirt' laughs—but at $1.75 and $2.25 prices. With an "olio," beer and pretzels, *The Drunkard* at this mid-century writing has lasted 18 consecutive years, almost 6,500 performances, over 2,000,000 customers who have consumed almost 4,000,000 bottles of beer. Jan Duggan and George Stuart of the original cast, along with Jackson Swales, the house pianist, are still with it. Mildred Ilse is the present producer; Gail Bell conceived the "revival" idea on July 6, 1933. *Life With Father* holds the legit long-run record with 3,224 performances. Incidentally, *The Drunkard,* when it was first produced at the Boston Museum in 1844 and ran 140 performances, had this authorship credit: "By W. H. Smith and a Gentleman."

Business was so good on Broadway in 1944 that not even a new Federal admission tax of 20 per cent—twice the old tax—could hurt the b.o., which showed a gain of between 10-15 per cent over the previous season. This was all the more remarkable in an election year, which traditionally cut into theatre revenues.

Billy Rose and Ben Marden took over the Ziegfeld Theatre, and then Rose bought his partner out for $100,000. He livened up the 1944 season with a champagne premiere of *The Seven Lively Arts* at $24 a seat. By shrewd publicity and advertising, the show had $350,000 in advance sales before the curtain went up, almost enough to underwrite it as a hit. But not quite, despite the Beatrice Lillie and Bert Lahr marquee names.

More and more producers began to divide up the risks and profits among a multitude of show angels, starting a trend which is still current. The Howard Lindsay-Russel Crouse show, *The Hasty Heart,* had no less than 41 investors in 1945. *Arsenic and Old Lace* was put on the boards in 1941 by the money of 27 backers.

For some reason both the Pulitzer Committee and the Critics'

Circle passed up *Winged Victory,* despite universal acclaim for the show, and refused to grant any play of the 1943 season the laurel. The Pulitzer Committee did give the nod in the direction of *Oklahoma!,* an unusual tribute since the award is rarely given to musicals. *Winged Victory,* in 27 weeks on Broadway, grossed $1,057,318 for Army Emergency Relief Fund.

$750,000 for 'harvey' pix rights   Boxoffice hits of the 1944 season included Mary Coyle Chase's *Harvey* (Frank Fay-Josephine Hull) which was to fetch the all-time record high of $750,000 for the film rights, spread over 10 years, from Universal-International; *I Remember Mama,* John van Druten's expert dramatization of Kathryn Forbes' *Mama's Bank Account,* with Mady Christians in the title role, ably aided by Oscar Homolka, Joan Tetzel, Richard Bishop and Ottilie Kruger; John P. Marquand and George S. Kaufman's *The Late George Apley* (Leo G. Carroll-Janet Beecher-Margaret Phillips-Margaret Dale); Philip Yordan's Negro play, *Anna Lucasta,* expertly acted by Hilda Simms, Canada Lee and John Tate; and two musicals. They were *Bloomer Girl,* with a cast comprising David Brooks, Joan McCracken, Celeste Holm (who had left *Oklahoma!* for newer horizons), Matt Briggs and Mabel Taliaferro. *Song of Norway,* with a score based on the Norwegian Edvard Grieg's melodies, was one of those rara avis —a hit "from the Coast" of which *Lend An Ear,* in a later season, was to be another. The idea of a West Coast tryout, because of lower production costs, revolved around the Edwin Lester type of California manager who, if he has anything, makes a deal with the Shuberts, or kindred more influential Eastern interests, and brings the show to Broadway.

Despite the boom, 11 musicals flopped badly, running into the red for a total of $1,735,000. The rush for theatre tickets turned the spotlight once again on the ticket agencies. Seven brokers had their licenses revoked within a brief period. Some were put out of business and three or four went to jail for flagrant violations. Most, however, enjoyed such lush business that they weren't tempted to step out of line on prices or short-change on Government tax.

While Mrs. Chase's *Harvey* took the 1944 Pulitzer Prize, besides a $750,000 film sale—also marking vaude-nitery comedian Frank Fay's comeback—the critics selected Tennessee Williams' *The Glass*

Menagerie (with producer Eddie Dowling, Laurette Taylor, Julie Haydon and Anthony Ross in the cast), launching Williams as one of Broadway's most promising new playwrights.

Despite excitement over the close of the war, Broadway enjoyed solid business through the next year. Theatres were at such a premium that the producer of *The Red Mill,* in order to move into Shuberts' 46th Street Theatre, had to pay a 5 per cent royalty on the gross to the Shuberts—a first in the history of theatre management.

Two political figures entered the 1945 season. Mayor LaGuardia stepped in and forced the play *Trio* to close at the Belasco because of the Lesbian theme. Clare Booth Luce left Congress long enough to play *Candida* in a strawhat, her first stage appearance; the drama critics agreed "There have been better—and worse—Candidas."

even vaude upbeats   Wartime vaudeville enjoyed the first upbeat it had known since its sad decline in 1929. In 1941, heavy Government spending filtered down to the public, permitting theatre managers to pay the price for stage shows and charge off increased budget costs to the public in raised ducats. Then, with the rapid spread of Army camps, a new demand for live entertainment caused a stage show revival.

Top headliners, both in theatres and in camps, were still the bands; and novelty vocal groups like the Ink Spots and the Andrews Sisters were knocking them dead via recordings and personals.

Outside of bands and singing teams, vaudeville was without a headliner of its own. The last of the tribe was Milton Berle, but in 1941 he was too tied up with 20th Century-Fox and a radio program. Some night club personalities, like Harry Richman, Jimmy Durante, Sophie Tucker, the DeMarcos and Carmen Amaya, played vaude dates, but only occasionally.

The major circuits were slow to respond to vaude's newly eager face. Loew's offered time only at the New York State and the Washington (D.C.) Capitol, plus a few one-night stands in New York neighborhood theatres. The best time offered was that of an independent booking outfit, the Eddie Sherman office, whose vaude jewel was the Steel Pier, Atlantic City, using name bands and vaude talent for 20 weeks in spring and summer.

Burlesque of 1941 was a monopoly combine of Izzy Hirst and the Midwest Wheel, which controlled 30 houses, booking most of the strippers in the business. Variety noted 35 traveling burly shows, another indication that the factory trade in the hinterland was getting cash in its overalls.

topical gags Vaudeville gag material of the year was built largely around air raid blackouts, air raid wardens, bomb shelters, the draft, Bundles for Britain and sundry other pre-Pearl Harbor headline currency. A favorite gag among actors was, "I just signed for 52 weeks with Uncle Sam—with options."

War gags were dropped quickly in 1942, by management orders, when the coming of war to America sobered the nation. Comics, desperate for timely material, switched to gags about "General Tim O'Shenko." Bands continued to hold No. 1 stage spot, with Kay Kyser getting $25,610 for a week at Detroit's Fox Theatre. Frank Sinatra, growing too big for the Tommy Dorsey band, left the outfit to go into radio and theatre work. His replacement was Dick Haymes, also destined to go into business for himself.

Vaudeville of 1943 found itself in a dilemma. The routes were there—domestic and overseas—in a copious abundance that was suddenly embarrassing. There just wasn't enough vaude talent to go around. What talent was unearthed in USO-Camp Shows was vaude's to have only temporarily, but not to hold. As soon as a promising new headliner appeared, he was optioned at once by either pix, radio or the big-spending niteries.

Only the bands were left as steady headliners. And they weren't vaudeville, but merely transplanted jukebox faves personaling in a theatre. The bands appealed almost exclusively to juve tastes, leaving vaude with very little ammunition for a genuine comeback.

New York was the focal point of the "comeback," such as it was. The Roxy spent as much as $37,000 for one show, including Danny Kaye, Beatrice Kay and Tommy Tucker's band, showing a handsome profit for the first two weeks. Shortly afterward, the Roxy, Capitol, Paramount and Strand bid high for name bands and headliners. Grace Moore got $20,000 solo at the Roxy; Jack Benny and Milton Berle later got twice that, as did Bob Hope and Martin and Lewis at the New York Paramount. As usual, headliner salaries shot up to impossible extremes, making the stage attractions top-heavy in theatre budgets. And as Broadway went, so went the rest of the nation. It was the same pattern of the vaudeville goose beginning to lay golden eggs—and getting his head chopped off.

By 1945 vaude's brief revitalization was being revealed as a zombie. Two top theatres, the Earle in Washington and the Cleveland Palace, dropped stage shows. Other theatres started to follow suit.

Even the unit producers were laying off. In 1945 the only major unit on the road was Earl Carroll's "Vanities." Lack of talent, as well as the heavy expenses of package shows, made producers unwilling to gamble with that type of entertainment. For what top vaude talent was available, it was a seller's market. The DeMarcos were paid $5,000 a week by the Roxy, a new high for a dance team.

For a few brief years vaude had put on its greasepaint again and pretended that the heyday of the Palace was back. It had knocked itself out, especially in the Army camps at home and overseas, thrilling to the huge roars of laughter, the whistles, the storms of applause. It felt proud that it was welcomed so eagerly by the young men in uniform who had been so apathetic toward it as civilians. It hoped that perhaps, after the war, they would remember. After the parades and the ticker tape, vaude put on its best suit and sauntered confidently toward Broadway—only to find that there was no place to go.

the money boom   The year 1941 was star-spangled for night clubs. Prewar jitters created a widespread urge to "eat, drink and be merry, for tomorrow. . . ." In night spots from New York to San Francisco, merry-makers would exchange the sentiments of the day. "You can't take it with you. . . ." "Inflation's coming" . . . "You're spending Uncle Sam's coin in the form of 'expenses'" . . . "If you don't spend it, you'll pay it in taxes. . . ."

Defense spending, of course, primed the pump. The boom began in the hinterland, then spread over both coasts like the overflow of flood waters. Horwath & Horwath, the rating outfit of the hotel and restaurant trade, revealed that the boxoffice for fancy supping and quaffing increased by 35 per cent in 1941. Successful cafes grossed between half a million to a million a year. Spots like New York's Copacabana thought $45,000 weekly grosses just fair; did over $50,000 a week with a Joe E. Lewis and a Jimmy Durante, the latter hitting a $62,500 mark one week. Straight eateries of a mass and class basis, like Dempsey's and Lindy's on Broadway, and Toots Shor's and "21," in New York, did $20,000 a week on straight food. The Stork jumped from $15,000 to $35,000 a week's take.

The trend in night club entertainment underwent a swift change. Formerly, emphasis had been on providing a lavish background with sweet music and luxurious lighting, against which the customers could make their own fun. Now, once and again there was the demand for flashy, elaborate floor shows and hoked-up gaiety.

The pace was not sweet, but hot. Monte Proser opened the Dance Carnival at Madison Square Garden, offering jitterbugging to triple dance bands—Benny Goodman, Larry Clinton and Charlie Barnett —at a scale of 44¢-66¢-88¢, with reserved seats for the intrigued at $1.10 and $1.40. The first weekend attracted 31,553 admissions for a take of $23,200. But the overhead was too heavy, and the attraction folded in less than a month.

One night club in San Francisco brought police, vice societies, and liquor control authorities swooping down as a result of its ad: "See Tommy Harris' Nude All-Girl Orchestra." Many faces were red when the "orchestra" proved to be one-dimensional, sand-blasted into a bar mirror. But it brought in the customers.

In its notes on night life of 1941, Variety revealed that gin-rummy and bridge corners were being set up in some of the popular boites; Harlem night life was suffering from the publicity given its crime wave; Judge Pecora upheld the legality of compulsory fingerprinting for cafe workers; and a "Friendship Club" in the Bronx was running dances with two restrictions—no one under 28, and no jitterbugging. In 1942 seamier night life items revealed some goings-on—2:30 A.M. curfews in war boom towns like Cleveland had inspired a rebirth of speakeasies; men posing as officers and plainclothesmen were shaking down clubs and personnel—a new racket; and clip-joint ballrooms and cheap cafes were bilking the service men.

The celebration department of show business was still in a gold rush by 1943, despite the difficulties of food ration points, and a new liquor shortage. Hotels shared the boom. Sinatra siphoned a heavy take into the Waldorf-Astoria's Wedgwood Room, while Carl Brisson—"the older girls' Sinatra"— had them fighting for seats at the Club Versailles in New York. Other standout attractions of the year were Hildegarde at the Persian Room of the Hotel

Plaza in New York, and the Hartmans (Paul and Grace) all over the place.

The croon-swoon cycle continued full swing. The Coq Rouge ran a Sinatra contest and came up with Martin Kent, one more to swell the ranks of Como, Haymes and Dean Martin, but little was heard of Kent thereafter. In the Danny Kaye tradition, Danny Thomas was slaying them at New York's La Martinique. The Copacabana was mopping up with Jimmy Durante and Joe E. Lewis. Ted Lewis made his *nth* "comeback" at the Hurricane, on Broadway, which also offered Duke Ellington. The Latin Quarter had Georgie Price. Both Billy Rose's Diamond Horseshoe and Lou Walters' Latin Quarter were in the $30,000-and-over weekly gross class.

The heavy spending in night clubs, bars, and other places of wassail was one of the reasons for the Government's salary withholding tax. "It's a certainty many of these saloonatics have little concern about the morrow," Variety said approvingly. "When mama goes back to washing the dishes, and the $110-a-week driller returns to his $30 white-collar job, they will have memories and a terrific hangover, no doubt, but seemingly, as of right now, that seems to be all right all around."

Night clubs were hit hard in 1944, when the Government clamped a 30 per cent amusement tax on the backs of the celebrators. Business slumped, with night clubs going down like tenpins, putting 20,000 out of work. The Government relented and cut the tax back to 20 per cent, which helped more performers get back to work.

By 1945 top night clubs were definitely in the big business brackets. New York's Copacabana took in an average of $45,000-$55,000 weekly, trailed by the Latin Quarter with $40,000-$45,000, and the Diamond Horseshoe and the Zanzibar with an average of $40,000 each. All groaned at a new midnight curfew for the amusement industry imposed by War Mobilization Director Jimmy Byrnes, who "regretted" the inconvenience. Any ordinance so vitally affecting night life inevitably inspires a flock of wisecracks, most cogent of which was boniface Toots Shor's now historic wheeze, in his own picturesque phraseology: "Any crum-bum what can't get plastered by midnight just ain't tryin'."

The curfew, of course, brought a wave of bottle clubs and post-Volsteadian "speakeasies," prompting Mayor LaGuardia to rule,

"New York is still New York; I don't like the curfew law" . . . and so he extended it to 1 A.M., which made everybody feel a little better. At least it didn't disrupt legit curtains, some having started earlier in order to give theatre-goers a little more post-theatre time for supper, a drink and a dance, à la the London idea of double-daylight time theatre curtains at 6 and 7 P.M., with supping —not dining—afterwards. It also advanced the niteries' "midnight" shows an hour, and thus crowded in some revenue, heretofore impossible under the 12 o'clock deadline.

Anyway, 1 A.M. was OK—it meant that you didn't have to go home on the same day!

53

Paeans of Victory—and Labor Pains

★

Soldiers off to war and workers to defense plants march faster and are stirred deeper with proper musical accompaniments. But World War II was not to produce another "Over There" although Tin Pan Alley rallied to all the Government's requirements—and then some—as they cropped up. Jimmy McHugh and L. Wolfe Gilbert contributed "A Grand Vacation With Pay" as a recruiting drive song. Later, McHugh and Harold Adamson were to prove more effective with their musical salute to the heroes of aviation, "Coming In On A Wing and a Prayer." Irving Berlin fashioned "Any Bonds Today," "Arms for the Love of America" (munitions), "Angels of Mercy" for the Red Cross, "There Are No Wings on a Foxhole" (infantry song), and of course "God Bless America," besides the notable *This Is the Army,* with its nearly-$10,000,000 yield for Army Emergency Relief.

Both the Army's Special Services division and the innate showmanship of Tin Pan Alley soon sensed that war songs, per se, never clicked with the GIs. Songs of sentiment, home, the girl back home, the miss-you theme, the completely happy-go-lucky, or escapist, such as "Hut Sut Song," "Don't Sit Under the Apple Tree," "Three Little Sisters," "I'll Be Seeing You," "White Christmas," "The Last Time I Saw Paris" and others, were the ones that the jukeboxes and the bands on the home front found most popular. There was enough oblique suggestion without punching it too hard on the nose.

The militant type of songs like "Remember Pearl Harbor," "This Is Worth Fighting For" and "Praise the Lord and Pass the Ammunition" occasionally were fraught with embarrassment, especially for 4F or "deferred" maestros. There were too frequent interrogations from pugnacious youths in uniforms and hyper-sentimental femmes who openly were heard to ask the bandleader, "Well, why don't you get into a uniform and fight, then?" Ecclesiastic circles didn't like "Praise the Lord" on the ground that religion and killing were an ungodly coupling, in prose or melody. Frank Loesser's song nevertheless clicked, as did his "Story of Rodger Young." (Loesser and Berlin were the Tin Pan Alley outstanders of World War II, even if never achieving the socko impact of George M. Cohan's "Over There.")

Apart from the personal sensitivities, the bands ducked fighting songs because they found the public generally wanted complete escapology when terping; besides which, the tempos of the "message" pops were poor for dancing and, anyhow, the ballroom was no place to arouse patriotism.

There was heated discussion as to the types of music soldiers preferred. Surveys by the Army's Special Services division showed that popular tunes, sweet or dance, won favor with 95 per cent of GI radio listeners. Swing—hot, scat and jive—was second with a 62 per cent rating. Third place went to old familiar music; hillbilly and Western music won the fourth nod; and lowest welcome was accorded classical music.

escapist hit paraders   By and large, the 1942 pop music crop—which rolled up the biggest sheet music sale in 15 years—was largely escapist. Many songs suggested the war, but slightly, such as "Bluebirds Over the White Cliffs of Dover," "My Sister and I," "The Last Time I Saw Paris" and "A Tulip Garden By An Old Dutch

Mill." Sentiment of a nostalgic order was the popular ring of Tin Pan Alley circa 1942. Hits of this nature were "Till Reveille," "Shrine of St. Cecilia," "She'll Always Remember," "Johnny Doughboy Found a Rose In Ireland," "I Left My Heart At the Stage Door Canteen" and "He Wears A Pair of Silver Wings."

The Japanese, of course, came in for due lyrical trouncing. The day after Pearl Harbor, two songs came out—"The Sun Will Soon Be Setting For The Land of the Rising Sun" and "You're A Sap, Mr. Jap." Later in 1942, Japan was the inspiration for "We're Going To Find the Fellow Who Is Yellow and Beat Him Red, White and Blue," "We've Got To Do A Job on the Japs, Baby," "They're Going to Be Playing Taps on the Japs," "The Japs Haven't Got A Chinaman's Chance," "The Japs Haven't Got A Ghost of A Chance," "Goodbye, Momma, I'm Off to Yokohama," "Oh, You Little Son Of An Oriental," "Wake Island Woke Up Our Land," "Slap the Jap Right Off the Map," "We Are the Sons of the Rising Guns," "To Be Specific, It's Our Pacific" and "When Those Little Yellow Bellies Meet the Cohens and the Kelleys."

The rest of the Axis was thrown in with "Put the Heat on Hitler, Muss Up Mussolini and Tie a Can to Japan," "Let's Put the Axe to the Axis," "Let's Knock the Hit Out of Hitler," "We'll Knock the Japs Right in the Laps of the Nazis" and "We Did It Before and We Can Do It Again."

Songs to stir up patriotic feeling were "Me and My Uncle Sam," a revival of "Ballad For Americans," Fred Waring's "Merchant Marine Song," and toujours "God Bless America," which became the theme song of Milwaukee night clubs where the German-American population liked everyone to think of them as unquestioned patriots.

Two songs were beamed at the wartime factory workers—"Don't Steal the Sweetheart of a Soldier" and "Rosie the Riveter." Another Rose was celebrated that year, "Russian Rose."

Songwriters responded to the call of the Music War Committee in 1943, and turned out a drove of bond-selling songs, including "One More Mile," "Swing the Quota," "The Message Got Through," "Has Hitler Made A Monkey Out of You?," "Get Aboard the Bond Wagon," "Unconditional Surrender," "While Melting All Our Memories" (scrap salvage), "Voices of the Underground," "Yankee Doodle Ain't Doodling Any Now," "Have You

Written Him Today?," "I Get That Democratic Feeling," "I Spoke With Jefferson At Guadalcanal," "West Of Tomorrow" (submarine song) and "In Business Since 1776."

Our Allies were celebrated in "My British Buddy" (again Berlin), which scored big in England, and Clarence Gaskill's "Franklin, Winston, Kai-Shek and Joe." The approaching capitulation of Italy was anticipated by "One Down and Two More To Go," which was ready for issue on the day of Mussolini's surrender. Hy Zaret wrote English lyrics to the "Garibaldi Hymn" to celebrate the occasion.

There was no great war song—the kind soldiers marched to— because it wasn't a marching war. The kind of song the soldiers sang was the favorite of the African campaign, "Dirty Gertie," which was cleaned up and offered in the United States as "Gertie from Bizerte." It never achieved its hopes as a second "Mademoiselle From Armentières."

allies adopt 'lili marlene'   Perhaps the outstanding real war song—unlike the patriotic "God Bless America" of Irving Berlin, and the sweet-sorrowful nostalgia of "The Last Time I Saw Paris" (incidentally the only non-musical comedy score song ever written by the late Jerome Kern and Oscar Hammerstein 2d)—was "Lili Marlene." It was "adopted" by the Allies from the Nazis during the North African campaign, and it was from the British that the American GIs picked it up. Originally a German ballad ("My Lili of the Lamppost"), this made it the first time in history that enemy troops both sang and enjoyed the same song.

(Postwar, the German songsmith Norbert Schultze sought an American visa, disclaimed being a Nazi but couldn't quite explain away his alleged "anti-Nazi sympathies" when he was spotlighted as the composer also of the 1941 Nazi victory paen, *"Wir fahren nach England"* ("We're Sailing Towards England"). Curiously enough, under American copyright regulations the Alien Property Custodian built up a sizable chunk of royalties for the errant Herr Schultze from the American sheet music and recording sales of the Anglo-Americanized version of "Lili Marlene." (This was the case, too, in the instance of the late Franz Lehar, thanks to a click revival of his *Merry Widow* on Broadway).

"Annie Doesn't Live Here Any More" suggested the upheaval that war production had caused in the lives of the people at home.

"When You Put On That Blue Suit Again" reflected the growing optimism of both civilians and soldiers at approaching victory, as did "Hot Time In the Town of Berlin," "When I Get Back To My Home Town," "Paris Will Be Paris Once Agan" and "There Will Be A Yankee Christmas."

Among "specific" songs were "The U.S.A. By Day and the R.A.F. By Night" (bombing pattern over Germany), "Johnny Zero (Johnny got a Zero today!)" (indicating a new attention to the Pacific theatre), and "Say A Prayer For the Boys Over There."

The songs of 1944 which made the greatest hit, however, were those in which the war theme was openly implied, with romance paramount, such as "I'll Walk Alone" and "I'll Be Seeing You." In a livelier vein were "G.I. Jive," "Shoo Shoo Baby" and "Victory Polka." Top favorites of all were pure novelty numbers, like "Mairzy Doats," "Milkman, Keep Those Bottles Quiet," "The Trolley Song" and "Don't Fence Me In." Escapist songs commanded the top money.

There was a revival of old sentimental favorites. Among the newly popular oldies were "I'd Climb the Highest Mountain," "I'll Get By," "Inka Dinka Doo," "Me and My Shadow," "Moon Over Miami," "Object Of My Affections," "Rainbow Round My Shoulder," "Whistle While You Work" and "Who's Afraid Of the Big Bad Wolf?" As revivals, the songs sold three times the number of copies they did when they were first published.

The Latin tempo was reflected by "Amor," "Let Me Love You Tonight" and "Besame Mucho." The Andrews Sisters started a whole new cycle of neo-calypso songs by taking an old Frank Loesser tune, "Sing A Tropical Song," out of an old Paramount film. Other off-syllable songs quickly followed, among the outstanding numbers being "Rum and Coca-Cola" and "Come With Me My Honey."

Fortune shone brightly for the music biz. Even the song-sheet sellers were frightened into good behavior, paying some $625,000 a year to the publishers and songsmiths for their lyric reprints. The big money for Tin Pan Alley, however, still came from radio—$7,000,000 for 1944, a new high.

petrillo—again War or no war, James C. Petrillo was battling to protect the interests of members of his American Federation of

Musicians. As in the 1948 debacle, five years prior thereto he was ranting against the phonograph recording as "the No. 1 scab" of the music business; and in 1943 he banned his AFMers from waxing for the "musical monsters which were killing employment" for the live musicians. But that didn't deter the oncoming of such pop disk faves as Bing Crosby, Perry Como, Frank Sinatra, Vaughn Monroe, Margaret Whiting and Spike Jones. And the combination of "middlebrow" musical tastes, along with the ballyhoo potency of pix and radio, zoomed such longhairs as Lauritz Melchior and José Iturbi into extraordinary platter sales.

In 1945 current events were reflected by "The President Harry S Truman March," "Don't Let It Happen Again" (a message to delegates at the San Francisco conference), "He's Home For A Little While" (furloughs), "I'll Be Walking With My Honey Soon, Soon, Soon" (approaching end of war), and Irving Berlin's peacetime paen, "Just A Blue Serge Suit."

Variety limned some notes of musical interest from abroad. The favorite song of the R.A.F. in England was a ribald ditty called "Roll Me Over In the Clover" by Desmond O'Connor. The United States Army stopped publication of "Berlin Will Rise Again" by Heinzo Gaze, after 20,000 copies had been printed in Germany without authorization by Allied occupation authorities. Berlin, meanwhile, was covered in the latter part of the year with Spike Jones' recordings of "Der Fuehrer's Face," a tune not exactly encouraged there in early 1945.

Bing Crosby tried to hit the 10,000,000 disk sale record that year, but Perry Como nosed him out with a Chopin tune, "Till the End of Time"—the year's best-seller—and "Temptation," "That Feeling in the Moonlight," "If I Loved You" and "I'm Gonna Love That Gal (as she's never been loved before)"—and none of his squealing admirers was under any misapprehension as to what those lyrics suggested. A few years previous, Tin Pan Alley had owed a tremendous debt to Tchaikowsky, giving rise to the musical observation, "Everybody's Making Money But Tchaikowsky," but in 1945 the larceny was perpetrated chiefly against Chopin.

Cole Porter's "Don't Fence Me In" snowballed to a sensational best-seller, the first song since "White Christmas" to go over the million mark in sheet sales. Another click was "Chickery Chick." "Bell Bottom Trousers" was popular, and also "When the Old

Gang's Back On the Corner (singing 'Sweet Adeline' again.)"

The boom in the music business led to an increase in recording companies until they totaled 130. Some counted on a new boom when plastic, nonbreakable records were put out to sell in racks like sheet music on newsstands.

Decca ran a big campaign on Crosby, to offset the Como menace, describing him as "the most-heard voice in the world," with no less than 75,000,000 of his records in private homes.

With the close of the war, songplugging and all its attendant evils began to make itself felt again. As Variety observed, "The manpower easement was manifested fast in the Lindy set. The pluggers are back from the war in droves, with the same ya-ta-ta, the same chiz and angle and dipsydoodle."

longhair goes middlebrow Edward Johnson, the new managing director of the Metropolitan Opera House, gave full credit to the people's medium, radio, for the relatively lush state of affairs of 1941 opera. The longhair field as a whole took $35,000,000 in receipts that year, with the opera latching on to $5,000,000 thereof. The Met had made one concession to the war in 1942—it dropped *Madama Butterfly,* with its quaint and flattering picture of Japan. It retained Wagnerian opera, indicating that the Met's artistic censorship was not because of the composers' nationality but more because of the libretto subject matter.

The intermingling of longhair and shorthair music continued through the war period. José Iturbi withdrew as conductor of the Philadelphia Symphony Orchestra in 1941 when Benny Goodman was a feature soloist. Iturbi's reason: "Beneath my dignity." Edwin MacArthur pinch-hitted on the cuff, declaring, "It is an honor and a privilege to conduct the Benny Goodman concert."

Longhair orchestras also resented the raids on their bandmen by swing outfits. In 1944 Jerry Wald's band burglarized six string men from the Cleveland Symphony. That year swing again invaded the concert field, when a handpicked group of top jazz musicians, under the baton of Eddie Condon, gave a concert at Carnegie Hall and turned 'em away. Hazel Scott also played Carnegie in 1945— while Artur Rubinstein did his chores before the cameras in Republic Pictures', *I Have Always Loved You.* Lauritz Melchior had long since gone Metro and jived the Wagnerian stuff on Fred

Allen and Frank Sinatra radio programs. Paul Whiteman, Phil Spitalny, Woody Herman, the Andrews Sisters, Mary Lou Williams, Duke Ellington, Victor Borge, Sigmund Romberg, and also Spike Jones, likewise went concert.

Agents began to take a second look at the concert field. Certain bands and acts, dressed with stylish showmanship, clicked handsomely in longhair emporia. And Toscanini, conducting a concert in the Hollywood Stadium, played on and looked with disbelieving eyes as a career-bent girl named Helen Faville, of Los Angeles, jumped onto the stage and danced across it—self-appointed ballerina for a night.

the hottest thing on ice   1941 was a sweet year for outdoor show business. The Ringling Circus went into Los Angeles for five days—10 shows—and left with a $230,000 gross, top coin in its 58-year-old history. Luna Park (Coney Island), offering many of the old New York World's Fair attractions, found the pickings equally juicy.

1943, however, found circuses and carnivals ready to quit because of gas rationing. In New York, two circuses opened at the same time. Ringling presented "Spangles" at Madison Square Garden, a one-ring affair which revived the circus parade in the arena. The Sunbrock Circus with three-rings opened on a lot behind the Roxy Theater, but folded quickly. The following year the Ringling show chalked up another record in New York with a gross of $1,500,000.

But 1944 was a year of disaster for outdoor show business. The Ringling-Barnum & Bailey show playing under canvas in Hartford, Connecticut, suffered a disastrous fire in the main tent. In the stampede that followed, 107 persons were killed and 412 injured. Disaster claims amounting to over $4,000,000 had to be paid off. The same year, both Luna Park and Palisades Park had fires doing $1,500,000 damage. Ringling's wound up 1945 still solidly in the black, however, cleaning up in New York, despite the lack of foreign importations which the war had made impossible.

The single outstanding star in the outdoor field was Sonja Henie, who grossed $280,000 at Madison Square Garden in 1942, and over $1,000,000 via a short tour of the nation's ice rinks. In the lecture field, war scribes and swamis raised the boxoffice in the spiel division to $800,000 in 1943; one of the outstanders being Burton Holmes, then 73 and celebrating his 50th season.

sunday legits   Equity, once firmly opposed to Sunday performances, was convinced in 1941 that these had proved a lifesaver for many shows. It therefore promptly endorsed the proposal that they be continued through the summer and into the fall season. Sunday shows continued to draw people into New York for weekends, benefiting film houses as well as legit. Once fearful that Sunday shows might seem a confession of boxoffice weakness, this soon proved a fallacy.

Frank Gillmore, Equity's head for so many of its turbulent years, died in 1943 at the age of 76. The organization had a fairly placid year, owing to the fact that so many of its younger members had left to play more dramatic roles in the war. The only flurry occurred during the election of councilors. Paul Robeson, although elected, refused to accept office, in protest against the slur on the Soviet Union implied by an anti-Red amendment in Equity's new constitution. There was no mistaking Robeson's Moscow leanings even then.

There were few jobless actors in 1945, with USO units crying for more talent, many summer musical stocks and a thriving road. Many retired actors returned and rejoined Equity, which began to have a recurrence of "ism" trouble when Frank Fay lashed out at the organization with cries of "Communism at the top."

A New York newspaper strike in 1945 reduced the size of the papers and cut out amusement advertising, merely listing the shows. Incidental music in a production of Shakespeare's *Tempest* (Vera Zorina-Canada Lee) brought a ruling from the American Federation of Musicians that it rated as a musical comedy, requiring upped salaries and a minimum of 16 musicians at $92 each, despite the fact that the music was scored for a 12-man orchestra.

War's unrest created other isms throughout show business. With labor's power asserting itself, its leaders sometimes abused that power, as witness the Willie Bioff-George Browne scandal in the picture business. These Chicago hoodlums, remnants of the Al Capone gangster tactics and in the worst Capone tradition, threatened to "tie up the entire motion picture industry by pulling out the boothmen" (projectionists) unless Hollywood "made a deal" with them. Hollywood was forced to. Between the courageous campaign of Arthur Ungar, late editor of Daily Variety and Westbrook Pegler's general daily campaign, Browne and Bioff and their cohorts, eventually got their just desserts via stiff prison sentences and fines.

Hollywood labor strife stirred anew via a jurisdictional battle between two American Federation of Labor unions—the Illustrators & Decorators Local 1421 and the International Alliance of Theatrical Stage Employees, as to which local would get the 72 screen set designers. This cost the studios many man-hours of time and money and tied up the sundry studios periodically through picketing and cross-picketing, walkouts and other demonstrations which led to much physical harm and other abuses. Although production continued, despite these hindrances, riots in front of studio gates resulted in severe strife, when the Hollywood gendarmerie was charged with siding with the IATSE men.

On a lighter note, the Rockefellers shuttered their glamor nitery in the clouds, the Rainbow Room, atop the RCA Bldg. in Radio City, when labor demands by waiters and cooks made an already unprofitable operation still more so—even for the Rockefellers. They just didn't think it was worth the trouble, and turned the operation over to the Union News Co. which runs the many other eateries, cafes and bars in Rockefeller Center. Incidentally it was something of a sentimental venture, since young Nelson Rockefeller had always fancied the idea of a "super nite club way up in the clouds." While at school he used to confide this to one of his tutors, a Mr. John Roy by name. So when the Rainbow Room debuted, the educator became a bistro boniface and John Roy found himself booking shows, hiring the bands and worrying about cuisine, waiters and service. Not until the fall of 1950 was an attempt made to reopen the Rainbow Room to the public, and then on an experimental cocktail dansant basis although it functioned all the time as a private luncheon club for Rockefeller Center tenants.

many showmen pass   The first year of the war period saw the deaths of three men whose obituaries were a shock to show business. All died in July 1941. They were Sam H. Harris, 69, one-time partner of George M. Cohan and producer of such

Broadway hits as *Dinner At Eight, Rain, As Thousands Cheer* and
You Can't Take It With You; Sam Scribner, 82, treasurer of the
Actors Fund; and Lew Fields, 73, whose partner Joe Weber was at
his bedside.

Joe Penner, born Josef Pinter, died at 36, cutting short a promising radio career that had paid him as much as $13,250 one week.
Another radio personality, Earl W. Grasen, "The Lone Ranger,"
died that year in an auto accident. Over 1,000 people paid him a
last tribute in Detroit.

The music world of 1941 lost Isidore Witmark, 71, founder of
the famous music publishing house; Ignace Jan Paderewski, 80,
who had earned between three and five millions in his 40-year career; Brig. Gen. E. L. Gruber, 61, who had written "The Caissons
Go Rolling Along"; and Bartley C. Costello, 70, author of the lyrics
of "Where the River Shannon Flows," a claim disputed by some.

Other obits of 1941 included Julian Eltinge, 57, greatest female
impersonator of them all; legit impresario Stuart Walker at 53;
Hugh Ward, 70, an American who had large theatre holdings in
Australia; vaudeville's "redhead" Irene Franklin, longtime part-
nered with her husband, Burton Green, in bigtime vaudeville, at
65; actors Eddie Leonard, 70, Richard Carle, 69, and George L.
Bickel (of Bickel & Watson, pioneer vaudeville comedy act), 70.
Playwright Eugene Walter (*The Easiest Way*) passed at 67; nitery
chanteuse and Ziegfeld star of *Show Boat* and the *Follies,* Helen
Morgan, at 41. Another premature death was Marie Saxon, musi-
comedy star at 37. She was married to Sid Silverman, the son of
Sime, who died in 1950 at 52.

Sam Morton, of the 4 Mortons, one of the first great vaudeville
family acts, à la the Cohans and Foys, died in his 70th year. Also
one-time Belasco star Blanche Bates, 69; Wells Hawks who press-
agented everything from circus elephants to battleships, at 71.
Steve Clow, publisher of the illfamed Broadway Brevities, a racketeering sheet which sent him to Atlanta, also died in 1941 at 68.

Among the show business pioneers lost that year also were Commodore J. Stuart Blackton, 66, one-time head of the Vitagraph
Pictures Corp.; Henry Burr, 59, one of the first ballad recording
artists; Fred Karno, 75, discoverer of Charlie Chaplin and Stan
Laurel (& Hardy), who worked in his Karno's "A Night In An

English Music Hall"; Mrs. Codelia MacDonald, 94, the original "Little Eva"; and Jenny Dolly, of the famous Dolly Sisters, who suicided at 48. [Whenever the Monte Carlo Casino needed a little publicity the story always went out that the Dollys had broken the bank, always a surefire revitalizer for the gaming tables.]

The outstanding obituary of the following year was that of the Number One man of the American theatre—George M. Cohan, who died at 64, and was laid to rest just 45 minutes from Broadway. The funeral took place at St. Patrick's Cathedral, where "Over There" was played for the first time as a dirge, and, incidentally, the first popular song ever played at the cathedral. Cohan left an estate of $712,393, a modest sum considering that the 10 per cent share he was given in *Yankee Doodle Dandy* netted $500,000.

Another great theatrical figure died that year, John Barrymore, at the age of 60, mourned as possibly one of the finest actors the American stage had ever known, despite his decline into buffoonery during the last years of his life.

Two pioneer radio commentators also died in 1942—Floyd Gibbons, who left an estate of $250,000, and Graham McNamee, 53, who set the pace for exciting sports announcers. Joe Weber, the other half of Weber & Fields, died at 74 only nine months after his partner. Morris Gest, famous producer of *The Miracle* and *Chu Chin Chow,* died at 61.

Other obituaries of 1942 included England's top managing director, Sir Oswald Stoll, 76; another famous legitimate actor, Otis Skinner, 83; Emma Calvé, a Metropolitan standout for 13 years and the greatest Carmen of her era, 83; Pawnee Bill (Major Gordon W. Lillie), who was once Buffalo Bill's partner, 81; Michel Fokine, famous ballet master, 62; and Addie Cherry, one of the famous Cherry Sisters—"the worst act in show biz"—at 83.

Hollywood mourned the death of Carole Lombard (Mrs. Clark Gable) at 32 in a plane crash while returning from a War Bond Drive in Indianapolis. An obscure obituary was Felix Powell, 60, who had written only one hit song in his life; as a staff sergeant in World War I he had entered a song contest with "Pack Up Your Troubles In Your Old Kit Bag."

The music world was hit hardest in 1943. Obituaries included Sergei Rachmaninoff, 70; Lorenz (Larry) Hart, of the famous Rodgers & Hart (American "Gilbert & Sullivan") team, 47—later celebrated in memorium by Hollywood's *Words and Music;* Vaughn de Leath, pioneer radio singer known as "The First Lady of Radio," 42; Ben Bernie, "the Old Maestro" who made his "Yowza" trademark a radio byword, 52; and Jules Bledsoe, the Negro baritone who sang "Old Man River" in the original production of *Show Boat,* 44.

Other music world obituaries were songwriters Joe McCarthy, 58, George Whiting, 61, and Fats Waller, 39; film veteran Hobart Bosworth died at 76; and Cecilia (Cissie) Loftus, noted mimic and legit actress, at 67. Writers passing were Stephen Vincent Benet, 44, and novelist Elinor Glyn, 78. Other deaths included producer Max Reinhardt, 70; Elmer F. Rogers, 72, manager of the Palace almost from its heyday to its decline; and James Madison, 72, the "American Joe Miller," who published his gag-filled editions of *Madison's Budget* for 40 years.

Actors headed the list of 1944 obituaries. Prominent among them were Lupe Velez, 36, whose suicide created sensational headlines; silent pix comedian Harry Langdon, 60; veteran Willie Collier and one-time Broadway sensation Yvette Guilbert; Richard Bennett, 72, famous actor in his own right and father of Joan, Constance and Barbara Bennett; and Wilkie Bard, 70, one of England's great comedians.

Death at 53 rang down the curtain on the glamorous gospel career of Aimee Semple MacPherson, who had brought the Mae West touch to the tabernacle for 25 years. Inactive for five years before her death, she still derived income from the Los Angeles and Oakland "temples."

Two famous authors, good friends, died in '44—Irvin S. Cobb, 67, and George Ade, 78, whose first show had been *Sultan of Sulu.* Novelist Harold Bell Wright, 72, who wrote *The Shepherd of the Hills,* also passed away. Other deaths included artist Nell Brinkley, 56, and a staunch friend of show business, and Republican Party nominee for the Presidency in 1940, Wendell Willkie, 52, who was chairman of the board of 20th Century-Fox at the time of his death.

f. d. r.   The greatest loss for all in 1945 was the passing of Franklin Delano Roosevelt, who had always had a high regard for show business, which had an equal affection for him. The night that he died, radio had its all-time peak audience—38,700,000—

except for the night F.D.R. had delivered his war message in 1941, when 62,100,000 were tuned in.

Theatres cancelled all matinees. On a 56-minute NBC show, almost every famous name in show business went before the microphone to pay a throat-choked tribute to the late President. For complete coverage of the sad event, the four major networks and independent nets cancelled commercial time worth some $10,000,000.

Reviewing F.D.R.'s relationship to show business, Variety recalled that his radio voice had first been heard in 1925, at Madison Square Garden, for Al Smith as the Democratic candidate for the White House, and again at Houston in 1928 for the same Happy Warrior. Roosevelt had always shown keen interest in the legitimate stage, Hollywood and radio. He regularly attended stock company plays, where he gladly talked to actors backstage.

Variety had always "reviewed" his talks from the time he first gave them from the Executive Mansion in Albany to the famous fireside chats of the White House. His physical condition had compelled F.D.R. to rely on the microphone, rather than on personal appearances, to win popular support—a fact which helped make him an outstanding broadcaster.

The three show business figures who missed him most keenly were his close friends Robert E. Sherwood, John Golden and Eddie Dowling.

The music world in 1945 lost Gus Edwards (64), Jerome Kern (60), John McCormack (61), Fiske O'Hara, another noted Irish singer (67), Erno Rapee, conductor of the Radio City Music Hall Orchestra for 12 years, also composer of "Diane," "Charmaine" and "Angela Mia," at 55, Moises Simons, Cuban composer of "The Peanut Vendor" and originator of the Latin-American trend in music, also 55, and Edward B. Marks (80), one of the most famous of all music publishers.

Widely mourned by actors, writers and critics, for he was all of these, was Robert Benchley, who died at 56. Actors who took their final curtains that year included Alla Nazimova (66), great tragedienne; famed film cowboy star William S. Hart, 80; Frank Craven (70), who scored so heavily in *Our Town;* Doris Keane (63), remembered for her role in *Romance;* and Charles Evan Evans (88), veteran comedian for 75 years, whose 3,600 performances of Hoyt's farce, "A Parlor Match," ran for 10 years starting in 1884, the longest theatrical run in history. Evans' partner was Bill (Old Hoss) Hoey; together they introduced "The Man Who Broke the Bank at Monte Carlo" and "Bicycle Built For Two." It was Evans who had brought Anna Held over from France for the first time in 1896.

Variety itself lost Joshua Lowe—*Jolo*—who died at 72 in London. An American longtime resident in the British capital, he had sat out the London blitz only to be hit by a taxi. Periodically *Jolo* would write letters to the home-office (usually after some severe aerial attack) that he "had to complain to the landlord again last night—too damn much noise upstairs." It was *Jolo* who originated the line, "Good for the big small time," and who also wrote the shortest vaudeville review ever to appear in Variety, as related in a previous chapter.

1950-51 obits included Fanny Brice (59), Vesta Victoria (77), songwriter Harry Armstrong (71), Ivor Novello (57), André Gide (81), Arnold Schönberg (76), Lou Clayton (Jackson & Durante) (63), Decca's Jack Kapp (47), Chi Hotelier Ernie Byfield (59), Damon Runyon (62), Eddy Duchin (41), Warner Baxter (59), John Alden Carpenter (75), John Erskine (72), Mayo Methot (47), Olive Tell (55), Jane Cowl (64), Carla (Mrs. Arturo) Toscanini (73), Variety's Ed Barry (*Edba*) (60), Ashton Stevens (78), Egbert A. ("In the Shade of the Old Apple Tree") Van Alstyne (73), Kelcey Allen (75).

PART SEVEN

VIDEO ERA

1946 - 195-

54

Veni, Vidi, Video, Vaudeo

★

"The Era of Wonderful Nonsense II is over," declared Variety at the close of 1946. "The past year was and henceforth will go down as The Awakening." Gone or going were the jackpots hit by furriers, jewelers, specialty shops and resorts, the wheels of which were spun with black market dollars. Gone or going were the defense workers in shirtsleeves in front row orchestra of the top hits; fabulous gambling in Saratoga and Florida; tipping in large denominations. "It's no gag," Variety observed, "that many a waiter up to now was on his second apartment house, and quite a few maitres can retire to Lake Como without worrying whether their Escoffier sheepskin is in jeopardy."

Although customers were still giving $100 tips for front places at Florida dice tables, war-inflated salaries slumped rapidly. A boxoffice limp was hurting all talent without a big reputation. Daily Variety in Hollywood carried a sign of the times with an ad in March offering an apartment for rent, including the owner's "talent and ability," in exchange for a movie contract. Another ad in an Atlantic City paper announced: WANTED—PIANO PLAYER WHO CAN OPEN OYSTERS AND CLAMS.

It was The Awakening, indeed.

Engaging the attention of show business circa 1946 were such phenomena as plays with dinner intermission; Mr. and Mrs. breakfast shows; 8:00 P.M. legit preem curtains to enable the A.M. newspaper critics to make deadlines; the gradual decline of whodunits on screen and radio, to make way for an upswing of psychological thrillers; the lance-tilting of England's J. Arthur Rank to capture American and world markets for London's celluloid produce; and the French invasion into the United States topflight chansoniers in the class bistros. The Gallic chirpers waxed as rich as French cooking. Edith Piaf, Charles Trenet, Jean Sablon, Lucienne Boyer, Suzy Solidor, not to mention Maurice Chevalier's one-man show as a legit touring attraction, further cemented Franco-American amity with a raft of Continental songs, such as "La Vie En Rose," "All My Love" (née "Bolero") and "C'est Si Bon."

New York's tugboat strike in 1946 played havoc with show biz. Mayor O'Dwyer set up a City Disaster Control Board to put the clamps on fuel-users. Restaurants were allowed to stay open; prepared food was permitted to be served, provided no extra fuel was used. O'Dwyer took to the air and headlines to tell New Yorkers not to go to work on the following day unless advised otherwise. He then shaped an edict shutting down every entertainment place in the city, which would have cost New York show business $2,500,-000. Suddenly, half an hour before it was supposed to go into effect, the order was called off. The strike lasted nine days.

Although the war was over, show business continued to stay in the front lines of patriotic, charity and general welfare work. The American Theatre Wing and USO-Camp Shows continued to play veterans hospitals. Walter Winchell's Damon Runyon Cancer Me-

morial Fund; columnist Ed Sullivan and the Heart Fund; Hollywood's Variety office dispensing free vaccination against a smallpox
epidemic for some 500 actors; $500-a-plate dinner tendered Al Jolson,
to raise funds for an Army hospital being built as a memorial to
Major General Maurice Rose, were part of the unslackening postwar
efforts.

commie probe   1947 was the year that Howard Hughes
made headlines with his Washington testimony; and the un-Ameri-
can Activities Committee probed key Hollywood figures, most of
them writers, for Communistic sympathies. Most of them got prison
sentences. Others, such as Fredric March and his wife, Florence
Eldridge, because of a normal wartime effort for Soviet-American relations, when we were allied against Hitler, found themselves pro-
fessionally embarrassed and forced to sue—and eventually won a
retraction—because the pamphlet, *Counterattack*, put them in a false
light. Edward G. Robinson, whose wartime work was beyond normal
expectancy, including a $100,000 donation to GI welfare, likewise
journeyed to Washington at midcentury to volunteer before a Congressional group as to his past record. Negro singer Josh White
dittoed as did Larry Parks, John Garfield, José Ferrer, and many
others—voluntarily or by subpoena.

As the anti-Communistic fever snowballed, there were needlessly
embarrassing incidents for any number of radio, TV, Hollywood
and other performers and writers, via the publication of their names
and pseudo-affiliations in the past with Communist-front organizations. Jean Muir's cancellation off "The Aldrich Family" TV series
by General Foods was a minor sensation in 1950. Gypsy Rose Lee
was forced to sue in order to clear her name. Ireene Wicker, vet radio
songstress with a son in the service, found herself "unoptioned" by
what she thought a strange "coincidence," on the heels of the *Red
Channels* "exposé." It was indicated that, in many instances, the
exposé sheet culled from erroneous data in *The Daily Worker* and/or
harked back to anti-Franco or wartime cultural alliances with
Russian artistic groups, at a time when those things were not only
unsuspicious but had a patriotic concept. That some, of course, were
insidious Communist-front groups is something which many
quickly discovered and exited, but the onus lingered, often to their
professional and economic embarrassment or hurt.

In 1947, too, a Boston jurist found the film version of *Forever Amber* so "pure" that he complained it "put me to sleep." Boston cropped up again three years later when it scowled on the Cole Porter musical, *Out Of This World,* with its Amphytrion libretto, and tabooed some of the lyrics and dialogue. A Broadway wag redubbed the show "Buttocks and Bows."

In 1947, also, came the cold war, with its front in Berlin. Watching the drama of the air lift, show biz decided to get into the act. Bob Hope, Jinx Falkenburg, Irving Berlin and others left for Germany to entertain the air lift boys for Christmas. On the home front it kept alive the "Purple Heart Circuit," as Eddie Cantor dubbed it, by supporting Veterans Hospital Camp Shows, the successor to USO-Camp Shows.

On the financial side, amusement stocks continued to skid. Shares had been dropping steadily from an average of $22.01 at the end of 1946 to $16.27 at the end of 1947. All phases of show business were beginning to cry the blues, with skating and bowling among the big war-boomers diving hard. The passing of the 5¢ fare in New York changed Coney Island from a "nickel Riviera" to a "10¢ St. Moritz." Steeplechase Park tried to minimize the upped fare by offering free video.

tv goes forward   By 1948 it was clear that the coming era in entertainment belonged to the new baby industry—television. TV gave rise to the most popular pattern of tele entertainment, at least in its initial phases—vaudeville on video, hence "vaudeo."

The first TV World Series was telecast in 1947. Broadway box-office suffered a 50 per cent slump, with matinees kayoed, but bars with television upped 500 per cent. This was the time that gags about "bartender wanted; must be able to fix television set" started. Eventually the World Series, in 1950, were to be sold for $800,000 to Gillette, its long time sponsor. (A subsequent 6-year contract calls for $6,000,-000 for the rights). Considering the fact that the Yanks murdered the Phillies four straight it made $200,000 per telecast pretty expensive sponsorship. Eventually, also, theatres were to attempt coping with major sports events by telecasting them into the cinemas, via large-screen, as part of the b.o. lure. It helped the grosses and the picture houses quickly contracted for "closed circuit," big-screen theatre TV events on an exclusive basis. The only video features that can get them into the theatre, obviously, have to be events not broadcast gratis into the home.

In Portland, Maine, the *Sunday Telegram,* which had published the names of purchasers of horseless carriages back in 1908, now began to do the same for posterity by reporting the locals who were going in for the newfangled video contraption. J. Walter Thompson was the first ad agency to hit $1,000,000 in sponsored tele billings.

Tele began to change the social fabric of the nation. Set owners complained of being deluged by neighbors who elbowed in, made themselves at home, and consumed a fortune in refreshments. Conversation at parties became a dying art, with guests sitting silently and staring at the tele screen in darkness. Women began to complain that when sporting events were being telecast, they were totally ignored—"video widows," *Variety* explained. Parents became frantic over the problem of how to tear Junior from the tele set, in time to get him to do his homework or go to bed.

Established branches of show business began to get really worried about the new medium. Radio examined with dismay a pulse survey which showed that the TV audience for baseball games outnumbered radio listeners by 33 to 1. Sports, the picture business, book publishers and others started to blame video for any and all ailments. Then they decided it might be better to co-operate with instead of fighting the new medium. To paraphrase Jimmy Durante, pretty soon "everybody wanted to git inta de act." Few were quite sure how.

The National Republican and Democratic conventions, both held in the summer of 1948 in Philadelphia, were accepted by tele as its first major challenge to do a better job than radio or newsreels could. Both radio and tele together spent $1,840,929 for the two convention coverages, with TV emerging as the wonder of the year, even stealing the spotlight from the stormy Democrats themselves. As a followup, 10,000,000 Americans saw President Truman take the inaugural oath of office through video, a total of more people than had seen the 31 presidents combined from Washington to Roosevelt.

There soon became no question that TV would be an influential factor in electing the next President of the United States in 1952. In 1950 TV achieved, for Governor Thomas E. Dewey, what nothing else could—it presented him in a more human light and did much to rid him of that onerous crack about looking "like the bridegroom on the wedding cake."

folsom on tv and politicos   TV helped re-elect Senator Robert A. Taft in face of much labor opposition, as the iconoscope reflected him for a sincere man and wiped out much of the invidious stuff written about him. As Frank M. Folsom, president of the Radio Corp. of America, observed: "He couldn't have been elected dog-catcher in face of the written attacks, but TV mirrored him more sympathetically, brought out much in a man's personality that couldn't be uttered, and Taft won. That figured in the case of Vincent Impelliteri, the successful New York City mayoralty candidate, showing him as a simple, sincere, folksy man. And, by the same token, it crucified others."

The growth of tele was fast and furious. The fashion industry announced it would take heavy time in video. The American Federation of Musicians lost no time in setting a scale for commercial video, which came to 75 per cent of the toll for radio network shows. United Artists became the first major distributing company for television films, via regular film exchanges. But a better b.o. idea was the usage by the Hollywood producers of TV spot commercials to merchandize their choicer new film releases,. as against the 10-and-more-years-old pix being telecast gratis.

All of Hollywood sat up and took careful notice when "Ultrafax" was unveiled at a sneak preview in Washington, and hailed as "the seventh wonder of the communication world." It proved the possibility of transmitting full-length movies simultaneously from a film studio to thousands of theatre screens. If this was to be the shape of things to come, the 1948 system of film distribution was doomed to obsolescence. Nobody knew for sure what was coming, but everybody was certain that the movies could not afford to ignore video as they once had radio. The Paramount in Times Square struck an experimental note by televising fights from the Brooklyn Y.M.C.A. on their regulation 18' x 24' screen.

Eventually the Broadway Paramount and the Fox, Brooklyn, started to telecast major bouts on their large screens, paying nominal experimental fees and finding it paid off socko at the b.o. Spyros Skouras, meantime, nurtured his pet idea of two-a-day televised programs, of super-boxoffice potency. Linking 20 Fox-West Coast Theatres up and down California to receive special big shows on a twice-daily schedule, in addition to first-run feature films, the showman figured he could achieve grosses of $500,000 to $750,000 weekly on a $1 top scale.

With that sort of b.o. revenue he figured he could play Merman, Crosby, Cantor; anybody; he could book *South Pacific* or the Metropolitan Opera. He knew that his theatres could never saturate the market, and that these theatre-televised shows—they'd never reach into homes or bars, being on a special wavelength—would also serve as boxoffice hypo to any big Broadway musical, the Met, or any top-flight variety programs.

It was too much to expect that Tin Pan Alley would let video pass without a calypso yowl or two, so Paul Specht promptly published a tune by Paul Rebere called "I Tell-A-Vision," while Harry Taylor wrote the ultimate in 1948 love songs, "Let's Build A Coaxial Cable of Love." He forgot to add, "Baby." Not to be left at the technicolor-TV post, Charles and Henry Tobias, with Nat Simon, in 1950 whipped up "A Colorful Little Couple" which was lyrically primed for all the spectrum love words.

TV also got its feet wet in libel and slander that year, when Elizabeth T. Bentley, videoed over NBC's "Meet the Press," charged suspended Department of Commerce official William R. Remington with being a Communist.

While vaudeo looked up, Loew's State on Broadway dropped vaudeville, but a flock of top names streamed to London to play the famous Palladium, most resounding being the smash impact made by Danny Kaye. Jack Benny, Dinah Shore, Betty Hutton, the Andrews Sisters, Sophie Tucker, the Ink Spots and Tony Martin also were among the big Yank hits in austere Britain, but at the other end of the British Commonwealth of Nations, vaude was laying an egg in Australia, with Variety reporting "slim coin and vague dates for United States acts." Eventually, however, Aussie's grosses also started to look up.

The year also saw giveaway shows hitting their peak on the radio. "Stop the Music" went personaling into the Capitol, and "Winner Take All" into the Strand, New York. But the vaude version of the radio jackpots flopped.

Joe Smith and Charles Dale, the oldest vaude team in show business, who were still doing their "Dr. Kronkheit" sketch, and working, celebrated their 50th anniversary together—slightly short of the records of Fox & Ward (58 years) and McIntyre & Heath (52).

Vaude was reduced to pointing with pride at Ken Murray's variety show, *Blackouts,* in Hollywood, which had survived for over seven straight years, passing the 3,224 performance record of *Life With Father,* but flopped in seven weeks when Murray brought it to New York. And to—shades of Willie Hammerstein!—Patricia "Satira" Schmidt, pardoned for the murder of her lover John L. Mee, who rolled up $6,500 on a percentage basis at Harlem's Spanish Mecca, Teatro Las Americas.

Upheaval in Radio

★

Emerging from the war as the nation's No. 1 news coverage source, radio strove to hang on to its halos. One of its biggest scoops of 1946 was its eye-witness broadcasts on the dramatic demise of Hermann Goering and the execution of 10 Nazi leaders. It also demonstrated its use as a public service in Minneapolis, when an outbreak of polio caused schools to close. Classes were held as usual, via radio.

In 1946, when the world was buzzing about the significance of the atom bomb, CBS, NBC, ABC and MBS pooled resources to cover the United States atom bomb test at Bikini. Variety ran a very terse and vivid review of the broadcast, to wit:

ATOM BOMB TEST
with Bill Downs, Clete Roberts, Don Bell, W. W. Chaplin,
Robert Stewart, Jerome Beatty, others
50 Mins.; 5:30-6:20 P.M. Sunday (June 30)
One Shot

Sustaining
CBS-NBC-ABC-MBS.

ZZZ ZZZ FFFTZ ZZZZM
ZZZ PFFFT ZZZZ ZZZZ
ZY PFTTT PFFFF ZZZZ.

Rose

As for entertainment, in 1946 the same radio names that spelled ether stardom 10 years earlier were still in vogue—Bob Hope, Fibber McGee & Molly, Red Skelton, Lux Radio Theatre, Edgar Bergen, Walter Winchell, Mr. District Attorney, Fred Allen, Jack Benny, Jack Haley, Bing Crosby, Eddie Cantor, Kay Kyser, Abbott & Costello and Amos 'n' Andy.

Variety estimated that the end of World War II found radio comics holding the bag for about $150,000 in unused and unusable war gags. Timely gags of the year centered around the railroad strike, coal shortage, under-the-table auto deals, the housing shortage, Kilroy, *The Lost Weekend,* fountain pens that wrote under water, the Brooklyn Dodgers, Petrillo, Truman's piano playing (later switched to Margaret's sopranoing) and Gromyko's U.N. walkout.

Radio humor also took a provincial turn, with increasing emphasis on Southern California, from where most broadcasts originated, and on intra-show biz "insult" gags. These local quips brought loud yoks from studio audiences on the Coast, but frequently left national audiences puzzled, lukewarm or bored. The La Brea tar pits, Mad Man Muntz, gopher holes, smudge pots, California weather, Sinatra's anemia, Fred Allen's nasal twang and the bags under his eyes, Benny's stinginess, Cantor's Ida and 5 daughters, Crosby's boys, clothes and horses, and the noses of Bob Hope and Jimmy Durante became trite and irritating gags of dubious mirth.

Crosby's tape-recorded shows for Philco, the first big-time deal on any network that allowed a star to do his stint away from the live mike, created a precedent. Other stars demanded that they, too, be allowed to wax their shows. Sponsors balked, feeling that they were entitled to live appearances in exchange for the heavy coin paid. They also feared a drop in ratings but eventually many capitulated. Filmed TV, however, was not countenanced until 1951—and certain comedy programs may always remain "live."

Among radio highlights in 1947 was the furore created by Ralph Edwards' highly successful "Who Is Miss Hush?" stunt on "Truth and Consequences"; Margaret Truman's radio debut in Detroit; the first soap opera with an all-Negro cast, sponsor and agency, "Here Comes Tomorrow," in Chicago; and the formation in that city of the first National Association of Disk Jockeys.

The ever-growing threat of television promised to capture the nighttime hours, leaving radio only soap-opera time when housewives were too busy to look as well as listen. Yet radio was still big business in 1948. Over 37,600,000 families were tabulated as listeners, enough to induce sponsors to part with an annual radio revenue of $663,000,000, of which $60,000,000 was net profit—an all-time radio high. ASCAP's cut of the radio melon amounted to $5,000,000. All this despite the Hooper survey that revealed that there was a *status quo* in the number of sets in use and in listening habits between 1940 and 1948, while other branches of show business had shown lush upturns.

radio jackpots   The biggest slugfest of the year was "Stop the Music" which blew the whistle for a giveaway orgy that turned radio into a perpetual "bank nite." Merchandise given away was estimated at $165,000 a week, the jackpot hitting $7,000,000 in only 44 weeks. The merchandise, services, transportation and vacations, were all contributed to the giveaway shows in exchange for free puffs. Frequently sponsors of the Santa Claus shows were hard put to tell who was sponsoring what.

Trouble began when listeners, hypnotized by the possibility of winning a fortune, dialed out old-time radio favorites. They slipped down the Hooper scales as the giveaways climbed up.

Fred Allen, hardest hit program because of the direct competition opposite "Stop the Music," led radio stars in ganging up in a campaign to laugh the giveaway shows off the air—and failed. Their gags were more than goodnatured humor; they had a sarcastic, always frustrated, bite. Allen's "insurance" policy, purporting to compensate any lucky listener called while tuned in to his show, had a reflex effect—in that it focused even more attention on the jackpot program.

Then a no-holds-barred raid by CBS on NBC's top stars highlighted radio in 1948. The raid had TV overtones in that Jack Benny, Amos 'n' Andy and the like were "bought" by CBS board chairman

William S. Paley with an eye to their TV potentials, in the event the AM medium became extinct or passé.

This was a departure for CBS which prided itself on building its own stars. It had a socko showman-salesman in Arthur Godfrey (his personal $400,000 annual gross, from $10,500,000 billings, attested fully to his merchandizing prowess) and was supposedly beyond star-raiding. This was the era of "capital gains" radio deals too. CBS ogled Walter Winchell, whose per-point payoff on his Hooperating made him a highly valuable commodity, but the American Broadcasting Co. kept him on its own network by getting Kaiser-Frazer to payroll a $1,352,000 contract for 90 broadcasts at the rate of $12,500 per 12½-minutes of WW gab on Sunday night.

Hollywood was still riding the crest of the wave in 1946, when $350,000,000 was spent making films. Earnings surpassed those of 1945, and popcorn alone accounted for a $10,000,000 revenue in film houses.

The 1946 film that copped most of the Academy awards was Samuel Goldwyn's *The Best Years of Our Lives*.

bing, bergman, 'bells,' 1946 boffs   The year's top-grossing stars were Crosby and Ingrid Bergman; the top-grossing film, *Bells Of St. Mary's,* which took $8,000,000, followed by *Leave Her to Heaven, Anna and the King of Siam, The Yearling, The Jolson Story* and Howard Hughes' *The Outlaw*.

As regards the boffo Bergman, not too long afterward, such being the mercurial boxoffice sensitivity, her flop *Joan of Arc* (the picture version of her hit Broadway play by Maxwell Anderson, *Joan of Lorraine*) was followed by another flop, *Stromboli*. Despite the Italian-made film's worldwide "advance campaign" (her unconventional romance with Roberto Rossellini, the Italian director who later became her husband), the public wouldn't buy it. Ingrid and Roberto were eclipsed only by the Rita Hayworth-Aly Khan escapade in the public prints.

When Daily Variety polled the Hollywood trade, at midcentury for all-time bests, Miss Bergman was second only to Greta Garbo as the top femme star. In the breakdown of sound pix (as against the silents), she ranked Bette Davis and Olivia de Havilland 1-2-3.

Incidentally, that poll voted *Gone With the Wind* the all-time best, Charles Chaplin and Garbo the top stars; the late Irving Thalberg best producer; and David Wark Griffith, best director. The latter's *Birth of a Nation* rated No. 2 in the half-century poll, with *Best Years Of Our Lives* third.

Ronald Colman and Sir Laurence Olivier tied for No. 2 in the best male star category, with Spencer Tracy runnerup. Behind Garbo and Bergman, came Bette Davis and de Havilland tied for third. Runnerup producer laurels went to Darryl F. Zanuck and Sam Goldwyn. Runnerup directors were Cecil B. DeMille and William Wyler.

A further breakdown in the midcentury appraisal of the best sound pix and the best silents rated Tracy, Olivier and Colman top men; Goldwyn, Thalberg and Zanuck top producers. (Obviously, Thalberg's edge in the silent era gave him the all-time award.)

In the best silent era category, *Birth of a Nation, Big Parade* and *The Kid* were the toprated pix; Chaplin, Valentino and Emil Jannings, male stars; Garbo, Gloria Swanson and Lillian Gish, femme stars.

The year saw the beginning of the cycle of psychological films. After the excitement of the war years, it was tough to hold film audiences with old formulas. The appeal was basically more adult and sophisticated. Another significant change in the Hollywood formula took place in Westerns, with the spurs-and-chaps boys dropping shooting irons and reaching for gee-tars.

The Westerns that flooded the screens from 1948-1950 included semi-historical expositions of epochal proportions. These actioners invariably prove good b.o., and even DeMille's *Samson and Delilah* was described in the trade as "a Biblical Western."

'adult' pix   The cycle for "adult" pix lasted a couple of years. Dore Schary made a short-budgeter at RKO, *Crossfire*, which fared well but Darryl Zanuck's *Gentleman's Agreement* clicked even bigger. Both dealt with anti-Semitism. Zanuck next tackled the Negro question with *Pinky* and clicked, as he did with *Snake Pit*, a picture about mental institutions. Stanley Kramer's *Home of the Brave*, also a Negro theme, registered but a later attempt for "adult" appeal, *The Men* (paraplegics), came a cropper at the b.o.

The cycle having run its course, exhibs suddenly started clamoring for "good, old-fashioned, solid film entertainment about boy-meets-girl, glamour, no 'problems.'"

In 1946 Hollywood began to take increasing notice of what was happening on English film lots. J. Arthur Rank won control of 20 out of 30 sound stages in England, and controlled 1,100 of 4,761 film theatres. All this, and a $220,000,000 combine, from films which started with a short subject against the demon rum! Rank roved his eyes over the American and foreign markets—and eventually was to experience a financial debacle, at least as far as his British production ambitions were concerned.

At first, the United States was highly indifferent to the British product. Even in 1947, when British cameras were beginning to turn out good stuff, Variety headlined: STIX STILL NIX BRITISH PIX. But the sticks were also nixing American pix that year. In Hastings, Nebraska, one exhibitor's marquee read: DOUBLE FEATURE—ONE GOOD SHOW AND ONE STINKER.

By 1948 cool winds were blowing in Hollywood. Hot stars with cold yarns gave the colony only lukewarm profits, which raised the question, "Are stars worth their prices today?" Profits slid 45 per cent, with the seven majors netting only $55,000,000. A wave of economy hit pictures, with heavy layoffs of studio personnel and East coast home office staffs. Producers were jittery, wondering whether this was the first impact of TV, the high cost of living, poor stories or an unhappy combination of all these factors.

There was little clue in the protests of theatre owners who listed sex, crime and costume pictures as the three biggest poison doses at the boxoffice. It was an old cry, and one which rarely stood up under analysis. It represented chiefly the exhibitors' "front" to appease the professional protesters. Hollywood took it with salt, just as it did audience votes for "single feature" programs. The customers invariably voted for one-film bills but went to double features.

divorcement   The situation in Hollywood during 1948 rapidly fouled up. The scared majors were afraid to produce for a declining market, while the independents found it hard to drag money out of the banks. The United States Supreme Court handed down its long awaited antitrust decisions forcing the major companies to unload most of its theatres, giving the Big Five a total of five years to get rid of the exhibition end. Paramount and RKO soon settled with the Government via a consent decree. Both divided into two separate companies as Warner Bros. was to do in 1951.

Howard Hughes' buy of RKO startled Hollywood. Few knew him intimately, or what could be expected of him. If he wanted anybody he would call them. If it was urgent, through a series of three 8-hour-a-day, round-the-clock secretaries one might get a message to him and he'd call back. Hollywood wits at first wisecracked, "Hughes will never buy RKO because he can't get it off the ground." But he did, and through the quick consent decree with the Government on theatre divorcement looked fair to cash in by ultimately selling enough RKO theatres to make his studio production and distribution organization purchase a comparative bargain.

The film industry's net profits for 1948 had dwindled from the 1946 peak of $90,000,000 to $55,000,000—still very fancy, however. Paramount's *Road to Rio* (Hope-Crosby-Lamour) was the biggest grosser, garnering $4,500,000. Warner Bros.' $22,000,000 net put that company second to Paramount.

The lowered nets stimulated anew the economy drives that placed emphasis on sharp production cuts, kayo of those fancy $250,000 up to $750,000 story and play properties. Great Britain's 55 per cent quota, and sundry money restrictions quickly influenced other foreign nationals to likewise embargo the American film industry. This forced Hollywood investments in foreign ventures, such as local pix production, hotels, theatres and other foreign-to-showbiz buy-ins, as a device to partially thaw out the piled-up frozen funds in Europe.

If films were on the downbeat, the nation's Drive-In theatres were thriving. Food and drink concessions yielded as much as 50 per cent of the profit. The public yen for outdoor films increased. Pix shown were cheap and profits were high. Some captious showmen called 'em "passion pits with pix." As the vogue of the ozoners increased, a Fly-In theatre opened in Asbury Park—room for 25 planes and 500 cars. A Canoe-Inn cinema was announced for Waltham, Massachusetts. The ozoners—eventually exhibitors preferred to call them auto-theatres—were the lone forward-moving light in the benighted exhibition business. They were a boon to the young marrieds (no baby-sitting problems) and the oldsters (invalids who couldn't navigate in a normal theatre were able to recline in the motors driven by their kin). Drive-in impresarios catered to basic needs by providing bottle-warmers for the infants; quick-lunch and soft drink dispensaries; playgrounds for the kids, some including even miniature zoos; laundromats so that, by the time they saw the picture, the family laundry would be done, and the like. This so-called by-product income accounted for a greater profit margin than the basic show business, and the distributors complained, not for naught, that they were entitled to a percentage on the popcorn and allied profits, since it was the Hollywood product that was the lure to draw the populace to the theatre, be it in or out of doors.

56

Disk Jocks and LP Versus 45s

★

The rise of the disk jockey is a postwar phenomenon of unusual proportions. Originally an economic device, chiefly associated with "one-lungers," as the low-watt hinterland radio stations were called, the turntable impresarios first became important on both coasts via Al Jarvis (Hollywood) and Martin Block (New York), with their "make-believe ballroom" technique of turning disks and making a sales pitch. By exercising a judicious ratio of platter and chatter it made them big-income merchandizers. It was the old medicine show on a larger basis, but with an intimacy that the major networks lacked when the super-shows attempted to sell nostrums, food brands, home equipment, motors, petrol and the like.

Eventually the deejay found himself the No. 1 key man in Tin Pan Alley. As one or another plugged a pet platter; or as such instances cropped up where an old Ted Weems disk ("Heartaches") became the bestseller through the single-handed plugging by a North Carolina disk jockey, music publishers and songwriters looked upon the jocks with new respect.

Incidentally, this al fresco method of creating hits and the uncertainty where the new hits will spring from, became part of the new

ASCAP dividend payoff system under the second Governmental consent decree. Newcomer songwriters benefited better than heretofore, where the multiplicity of plugs was the factor, but it hurt the veteran songsmith who suddenly found his backlog catalog not as valuable for royalty dividends as in former years. This was viewed as an inequity by both factions. Even the newcomers now recognize that, if in future years they had no "active" songs being prolifically performed, they too would suffer on the annual ASCAP royalty melons. A more equitable balance is being worked out within ASCAP and in collaboration with the Government.

The decree, however, makes it easier for ASCAP writers to work with BMI firms, and vice versa. Already there are several music publishers who have both ASCAP and BMI catalogs.

As the public became selective in its plays and pix, so it was on the disks. It cared little if it were a major label like Victor, Decca or Columbia or some obscure brand. The interpretation counted, and that's where the deejay came in. He played them all and plugged those he liked. Sometimes the plugs had a payola connotation but since the public always decides in the final analysis, any artificial respiration can give impetus but never insure acceptance. Thus, a relatively obscure artist like Bill Snyder came to the fore with his unique version of "Bewitched"; Frankie Laine with "Cry of the Wild Goose"; Patti Paige with "All My Love" (nee the French "Bolero"); Red Foley with "Chattanooga Shoe Shine Boy"; Eileen Barton's "Bake a Cake"; Teresa Brewer with "Music, Music, Music"; the colored Billy Eckstine and Billy Daniels, via disks, nitery and vaudfilmeries; the Ames Bros. with "Rag Mop"; and hillbilly singers Tennessee Ernie, Jimmy Wakely and Ernest Tubb with their sundry items.

The deejays soon were wagging the dog. Tin Pan Alley welcomed the development of television which, by its production values, looms as the more logical stimulant to music. The cycle was certainly completed in 1950. The yesteryear, silent movie illustrated song-slides became glorified productions as endowed by Lucky Strike on its Hit Parade video series.

The pop music business boom reached its peak in 1946, collecting $10,000,000 in phonograph royalties and countless millions from sheet music, but subsequently skidded, with the economic downbeat. However, basic copyright values of songs continue to mount in value, in light of new-found incomes from synchronization (film) rights, TV's future values for production rights, and the like. Metro-Goldwyn-Mayer recognized that by buying out its 28 per cent minority partner, Jack Robbins, for $500,000, thus (with 20th-Fox) controlling 100 per cent of a giant copyright pool in the Robbins, Feist and Miller Music holdings, along with their subsids.

Songsmiths found their careers more frequently celluloidized in lavish filmusicals such as Bert Kalmar & Harry Ruby (Metro's *Three Little Words*), Jerome Kern (Metro's *Look For the Silver Lining*), Richard Rodgers & Lorenz Hart (*Words and Music*, again Metro) and Vincent Youmans (Warners' *Tea For Two*). The same was true of Fred Fisher (20th Century-Fox's *Oh, You Beautiful Doll*) and Joe E. Howard (20th's *I Wonder Who's Kissing Her Now*).

battle of the speeds An evolution of the internecine battle between the two giant networks—CBS' raid on NBC's talent, with the capital gains as the gimmick—was the battle of the speeds. A nation which had been content to get its platter music on 78 revolutions per minute was suddenly in the midst of LP versus 45s. That meant Long Playing (Columbia Records' 33⅓ rpm pattern) as against RCA Victor's 45 rpms. The RCA record is a 7-inch, plastic job (of vinylite texture), with a large spindle hole. The records are tinted, to facilitate ready identification for pops, red seals (classics), hillbilly and blues. RCA propagated that theirs wasn't merely a new record but "an entirely new system of recording"; that experimentation had convinced them that only a certain portion of the band on the 45s reproduced the "truest" music—thereafter it became distorted to the sensitive ear.

Eventually, after the record business experienced a critical year, the transition was made in 1949-1950 into two broad categories—LP (33⅓ rpm) for the classics and the musicomedy scores, and 45s for the pops. Since there were still an estimated 12,000,000 to 16,000,000 oldfashioned 78 rpm players in the market, the 78s continued manufacture, but the rich metropolitan markets, which more consistently supported the record business, soon converted into "three-speed" machines, either alone or in combination with the boom of television which, by 1951, saw nearly 15,000,000 TV receivers in American homes.

The universality of music, as a language which everybody understands, placed music values more and more to the forefront of show business. American jazz (Duke Ellington and Louis "Satchmo" Armstrong) once again invaded Europe, and conversely Edith Piaf and Maurice Chevalier found few linguistic barriers with successful engagement in the United States. Jazz invaded New York's Carnegie Hall and Town Hall anew at $3 top.

On the longhair side, the Metropolitan Opera House imported Rudolf Bing to succeed Edward Johnson as managing director and, with the assistance of "the Broadway touch," via legit stage directors such as Margaret Webster and Garson Kanin, the Met's 1950-1951 season reopened with Miss Webster's production of Giuseppi Verdi's *Don Carlo* to an all-time record gate of $50,000, easily the top one-night gross in history of all show business on a straight per-ticket basis, with the exception of some mammoth charity.

Ironically, the sensation of the Met 1950-1951 season was not a longhair attraction at all, rather a modern version in English of the ever-popular Johann Strauss operetta, *Die Fledermaus,* with a new book by Garson Kanin (author of *Born Yesterday*) and new lyrics by Howard Dietz. Staged by Mr. Kanin and sung by a top-drawer cast of Met artists including Ljuba Welitch, Patrice Munsel, Risë Stevens, Set Svanholm, Richard Tucker and John Brownlee, *Fledermaus* proved the wisdom of the Broadway legit touch at the Opera House. A boxoffice socko from its preem performance, the Strauss favorite vied with smash Broadway musicals for top pop stage appeal during the season and was the most frequently repeated opus in the Met repertory.

talent raiding   With the battle of the speeds, talent values boomed. Decca snagged Lauritz Melchior, Frankie Carle and Tommy Dorsey; RCA took Ezio Pinza away from Columbia and Columbia retaliated by snaring Leonard Bernstein, Dorothy Kirsten, Pablo Casals, Sir Thomas Beecham, Bill Lawrence and Sammy Kaye. RCA, in turn, annexed Dinah Shore, Risë Stevens, Helen Traubel and Gregor Piatigorsky.

The vogue for "original cast" albums by the disk companies became complicated by Decca's holdout on Ethel Merman, its exclusive contractee, despite the fact RCA had 100 per cent bankrolled the

Irving Berlin musical *Call Me Madam,* in which Miss Merman starred.

There was a vogue for duets which soon ran its course, only to be revived again when Mary Martin-Arthur Godfrey and Ethel Merman-Ray Bolger clicked with their novelty "Go To Sleep" and "Dearie" diskings. There was another type of "duet" vogue when Bing Crosby and his son Gary clicked with "Sam's Song" (Decca), followed by Mary Martin and her son Larry dittoing two duets for Columbia. But for a spell, it was a succession of duets by Doris Day-(the late) Buddy Clark, Jo Stafford-GordonMacRae, Margaret Whiting-Jimmy Wakely and Bing Crosby-Andrews Sisters, although he was variously paired with Patti Andrews singly, as well as Ella Fitzgerald, Louis Armstrong, Ernest Tubbs and others. Kay Starr-Tennessee Ernie were another odd coupling of a rhythm singer with a hillbilly specialist, but the folk song vogue was such that anybody and everybody did 'billy tunes as well as the livelier tempos. Fran Warren-Tony Martin were RCA's romantic defi to the Day-Clark and Stafford-MacRae vogue. Incidentally, the platters catapulted both Doris Day and MacRae to Warner Bros. film contracts.

Novelty duets reached "gimmick" proportions as diskeries became imbued with the idea that the more freakish the tunes and/or talent couplings were, the better sales would be. Sometimes it worked. Mario Lanza's surprise boffola, *The Great Caruso,* with its longhair hit parade music, catapulted a wave of middle-and-highbrow music.

RCA Victor's rebuttal was to couple Ezio Pinza with The Sons of the Pioneers in a prairie number titled "The Little Ol' State of Texas." However, his rich basso proved unconvincing when chirping about the wide open spaces. More effective was the pairing of Helen Traubel with Jimmy Durante in the pranksome "A Real Piano Player" and "The Song's Gotta Come from the Heart."

Riding the pop hit paraders were Patti Page, Nat (King) Cole, Frankie Laine, The Weavers with their folk stuff, Rosemary Clooney and Kay Armen. Both of the latter got attention with "Come On-a My House," a little Armenian folk item whipped up by William Saroyan in collaboration with Ross Bagdasarian, who also disked it for Coral.

The 1948 musicomedy season was so sparse that the "society" bandleaders complained there wasn't a good new show tune, and that the most popular requests were the Al Jolson-Decca album tunes, inspired by *The Jolson Story*. Accent was given to the fact that such Tin Pan Alley greats as George Gershwin, Jerome Kern, Vincent Youmans, Walter Donaldson and Con Conrad were gone, and that the bulk fell on the perennial Irving Berlin, Cole Porter and Richard Rodgers. But soon Rodgers & Hammerstein's *South Pacific*, Porter's *Kiss Me, Kate,* Frank Loesser's *Guys and Dolls* and Berlin's *Call Me Madam* scores more than took up the musical comedy slack.

But the music business had to concede that its pop song hits no longer came from the greats. Some hillbilly or newcomer, and many of them via BMI, rather than the lordly ASCAPers, could turn out hits like "You're Breaking My Heart," "Room Full of Roses," "Jealous Heart," "Nature Boy," "Rudolph the Red-Nosed Reindeer," "Careless Hands," "A Little Bird Told Me That You Loved Me," "That Lucky Old Sun," "Don't Cry, Joe," "Riders in the Sky," "Powder Your Face with Sunshine" and the like.

The deejay impact made it open season for all types of songs and songwriters. Just because you were a vet ASCAP songsmith or publisher was no guarantee against some upstart hillbilly song and/or tunesmith from the hinterland bobbing up with such oddities as "Mule Train," "Chattanoogie Shoeshine Boy," "Slippin' Around," "Tennessee Waltz," "If I Knew You Were Comin' I'd Have Baked A Cake," "Cry of the Wild Goose," "Wedding Samba," "Dear Hearts and Gentle People" and "Rag Mop."

broadwayites go hillbilly   The Brill Bldg. and Lindy's set of professional music men who deprecated the oddity of these "awful" songs becoming hits were given the brushoff by Irving Berlin, in a *Variety* interview, that "any song the public accepts is a good song; and perhaps it is the too sophisticated professional writers who are at fault for turning out their own brand of 'bad songs,' otherwise the public would have reacted more favorably to them." The continued acceptance by the masses of the simple, folksy tunes—the hillbilly genre—didn't leave the ever resourceful veteran songwriter and publisher too smug for too long a period of time, because they did an about-face and started fashioning songs with a Western, folk or hillbilly flavor. What's more, they found them more acceptable than the too hep stuff they had been writing of late.

All this—for there is an affinity between the nation's songs and the state of the nation—was part of the yearning by mass Americana, circa 1948-1951, for a return to the yesteryear *gemütlichkeit*. If the threat of Communism the world over was distressing all hemispheres, at least in their native habitat the Americans seemed to yen for the simple and romantic, as witness these samples of the recent crop of pop hits. From a dispersed people America borrowed and accepted "Tzena, Tzena"; from Huddie Ledbetter ("Leadbelly"), with an assist by musicologist John Lomax, they borrowed "Goodnight Irene." From Italian and Germanic paraphrases came "There's No Tomorrow," "Forever and Ever" and "You're Breaking My Heart." Just as the French impact left its mark on the Hit Parade, the British, too, contributed their quota of international hits with "Galway Bay," "Cruising Down the River," "Hop Scotch Polka" and "Now Is the Hour," although, from London's Denmark Street—the British counterpart of Tin Pan Alley—came protests of the too dominant "Americanization" of English popular music tastes. Periodically, the British Broadcasting Corp. is besieged to "ration" songs so as to give home-grown pop product better representation.

That didn't mean that the songsmiths had forsaken the classics. After the Tchaikowsky, Chopin and Grieg binge of the mid-1940s —Perry Como in 1945 put Chopin on the Hit Parade for many weeks, viz., "Till the End of Time"—the boys were digging into the Italian and mittel-Europa folksongs. Johann Strauss had long since been exhausted, reprised, revived and discarded once again. The refugee, whose first impression of America was that "the people here are all so classical-minded; they whistle the masters and sing and dance to fine old melodies" about summed it up.

Styles in music were chameleon. "Enjoy Yourself (It's Later Than You Think)" became a sort of nitery spending theme song, with the bands propagating the free-spending philosophy. There were attempts at saucy songs which occasionally got network frown or taboo, as for instance the Arthur Godfrey-Mary Martin version of "Go To Sleep." The nation's nostalgic yen for a hark-back to the "good old days," which made the Prohibition era's Jazz Age almost a picnic compared to the Stalin-fomented world unrest, inspired a comeback for the Charleston. This was aided on both coasts by regular Monday night "Charleston contests" at the Mocambo, Hollywood nitery, and by the 1920s theme of the musicalized version of Anita Loos' *Gentlemen Prefer Blondes*. The polka also had its vogue, and with it the zither cycle, inspired by the click of "The Third Man Theme," from the Korda picture of that title. The Dixieland style of dansapation followed the nostalgic urge, and Benny Goodman is in the throes of a swing revival at this writing. Bebop flopped.

passing of many greats   The post-World War II era is notable for the passing of a Who's Who of names, who by their fame or achievement, contributed so much to the American scene or to the scene of world entertainment, letters, music and the other contemporary lively arts.

Somehow there is more than a usual quota from the field of music. The names are reprised, chronologically, not so much as a mass recording of obits but for their accumulative name-power and the voids they must leave, excepting where their works have durability or have been recorded for reprise in posterity, be it a George Bernard Shaw or an Al Jolson.

Literary giants like Theodore Dreiser, 74, E. Phillips Oppenheim, 79, Booth Tarkington, 76, Gertrude Stein, 77, and H. G. Wells, 79, were among the 1946 obits. Capt. James Medill Patterson, publisher of the New York *Daily News,* one of the most successful tabloids in the world, died at 67. Others included actors George Arliss, 77, Lionel Atwill, 61, comedians W. C. Fields, 66 and Joe Keaton (Keaton Family), 79, Al Reeves, who discovered Charles Chaplin, died at 77. Others who passed on were film tycoon Jules Brulatour (Eastman Kodak), 76; legit producers George C. Tyler, 78, and William Harris, Jr. 62; Major Edward Bowes, the radio "amateur hour" impresario, 72, and George Foster, 82, founder of England's biggest talent agency. Rose Melville died at 68 (she played Sis Hopkins to 5,000,000 people in 5,000 performances) and Florence Turner, early-day silent film star, died at 61.

al jolson   When "the king," as even the other show biz greats called Al Jolson, died in the fall of 1950, this marked the end of a golden era. The surviving wearers of the purple, such as Eddie Cantor, Jack Benny, Fred Allen, Ed Wynn, George Jessel, George Burns and Jimmy Durante recognized it as something historic.

When Jolson went out "like the headliner he always was," by willing his entire $4,000,000 estate to be equally divided among Protestant, Catholic and Jewish charities, he was the subject for acclaim in press and pulpit, as with the public in his rich career of nearly 50 years in all branches of show business. He pioneered *The Jazz Singer* into making the talkers the lifesaver of the silent pix era, and he pioneered stellar entertainment for GIs in World War II, and again by being the first star to go to the Korean war area in 1950. At the memorial service for Jolson in New York the crowds were terrific. Eddie Cantor, who delivered the eulogy in New York, as did Jessel at the actual services in Hollywood, observed, "Jolson turned them away again."

The Government officially recognized Jolson's greatness by awarding him the Legion of Merit. Admittedly Jolson was as much a war casualty as the soldier in battle.

Himself a songwriter, for years he had instructed the American Society of Composers, Authors and Publishers to cede 50 per cent of his income direct to the Northwoods Sanitarium, at Saranac, New York.

sid silverman   The 1950 year's mortalities included Sid Silverman, publisher of *Variety*, and son of founder Sime Silverman, who willed his dominant ownership in the paper to his 18-year-old son, Syd, now a Princeton undergraduate. Harold Erichs, business head of the paper, and Abel Green, its editor, are the lone individuals owning equal minority shares in Variety, Inc. While an absentee publisher for over a decade, Sid Silverman was very much attuned to the sundry nuances and variations brought about in show business, and with the upcoming of television he was one of its keenest observers and interpreters right until his death at 51.

Other giants of the stage who passed on in 1950 included producers William A. Brady, Arthur Hopkins and Brock Pemberton; stars such as Jane Cowl, Walter Huston, Julia Marlowe, Sir Harry Lauder, Pauline Lord and Maurice Costello; Sid Field, England's No. 1 comic, and Cyril Smith, another w.k. English comedian.

Showman Sid Grauman, notables like Buddy de Sylva, Kurt Weill and Nijinsky, agents Max Hart and Ralph Blum, Lou Clayton (Jackson & Durante), Jack Dean (longtime married to Fannie Ward), Whispering Jack Smith, Alan Hale, Aunt Jemima (Tess Gardella), Tom Patricola, Bull Montana, Hobart Cavanaugh, Lew Lehr, vet New York *World* drama critic Charles Darnton at 80, Col. Lemuel Q. Stoopnagle (of radio), Joe Yule (Mickey Rooney's actor-father), Arthur Ungar, editor of Daily Variety, songwriter

Joe Burke, playwright Edward Childs Carpenter (*Whistling in the Dark*), producer A. B. Marcus (in his prewar "Marcus Shows," which toured the Orient, Danny Kaye first got his real professional start), author Sam Hellman, William M. McBride (the theatre ticket agency man), Eugene O'Neill, Jr. (a suicide at 40) music publisher Jay Witmark, author Edgar Rice Burroughs (of Tarzan fame), silent-screen director Rex Ingram (*Four Horsemen of the Apocalypse*), author Robert S. Hichens (*Garden of Allah*) at 85, Lady Mendl (Elsie de Wolfe), and actor Pedro de Cordoba swelled the mid-century obits.

Composer Herbert Stothart died in 1949 at 64, as did Herman DeVries, 90, dean of Chicago music critics; Congressman Sol Bloom, at 79, who started as a music publisher and whose daughter, Vera Bloom, is a songsmith. Singer Buddy Clark met an untimely death at 38, in a chartered plane crash while returning to Hollywood from a San Francisco football game.

Other 1949 obits comprised Joe Cawthorne, Charles Hanson Towne, producer Crosby Gaige, A. Atwater Kent (pioneer radio tycoon), Sir Seymour Hicks (British stage star), Wallace Beery, Maurice Maeterlinck (author of *The Blue Bird*), Patric J. Cain (Cain's Warehouse), Robert L. Ripley, A. P. Giannini (the California banker so prominent in film financing), David Balaban (& Katz), Mrs. Chauncey Olcott (a playwright in her own right), Frank McIntyre, Al Shean (Gallagher &), George Moran (& Mack), Charles Feltman (Coney Island), Richard Dix, Frank Morgan, Ed Ford (4 Fords), Max M. Dill (Kolb &), Rex Beach, William J. Kelly and Ralph Spence (pioneer silent film gagman).

In 1948, J. Keirn Brennan (74) followed his longtime songwriting collaborator Ernest R. Ball into the beyond, as did Clarence Gaskill ("Minnie the Moocher") 56; Oley Speaks ("Road to Mandalay" and "Sylvia"), at 74; Vernon Dalhart ("Prisoner's Song") at 65; Franz Lehar (the *Merry Widow* composer) at 78; music publisher F. A. (Kerry) Mills at 79; and versatile composer-producer-playwright Earl Carroll, who was killed in a plane crash, at 56, along with his "heart," Beryl Wallace, who was the No. 1 beaut at Carroll's theatre-restaurant in Hollywood. His will requested joint burial, and special municipal permission had to be obtained in Los Angeles for the artistic nude the showman specified over their joint tomb.

The year also saw the passing of David Wark Griffith, the film pioneer; Burns Mantle, the dean of New York drama critics; King Baggot, another early film idol; Carole Landis, a suicide at 29; Elissa Landi; Mary Nolan (Imogene Wilson); Fred Niblo, vet pix director who megaphoned the silent epic *Ben Hur;* Vera Gordon; Viola Allen, Frohman star of yesteryear; Dame May Whitty; Bessie Clayton, the toe dancer, playwright Max Marcin; and Rupert D'Oyly Carte, founder of the great Gilbert & Sullivan opera co.

Harry K. Thaw, the Tommy Manville of his era, died in 1947 at 76, as did J. Herbert Mack, pioneer burlesque impresario, at 91; J. C. Nugent; Lewis E. Lawes, the warden at Sing Sing; Lucille Webster (Mrs. Jimmy Gleason); humorist John P. Medbury; columnist-producer Mark Hellinger; Will Fyffe; pioneer Western star Harry Carey; poet-playwright Richard LeGallienne (father of Eva); Lucius Boomer, the Waldorf-Astoria bossman; J. Warren Kerrigan, silent movie matinee idol; songwriter Bert Kalmar, at 63; Eva Tanguay, vaude's great song interpreter, at 68; Grace Moore, another songbird of a different caliber, at 45; Walter Donaldson, 54, another Tin Pan Alley great; Lieut. Gitz Rice, the Canadian war hero and songwriter ("Dear Old Pal of Mine"); and A. Seymour Brown ("Oh You Beautiful Doll").

The year 1945 saw the passing of such songwriting giants as Jerome Kern, Gus Edwards, Edward B. Marks, James V. Monaco and Al Dubin. A year later Harry Von Tilzer (73); Moritz Rosenthal (83), the Polish pianist-composer; and former Mayor James J. Walker ("Will You Love Me In December As You Did in May?") at 65 joined them in the musical beyond.

Other 1945 obits included the great minstrel man, Al Fields; Billy Watson (né Isaac Levine) of the famed Watson's Beef Trust; playwright Richard Walton Tully (*Bird of Paradise*); Johnnie Jess, 83, another burleycue pioneer; actor George Sidney; musical comedy's Gus Shy; Winfield Sheehan (William Fox's chief aide); producer Oliver Morosco; Charles Coburn (not the actor—né Colin Whitton McCallem English, he wrote "The Man Who Broke the Bank At Monte Carlo"); Albert Geyer, 85 ("World's greatest acrobat," of Geyer & Delhauser); bandleader Glenn Miller (the United States Army officially "presumes" he is dead, victim of a wartime air crash); playwright William Carey Duncan (*Royal Vagabond*); William J. Ferry ("The Frog Man," a vaude and circus great); Kitty Sharp (90), last surviving cast member of the original *The Black Crook*

Company); Julius Keller (81)—he was the first to introduce the cafe floor show to Maxim's, New York, and the first to supply gigolos for lonely ladies at Maxim's tea dansants); newspapermen O. M. (Monte) Samuel (60), Variety's oldest mugg, he started with the paper's founding in 1905; Hype Igoe; Joseph V. Connolly (King Features head); and essayist-critic Benjamin deCasseres.

57

The 'Monster'

★

Show biz already was calling television the "monster," and the continuing $64,000,000 question is, will TV eventually swallow up practically all of show business? The 1951-52 season is undoubtedly the year of decision. Already both Hollywood and TV have decided to go steady. The pix biz figured as long as it can't fight progress it might as well join it, and virtually every major film studio agreed to rent studio space for TV film production. However, film moguls still held out on releasing any relatively recent films to video despite the issuance of lesser if slightly newer British pix. On the other hand, if indie producers want to use studio space for specific vidpix production, the majors are willing to rent their facilities.

But this attempt to protect the 18,000 exhibitors, the long-time customers of the producers, was constantly losing ground. Bill Boyd's Hopalong Cassidy was doing so well with oldie pix that Roy Rogers and Gene Autry got similar ideas for theirs.

United Paramount Theatres dramatized the situation most vividly by a merger proposal with The American Broadcasting Company, and retaining a number of key network executives. Par Theatres' prime objective was to insure TV outlets in 5 key markets, the limitation under existing FCC restrictions.

The show biz axiom about there "being nothing more certain than change in this business" witnessed several changes, shifts, moves, and mergers—all pointing to TV. Henry Ginsberg, former production topper at Paramount, joined NBC as "production coordinator," an ambiguous post at first but keyed to ultimate vidpix production. Billy Rose became a $100,000-a-year TV consultant to NBC. David O. Selznick's Dan O'Shea became an important cog in the CBS top echelon. Louis B. Mayer resigned from Metro-Goldwyn-Mayer, the company he helped found some 27 years ago, in a policy scrap with "the General," as Loew's, Inc.'s prexy, Nicholas M. Schenck, is called. Latter favored production economies and new blood, symbolized chiefly in Dore Schary, the relatively new production boss at the studio. M-G-M is now minus both the Goldwyn (long since gone indie) and Mayer names.

An abortive $25,000,000 deal—at $15 a share for the Warner freres' 24 per cent control—continues to have TV repercussions. Warner's Burbank plant is streamlining its holdings by offering to sell accumulated, heretofore unproduced, scripts, to TV. The Brothers renamed their Broadway Strand showcase the Warner Theatre, in celebration of the "25th Anniversary of Sound," and became the first Main Stem de-luxer to install RCA big-screen television production equipment. The N. Y. Paramount already had its big screen TV equipment. Even the holdout Loew's Theatre chain is following suit along with other circuits.

subscription television   The click of the Joe Louis-Lee Savold fight, and the "Irish Bob" Murphy-Jake LaMotta fisticuffs exclusive TV showings at theatres sparked renewed interest in "subscription television."

These innovations brought the industry back to Commander Eugene F. MacDonald, Jr., president of Zenith Radio Corp. and proponent of Zenith's subsidiary, Phonevision. Phonevision enables viewers to screen motion pictures at home, the $1 fee per new picture being charged to the individual's telephone bill.

The results were good for the 90-day Phonevision experiment which took place with a special FCC license. This was an about-face for the FCC who had previously frowned on "subscription radio." But new modes and moods brought new rules. Paramount bought control of the Telemeter subscription idea; the Skiatron Corp. had its own Subscribervision system. Based on a coin-in-the-slot principle, the machines unscramble distorted patterns on a special channel. Telemeter claims a unique gauge which automatically records which feature earned which fee, so that it can accurately compute what percentage split goes to what entertainment medium.

The color hassle continued bubbling. CBS got into the field first with a commercial chain telecast, which restricted its own audience because of the complicated CBS system. Later, to offset this difficulty, CBS began manufacturing special colorvision sets. RCA followed with its "compatible" tube system which enabled any black-and-white TV set to receive color. CBS color is a blur when received on an ordinary black-and-white TV set. Somehow manufacturers are sticking with RCA's system, despite the governmental agency's partiality to the CBS system.

The closer affinity of video with the stage, rather than with Hollywood, is figured to hypo the "live" theatre. The plenitude of ballet on TV may or may not be an influencing factor in the fabulous grosses which ballet companies like Sadler's Wells, Roland Petit and his Paris ballet troupe, and others have enjoyed. The English Sadler's Wells ballet netted $134,769 sans tax, in eight shows which exceeds the record set by the national touring company of *South Pacific,* for instance, whose high-water mark was $112,368 in Dallas, and even the still higher gross that *Oklahoma!* did in an Oklahoma City week with $119,811. The Sadler's troupe had over $1,000,000 advance before its second United States tour in 1950—an all-time record in the history of the dance.

Greats, some of whom started in vaudeville and achieved world renown in radio segued into TV and clicked, include Jimmy Durante, Dean Martin & Jerry Lewis (who didn't fare well on radio), Eddie Cantor, Arthur Godfrey, Bob Hope, Jack Benny, George Burns & Gracie Allen, Ed Wynn, Ken Murray, Danny Thomas, Bobby Clark, and Abbott & Costello.

Unlike the more slowly pioneering radio, which was content with such early-day favorites as the Happiness Boys (Billy Jones & Ernie Hare), the A & P Gypsies, Vaughn de Leath, Whispering Jack Smith, Little Jack Little, band pickups such as Vincent Lopez, B. A. Rolfe, Paul Specht and Ben Bernie, TV was big time in no time.

Video interests realized that only big league entertainment would sell receiving sets costing $300 to $500, and more, and sell valuable time to sponsors on the TV networks, so it set out to buy up as much important marquee talent as possible.

Both the William Morris agency and the Music Corp. of America, as well as other talent agencies were equally quick to realize that the pioneering, low-cost era of video would be fleeting. Important money soon became the vogue. Bob Hope's $40,000-a-week (his first Frigidaire-sponsored package was a $130,000 item) set the pace. For the more consistent once-a-monthers such as Eddie Cantor and Jimmy Durante, the "packages" brought $50,000, and with overtime (which the sponsor and network absorbed in part) for rehearsals the shows ran closer to 60G. While the stars could net $20,000 to $25,000 for a month's wages the nature of video is such that more intensive scripting, preparation and rehearsal is necessary. The actor who comes to the radio studio an hour before curtain-time and reads his "ad libs," cues in his songs (with an expert piano accompanist, who anticipates every nuance), or even reads a dramatic script, is a thing of the past. That was AM—not so with TV.

tv's own stars   Meantime TV has been making its own new stars—Sid Caesar, Imogene Coca and Dave Garroway; "plunging neckline" personalities like Faye Emerson, Maggi McNellis, Dagmar, and Eva Gabor; grownup quiz kids, of the Oscar Levant genre, such as Eloise McElhone; and Ken Murray, Clifton Fadiman, Milton Berle, Arthur Godfrey and Ed Sullivan became kingpins as vaudeo entrepreneurs; Ted Mack took the "amateur hour" technique successfully from AM to TV; marionette stars like Kukla, Fran & Ollie and Bob Smith's "Howdy Doody" came to the fore.

By buying back control of his old "Hopalong Cassidy" pix for TV, Bill Boyd put himself into income brackets such as he never before knew. The subsidiary income from "Hoppy" Western regalia and its by-products is astronomical. An example of Boyd's boffo b.o. occurred at the Liberty Theatre, Chicago, which presented "3 Hopalong Cassidys Never Before Seen On TV!"

Godfrey brought back the ukulele to such an extent that music publishers had to reincorporate special uke arrangements on their new sheet music—a practice abandoned after the F. Scott Fitzgerald "Jazz Age" era when raccoon coats and ukuleles were standard flipper-and-flapper equipment.

In line with sophisticated video entertainment—the s.a. gals, adult dramatic scripts, nitery comics' flip gags and the like—there was concern on two fronts. TV wanted to insure itself against any FCC frown by self-regulation; and pix, seeking an alibi for their partial b.o. eclipse, wondered if the "Production Code" (known as the "Joe Breen office" in the trade) should not be relaxed to conform to more "adult" standards. The video cameras have, unquestionably, on occasion, been too revealing, although sometimes accidentally so. There is the instance of the rather prim newspaper gal who appeared on TV in a white decolleté, which through a quirk of the camera, gave her an overall Gypsy Rose Lee appearance. Certain comedians, particularly those from the cafes making guest-shots on the vaudeos, have slipped over an occasional indigo nifty. The dramatic scripts, betimes, also might have gotten "the Joe Breen office" frown if done in Hollywood.

color tv   With the atomic development of post-World War II video, color TV loomed large and menacing in 1950. The two giant networks, CBS and the Radio Corp. of America and its National Broadcasting Co. subsidiary, crossed electronic swords. The Federal Communications Commission's OK on CBS' color TV method over RCA-NBC's touched off an intra-trade and a public battle which made a road company out of their two previous feuds, talent raids and record speed battles.

It is generally agreed that with the coaxial cable now reaching from coast-to-coast the color controversy will catch up with TV's scientific developments, returning the medium to show biz's fundamental—what's the attraction?

TV's importance created another Broadway phenomenon. The easterners who joined the Hollywood pix and radio gold rush came back home. Some sold their Bevhills homes and gave up memberships in the Hillcrest and Lakeside country clubs; most re-established apartments in New York. The Lambs, Friars and NVA club rosters zoomed again as old members returned and lapsed memberships were reactivated but not for long. Already Hollywood is reclaiming some of its lost glory now that the coaxial cable is here.

Fact is that Hollywood, with or without the TV-inspired downbeat of top names—so many of whom hurried back to Broadway, as did scripters and directors—is one of the top datelines in the world. Over 300 correspondents accredited to the "Eric Johnston office" alone attests to that.

Meantime the question of new talent is a continuing one, especially as TV has been devouring so much of it. But somehow new values seem to assert themselves. The mountain summer resorts in the Catskills (New York) and Poconos (Pennsylvania), broadly grouped as the borscht circuit, come up with talent season after season. That, along with niteries and what is left of vaudeville, which heretofore, along with burlesque, was the biggest proving ground for talent, constitutes about the most fertile fountainhead for new faces.

Noted in recent years by Variety's New Act reviews is that over 80 per cent deal with song-and-dance and acrobatic turns—very few comedy acts and talking turns. In vaude's heyday the ratio was about 90 per cent talking acts, and 10 per cent dumb acts or straight singing turns. Yesterday's dumb acts were openers or closers, or an occasional "deuce spot" (No. 2 on the bill). In video, today, they get important spottings. Too often, of course, they're utilized as foils for a Milton Berle comedy antic, for example. But it does pinpoint the paucity of the truly great comics—that's why the few remaining Cantors, Berles, Allens, Bennys, Hopes, Durantes and Wynns must be so carefully rationed around the iconoscopes, on a once-a-month, or even less frequent schedule.

In actuality, video is a blend of or an inspirational force for almost every branch of show biz. Vaude went into the niteries, radio and now video. Legit and ballet, puppets, Little Theatres, circuses and carnivals, musical comedy and revue—all these are now part and parcel of TV. The cycle thus has completed itself, save for minstrelsy which has long become extinct and lingers only in makeshift amateur entertainments by lodges and fraternal organizations.

TV now has permanent circus features as bait for the juveniles, and as an antidote to the Hopalong Cassidy vogue that first seemed to dominate the 5-7 p.m. slots on TV. As regards major outdoor attractions, the Ringling-Barnum & Bailey Circus found TV a boon rather than a b.o. bane, as evidenced by the $6,000,000 record grosses in 1949 and 1950, of which $1,500,000 was from Madison Square Garden alone.

Video's inroads on sports are being offset by underwriting major fights, ball games and the like. TV has helped basketball and hockey, revived wrestling into a clown type of showmanship-sports event, and created popularity for a new sport, the roller derby. Percentage of the TV coin to baseball players, pro gridders, fighters and the like is figured to take up the slack, besides proving a continuing ballyhoo medium for these sports.

Radio's status, meantime, has gone through a gamut of super-shows, such as a 1½ hour, Tallulah Bankhead all-star galaxy that NBC inducted in late 1950 to "knock off Benny at 7," to the petering-out of quiz and jackpot shows. However, the Stop the Music type of show, at its height, did achieve a k.o. on such stalwarts as Fred Allen. For all his fulminating against "radio which makes a frig-idaire the headliner and jackpot the prime entertainment," Allen was forced into retirement, although not for long.

The giveaways assumed staggering and ridiculous proportions until the money and prize-award shows graduated into engaging such expert conferenciers as Groucho Marx, Ralph Edwards, Jan Murray and Joey Adams who merely used the prizes for comedy entertainment values.

The gambling instinct basic with people, combined with the something-for-nothing appeal, gripped the American public. Spon-sors latched on to the millions of phones in American homes as a device for a legal form of a quasi-lottery, and in no time Winchell, the radio columnists, and others were assisting in "the key to the mystery melody" and other inside info, like tipstering sheets.

Amidst the TV hoopla, radio refused to concede defeat and the continuance of AM billings attest to that. Radio is still rich, lush, and thriving. Hinterland independent stations accused the chains of be-coming so big-city sold on TV that they were sabotaging radio, which still paid the freight for all of TV's new excitement. NBC conceded that only 3 of its 5 stations in 1951 were making money, and that the others were only at break-even points.

As for "the monster" taking over all of show biz, Brigadier Gen-eral David Sarnoff, board chairman of RCA, didn't think so. He told Variety, "Television would be a big hit if it only reflected the march of life. In other words, were TV to show only milling crowds in Rockefeller Center, The Loop, or on Market Street, people would want to look at them. It brings the excitement of our world right into the home. Witness the Kefauver committee's investigations, General MacArthur's address to Congress, and major sports events and big entertainment programs."

legit's boom   That fabulous invalid, legit, proved really socko at midcentury. As with all postwar selectivity, you couldn't get into the hits and you couldn't give away the in-betweeners.

The road sagged, but two Rodgers & Hammerstein honeys were continuing to mop up. *South Pacific* bid fair to top the fabulous *Oklahoma!* which, in seven years, rolled up a $4,185,500 profit on the road. In its first year on Broadway, *South Pacific* set a new mark with its $2,635,000 gross, topping Ziegfeld's *Show Boat*.

R & H refuse to have their shows filmed. On Broadway and on tour *South Pacific* and *Oklahoma!* have done more profit than a smash picture which, if costing $1,500,000-$2,000,000 and if realizing a gross twice that amount, is deemed highly profitable. A legit musical's investment today averages $200,000-$225,000 although, of course, the continuing weekly overhead cannot compare with the single-cost investment that constitutes a film's over-all "nut."

Just as *Abie's Irish Rose* was the smash of the 1920s, and *Tobacco Road* with its many road companies was the 1930s topper, so were *Life With Father* and *Oklahoma!* the highlights of the 1940s.

Abie ran on Broadway from 1922-1927 and grossed $2,500,000, garnering its real gravy from myriad road companies, including England, Australia and South Africa besides several national touring troupes in the United States, which piled up another $17,500,000. However, *South Pacific* on its first year grossed $2,635,000. In the comparisons it must not be forgotten that the $2 scale in the 1920s for a light comedy that spelled a $10,000 weekly gross meant a lot of profit.

Tobacco Road grossed $4,300,000, of which $1,820,000 came from its second-longest-run on Broadway record (1933-1941). *Oklahoma!* grossed $12,115,869 all told, and *Life With Father* clocked $9,908,000. *Oklahoma!* as a champ Broadway long-runner is fourth only to *Father, Tobacco Road* and *Abie,* the all-American long-runners on Broadway with 3,224, 3,182 and 2,327 performances respectively. Both *Road* and *Abie* also enjoy the dubious distinction of having been roundly panned by the critics but survived the scriveners' barbs, a commentary that is significant in light of recent years when, managers aver, "unless you get a good set of notices you're dead." *Oklahoma!* with 2,248 performances, *Hellzapoppin,* 1,404, and *Annie Get Your Gun* with 1,147 performances are the only three musicals in the top 12.

On the subject of long runs, those wonderful old melodramas of the 19th century, Denman Thompson's *The Old Homestead,* Harriet Beecher Stowe's *Uncle Tom's Cabin* and Lottie Blair Parker's *Way Down East,* really make *Father* and the others look like short-runners. Thompson played in his *Homestead* for 20 years after its first production in 1896. *Tom* troupes roamed the country and the riverboats for decades after its dramatization in 1852. *East* has been a stock company standby for decades after its 1898 premiere.

rodgers & hammerstein George and Ira Gershwin cornered the musical comedy market in the 1920s with words and music for George White's *Scandals,* Alex Aarons & Vinton Freedley shows (Gertrude Lawrence in *Oh, Kay!*), the Astaires, *et. al.,* but the 1940s and 1950s belong dominantly to Rodgers & Hammerstein & Co. Whereas George Gershwin wrote jazz rhapsodies, jazz operas, and musical comedy scores at a highly accelerated pace during his 38 years, Oscar Hammerstein, 2d, and Richard Rodgers are having richer, fuller careers.

They and their associated stagers, directors, coauthors and coproducers account for a rich heritage in the American theatre, *Oklahoma!* was a signal turning point in the Rodgers & Hammerstein career. It was their first joint effort and it proved a real sock, on the heels of the death of Lorenz Hart at 47 in 1943. Dick Rodgers & Larry Hart had been spoken of as "the American Gilbert & Sullivan." Hart's lyrics were clever and sophisticated, but with the more gentle and poetic Hammerstein, Rodgers was to fashion his even richer scores and to figure as coproducer in some of the best straight comedies.

While the Theatre Guild produced their *Oklahoma!,* the songsmiths in collaboration with Leland Hayward and Joshua Logan, produced *South Pacific.* Alone they presented *The King and I* (Gertrude Lawrence-Yul Brynner). As a production team they also accounted for *I Remember Mama, John Loves Mary* (the latter with Logan), *The Happy Time,* and another fabulously successful musical, *Annie Get Your Gun,* which starred Ethel Merman, with an Irving Berlin score; this was Berlin's takeover of a Herbert & Dorothy Fields book following the death of Jerome Kern at 60 in 1945. Kern was originally to have tunesmithed *Annie.*

The Rodgers & Hammerstein alliances all prospered, as witness the Berlin-Merman musical, *Call Me Madam*, under Leland Hayward's aegis. Hayward, a Hollywood 10 per center turned legit producer, successfully impresarioed *A Bell for Adano, State of the Union, Mister Roberts* (coauthored with and staged by Joshua Logan), *Anne of the Thousand Days* (in association with the Playwrights' Company and authored by Maxwell Anderson). Logan, in turn, was author (from the original *The Cherry Orchard* of Chekov), director and coproducer (with Leland Hayward) of Helen Hayes' *The Wisteria Trees*; coauthor and director of *Mister Roberts* and *South Pacific*; and stager of *I Married an Angel, On Borrowed Time, Two for the Show, Knickerbocker Holiday, Higher and Higher, By Jupiter, Charlie's Aunt, Annie Get Your Gun, Happy Birthday,* and *John Loves Mary*.

south pacific & oklahoma!   The fabulous Rodgers & Hammerstein saga reflected by that sordid economic basis which show biz best understands—the b.o.—is best pointed up by the hit, *South Pacific*. Now in its third year, *Pacific* earns over $20,000 weekly from two companies, over $1,000,000 annual profit. It has already distributed a total of $2,200,000 in profits to the lucky investors.

Oklahoma!'s melon has been $4,275,500, including $60,000 from the 1950-51 season's road tour, as well as British and other foreign managements' rights, record sales, etc. Stock rights have not been leased and there are no picture deals. Ditto *South Pacific*. Rodgers & Hammerstein just can't see undermining their living theatre property by selling celluloid rights.

While it's a Rodgers & Hammerstein era all right, Hayward's *Mister Roberts* didn't do badly, with $1,150,000 in distributed profits so far, and $85,000 in the kitty for cash reserve. And the lucky angels are awaiting another cutting of the melon.

Like Irving Berlin who was accused for 10 years following his marriage of having "lost the common touch" and "the feel of the people," Hammerstein, after a succession of flops, finally wowed 'em with *Oklahoma!* In 1944 he took a memorable ad in Variety telling show biz, I'VE DONE IT BEFORE AND I CAN DO IT AGAIN! And instead of listing *Oklahoma!* or any of his previous successes, Hammerstein's self-kidding ad reprised some of his undistinguished but highly memorable flops, such as *Very Warm for May* (7 weeks), *Ball at the Savoy* (5 weeks), *Sunny River* (6 weeks), *Three Sisters* (6 weeks), and *Free For All* (3 weeks).

It was poetic justice, therefore, that his two outstanding flops—*Ball at the Savoy* and *Three Sisters,* both at London's Drury Lane Theatre in 1933-34—were later wiped off the slate by his being established as the Drury Lane's "longest-run author" in the history of that 288-year-old London theatrical landmark. First came *Oklahoma!* in 1947, which ran over three years (1,343 performances), and *Carousel* in 1950-51 which will have run 1½ years by the time Mary Martin re-creates her *South Pacific* role in the West End in the fall of 1951. (For Miss Martin, too, *South Pacific* is a kind of challenge. In 1946 she flopped in Noel Coward's *Pacific 1860* at the Drury Lane and the comedienne swore she would come back to London and redeem herself.)

Carousel's career at the Drury Lane made it the fourth longest run in the theatre's history, topped only by *Oklahoma!* and two 1920 operettas, *Rose Marie* and *The Desert Song,* on which Hammerstein also collaborated.

$50,000,000 legit biz   As Variety's legit statistician, Hobe Morrison, computed, the legit gross for 1950-51 was $48,216,600, of which $27,886,000 was done on Broadway and $20,330,600 on the road. The 1949-50 season's gross was $49,015,800, of which Broadway contributed $28,614,500; and the year before, legit in the U. S. and Canada grossed $52,498,600, comprising tickets worth $28,840,700 on Broadway and $23,657,900 on the road.

Lemuel Ayers' and Saint Subber's *Kiss Me, Kate* cut up $996,000 in profits and has about $90,000 in other liquid assets. The relatively newer *Gentlemen Prefer Blondes* has cut up $440,000 on a $200,000 investment, with more to come.

Coproducer Joshua Logan, himself an ex-GI, waxed plenty sore at General Thomas T. Handy who banned *Mister Roberts*—which had "soothed" President Truman—from his European command. General Handy's wife thought *Roberts* "too rough" for our German Occupation Army GIs!

Cole Porter's 1951 season entry, *Out of This World,* proved the reverse of *Kate.* It lost $179,000 on a $250,000 production investment. Where the Bard was boff on Broadway in an earlier era, Olivia de Havilland's *Romeo & Juliet* represented a $330,000 setback. *The*

Green Pastures revival cost $200,000; *Billy Budd* gave up with a $105,000 loss; *Make a Wish* was a $250,000 casualty. *Wish* was a handsome production but lacked a good score. Comedian Phil Silvers cracked "Soooo all right, the people will go out humming the costumes!"

The 1951 legit season was notable for the producing team of Feuer & Martin (Ray Bolger's *Where's Charley?* and the Damon-Runyon-inspired *Guys & Dolls*), and, coincidentally, the growing stature of Frank Loesser, composer of both scores.

an actor's year Recent developments indicate that, more and more, "it's an actor's year on Broadway." With Ethel Merman and *Madam*, Carol Channing and *Gentlemen*, Shirley Booth and *A Tree Grows in Brooklyn*, John Gielgud and Pamela Brown in *The Lady's Not for Burning*, Frederic March and Florence Eldridge in Lillian Hellman's *The Autumn Garden*, Celeste Holm in *Affairs of State*, Rex Harrison and Lilli Palmer in *Bell, Book and Candle*, Paul Kelly and Uta Hagen in Odets' *The Country Girl*, Richard Whorf and Nancy Kelly in *A Season in the Sun*, Louis Jouvet's company, Claude Rains with *Darkness at Noon* by Sidney Kingsley, Gloria Swanson and José Ferrer in the MacArthur-Hecht *20th Century* revival, Gertrude Lawrence and Yul Brynner in *The King and I*, Maureen Stapleton in *The Rose Tattoo*, Charlotte Greenwood in the ill-fated *Out of This World*, Louis Calhern's *King Lear*, Barbara Bel Geddes in *The Moon Is Blue*, Bert Lahr and Dolores Gray in *Two on the Aisle*, et al.

critics' box score 1951 was the year Variety finally acceded to the Legit Critic's long-pending beefs against the Critics' Box Score, and dropped it. Variety pointed out anew that a daily paper's critic's prime function should be to advise his readers whether or not to spend from $3.60 up to $7.20 for a ticket and that pure critical appraisal should not blind the reviewer to the box office objective. Anyway, as Variety pointed out, its 26-year-old box score achieved its purpose: (a) It got reviewers off the fence, because most of them were giving definite opinions; and (b) if there was any backsliding and recourse to fence-sitting it could always be reinstated. In an informal reappraisal of critical opinion, which Variety continues to keep for intraoffice information, it was noted that there were fewer "definite maybes" given than ever before; that the critics were sincere in their efforts to state definite opinions. Their papers went further by broadsiding this dubious acclaim by institutional ads on delivery trucks, office ads in the newspapers themselves, and the like.

at midcentury As show biz rolls into the second half of the 20th Century, it harks back and wonders. First it was vaude. Pix knocked that off. Sound knocked off the silents. Radio almost dittoed, but, somehow pix and other general entertainment entities were able to capitalize on radio ballyhoo and build-up for b.o. benefit. Now comes video, something unique unto itself. Sight value, added to sound, brought into the home, and what it does to baby-sitting problems, are all staggering plusses for TV.

Hold on to your hats, boys, this is where we came in!

Glossary

Admish—admission price.

AM—amplitude modulation radio reception; antithesis of FM

Angel—show-backer.

Anzac—an Australian.

ASCAP—The American Society of Composers, Authors and Publishers.

Aud—auditorium.

Balto—Baltimore.

Belly laff—big comedy reaction.

Big time—big league.

Biz—business.

Blue stuff—dirty comedy or risqué stage business.

BMIer—member of Broadcast Music, Inc., radio's ASCAP counterpart.

Boff—a hit

Baloney—spurious.

Booners—talent scouts, derived from Daniel Boone.

Borscht circuit—broad connotation for Catskill (N.Y.) Mountain resorts booking talent.

B.o.—box office.

B.r.—bank roll.

Brit flick—British film.

Brodied—flopped; derived from Steve Brodie.

Brush-off—to ignore or brush aside.

Budgetitis—trouble with the financial budget.

Burley or burleycue—burlesque.

Caviar set—snobby circle.

Chi—Chicago.

Chiller—melodrama.

Chiz—chiseler; a gyp.

Chowmeinery—Chinese restaurant.

Chump—Broadway sucker.

Cincy—Cincinnati.

Cleffer—songwriter.

Click—a rousing success.

Cliffhanger, or cliffer—melodramatic serial; derived from habit of ending chapters with hero on brink of disaster.

Cocktailery—cocktail lounge.

Coffee-and-cake time—bush league.

567

Coffee Pot Canyon—Times Square, because of the large number of all-nite drugstores and cafeterias there.

Coin happy—hungry for money, to make money.

Competish—competition.

Crix—critics.

Cuffo—on the cuff; for free.

Damp blanket—bad reviews.

Dancery—dancehall.

Dansapation—syncopated music.

DC—Washington, District of Columbia.

Deejay—disk jockey.

Diskery—phonograph record manufacturer.

Divvy—quarterly dividend.

"Downtown end"—Wall Street, as used in relation to financing a big amusement deal.

Drive—artificial campaign to plug a song into popularity.

Dualer—house playing two films.

Eatery—restaurant.

Emcee—master of ceremonies.

Exhibs—Motion picture exhibitors.

Fanner—fan dancer.

Femcee—mistress of ceremonies.

Femme—female.

Femme looker—pulchritudinous woman.

Filmusical—musical picture, sometimes called tuner.

Finale bend—final bows.

Flesh—live actors.

Flivved—flopped.

Flopped—performance didn't get over.

FM—frequency modulation radio reception; antithesis of AM.

Foldee—a show that folded.

Freeloader—a chiseler; from one who loads up on free drinks and food.

Frisco—San Francisco.

Frolic—performance.

G—$1000.

Gabber—radio commentator.

Gower Gulch—See *Poverty Row*.

Grind—stripteaser's pelvic gyrations.

Grind house—continuous performance theater.

Grunt-and-groaners—those phony TV wrestlers.

Guestar—TV or radio guest artist.

Gyp 'n' take—larcenous show, carnival, etc.

Hand-to-hand music—applause.

Heave-'n'-grunter—wrestler.

Hebe comic—Jewish comedian.

Hip-flinger—cootch dancer.

Hoofery—dancehall.

Hosp—hospital.

Hoss opry—Western film.

Hypo—to stimulate b.o. receipts.

In the test tube—play tryout.

Indie—an independent exhibitor.

Inside stuff—the real lowdown.

Introed—introduced.

Irish justice—burlesque term for skit where judge hits defendant with rubber bladder.

It's the nuts—Sime's brushoff to anything spurious.

Joebreened—script that has been cleaned up; from Joseph I. Breen's, film industry censor.

Joint—nite club, hotel or restaurant, no matter how exclusive.

Juve—juvenile actor.

Kill time joint—cocktail lounge.

Knocked 'em bowlegged—rousing success.

L.A.—Los Angeles.

Laid an omelet—variation of "laid an egg"; a flop.

Layoff—unemployed actor.

Leblang—from Joe Leblang, king of cutrate ticket brokers. When a show goes over "with a Leblang" it profits through cutrate ticket support.

Legit—legitimate theater.

Legmania—acrobatic or intricate dancer.

Life of the party—generally borscht circuit m.c. whose job is to "laff it up" for the resort patrons.

Looker—beautiful woman; in TV dept. could also mean people looking-in on video.

Loop—Chicago's well-known theatrical sector.

L'ville—Louisville.

Mag—magazine.

Mazda Lane—Broadway.

M.c.—See *emcee*.

Megger—Film director; hangover from days when directors used megaphones.

Meller—melodrama.

Mesa meller—Western film.

Mesquiter—Western film.

Met op—Metropolitan Opera Association.

Milk man—actor who "milks" audience for extra laughs.

Mitt-reader—palmist.

Mugg or *Variety mugg*—a Variety staffer.

Muny op—municipal opera.

Mustang meller—Western film.

New faces—new talent.

Nice people—vaude agents' appraisal of actors who gifted them with more than 10% commissions.

Nitery—nite club.

Nix—no, veto, thumbs-down.

No cov joint—joint that doesn't charge cover or minimum.

N.s.g.—not so good.

N.s.h.—not so hot.

NY-to-LA—Broadway to Hollywood.

Oater—Western film.

Obit—obituary.

Ofay—Harlemese for white man.

Oke—OK.

Oke fodder—commercial show; good b.o.

Olio—scenery, in front of which an act, generally a "sidewalk comedy" team performs; also specialties performed between acts in burlesque.

O.o.—once-over.

Op—operation.

Opposish—opposition.

Orange Juice Gulch—Times Square, because of the large number of fruit juice stands there.

Org—organization.

Ork—orchestra, dance band.

Ozoner—drive-in theater.

P.a.—press agent; also personal appearance and public address system.

Pacted—signing of contract or pact.

Pan-Aired West—took Pan-American to Hollywood.

Palooka—an oaf.

Panicked the house—big hit.

Payoff—end result.

Peasants—"unhep" audiences.

Peeler—stripteaser.

Philly—Philadelphia.

Pitmen—musicians in the orchestra pit.

Pitt—Pittsburgh.

Pix—motion pictures or motion picture business.

Platter—phonograph disk.

Plugger—songplugger or music exploitation man.

Plushery—class joint (hotel, nitery, eatery).

Poverty Row—Gower and Sunset in Hollywood, headquarters for quickie producers. See *Gower Gulch.*

Pratfall—comedy fall.

Preem—theatre première.

Prez—president.

Prima—prima donna.

Pro ams—professional amateurs, those pseudo-tyros who constantly appeared on so-called amateur radio and vaudeville programs.

Prostie—prostitute. Variety's sensitized way of describing female characters comparable to those in early Mae West plays.

Pub-ad—publicity and advertising dep't.

Pushover—easy touch or easy make.

Quickie—cheaply made film.

Rave—top critical notice.

Reorg—reorganization.

Risley act—acrobatics that feature foot balancing.

Round actors—See *flesh*.

Round heels—a pushover.

S.a.—sex appeal.

Sagebrusher—Western film.

Schnozzle—nose (viz., Jimmy Durante).

Scram—exit.

Shoestringer—inexpensive or cheap theatrical operation.

Show biz—show business.

Shubert Alley—private street off Broadway, between 44th and 45th, where legits congregate.

Silo circuit—strawhat circuit, summer stock companies.

Situash—situation.

Small time—bush league.

Songplugger—exploiter of songs.

Spec—a spectacle; occasionally, ticket speculator.

Staffer—reporter.

Starrer—starring vehicle.

Stoky—Leopold Stokowski.

Stooge—grotesque comedy aide to a comedian; also a foil.

Strawhat—summer stock company.

Stripper—striptease dancer.

Stubholders—audiences.

Super-Chiefed east—went to New York on the Super-Chief.

Tab show—tabloid version of a musical.

Tad comic—Irish comedian.

Talkers—sound films; rarely called "talkies" in Variety.

Tea-reader—fortune teller.

10%er—theatrical agent.

Termer—a term contract.

Terpery—dance hall.

Terps—dancing.

Terp team—ballroom dance team.

They-went-thatawayer—Western film.

Third sex—a homosexual.

Tin Pan Alley—Music publishers' row, derived from the open-windowed brownstone houses west of Broadway on New York's 28th St. in the early 1900s when show business activities were focused between Union and Longacre (later Times) Square. Theatrical reporter Monroe H. Rosenfeld is credited with having coined the term in an interview with songwriter-publisher Harry Von Tilzer, and from that interview stemmed the legend that Von Tilzer coined it. TPA is still used because of its color although the music business has moved largely to the Brill Building uptown at 1619 Broadway; also Radio City.

Tinter—Technicolor film.

Took a bath—went into bankruptcy.

Took the veil—retired from public life.

Torcher—torch singer.

Torso-tosser—cootch dancer.

Toscy—Arturo Toscanini.

Trench unionist—musician in the orchestra pit.

Tuner—musical picture, or filmusical.

Turk day—Thanksgiving.

TV—television.

TVA—Television Authority.

TWA'd to the Coast—flew to Hollywood via TWA.

Vaudery—vaudeville theater.

vaudfilm—house showing films and vaudeville.

Ventro—ventriloquist.

Video—television.

Vidpic—films especially made for television.

Whodunit—mystery show.

Wickered—wastebasketed.

w.k.—well known.

Wowed the customers—big hit.

Yocks—big laughs.

Index

573